DELIVERY

DELIVERY
A Nurse-Midwife's Story

Jennifer Crichton

WARNER BOOKS

A Warner Communications Company

A Warner Communications Company

Printed in the United States of America

First Printing: October 1986

10 9 8 7 6 5 4 3 2 1

Designed by Giorgetta Bell McRee

Library of Congress Cataloging-in-Publication Data

Crichton, Jennifer.
  Delivery : a nurse-midwife's story.

  I. Title
  PS3553.R478D4   1986   813'.54   85-40915
ISBN 0-446-51331-8

The main character in this book, Holly Treadwell, is a created figure, constructed from what I learned about midwives, from midwives, over the course of a year. The incidents described here are based on true case histories, but I've taken the liberty to alter details and graft on information, both to protect the privacy of those who actually lived through these events and to give the reader a good sense of what a midwife does, and how she does it.

Acknowledgments

I'd like to thank all the nurses and widwives who were so forthcoming in describing their professions and how they live them. Almost every one had enough to tell to write a book of her own. None had the time to write it.

I'd also like to thank the women I met while they were in labor. I'm sure they don't remember me. I'm sure book-writing was the last thing on their minds. Good luck to everyone—the babies in particular.

olly Treadwell snaps down the bottom of her bathing suit, a bleached-out suit she found in the bureau of her old bedroom; it smells of wood from having sat for such a long time in the drawer.

She dives into the pool and emerges at the other end. She never swims in New York, and she misses it. The weightlessness of it. The silence. When she swims, she forgets herself, and she starts to remember only when she's back on solid ground.

Floating on her back, she stares up at the huge old trees that border the pool with a rich green color and thick, fanlike leaves you don't find in New York. She likes the rushing noise of the wind through the trees. That's the sound she misses the most, living in the city. The sky has turned gray in the twilight, and clouds catch and hold the last light of the day.

On a chair by the pool, beneath a towel, is her log of births. The journal's corduroy cover is ragged and frayed. This is her second log. She started her first when she was a midwifery student and worried that all her deliveries would wind up sliding together in a shapeless stream if she didn't hold them fast to the page. The point of the log is to testify, to bear witness, but most of all to capture each birth before it has the chance to slip away. Births slither off if you don't pin them down. Without the log, Holly's selective memory forgets the bits of pleasure and the small joys, and just summons up the rough work of nature gone awry: the disasters, crises, bad babies, and sick mothers.

Midwifery is an odd, hard way to make a living.

This morning, one of her parents' neighbors asked, "What are you up to these days, Holly?"

"I catch babies."

1

She catches babies.

Babies fly through the air and land in her hands. Babies spiral out of the water and rocket into her hands. Babies wait, silent and still, for Holly's hands to pull them out into the land of the living.

Holly's school friends from here, on the Main Line, the strand of villages outside Philadelphia, are now corporate lawyers and advertising executives. They're housewives with pools, entire days spent in Ellesse tennis wear, winter vacations in the Caribbean, and babies of their own that were delivered by obstetricians. "I thought of going to a midwife, Holly," they'd say apologetically, "but then I thought, what if something goes wrong?"

What if something goes wrong? But midwives know what to do when things go wrong, because something always does, one way or the other.

A strange profession, pulling little creatures out of darkness and fluid into the dry world of air, light, and heavy ground. "What do you do?" I attend the passage out, Holly could say, if she wanted to get pretentious about it.

Holly dives down to the bottom of the pool and touches the round drain for luck. A piece of magic she picked up as a kid. Then she shoots back up and resurfaces, out of breath, into the cool evening air. September means warm water, chilly nights. When she went underwater, it was still twilight. But now it's night.

Night falls fast here, she thinks, and pulls herself out of the pool, walking barefoot across the wide lawn with its thick-bladed grass, towel in one hand, her journal in the other. She is ready to go into her parents' big white house. In the pool, she forgot herself. But when she walks into her parents' house, she'll become just a daughter again and her life as a midwife will be left outside in the dark, with the rustling trees.

MORRISON HOSPITAL

CHAPTER 1

Holly feels at home on Seven-B. Labor and delivery. She hates it, plenty of times, and wants to be somewhere else, and views it as a whirlpool or a swamp of despair or a cesspool or a trap—none of which makes it feel any less like home.

If the locker room didn't exist, Holly would have invented it. It's the bridge from outside to inside—the changing room. Here, Holly changes.

She never opens her locker door as far as it can go, as the locker is filled with leftover gear she doesn't want to see spill out onto the floor. It's stuff she doesn't even want to think about. Figuring out what junk is worth keeping and what she should throw out would require a degree of decision-making that is, at present, beyond her. Maybe next year. This year Holly knows how to stop a woman from bleeding out, but she's not sure what to do with the green sweater, spotted with bloodstains, lying at the base of her locker. Or what to do with the anonymous note someone slipped into her locker a year ago. Her first and only piece of hate mail. "Holy Tredwell you are a c - - t." As Holly's friend Denise, an OB nurse on Seven-B, told her, "I guess the person doesn't know how to spell it out."

"Do you think I'm a c-dash-dash-t, Denise?"

"Only when you're not being a b-dash-dash-dash-h."

Holly keeps her hairbrush, barrettes, hand cream, and lip gloss in a kidney-shaped basin she appropriated from a delivery room and drafted into her personal service. She awaits the note that reads: "Holy Tredwell you are a t - - - f."

Holly puts up her blonde hair, releasing some wisps for that romantic-maiden look—cascading tendrils—that will shortly be replaced by the slatternly-fishwife look that inevitably follows a few hours on the floor.

5

She pulls on her scrubs. Like most of the crew, she disdains Morrison-issue scrubs. They never fit right and are that color green that makes everyone look fatigued, depressed, hollow-eyed. All variety of washed-out colors move about the labor and delivery suite to put the lie to the word "uniform." Holly's scrubs consist of lavender baggies she's had since she was a maternity nurse and a blue surgical shirt. To match her eyes, sort of.

When Holly drops her Italian shoes into a heap at the bottom of the locker, their fall is cushioned and noiseless, one advantage of the locker-as-dump principle. From the top of the locker, she pulls down her Dr. Scholl's sandals. Their leather straps hold the faint echo of blotches: bloodstains that have almost been scrubbed out but are irrevocably sunken into the grain of the leather. The stains are coffee colored now, and the rubber heels have worn out, leaving raw, splintery wood. White running shoes are now the Morrison footwear of choice, giving the hospital an erroneous image of being staffed by fit, healthy workers. Holly sometimes considers buying a pair herself, but she doesn't want to give these old sandals the heave-ho. They've brought her semigood luck. At least, she's never lost a patient—not an adult one, that is. And Holly is superstitious. When she wants to touch wood, she taps her foot on the floor. She taps her foot now.

Once Holly has on the Dr. Scholl's and starts to clatter like a horse on a cobblestone street, she knows she has become Nurse-Midwife. It's almost eight o'clock in the evening, and she'll be a midwife until eight in the morning. Twelve hours of looking alive.

Before she bails out of the locker room, she checks her hair. She's twenty-eight years old, and she's been at Morrison for three years. She's an old-timer, a veteran, full of war stories from the trenches. At the mirror, she looks fresh and composed, but she'll lose it pretty soon. Now she grabs on to whatever girlishness she has left and hangs on tight. Because she'll have to let it go. When you plunge into the birth of a whole other being, your own girlishness just stands in the way. The long haul of labor-sit grinds it down. An all-consuming disaster reduces Holly to a pair of hands and a quick mind. Maybe that's what Holly likes about Morrison, Seven-B. Maybe that's what makes it feel like home. It's here that the essentials come clear and life comes clean. In a way.

CHAPTER 2

Levy, the fourth-year resident, leans back against a wall by the nurse's station. He scribbles on a chart. When he first got to med school, they told him that he'd spend half his working life marking down observations for posterity. He didn't believe them, then. People who haven't met Levy assume from his name that he's Jewish. Maybe he is, but he's also and principally a black man. In scrubs and white Adidas tennis shoes, he strains to be taller than five feet seven—and he always claims to be five feet nine, although that is a patent falsehood. With almond-shaped eyes, he borders on being pretty and tries to mitigate his soft handsomeness by adopting a swaggering, cock-of-the-walk machismo. Holly is never sure if this is meant to be a put-on or deadly serious. Either way, it's laughable, if appealing, some of the time.

Three labor rooms run off from the nurse's station, two beds to a room, each bed separated by a curtain. The beds are full tonight.

A moan pushes out to the station, drifts down the corridor, and is stopped by the heavy metal doors marking the end of Seven-B. Only screams make it past the metal doors, all the way to the elevators, but screams are discouraged. Midwives' patients sound the best, Holly thinks. They make resonant noises—growls and grunts.

"I want you to sound like an animal," Holly tells her patients. Screams tighten the chest, the neck, constrict everything, constrict the cervix, tense up the pelvis.

"But I don't want to sound like an animal," a patient once said.

"Just for tonight," Holly said, "then you can go back to sounding humanoid."

By the elevators is a small waiting room. When Holly was a maternity nurse in a private hospital, the waiting room there was called the Stork

7

Club and done up to look like the 1950s ideal of an all-American man's den: couches upholstered in plaid; framed prints of trout flying out of streams; huge brown unbreakable ashtrays for all the anxiously smoked cigarettes and cigars; copies of *Sports Illustrated* mingled in with crumpled pamphlets on baby-care: *What You Should Know About Your Baby: A Dad's Guide.*

The waiting room at Morrison benefits from minimal interior design. The only thing the Morrison waiting room has is four walls, a bare radiator, and a window nailed shut. There had been a wooden bench once, but somebody—an "anxious dad," no doubt—smashed it up. Crowley, a Jamaican nurse, was the first to discover its remains.

"What sort of person would do this?" she asked Holly as they bent down and picked up stumps of the bench together.

Holly examined a foot-long shard. "Breaking this bench was a job of work," she said. "It must have been a highly motivated personality."

"Is that what you'd call it?" Crowley said. "How interesting."

The waiting room is painted every two months, and the fresh coats of paint are irresistibly seductive to the graffiti artists who come here to wait for their offspring to be born. This month, the wall sports two cartoon figures. Each has a potato-shaped nose, Big Apple cap, and rounded feet that most closely resemble inflated inner tubes. One figure is taller than the other, and they hold hands as they bop down an imaginary avenue. "Hello Newest Homeboy on the Block," the caption reads. "Love from You're Homeboy Pop." That's love.

Save for graffiti artists, nobody waits in the waiting room. Instead, they sit near the elevators, propped on the windowsill, the radiator, and the standing ashtray, which has been covered by a plank of wood. The one chair—old, molded-plastic, aqua colored—always seems occupied by an older woman who smokes cigarettes with the fatigued air of having been here before.

As the door to Seven-B swings open, a transport orderly saunters through, pushing an empty wheelchair, and a moan spills out before being dammed off, in midstream, when the door swings shut again.

The groans aren't really heard on Seven-B. They're part of the ward's aural landscape, like chain saws in the woods in autumn, birdsong at dawn, police sirens at night in Brooklyn. The nurses, residents, and midwives learn not to hear them at all. Instead, they train their ears to pick out sounds of big trouble and can detect, with half an ear, the moan that signals a brand of distress above and beyond the run-of-the-mill variety.

The Seven-B nurses are especially attuned to the high-pitched moan that threatens to escalate into a scream. Screams must be nipped in the bud. They are counterproductive, tension producing, but a scream's chief danger, as the nurses perceive it, is its contagious power. A scream is fear and pain transformed into sound. As such, it terrifies other patients, who are then inclined to scream. A scream is a dam that has burst to flood all the labor rooms, drenching everyone with distress. A scream demands crisis intervention, which is its purpose since most women scream to be heard, to be helped.

"No screaming, dear," a nurse tells a patient now. "Breathe, dear, slow, dear, breathe, baby, slow. You don't want to scare the baby, baby."

Holly taps Levy on his head and makes a hollow-wood sound with a click of her tongue. Levy isn't amused.

"What's up?" she asks. She pronounces "what's up" like the young orderlies do, as one word: "T'sup?"

Levy gives Holly a cold look, then returns to his chart-busting. "Nothing you'd be interested in, Treadwell."

"Try me, Levy. You fascinate me. I'm always interested."

"Well, if you must know," he says wearily, "we zapped a lady with a bit of Pit, and whammo, she's hyped."

Pitocin is the pharmaceutical equivalent of oxytocin, the natural hormone that induces and sustains uterine contractions. It's a powerful and violent drug, and too much of it can hyperstimulate the uterus, causing it to contract without pausing. At Morrison, Pit is pumped slowly, one drop at a time, into a dextrose solution, which is administered intravenously.

"Did you pull the Pit?" Holly asks.

"No, Treadwell, I upped it. Took it to the max. Pumped it up." Levy leers. Not an attractive sight. "And on my days off, I put cats into clothes dryers to see them spin. Anything for a kick. Any more questions?"

"How were the contractions spaced?"

"Would they *were* spaced. There was barely an eyelash of time between them."

"Christ, Levy, you'll rip that uterus to shreds."

"Thanks for the consult, Treadwell. Your interpretation of events is always so illuminating."

Holly steps into the hall, a fifty-yard dash covered countless times each night by the OB staff. As Denise, who is twenty-four years old, black, and from Brooklyn, told Holly, "What we really need are roller skates to zip and zap and hip and hop and roll and rock, just like that." She snapped her fingers. Denise has rhythm in a big way.

Here she is now, hurrying down the corridor with her hips swiveling like a Roto-Rooter and elbows snapping back like pistons. Denise considers running conduct unbecoming to a nurse. A nurse should *anticipate* so that running isn't necessary. A good nurse is like a good basketball player: she shimmies into position at the right moment to catch a pass and take a shot. But Denise can't always live up to her own no-running code and she compensates with an impressive racewalk, covering territory faster by walking heel-toe than Holly can in her adrenaline-fueled bolts.

Denise points at the operating room. "Scut," she calls, pumping her way into the OR. The OR, next door to the two delivery rooms at the end of the hall, has to be set every four hours with sterilized equipment, even when it hasn't been used. Denise has pulled this particular scut work, and Holly laughs lightly. She doesn't need to do that scut work anymore. She's moved on to higher levels of scut. Drawing bloods from a pregnant bag lady. Mining for accessible veins in an obese teenager. Starting an IV for Levy in exchange for a favor. Scut is the currency of the realm. Trading scut work is serious barter that demands careful calculation and tactful negotiation. Nobody ever feels satisfied with the deals they make. Everyone always feels slightly . . . shafted.

Both DRs are empty. Four o'clock in the morning is the estimated time of arrival for Morrison babies. Nobody gives birth this early in the evening. It just isn't done. Most of the time, that is. Midwife's law: When you think you know everything, you don't.

Beyond the DRs is a storage room: an expanded closet filled with things the staff doesn't need (twenty thousand pressure catheters, to gauge the strength of contractions) and lacking the one thing they do (a Foley catheter).

The room next door was intended as a storage room, and it was one, until the nurses commandeered it as their private lounge.

It's a sacred, hallowed ground of vital fluids: coffee and IV solutions. Wobbly, transparent bags of IV solution (the dextrose DW5 is most popular) are piled on open shelves. Competing for attention across the room is a Mr. Coffee machine standing next to a sink with a leaky faucet. The faucet has dripped for years. In an enormous hospital staffed by specialists of all kinds, no one seems equipped with the Industrial Age skill to replace a faulty washer. Chairs salvaged from a street dumpster and appropriated, late at night, from an administrator's office ("It's time he redecorated anyhow") serve as buffers between the two sets of vital liquids. The chairs sit in the middle of the room, the decorator's equivalent of a bad penny, and never look quite at home there.

The lounge, as the storage room is called, is remote and calm, a cabin in the mountains, compared to the nurse's station next door.

The station is the hub, the engine of the floor. To one end is the admitting desk, the tollgate to the L&D ward, commanding a view of the entrance and stacked with all the necessary papers, the kind a woman can't have a baby without. Forms for blood tests, the admitting interview, labor charting, informed consent permission, birth certificates. Then there are the booklets, which mostly go unread but are required by law to be conspicuously accessible, detailing in English and *español* a patient's rights.

"Do you have this in French?" a young Haitian woman asked one night after the admitting nurse handed her a Spanish booklet. No French translations yet. Each year, Morrison sees more Haitians, recent émigrés to Brooklyn, and the shift in demographics has taken place just as Holly's high school French, lingering for years as a kind of cerebral vestige, at last has atrophied away from disuse. Rudimentary Spanish—a thousand times more useful for a midwife—supplanted her French, and now that Holly can conduct primitive communication with her Hispanic patients, the French that her mother told her would come in handy someday is coming in handy. Or would, if Holly were able to remember any of it. But she is pretty sure her mind can't house three languages at once. It's just too small for that. She's afraid her French is permanently excised from her mind, lost to the brain's slag heap, where the laws of calculus and the details of the Thirty Years War have also been relegated.

At the other end of the nursing station is the Board. The Board is just a long chalkboard, but it's invested with a degree of authority accorded to nothing and nobody else. The Board has a presence. It's almost a *personage*. The Board lists the patients in labor, their ages, the time of admission, the status of cervical dilation, blood pressure, medications given, and procedures performed, special conditions that need to be watched, and each patient's parity (a four-digit number representing a patient's obstetrical history in shorthand, indicating the number of children and miscarriages she's had).

The Board is always watched. The staff gives it the once-over as they pass, reading it with well-developed peripheral vision, because the Board is the one reliable source of information. The Board explains what's happening on the floor, and unlike any other staff member, the Board is exempt from confusion.

Holly studies the Board. She wants to know who Levy zapped to the brink before he retreated. She leaps into his impatient mind-set. Which patient did he Pit into hyperspace? A poky customer, most likely, whose labor didn't scamper up the Friedman curve of labor—the graph that demonstrates in one fell swoop the typical length of labor—like a mountain goat.

Holly squints. Butler. Has to be. Butler was admitted seven hours earlier and has dawdled at six centimeters. Slow for a multip. ("Multip" from the word *multipara*, meaning a woman who has given birth at least twice, but the term is used informally to mean a woman giving birth for at least the second time. "Grand multip" signifies a woman who has given birth many times. "Primap," from *primipara*, is used at Morrison to mean a woman giving birth for the first time; formally, it means a woman who has given birth once. "Nullip," from *nullipara*, is the correct word for someone giving birth for the first time—but it's never used to mean that, signifying instead a woman who has never been pregnant.)

Butler is twenty-seven years old, old for Seven-B, and she's moving slowly, even by Holly's relatively generous standards. Multips who aren't well nourished or in good physical shape can lose much of their uterine muscle tone. When the flabby muscle won't compress with the taut force it might have, the first-stage labors can be plodding affairs—the less efficient contractions don't press the baby's head against the cervix with the hard, regular pressure the cervix needs to draw up into the uterus and open, letting the baby out.

Once the cervix is fully dilated, though, and labor enters the second stage (the pushing stage), a multip usually has the advantage over the primap, as her pelvic inlet and birth canal are more relaxed and the baby has an easier time descending the canal to slide on out.

Holly doesn't move a primap to the DR until the baby's head appears at the vaginal outlet. But as soon as a multip's cervix dilates to ten centimeters—which is as far as it goes—Holly transfers the patient onto the champagne trolley and sends her flying to the nearest DR. Then Holly crouches at the end of the delivery table and waits to catch a baby on the move.

Levy emerges from Butler's room.

"Levy, she'll sneeze and that baby is going to be born," Holly says.

"Who?"

"Butler."

"How'd you know it was Butler?"

"Because." *Tact, Treadwell, shut your yap.* "Because."

Because, Levy, you're impatient with the variable pace of labor, that's why.

When you go into OB or midwifery, the slowness of pregnancy and labor comes with the territory. It's a precondition, an essential part of the working environment. Working with pregnant women means a laborious pace broken by a flash of a baby's head or a catastrophe that sends you diving and reeling in different directions like a small fish come gill-to-gill with a toothy barracuda. Slowness is labor's working material, but Levy hasn't learned to work with it. It makes a certain kind of sense that a hyper guy like Levy winds up hyperstimulating some unhyped lady.

He tosses his clipboard down onto the desk. "Okay. So it's Butler. You're right."

He can hear the charge Holly left unspoken and knows it's true and is ticked off with himself. He's inclined to manage labor instead of letting it take its course, and he can't or won't change. At least, not now. Not yet. What he can't admit is that with every crisis, he gets the chance to practice his skills—maybe he doesn't do everything possible to avoid crises from developing. It isn't an entirely conscious or intentional method of self-education, but more of an accidentally-on-purpose syndrome.

Holly would hate Levy, except for the fact that she likes him. The trouble is, he likes her. The fact that he likes her makes her spoken and unspoken charges stick and sting and melt down in his mind. The chemical problem of having an adversary you like: that's not taught in med school either.

A look passes between them. All their years spent capped and masked in hospital DRs have taught them how to speak with their eyes. They both have a few more lines on their foreheads than other people their age—all those raised eyebrows and widened eyes, animated in the exposed slat of skin between mask and cap—and when Holly's blue eyes meet Levy's soft brown ones, there's a weird kinship. With a little less self-control, they'd either come to blows or jump on each other's bones in lust. They don't know which. It can go either way.

"I want Butler," Holly tells Levy. He's responsible for making patient assignments.

"Why?"

"She needs a break. Some midwife's TLC."

"Can't happen," says Levy.

"Levy, you owe me Butler.'

"Why do I owe you?"

"Remember that man-hating hypertensive we had in here a month ago? Young lady with a nasty social history?"

A major scut exchange.

Until now, Holly hadn't thought of her, the memory almost ashes in the Obnoxious Patients Incinerator of her mind. An alarming patient. The woman had a square head that looked to have been molded in a vise and a square haircut that made the blockhead look even blockier. Some people have rounded bowl-cuts, but the Blockhead had a kind of box-cut, as if her hair were cut with a box stuck on her head. She looked like one of those stone icons found down in South America: the square-headed grim gods that demand human sacrifice.

The Blockhead didn't want a man to touch her, and Madeline, the one female resident, had been off that night, as she is tonight. Holly had been swamped with clinic patients—nice women who made an effort—when Levy swaggered up to say, "How'd you like to take a man-hater off my hands?"

After introducing herself (a formality many residents dispense with), Holly tried to inset an IV catheter into the back of the Blockhead's hand. The way the Blockhead glared at Holly was unnerving, and Holly took a bloody tap. The catheter jumped back a few crucial millimeters, and a spurt of blood gurgled forth in a tiny fountain. "Watch it, bitch!" the Blockhead hissed.

Which is when Holly realized the Blockhead wasn't a man-hater, but hated everybody. Holly wanted to put a mask of inhalation anesthesia over the woman's face, grab the baby out of her with a two-handed yank, and pitch her into the street. Buff and turf her into another time zone. Holly figured this was how some residents felt about all the patients all the time—all their patients seeming to them to be this uncooperative, this unappealing, and deserving of a revival of the time-discredited medical tradition the scope cocktail (scopolamine, or twilight sleep, mixed with Demerol) to hurl them into a black hole to be crushed by limitless, nameless quarks.

The Blockhead brought Holly a cynical revelation. For that mind-altering experience, Levy definitely owes Holly.

Levy scratches his head. "Wasn't that man-hater named Holly Treadwell?"

"You're so clever, Levy, but you know I only hate men on a selective basis."

"So you had to deal with a nasty lady. Hold the presses."

"I took over for you, Levy. And one of your statements is lodged in my memory bank. The statement is, 'Treadwell, I owe you one.' I love it when you're in my debt, Levy."

"Never happened," Levy says, shaking his head. "I'd never be so crazed as to actually say those words, Treadwell. I might as well have written out my death certificate while I was at it."

"You said it, Levy, and you owe me. You did your number on Butler. Now let her off the hook and give her to me."

"Can't be done. I have other considerations to consider."

"Such as?"

"Such as Scott."

"The Citadel closes ranks, and it won't be the first time," Holly says glumly. "Butler has gone through the wringer and now you want to throw her to Scott? Is there no justice in this world?"

"He's capable," Levy says defensively.

"Sure, he's capable. The question is, capable of what?"

"The scene gets ugly," Levy says. "So this is the end of the discussion, Treadwell. Scott is assigned to Butler. C'est fini. You'd better return to your clinic patients. I understand they need a lot of that midwifery TLC."

CHAPTER 3

Denise stands behind Holly and sings into her ear. "Scott the red-hot proves that an MD can be bought. His daddy has the money, he bought the school for sonny, Butler's kid is gonna look funny, and that's the story, honey."

Holly turns and smiles. "You have what the Irish call the gift of gab."

"That's not gab. That's *rap*. And we finish it off with a little saying."

"What?"

"Bust that!" Denise laughs hoarsely.

"Bust *that*," Holly says, nodding in the direction of the Sneaker.

The anesthesiology resident, the Sneaker, prowls the halls, advancing noiselessly in tennis shoes, relentlessly looking out for hard-luck cases. His phrase that pays is, "Anything bad happening?" which he asks with a hopeful tone.

Everyone feels free to despise the Sneaker. He's short, with bright red hair and colorless eyelashes, and from a distance, he reminds Holly of her brother Michael. Up close, he has strange, bright eyes that seem to jump out of his chalky skin. It has occurred to Holly more than a few times that the Sneaker does some drug accessible only to an anesthesiologist.

The Sneaker's shifty eyes peruse the Board.

"Anything bad happening, ladies?" he asks with a smile.

"Nothing bad," Denise says. "But give it time."

"I shall return." The Sneaker creeps silently down the corridor to other, more fertile fields of anesthesiology.

"Forget the name 'Sneaker,'" Denise says. "He is the *Creeper*."

"How can anyone walk so quietly?" Holly asks, amazed.

"That's a characteristic of Satan, you know."

"Go on, Denise! Are you for real?"

"The Devil never makes noise when he moves. Didn't anybody ever tell you that?"

"He does have that Angel of Death aura," Holly says, considering the Sneaker/Creeper as he swings through the fire doors at the end of the hall.

"The way he hovers and looms. You can just about hear his big wings flap-flap-flapping." Denise shudders.

"You ought to have kids. You could tell some spine-tingling ghost stories."

"I don't have to tell no ghost stories. I *live* them."

"Speaking of ghosts," Holly says, "since Scott has vanished to the great unknown, I'm going to take a look at Butler."

High-risk patients and grand multips are put in the A beds, closest to the door, for quick getaways to the DR and easy observation by nurses passing by. Lelia Butler is in an A bed. Levy pulled the Pit half an hour ago, and since Pit's effect on the uterus fades out three minutes after it's been discontinued, Butler isn't hyperstimulated anymore. At least, her uterus isn't. But the rest of her body suffers aftershocks. Her body shakes like a sapling in a high wind with its leaves trembling. This looks like transition, when first-stage labor passes into second stage. But it's not. Butler has been zapped to the brink. She hasn't gotten back yet.

Reflexively, Butler lifts her hand and flattens down her hair, which has gone wild. Holly can tell that at the start of her labor, her hair was braided; she has loose, vague loops of hair that no longer weave together but seem to want to. Her hair stands out on end like a cartoon character's after he has stuck his finger in a light socket. Butler's instinctive move to smooth her hair is that of a woman on automatic.

Modesty and vanity are the flotsam and jetsam of the birthing process. When the passage gets rough and exhausting, and priorities are rearranged, vanity is one of the first particulars of personality jettisoned overboard to lighten the load. Hauling vanity into rough sailing like labor takes up too much energy.

But vestiges of vanity always remain, as if the law of self-preservation stops a woman from disappearing without a trace of her normal self into the all-consuming process of labor. Her past self includes her vanity. At Morrison, the labor rooms have no mirrors. Maybe budgetary constraints have to do with their omission, but more likely, someone decided that no woman wants to see how labor has put her through the mill.

A woman who worries about her looks during labor is trouble of a genteel sort. When a woman is concerned with being ladylike, she keeps her knees tucked together and her legs crossed, literally and figuratively. Labor slows in deference to her resistance. Parlor manners don't sit well in the labor room. Neither do tired old ideas of female weakness that encourage women to collapse early on in the ordeal, overwhelmed by pain.

Holly regrets that Butler lifted a shaky hand to brush down her hair. But she sympathizes, too. She'd have done the same thing herself. "Forget it," Holly would like to say. "Your hair is messed up in a major way, but you look fine anyhow." Holly will have to wait to say it, when she knows Butler a little better. You don't build trust by storming in with a torrent of free-floating compliments.

Holly touches Butler's shoulder with a light hand, and her shaking stops. Holly lifts her hand. The shakes, with chattering teeth and clattering bones, begin again. Holly touches Butler. The shaking stops. Holly's touch—or anybody else's, really—can turn the fear and trembling on and off. The human touch is strong medicine. If it weren't, half the patients on Seven-B wouldn't be here. Wouldn't ache for a man's touch, wouldn't want that touch to go on, wouldn't ache for the oddly strong clasp of a baby.

Holly presses firmly on Butler's abdomen, walking her fingers along the uterus in search of tenderness that would mean a tear in the uterus's muscular fabric.

"How does this feel?"

"Feels all right."

"Feels good?"

"I wouldn't say that," says Butler.

"Good," Holly says. "It shouldn't feel too good."

A bad sign if it felt good. When the uterus ruptures, blood and amniotic fluid run off. Pressure is released, the abdominal cavity is swamped in a warm, dangerous bath, and the patient sinks into shock and lets go. The drowning feels good.

Holly listens to the fetal heart monitor The galloping blips. If the uterus has ruptured, the first signs of shock, as the mother bleeds out, appear in the fetus. When trauma hits a pregnant woman, nature spares her at the expense of the baby—a gloomy law of nature designed for the survival of the species. Because our bodies are still organized as they were in prehistoric days, they respond to trauma in a manner fashioned for those harsh circumstances. If a baby dies, that's the loss of one life. But if a mother dies, she takes two lives—her own and the baby's—and all the lives she could bear in the future. In prehistoric times, a motherless baby (while theoretically a future procreator, just as its mother was) had to be presumed lost. A certain bleak logic governs nature's taking the baby first.

Following this rule, you gauge trauma in a pregnant woman by tracking the fetus. With the internal fetal monitor in place, screwed into the fetal scalp, you don't rely only on the mother's vital signs to detect what's happening in her body. You study the baby instead, who'll show signs of blood loss before the mother does.

"You're doing good," Holly tells Butler.

"I wonder how I got into this," Butler says, rolling her eyes. A sense of humor is one of the most valuable things a woman can bring with her to labor. It lightens the load for those who care for her—a good tactical maneuver, as people are more inclined to help out likable patients. But humor means more to Holly. It shows a reserve of vitality to see a woman through hard times. A life force. A will to live. Butler is the kind of patient Holly wants.

CHAPTER 4

"Here comes trouble," Denise says under her breath. Scott, the second-year resident. Still the inept intern. Ineptitude in an intern is not only tolerated but expected. What makes Scott singularly menacing is that his own ineptitude fails to frighten him, as it should. In his four months here, he has shown no talent for the pursuit of obstetrics, and his apathy appears pathological.

"He's just worn out from doing time in the ER," Levy said at first. "Battle fatigue. Shell shock."

The floor awaits his recovery.

Scott has frequent, irresistible urges to lie down and take a nap. He is continually prone on a bunk in the residents lounge and most often appears as he does now: blinking awake in the corridor, his eyes crusty with sleep, his hair mussed, his scrubs hanging loose from his tall frame. The overall look is that of an overgrown kid dragged out of bed in pajamas handed down by a more filled-out older brother.

"He has a cute face," muses Holly, as Scott shambles forth.

"What a waste," Denise says. "He's the boy who puts the *dense* into *residence.*"

That Scott appears likable only confuses matters. He looks like the kind of kid Holly might have grown up with, the kind her mother would get a crush on and want Holly to go out with, the kind of boy who always scuffled into other people's kitchens looking for something to eat. While the staff wants to hate him for his inertia, he looks as if he doesn't deserve it.

What's hateful is that he doesn't bother turning on the charm for anybody. It's insulting, and worse. His failure to flatter the nurses is viewed as a serious defect of character and intellect. A poor career move. Sheer folly. Scott knows that the practice of medicine is a thing apart from textbook knowledge, but he hasn't quite gotten the picture that you can do without textbook learning if the nurses are on your side, but you can do almost nothing with it if the nurses are against you.

Holly greets him by saying, "Levy has an interesting patient for you."

"How interesting?" he asks, startled.

"As interesting as you'd care to make it, I suppose. A multip, para three, hyperstimulated via Pit at eight-thirty. A groovy, swinging chick."

"She worked up yet?" he asks, even more alarmed.

Holly sighs. "Nothing for you to do but catch her baby."

Scott's body relaxes; his panic recedes. He's ready to catch a baby, but starting an IV line makes his spine arch. Now he can return to his usual slouch.

Two hours later. Holly is moving a primap to the DR when Denise bursts in, racewalking like crazy. "I can't find Scott anyplace. I guess he's sightseeing. That's my name for him now. The Sightseer. All he needs is a pair of binoculars, Bermuda shorts, and a guidebook."

"Birth as a spectator sport."

"But this is serious," says Denise. "Lelia's ready to go."

"Lelia?"

"Butler to you."

"I can't leave now," Holly says.

"She's next door. I want to know if I'm only imagining she's ready to go or what. I want you to take a peek and tell me where she's at."

"Mind if I wash my hands first?"

Holly runs around the corner to the next labor room and does a quick exam. Loudly and for Butler's benefit, she says, "She's at nine and counting." But she doesn't unglove. Straightening up, she whispers to Denise, "Damn that Scott. Lelia has an edematous anterior lip the size of a golf ball."

An edematous lip is usually caused when a woman pushes before she's fully dilated. The baby's head presses the anterior lip of the cervix against the pubic bone so that the lip swells up. The swollen part won't retract with the rest of the cervix, and its presence will block the baby's descent, a flap of flesh lying in the baby's path. There's also the chance the cervical lip will be lacerated by the baby's pushing against it, and unnatural communication will be established between the cervical canal and the bladder. In a worst-case scenario, the lip can separate entirely from the cervix, just as a person who bites his lip for a long enough time will eventually bite part of it off.

"It told her not to push," Denise says, in her own and Butler's defense.

Holly isn't angry with Butler or Denise, but with the resident who failed to manage Butler's labor. She slips her fingers inside Lelia again and finds the swollen, mushy lip. A contraction begins—Holly feels it as if her hand were at a deep layer in the earth at the start of an earthquake—and as the baby's head is forced down, Holly tucks back the lip, keeps it pressed above the *symphisis pubis* (the pubic bone), and waits for the next contraction, to make sure the lips holds.

"Maybe the lip started when Lelia was hyped," Denise offers softly.

"*Quién sabe?*" Holly says, shaking her head. "It wasn't your fault, old girl."

Denise wipes Lelia's forehead with a damp cloth and shouts, "You're almost there!" as she hugs Lelia quickly around the shoulders.

"Don't shout, Denise," Holly says, slipping out the door. "You'd better find Scott. It's time you all moved to the DR."

Denise looks up. "Find the Sightseer? Huh!" She snorts. "He's probably in the Pavilion of the Future at Epcot Center, or some such attraction." Turning to Lelia, she gives the perennial command: "Don't push yet, Lelia! Don't push!"

"But I'm ready," says Lelia. "I'm ready."

CHAPTER 5

In the DR and Lelia is ready. Frances, the nurse's aide, stares at Butler's crotch. This is something of a habit of hers. She's transfixed by the sight of a vagina that is wide open, rounded, not shuttered up by labial folds. Holly finds pretexts to send her out of the DR when a woman is delivering, but now Frances—short, dark, silent as a mute—is all the assistance Denise has as she yells at Lelia to pant and not to push. "Frances, you watch Lelia for a minute." This is something Frances can do.

Denise racewalks across the hall, elbows pumping, to find Scott in DR1. He has lumbered in to view the birth of twins and is tying on his mask as he slips across the floor in blue paper booties—they're too small for his big feet and fit like a pair of women's Peds, like half-socks.

Scott is ready for the big attraction. Twins draw a crowd. Seven-B is used to twins, but not bored with them. Twins galvanize affairs. Twins double the electrical charge of ordinary births and make single deliveries seem lonely, boring, lacking, and impoverished in contrast. When twins are about to deliver, nurses find reasons to enter the DR, orderlies appear from nowhere, sleepy residents bestir themselves, and Levy hustles down to the sono office and wheels in a portable sono as if it were a supermarket cart, in search of the position and presentation of the second twin.

Holly tries to ignore twins. She's not allowed to deliver them, even though she knows she could do it as well as anyone. She's envious. And twins make all other births seem anticlimactic in contrast. Which means her patients get short shrift.

"Dr. Scott," says Denise, tugging at his sleeve. She can't bear to call him by his last name and give him that much respect. Scott looks down at her, his eyes expressionless and disinterested, as if he doesn't recognize Denise, as if he's looking at a stranger. "Lelia Butler is ready to go. No lie. She's about to crown."

Scott looks up, surveying the DR scene. Preparations. Levy is squinting at the woman's crotch, then adjusts her legs in the high stirrups. Her legs are invisible beneath the blue sterile drapings and leggings that leave just a window of flesh visible. A sterile field, just barely alive.

"Scott!"

"In a minute," he says. Scott has learned this at least: the voice of the put-upon superiors. "The second twin is breech. I got to watch Levy do it."

The lost art of breech birth, practiced only with twins these days. The breech might arrive ten or fifteen minutes after the first twin, the first twin is not yet born, and Butler is ready to go. Lelia will go it alone, deliver alone, if she has to. It's been done before, and it'd be in keeping with the rest of her treatment: the hyperstimulation, the anterior lip.

Frances wanders silently into DR1. Twins draw a crowd. And if Frances is going to stare at somebody's crotch, this one, about to open up for two babies, is pay dirt in the curiosity department, a boffo show for all interested sightseers.

Denise glances at Scott and at Frances. Useless. Fuck racewalking. She takes off across the hall and makes it to Lelia's side in three bounding leaps.

CHAPTER 6

"All right, girl, it's just the sisters tonight. Put your knees up, sweetheart."

Lelia raises her head. "Where's the doctor at?"

"We'll be fine, girl. I've done this hundreds of times."

Denise has the jitters. She's always been a high-strung person. As she told Holly, when she was little, she burned calories so fast, she couldn't keep any meat on her bones. Her hair was neat, her clothes were clean, but she looked emaciated. A neighbor called the human services department to lodge a complaint against Denise's mother, and an inspector came to the house to make sure Denise's mother wasn't depriving her of food.

"Eat up, girl," her mother would say. "People think I'm starving my own child. Don't move around so fast. Eat those bananas."

Lelia reminds Denise of her mother. Had Denise been born like this? A white resident from the suburbs letting her mother lie all by herself, to come in at the last minute, frame her black ass with draperies, and yank tiny, skinny baby Denise out of her poor mother?

"I can't pant no more," Lelia says.

"No, I know you can't."

Denise has hauled out the stirrups, brought up from Sterilization and still wrapped in brown butcher paper. She was going to twist them into the delivery table like oversized pieces from an Erector Set. But she puts them down on the radiator, instead, a distinctly septic field.

Her obstetrical taste has changed, and stirrups look creepy to her now, reminding her of prosthetic limbs. She doesn't like the way ladies look, straddling the things. When she sees them now, she thinks of the porno movie her boyfriend talked her into seeing. ("Don't call it porno, baby," he'd said. "Call it triple-X.") In the movie, a girl's hands and legs were

24

handcuffed to a four-poster bed and stupid-looking men took violent possession of her in various ways. Toward the end, a stupid-looking man dragged the girl's feet up and propped them against the bedposts. "The lithotomy position," Denise told Holly later, "stirrups." She bolted out of the theater. It was like her stomach permanently turned, and turned against stirrups.

Even when the stirrups don't look like a piece of wickedness, they look dopey and babyish, like training wheels on a bike, and Denise wonders why the docs don't feel embarrassed to be seen using them.

A stirrup clatters to the floor and Denise lets it fall.

In part, Holly is to blame for Denise's new squeamishness. Holly was the first midwife Denise ever worked with, and she's the midwife Denise trusts more than any of the others. Denise hadn't known what to expect when she first assisted Holly. Midwives were old-time grannies or New Age hippies, and Holly struck her as being more of the latter than the former, what with her straight blonde hair and lavender scrubs. Did she chant and pray? Sprinkle herbs all over the room? Holly didn't act like a hippie, but how could you be sure she wasn't a hippie in disguise?

That first time, Denise had started to work the stirrups into the table, wending them in with a clank here and there, before Holly cut her off.

"That's okay. You can put those things down."

What things? These things? But you had to have 'em! Couldn't see otherwise, if those legs weren't all the way up there! Need that high visibility and those high legs for the baby to get out!

"This won't be a heavy-metal birth," Holly said. "Let's keep this real low-tech. I don't need those stirrups."

Heavy-metal? Low-tech? Denise shrugged. "Whatever you say, ma'am." And dropped the stirrups on a counter with a loud bang.

Holly got the lady to scoot down to the end of the table and bend her knees, which was how you delivered a lady by *accident*, when you didn't have time to *prepare*. Holly was setting up for an ad hoc birth. It was bizarro.

When Denise handed Holly the episiotomy scissors, for the cut on the perineum (the length of skin and muscle running from the vagina to the rectum), Holly shook her head. Emphatically no.

Denise double-checked. "You ain't going to cut a 'pis?"

"Not planning on it."

Denise watched the lady's perineum and willed a giant tear. She wanted her worst fears confirmed. Why? That was her instinct. She liked it when things were done the old way.

It was weird, the way Holly didn't even holler at the lady to push. To the contrary! Holly talked to the lady as if she were directing a car into a tight parking space.

"Easy. Easy now. Slow. Beautiful. Perfect." The baby slid out cautiously as if to avoid a crushed bumper to the rear, a smashed headlight to the front. "That's right. You got it now." No one in a hurry. This birth was like an old lady out for a Sunday spin in her 1962 Buick. To keep the metaphor going, it wasn't your normal cop-show action, with cars peeling out and skidding in, babies popping out of ejector seats, and sirens screeching.

This kind of birth had a strange sex appeal. It wasn't arousing at all, but it was closer to the way the lady had probably gotten pregnant in the first place—more of a soul ballad than a heavy-metal number. Drawn out and smooth and gentle. Not wham-bam-thank-you-ma'am. It was weird. Mucho bizarro. It was nice.

Holly explained later that the word *lithotomy* literally means the removal of a kidney stone. In the nineteenth century, obstetricians borrowed the feet-in-stirrups posture that surgeons used when taking out kidney stones. When they took the position, they took the name as well. The prefix *litho* comes from the Greek and means stone. The only other time the prefix is used in English is in the word *lithography*, the printing process that involves etching stone.

"I'm a midwife," Holly said. She was pontificating. "Whenever feasible, I don't remove stones. Stones have lousy Apgar scores. Stones mess up our outcome stats. Stones are boring. They aren't cute. That's why I don't like to deliver my patients in the stone-removal position. I like babies, and I don't like stones."

"You goofing me?" Denise said, studying Holly warily. Holly was proving to be a more consummate flake than Denise had dreamed possible.

"Maybe," Holly said.

The lithotomy position has its benefits. Once the baby has crowned, you can get him out in a hurry. Holly uses the position in about one out of twelve births, when the baby is in trouble.

"But it's not really convenient otherwise," Holly had explained to Denise. When Holly snags a possible midwifery convert, she doesn't let go. It's less missionary zeal and more a law of survival. Midwives need all the support they can manage to scare up. "The birth canal is shaped like a *J*. The baby moves down, then up again at the end."

The curve of Carus, it's called: the birth canal as cylinder through which a baby struggles to be born. "Birth is uphill as it is, without stirrups complicating matters, tensing up a lady with all that cold steel, wreaking havoc on her varicose veins, putting all the weight on her belly, crushing the major aorta behind the uterus. Need I go on?" Maybe Denise didn't need her to, but Holly needed to. "You can't deliver in stirrups without cutting an episiotomy or letting the lady tear pretty bad."

"But everyone here gets a 'pis, anyway," Denise said.

"Not my ladies," Holly answered pointedly, self-righteously.

It was the first time it had occurred to Denise that birth without an episiotomy was possible.

What else did you learn from Holly? Denise asks herself now, as she is about to catch a baby herself. To glove up. That's always a good idea. A sign, taped to a supply cabinet, reads: "Nobody ordered infection. Wash hands frequently and well." Of course, it's written in the commanding hand of Sparks, the head nurse, who tries to leave her mark in some way or another in every room on the floor.

Denise pulls on a pair of size fives just as her mind registers what her eyes picked up a moment before. A baby's head. The dark coils of a black baby being born.

"I'm burning down there!" Lelia cries. "What's happening?"

"You're s'posed to burn! Hang on! Almost done!"

Denise cups the baby's head, in case it shoots out like a cannon shot. "There's a scrunched-up little prune face here." The baby's head pushes out. Christ, can he move! Strong little bugger! The face is downward, pursed lips and puffy eyes, considering his next move. He rotates forty-five degrees in what seems like slow motion, Denise's hand pressed lightly on the crown of his head. She's scared that if she applies too much pressure, he'll stop. He won't turn. He won't come out. His shoulders will stick. He'll wither away and die on her.

It's a slow spin in external rotation, but the baby grinds to a halt. Ready to be born. Denise has seen this a thousand times, but now she doesn't know how to get the baby out. Holly doesn't like it when the ladies push now—she likes to control the delivery—but Denise doesn't know how to proceed. She just wants to catch the baby now. She's not into style. She's not going to control it, anyway, no matter what she does.

"Push, Lelia, honey! Push!"

With a grunt and a face crunched up with effort, Lelia bears down, her thick, white-skinned heels tearing the sterile paper below her. With a gush of fluid and a spurt of blood, the baby slips out into Denise's hands. She's had one hand on the head and another hand on a shoulder, and now the whole goddamn thing is in her two hands. A boy.

"Shoot, I didn't check for the loop-de-loop," Denise says aloud. Terror object number one for expectant moms. The cord around the baby's neck. But a nuchal cord is one thing even a diploma nurse like Denise can finesse. Just whisk the thing over the head. About a third of all babies have the umbilical cord around their necks. But Denise lucked out. Lelia Butler's baby's neck was free.

Denise looks up at the peeling plaster on the ceiling. "Thank you, Lord," she says quickly, then looks back down at the slippery, extravagant bit of protoplasm in her hands.

"Shoot, he's here!" She wipes his face, keeping him in her arms in a football hold. But he's not saying anything. She suctions his mouth and nasal passages with a bulb syringe. Denise wants to hear big noise from this baby. A loud baby cry. "A lusty cry," she says out loud, then turns him over and whacks his bottom. This isn't standard operating procedure anymore, but more than she wants to do things right, she wants to hear the kid hollering.

"Let me see!" cries Lelia.

And the baby screams.

"It's here!" Denise says again, in disbelief.

"It's a girl, isn't it?"

Not with those huge, hormone-pumped testicles.

"Good Lord, I hope not!" Denise says, laughing. "Check this!" And points at the baby's genitals.

"He's so big!" Lelia says, with a hoot, pointing.

"You have two boys at home. You've seen this before. You know they're big when they're first born."

Denise wraps the baby in a receiving blanket, and Lelia starts to laugh as she takes him in her arms. Denise works a little receiving cap, which looks like a ski cap for a doll, onto his head. The DR is cooler than the labor rooms, and the little babies get cold. They burn calories at a manic rate and can lose two hundred kilocalories in a minute in their effort to stay warm. A newborn baby really cooks. The nervous system grabs for the deposits of brown fat found on the baby's back, which is the anatomical parallel of cheap fossil fuel: it's readily available and burns fast. The baby also has stores of white fat, the adipose tissue in such great supply in the adult world, but it's higher quality fuel that takes a longer time to metabolize. No matter how much milk a baby drinks, he'll be a few pounds lighter after delivery than he was at birth. In part, the weight loss represents the excretion of fluids that have saturated his water-logged body, but mainly it's the reserves of fat burned up as the baby keeps stoked during his first days in the cold world.

The receiving caps are the innovation of the year. Morrison Hospital has at last drawn the universally recognized conclusion that body heat is lost when the head goes uncovered—and decided that this principle might apply to infants as well. As Denise said to Holly, "No shit, Sherlock." The caps are this year's fashion statement, an accessory to increase each baby's lovability quotient. All babies, even the homely, gray-colored ones, look jaunty and comical wearing them.

The two women gurgle with laughter as they admire the baby. Black women who did it by themselves.

"He's so white!" Lelia says.

"Not for long. That's just the goo he's covered with in the womb so he doesn't pucker up too prunelike."

Vernix could be bottled and marketed as the world's most effective body lotion. It's a sealant, a natural Scotchguard, to keep a baby from becoming completely water-logged. Postdates babies are usually particularly ugly, as the vernix, not designed to last longer than forty-two weeks gestation, has shed off before birth, leaving the babies more puckered, wrinkled, and unappetizing-looking than the average one-minute-old neonate.

"Just wait till you put him in the sun and let the pigmentation rise," Denise tells Lelia. "He'll be a good-looking black fellow." She addresses the baby: "You'll be the first black president in America."

"A black president from Brooklyn?" Lelia asks softly, staring at her baby to discover these invisible properties and possibilities.

"Little acorns, big oaks. All that business. Somebody's got to do it. And I delivered him."

Denise pulls off the baby-blue paper draping around Lelia's hips and thighs and slips a fresh Chux pad under her bottom. The placenta slips out just as she's crumpling up the old paper. Plop. Right onto the table. A fat piece of liver.

"Well, that's over," Lelia says, lifting her head and peering between her legs. "Good riddance."

The baby's umbilical cord is no longer attached to Lelia Butler but is now attached strictly to this red blob of veins and glossy tissue. There's a little rush of blood out of Lelia's stretched-out vagina, and when the possibility of hemorrhage occurs to Denise, she wills the blood to stop. It stops.

She studies the placenta, looking for any holes that mean bits have been left behind in the uterus, and puts a hand on Lelia's abdomen, massaging it, stimulating it. The abdomen hardens in a contraction, and Denise glances up. The mesmerized Frances is staring mutely from the doorway. The multiple gestation in DR has its appeal, but a nurse delivering a baby gets points for sheer oddness.

"Stop your gaping, child," Denise calls. She's tired, suddenly, of being on her own. She is scared for what might have happened and what might happen yet. "Go find somebody who knows something about something. Go tell somebody I just delivered a baby."

CHAPTER 7

"Well, this is a fitting end to the hyperstimulation that started the evening off with a bang," Holly tells Levy.

"What do you mean?"

"I mean, if there was a woman at risk for hemorrhage, it'd be the hyped multip. Uterine atony. Maybe you've heard of it. An overworked uterus that has bopped till it's dropped."

"No need to get testy, Treadwell."

"Merely an acknowledgment of the importance of teamwork. That doctors have their place in a hospital setting at certain moments. I begged you to give me Butler, but you gave Butler to Scott. Where was he when Butler was about to bleed out?"

"What was the EBL?" Levy asks. Estimated blood loss, that is. "Butler didn't bleed out, right?"

"Levy, that's not the point and you know it."

He scratches his head, and the grating sound of the scratch irritates Holly. She is ready to snap and takes a deep breath, then exhales. Lamaze in professional relationships. Breathing to divert her mind from the source of her discomfort.

Levy sighs, then yawns. "Scott's a little absentminded."

"Scott's more than a little absentminded. Scott's *absent*."

Holly hip-checks the locker room door open. It's six in the morning, time for morning rounds, but Holly will first sneak a cigarette. Cigarettes are a perversity. They warp the midwifery ideal of self-help, of taking responsibility for one's own health. They flout responsible health care. They're less of an addiction than a bad habit, and when Holly smokes, she sips the nicotine as she'd sip a glass of whiskey. Consciously, with guilty pleasure.

30

The locker room is both calm and chaotic. Empty stethoscope boxes lie collapsed in the corners. Torn stockings hang from open locker doors. Dust-encrusted winter coats are abandoned in the bottom of lockers that belong to no one. Half-filled cans of soda and junked shoes are scattered on top of the lockers, unclaimed and forgotten. Memos written by the administration a year ago litter the linoleum floor, with a reminder to "double-glove" when handling hepatitis patients overlapping with an explanation of a change in retirement benefits. Both are smudged by footprints. The linoleum is cracked, with crevices revealing an unidentifiable black crust below. A bottle of Betadine microbicide, stained with drips that obliterate the label, stands on a shaky card table beneath a speckled mirror.

A photocopied cartoon of Snoopy atop his doghouse is taped to the mirror. The caption reads: "Your mother doesn't work here. Please clean up after yourself." Some well-intentioned or bossy hand—Sparks, probably—tacked it up a year ago, when it was read once by everybody, then promptly ignored.

The staff learns to ignore everything. They barely notice the locker room mess. And nobody is aware of the poster of gulls wheeling through a golden sunset or the close-up shot of a dewy daisy in soft focus that one day simply arrived on the locker room wall. Somebody in Administration had read about the morale-boosting, productivity-increasing effects of eye-pleasing surroundings and ordered the posters. But the posters have long since disappeared into the walls, as far as the staff is concerned.

Denise racewalks into the locker room. She wants her morning cigarette, too, and Holly passes her one.

"You're an honorary midwife now, Denise."

"How'd I do?"

"You did good. Next time, support the lady's perineum more, and she won't tear so bad."

Holly had delivered a primap over an intact perineum, without a skid mark on her, in Recovery, the only available space, and Frances had fetched her to the DR to stitch up Lelia Butler's few small tears. They were jagged little rips, like when you snag a sweater on a tree. Holly was tempted to let the tears heal up on their own and to advise Lelia to keep the perineum clean and sit on cold packs. But Morrison is a nest of infection, and you close up everything you can.

Scott turned up in the middle of the repair, and Holly didn't need to look up to know who hovered behind her, like a shadow, watching. She can recognize almost everyone on the floor now by the sound of their footsteps, and Scott has a distinctive shuffle.

"Forget it, medical student," she said, not looking up. "Everything's under control now."

Scott hovered a few seconds longer, then pivoted soundlessly out the door. The rebuffed sightseer had lost his patient by default.

If Levy is the quintessentially meddlesome obstetrician, Scott is the extreme in hands-off care. Holly feels as if she's running from one end of a seesaw to the other, trying to get it all balanced out. A futile pursuit.

She inhales her cigarette and starts to explain fundamental hand skills to Denise. "You put your right below and keep it there until the baby's head is out. You'll do better next time."

"Next time!" Denise says with a snort. "There isn't going to be a next time!"

"Sweetheart, you're an OB nurse. There'll be a next time, believe you me."

Holly drags on the cigarette and lies down on the card table, which feels just right under her back, as if it were built to support tired midwives. She touches the keys that dangle from a safety pin clipped to her shift right above her chest and makes sure they're all there: the key to the nurse-midwifery office; Sono; the narcotic chest, where all the hard-core drugs are kept; the locked cabinet with the hypodermic needles.

"There'll be a next time," Holly says again. "No doubt about it." She props herself up and sits on the edge of the card table. "Ever think of becoming a midwife?" she asks Denise with the forced casualness she always uses when she doesn't want to scare off a flighty character by a direct approach.

"Why do you ask?" Denise says, startled. "Just because I birthed one itsy-bitsy baby?"

"How do you think I started?" Holly asks.

"Like this?"

"Like that." And Holly snaps her fingers.

CHAPTER 8

It had been Holly's first year as a maternity nurse in a private hospital in Manhattan. She'd tried to get into the combined RN/midwifery program at Yale but hadn't made it. The way to become a midwife, then, was for Holly to do an RN program—at the University of Pennsylvania—then hit the maternity wards for a couple of years before applying to nurse-midwifery programs, the best of which required two years' labor and delivery experience.

Holly wasn't at all sure she wanted to become a midwife. Maternity sickness was a happy field, everyone said, with hardly any sickness and almost no death. In maternity care, everyone whistled and sang happy tunes. But Holly had vague ideas of joining the Peace Corps or a public health program, of traveling to distant lands, heading into the bush, saving little African children. She was twenty-three years old, and she didn't know what she wanted to do. She was just marking time in the maternity ward.

It was the Fourth of July, and fireworks were blasted off in New York Harbor. Tall ships sailed and motored up rivers dimpled with trash. The city seemed to have emptied out, removed itself from the middle of Manhattan to gather at the end of the island, where a mass of New Yorkers simultaneously gazed at and created the spectacle.

In the midst of the crowd, an obstetrician elbowed his way through the huddled masses. His beeper had beeped, his wife was frowning, and his kids looked peckish. He pushed away to try to flag down a cab, to get to the hospital to deliver a baby. Cabs were on the streets, but they were all parked and locked, the drivers having abandoned them to join in the event, so the doctor scurried into a subway station. He hadn't taken a subway for years, maybe decades, and when he got on a train, he found it was taking him for an express ride in the opposite direction from the hospital. For the first time in recent history, the obstetrician had gone to Brooklyn.

Holly had come into the hospital at six o'clock. Earlier, she'd been at a barbecue on Long Island, at an uncle's house. When she'd had to leave, everyone had made loud, not-really-funny jokes about it. "Can't those babies wait until tomorrow? Don't those pregnant ladies ever give you a moment's peace?"

They can't and they don't.

The hospital had two delivery rooms—one with a window and the other without. It was the delivery room without a window where Holly would catch her first baby, thus setting a dangerous precedent. She was fated to deliver in rooms without views. It was unfair, on this night, because the scene would have benefited from the drama of fireworks exploding as the baby entered the world, squalling as babies do in movies, perfect blossoms of cascading fireworks lighting up the night sky.

The camera could move in for a reaction shot of Holly's radiant face—she'd look like a young Ingrid Bergman—as she makes the decision of her life. The look of a brainstorm, a moment of illumination, would flicker over her face. "That's it, by gum! I'll become a midwife! For sure!" Then more footage of the fireworks and soft focus on the trinity of mother, child, and Holly Treadwell, midwife-to-be.

Destiny is clumsier than that.

The air-conditioning was lame, and the air seemed to limp. Both Holly and Mrs. Strasser were slick with sweat, and Holly's object was to prevent Mrs. Strasser from giving birth, which is much harder than actually delivering a baby.

"Keep your legs together, Mrs. Strasser. Pant!"

Mrs. Strasser panted so much, it seemed probable that she'd pass out before the baby was born. Holly loomed over her, shouting, "Pant like a dog!" and panted along with her: huh huh huh huh huh. Mrs. Strasser was an admirable rapid-shallow-breather. Holly wondered if she'd hyperventilated a lot in her past; she seemed practiced.

"Just pant through the contractions, Mrs. Strasser!"

But Mrs. Strasser didn't respond. She was panting in earnest. Unstoppably! Maybe she *was* hyperventilating! Holly looked around the room for a brown paper bag—or a white paper bag—how about a plastic bag? Then imagined the next day's newspaper headlines: DISGRUNTLED NURSE SMOTHERS MOM, BABY. The Saran Wrap Murders.

Holly pushed Mrs. Strasser's thighs together. "Take a deep cleansing breath, Mrs. Strasser!"

Mrs. Strasser opened the eyes she'd clenched shut. Every fiber of her being was strained to let go, to push. She was living a physical paradox, holding the baby in, and she was concentrating on the sound of her own panting so she wouldn't go crazy.

"I'll breathe only when you let go of my legs," Mrs. Strasser said, enraged.

Holly let go. Clamping Mrs. Strasser's thighs together with her hands was the most unnatural act she'd ever performed. I don't want to do this again, she thought, not ever.

Mrs. Strasser had wanted her to let go, but now that Holly had, she looked scared. She was a pretty woman, with rich chestnut hair and a smooth, marble-complexioned face, but her forehead was wrinkled up now and considerably shortened in length, as though gathered by a string pulled in the center. Mrs. Strasser opened her eyes wide and cried, "The baby's coming!"

In a world of fluctuating variables and shifting values, the one sure thing is that when a woman says, "The baby's coming," the baby is coming. When a woman says this phrase or expresses a similar sentiment, give her space, cup your hands, and prepare to catch. Take off your shirt or jacket: the baby will need to be swaddled. "The baby's coming" means a kid is about to exit the intrauterine environment for the extrauterine world, and no matter how tightly the mother clenches her thighs, or how strenuously she pants or wills the baby back, a force of nature is unleashed. Baby as unstoppable force.

Holly briefly wondered what would happen if she stood Mrs. Strasser on her head. Would the baby slide back in? An idea borne of desperation. An inversion that would constitute the medical equivalent of a black mass.

A nurse trotted in to cannibalize the room's supplies. These were the old days of medical marketing, when there were no prepacked OB kits, with delivery drapes and cord clamps all together in one convenient place. Even after the introduction of these self-contained units, nurses tore around, pivoting and lunging for some essential item that the doctor had managed to drop on the floor.

"Sharon!" Holly almost shouted. "Isn't there a resident around?" In those days, Holly rarely bothered to whisper or lower her voice, as if patients were impervious to the hospital business swirling around them.

"He's in a labor room, which is where I'm going," Sharon said, spinning out of the room.

"Labor room?"

"It's zooey out here, Holly. We're delivering in two labor rooms at once."

"The resident must have long arms to deliver in two rooms at once," Holly said to Mrs. Strasser, joking.

Mrs. Strasser didn't laugh.

"Okay," Holly said. "You're here now." She considered what was happening. "I guess you want a baby out of the deal." And she lifted Mrs. Strasser's feet up to the stirrups.

Holly hadn't prepared Mrs. Strasser earlier because she hadn't wanted to open her legs. But Holly began now, dousing the shaved pubic area with Betadine, which dropped like bloodstains onto the sterile field below. She swabbed Mrs. Strasser's thighs with zigzag strokes, tossing four-by-four gauze pads to the floor as she finished. Then she saw the baby's head at the vaginal outlet. The part of the baby's head that she could see was the size of a quarter, but it was there, and without thinking, Holly took Mrs. Strasser's feet out of the stirrups and pressed her legs together, flashing on the story of King Canute she'd read as a kid—the medieval king who claimed his divine power could stop the ocean tide. She remembered the illustration: the old king standing waist-high in the ocean. The tide didn't let up for him, and this tide wouldn't let up for Holly either. It was engineered by nature's power. It had to come. Forget the Betadine. At this point, it would only stain the baby's head brown.

"Put your legs up and your feet in here." Holly cracked open a package of sterile leggings, but then let them fall to the floor. This was birth during wartime.

"Don't worry," she told Mrs. Strasser doubtfully. "I'm right here."

Catastrophes erupted in Holly's mind. Shoulder dystocia, with the kid's shoulder stuck inside. Hydrocephaly, with the kid's head too big to get out. Undiagnosed twins. Third-degree tears on the perineum. Spina bifida. And her own clumsiness. Don't drop the baby. That was the first rule. Headline news: NURSE DROPS BABY. UTERUS FOLLOWS.

"When you feel like pushing, push," Holly said. "But don't do anything rash."

By anything rash, she meant actually letting the baby out.

Mrs. Strasser wouldn't do anything rash. She wasn't in any great hurry to let the baby fall into the hands of an untried nurse.

Noise drifted in from the DR across the hall. Over there, they not only had a view of the fireworks but what sounded like gangs, mobs, masses of people. Loud voices chanted, like rowdy voices at a football game. Hopped up. Aggressive. Eyes trained to the finish line. "Come on! You can do it! Push! Push!"

Holly felt like she was at the wrong New Year's Eve party. The real fun was next door; here there was just awful, silent waiting. If the other delivery room was a football game, this was a yoga class. The two women concentrated quietly, almost meditatively. Mrs. Strasser didn't seem to be the stoic type, but Holly had never seen a woman deliver with so little fuss and noise. She gave a solid, low grunt, and the round of the baby's head pushed out. It was slicked-back hair, like patent leather in the DR light, and it retreated as if the baby, like all babies, had suffered a change of heart: "Nope, not going out there. I'll stay here, inside."

"He's ready now," Holly called, despite appearances to the contrary. "He's coming now."

The baby's head turned, rotating, and then the entire head popped out, the color of the moon. A spurt of blood. Mrs. Strasser had torn. Damn, Holly should have cut an episiotomy! Never mind that she didn't know how! How hard could it be to pick up the scissors and make a snip on the perineum? An episiotomy wasn't a major operation, but a simple incision, like trimming your bangs.

Holly's mind darted about, chasing down the procedures of delivery. With the bulb syringe lying on the tray at the foot of the delivery table, she sucked out the fluid trapped in the baby's nose and throat—mucus and amniotic fluid absorbed on the trip out. There was no sign of meconium—no green clumps or fluid—which might have meant some degree of infant compromise. A baby passes meconium, its first stool, when suddenly deprived of oxygen. But there had been good oxygen and no meconium.

Go on, Treadwell.

The baby's head was out—the largest part of the body. That huge head is way out of proportion—one-third of the baby's body. For a six-foot-tall man to have such a big head, his face would have to be two feet long. Not a pretty sight.

In true obstetrical fashion, Holly tossed the bulb syringe on the floor. Let someone else take care of the niceties; I'm doing important work here. She got both hands on the baby's back and chest and pulled the baby down, then up, in a sort of arc. A bird-flight in miniature, as she lifted and swooped the baby into life.

She almost said aloud: "I didn't drop him."

Don't pull the cord, Treadwell.

Mrs. Strasser stretched out her arms, sitting up to get at her baby.

"Your legs," Holly said. She eased one of Mrs. Strasser's feet out of the stirrups, then the other. The thought crossed her mind: "You're not a patient now, Mrs. Strasser. You're a mother."

A baby boy. The purest object in the universe. What made him really brilliant was that he was breathing, which was even more important than the fact that she hadn't dropped him. He wasn't bluish in the slightest, not even around the edges.

Mrs. Strasser cried, relieved that Holly hadn't dropped the baby, that she'd managed to bring the baby out safely. But Mrs. Strasser was crying mainly because she was happy. Her baby was born, and she loved him already and always would. Even if he went berserk as he grew older and mugged old ladies or committed high treason or embezzled company funds, she'd love him anyway.

Now here he was, the blank slate whose first knowledge of the world was Holly's gloved hands and the sea-green walls of the delivery room. Holly felt a sense of loss because he was not her baby, although she felt as though he ought to be by now. She was tempted to give in and cry with Mrs. Strasser, out of sheer relief, and a flood of tension exploded, released, through her back and shoulders. But she resisted, not being a crier. Then she cried.

"Gosh, he's cute!" Holly said, drying the baby off with a towel. Holly was in love. Usual hospital procedure was to cut the cord immediately after delivery, race the baby to the radiant heater, dry him off, wrap him up, and lower him into a portable Isolette to be shunted off to the hothouse confines of the nursery. The doc would wave the baby over the mother's face before whisking him away, so she could track her baby as she'd follow the path of a shooting star: an exhilarating, exasperating vision, a baby as a gorgeous, inaccessible thing. But standard operating procedure wasn't in force. This was a holiday birthing, skeleton-staff style.

When she hadn't had time to think, she couldn't entertain doubts. But now her uncertainty built into a limited form of panic. She'd digressed from routine, and any deviation from standard procedure struck her as risky. She had the faith of youth in institutions: authority knew what it was doing, and institutions, being privy to wisdom higher than her own, had to know more than she did. Protocols, like the quick cutting of the cord, must have been drawn up after stringent research and long contemplation of the facts and arrived at through logic that couldn't be successfully challenged by someone like a nurse.

Which is why Holly became terrified when she realized she'd broken protocol by not yet cutting the cord. How dangerous was it to delay cord-clamping? Many docs snipped the cord before the shoulders were delivered—Holly had let three minutes pass. She lunged for the cord clamps on the delivery tray, little plastic things that looked like clothes-pins with serrated edges, and snapped the suckers on, putting a lock on the coiling umbilical cord, which was as translucent as mother-of-pearl. She stared hard at what she'd done. Were they in the right place? Too close to the baby? Too far?

Holly doubted everything now, sure of nothing. But she didn't want a doc barging in to save her. Now that she'd delivered the baby, she felt this was her territory—nobody had the right to trespass now. She didn't want to be relegated to competent but essentially irresponsible nurse, scurrying around to follow a doctor's orders like a well-trained higher primate.

And she'd discovered she was tired of the way the boys started up with all their loud boys' stuff. That's how she thought of it. Boys' stuff. Hearty laughter. Backslapping jokes. It was odd, because she'd always liked boys' stuff. She had two brothers, and as a kid she'd always tramped around with the guys, and kept up with them, too. She'd always liked being where the boys are.

But now she didn't want the boys roughhousing with something like childbirth. Enough hue and cry, as if everyone had to imitate kettle drums, cymbals, and tubas for a birth to come out right. Suddenly, as when Denise saw Holly deliver for the first time, Holly viewed birth as a romantic thing.

You're turning into a gentle-birth person, Treadwell.

That gentle-birth stuff was babyish coddling. Sissy and mushy. It was malarkey. But it made sense. It was rational. You couldn't be in favor of birth without violence until you saw a violent birth. And you couldn't see the violence of those births until you'd seen a birth without violence.

Holly saw her first birth without violence by accident, and she was responsible for its gentleness.

Mrs. Strasser's OB walked in, wilted from the heat, face gleaming with sweat from his romp on the subway through the Fourth of July night. "What have we here! A baby! And a boy to boot!" He gave a job-well-done slap somewhere between her shoulder blades and rear end, and flashed her a wink. Holly smiled back, which was how any good-natured nurse without a feminist chip on her shoulder responded in those days.

But as she smiled, what she thought was, "Who's going to sign the birth certificate for this baby? Who delivered him?"

She glanced across the hall into the DR with the window, which was now vacated and full of the remains of the delivery. The room looked like a slaughterhouse. Blood had dripped onto the floor, and the once-sterile blue fields of the drapes were crumpled on the table, where the mother had been, and stained with Betadine and blood. A curling piece of umbilical cord lay in a corner of the room. It had been essential, but now it was useless, lifeless garbage. It was trash. Holly stepped farther across the hall, straining to see fireworks. Fireworks would climax everything. Fireworks would make the day seem auspicious, prophetic, full of meaning.

Sharon passed by, and Holly grabbed her arm.

"Hey! Don't I have enough trouble without you attacking me?" Sharon said, jerking her arm away.

"If I did the delivery, who signs the birth certificate?" Holly asked urgently.

"Don't be a chowderhead, Holly. The attending signs it. Who else?"

"I don't know. I thought maybe..."

"You thought wrong."

"Christ, Sharon, if the doc signs the certificate, I'll feel like a ghostwriter or something. I supply the material. He gets the credit."

Sharon rolled her eyes. "How green are you? You were expecting what exactly? Wake up and welcome to the beautiful world of nursing. Don't be a sucker-chump. If you don't like it, become a midwife."

"A midwife?"

The moment of illumination. The fevered brainstorm. Ingrid Bergman beatified, as played by Holly Treadwell.

"Yeah, a midwife," Sharon said. "Then you can write out as many birth certificates as you have babies. In the meantime, let go of me, will you?"

Holly leaned against a supplies cabinet in the vacated DR. The New York City sky glowed its peculiar shade of orange: the color of an average city night as pollution trapped the reflection of millions of lights and the light collected in an orange haze. The fireworks were over.

Don't be a sucker-chump. The doc was the legal author of the delivery. Holly was the ghostwriter who couldn't take any credit, but she wouldn't take any blame either. Besides, the attending had to stitch up the tear she'd caused by her inexperience. If she'd known how to cut an episiotomy . . .

Holly remembered that in some states, the person who cuts the cord is legally the person who delivers the baby. Holly hadn't cut the cord. The attending had, handing her the cord without ceremony for disposal. Just pretend that New York is one of those states, Holly told herself. But the tactic didn't work. She couldn't fool herself. She'd delivered the baby, and she knew it.

Holly backed out of the delivery room, but as she turned, she could see through the little window in the scrub room, off to the side. A rocket of sparks filled the sky and spiraled down. The fireworks weren't over, only shooting up and tumbling down from a different angle, arcing from another point of entry.

Now there's a decent omen, Holly told herself, and swung back into the DR across the hall to play the role of nurse.

A year later, when she applied to midwifery school, a nurse asked her why she wanted to become a midwife. "I want to write birth certificates," she said. "That's what midwives do."

CHAPTER 9

Denise doesn't take too well to the idea of becoming a midwife. She laughs in Holly's face; she smacks her thighs with her hands. "You want me to bust my chops, get paid pitifully, take truckloads of grief, and be despised by one and all?"

Holly looks injured. "It doesn't have to be that way. Who despises me? You? Lelia Butler? Not even Levy hates me."

"That's because he's after your white ass."

"And even if you were a midwife, he'd like you because of your black ass." Holly considers the problem of being in a professional minority. Then she says, "It's true that when you're a midwife, you have to earn your friendships. Pull teeth to get some respect. You have to be a stubborn cuss, but you're a stubborn cuss to start with—it comes naturally. You're a fighter. And I do mean that as a compliment."

Denise looked up shyly. "My mother would have a fit if I became a midwife," she says, looking down again and shaking her head.

"How come?"

"Midwives are—you know, they're old timey. They're for Southern trash, y'know."

Holly sits up on the card table, dangling her legs over the table's edge, and taps Denise's hand. "My mom had a fit. Everyone's does. Pam's mother is first-generation Irish. She still won't tell her friends what Pam does, because midwives are old country—ignorant crones only poor relations used. Midwives are from poverty city. From hunger. Everything Pam's grandparents came to America to escape. But now is now. Doctors may be the great American dream, but they're only a dream.

"And as for the granny midwives, the old-timey black ladies from down South are part of the nurse-midwives' heritage. We respect them more than anyone else. They birthed babies as a calling, a vocation, out of

41

compassion and charity and duty. And they did it well. They had faith in nature. They had faith in God."

Grannies knew how to handle breeches without sonograms, how to deliver twins without transforming it into a Madison Square Garden event. An old granny had impressed the importance of ambulation in labor when she told Holly at the nurse-midwives' convention she attended as a student, "I keep the ladies stirring. Keep them moving! And the babies will come out."

"Grannies provided health care when nobody else would," Holly tells Denise.

"That's the point, Holly," Denise says. "Midwives are from the bad old days when there weren't any hospitals. My grandma went to the hospital to deliver my mother, and they turned her away. She had to walk the five miles back home with my granddad. She had to deliver at home because she was just a black dirt farmer, not because she wanted to. Nobody wants to remember the bad old days when all there were were midwives."

"Are these the good new days for black women, then?" Holly asks. "If your grandmother were giving birth to your mom today, she'd be admitted to Morrison Hospital. What a privilege! Are these the good old days?"

Denise shakes her head and smiles. "What days are going to be good for black women anywhere?"

"One never knows, do one?" says Holly, sliding off the card table. She points a finger at Denise. "Midwifery wants you."

"I don't know why." Denise leans against the window and watches the dark day crack into a gray-blue color, a thin strip of orange dawn chopped off by the hulking bulk of Morrison's other buildings. Down a sidestreet, a car's engine roars to turn over in the cold morning air but fails to catch, and the roar dies out. "Why does midwifery want me?" she asks.

"You're prime midwifery material. You're bright. You're bored with what you're doing. You don't want to wind up twenty years from now in the same place you are now. You're aggravated. You don't want goons like Scott delivering women like Lelia. You're secretly a nice person. You care about the patients and have a good rapport with them. You get a kick out of catching babies. You think it's cool."

"Anything else?" Denise says, laughing nervously. She can handle flattery from men, accept it, toss it back and play with it like a thrown Frisbee, but a genuine compliment is more like a swarm of midges. It makes her uneasy—something to swat at and run away from.

"That's enough for one shot," Holly says, tossing her cigarette butt into an old Coke can in a corner.

"How come there aren't more black midwives anyway? How come all of you are such a white-bread crew?"

Holly scratches her head. "I guess black women who want to go into obstetrics figure that if they climb another rung of the upward-mobility ladder, they might as well go on to medical school. Maybe there hasn't been enough recruiting of black talent. I don't know. You tell me."

"Maybe they don't want to walk into another heavy case," Denise says. "Maybe they're tired of people assuming they're inferior so they have to prove them wrong, like the midwives have to do with the docs. Maybe they're tired of the same old shit."

"Maybe so." Holly sighs as they step out into the corridor. "Maybe the midwives' motto should be 'Proving It!' At least it's better than the docs' unofficial motto."

"What's that?"

"*Primum non nocere.*"

"Translation?"

"First do no harm."

"Bust that," says Denise.

"See, you're a born midwife."

"You're a con artist."

"I'm not a con artist," Holly says, frowning. "When you're a midwife, you'll see what I mean. This is evangelism. Pass the ammunition."

"Sounds like war to me," says Denise.

"Yeah, but you knew that already."

CHAPTER 10

Morning rounds take place at dawn. The postpartum floor is on six, which is Holly's neighborhood but not her home. The ward is old-style: rows of beds separated by half-drawn curtains.

This morning, two young girls sit together on a bed, cross-legged in pink nightgowns, fixing each other's hair, giggling. They're mothers.

All these patients have to be papered—given brochures on postpartum care, breast-feeding, maintenance of a circumcised infant—and taught—verbally walked through the brochures' contents. Nobody gets out without being papered and taught.

A young girl scuffles down the hallway on her way to the bathroom, wearing her hospital gown and cobalt blue socks.

"Oh, mother! Mother!" a nurse calls out to her. It's against hospital regulations to walk around without slippers, and the hospital will supply a pair of olive-green foam numbers for women who don't have a pair of their own.

The girl in the cobalt blue socks keeps scuffling on, and the nurse shouts again, "Oh, mother!" At last she hollers, "Young lady! You, girl!"

The girl stops in her tracks, turning slowly. "You talking to me?"

"Of course I'm talking to you, young lady!"

"Damn, I didn't know *who* you were talking to!"

She's not more than sixteen years old. Why would someone call her "mother"? Holly wonders when the girl will take the leap and know inside that she is identifiably a mother. That will be the longest step.

Most of the mothers are still in bed. Their babies are born, and the mothers sleep soundly or fitfully, depending on whether they've been medicated or how hungry they are. The thought that they are mothers must weave through their dreams to wake them with the realization:

"Oh, I'm a mother." As Holly walks into a room on the postpartum ward, she sees women staring into the darkness, their eyes wide. "The baby is here," the eyes seem to say. But the baby isn't here, but elsewhere, in the nursery. The mother is left to lie awake in the dark and wait for morning, not sure if what she wants is her baby or breakfast.

Lelia Butler waves wearily to Holly as Holly finds Gloria Sanchez. Problem patient. Spiked a fever on Day One, as the first postpartum day is called. Now she's Day Eight, which is five too many days for her to spend at Morrison. Her hematocrit, the index to the percentage of red blood cells in her blood, is down to eighteen. Ladies don't leave Morrison with such a low 'crit—at least, not with physician consent. Now it's up to Holly to persuade Gloria Sanchez to accept a transfusion to up her flagging 'crit.

Gloria is awake, dressed, and sitting on a chair by her bed.

"How are you feeling today?"

Gloria shrugs, thin in her blue jeans and ready to go home. She has big brown eyes that she turns up to Holly in a doleful way. Her wings are clipped by her IV: ampicillin to combat the unknown infection.

"You're not having much fun, are you?" Holly asks, putting a foot on the bedstead. Ahhh. Her feet hurt at six-thirty in the morning.

"No. I'm not."

"A lot of people think that if you had a blood transfusion, you'd have the strength to get over your infection."

Gloria crosses her arms. "No way," she says, laughing in a low tone. "That blood it'll kill you."

"Naw, it'll help you get well."

Holly is too tired for this, to push against someone else's will. And after a minute's cajoling and consolation, she presses on. It's time for Morning Report.

The residents, midwives coming onto the day shift, and Holly meet with the chief resident in the OB conference room on Seven for the changing of the guard. The meeting is already under way by the time Holly swings into the room and shrinks into a chair toward the back. Her last mission of the day—to persuade Sanchez to accept a transfusion—has failed.

Levy is intoning about Butler. "Para three, BP normal, slight edematous lip, left labia a little soft." He glances up at the still-sleepy but relatively fresh-faced residents drinking coffee. "This was a nurse delivery, actually."

They all exchange looks of surprise. "Did she cut a 'pis?" one resident calls out.

"With cuticle scissors," another says.

They laugh, and Levy looks at Holly, expecting an indignant response in defense of Denise. It doesn't come. Holly is flipping through her Card-tex file, ready to report, and as she doesn't want to slip up in front of the residents, she doesn't care anymore about Butler's delivery. That's what she'd like Levy to think, at least.

"Baby was delivered without incident," he says, which is his way of coming to Denise's defense.

Holly reports, and then brings up Sanchez, reviewing the history in a quick, staccato way. They all know the story by now, because Sanchez is Day Eight and they have heard this particular story every morning for a week. Holly is obliged to run through it anyway. Protocol. "Problem patient. Day Eight. Spiking. On Sifoxin. Then Genta. Them Ampi. Last spike was one-oh-three point four. No uterine tenderness. Her crit down to eighteen. A few days ago, blood was ordered, but the offer was withdrawn."

"The offer was withdrawn?" the chief resident asks. He is Willard Sovern, and he is white faced, red nosed, and prematurely gray haired. Willard hides a lot, is into low visibility, but he asks questions at Morning Report.

"She refused transfusion at that time," Holly says. She wasn't even on at the time, and she glances for support at the midwives who have just come on duty.

"She thought she was going to go through with it, but then she refused and we didn't push her on it," one midwife says uneasily.

"Document that transfusion was advised but patient refused," Willard says to Holly.

"We were afraid to transfuse with the temp, because we wanted to see if there was a transfusion reaction," the other midwife adds.

Willard turns wearily to Holly. "She's not going to have the white blood cells to fight infection unless she's transfused, and the temperature isn't going to come down without the white blood cells. Fuck the transfusion reaction. Get some blood into her."

"I tried this morning, Willard," Holly says. "She's pretty adamant."

"Scare her pants off then," Willard says. "Tell her she's at death's door. Do we even have a working diagnosis for this thing?"

"The Sanchez baby has been in the nursery so long," a pediatrician pipes up, "they're going to promote her to head nurse."

"It was endometritis," Holly tells Willard. Holly doesn't like infections, because they rarely know exactly what it is. It could be endometritis or amnionitis, but the same thing happens, no matter what. One antibiotic after another is blasted into the system, and if one doesn't hit the infection, another is mustered into action.

"Oh, Christ," Willard says, lowering his face into his hands. "It's not endometritis without fundal tenderness."

"How about plain old childbed fever?" Levy asks.

"Care to document that, Levy?"

"If Holly puts her name to it, sure."

Everyone laughs.

"Let's look at her bloods today and decide later how we're going to get her crit up," Willard says. He is eager to go on, but Holly has an argument to make.

"We keep bleeding this woman. How's she going to get better if we bleed her every day? And she's going to lose all her veins if we keep pumping in the antibiotics."

"You have a better suggestion?"

"Get her two trays. Pump up her protein. She's malnourished."

Willard looks unimpressed. But he's impressed. "Fine," he says indulgently. "You get her two trays, and we're sure to beat childbed fever with an extra slice of bread. Are you finished now?"

"I'm finished now," says Holly, snapping her Card-tex shut.

CHAPTER 11

Holly is now wearing her Italian shoes, her sole purchase of the month. She can barely hold herself back from looking at her feet as she walks. They give her shivers of pleasure. She's about to push through the metal doors to the elevators when out of the corner of her eye she sees Crowley extending a birth certificate to Scott, for him to sign, and his long fingers double over to sign the thing. Lelia's baby. The Butler baby is officially born, now that a doctor's hand has put his seal to it.

When Holly made it to midwifery school, she did her clinical work in a hospital whose policy was that birth certificates were signed only by docs, which meant that midwife-managed births went unreported. The midwives need those absent statistics to defend their professional competence when questioned. Statistics make their case. If the charge runs that nurse-midwives aren't safe, the stats prove they are.

As a student, Holly was working toward the thirty births required for certification by the American College of Nurse-Midwives. One day, she managed a difficult labor with a long, tricky second stage, but she got a good baby out of the rough haul, and her instructor told her, "You done good, kid," and left her to mop up. Just as the placenta was being expelled, a resident scuffled into the DR, scrawled his name on the birth certificate held for him by a nurse, nodded at Holly as his acknowledgment of her efforts, then shuffled out again.

The nurse looked at Holly, shook her head, and tore the certificate in half, then ripped it again and again until nothing was left but bits of meaningless paper shredded on the ground. The nurse smiled, looking down at the litter. "Gee, Holly, something happened to that birth certificate," she said. "You'd better write out a new one."

"I guess I'd better," Holly said.

Because that's what midwives do.

CHAPTER 12

The slap of cool air feels good. The hospital starves her skin of fresh air. Even in the depths of Brooklyn, where houses turn the color of mud and coal dust, the mornings manage to smell fresh as the sky struggles to stay blue while huge clouds, sailing fast inland from the ocean, overtake it in bursts of white before passing on.

Morrison Hospital occupies about five acres of Brooklyn. None of the acres is green. This isn't the Brooklyn of quiet, shady streets lined with historic brownstones that catch the spillover of young professionals from Manhattan—the neighborhood where Holly's boyfriend lives. It's not the Brooklyn sprawling out in the farther reaches that achieves a respectable simulation of the suburbs, with one-family homes and well-tended lawns. This is urban nightmare Brooklyn. The kind of place where you don't want your car to blow out a tire at night. Where you check to make sure the windows are closed and the doors are locked. Where you mentally rehearse what you'd do if a maniac hovered over your windshield wielding a sledgehammer—you decide you'd find the nerve to mow him down without too much hesitation.

The physical plant has the grim look of a Soviet office building or the sooty look of an Industrial Age prison in a steel town, depending on the weather. Today it looks like a federal penitentiary or a particularly cruel orphanage. You half expect to see chimneys smoking, pig-iron bubbling, and chained men in gray uniforms trudging through the dusty yards with heavy burdens on their backs.

Morrison is known for its trauma unit—one of the city's best. If you are going to be shot in the stomach or clubbed on the head, you'd do well to be assaulted near Morrison and many people are. But if your plaint is less than major—say, a mysterious respiratory illness or a seizure

49

that has struck, abated, and requires investigation—a smart move is to keep driving and bypass Morrison.

Once, a television news reporter asked a hospital administrator, "Is it true that hospital workers refer to Morrison Hospital as Morbidity House?"

The administrator sat back in his seat, smoothed his thinning hair, and clasped his hands together in something resembling prayer. He had to compose himself to field a tough question like this. "Most hospitals do find themselves in receipt of affectionate nicknames. It's one way for our employees to express their emotional affiliation to their place of work."

Hospital employees express their emotional affiliation by going else-where for their own health care. They give birth at St. Vincent's, have hernias closed at Roosevelt, and go to New York Hospital for CAT scans. As an exception to the rule, one pediatrics nurse knowingly and willingly admitted herself to Morrison for not one, but three cesarean sections, thus shocking people who had previously considered themselves beyond shocking.

Out the gates, Holly swings around to look at the five massive buildings that make up the hospital. Out! Amidst the tenements are a few two-family homes, barricaded behind Cyclone fences and padlocked gates and signs warning of dangerous dogs. An old woman is at work in her tiny square of garden, picking up sticks in her slippers, a coat thrown over her nightgown. Her mangy and dangerous-looking dog eyes the stream of hospital employees who trudge past this armored truck of a house as its mistress studiously ignores them. Sparrows bob along chain-link fences and soot-covered cars, part of nature not even the city's abuses can repel, and birdsong percolates to the left and right from invisible sources.

As Holly watches the morning shift walk slowly to work, her step lightens as she walks the five blocks to the subway station. She feels an illogical sense of freedom, having captured the day for herself, as if she doesn't have to put in the same number of hours that the day staff does, those people who barrel and bully their way up the subway steps as she elbows her way down.

The subway to Manhattan, where Holly lives, is packed with Brooklynites on their way to jobs on Wall Street and in midtown. Young execs, athletic builds sheathed in well-cut suits, unlined faces revealing nothing but good humor, so bright-eyed and bushy-tailed as to be conspicuous, ostentatious, annoying, and impossible to reproach.

The other passengers are worn-out specimens of human nature, which makes Holly a little more comfortable. They wipe sleep from their eyes, doze off with their chins pressing into their chests or with their backs straight and only their eyelids dipping down, or yawn widely into the Ann Landers column in the *Daily News.* They look less fresh than Holly, who hasn't been to sleep since one o'clock yesterday. The giveaway that exposes Holly as less than fresh is the bits of mascara that have, during her shift, flaked off onto the uppermost stretches of her cheeks.

Their fatigue is barely wound up, but hers is keyed up in the extreme. They are creaky, cranky, and take the subway's fluorescent lights as a personal affront. Their exhaustion is all in their heads, unearned, a banal complaint, while her exhaustion is accomplished. New lives kick, cry, and sigh in Holly's wake. The chief thing is that Holly is on her way to bed, while they are taking a completely opposite direction on the same train.

Home, in Greenwich Village, is warm, silent, still. The morning sun lies in a flat horizontal strip across the living room carpet. The refrigerator hums. The harmless shrieks of kids too young for school drift up from the street. A half-drunk mug of coffee sits on the foyer table. Holly wonders if she should drink it and decides not to. Yesterday's coffee.

She slips out of her sweater and her blouse and into an extra-large T-shirt stolen from her boyfriend, Matt Daily. It smells like him, but Holly doesn't know what the smell is, exactly. The bed pulls at her with magnetic force. She is ready for sleep. But first it's time for *Donahue*. A debate on the need for, or needlessness of, most hysterectomies.

Holly would like to call in and testify. To the uteri plucked out, thrown away, women made barren in a minute flat. Testify to the doc she once knew who was supposed to do a tubal ligation but changed his mind and decided to do a hysterectomy. "Fibroids," he said, but really he wanted to do the hysterectomy so the resident bugging him for more surgery experience would lay off. Giving the kid a chance was easier than resisting.

"Those fibroid tumors will have to come out," the doctor says. The patient hears the word *tumor*, and her blood pressure shoots up as she counts the days to her imminent death. "If you say so, doctor," she says and shuts her eyes, and her uterus is gone for good.

Yes, Holly would like to bear witness.

"Is the caller there?" Donahue would shout, and Holly wouldn't waste time admiring Donahue's show.

"I'm a nurse-midwife," she'd say. "And this is what I've seen."

Donahue would pace the floor and say, "Keep it short. We don't have much time."

Holly would wax eloquent with an expressiveness that has escaped her until now as the doctors in the viewing audience would be reduced to tears, fall on their knees, plead forgiveness. When her eloquence had dried up, Holly would turn fierce. "You know, Phil, there's on OB we used to call the Pickpocket."

"By pocket, you mean womb?" Donahue would ask.

"That's right, Phil," Holly would say. "Sort of a double entendre, with the money connection, see."

But that's not empirical evidence. That would never do.

It's all a fantasy, and it pulls Holly down, with its particulars of sweet revenge, into sleep, the midwife's haven. Threads of sunlight run through the slats of the venetian blinds. She can smell Matt in the pillow. Why do men have their peculiar smells? Why does she like these smells? In the mysteries of life, she sleeps.

CHAPTER 13

The midwife who reports to Holly when Holly comes onto her shift is Katrina McLeod.

Katrina appeared at Morrison a year ago, as an Integration student. Integration is a residency in miniature: three months of clinical work to incorporate everything a nurse-midwifery student has learned in school. After Integration, the students take their boards to obtain—or to be denied—certification by the American College of Nurse-Midwives.

The core competency successfully navigated and negotiated in school is put to the hard-reality test under the supervision of a preceptor. As it happened, Holly was Katrina's preceptor, although she didn't want to be.

"Holly, be a sport. These students really keep you on your toes," said Pam, one of Holly's best friends among the midwives. "Inquiring minds want to know."

"I'm on my toes enough as it is. My mind inquires fine on its own."

"But we need more students to sucker into coming to work here. How many midwives do we lose every year? Two or three? We have to keep the pool stocked. Besides, a student for us is what a resident is to a hospital. Nearly unpaid slave labor. What more could you ask?"

Holly looked at Pam with suspicion. "You promise me she becomes my personal slave?"

"Sure. Why else be a preceptor?"

"I always wanted a slave," said Holly.

Katrina brought new meaning to the word *mousy*. Sneaky, quick-moving, and cute, in a rodentlike way. On a cold winter's night, she appeared wrapped up in what looked to be her grandmother's camel hair coat. In it, she was lost. Tiny little chin, tiny little nose, tiny little button-eyes poking out from thick brown bangs. The eyes worried Holly, as they were soulful and sensitive-looking. Holly wasn't sure if Seven-B had any openings for another thin-skinned midwife.

"You mean to stay then?" Holly said. "You didn't take one look at the locker room and decide to leave?"

"I'm not one for taking off."

"How come you're on Integration now, instead of in June or July?"

"I finished up last May, but my father was sick. I took off time to stay with him."

The explanation for the' troubled, soulful look in the eyes. But Holly didn't think she was supposed to get mushy about it. She was supposed to play crusty old salt with heart, the drill sergeant. Everyone she'd ever learned from played that role to the hilt, and now it was her turn to give it a try.

"I'm Holly Treadwell. You have the dubious privilege of working under my expertise. This is life in the trenches. Keep your eyes open and your head low. Watch out for flying bedpans." She squinted at Katrina. "I hope you're handy with IVs. We do a lot of work with IVs. Lots of lines here. And some of the residents are sort of... limited. Limited to the hunt-and-peck method of catheter insertion."

Holly was pleased with her tough-guy routine. She was actually pulling it off.

"I'm handy with an IV," Katrina said easily, surprising Holly by her confidence, which students aren't expected to have. They're supposed to be shy, nervous, grateful for a kind word. But Katrina pushed on, explaining, "I used to work in an NICU."

Holly is blindly admiring of anyone who works in neonatal intensive care. She can hardly bring herself to stick babies, and one benefit of being less than autonomous at Morrison is that she doesn't have to do basic neonatal care: PKU test, blood glucose. There are nurses to do that and pediatricians to do the rest. Holly has a hard time breathing within the confines of an NICU, where rows of Isolettes are filled with the most vulnerable creatures in the world, tiny babies who could drown in a teacup and who could, and do, drown in their own fluids.

Holly worked for a time in adult intensive care during nursing school. The patients died there when a flick of an eyelash became too much for them and gave them the last push over the edge. But even in an adult ICU, where life hung on the force of an eyelash, existence didn't seem as tenuous, as dependent upon the graces of an invisible, impossibly delicate balance, as it did in the NICU. To Holly, the hydrocephalic babies and three-pound premies seem as exposed and threatened as if they'd been left alone on a mountaintop in a cold wind. But more than any other humans, those babies make clear what's best about human nature: the incalculable will to live, a kind of forward-looking resilience.

As a nurse, Holly admires the NICU nurses for working in a place where everything is always on the brink. As a midwife, she admires their hands, which move quick and steady, like hands trained to dismantle bombs.

"After sticking the tinies, you'll be able to deal with the ladies here,

I'm sure," Holly said, returning to her drill sergeant act. "You can drive a truck through our patients' veins. Veins like the Holland Tunnel."

Katrina laughed politely, as a student should when her preceptor cracks a pathetic joke, while Holly briefly studied Katrina's hands. Holly doesn't have a distinct set of criteria to judge hands by, but she's always curious about another midwife's hands, just as a carpenter might be interested in another carpenter's tools. In the end, midwifery is a test of manual dexterity, a handicraft. Katrina's hands were chapped and red and her fingers stubby. They had been around the block.

Emboldened, Holly decided to hector Katrina. With hands like those, she could take it.

"Ground rules. You know more than the interns and medical students. You know more than the residents. But this is a covert war, guerrilla warfare. We're the guerrillas. We run in, do our thing, take off again." Holly's boss, Mrs. Gruener, who worked exclusively at the clinic on Howard Street, would be proud. This was what she'd told Holly many times before. "But if the docs find out how well we're doing in this war, they'll step up the offensive. And they're offensive enough as is."

More polite laughter from Holly's captive audience, and Holly paced up and down the locker room, surprised to find how natural it is to pace while hectoring. She forgave all her professors in college, who had hitherto struck her as pretentious and cornball. Pacing helped her hectoring's rhythm and forced her audience of one to keep her eyes fastened on her.

"The big rule is, you know more than all them dopes, but don't let them in on the fact. But the most vital rule is that you don't know half as much as I do. Now, maybe you've heard that we don't do groovy births here at Morrison. So leave your high expectations parked outside the door. No holistic or homeopathic or naturopathic or good-vibrations midwifery here. It doesn't survive in the Third World, which is where you now are. The last low-risk patient here was admitted before my time—in fact, the year I was born. The best we can hope for is a patient of questionable risk, for whom we run the high-risk protocol, *just to make sure*. The patient carries the burden of proving that she's low-risk. Hard for her to do when she's hitting transition and throwing up on your shoes. Did you happen to notice the birthing room when you came in?"

Katrina looked up. She had started knotting the tie on her scrubs, but the scrubs, the smallest issued by Morrison, were too big and gathered around her ankles. "Not the prettiest birthing room I've ever seen," Katrina said diplomatically.

"Don't worry about it. You'll never see it again. The room exists primarily for contagion control. We turf all the infectious hepatitis-B patients there. Maybe you noticed there's no mattress in there at present. That's infection control, too. A hepatitis patient bled out all over the bed, and some guys wearing uniforms borrowed from the Atomic Energy Commission—helmets, space boots—hauled the mattress to the incinerator. You got the picture, Katrina?"

"Sure."

Holly noticed that the green of the scrubs had reflected onto Katrina's face to make her look even more mousy and pale. "You can bring your own scrubs if you want," Holly said, lapsing into a normal tone of voice, a bit exhausted by the exertions of hectoring. "Green isn't everyone's color."

"Neither is lavender," Katrina said, glancing at Holly's scrubs.

Which is why Katrina brought new meaning to the word *mousy*. She looked it, but she didn't act it.

Katrina turned out to be a gifted but hardass midwife. She had principles, the hardest thing to integrate into her Integration at Morrison. She carried around a copy of *Midwifery: Heart and Hands*, an informal textbook for lay midwives, so she wouldn't lose touch with what a real midwife is all about. She didn't give two cents if anybody on the floor liked her or not. She never got impatient. She never seemed flustered. That's why Holly thought of her as a hardass. She was a better midwife than Holly in many ways. And one thing that seemed true of midwives was that each one thought she was the best. But here was a girl just as good as, if not better than (infinitely superior in starting IV lines) Holly was. If Holly hadn't liked Katrina, she'd have hated her.

Which is how Holly feels about her now.

"Holly, I have to leave early tomorrow. Can you come in an hour early and cover for me?"

"Say what?" Holly has a hard time seeing Katrina as an equal. She still feels as though she should act the crusty old drill sergeant routine—not let these greenhorns flake out or take off or blow away breezily when the mood strikes. As Holly's preceptor told her during her own Integration period, "Death is the only reason you won't be here."

"Death in the family?"

"No, your death," her instructor said.

"I have to go somewhere," Katrina says, dipping her head.

Putting her hand on her hip, Holly takes on what she believes is a doubtful expression, although the rest of the world might view it as a smirk. "Where, precisely?"

"I'm a paid model in a pelvic exam seminar for medical students."

"The one here in Brooklyn? The one organized by Leah Stern?"

"Yes. That's the one."

The pelvic exam seminar was an innovation, is a revelation. It's crisis intervention, the point being to better prepare medical students to perform pelvic exams before they actually go out and do their first exams on poor, relatively inarticulate women in hospitals like Morrison. Holly knows Leah Stern, who founded the seminar. The last time she talked with Leah, Leah had successfully offered it as an elective to a few medical students. "Some of the schools thought it would make a decent require-ment, but I don't want it to be a required course," she told Holly. "I don't want to deal with guys who don't want to be there."

But many of them want to be there.

Students dread doing their first exams. First and foremost, the pelvic exam is a sexually charged event. According to Leah, "Even at their best, med students tend to be competitive and anxious types to start with. The seminar's whole purpose is to let them learn how to do this without flipping out with anxiety. I've seen them faint, even at the seminar. When they do their first exam in a hospital, they're expected to be the knowledgeable doctor. If they don't know what they're doing, that's something they have to hide.

"In the meantime, they're so scared, they don't voluntarily talk to patients. So they don't know what kind of physical effect they have on a patient—a patient who doesn't feel she has a right to speak up or who speaks up so much you don't know what to believe. To reduce their own anxiety about examining naked women, they reduce the body to a thing. They purposely dehumanize both themselves and the patient.

"At the seminar, they don't have to pretend they know what they're doing. They can ask questions as they go along. And the models don't just lie there in numbed silence. They talk back, in specific terms. They don't figure the doctor knows best. They know what's supposed to hurt and what isn't. We have to start from hello-hello with some of these guys, teach them to maintain eye contact with the patient so that the patient doesn't misinterpret what's going on. That's hard for these guys. We teach them things midwives take for granted, like talking their way through the exam: now I'm examining the tissue and folds. Now I'm palpating the ovary, and it's nice and firm."

"What do you tell them about draping?" Holly had asked.

"Draping is another charged issue. We tell the guys—they're not all guys, actually—that draping should be up to the patient. But the guys feel as if they need the draping, particularly on the woman's lower half, so they can disconnect from the idea that they're examining a woman. And they hide behind it. But our models decide what they want to do for draping, and the students have to work with that. God, they look seasick when they start, these guys."

"They must go nuts when they examine someone they actually know," Holly said. "A classmate or something."

"It blows them away. But once that's over, they get comfortable. By the second class, they're a whole different breed of cat. What's great about the whole thing is that nurse-midwives are actually working role models for these guys. We really change the way they practice medicine."

"I like it that women who are supposed to be getting health care at a hospital like Morrison might not have to be reduced to the level of experimental guinea pigs for med students."

"That's the deal, Holly. That's the point."

When Holly learned how to do a pelvic exam, her midwifery program offered a pelvic seminar before any such thing existed. A week of anxious pelvics and of anxious pelvises: the students practiced on each other, giving one another speculum exams every evening for a week. Until the first night, Holly hadn't realized she'd have to examine her instructors, too. "I guess that really brings a professor down to earth," said Holly's boyfriend at the time. True.

She managed to avoid the instructor for the first few evenings. The first person Holly examined was a sweet-tempered classmate who said little and practiced visualization and relaxation techniques as Holly poked around inside her, staring for reference at the plastic pelvis that stood, dusty and grimy, on the radiator in the classroom. She thought she was doing all right until her hands suddenly lost all their bearings. Nothing felt right to her, and she had a moment of panic you sometimes feel in pitch darkness, the wild panic of momentary blindness. Holly's victim—er, her model—shut her eyes and did circular breathing.

The student who practiced on Holly was clumsy and rough and didn't improve even when Holly winced demonstratively. Keeping this exam in mind, Holly was even more hesitant and fearful the next time she practiced and kept asking the girl she was examining, "Are you all right? Am I hurting you?" Anxiety didn't help her hands.

"For God's sakes, Holly," her instructor said, hovering near her. "If you're scared of hurting someone, do what you're going to do, do it quickly, and get the hell out."

After the seminar, one of Holly's friends said, "Act like you know what you're doing. Even when I don't know what the hell I'm doing, I keep up a kind of professional manner and do the task and always wind up okay. It's like I bluff myself, and when I act more professional, I actually become more professional."

By the end of the week, Holly's hands had learned to see. She could fell the texture of the vaginal walls and understand the structure, palpate the Bartholin's glands and the ovaries, and visualize what size diaphragm each woman would use, if they were all to use a diaphragm (which most of them did). In short, Holly was learning her way around.

Everybody else in the class—there were only eleven students in the entire nurse-midwifery program—had made progress, at a price. By the end of the week, they were all saddle-sore, students and instructors both, and walked somewhat bowlegged for days, and Holly was not at all in the mood for sex.

It's a brave woman who willingly serves as a model patient for nervous medical students.

"Where do you find your models?" Holly had asked Leah Stern.

"They're women from our women's health group. Or we pass the word around. They do about four a year. After a point, they numb out. Get desensitized. Fifteen dollars for each session. They earn it, too, because they're the real teachers in the deal. We give them the choice of having a rectal exam each time."

"What do most of them do?"

"Most of them have the rectal each time," said Leah, "because they don't want the students to get away with anything."

Holly now tells Katrina, "I'll come in to relieve you whenever you want me to. But do a favor for me."

"What?"

"When you go to the seminar, take Scott with you."

CHAPTER 14

"Why does Triage do this to us? She's just a fingertip. I want her to go home and come back."

"Triage is a sieve," Crowley says, shrugging. "Getting admitted is the easy part of labor. Anybody can do it."

"And everybody does."

Holly keeps a running list of Subjects About Which to Harangue Patients, and the question of when women should leave for the hospital tops it. During the childbirth classes Holly teaches at the Howard Street Clinic, she tries to drill in the point that it's deleterious for patients to admit themselves to the hospital too early. But the idea that the hospital might be a dangerous place, rather than a safe one, is too contradictory for her patients to accept wholeheartedly. This doesn't stop Holly from trying.

"Beat them at their own game," she tells them. "Go at the last minute, so they don't have much of a chance to mess with you. When you go into the hospital, you'll wind up lying flat on your back. And what don't we want to do during labor?"

"Lie flat on our backs!" the class shouts back in this well-rehearsed call-and-response.

"Lying on your back makes labor last longer," Holly goes on. "The baby will have a hard time getting out that way. Since labor's no fun, you don't want it to last any longer than it has to. So don't go into the hospital too early." Then Holly employs another tactic: scare them with needles. "If you go into the hospital too soon, the needle will hurt when they stick you for the IV. But if you go in during labor, you could care less about the needle."

The class nods knowingly, but at the end of the session, a hand always shoots up with the question: "What if my bag of waters breaks?"

58

"Look at the water." Holly waits for the class's disgusted exclamations to wane. "It sounds *muy disgusto*, but do it. Look at your underpants or your pad, if you're wearing one, and if what you see isn't green, if it isn't pickle juice or pea soup, stay home. Listen to music. Walk around. Chill out. Because no matter how crummy you think your own place is, the hospital isn't going to be any better." Holly then turns to one of the pregnant women. "What do you do when you think you can't stand it any longer?"

"Wait one hour and then go to the hospital," she'll dutifully respond.

For every patient who hears Holly's message, there's always one who misses it entirely and turns up at Admitting with the first flutter. Most hospitals won't admit patients in early labor ("Four centimeters is the price of admission"), but Morrison worries about the liability problem in turning away high-risk patients. And as almost all Morrison patients are high-risk, low socioeconomic status being a major risk factor, women in labor are rarely turned back.

Why do pregnant women come in so early? They panic. They listen to their mothers, who advise them to go straight to the hospital with the first pain. ("Sometimes I think the mothers are our enemy," Pam once told Holly. "They have the patients their whole lives. We have them for only a day or so.") Or the women in labor mislead themselves into imagining they're farther along than they really are.

Most of the women who admit early present with PROM, premature rupture of the membranes, premature because the waters break before the onset of labor. The Morrison midwives tell their patients to come into the hospital twelve hours after the membranes rupture, if labor hasn't started. But other maternity services in other poor neighborhoods recommend that the women come in as soon as their waters break, operating under the principle that the women's own homes are too nonhygienic and make infection too probable.

According to Triage, Flood is a "PROM." The PROMs Triage sends up are often questionable, meaning that Triage considers itself too busy to perform a nitrazine test to put the question to rest. At least one-quarter of the admitted PROMs are false PROMs. What the pregnant women believe is amniotic fluid is actually leaked urine. When the baby's head engages in the pelvis, it squeezes the bladder to the size of a silver dollar, and women might experience incontinence without realizing it, until they discover their underwear is wet.

"Mrs. Flood, I'm going to test you to see if your waters really broke."

"Oh, they broke all right."

"Well, I have to check to make sure."

Holly does the high vaginal swab in DR2. This is a speculum exam, and it's hard to see the cervix for the blood, as blood vessels break in the cervix from the pressure of the baby's head. Holly opens a packet containing a long cotton swab and rubs it against the bloody cervix, as

Crowley holds out a strip of nitrazine paper, which is used so often, it comes on a spool, like Scotch tape.

"You're not going to get any kind of result from that," Crowley murmurs as Holly touches the swab to the nitrazine paper. The swab is bloody. Maybe there is amniotic fluid leaking from up there, but the blood has vitiated the sample, and the paper won't yield any workable result.

"Maybe I should try to swab some of the blood away," Holly suggests.

Crowley bends over, pulls down the light so it shines into Flood's vagina, which is wedged open by the speculum, then shuts the light off. "Don't be stubborn, Holly," she says, with a smile and a shake of her head. "She is really too bloody for you to do anything. She looks about two or three fingers as it is. Admit her." She puts a hand on Flood's calf and calls, "Are you ready for a baby, darling?"

"Am I having it now?" Flood answers.

In the corridor, Holly tells Crowley, "I think it's terrible, the way you can tell how far a lady is dilated just by taking a quick glance."

Crowley lifts her head in her indulgent, regal way. "When a lady is two fingers, she's two fingers. No need to be a genius to tell."

Sparks, passing by, snaps, "We don't talk about fingers anymore."

"Oh, no, Miss Sparks?" Crowley asks.

"We talk about centimeters. That's the modern way."

Levy, who has just stepped out of the labor room, smiles. "We don't talk about dilation in terms of fingers, but that's how we think of it."

Sparks glowers at him. "Centimeters, Miss Crowley." She enunciates the word scrupulously to drive home her point. "Cent-i-meters."

Holly mimics her. "Cent-i-meters." When she realizes what she's done, she runs away and hides by Flood's bedside.

Six hours later, Holly glances at the Board with half an eye, then turns away. But she has the feeling that something isn't right. Her mind is flashing alert signals at her for a reason she doesn't know yet. She studies the Board again, with both eyes, in hard concentration.

Somebody, some ape's hand, has erased Flood's dilation status, which Holly chalked in an hour earlier, and replaced it with an entirely different number. When Holly did her last exam, Flood was at six centimeters. Now, according to the Board, Flood is only five.

"Time for graphological analysis," Holly says out loud. But she doesn't need to be a handwriting analyst to make out who that excessively round, shaky, and sketchy writing belongs to and who can be credited for a faulty dilation status.

His name is Scott.

Three hours earlier, Flood was at four centimeters. For all intents and purposes, the charts now show she's progressed only one centimeter in three hours. It's the labor and delivery version of Dorian Gray. As the hours tick on, Flood's labor moves in reverse. In another month, she'll be only eight months pregnant. . . .

Two different sets of hands have arrived at two different sets of understanding. One centimeter is a small discrepancy that matters.

Holly looks down the hall as Scott lumbers out of the residents' lounge. To forewarn him, she puts a hand on her hip in a bit of aggressive body business. She's always been partial to tall, rangy boys, as her brothers are tall and rangy and so is Matt. But now Holly has the fleeting impulse to fire a BB gun in the direction of the resident's slightly hunched back. Failing that, the impulse to slap his face with a dead fish. What could have been shambling charm on Scott's part is now just the sense that everything he touches falls in shambles.

"Can I see you a minute, Dr. Marrow?"

Scott pales and shuffles forth with his head bent down, hangdog style.

"Is Flood my patient or yours?" Holly asks.

Scott sighs and looks up at the ceiling. "Levy told me to check Flood, so I did."

"Levy was wrong. Flood is my patient. You might have noticed that when you looked at her chart."

Scott shrugs. "I'm not interested in stealing your patients, Treadwell. Levy told me to do something, and I did."

"Let me look at your hands, Scott."

He hides them behind his back. "Why do you have to be so confrontational?"

"Why don't you just call me a ball-breaker and be done with it?" she says, knowing she's being a confrontational ball-breaker.

"Okay," Scott says, smiling. "Why do you have to be such a ball-breaker?"

"Let me see your hands first."

Scott extends his hands, palms up, warily.

Holly peers at them. "They don't *look* peculiar," she says.

"Why should they?"

"It's pretty nervy to change the dilation status on Flood so that she was going back in time, Scott."

"She was five centimeters. What do you want me to do? Lie?"

"Did it occur to you that your fingers are different from mine? That you might have been wrong?"

"She was five centimeters," Scott says, defiant and surly now.

"Look, Scott, I don't care about my professional pride—" Holly stops when Scott laughs. "All right. I care about my professional pride. But right now I care even more about Flood. I don't want her Pitted out just because your fingers can't gauge centimeters within a two-finger margin of error."

"Don't dress me down, Holly," Scott says, withdrawing his hands. It's a plea. Leave me alone, is what he's saying. "It's not your place."

"I have a suggestion," Holly says, softening. The tension that had been running through her jaggedly, putting her on a mean-spirited course, runs out of her. She's derailed, calmer now. "When I was in midwifery school, I used to practice figuring out diameters and circumferences with my fingers. I'd go around with a tape measure in my pocket and measure everything with my fingers. Coffee cups, ashtrays, pickle jars. I taught my fingers to see, to read surfaces. They became a tape measure on their own. Know what I mean?"

"I know what you mean," Scott says, kicking at the floor. "You mean you're God's gift to obstetrics." He looks her in the eye. "I'm too tired to measure pickle jars. I'm too tired to even eat a pickle."

"Too bad," says Holly. "What are we going to do about Flood? She's falling behind on the Friedman curve."

"At this point I don't give a damn what happens to her."

"Can I presume she's my patient once again?"

"I don't give a fuck what you presume!" Scott throws his arms in the air so that they look like sticks flying. "Christ, I hate OB. I hate midwives. I hate fucking pregnancy." He flaps his arms against his sides and swallows hard, his Adam's apple bobbing.

Holly feels sorry for him. "Why don't you cut your losses and run, boy?" she says quietly. "Just get out. That's what I'd do. You're miserable. Anyone can see that. Bail out."

Scott draws a deep breath, ducks his head, and looks behind him down the hall, through hooded eyes, to see who might have overheard him. "If I go down, I'm taking someone with me."

Holly frowns? What is this? A threat or a suicide/murder deal? The boy is flipped. Holly touches his arm. "You seem like a decent guy," she tells him. "So if you're going to take somebody with you, take Levy." She'll stay here, with Flood.

CHAPTER 15

Levy is taking a lie-down in the residents' lounge. The lounge is across and down the hall from the nurse's station, equipped with a bunk bed, countless numbers of unmatchable and untouchable, soggy and crusty old socks. Month-old newspapers, a bloodstained copy of *Obstetrical Emergencies*, and an ancient black-and-white television set. The television is notorious for its imprecise resolution and is, appropriately, called the "auxiliary ultrasound," as it picks up only the vaguest outlines and images, which is all one can hope for from Morrison's creaky ultrasound equipment as well. The ultrasound was state-of-the-art ten years ago, but by high-tech standards, it's now considered a useless antique.

The residents' lounge is called the Not-O.K. Corral, a nickname usually shortened to the more on-point diminutive the Not-O.K. Folk etymology has it that the name found currency when one resident said to another, one too many times, the fundamental truism, "I'm not O.K. You're not O.K. We're all not O.K." Who those residents were or where they are now isn't known, but one thing is sure. There are always more residents where they came from.

There's no stopping the residents. Every first of July, residents are spirited out of their homelands and pushed into the forced exile known as residency, to be held under house arrest. In July, fear and ineptitude stalk the hallways. Fear, ineptitude, and exhaustion verging on collapse always have a place on the Morrison landscape. The difference in July is that the place they hold becomes dominant.

Of course, as Holly gets older, the greenhorns look more baby-face and arrogant, frightened and frightening, with every passing year. And no matter how many babies Holly has delivered or how many years she works as a midwife, the smooth-skinned residents will still have first dibs on patients and last say on patient management. In short, these lamebrained greenhorns are her superiors. Having been through the med school mill, a resident is always considered better qualified to manage births than a certified nurse-midwife, even if she performed the dubious achievement of catching him as he slid from his mother's womb twenty-five years before.

This thought makes Holly tired and worried. For some reason—maybe to be reassured that this isn't such a bad thing—she seeks out Levy in the Not-O.K.

He is flat on his back on the lower bunk, hands beneath his head.

"Christ, Levy, I think I caught you in the act of thinking."

"Wrong, Treadwell. I'm sleeping with my eyes open. Doctors can do that, you know."

"I noticed."

Holly decides to climb to the top bunk, as she's never been there before, and as she climbs, she threatens to smash in Levy's face with her stockinged foot, holding it an inch or two above his head.

"Quit that, Treadwell. We're professionals."

The official credo of the room has been scrawled on a fetal heart monitor strip and tacked up on the wall. "I'm not O.K.—You're not O.K." The college banner for a school of misfits. Below that is a wrinkled advertisement from a magazine that has seen Levy through his undergraduate years and accompanied him here, to his final training ground. It's a famous old ad: "You don't have to be Jewish to like Levy's." It shows a cute black kid biting into a sandwich too big for his face. Holly used to think the ad summed up Levy pretty well—a cute kid biting off more than he can chew. Now she's not so sure.

Holly shuts her eyes to snag a bit of sleep. She opens them quickly. "It stinks in here, Levy. Doesn't Housekeeping venture in anymore?"

"Nobody invited you, Treadwell."

Silence.

"Hey, Levy," Holly says, not loudly enough to wake him if he's found his way to sleep.

"What, Treadwell," he says wearily. He's on the eighteenth hour of his shift. He's never gotten comfortable with exhaustion, although that is the way to learn medicine: to fatigue the brain so that it learns to work in cunningly laborsaving, nonanalytic, and reflexive ways. As the aprocryphal resident said, from the depths of his exhaustion, to the patient who is taking too long: "Aren't you ever going to die?"

"Levy, are you really planning on treating rich ladies when you leave here?"

"The richer the better, Treadwell."

"You could treat rich women four days a week and buy your Mercedes, then spend a day or two doing clinic work to pay back your debt to society and all. Ease your conscience."

Holly lies on her back with her arms beneath her head and her blue eyes wondering. She tries to picture Levy in a different world. In *la dolce vita.*

Levy juts his head out, looking up at Holly on the top bunk as she lets her head fall over the side of the bed and stares him in the eyes.

"You don't understand anything, Treadwell," he says, the cords on his neck standing out from the strain of speaking in this position. "You think I'd buy a Mercedes at this point? Too obvious. Passé. Nouveau riche. It'll be a BMW for me—or nothing at all."

"I could spit in your face from this perspective, Levy," says Holly. "Lucky for you, my mouth is dry."

Levy retracts his head.

They fall into silence and the fractured, floating kind of snatched sleep that's the purported function of the room.

"Hey, Holly," Levy calls softly. "You think rich white ladies would actually spend big bucks on a black OB like me?"

Holly pauses for a moment. "Hell, yeah. If you quit those meddlesome obstetrics, I'd refer all the rich and semirich ladies I know to you."

But that's not the question. Holly isn't so sure how rich or semirich white ladies will feel about going to a black OB. Since becoming a midwife, Holly has learned how hard it is to gauge prejudice and its depths. Prejudice lies low in hidden quagmires that you don't see until you fall in, face first.

Nurse-midwives have spent decades fighting for a toehold in organized medicine. Fighting against the reputation of midwives as superstitious peasants. Fighting physicians who didn't welcome a threat to their economic turf, who had a vested interest in discrediting nurse-midwives and so perpetrated negative stereotypes of them, hindering their acceptance by the public. Fighting for fair licensing requirements that didn't restrict nurse-midwives' practice—even though the licensing was set by boards of medicine dominated by physicians. Fighting for low-tech labor and delivery methods in high-tech settings like Morrison, where labor is interfered with as a matter of course.

The toehold nurse-midwives have gained is still precarious. Nurse-midwifery programs scrape by on bare-bones funding, as there are no wealthy alumnae to lead endowment drives, or contributions from pharmaceutical houses or medical-technology companies (not for a program that advocates minimal use of medication and technology), and universities see no great advantage to their reputation or status in boosting and bolstering their midwifery programs. The future of nurse-midwifery programs always seems uncertain, as midwifery students compete with medical students for access to indigent patients—the basic educational resource and learning material on which both the medical and midwifery students depend to get their degrees—and often get short shrift.

While nurse-midwives can be found at hospitals like Morrison as a cost-effective solution to the management of indigent patients, until recently in New York State, access to private patients had been limited by the fact that third-party reimbursement by major insurance companies wasn't mandated by law. Which meant that a middle-class patient, the backbone of the obstetrics profession, wasn't necessarily able to pay for midwifery care through Blue Cross or another insurance policy—and so had to be seen by an OB, even if she preferred not to.

To add to the precariousness, some states are attempting to require all nurse-midwives to have a master's degree, meaning that any nurse interested in becoming a midwife must acquire a BSN degree; graduation from a certification program not being adequate. Already-certified nurse-midwives without master's degrees would be "grandmothered" in. But if the legislation passes, the pool nurse-midwifery draws its candidates from will shrink. And will shrink anyway, if the Nurse Training Act, which supplies financial aid to women who want to become nurses, is cut. This will decrease the number of nurses generally and the number of women going for their BSN degrees in particular. Fewer BSNs meaning fewer nurse-midwives.

And Holly is surprised that she has to fight little fights every day. Sometimes the struggle takes the form of having to prove her competence to a physician. But always the struggle takes the form of explaining what a midwife is to anybody and everybody who expresses the slightest interest. Nurse-midwifery is a profession that compels you to have an eloquent explanation at the ready. To be prepared with a line of defense, a spiel, a shtick. When she's tired, Holly evades the line of inquiry by simplifying: "I'm a nurse."

But she simplifies guiltily. All nurse-midwives understand that they're responsible for spreading the word, educating the public, furthering the profession. This is what Holly's instructor—and Mrs. Gruener at Howard Street—mean by the term "change agent." Being an agent of change carries special responsibilities. It means explaining what nurse-midwifery is to a cab driver, an old lady on a bus, the dental assistant who cleans your teeth. Most midwives learn how to speak in public, and some welcome every chance to explain nurse-midwifery, no matter how tedious the Speech has become. Holly is an ambassador from a foreign country, representing a beleaguered, misunderstood nation.

The number of misconceptions about midwifery that Holly fields every day is disturbing. She keeps expecting the questions to diminish with time, the ignorance to be less glaring. It seems as if she's explained midwifery to so many people by now that everybody must have heard already. But every day she's proved wrong.

"What does a midwife do exactly?" is usually the first question. But then there are the people who have no knowledge of midwifery but have managed to obtain strong opinions about it. "Midwifery is nice, but personally I'd want a doctor. What if something happened?"

Something happened. The specter of unknown obstetrical horrors sweeps through the questioners' minds. They don't know what these *somethings* are—only sure that they happen and that when they do, only a doctor is capable of doing anything about them. She explains that there are fewer obstetrical emergencies than people imagine and almost all of them can be foreseen. She explains how midwives work in collaboration with physicians.

But even after Holly gives her reasoned argument, the questioners resist believing her. Holly can see them holding back, hanging on to their convictions, nodding out of politeness, maybe progressing to the point of agreeing that midwifery is all right for others but somehow not good enough for them or their wives or their friends. After all, Holly has been able to convince only a few friends to go to midwives to have their babies; to convince them to see midwives for a GYN checkup is to pull teeth.

At first, Holly wondered if this was the failure of her powers of persuasion. But now she sees it differently, as a deep-rooted belief in the superiority of doctors that can be shaken only by some breach of faith on the part of a physician.

The older women to whom Holly speaks about midwifery are most open of all to the idea of it; because they've lived too long to keep blind faith with doctors and hospitals. They gave birth in the production-line style of the 1940s and 1950s and are glad, now, that there is a more humane way of delivering children, and they tell Holly as much. "I was so scared. I was so lonely. It was awful." They can't believe any longer that doctors and hospitals are infallible; but many young women can, women who haven't had their beliefs tested yet.

Holly wonders how Levy will prevail in a world where open-mindedness is sometimes a veneer that conceals prejudices and convictions more dangerous than truth. She doesn't know how many women might have unvoiced opinions, something like, "He seems so nice, but I want a white doctor, *just in case.*" She guesses she'll never know.

As for recommending Levy, Holly meant what she said. Any reluctance to recommend him would have nothing to do with the color of his skin and everything to do with his acceptance of the technological model of childbirth. In good faith, Holly can't suggest a doctor who's impatient with the slow pace of labor, who cuts episiotomy as a matter of routine, and who does vaginal exams every hour to satisfy his own curiosity.

Levy's problem is that he doesn't know what he wants. His conscience is strong enough to prevent his ambition from dictating his medical philosophy, but he's too driven by ambition to allow his conscience to form his guiding principles. Levy is a man in crisis. Maybe he doesn't realize it, but Holly does. Levy is a man full of doubts and regrets.

She swings down from the top bunk, her blue scrub shirt riding up to the level of her breasts in the process.

"I dunno, Levy," she says, standing in front of him. "Life certainly is a bitch. They don't tell you what it's going to be like when you're in school."

"That's because they don't *know* what it's going to be like," Levy says, propping himself up on his elbow. "It's different for everybody. Besides, it'd be boring if they told you exactly how it is out here."

Holly looks at Levy, struck by his good looks, his philosophical approach. Lying on his side like he is, he looks about ten years old. Holly can just imagine the curious little boy he must have been—the kind of kid who examines worms under microscopes, performs science experiments in the kitchen, and accidentally dyes the sink green when he does so. "You're right, Levy," she says, with new appreciation for the man. "You really are right."

"But I know something," Levy says. "Something good. Something that really helps a guy keep the faith."

"What's that?" Holly asks because she wants to know. She wants to know something good that will help to keep the faith.

"You're wearing a red bra," Levy says, smiling. "That's what."

Holly turns and clatters out the door in her bloodstained Dr. Scholl's. She's wasted too much time as it is.

CHAPTER 16

Sparks catches Holly by the sleeve. "A midwife is wanted in Triage."

"What's the disaster?"

"They called for a social worker first, but when they couldn't find her, they decided to settle for a midwife."

"I'm second fiddle to a social worker?"

"You always are," says Sparks.

Holly pulls on her white lab coat so that people downstairs won't think she's a nursing student. The coat gives her the air of authority she apparently lacks by nature. In her violet scrubs, Dr. Scholl's, and rhinestone earrings, Holly once hit Triage to collect a distraught woman in labor whose husband had dumped her at the hospital entrance and taken off. The woman screamed at the resident attending her, "What? You want me to go with that *girl?*" as if Holly were some schoolgirl who just happened to be up late that night.

Holly guesses that some psychotic pregnant person is going off down there. Exploding into a million bits. It's always good to get some exercise before facing a whacked-out specimen of humanity, so Holly decides to run down the seven floors to the first. The stairwell acts as a wind tunnel and perpetually holds a breeze. Holly likes to run straight through it, as if she were charging down the funnel of a cyclone. It feels good to be alone.

But one flight down, there's a couple standing on a landing. Holly recognizes her from Postpartum, a young Puerto Rican woman in her green-foam slippers and nearly transparent nightgown. She leans against the cinder-block walls in curlers and smokes a cigarette while her boyfriend kisses her, in between puffs. They look up, startled, at Holly. It's three in the morning. Not exactly visiting hours. But Holly looks at

69

them, shrugs, then takes off again. When she's down a flight, she hears the kisses resume: loud, smacking kisses caught in the echo chamber of the stairwell.

Because the stairwell is usually empty, Holly moves fast through it—not necessarily to save time but because you never know who might be waiting to jump out at you. Holly likes a little danger. She likes to take off on a full-bodied adrenaline drive. It's like blowing out your engine on an empty freeway late at night. Restorative and reckless at the same time.

When Holly pushes out and turns the bend into the ER, she sees the problem right away. An at-term black woman holds on to an orderly's arm for support, while he looks up at the ceiling for the same reason. She's in a housedress and surrounding her, a merry-go-round of children: four little kids, none of them taller than the woman's waist and all of them hopping up and down.

The woman has nobody to take care of her kids. Or nobody she trusts enough to take care of them. Or nobody who'll take care of them at a fee she can afford. Triage wanted a social worker to find a receptacle for the kids, since nobody can "street" a grand multip like this, who'll probably deliver in minutes, and nobody can turn out a passel of kids either. Triage doesn't know what to do, which is why Triage summoned a midwife.

"You the nurse-midwife?"

Holly looks down at the young nurse, triaging patients into Triage, gazing up at her. She's pasty-faced, just getting over a bad case of acne, and looks like she wishes she were getting older someplace else.

Holly glances down at the nameplate on her jacket. "I am," she says, "most of the time, at least."

The nurse is not amused and says dully, "What are you going to do about this?" She waves a pen in the direction of the woman and her phalanx of children. "These kids aren't in my book." The nurse pokes at her black binder of ER protocols with her pen, which seems to be a supranormal extension of her primary digits.

"How far along is the lady?" Holly asks, stealing a look at the woman with a corner of her eye. She doesn't want to stare directly until she's figured out what the hell she should do.

"Four centimeters. The resident says she's going to spit the baby out and crush the kids if we don't get them out from under pretty damn quick."

Holly knows the question is fruitless, but she asks, "There's nobody to take the kids?" A fundamental rule of midwifery: start stupid and think simple. Start with the most obvious questions and the most obvious resolutions and proceed from the land of the stupid and simple into the land of the stupid but complex.

"Maybe you noticed we don't have day-care here," the nurse says with a sarcastic smile. "Especially at three in the morning."

"No relatives or friends?"

"She says she has a sister who moves around all the time. She can't find her now."

Holly studies the woman, who is groaning as the orderly stares up at the ceiling. Holly wonders about the woman's personality. Unless she's just moved here from another city, wouldn't some neighbor be willing to hang on to the kids for a time? Then again, how many neighbors does Holly have who'd take four kids, all under the age of six, for a few days? Holly presses her temples with her fingers. She squeezes too hard, and tears spring to her eyes.

"You called the BCW?" Holly asks the nurse. The Bureau of Child Welfare.

"You ever try to find shelter care for four kids this time of night? Besides, the mother doesn't want them in shelter care. And if they have to go, she doesn't want them split up. The oldest girl is like the little mommy of the group."

The little mommy is belting a little boy with a plastic handbag.

"The resident is right," Holly says finally. "She's going to drop the kid on the floor if we don't get a move on."

"You mean, *you* get a move on," the nurse says.

"Don't I need a shepherd's crook for this operation?"

"They're little ducks," the nurse reassures her, happy now that the problem's off her hands. "They follow whatever is big and waddles."

"I should bring Sparks down here then," Holly thinks aloud.

Sparks looks like the queen of the Amazons as she blocks the doorway leading to the admitting desk and the labor rooms beyond, which have taken on the aura of the promised land. "You can't allow these little children onto the labor floor!" she says explosively, as Holly stands next to the woman, who is now confined to a wheelchair, the kids hiding behind Holly as she told them to, to lessen the visual impact of their mass. A manipulation that has failed.

"There are special, extenuating circumstances—" Holly starts to say.

"Don't talk to me of special, extenuating circumstances! You take those children *out out out*."

The littlest boy, in pajamas and sneakers with untied laces, belts his eldest sister in the back and sings, "*Out out out*."

Grabbing his pajama top and almost lifting the boy into the air, she says, "You shut up, you doofus!"

The kids notice that a woman is lying in the hallway, with her baby beside her, in a transport unit. The cart the woman is lying on is too high to admit examination, but the unit with the baby is exactly at their eye level, and the baby becomes some kind of science exhibit, a diorama in a natural history museum.

"It's a baby! A little baby!"

"Little—nothing! It's tiny!"

"What is that?" the second smallest boy says, pressing his nose against the plastic wall of the transport unit.

The oldest girl says, "A baby, doofus."

And the oldest boy says, "Fresh! That baby is fresh!"

"You children, get away from there!" Sparks says, pulling them off.

But the kids are in the door.

The postpartum mother looks down with sleepy eyes, not sure what to make of this. You go through all this labor and delivery shit and you come to the other side . . . to a screaming bunch of kids?

"Miss Sparks, can't we put the kids in the ABC?" Holly says, interceding. She's talking about the alternative birthing center—a room with nothing but a bed, right next to the Not-O.K.

"Who's going to baby-sit these terrorists?"

"They'll sack out. We'll put blankets down for them."

Denise butts in. "A phenobarbital split four ways. That'll quiet them down. That's TMM. Trashy Mother Method."

"Denise!" says Holly.

"This doesn't sound kosher, any of it," Sparks says. "And I'm going to consult with Levy."

"Tell him our only other option is to stuff them in a cab and send them to an empty apartment," Holly tells her. "You tell him that."

"You kids stay down from there!" Sparks barks.

The kids huddle against the wall, the two littlest ones staring straight into it. Sparks examines them, pulling them this way and that by their collars. "They might all fit into one bed. They're little creatures." She shudders and straightens up. "All right, you children, you march into that room."

"Where? Which room? Say what? Where? Huh? Which room? Miss, I got to go to the bathroom. You hush up, you stupid stoop! Don't!"

They are all piled, like a litter of puppies, on the bed in the ABC. They sleep horizontally on the bed, a tumble of kids. Holly pokes her head in, bringing a shaft of light with her. One of the kids stirs, then the next. Like dominoes, they all shift around as soon as the first one does. "What?" asks one of them.

"Go to sleep," Holly says softly, and shuts the door.

At Morning Report, Holly gives the story. "Grand multip, aged twenty-five—"

"A grand multip aged twenty-five? Wowee-zowee," says a resident. "How grand is she?"

"This is her fifth. Presented last night four centimeters dilated and four kids."

"The kids are part of the presenting complaint?"

"If you saw them tearing the ER apart last night, you'd know they are," Holly says, looking up from her Card-tex file. "NSVD"—normal

spontaneous vaginal deliver—"baby boy, seven pounds. Wants him circed"
—as in circumcised—"wants him to be a girl generally. That's it. Oh,
yeah. The kids are still presenting."

"What are you talking about, Treadwell?" the chief, Willard, asks
wearily.

"The kids are still here. They spent the night in the ABC, where they
can now be found eating breakfast at the taxpayers' expense. They don't
like eggs, so they're eating All-Bran."

"Doesn't this city provide something like shelter-care?" Willard asks,
searching the room indignantly for someone who'll defend the city.
Nobody does.

Holly says, "I got in touch with the social worker at six this morning,
and she's working on it now. I suggest that if the lady's bloods check out,
and she's not spiking any fever, we discharge her this afternoon."

Willard waves a finger at Holly. "You paper her and teach her. And do
it well."

Holly nods.

"How many cans of foam you usually hand out to the ladies?" Willard
asks, referring to the contraceptive foam Holly and the midwives pass out
as a good-bye prize.

"Two," she says.

"Make it eight," says Willard.

"Where am I going to get all that foam? The pharmacy won't—"

Willard reaches into his pocket, takes out his wallet, pulls out a
twenty-dollar bill, leans across the table, and smacks it down in front of
Holly. "Here," he says. "And that's my contribution to society."

CHAPTER 17

When Holly unlocks both locks on the door to her apartment and swings the door open, she knows right away somebody's there. She can hear the rush of water, and then the water being turned off.

"Hello?"

She stands in the doorway, ready to make a break for it.

"That you, Holly?" comes Matt's voice from the kitchen.

He must have let himself in after Holly left for work. He emerges from the kitchen, wiping his hands on his pants. He's tall, with the almost-gaunt face of a long-distance runner and short brown hair, cut in a corporate New York way.

"Don't kiss me," Holly says, stepping back into the hallway. But when Matt steps forward, she says, "I changed my mind. You can kiss me."

"Do you smell of blood and guts?"

"No, I smell of birth."

"That's what I said. Blood and guts. But I'll kiss you anyway since not every guy gets to kiss a girl who smells of blood and guts. At least, not this early in the morning."

"I missed you," Matt says. They're sitting up in bed, their clothes piled on one half of the bed, with Holly's bag at the foot of the bed. Matt pulls the bag up and puts it in her blanket-covered lap. "Christ, I always thought this was a book bag from your high school or something," he says, studying it. "What is this seal exactly?"

Holly snatches the bag from him. "Don't make fun of my midwife stuff."

"Well, what's this seal about?"

They can just make out the seal of the American College of Nurse-

74

Midwives, which has been nearly washed away by hundreds of launderings. The seal is elaborate, a crazy quilt of symbols contained within a circle. There are three intertwined circles, like a truncated version of the Olympics symbol, supposedly representing the family. The compressed rendering of the stars-and-stripes is the ACNM's pledge of allegiance to the United States. A banner bisects the shield with "Vivant!" emblazoned on it. And below the banner is a smoking caldron.

"What's with the caldron bit?" Matt asks. "Does it represent the witchy past of ye olde midwives?"

"Naw. Are you nuts?"

But Holly can't remember what it's supposed to represent. Of course a smoking caldron brings to mind witches and covens. What were those nearly nurse-midwives thinking of when they put that symbol on their shield?

"Probably it means the ever-burning flame of midwifery or something," Holly says, staring at it. "Or the life force itself. I'll look it up."

Holly gets out of bed and pulls on a T-shirt.

"You work with naked people all day and you can't even walk across a room naked," Matt says.

"Different context." She pulls her old nurse-midwifery textbook from her bookshelf. "We were both wrong," she says. "The smoking caldron is really a tripod to symbolize 'continuance and warmth in dedication to the American family.'"

"I'm moved," he says, lying back, "to throw up."

"Our interpretations were better," Holly says, slamming the book shut and jumping back into bed, just as Matt gets up to shower for work. One month working nights at Morrison, one month at the Howard Street Clinic, then one month working days. He's always glad to see her return to a day schedule.

They've been together for two years.

"Holly, have you thought about getting serious?" her mother has asked.

"Yes."

"And?"

"I've thought about it."

"Have you thought about it with Matt?"

"We might have thought about it together."

Maybe they have thought about it together, lying silently side by side. They just don't like to talk about it. They don't even live together, although that's more a function of the tight New York real-estate market than representative of their feelings for each other. Neither wants to give up a tolerable apartment for less than a sure thing.

Matt's a lawyer, she's a nurse-midwife, they're both busy, and sometimes it's as if they live in different cities, an arrangement that suits her. But they've both changed since they first met, and as they don't see each other more than three times a week, it's hard to say how they've changed exactly.

When Holly first met Matt, he was a law student and a soccer coach at a private school in Brooklyn. The headmaster had assigned Matt to teach the health course: the class that is nothing but a seminar on sex and drugs. Matt didn't know where to begin. Everything he knew about the reproductive process had been garnered from the *Playboy* Advisor, *The Joy of Sex*, and a girlfriend's copy of *Our Bodies, Ourselves*, which he read, sporadically and furtively, during his sophomore year in college, abashed by his curiosity and surprised by his ignorance.

He lacked a base of knowledge that could withstand a semester's onslaught of adolescent inquiries. A friend of Matt's knew Holly and suggested he call her—maybe she could give him a crash course in ovulation and the mixed blessings of the rhythm method, or send him, at least, to the proper sources.

When Matt called, he and Holly made a date to meet at her apartment. One of her worst suggestions, as she didn't feel comfortable talking about sexual things with friends and tended to blush when she did, even if she could sit in her office on Howard Street and talk about condom use and rear-entry intercourse. She should have met him someplace public—the intimate confines of her apartment seemed... suggestive. That they were attracted to each other right from the start didn't make anything easier. Having set eyes on him, she almost said, "Nobody told me you'd look this way." From his look of surprise and the way that he stammered, she knew he felt the same about her.

That night, they didn't talk about sex, but drank beer and talked about everything else. Neither had learned to dress in a sharp, urban way. They wore almost the same clothes: Levi's, polo shirts, and tennis shoes. With the exception of discussions about sex, they felt easy with each other, as if they'd known each other a long time. For the second lesson, they went to bed. After that, they could talk about sex because they had no desires to conceal. They'd made their desires plain.

They had a great first year together. When Holly's odd hours meshed with Matt's odd hours, they had their time to themselves, conducting their courtship in the off-hours. Their romance was private, isolated, and exclusive, as if they were vacationing somewhere in the off-season—an arrangement that particularly appeals to new lovers.

Matt appreciated midwifery's legal problems, and he explained the concepts of liability, and negligence, and the need for diligent documentation, with more subtlety than Holly had ever encountered. Although Matt had barely even heard of midwives before meeting Holly, he became a tremendous midwifery advocate, indignant on behalf of all the women deprived of a midwife's services. He talked to pregnant women on buses and subways and asked about their delivery plans, was thrilled to meet women who'd delivered at Morrison, and cooed over babies on the street.

But Matt has changed since that first year, now that he works in a corporate firm in midtown. He worked hard in school, but he was working toward something. That had made the work tolerable. But now he isn't sure what he's working for, and without a purpose underpinning the long hours of relentlessly detailed and thunderously boring work at the firm, he's become bitter, edgy, and confused, although he doesn't look like he's any of those things. He whizzes off to work in the morning like every other rising young man who's ever risen in New York—in Brooks Brothers suit and with a haircut resembling a flattop. But his high spirits seem to exist only to stave off the sinking feeling that things aren't turning out as he'd planned—not nearly as interesting or free as he'd dimly imagined for himself. He has discovered he likes money more than he thought he would, and when he spends it, he can numb himself to his sense of loss. But when exhaustion has destroyed his defenses, a feeling surrounds him—that he's lost something of himself. Holly has noticed it. Matt has lost some of his sweetness.

Matt returns to the bedroom now, toweling himself off after his shower and pulling on his trousers. "So, old bobcat," he says, combing his hair, "now you smell like birth and sex. The all-purpose scent."

"I smell like you, too," Holly says. She's almost fallen asleep and can hardly wait for him to leave so she can keep falling.

"Birth, sex, me."

"Yeah."

As he buttons up his shirt, he says, "What does death smell like, I wonder?"

Holly's eyes open at the question. As a nurse, she's smelled death. She's smelled death at stillbirths. What does death smell of? Smells without a human behind them, smells remaining after a human has checked out. Dead babies smell like babies...almost. Almost. "Death smells like a hospital," she answers.

Then she goes to sleep and leaves Matt alone in the room, wondering.

CHAPTER 18

A young black kid knocks on the labor and delivery ward door just as Holly comes on her shift. He pushes the door open halfway and pokes his head around. He is about fifteen. He hasn't reached his growth spurt; his feet are like a puppy's paws—disproportionately long and wide—and shod in Pumas with red "fat laces." His eyes are bright and amused and scared.

"Who's that knocking?" Sparks snaps. "Why, what do you want, young man?"

"I'm looking for Henrietta Harrison."

"Henrietta who?"

"Henrietta Harrison."

From Recovery comes a roar: "Tell him Henrietta Harrison is in here and I'm comin' out!"

Henrietta is a big girl, about five feet nine and, postpartum, weighing in at about one hundred seventy-five pounds. An hour ago, she gave birth, and now here she comes in a bright yellow nightgown and bright yellow slippers that make a shuffling sound, and she steams toward the kid wagging a big finger. "Why, you . . ." And then that big finger curls under and gets replaced by a fist waving in the air and a huge smile on Henrietta Harrison's face.

"What you doing out of bed?" the kid cries, voice cracking.

"I'm comin' out to get you, that's what!"

The boy looks up at Sparks. "Miss, I'll come back later, when Henrietta is asleep." Then he pulls open the door and makes for the stairs, sneakers squeaking and screeching on the polished floor.

Henrietta, sore from childbirth, shuffles as steady and strong as a steamship out into the hallway and hollers down the stairwell, "All right!

Be that way, Calvin Billings!" When she returns to the ward, she looks Sparks in the eye. "Is that what you'd call a daddy?"

"Young lady, I'm still wondering if that was a human being."

There is a new resident and he's a terror. He has a name that Holly considers scary as well: Gus. Gus is a second-year who did his first year in residency in Cincinnati. Cincinnatti is a place, Gus makes it known, where they do things right. How he wound up at Morrison, if he is such a hotshot, and wound up at Morrison in the middle of the year, is a mystery that gives rise to interesting speculations.

"There's no doubt in my mind," Denise said to Holly. "A psychotic like that can't get over on someone like me."

"What do you not doubt?"

"Obviously he killed somebody in Cincinnati."

"Accidentally or on purpose?"

"First accidentally and then, to cover it up, on purpose."

"Why would Morrison want him then?" Holly wanted to know.

"He's probably paying *them* to work here." Denise made a clicking sound with her tongue. "Understand me now?"

Holly's personal belief is that the man is manic-depressive and has probably been ordered to a psychiatric specialist in New York City; the Cincinnati shrinks were helpless to treat him. It's Morrison's misfortune that Gus is presently in his manic phase. In contrast to the inert mass, Scott, Gus is hyperactive and into everything. He cannot be contained.

One of Morrison's newest innovations is pH scalp sampling. Before scalp sampling, if a fetal heart monitor showed signs of fetal distress, a section was ordered STAT. Scalp sampling is run to make sure a monitor's indications of distress aren't false alarms—the result of a malfunctioning monitor or a misinterpretation of the monitor strip—or to discover that the baby's aberrant heart rate is essentially benign and is having no ill effect on the baby. The fetal heart monitor, once the definitive arbiter, has now been relegated to an early-warning system as scalp sampling becomes the final test of a baby's fitness or lack of same. This makes Holly glad.

A blood sample is drawn from the fetus's scalp and analyzed, in minutes, on a desktop machine that calculates the pH levels in the baby's blood, determining if the baby's oxygen supply is adequate and if the baby is fit enough to continue labor.

Scalp sampling isn't a pretty procedure. With the fetus's head visualized by a cylinder of light (fiber optics) inserted in the birth canal, a doctor nicks the head with a lancet, then cups the wound with a thin tube to draw the sample. Once the baby is delivered "abdominally" (as the medical euphemism for a cesarean section goes) or vaginally, a scab forms on top of the baby's head. This isn't pretty either, but the beauty of the system is its effectiveness and the number of unnecessary sections it has prevented. Since pH scalp sampling was introduced at Morrison half a year ago, the section rate had dropped from twenty percent to fifteen percent of all deliveries. Scalp sampling puts the lie to the fetal heart monitor.

Holly's one regret is that midwives aren't allowed to perform the procedure. And now, when Velez's baby shows signs of distress, Holly has to find a doctor to take the sample. Levy is delivering in the DR. Holly can't bring herself to call Scott. And that leaves Gus.

"Denise . . ." Holly begins.

"Need a scalp?"

"Need a resident."

"Maybe we can wake the chief."

"I don't think that'd look good on .iy record."

"Maybe we could call over to King's County and ask for a loaner."

"Maybe you'd better find Gus," says Holly.

Holly is leaning over Velez, explaining the procedure and its significance, when Gus charges in. He has hair the color of a blackbird, cut in a spiky way that would be hip if Gus had intended it to look that way. But Holly figures that while in a manic state, Gus stares into a mirror, then swipes away at his head with an electric razor. She has a feeling he'd perform the scalp sampling in just that way as well.

Gus is out of breath and holding a lancet upright in his hand. "Where's the kid to be scalped!" he booms out. "I'm here to scalp some kid!"

He meets Holly's eyes, and she meets his. The man must be on a world-class amphetamine. That's why he left Cincinnati, she figures. Busted at the narcotics chest. His eyes are popping out of his head. Hypertension, she'd think, if it were anyone but Gus.

"All right, midwife. Let me at 'em!"

Holly doesn't want to let him at anybody. She stands in front of Velez's bed and crosses her arms. "It's a shell game, Gus," she says. "You gotta lift the shell off every pregnant lady to figure out which one it is."

"You're mixing metaphors, nurse. Now let's boogie."

He steps forward, and Holly blocks his way.

"Chill out," she says.

"I called you *nurse*, didn't I?" he smacks his hand on his forehead and pulls it down over his face in a slow burn. He makes an agonized expression, genuflects, and doesn't come back up. "Shoot me. You're one of *them*. I forgot. Do forgive me. Please!" He is shouting. Now he stands up and says, "Which one is it? Who needs to be scalped?"

"Cool out," Holly whispers. "Don't go hollering about scalping the kid. It scares the ladies."

Gus rolls his eyes. "Madame, I'm a doctor," he says, caricaturing an expression of exasperated patience. "Let's not start with the sissy stuff. I'm here to render medical services, if you don't mind."

"It's Señora Velez."

"Señora Velez. We need Hispanic pH then. I believe *pH* is spelled with an f in *español*. Lead the way." He shoves Velez's gown up toward her chest. "Let's see what we can see," he says. "Ah-ha." He can see nothing. Velez's legs are pressed together. "Midwife, get the patient into left-lateral position, please."

Velez looks anxiously at Holly. "Don't worry," Holly says soothingly. "It won't hurt. Just pull your leg up like this." Velez bends her right leg over her left. "You'll have to lift your left leg, when it's time. You can put it on the rail right here." Velez follows Holly with her eyes.

"Let's go!" Gus bellows. "A baby might be in big trouble here! Trouble to the max! Mega-trouble!"

"Let's try to keep the talk reassuring," Holly says.

"Let's visualize!"

Holly holds the endoscope, the cylinder that provides light and relays an image back, so Gus can see the dilated cervix. Gus says, "Let's go with the blade." Denise hands him a fresh lancet, and he grimaces broadly as he makes the incision in the fetal scalp. He pulls the blade out. "Capillary tube, somebody," he says. Denise hands him the thin tube. He looks up for a second. "Mmmm, chocolate," he says. Holly can feel the seismic shock that runs through Denise. She meets Denise's eyes, and they both shake their heads.

"I'm nobody's chocolate," Denise says loudly.

"All right. We're scalped! We got the bloods!"

Gus pulls the light source out of Velez. A gush of fluid follows.

"What's that from?" Holly says, pointing at the meconium-stained fluid that has hit the Chux pad beneath Velez's bottom.

"What do you think it is? The tears of Mary Magdalene," Gus says with a snort.

"He blasphemes on top of it all?" Denise asks in disbelief.

"Don't blaspheme," Holly says to him coldly. "Don't mess with religion around here."

"Excuse me!"

"Excuse me," Holly says, "but where's that fluid coming from?"

The amniotic sac has already been ruptured for the insertion of the internal fetal monitor. But some of the backwaters from the fundus (or top of the uterus) might have been released if Gus tipped the baby's head when he took the sample. This stream represents a lot of amniotic fluid.

"Gus, did you feel the baby's head move when you took the sample?"

"Hell, no. I have million-dollar hands." He waves his hands in front of Holly's face.

"Get your hands away from my face, please. Was the head floating?"

"A floating head? Naw. Never happened." Gus looks down at Velez and slaps her thigh. "Okay, we came, we scalped, we conquered." He trots out of the labor room, holding his Vacutainer aloft. "Here come the bloods!" he shouts in the hall. "Here come the bloods!"

Holly dries off Velez around the thighs, then pulls down her gown. "Sorry about that, señora. He's kind of an eager-beaver type."

"He's whacked. That's what he is. Whacked."

"Yeah. That too." Holly washes her hands and breaks out a pair of gloves she had in her pocket. "I've got to put that monitor back in. More poking around, I'm afraid."

"Better you than him," Velez says with a grunt. "You sure he's a doctor?"

Holly blinks. Christ, what if Gus is an impostor? No, she's not sure. "Sure," she says. "It's just that these residents get antsy when they keep weird hours."

"You said it," Velez says. "Weird."

Holly's left hand passes up the vagina to the cervix, and her hand has to stretch to find the baby's head. She curses her short fingers. Then she curses Gus. The head has lost its engagement. It has drifted upward, dislodged, and is floating. Well, that sets labor back and increases the changes of a section and of cord prolapse, the dangerous occurrence when the umbilical cord drops down before the baby's head. A floating head is not nice, not in the least.

"Yeah," Holly says, mainly to herself. "They get antsy, they do." She straps an external monitor around Velez's abdomen and tunes in to the baby's heart. Thump away, baby. And tells Velez she'll be right back.

Holly heads down to the nurse's office at the end of the hall, where the pH machine is. Gus hums as he reads the printout, which looks like a cash-register receipt, and bursts into song, singing, of all things, "Down by the river, I shot my baby."

"What are the numbers?" she asks.

"Satisfactory."

"The reason I ask is, if she's going to be sectioned, let's do it now. The head's not engaged, and I'm worried about a prolapsed cord."

"Borderline," he says, spinning his head around. "Borderline numbers."

Borderline psychotic, she thinks.

"Someone ought to hang tough beside her," Holly says.

"Ah-so," Gus says, crumpling up the printout and tossing it in the trash.

"Yo, Gus! Are you bonkers? We got to staple this to the lady's chart."

"Oh, right," he says and pivots out of the little office as Holly bends down to find the printout. An impostor. The thought has the ring of truth, and Holly wonders if there are actually any numbers on the slip of paper. What if he's just bluffing? Holly finds the wad of paper and straightens it out. As the ribbon is worn out on the machine, Holly can only just make out the numbers: 8.7. Borderline indeed. At least Gus knows how to work up a sample.

Holly clatters down the hall, passing Denise.

"T'sup?" Denise calls.

"We've been scalped," Holly calls back.

When she gets to Velez, she looks at the monitor strips. "Cripes!" Weird decels. The term "fetal distress" is bandied about a lot and sometimes manages to encompass any condition that is less than maximal, that shows the slightest hint of fetal compromise. In most cases, true fetal distress is caused by one thing—cord compression—which looks distinctive on a monitor strip because of the herky-jerky dips known as variable decelerations. One look at the strip tells Holly that the decelerations don't bear any connection to the onset or duration of the contractions as they should. And the decels are inconsistent in their length, not lasting the same amount of time each time. And there are signs of tachycardia, which occurs when the baseline of the fetal heart rate rises above 160, indicating a baby under stress.

Variable decels. A tachy baby. A floating head. Holly doesn't bother to wash her hands. She breaks out yet another pair of size sixes and roughly pushes her left hand up to Velez's cervix. "Sorry, honey," she says. Then she feels what she doesn't want to feel. A dropped cord. Nature abhors a vacuum. Where there was baby, so shall the umbilical cord be. Her hand keeps going, and she finds the baby's head. A contraction is starting. She can feel the internal rumblings. She puts four fingers on the baby's head. That head can't come down with the next contraction. No. It can't. Holly won't let it.

"Nurse! Help!"

Having been powerfully influenced by "Peter and the Wolf" as a child, Holly doesn't yell much. When she does, she means it—and everybody knows it. Denise runs in, followed by another nurse.

"Denise, prolapse. Drag Levy away. Let's go OR. Section STAT."

And Denise is gone.

Velez lifts her head. "What?"

"You'll be all right, señora. The umbilical cord has dropped a little."

"It's dropped?"

"Here's what you do, and the nurse will help you do it. I have to keep my hand in, so you must turn onto your left side and put your right leg up, like we did before. Let's go. Let's do it now." The left-lateral position reduces the pressure of the baby's head on the cervix—or Holly's fingers—as well as improving blood flow to the fetus.

The nurse helps turn her over, and Holly must follow this internal rotation, bending over, never letting go of the baby's head. The nurse drops the guardrail on the bed.

"We have a trolley on the way?" Holly shouts out to the hall.

"One second, midwife!" a male voice says. "We're coming!"

An orderly works a trolley into the labor room. The nurse squeezes herself into the space between the wall and the big, boxy fetal monitor.

"Nurse, you've got to help our man with the señora," Holly says. As Velez inches onto the trolley, Holly stays to the side, keeping her hand inside the patient, keeping hold of the head. Another contraction begins, and the baby, part of a natural force, wants to move down. Holly won't let it.

Levy pokes his head in. "Hey, Holly. OR's ready to go. Sneaker's waiting out here. How many decels before you caught it?"

"Don't know, buddy. How about some Maalox here?"

The antacid is to neutralize the stomach acids so that Velez doesn't throw up under general anesthesia—one of the big risks of emergency sections. Even if the stomach is empty, the stomach acids can be regurgitated and aspirated into the lungs.

Denise swivel-hips her way through the door. The bulky group attempting to pass through the doorway resembles nothing so much as a transverse lie. They'll never get through the pelvic brim at this rate. The nurse grabs the IV bag and holds it aloft, the orderly pushes the trolley, and, of course, Holly with her hair in her eyes and her hand still inside Velez—all try to push through the door at the same time. Holly gets at the end of the trolley and leans her elbows on the bed, in a space between Velez's knees.

As soon as the caravan makes it into the corridor, Denise scurries to the trolley with a medicine cup full of antacid. "Stop this train," she hollers. "Open up, dear—this is to settle your stomach." Velez opens her mouth, Denise pours in the chalky white fluid, and Velez wipes her mouth. "Yuck!"

"Yo, I'm not finished yet!" Denise shouts, waving an orange informed consent form and a pen, chasing the trolley into the chilled precinct of the operating room.

"It's like ice," Velez murmurs. She looks up at Holly. "I don't want to go."

"I'll be with you every step of the way."

Velez crosses herself. "I'll miss it. I'll miss my baby."

"When you wake up, you'll be with your baby."

"I won't even see it."

"You'll see him a lot, a lot." Holly wipes away residual Maalox that has gathered at the corners of Velez's mouth.

"I'm all right?" Velez asks.

"You're all right," Holly says.

The Sneaker takes Velez's arms. "Hullo. I'm Gary Allbright."

Allbright, Holly repeats in her mind, that's his name. Christ, what a name. But then again . . . she's Treadwell.

"I'll be watching you all the time," says Gary Allbright, "to make sure everything's okay. Here's the blood pressure." Denise takes the BP, then ties a mask on Holly and fits a cap over her head. "Your head is big," Denise says. "All them brains of yours."

"Holly," Velez says. Holly puts her face near hers. "Who's the doctor?"

"Meet Dr. Levy. One of the best."

Levy smiles with his eyes. "Nothing to be scared of."

"He's right," says Holly, hoping she's not tempting the gods. "Nothing to be scared of."

"When I put this mask on your face, you inhale slowly," the Sneaker says in an unctuous, almost seductive voice. This must be his real instrument, Holly thinks, finding herself slipping into the smoothness of that voice, wanting to trust it. This is the hypnotic intonation Holly always tries to produce vocally herself, and here it comes out of a guy with suspiciously pale lashes and pale eyes and a generally mild appearance that could only mean, in the halls of Morrison Hospital, a viciousness at his core. The pale eyes are settled calmly and watchfully on Velez's face as his right hand adjusts the gauge on the tank of gas. "Are you ready, señora?" he asks gently.

"Yes."

Holly leans way over and gives her a peck on the cheek. "See you in the morning."

Velez smiles faintly and shuts her eyes.

"Count to ten," the Sneaker says. "In *español*, if you like."

"*Uno, dos, tres, cuatro . . .*" She fades out at "*ocho.*"

As soon as she's out, the OR explodes with noise. Denise has swabbed down Velez's belly, and Velez is draped and ready to go. The general anesthesia will hit the baby in minutes, so they have to move fast.

"Let's attack the window of vulnerability then," Levy says.

"Start slow," Holly says, worried that Velez might be semiconscious. She braces herself for a scream, remembering a section she attended where the woman was given an epidural—the spinal anesthesia that is supposed to numb the lower body but keep the patient conscious—that didn't take. The first move of the scalpel . . . They don't use epidurals for sections at Morrison.

"She's gone," the Sneaker says.

"Well, for Christ's sakes, let's use some positive imagery. She can hear you subconsciously," Holly says, irritated, bringing her midwife's sensibility into the doctors' domain. It's not wanted here. *You're a nurse, Treadwell, a nurse. Try to act like one.* "Contraction," she informs them. She feels it in her hand.

Levy starts slow. He is doing a classical section, straight up and down, a long scar for Velez to show the kids back home. He slices the skin to pull it back. There's the sinewy, glossy muscle of the uterus during a contraction. Taut, gripping. "Prepare for the flood," he says. "The whale is going to spit Jonah the hell out of here." He looks down. "Shit, didn't you catheterize the patient beforehand?" he asks Holly.

"I had my hands full, Levy," Holly says. Her arm is tired.

"Nothing like keeping a hand in, Treadwell," he says.

Everyone laughs.

"Well, hurry it the fuck up," Holly says.

"'Fuck up'?" Levy says. "I guess we have to get you into the OR for you to curse."

"Or you have to fuck up real bad," she answers.

"We can manage that." Levy cuts into the uterus itself, and there's an outpouring of fluid and blood that rolls off the operating table right onto Denise's scrubs, or what she calls her "fatigues."

"Who's gonna pay this cleaning bill?" Denise cries.

"Hey, it's a baby," Levy says. "Push up, hand of Treadwell."

"Christ, I don't like my hand being here," she says.

They can't see the head. The open womb is framed by the blue sterile drapings. All they see is the white strips of uterine muscle, and arms, and an extended umbilical cord, and the curves of the baby's curled-up bottom and legs.

"Push up, Holly," Levy says gently.

She pushes the baby's head up with her hand, and as the baby ascends, a pediatrics resident leans over the table and suctions the baby's nose and mouth just as Levy gets hold of the baby's feet.

"Scott, cut the cord, fisthead," Levy says.

Scott steps forward, cuts the cord. And the baby is born.

Velez lets out a rolling snore. Everyone stops for an instant. Then nothing.

"All right!" Levy cries.

He hands the wet baby to the pediatrics resident. He's a bluish-looking baby boy.

"Yo, Holly, you can remove your hand now."

"It won't move," she says. "It's numb." She pulls it out. Her arm is free now. She looks at Velez's sleeping face.

Holly can move away, into the middle of the OR, into the corridor, anywhere she likes. She has been linked to Velez for only fifteen minutes—fourteen minutes flat, by her somewhat moistened wristwatch, which must be some kind of section record here at Morrison—yet Holly feels as if she's been bound in chains for days. She doesn't go far. She watches as Levy pulls the placenta from the uterine wall, peeling it off as if it were a label, then dropping it into a basin.

"Gonna help me close?" Levy asks, glancing up, eyes shining over his mask. He did a good job.

"Naw, Levy. I'm just a midwife."

"How 'bout mopping up?"

"I'm a midwife," she says. "Bringing damaged babies into the world. That's my game."

"Accentuate the positive," Levy says, mocking her, his words muffled behind his mask.

Holly moves toward the OR door and pulls off her mask, which seems only to redirect whatever is propelled from her mouth and nose in a less direct rout to the OR atmosphere. "I'll catch you later, my man, for a heart-to-heart," she says.

"Your heart or mine?"

Denise says, "Watch where you're sewing, Marcus."

"Girl, you grab that retractor there."

"I ain't no doctor."

"Well, hell, what makes you think I am?"

Holly finds Levy in the medicine room. It's a private place, as nobody can possibly be in the room besides them without their knowing. By the same token of intimate confinement, there's no place for Holly to stand where she is any more than two feet away from Levy. They are not wearing masks. They are speaking virtually mouth to mouth. Or, as Levy would have it, "Lips to lips."

"Good choice of a trysting place," he says with a smile. "Keep up the good work."

"Levy, I thought you were bad. But compared to Gus, you're just minor-league meddlesome. This dork is a menace, Levy. Armed and dangerous."

Levy winces. "I'm not crazy about the boy myself."

"I mean, prolapsed cord, cord compression, pathetic Apgar scores for the baby. That kid might be Willowbrook material just because some whacked-out second-year stuck his hand in too hard and too far."

"These things happen, Holly," Levy says. "OB is a high-risk specialty. Et cetera. Multip with a big, roomy uterus and a little kid. Engagement isn't maintained."

"Levy, that's a crock."

Holly turns toward a cabinet and presses her forehead against the cold metal door. She is starting to cry. Holly Treadwell does not cry. Precipitous weeping. She was not expecting this.

"Oh, Treadwell, don't do this to me. Don't get all teary-eyed." Levy puts a bashful hand on her shoulder. He has the chance to take advantage now and make some moves. But the truth is, Levy is something close to being a decent guy. Levy is a gentleman. Levy is a good guy, when everything else boils down. "It's not that bad," he says.

"Oh, it's bad. When you think about it. When you imagine what might happen to that poor little baby just because...I don't like it, Levy. A whole life wrecked just like that, one or two fingers knocking over the whole house of cards. Everything's so precarious. There's no justice."

She turns around and finds Levy nodding, eyes downcast.

"You're right," he says, lifting his shoulders, then lowering them slowly. "There's no justice. It's not fair."

"We're dealing with lives here, Levy. It's not that I usually forget it, but sometimes I remember it better than I do at other times." Holly thinks a moment. "Maybe I should tell that lady to sue."

"Treadwell!"

But Holly is enough a member of the brethren to know she can't do this. That she'll never work again in a major hospital if she does.

"Holly, the statute of limitations for bringing suit is twenty-one years. Velez should be able to figure it out for herself in twenty-one years. All you have to do is turn on the radio to hear an announcer saying, 'If your child has suffered brain damage or cerebral palsy at birth, or you think in your wildest dreams that he has, contact us, the ambulance chasers of the tri-state metropolitan area.' She doesn't need you to drop the big hint."

"So what are we going to do about Gus the Butcher?"

"I don't know yet."

Holly wipes away her tears with the back of her hand. The tears are black, from mascara, and she bends now to study her face in the reflection of the hematocrit centrifuge. "In the meantime, can't you prescribe a sedative for the guy?" Holly asks. "Put the man on downers before he can kill again."

"I'll have a talk with the boy," Levy says in a baritone voice, hooking his fingers into his armpits. "And then I'll shoot him."

"That's what I call managerial flair," Holly says.

CHAPTER 19

On morning rounds, Holly starts on the cesarean ward. This is Holly's least favorite place to do her rounds. Not the happiest of places. During the days, the women tend to lie back and stare dazedly into space in a Demerol haze with a vague sense of loss, when in fact they have lost almost nothing. To heal faster, they are encouraged to walk around, a practice they generally resist. Periodically a nurse sticks her head in to shout, "You mothers must walk!"

Because the physical conditions of cesarean mothers don't fall within the purlieu of normal birth, which supposedly is Holly's area of expertise, Holly acts less like a medical personage during these rounds and more like counselor and comforter.

"Remember what we talked about in class?" Holly will ask a mother she knows from Clinic. "Remember that the point of all those preparations is to get a healthy baby out of the deal?" The young woman might nod tentatively, as if she doesn't quite believe it. "Now you have a terrific, healthy baby," Holly will say brightly.

And the young mother might say, "But where is he?"

Morrison Hospital, a lumbersome, cumbersome animal, is slow to change and has yet to follow the lead of other hospitals in permitting mothers liberal access to their babies. These cesarean mothers see their babies for an hour in the morning and an hour in the evening, and sometimes, through logistical mishaps, they go a whole day without seeing their babies at all. One woman once said to Holly, "I wouldn't know my baby if I saw him."

When Holly works days, she has the whole day in which to fit all her postpartum rounds, scooting downstairs when she has a few minutes to spare. Sometimes she has to fish her patients off the sun porch, a cinderblock structure painted canary yellow that catches an hour of hard,

88

solid sunlight in the morning. It's the place where patients watch soap operas as they soak in the rays.

The sun porch television plays tricks on its captive audience. Every hour, a hospital-produced program on birth control or postpartum care or breast-feeding breaks into regular programming. Patients who sit on the sun porch benches, anticipating *General Hospital*, are not pleased when gynecological information floats out of the box instead, drifts into the sunbeams, and washes over them like motes of dust. This is no way to get patient compliance—to preempt *General Hospital*.

Holly is guilty of aiding and abetting these programs. She even appeared—no, starred—in one of them. It was called *Your Annual Checkup* and walked the viewer through the steps of a GYN checkup to demystify the process. In the video, Holly plays a nurse-midwife, a hard role to play normally and even tougher to play when the camera follows you, while a Jamaican nurse-midwife, no longer at Morrison, plays the patient. Everyone smiles all the time. Holly appears at the Howard Street maternity services doorway waving and grinning madly as her patient bounds into the examining room with uncontrolled enthusiasm.

Holly had been slightly shocked to see herself on screen—her legs were stockier and her ears, holding back her hair, bigger than she'd ever imagined. But all in all, she presents a friendly, inviting presence—yet not an enthralling one, to judge by the number of new mothers who use the break from the soap operas to tend to other affairs: doing their nails, calling their friends from the pay telephone, reconvening around the television only when "a real show" returns.

At night and in the early morning, as now, the sun porch is empty, the wards dark. Holly looks down the rows of beds, searching out Velez, who was moved here from Recovery an hour earlier. For every woman asleep, one is awake, staring into the darkness, wondering and waiting. Down the hall, the nursery is ablaze with light and busy with nurses handling babies who exist only behind Plexiglas and clutch at air.

"*Señora . . .*"

Velez opens her eyes in a stupor. "The baby?"

"You had a boy, remember?"

"Remember . . ." She puts a hand on Holly's forearm. "How is he?"

"He's fine."

"My husband . . ."

Holly finds Mr. Velez. He is the man asleep on the floor in the empty waiting room, his head on a folded newspaper. How do you wake a sleeping man you've never met before? Very carefully. Holly shakes his leg; even that strikes her as overly intimate.

"Wha . . . ?" he says, looking up, confused.

"Congratulations," Holly says.

Holly steps off on Six, Postpartum, before heading home. A young black teenage boy leans against the reception counter and says, "I'm looking for Henrietta Harrison." He leans over the counter to study the floor plan for himself, and the nurse swats him on the shoulder with the *Daily News*.

"Back," she says. She looks at the floor plan. "Henrietta Harrison. Three-A."

Henrietta must have heard his sneakers squeaking on the floor, because a shout comes from down the hall. "Is that you, Calvin Billings? You're not getting away this time!"

Calvin Billings looks down the hall and sees Henrietta coming at him, hand folded up in a fist and a smile that makes her eyes shine.

"Henrietta!"

"Where have you been, Calvin Billings?"

Henrietta approaches in a slow, steady shuffle.

With a squeak and a rush of wind, Calvin Billings has taken off again.

CHAPTER 20

Sometimes, when Holly leaves Seven, she expects to come downstairs to a hospital that has emptied out to start fresh. But it's always the same, as if the hospital's slogan is: Disease Never Sleeps.

In the ER waiting room sit poor families of all colors and nationalities, exhausted beyond anger or angry beyond exhaustion. A television, bolted to a shelf close to the ceiling, flicks out B-movies from the 1960s on a skewed color tube, the kind of movie that stars John Derek, as if the hospital has a satellite dish that catches television rays that were lost in space and then siphons the worst of pop culture into the waiting room. The sound on the set is usually set too low for anyone to hear, or so high that the shrill noise pinches all the overworked nervous systems within a fifty-yard radius. Only a few people bother to lean their heads back, planetarium-style, and stare at the television screen. The rest gaze at the floor, littered with brochures on patient's rights and tuberculosis, breast self-exams and diabetes, and candy bar wrappers. Today, a pool of spilled soda pop lies in one corner and gels into a tough film.

Holly hurries through the lobby. She just wants to get home. Home, where it's cool and calm and airy, a big bed with clean sheets, a breeze brushing through the curtains... Maybe she'll have a beer for breakfast and drink half of it as she reads the morning papers before falling slowly asleep.

She's living in her dream as she trots up the street, her tote bag slung over her shoulder. But the dream collapses three blocks from the subway stop as her name is called in a peculiar way.

"Miss Treadwell? Nurse?"

"Sheila!"

Sheila steps down from a stoop, ducking her head shyly. She has never

91

learned to do her hair right. She's fifteen and friendless, and her mother doesn't seem to help. Her black hair is straightened but left unshaped, so that it bunches out aggressively from her head in a bushy way. Sheila would look pretty in a natural hairstyle, Holly thinks, with her rich, dark brown skin and sweet eyes. But nobody has helped her out. Nobody has helped her out with the shiny blue blouse that barely closes over her big, pregnant belly and opens slightly to show the thick white bra girdled around her chest. A heavy black wool skirt falls past her knees and skims the top of her knee socks. She is wearing white patent-leather pumps. If only Holly had a few hundred bucks to spend on the kid!

Sheila had wanted an abortion, but her mother, a strict Roman Catholic, forbade it. The father of her child is her older brother's friend, and Holly can't figure out whether Sheila was raped or seduced, or a little of both. Either way, the father had his way with Sheila, as they used to say, and it was Sheila's first and only time, sexually. Sheila should not be a mother. Not only is she young and poor, but Holly thinks she might be completely crazy. She talks to herself when she comes to the clinic and bursts out laughing when she is facing a wall. In cold weather, she wears sundresses. In hot weather, she wears a hooded ski jacket. She always dresses as if she and the rest of the world don't live in the same place or occupy the same space.

Sheila doesn't go out much now. She doesn't like to be seen. She'll call up right before an appointment. "Holly, I can't come today."

"How come?"

"I don't feel well."

"If you don't feel well, that's a good reason for you to come in, not stay away."

"I just can't today, Miss Treadwell."

And Sheila will turn up the next day, standing furtively outside Holly's door, and Holly will take her, even though she has no appointment. So Holly is surprised to see Sheila standing out in the open, as she's doing, and she knows that Sheila must be standing there just to wait for her.

"Hanging out, Sheila? Conveniently close to the hospital in case you go into labor?"

Sheila lifts her head glumly. "There's something wrong with my baby," she says in a low voice.

Holly sits down on the stoop. "Why do you think that? Have you been feeling ill?"

Sheila sits down beside her. Her head hangs low. Her back curves over, and she rests her forehead on her big belly. Speaking into the thick wool skirt, she says, "It's going to be ugly. A nasty, sick thing. Something's wrong with it. I can feel it in my bones."

This is the kind of anxious sentiment that isn't peculiar to teenage mothers, particularly at about the seventh month, where Sheila is now. Holly puts a hand on the back of her neck. "It's going to be a beautiful little baby," she says. "Remember the sonogram pictures I showed you? How big and healthy it looked?"

"I couldn't see nothing. It wasn't nothing but a blob."

"But I can see things," Holly says, pointing at herself. "I know it wasn't a blob. It's going to be born in January, which is a lucky month to be born in, because everything is just beginning. Labor will be hard, but you'll be able to do it, because you're a strong and good girl."

"No," Sheila says, letting her face fall into the lap of her skirt. "I'm not a good girl, and everyone can see I'm no good girl. I'm bad. That's all." She pulls her head up, and Holly smooths down her hair where it stands out awkwardly. Sheila jerks her head away, her eyes red and her face puffed up and thick.

"Sheila, have you gone to see the social worker again?"

"She can't change my badness."

"She can show you your goodness, if you can't see it yourself."

Holly had referred Sheila to the Howard Street social worker on her visit. Even then, Sheila had seemed suicidal, self-hating, confused in her thought processes.

Sheila turns her face to steal a look at Holly, her eyes scared, and dips her head again. "What if the father of my baby is the Devil?"

Holly feels her heart break. Before she took this job, she'd never felt that sensation before. A tinge in her chest. Something snapping. The way she responds to heartbreak is to let her adrenaline loose on it. She cups Sheila's face in her hands, as if she's delivering the head of a baby, and directs Sheila's face to her own. She wants Sheila to look her straight in the eye. "I know all about these things," she says. "And about the Devil and all. The Devil isn't going to get to you because I can see into your heart, and I happen to know that it's good. And all babies are good, because God loves them more than anything else in the world. All babies want is for everyone to be happy, just like you do. Your baby will be sweet and beautiful, just like you are. There's nothing wrong with your baby. And there's nothing wrong with you that a little hopefulness and cheeriness can't cure."

Holly lets go of the startled girl's face. Holly beams into her eyes, wishing she had hypnotic, healing powers that could set everything right.

"I want you to see the social worker again," she tells Sheila. "When I get home, I'm going to call her. Then I'm going to call you." Holly stands up. "Now, have you thought about names for your baby?"

"If it's a boy, Damien," Sheila says, looking up at Holly slyly.

"Isn't that the name of the devil-child in the movies?"

"Maybe," Sheila says, shrugging. Then she smiles slightly. "I don't know." She knows, all right.

"You'd better go home and think up a nice name for your baby, one that makes you happy just to hear yourself say it. You'll be saying it a lot. Now, come with me. I want to buy you a frozen yogurt. If I know babies, yours is hungry right now, no matter what his name is."

Which is how Holly leaves work.

CHAPTER 21

Back. A still night, and the noises on the ward are in order. Groans from the labor rooms, the joking arguments of nurses sipping coffee and eating sandwiches in the lounge, the muted flush and whir of the hopper.

The hopper, where the contents of bedpans are heaved, is set into the wall, like an incinerator, right by the admitting desk, and a faintly fecal odor penetrates out to where Crowley sits, drawing up next month's schedule. (The constantly vibrating hopper is the price paid for the confinement of patients to their beds and reliance on bedpans and the routine enema—at least the enemas are no longer 3-H: high, hot, a hell of a lot.) You forget the smell after a while, as Crowley manages to forget it.

A cockroach runs along the floor, then scurries out of sight, running under the dolly bearing the filing cabinets—the records for past and present clinic patients—that are transported every evening from Howard Street and will be wheeled back downstairs, put in a van, and taken back to the clinic in the early morning.

Record-keeping can be a complicated enterprise. One night, a woman was admitted who said she'd been given antepartal care at Howard Street three years earlier. She'd been an illegal alien then, and had been afraid to give her real name. She had taken an alias, which she couldn't remember. "The name of a town in Puerto Rico," she said.

"You wanted it to sound like you came from Puerto Rico?" Holly asked.

Yes, emphatically.

A Puerto Rican nurse listed all the names in Puerto Rico she could remember. "Coamo," was the last one. "*Sí*, Coamo," the woman said.

And there she was, in the files, listed under Coamo, as was her son, Luis Coamo.

Crowley sets eyes on the roach but doesn't see it as it scrambles up the wall, across a sticker advertising a suicide prevention hotline (a joke, maybe), and disappears into an old log of births stored on a shelf over the desk. She doesn't notice that the roach stays there, where all babies go when their weight is recorded, their sex noted, and their existence acknowledged. Crowley is far too engrossed in the ultimate Crowley job to notice. Scheduling is the quintessence of straightening things out and up.

Crowley likes scheduling, which has everything to keep a busywork addict like her happy, with its fussy organization and manipulation of names, the satisfying placement of staff members in the proper places. A sense of calm and well-being fills the ward, as it does almost every night for a time; a seductive deception. Quiet is not to be trusted.

Sparks will do something about the quiet. Sparks isn't comfortable about a calm. Both Crowley and Sparks are West Indian, tall, handsome women, although Crowley has, deservedly, the sweeter face. They took their nursing training in Jamaica, where nurses are trained in midwifery and considered by the public to be synonymous with midwives. But their careers as midwives stopped as soon as they entered the United States. To become certified nurse-midwives here, they'd have to take a refresher course. Both having large families and neither the time nor the financial wherewithal, neither could take such a course. And now that they have more time, spare energy, and extra money, the one refresher course in the entire country—not to mention the state—has closed, which means that foreign-born nurse-midwives will have to take a full midwifery course if they want to practice here. Crowley and Sparks will always be nurses.

They have identical work habits: both in perpetual motion, into everything, straightening whatever can be straightened. Legend has it that one night Crowley smoothed the wrinkles on a patient's gown with an absentminded hand when a baby's head popped out below. Crowley knew what to do. "Babies play tricks on old, tired nurses who think they've seen it all," she tells Holly about once a month. "Remember, just when you think you know everything, the baby plays a trick on you."

Like other West Indian nurses, Crowley and Sparks insist on being called Miss Crowley and Miss Sparks, even though they're both married and officially are "Mrs." One night, Holly asked Sparks what her first name is. "Miss Sparks," Sparks said.

Of course, since Crowley and Sparks are so much alike, they constantly argue. Now Sparks is arguing with Crowley, who she thinks has admitted a patient incorrectly. The patient's name, says Sparks, is Standre, but Crowley has admitted her as St. Andre. Sparks pushes the patient's plastic Addressograph card with her finger and then thrusts the card in front of Crowley's face. "See, downstairs they know her name is Standre," Sparks says.

Crowley flinches slightly. Her version of a flinch is a slow, irritated blink. "It's not Standre," she says, drawing herself up. She wears purple eye shadow and gold earrings shaped like seashells, and appears regal to everyone but Sparks. "It's St. Andre," Crowley says, "like the saint. You just don't understand."

"Her name is Standre, Miss Crowley. Standre is on the card. Standre is what she signed on the form. And Standre is the name the baby will take."

"What she signed on the form!" Crowley repeats indignantly. "You know the Haitians can barely read or write!" Every ethnic group at Morrison—where there is almost every ethnic group—has its particular prejudices. Crowley and Sparks happen to feel superior to their French-speaking West Indian neighbors, the Haitians. As always in America, the newest immigrants are most likely to be the objects of prejudice, and the Haitians as a sizable population are relatively new to Brooklyn, where Jamaicans are well established. "There's one way to settle this," Crowley declares, and she gets up and marches into Labor Room 2, to the bedside of the pretty young Miss Standre/St. Andre.

"Miss," Crowley says, "baby, what is your last name exactly?"

"Saint Andre," she says cheerfully, pronouncing the name in the French way.

Sparks stands in the doorway with her arms folded, glowering. "She should have put an accent on it. That's what she should have done. An accent mark over the e and this perplexity would never have happened."

Crowley wishes to gloat a bit longer. "It's not Standre?" she asks sweetly.

"No. Saint Andre. Like the *catholique* saint."

"How do you spell that?"

"S-T-A-N-D-R-E."

"But that's two words, baby, isn't it?"

"Yes. Two words."

"Well, I'd better hurry and get you a new card or else the baby will be called Standre."

The Haitian woman pulls herself up in bed, looking stricken. "But the baby is not St. Andre."

Crowley freezes in her tracks. "Not St. Andre? Didn't I ask you what the baby's name is going to be when you were admitted, honey?"

"I didn't understand. My husband isn't . . ." Mlle. St. Andre is at a loss for words.

"He's your husband," Sparks offers from the doorway, "but you aren't married."

"Yes," St. Andre says, much relieved.

"Just what is your baby going to be called, Miss St. Andre?" asks Crowley, much put out by the altered name. The hospital is supposed to have an affidavit from the purported father to the effect that he is, in deed as well as intent, more than just purported.

"Bourget," St. Andre answers.

"Bourget," Crowley repeats.

Flapping her arms and leaving the room, Sparks mutters hatefully, "Bourget."

In the corridor, Crowley says, "I was just beginning to understand the Spanish names."

"And you never understood those Spanish names as well as you might imagine," Sparks says.

Before they come to blows, they move, instinctively, away from each other, straightening as they go. Crowley goes downstairs to Admitting for a new Addressograph card as Sparks takes the damp rag from the ledge beneath the Board, erases the name Standre, and chalks in the correct name, flicking an accent over the final e in St. Andre. Thus moves the world of medicine.

Names.

Standing at the Board with Holly, Levy asks, "Recognize any of these names from Howard Street?"

The rotation of midwives has Holly at Clinic, one month every other month, and some names should have sunk in by now. But Holly stares hard at the Board and blanks out in a blur of names as significant as a phone book listing. Her head swims with names as every day there are more names, of patients, babies, nurses. Holly can remember faces or names, but not both, not all the time.

"No," she answers.

First names are easier to remember than last names, which aren't personal enough to ring any bells. On the Board, only last names are used, with the first names in initials. One night, three women named Hopkins were on the Board, and two of them were B. Hopkins.

Names. "No, I don't recognize any of these names," she says, turning to Levy. She can remember a cervix, a voice, a face, but she can't remember names.

Sparks taps her hard on the shoulder. "Maybe you'd like this," she says coolly, holding out a green envelope.

"Maybe I would."

The envelope is addressed to Dr. Holly, Day Shift, Maternity Ward, Morrison Hospital, Brooklyn. Inside is a card illustrated with a maniacal St. George smiting a comical-looking dragon that seems to have been modeled after an alligator, with the artist adding horns for the complete dragon effect. A fountain of blood shoots out from the back of the impaled dragon.

Holly opens the card and reads, "Dear Dr. Holly, I have thought of you often since the time I spent in the hospital. I thank Jesus for you and put you in my prayers because you are one of the blessed, I am absolutely sure of that. Thank God for the thirty days. God bless you." The card is signed, "Mrs. Ismenia Herrera and little Ray."

The name means nothing, but the reference to the thirty days means everything.

Ismenia was a short, pudgy woman with hair dyed copper and penciled-in eyebrows. "No more children!" she'd cried. "No more men! *No más!*" She'd been in labor for fifteen hours, second stage—the stage that usually lasts only fifteen minutes in multips—for over an hour. The baby was high up, only at −2 station, and Holly and the hospital had tried everything. Pit run. Artificial rupture of the membranes (AROM) to help the baby descend (which led to the first signs of bradycardia, the slowing of the fetal heart rate, in little Ray). Demerol to ease the pain of the violent Pit contractions and help Ismenia loosen up some. And ambulation. Ismenia stood pressing her arms against the wall as Holly pulled back her gown for peeks at the perineum, hoping to see bulging there, bulging of the baby's head propelled downward by the contractions and gravity.

"I'll never go through this again," Ismenia moaned. She'd given up. She lay on her left side and stared at the fetal monitor tracings, dipping, peaking and dipping again. "I won't let a man near me ever again, I promise you that."

Second-stage arrest. It was time to let Ismenia off the hook. She was worn out. Her uterus was on the brink of hypotonia: sheer exhaustion. The labor had put her through the wringer. And the intermittent bradycardia was troublesome. The choice was forceps or cesarean, and Holly let Levy decide. Holly's preference was for section, since there was less trauma to the baby than with high forceps. Levy agreed. No grip-and-flip forceps action that night. Ismenia was ready to go.

While Ismenia had already signed an informed consent on admittance, she needed to sign another form consenting to surgical treatment.

"I'll sign anything. Anything. Just put me under."

"I want to explain the risks, Ismenia," Holly said. Loss of blood. Going under general anesthesia entails risk. Infection. Blood pressure might drop . . .

"Fine. Blood. Whatever. Give me the pen. I'll sign."

As Holly hurried away with the informed consent in hand, Ismenia called, "When my sister was cut, she had another operation. One for no more children. Not after the operation."

"Her tubes were tied?"

"*Sí.* Her tubes were tied."

Holly stepped forward. "*Señora*, it's against the law to have your tubes tied during an emergency section." Holly's not sure she should even use the expression "tubes tied," as it's misleading. In truth, the tubes are cut. Saying they're tied gives some women the sense that they can just as easily be untied, like shoelaces.

"Against the law?"

"If you want your tubes tied, you'll have to wait at least thirty days."

"But my sister did it! She had a cesarean, then she had her tubes tied. Everything is down there! It's easy!"

The law exists just because it is easy.

Sterilization abuse ranged from the actively malign to the paternalistically thoughtless. A physician might decide that a woman, being poor or unstable or perceived to be of inferior stock, shouldn't be burdened with any more children or allowed to burden the state with any more children. To this end, tubal ligation was sometimes proposed to women in the thick of labor. For women in labor to vow never to sleep with a man again, never to become pregnant again, never to want another child is historical tradition. Holly and other midwives call it "singing the right song." The oaths of a woman in labor aren't ones that anyone takes seriously, but more of a forced confession, made under extreme duress.

Sterilization abuse laws were enacted nationally in 1977, requiring a thirty-day wait during which a new mother could safely experience a change of heart. But before those laws were in place, hospital staffs proceeded, at times, as if the pledge to have no more children were a considered decision, and performed ligations as if in service of their patient's wishes. The ligations turned the fleeting emotions of labor permanent.

Ismenia Herrera couldn't have a tubal for thirty days.

"Señora, when you're up and about, come visit me at the clinic. If you want your tubes tied then, you got it."

Ismenia sank her head back into the pillow and tried to escape. Escape the closed-in room, the orderly readying the cart on which she'd be wheeled to the OR, the force of the contractions. "You tell them I'm ready," she said faintly. "I'm ready to go to sleep."

Holly wondered how many laws designed to protect people infuriated the people they were designed to protect.

Now here was a card of thanks. Of blessing. Thanking Holly for doing nothing. That's all right. Holly will take thanks of any kind. She slips the card into the loose pocket of her scrubs, and as she moves, it rubs against her leg. For the rest of the night, it'll serve as her talisman, her relic, her heart.

CHAPTER 22

"Nothing bad," Levy says. His way of introducing an unappealing patient. "Just a pain in the ass."

"You have an invisible protocol working in your head that refers pain-in-the-ass patients to me," Holly says. "Do I read you right?"

"You're nothing if not astute. Birds of a feather and all that. One pain in the ass deserves another."

Camilla Ortiz is a pain in the ass who doesn't like answering questions. "I've had them all," she says, waving her hand and fanning herself with the neckline of her gown.

"You've had all the childhood diseases?"

"Sure."

"Diphtheria?"

"Probably."

When Holly performs the Leopold maneuver—abdominal palpation to discern the lie and estimated weight of Camilla's baby—she has one of the two things the black book of protocols, found near the admitting desk, says she needs: "Start with warm hands and a cooperative patient." She has the warm hands.

Holly is trying an experiment. She's going to act professional and cool and try to intimidate Camilla enough to get her to toe the line. She's going to play doctor. "You're para four," she says. "Who's staying with the kids now?"

"They're staying with themselves. They're used to it."

"How old is the oldest?"

"She's ten. A mommy already."

"Not literally, I presume," Holly says nastily under her breath.

Plenty of Morrison's patients leave their kids on their own, but usually the mothers express some regret or worry about doing so. Not Camilla.

She's the kind of woman Holly thinks of as "borderline," a category Holly doesn't talk to other midwives about, since it's a personal pigeon-hole to label women she thinks might wind up to be bad mothers and a judgment call that derives from prejudice, instinct, or common sense, but not any clinical evidence. It's an assessment Holly figures she might be in the wrong about. The borderline women are the ones who need midwifery care the most, the people inclined to look on the negative side. A midwife has to alter the values, to shove, by dint of will, the negatives into the realm of the positives. It's like pushing a boulder. Holly's not sure she's up to it. She isn't in the mood for altering values. In fact, the values seem to be altering her.

At three centimeters, Camilla is wailing. Holly tells her, "From your stomach. Low, keep it low." But Camilla carries on at her high pitch. "We don't mind if you don't sound like a lady," Holly says. "We like it when you don't."

This distinction fails to penetrate. "*O Dios mío!*" Camilla moans. "The pain! The pain!"

Crowley is disdainful. "At three centimeters! Really!"

"*O Dios mío!*"

Holly doesn't like that expression. Of all the things a patient might say, "*O Dios mío*" strikes her as the worst, an operatic phrase that lends itself to being drawn out—"*O Dios mío-o-o-o-o!*"—and elaborate styliza-tion, so that it can take almost a minute to articulate. As expressions go, it's a menace.

"Give me something for the pain!"

"I can't," Holly says.

Camilla's labor is speeding along, so that any medication Holly gives her now won't wear off until after the baby is born and the baby will be born droopy. But resisting Camilla's plea for medication is a job of work. Camilla falls to her knees on the bed, tears at her short brown hair, and contorts her face into an expression of anguish as she clasps Holly's hand in supplication. "I beg you! Please! The pain! O Dios mío!"

It's no fun being cruel to be kind. Holly doesn't like to see women in pain, and most of the labors Holly sees involve pain rather than discomfort. But as a midwife, she's as much the baby's advocate as she is the mother's and has to look out for the interests of her other, invisible patient. That's why she tells Camilla to relax, breath deep, go slow, and shut her eyes, and leaves the Demerol in the cabinet.

Holly is doing some paperwork by the nurse's station when a nurse says, "Ortiz is screaming for Demerol."

"Too bad."

"But she's such a pain in the tail without it."

"I'm not going to be blackmailed," Holly says. "I don't care if she screams her head off. The baby's going to be here any minute."

"You tell her," the nurse says. "I think she might throw something at me."

Whenever a resident or nurse passes by, Camilla raises her voice to wail even louder but then quiets down as soon as they're out of earshot. Cynical and manipulative complaints, Holly thinks sternly, not able to restrain her urge to judge. She can't open her heart to everyone, and she doesn't happen to care that Camilla has a low pain threshold. That's her problem, her fault, her weakness. Tough it out! Holly doesn't feel up to giving the tender loving care midwives pride themselves on. The best she can do is care enough not to give in to Camilla and not dose her up to keep her quiet. This is hard, because part of Holly would like nothing more than to see this bundle of negative energy nodded out and shut up.

"Think of the baby," Holly tells her. "It's almost over." Dilating two-and-a-half centimeters an hour, Camilla is going through a labor that is the equivalent of sledding down an icy slope on a toboggan. It's as fast as any woman could hope for.

"It's not fast enough!"

"Try and think positively," Holly says, not at all persuaded that her words will have any reasonable effect. "Each pain brings you closer to your baby."

"I don't care!"

"Do you know what you want?" asks Crowley, to warm her up, take the focus off her pain and put it on the baby, which is the purpose of all this. "A boy or a girl?"

"I don't care, as long as it comes out—and soon!"

But the baby is coming now, and they have made the move to the delivery room. Crowley positions a mirror on a stand at the end of the delivery table. Having a theory that patients are more receptive to watching television than themselves in a mirror, she says, "Watch the TV, baby." Camilla watches the TV. She's never seen her own children get born before, and Holly watches Camilla watch herself, absorbed in what she is: a woman bringing a baby out of herself, on her own.

Holly delivers the head in a Ritgen maneuver, supporting the head with a doubled-up towel as she forces it out with as much firmness as gentleness. Meconium-stained fluid gushes out with the feet, but since the forewaters were clear, there's little chance the baby inhaled meconium on his rush out.

"He got excited," Crowley murmurs, looking over Holly's shoulders at the baby's thick legs splattered with meconium, as if he'd walked through a mud puddle to get here. "He got all worked up about getting born."

Camilla is studying the mirror with a facial expression somewhere between a smile and a grimace, which Holly imagines tends more toward a smile. The baby has been pulled, whole and intact and a boy, out of the birth canal and into the bright lights of the cool DR.

"I wanted a boy," Camilla says as Holly lowers him into Camilla's arms. "I just didn't want to hope, that's all."

"Always hope, honey," Crowley says. "Hoping is all right."

*　　　*　　　*

DELIVERY 103

It's been ten minutes since delivery.

"I don't like this part," Camilla says, as if she'd liked any other part of labor and delivery. "The waiting."

Camilla has warmed to her baby. "Man, he sucks hard!" she says admiringly, having put her little finger in the baby's mouth. With a clear conscience, Holly can check the square on the intrapartum chart that indicates "excellent bonding." PRESS HARD: YOU ARE MAKING COPIES. Excellent bonding, against the odds, in quadruplicate. A midwifery victory that pushes back the borderline and alters the values.

A woman like Camilla needs bonding exactly because she's a poor candidate for it. Levy views bonding as a sentimental gesture. When he provides time for it, the bonding is a sop tossed in the direction of fashionable thought. He gets antsy. He suffers through it. He needs to be rewarded for it.

"What did you think of that bonding, Treadwell?" he asked a few months ago, as pleased with it as he would have been with a Ralph Lauren sports coat.

"It only lasted three minutes, Levy."

"Hey, baby, you'd be amazed at what three minutes can do. If you give me the chance, I'll show you."

"Let me imagine it instead, Levy. I'm not ready for the real thing yet."

"Dream on, Treadwell. But remember, reality can only improve on the imagination."

For his sake, Holly hopes so.

Holly likes bonding more for its practical application and implications than for its trendiness. In a surveyed group of abused children, the majority had had no bonding time with their mothers directly after birth. And of that majority, most had been cesarean or premature births and had been separated from their mothers for long periods of time after delivery.

As far as Holly can tell, basically good mothers can survive an absence of bonding. The women Holly thinks of as "good mothers" who don't bond with their babies may have a higher incidence of postpartum depression than women who do bond, but they will beat up on themselves rather than on their babies, who will suffer indirect, psychological harm rather than direct, physical harm. Holly doesn't undervalue the seriousness of psychological trauma, but if she had to choose between a good mother or one she considers borderline to bond with her baby, she'd choose the borderline mother every time.

The bonding always happens like this, even in the touch-and-go cases—the women not particularly thrilled by having another kid or who say they want a girl but get a boy and show their disappointment from the start—as it happens now to Camilla. The mother puts a finger on the baby's head, as if the baby were a fragile, foreign thing. Then she trusts herself enough to place her whole hand behind the baby's head, eventually letting her hand travel over the baby's whole body to lay claim to her child. She looks the baby in the eye, and if the baby hasn't had too many drugs in utero, it looks back at her and gets to know her, too. When the mother bonds with the baby, the baby has bonded with her.

The women who need bonding aren't downright wicked, but the kind who are swept up in their own problems and hurtled into emotional confusion. Holly tries to sweep away that confusion and make the connection between the mother and child a clear, uncomplicated thing, for the baby to seem like the genuine article, and not just a hypothetical burden that hasn't quite materialized. Bonding helps a woman feel like a mother right from the start. A mother who has bonded rarely develops the obsessive fantasy that her baby has been switched in the nursery or that she's been given the wrong baby on leaving the hospital. She knows her baby is hers and nobody else's.

Of course, after the bonding connection is made, everything at Morrison seems to conspire against it. Every so often, there's an occasional stir of activity to loosen up the nursery's limited visiting hours. But the hospital has yet to initiate more lenient hours. As one mother complained to Holly, "What do I have to do to get to see my baby? A special dispensation from the pope?" No, Holly wanted to say, you have to get out of here. You have to go home.

Things like the placenta expulsion time limit don't dò much to nurture the bonding process either.

In the corridor, Sparks snaps at Crowley, "When was that baby born?"

"Ortiz?"

"Ortiz."

"I don't know, Miss Sparks," Crowley answers protectively.

"I do. It was fifteen minutes ago." Sparks appears in the doorway and calls out, "Fifteen minutes, Holly!"

Holly doesn't need Sparks to remind her of the time, and Sparks knows it. It's Sparks's way of needling Holly. Sparks probably enjoys a delayed placenta expulsion, particularly if Holly is managing the delivery. Crowley knew what she was talking about when she said to Sparks during one of their tiffs, "You thrive on strife, Miss Sparks." Holly hasn't been able to shake the remark from her head. It pulsed with truth. Sparks thrives on strife.

Sparks had called time, but what player would leave the field now? A mother has given birth, her baby boy is in her arms, and no placenta is in sight. The cut umbilical cord leading back up to the placenta doesn't twitch at all, to give the sign the placenta is on the way, even though fifteen minutes have passed since delivery. In short, nothing is stirring: conspicuous inaction is a crime peculiar to Morrison Hospital.

Holly isn't fearless enough to turn and glare at Sparks, so she gives the nurse a modified glare: a quick, hard look. With her customary sixth sense, Sparks knows not to pay any attention to Holly's surreptitiously hostile gesture. She is putting the finishing touches on a labor-progress chart, signing her name with a swooping flourish that takes up more than its allotted space on the form. This strikes Holly as a metaphor for Sparks generally. Self-aggrandizing. She doesn't keep to her allotted space.

Sparks slides her chart into the patient's folder, making sure she's put it in the proper order. Sparks's record-keeping is exemplary, and she's in charge (a position she appointed herself to) of teaching younger nurses the fundamentals of meticulous chart-keeping. It's hard to fault Sparks in terms of her nursing, and her diligence is infuriating. Holly wishes Sparks would screw up royally just once. It'd be even nicer if she screwed up really badly twice.

Sparks jams her pen into the chest pocket of her white uniform. She needs a plastic pen guard, the kind that nerdy engineering students used to wear in college, because streaks of ink flare out from her pocket. An odd and trivial flaw, but worth squirreling away as possible ammunition for the future. The ink stains draw Holly's eyes to Sparks's substantial bosom. Now Holly drops her eyes. The last thing she needs is to be caught staring at Sparks in the wrong place.

"Yes, Miss Sparks," Holly sighs. "It's been fifteen minutes."

Sparks glances at the clock. "Eighteen minutes actually."

The main problem with working with Sparks is that she believes she's better qualified than Holly is. Sure that she knows as much as, if not more than, Holly and the other midwives, Sparks gives advice without having to take responsibility for the consequences. Her education has been out of date for years, and whatever midwifery principles she may have learned in school decades ago have long since been eroded by the poor examples set by Morrison Hospital doctors.

Holly has overheard her tell a patient, "Drinking wine during pregnancy, that's good for you—plenty of iron in it." She discourages breastfeeding by saying, "The formula you give your baby in a bottle has everything. You can be sure your baby is getting all the vitamins and minerals he needs." The midwives try to discourage circumcision, so, of course, she heard Sparks tell a woman in Recovery, "The boy will get diseases if he's not circumcised." Holly has to untangle the webs of confusion Sparks has cast over suggestible patients.

Sparks scares more patients single-handedly than the entire staff combined. "If you can't push any better than that," she told a young girl, "you'll have to have forceps." The girl's pushing went straight to hell and didn't come back, and the baby was born with forceps. When another patient had trouble getting the hang of pushing, Sparks told Holly to pull down on the bottom portion of the woman's vagina. "That'll get her going," said Sparks. True, putting internal pressure on the perineum triggers the pushing instinct, but Holly doesn't put her fingers in a patient unless she absolutely has to. She has never found the right time to explain this to Sparks, as the right time doesn't exist. The truth is, Holly is scared of Sparks, which makes Holly more angry than anything else. Sparks has gotten to her. All that intimidation really works.

Sparks knows this and resists taking orders from the midwives who are too shy to press the issue. She plays deaf and forces them to shout at her or to give up and do what they want her to do themselves. Sparks apparently takes the *nurse* in *nurse-midwife* seriously.

"I don't understand," Denise said one night in the nurses' lounge. "The residents don't make much more a year than the midwives do. Why are midwives supposed to be the better bargain?"

Sparks explained her perspective. "The residents perform only the function of a physician and must have the nurses perform the nursing function. But the nurse-midwives do both. That's why they're a bargain."

"Miss Sparks, I'm not sure the midwives are supposed to take care of all the nursing duties," Holly put in softly, fearfully.

"But of course you are. Don't be a silly goose."

Sparks acts as an extra pair of hands for the midwives only under duress, with the most resentful air. She can get away with being mean-spirited because she would gain nothing by hiding her feelings except harmony on the floor, which doesn't interest her. Morrison is a city hospital that pays its nurses low wages, and nobody is going to fire a capable nurse like Sparks just because her attitude toward the midwives is less than friendly.

Holly thinks of residents as inexperienced greenhorns, strong mainly in book-learning and too stupid to recognize how inferior they are to her. This is how Sparks thinks of Holly and the other midwives. And the way the residents sometimes feel about Holly—she's a half-educated bitch, a paraprofessional posing as professional who grasps at more power than she's entitled to—is how Holly feels about Sparks. This is how team obstetrics at Morrison Hospital works.

Sparks now cranes her neck to study the clock on the wall, right above the babies' footprinters. Sparks's wristwatch works fine, but staring at the wall clock makes a more dramatic impression. Taking note of the time, Sparks clucks her tongue and with a loud sigh sorts out the samples of cord blood drawn from the cut umbilical cord.

Holly would like to shout, "The placenta may be late, but placentas don't move like clockwork. What do you plan to do about it?"

Holly knows precisely what Sparks will do about it. She'll tell Levy, who will then spoil Holly's midwifery victory.

Hospital protocol directs that if a placenta isn't delivered fifteen minutes after the baby, a doctor should perform a manual removal, with the patient put under general anesthesia. For a manual removal, the doctor puts his hand into the uterus and peels the placenta off the uterine wall. The very definition of "invasive procedure." A manual removal might contribute to greater blood loss than if the placenta were shed naturally, by the force of the contractions. The procedure's invasiveness would require a prophylactic antibiotic treatment. And the patient would have to stay on a glucose IV during recovery, as a cesarean mother would, because the anesthesia would make her bowels too sluggish to digest solid food. The blood loss, the disorientation produced by the anesthesia, and the possible infection would all lengthen Camilla's recuperation, as would the IV, which inhibits movement that would speed up recovery and reinforces the woman's image of herself as sick.

Worst of all, general anesthesia would break Camilla's bond to her baby, the threat of which makes the bond—a thin, transparent thread linking mother and child—seem more fragile than before, as if it'll break with a snap as soon as the gas mask is lowered onto Camilla Ortiz's face. Manual removal would push a borderline patient over the limit, and Holly can picture how it would happen: Camilla blanks out, forgets her delivery, forgets her baby, wakes up and returns to how she was when she was first admitted—bugged out and pissed off and not liking labor or delivery or babies.

Most midwifery textbooks permit a lag time of forty-five minutes from the delivery of the baby to the spontaneous delivery of the placenta. "I heard about one lady who had a baby in 1975," Denise told Holly. "In 1977, she was in the shower, looked down, and said, 'What's this fallen between my legs?' Yes, ma'am. That was her afterbirth, very much after birth."

There's no medical indication that late expulsion of the placenta is harmful to a just-delivered woman. The fifteen minutes Morrison permits is short shrift, a length of time that seems to have been chosen at random. Or, when Holly puts a cynical light to it, to have been designed to keep the DR turnover moving along at a fast clip.

Fuck them, Holly thinks. She isn't going to put Camilla Ortiz under general anesthesia just because the DR needs to be cleared out for the next patient. Let them deliver in bed. She'll just have to outfox the placenta time limit. All she has to do is figure out how.

Hospital protocol orders thirty cubic centimeters of injected Pit following the placenta's delivery to make sure the woman's contractions are strong enough to clamp the uterus down upon itself and act as tourniquet on the blood vessels left exposed by the expelled placenta. This suits Holly fine, as she's seen enough hemorrhages in her time to not want to risk any. The Pit may be uncomfortable for the portpartum woman, but at least the baby is out of harm's way.

Holly considers giving Camilla the Pit before the placenta delivers—to invigorate the contractions and shake the placenta loose—but decides against it. Without pressure from the baby's head, the cervix may start to close up, which wouldn't be helpful. If she had time, she could do a Pit run and follow a third-trimester abortion protocol on the placenta. But she doesn't have time. She wants the placenta out of there before Levy catches wind of the delay, warms up the OR, and pages the Sneaker. Holly can just see it—the Sneaker padding through the hallway, asking hopefully, "Anything bad happening?"

"You're going to have to bear down even harder now when you feel the pains," Holly says tensely as the future unfolds and unravels in her mind's eye. "You have to push."

Sparks comes in for the baby. "It's been twenty minutes," she says, feigning indifference, although no one who's kept such close track of time could be indifferent.

"Let's get it out now," Holly tells Camilla. "Just as if it's a second baby."

Camilla isn't listening. "Ronnie," she says, following the baby out of the room with her eyes. "I'll call him Ronnie."

Lousy name, thinks Holly. "Big push," she says, straining to make contact with Camilla. "Big push." She sounds tough now. She wants Camilla's face to bunch into a hundred folds with the effort of pushing. She wants to hear grunting. She wants Camilla to hang in, bear down, push it out.

The clock on the wall doesn't tick, but Holly imagines that it does and that it ticks loudly. She always knew that the placenta time limit leads to mismanagement of the third stage—the kind of mismanagement that's responsible for most postpartum hemorrhages—but she never thought she'd be susceptible to mismanagement, the things midwives and doctors do when they should really do nothing.

She is about to become a meddlesome midwife. She's going to give cord traction a try, hoping to coax the placenta from the uterine wall. Clamping a pair of ring forceps around the end of the cord, she puts one hand on Camilla's abdomen to steady the uterus and pulls lightly to test the cord's give. Then she rotates and twists the corkscrewlike cord. Cord traction isn't recommended anymore, but it's practiced all the time anyway. You can break a placenta apart by pulling the cord too hard, leaving half behind in the womb, still attached. You can snap the cord off the placenta. And too much pull can draw the entire uterus out of the body, so that it inverts like any loose bag and the top of the uterus appears at the vaginal introitus.

Holly doesn't like what she's doing. She wouldn't be doing it at all if time didn't bind around her in a stranglehold. The cord traction creates a basic anxiety, a sense of dread. One of midwifery's first laws is, "Don't cause what you can't cure." Holly can't cure what cord traction might cause, and she listens to her instincts and drops the ring forceps, with a clang, into the basin.

Just two months before, she had criticized Levy for being too aggressive with cord traction. He'd performed it without anchoring the uterus with his left hand.

"You're gonna pull the uterus straight out of there if you don't watch it," she whispered to him. His eyes crinkled into a smile above his mask. "What's so funny?"

"I was remembering when I was an intern in Connecticut," he said, twisting the cord with the forceps. "This old attending was doing a manual removal, and he pulled the whole goddamn thing out. Know what he did then? Just shoved it right back in. 'Son,' he said, 'the procedure here is to punch it back into place. She'll never know the difference.' It worked fine." Levy laughed.

Holly stuck her hand on top of the patient's fundus to stop the uterus from moving. "Whatever you do," she said to Levy, "don't tell that story to any of the first-years, all right? They'll think that's standard operating procedure for manual removals. Yank the uterus out, pull off the placenta, and shove it back in."

"Just pushed it right in," Levy said, musing. "Awesome. Positively awesome."

Holly now stares at the cord that extends, inert, from the introitus. She doesn't like the umbilical cord's looks. It doesn't look fit. Its blood vessels seem weak and thin, and she compares it with a cord she saw a month ago that's lodged in her mind as the ideal cord, an umbilical cord great.

It had been a beautiful thing, thick and hearty, blood vessels a strong purple-red color, twisting through the cord's body like stripes on a candy cane. When that cord had pulsed, it had pumped and throbbed. Camilla's baby's cord is dull and gray, and when it was still pulsating, right after delivery (and Holly rarely cuts the cord until it has stopped pulsating), it looked lifeless, the circulatory equivalent of a limp handshake. In midwifery school, a nurse once complained to Holly about how hard it was to take blood from an unhealthy umbilical cord, draining the umbilical veins into tubes for exam by the lab. "The veins are all schmoozy," the nurse had said.

"Schmoozy?"

"Don't you speak Jewish? They're *schmoozy*."

The veins on this cord are schmoozy, too.

Holly wonders if the cord's thinness influenced the baby's infrequent bradycardia—depressed heart rate during contractions. Another idea for Holly's "Great Ideas File," to be ransacked when she finally gets around to increasing her midwife's value by putting together a publishable bit of research. The report could be called, "Correlation? An Umbilical Cord's Fitness and Its Connection to Incidence of Bradycardia."

Leaning against the delivery table, Holly becomes conscious of her aching feet and that she's slipped out of her bootie-covered Dr. Scholl's without ever realizing it. She is standing on the delivery room floor in her stocking feet. Guiltily she slides her feet back in and realizes how tired she is. She gets more tired when there's nothing to do but wait, and when she has too much time to wait, she worries. She worries that what they have here is a placenta accreta, the cotyledon of the placenta—its anchoring roots, essentially—having implanted too far and deep into the uterine wall. And she worries that she's caught the hospital hysteria so that a delayed placenta has begun to look downright pathological.

In her fatigue, Holly doesn't care what happens to Camilla. Let someone else take this patient, destined from the start to be a pain in the ass. Judging by the cord's appearance, the placenta will probably be in lousy shape as well. Something bumpy and dull-looking that will fail to navigate the birth canal in one piece, leaving chunks behind so that Holly will have to do a uterine exploration and pull out the placenta's remnants and debris—almost as invasive a practice as manual removal and nearly as painful. So let Levy take Camilla away. Holly doesn't care. She's tired, and she wants to sit down.

Holly bucks up and stands up straight. Her fatigue is dangerous, like metal fatigue on an important machine—she's worn so thin that the slightest pressure will snap her and send her crashing, and soon she'll be like the residents and need someone to do her thinking for her.

A blip swims into her field of vision, a form taking shape in the corner of her left eye. This blip, the form, is Levy, standing in the doorway and pushing back his surgical cap to scratch his head. Smiling lightly, he leans casually against the wall, in a rush but not in a rush at the same time. He is standing there to remind Holly that she is still standing there.

"Finished bonding?" he asks.

"The baby's in the nursery."

"Doing episiotomy repair?"

"She didn't need one."

"Ah-ha." Levy smiles broadly. "Nothing much seems to be happening here."

"The placenta hasn't delivered yet." Holly knows Levy knows the placenta hasn't delivered. He's playing cat-and-mouse with her, tickling her with a paw, rolling her over, curious to see how she'll try to scurry away.

"How long do you think you'll be?"

Holly shrugs. *Casual, Treadwell, be casual.* "A couple of minutes."

"Promise?"

"Do I have to promise?" she asks.

"I need the room, Treadwell," Levy says, not smiling any longer. He nods at the hall. "Other ladies would like to have their babies now."

"Ten minutes then."

"No, Treadwell, five minutes."

Holly moves toward Levy. "Eight minutes. Please."

Levy snorts. "No, Treadwell, no haggling tonight."

"Me? Haggle? I'm from Philadelphia. We don't haggle." Holly strains for a merry, flirtatious tone. But the strain shows, and her words sound shrill. She's desperate now, and she's lost the energy to flirt.

"Maybe you Philadelphia ladies have a different word for it," Levy says, crossing his arms. "But you're haggling. Five minutes. Because I like you."

"Thanks, Levy."

Levy has just implied that if he didn't like Holly, Camilla would be long-gone in the OR, taking in the gas as her arms are stretched out, with Sneaker monitoring her BP and studying her sallow complexion,

Levy sponging down her vacant uterus after the manual removal, a nurse gently prodding Levy not to forget the sponge in utero. "Sponge, Dr. Levy," she'd say under her breath.

That's how Camilla's fate is decided, by whether or not Levy likes Holly Treadwell. What will happen when Holly is old and haggard and the residents don't like her as much as they do now, which is not terribly much? What will happen to Holly's patients then, when their labors are managed by a middle-aged midwife who has lost the power to charm?

Holly explains the manual removal procedure to Camilla. Prepared childbirth, Morrison-style.

"I go under the knife?"

"No knives, no stitches."

"But I go to sleep," Camilla says, double-checking.

"You go to sleep."

"I don't want to." She shudders.

"There's still time for you to bring it out on your own. I'll crank the table up higher to help move the placenta down." Holly believes in the power of positive thinking. The placenta is about to dislodge itself, and Camilla will bring it out on her own. "With the next contraction, push with all your might, as if this is a whole baby you have to get out."

"I'm tired."

"If you get it out, you'll be eating breakfast in bed soon."

"When will it be over?" Camilla has returned to the whimpering state of her predelivery hours. Her baby isn't there to offer his good example: his placid acceptance, his easy love. She no longer has her baby at all.

The scrub room has a small window looking into the DR, so that physicians can keep their eyes on their patients as they scrub. But as Levy scrubs up for the manual removal, he keeps his eye on the midwife, not the patient.

This is now a midwife–doctor fight. Holly promised herself that she wouldn't let politics interfere in the care of her patients, but she's sucked in. She cares more about winning this as a professional game now than she does about what happens to Camilla. The only saving grace is that her sense of professional competition doesn't run contrary to what's best for the patient. She wants to defend the touch-and-go bond of Camilla and her Ronnie, but she also wants to beat Levy but good.

"Push!" Holly shouts at Camilla, and the shout almost doesn't sound like her voice. She sounds angry. Holly clamps the cord with the ring forceps, but when nothing happens, gives it up and tosses the forceps, with a clanking clatter, into the basin. The basin contains the small amount of blood that came out with the baby, the product of broken blood vessels in the cervix, and the blood is clotted and dark now, a sign that it's been a while since the baby was born. Holly fights off despair by marshaling her mental powers and willing the placenta out. She shouts again in an anxious voice, almost annoyed that Camilla doesn't know what's at stake, for her or for Holly.

Levy appears in the doorway in a fresh surgical cap and mask and long gloves that run up his forearms. He's ready to go. He stretches his arms up and out in front of him so the gloves' sterile field won't be compromised by touching any septic material thing, and in a low, cool voice, he says, "Looks like an accreta to me."

"A tardy placenta," Holly says without turning. "How do you make a differential diagnosis between a tardy placenta and a placenta accreta?"

"You look at the clock," says Levy. "That's how you make a differential diagnosis."

An orderly with a hand truck for garbage squeezes by Levy, followed sheepishly by a worker from Housekeeping with a cleaning unit, now dressed in a yellow visitor's gown, having been hollered at by Sparks: "You, Housekeeping, where is your yellow gown?"

"Looks like closing time," Levy says genially.

"Or a public exposition," Holly says. She turns to the men. "Maybe we could have some privacy here," she says, blocking the view of Camilla with her body.

The men glance at each other.

"You mean me?" the orderly says.

"I mean both of you. You can come back later."

Holly understands the real purpose of the drapes used in delivery, which have long been proved to be of no help in infection control. Those drapes to the hilt don't provide sterility so much as privacy, a peremptory means of salvaging the trespassed modesty of patients without inconveniencing the hospital employees. Instead of keeping employees away from women who are, for the most part, naked, the hospital works for its own convenience and makes the women less naked so the employees can move about freely.

Except in Holly's delivery room.

The orderlies leave, grumbling, and Holly feels sick. Sick of the laws designed for the good of the hospital, under the pretense of being good for the patient, which are in fact detrimental to the patient. Sick of Morrison and Levy and the way they've made her become a hard-nosed bitch. Sick of the fifteen-minute placenta rule and of fighting and what the fighting is doing to her. "Christ," she thinks, with a spasm of terror, "I'm twenty-eight years old, and I'm burning out."

"Ooof!" Camilla's mouth turns down like the mask of Tragedy, with impossible elasticity and informed by her gift of theatrics.

Holly is irritated. "What now?" she thinks. Did she throw a pair of scissors onto Camilla by accident or stab her with a needle? That kind of luck would be apt: an iatrogenic stab wound on top of everything else.

But, no. The umbilical cord has jerked. It's doing its little dance, shaking, quaking. . . . Holly picks up the ring forceps to grab hold of the cord, but as she prepared to clamp, she loses her chance and knows it and grabs the basin instead. Plop. A fat placenta, like any other organ that has lost its way and is out of place, has arrived exactly where Holly wants it, in the basin of congealed blood, on the loose in the big, bad world but trapped all the same. It has splashed, to Holly's benefit and loss, splattering Holly's scrubs with fresh and old blood, but that's all right. Because there it is, the placenta, which has died for good, in the right place, in the right hands, and at what now seems to be exactly the right time.

A roar comes from the hallway as the man from Housekeeping revs up his machine.

"Aren't you great, Camilla!" Holly calls as she holds the basin to catch the fresh blood still streaming in a sporadic trickle out of the uterus. The placenta is intact, with no holes, no chunks missing.

Levy scuffles to the delivery table, fixing Holly with a long look, and peels off his surgical gloves, which he lays on the rim of the basin. "These are for you, dollface," he says, and shuffles out again.

"Levy?" Holly calls when he's almost out the door.

"What now, Treadwell?"

"You're a good buddy."

"I bet you say that to all the boys."

"The funny thing is, I don't."

The funny thing is, now that the threat of manual removal has been withdrawn, Holly actually likes Levy again. She likes Camilla. She almost likes Sparks.

No. She doesn't. By her sixth sense, Sparks has deduced that the placenta is delivered. She enters the DR as if she's not the least bit surprised to see the placenta, in its brick-red glossy mass, contained within the basin.

"Are you through with the placenta, Holly? I must pack it up to send to the university lab."

They used to have to save umbilical cords as well, sold to the labs for fee based on length, and memos went out encouraging midwives and doctors to "maintain lengths as long as are medically feasible." Holly purposely cut the cords needlessly far away from the baby then.

Sparks is always the first person to collect the placentas, and Holly wonders if maybe Sparks is what people used to think midwives were—a witch—and steals them to make potions from them. Maybe there's a rite that demands a steady supply of fresh afterbirths, and witches have infiltrated all the maternity wards in the country. . . .

"I'm through with the placenta, Miss Sparks. Thank you."

Holly sponges Camilla around the perineal area with soapy water, then pats her dry, lays a Chux pad beneath her, along with maternity pads, Kotex-like pads a bit longer and wider than the ordinary pad, tosses away the draping mounded on top of her, and pulls down her hospital gown. Holly likes cleaning up a woman after birth. Everything tidy, clean, comfortable, settled in a real bed, more or less.

Sparks puts the placenta in a plastic bag and ties the bag with the kind of twist-tie found in boxes of Baggies. If Sparks doesn't take the placenta home, it'll go into the placenta freezer to be sold in bulk with all the other placentas to the university, where it'll be dissected and analyzed and discarded again.

Holly doesn't mind seeing the placenta go. Because now Camilla and Holly are alone in the delivery room. Soon they'll leave the DR behind, too. They've been there too long already. Levy is gone. Sparks is gone. The baby is gone. The placenta is gone. They have nothing but themselves. That's all right. Because in the morning, and it's almost morning, Camilla will wake up, sit up, eat breakfast, and then see her baby, Ronnie.

CHAPTER 23

"**A**m I waiting to go to the recovery room?" a new mother asks, lying on a cart in the corridor.

"No, baby, this *is* the recovery room," Crowley answers. "From here, you go straight to bed, say your prayers, and eat your breakfast. We just keep an eye on you for a while."

If Seven-B isn't going nuts—isn't in the throes of hectic, zooey times—postpartum patients wait it out in the hallway, hard by the alternative birthing center and across the way from the admitting desk.

There *is* a recovery room, next door to the OR, but it's not in the swim of things and is mostly used for section patients, heavy-duty hemorrhage cases, or women who have suffered stillbirths and need some kind of quiet and privacy.

As the convenience of the staff is the principal impulse behind nonvital hospital functions, the rest of the mothers recover as they deliver, in public. After giving birth, they're wheeled into the corridor and left there for forty-five minutes before being sent to the dark enclosures of Postpartum. It's easier to check them for signs of hemorrhage when they're smack-dab in the middle of things than when they're cordoned off in Recovery, off the beaten track.

Strolling by, nurses, midwives, and residents massage the patients' bellies and tell the patients to do so themselves—this stimulates contractions and checks for mushy "bogginess" that indicates a blood flow that has been obstructed by clots or bits of placenta lying over the cervical opening. And if a lady gushes blood, she'll gush it in the hallway, where a radical flow of blood can't be overlooked.

Most of the mothers don't seem to mind being exposed during recuperation. Peering in the labor rooms, they watch as other women are moved to the DR, with the perspective of survivors and the great relief of knowing the worst is over. If the mothers are primaps and didn't know what to expect, they know now, and there's a certain gratification in watching other women get wheeled away for initiation into these widely held mysteries. Holly has noticed that when postpartum mothers are confined in Recovery without the advantage of contrasting themselves with those women about to give birth, they lose their justified sense of specialness, having become simply postpartums among other postpartums. They've become commonplaces.

The recovery room might be preferable to the hallway if it were a pretty, airy place, but it's not, and it has little to recommend it over the kinetic virtues of corridor recovery. Hungry, thirsty, still hooked up to their IVs, they lie on their sides and study their babies in the transport cribs beside them. The two tubes of cord blood, propped up against the babies' swaddled bodies, are almost half the babies' lengths.

Fathers and mothers' mothers, forbidden to attend deliveries, return from exile by the elevators to meet the babies. The fathers clutch the new mothers' hands as they try to soak in the change. Some of them are pretty tough nuts, but they almost all seem moved. What is more common and stunning than a birth? Than a father seeing his baby for the first time? Men have always come back from outside a room to find the baby there, a human being that never existed before. Holly wonders if hope is an instinct, like other self-preservation mechanisms, that rises up without even willing it. Under the worst conditions, babies embody hope. Maybe this is the baby, the one for whom everything will be different. . . .

The young mother asks Crowley, "Why do all the babies come out at night?"

"The babies take their own time," Crowley says, touching the baby's forehead with a light fingertip. "They like the company of other little babies, and they won't come out until they know the other little babies are out and about."

This doesn't seem farfetched to Holly, as babies are almost nothing but adrenaline—a newborn's adrenal gland is his largest organ and is as big as an adult's adrenal gland. After birth, the adrenal gland shrinks away, only to grow back as the baby grows, but at birth, it's like a huge engine, linked up in the labor and delivery process in ways nobody quite understands yet. Who is to say that the baby doesn't hear other babies cry, which triggers his adrenaline, which sends him reeling out of the womb?

Crowley admires the baby. She always stops to admire the babies. She doesn't get enough of them, for the babies are hardly here on Seven-B at all before they leave the nursery, so Crowley admires them when she can.

Crowley knows just how vulnerable and suggestible young mothers and fathers can be, and as the mother's boyfriend stands over the crib, looking at his baby with wonder, Crowley tells him, "I believe the baby looks just like you."

The purported father lights up. "You think so?"

"I certainly do," she says. "Look at the eyes." Nurse as definitive authority.

Holly glances up from some paperwork, wondering how much Crowley does on purpose to improve the ward's vibes and how much just comes naturally—Crowley always leans in a positive direction. Her casual observation that the baby looks like the boyfriend could have incalculable influence. What if the man wasn't sure the baby is his? Maybe Crowley put an end to his doubt for good, and changed the way he felt about the kid. He can always remember what the authority figure in the hospital told him, that the baby had to be his, the likeness was that strong.

A young woman comes into the ward, uneasily, to be admitted. She's not used to Seven-B's sights and sounds. Holly can tell she's scared. The new mother, lying near her baby, holding her boyfriend's hand, is reassuring, smiling in a weary but happy way, and the baby is cute in his receiving cap, wrapped up in all those itsy-bitsy blankets. It takes some of the terror out of it, to see what the point of the long, tough haul really is. In a minute, the young woman's boyfriend joins her. It's someone Holly knows. It's Nigel.

Holly first met Nigel two years ago at a teen fathers' discussion group, which was the social worker's province; Holly was there to answer questions about pregnancy and birth control and take stock of the people she viewed as her constituency. Or, more accurately, the guys who produced her constituency. The social worker asked them, "How many of you think it's cool, that it proves you're a man, to get a girl pregnant?"

They all shook their heads and said what they were supposed to say. "We know it ain't cool." "Everyone knows it's the manly thing to be responsible about birth control." Then Nigel took the floor. "Let's not BS the ladies, all right? The macho thing is to put a baby in the oven. It means you got what it takes, where it matters, and you know we be bragging on it, too, on our manhood." Natural leadership ability. "If you can't do anything else, at least you can do this."

During the labor of his then-girlfriend, Nigel was a trouper. (Teenage fathers with strong father figures in their lives stand a better chance of behaving well than those without. Nigel's uncle lived with his family and set down a code of behavior for Nigel, which he followed pretty well.) Nigel stayed in school, wearing a locket with a picture of his son in it. One day he came to see Holly at the clinic—the one and only boyfriend of any patient who did that. "I don't have nothing to give my kid," he said. "I don't have no money to buy things for it."

The young dads seem to love their kids, but they think in concrete terms. If they don't have anything to bring their kids, they figure they have nothing to give and that they've failed to provide. This demoralizes them, while their girlfriends are demoralized by the boys' limited view of their role. "All he does is bring little Smurf thing-a-dings and little bears and all this nonsense when all I want is a little help now and then. All these little nonsenses he does!" was what one teenage girl once told Holly.

The thing to do is catch the demoralization before it sinks in too deep. But Holly doesn't know who is supposed to do that. Or how to avoid demoralization herself.

"First of all, Ni, your baby isn't an it—it's a he or a him, and you should call him by that. Second of all, imagine yourself when you were a little kid. What would you have wanted from your dad, if he'd been around?"

Nigel laughed. "For him to be around. Period."

Holly looked at him and let what he said kick in. "You think your son is going to be any different?"

"No."

"You know the old song, 'I Can't Give You Anything But Love, Baby'?"

"No."

"Well, that's the name of that tune. Stay in school. Work hard. You'll get a good job one of these days, because you're a smart guy, and you'll be able to help out more financially. But until then, your baby needs your love, attention, and care. You can give him that much."

"Yes, I can," Nigel says, beaming from her compliments.

Now Nigel is rushing over to Holly, Sparks hollering at him to put on a yellow visitor's gown, and as Holly helps him into the gown, he says, "I tried to get Cherie to go to you all at Howard Street, but she wouldn't listen. I messed up when I said Samantha went there." Samantha is the mother of his first baby.

"All's well that ends well," Holly says gently. Then she smacks him on the arm. "Did you plan this out? Or was this a surprise?" Surprise pregnancy is what the Howard Street midwives call unplanned pregnancies. Maybe the pregnancies aren't planned, but they're not accidents either. Or if they are accidents, that's too negative a way to phrase it.

"She surprised me, believe me!"

"Didn't you have anything to do with it?"

Nigel lifts his hands, protesting his innocence. "She told me . . ."

"You've had enough surprises for one lifetime, Nigel."

He smiles sheepishly. He's sheepish because he's pleased with himself. Holly doesn't know how to go up against that, or if she's the person to do it. It's too hard for her, as a twenty-eight-year-old white woman, to tell an eighteen-year-old black guy how he's supposed to run his life, since she doesn't know the half of it.

She pats him on the arm. "I miss you. Come and visit me sometime, when you want to talk."

He nods and smiles. Their eyes meet, shyly. She knows he never will.

Holly is on six. Calvin Billings sidesteps the receptionist's desk altogether. He has a bunch of furled-up flowers in his hand and wears a

Windbreaker zipped up tight over a sweatshirt, the hood hanging out down his back. He walks silently in his Pumas, but from behind him comes a strong female voice that says only: "Calvin Billings!"

Calvin Billings jumps all the way around, without touching the ground, like a cat. "Oh. Busted."

Down the hall are Henrietta Harrison and a woman who must be Henrietta Harrison's mother. She looks just like Henrietta, only older.

"You come over here!"

In the arms of Henrietta Harrison's mother is the baby, wrapped up in a bright yellow blanket.

"You're out of bed, Henrietta," Calvin says, approaching with unnatural slowness.

"Yes, Calvin," Henrietta's mother says.

Calvin Billings bows, holds up the bouquet, and for the first time in history, sees his son.

"Here, Calvin Billings, you take this," Henrietta says, handing him a flowered overnight case. When an elevator arrives, Henrietta yanks him into the car by his hood.

Calvin Billings stares to the front.

As the doors close, Henrietta says, "Now where have you been?"

Calvin Billings sneaks a glance at the baby in the yellow blanket. "Word up, Henrietta," he says. "Does the little dude look like me?"

And the elevator doors close.

That's all Holly ever sees of Calvin Billings.

CHAPTER 24

Holly is in bed with the windows open, a cool breeze twisting up the light curtains in her bedroom. Matt seems a distant memory she misses only vaguely. She dips in and out of sleep, dreaming of other lines of work. She could be a florist, arranging bright, sweet flowers all day. She could become intimate with pale-green stems and deep-green leaves shaped like tubes. She could be a baker, icing cakes with a flourish of her hand, kneading dough before anyone else is awake. . . .

When she wakes up fully, she thinks, "Why are all these jobs manual work of one kind of another? Work with my hands? I'm college-educated. I should think about investment banking."

But who lies in bed and dreams of investment banking? Besides, she knows that can't be her way. She must do good things with her hands. It's her nature.

She puts her hands under her head and rolls back to sleep.

The phone rings. It's about time something roused her out of the old midwife hibernation restorative-sleep cure for the emotionally drained.

"Speaking," Holly says.

"I'm glad you are able to do that much," says Mrs. Gruener, the head of the midwifery service, in her German accent.

"Oh, hello, Mrs. Gruener." Holly sits up straight and brushes back her hair. "What brings you to—"

"It so happens that Pam will not be able to attend Convention. Her mother is going into the hospital tomorrow. Your name is on the waiting list of midwives who desire to be set loose in Houston. Do you still desire to go?"

"Of course I desire, Mrs. Gruener. Convention is carnival." Holly slaps her own face. This is not the thing to say to someone who is already fairly convinced that Holly is frivolous, trivial, and childish. "And I'm really looking forward to the continuing-ed seminars," Holly says.

"I am sure you are," Mrs. Gruener says. "And I look forward to seeing you there, at every single one."

Click.

"My bags are packed," Holly says, into the dead line.

CHAPTER 25

Scott has made a big career move. For the first time, he has actually taken the initiative. He poked his tousled head out of the Not-O.K. and saw a patient pushed in a wheelchair by her mother toward the admitting desk. Then he did the unexpected, radical thing. He stepped forth and approached the desk *of his own volition*. This diverges remarkably from the classic Scott response, in which he'd retract his head, slam the door, and hide, more or less, under the bed, with the candy wrappers and dustballs. Holly wonders why he has changed, whether it's confidence, courage, a sense of responsibility, or the awareness that Levy is probably going to demolish him when it comes time to write up reports.

In any case, Scott has volunteered to do the workup; whether or not he sticks it out to the end is another story. Sometimes he leaves a workup in the middle, the history taken but the bloods not drawn, or the bloods drawn and an IV in place but no exam done.

Holly is labor-sitting an upset woman, monitoring the possibly tachy baby, and can see Scott and his patient when she leans against the radiator. At first she watches him absentmindedly, hardly aware that she's watching him at all, the white of his jacket just a plain field to rest her eyes on. But now that he's trying to wangle a catheter into the back of the girl's hand, her interest is piqued. *Say hey, Treadwell, look alive and watch this!*

The purpose of most IVs is to keep a pipeline open to the patient's veins. The dextrose solution maintains maternal hydration and gives the patient energy, but a bowl of ice chips and a few hard candies would finesse this need just as well, with less discomfort and at less expense. The point of running a dextrose solution isn't that. It's to ready a transport system for wartime, for disasters, when you have to slam something other than dextrose into the veins. The transport system runs idle in neutral, with dextrose solution.

IV preparedness is a pain in the ass. Too many working hours go into it. Too much time spent finding a hospitable vein, only to see it roll beneath the needle. Too much time searching the forearms for a usable vein, only to give up and resort to the back of the hand, where veins are more accessible but the sticking causes more pain. Too much time stretching the skin out around the vein so the skin won't pucker up, because once the skin puckers, the catheter won't glide in, and if you're reduced to working a catheter into a vein, you might as well give up—you've lost it. Holly spends too much time sticking her patients twice, just at the moment when it's most important for her to establish a rapport with her patients, when she wants them to relax, trust her, and feel comfortable, in a fashion.

What a novelty it'd be to have a labor and delivery free of needles. A friend from midwifery school now works in a home birth practice. When Holly asked her if she was happy doing home births, the woman said, "Oh, yeah! Almost no needles of any kind!" No IVs, no Pit, no episiotomy repair, no glinting needles, no rolling veins.

Scott sticks his patient once, twice, three times. Each time, the catheter springs out of the blood vessel. This is proving to be more than minor discomfort for the patient. This is starting to hurt her, which is clear enough when Holly steps forward and the woman catches Holly's eyes with a frightened expression. I'd be scared, too, if this ape were sticking me, Holly thinks.

Assuming what she thinks is an officious yet friendly voice, extending an officious yet friendly offer, Holly asks Scott if he needs a hand.

"No, thank you," Scott says with determination, not turning around. "Everything is under control, thank you."

"We have a saying in midwifery," Holly says softly, standing by his bent back. "Three strikes and you're out. Sometimes you get jinxed and just can't swing it after three tries. . . ."

"I'm not in midwifery." Scott plunges the needle in for the fourth time, but the vein rolls, the needle falls, useless, on the woman's forearm, and a short stream of blood spurts out. "Damn!" He mops up the small pool of blood. "All right," he says sternly, "let's try this hand." He sticks the patient in the right hand. "This isn't midwifery," he says coldly. "This is medicine."

"Well, I guess it is."

But the point is moot for now, as Scott has made it this time.

CHAPTER 26

Levy grabs Holly's arm. She has just finished taking a woman's blood pressure and is wrapping up the cuff. Now Levy is shoving Holly toward a window. "Look over there," he says. He points at Building B, a grim building with barred windows that houses the psychiatric ward. "What do you see?"

"Leavenworth Federal Penitentiary?"

"No. Look again."

"I don't see anything. Nothing."

"That's right. Nothing. You see nothing because the entire building has emptied out and is coming over here."

"The nut cases have left Building B for the L and D ward?"

"This is correct." Levy glances at his watch.

"Did you guys synchronize your watches?" Holly asks.

"Just about. In three minutes, they should be here."

"Should I batten down the hatches? Ready the Thorazine? What?"

"Hide your shopping bags. A bag lady is on the way. A paranoid schizophrenic—but then, they say that about all the gals over there. Last known domicile was the sidewalks and gutters and piss factories of New York. Yes, a bag lady is about to deliver two bag babies."

"A paranoid schizophrenic and multiple gestation?" Holly asks. Triple whammy. "What are the ramifications here?"

"Two options," Levy says. "First option is that you and I turn the fifth-floor supply room into our private love nest, our lair of joy."

"What's the second option?"

"You take over all the residents' patients as we residents live and earn— excuse me—*learn* from an experience which, in all probability, will uncannily resemble an inner circle of Hell. Exactly which circle is not yet clear."

"The residents are going to Hell?" Holly exclaims. "I can deal with that."

"Hark!" Levy puts a hand to his ear. "I believe I hear the lady in question approaching."

A woman's voice is bellowing down the hall with the kind of power that seems summoned up only by the insane. This is a voice devoid of gentility. This is a voice that does not give a damn how it sounds to others.

"Goddamnit!" the voice bellows. "God, goddamn you, give me a break, will ya! Just one goddamn minute! Please! Ohhhh, God! Just give me a goddamn break!" The voice nears. The voice is quite irritated now. "Knock it off already! How many times I gotta tell ya? Enough is enough! What kind of joke is this? What's wrong with you, God, you got your head up your ass?"

"Christ, Levy," Holly says, turning to him, eyes wide. "That's not nuts. That's blasphemy."

"I think she's being kind of reasonable," Levy says, moving toward the swinging doors. "Anyway, I warned you that Hell is on its way. Keep the fifth-floor love nest in mind as a last resort. Heaven. It could be heaven."

There's a phalanx of attendants guarding, steering, blocking the gurney that carries the madwoman forth. A social worker, a psychiatrist, an orderly from the psychiatric ward, psychiatric nurses, residents. Gus is worked up. He keeps sticking his fingers in his hair, as if he can just barely contain his excitement. It seems like he's about to burst. "Let's do it!" he keeps shouting. Do what?

Holly can barely catch a glimpse of the madwoman in labor. A chink in the wall of people breaks through. Holly sees a bushy-haired woman with the gray, ravaged face of a sixty-year-old. She is an old crone. That this old crone is about to give birth is a paradox that sends Holly's mind reeling. Part of her believes what she sees; another part denies its existence. The pregnancy is the only element of youth that seems to have lasted. Mental illness and street living and incarceration in Building B have stripped her of any physical characteristics that could possibly say "youth."

Her skin is old; her face, her hair are very old. Everything is old except that big belly, which looks, under the circumstances, to be nothing but a tumor gone wild. Her feet are bare and swollen, full of sores and scabs and scratches. She literally tears at her hair as she hollers at God to "just quit it already, will ya? Give a goddamn girl a break?"

The woman has done all her laboring in Building B to spare the labor and delivery ward from her wild complaints. She has been brought over at the last minute, now that she is completely dilated. When Holly was in high school, she held the romantic belief that crazy people had more wisdom than everyone else, that they saw through the world's hypocrisies and wouldn't accept them. But now Holly wonders if maybe mad people see the world's truths and won't accept them either. Which is not such a romantic approach. Holly has never seen anyone fight labor as this woman is doing.

In the delivery room, the residents and the social worker and the psychiatric nurses crowd around her, bellow at her, outdoing her own bellows. "Push! Push! Push!" They are trying to connect with a woman who, for all intents and purposes, is disconnected. "Push! Push! Push!"

She hears them. "I'm pushing already! Enough already! Just a minute, God, I have to catch my breath!"

A nurse stands by Holly in the doorway. "You know, when I had my first child, I used those very same words."

"I bet nobody called you crazy when you shouted like that."

"Oh, yes, they did. They had to give me twenty-five milligrams of Demerol before they could get me to shut up."

The crazy woman delivers two boys. They're blue—cryanosis—and both of them have one-minute Apgars in the four to six range, which is not good. They look to weight about five pounds each.

"Is it over? Is it goddamn over? Are there babies?"

But nobody answers. "We're almost ready to go home now," the psychiatrist says.

"Is it over?"

Holly wonders what the fate of the bag babies will be, now that they're wards of the state. What will their future be? Was their mother on Thorazine when she first conceived? How long did she walk the streets, pregnant, barefoot, sick?

It's not your problem, Treadwell. You can't do anything about it.

I can adopt them.

No, you can't.

The bag lady is yelling at God. "Get me outta here, God, on a magic carpet, will ya?"

She has stopped asking about the babies. Maybe the babies will be one chapter in a long saga of hallucinations, an ephemeral image stuck, in her mental chain of events, somewhere between talks with Jesus and a flight across town on the wings of an angel. Or will the birth be recalled as the one flash of irrefutable reality? Maybe the crazy woman's mind will tell her, "That was legit. Those babies really happened."

The babies are born into life as wards of the state, motherless as soon as they are yanked out of the crazy woman by Levy. They were motherless even before they were born.

Scott shambles out the delivery room door, knocking into Holly and the nurse en route. He peels off his cap and says, "I'll tell you one thing. When she complains, she goes right to the top."

"I don't think God can hear her from here," Holly says to no one in particular. "I don't think prayers ascend from Morrison very easily."

"Why do you say that?" the nurse asks, offended, and turns away.

"Thank you, God!" the woman shouts as the placenta is delivered, Levy twirling it from a pair of forceps. "I am now released."

The social worker and psychiatrist and orderlies and nurses prepare to wheel the woman back across the cold, dark courtyard, to Building B, where she will stay in a postpartum unit of one.

CONVENTION

CHAPTER 1

Holly lies on the bed, taking a short lie-down before heading out to Newark for the flight south. Matt is beside her. "I guess I don't have to worry about you," he says, stroking her hair. "Straying, I mean."

She pulls back. "What do you mean? Of course you have to worry about me."

"How much trouble can you get into, with five hundred midwives?"

"Plenty," Holly says, indignant. "Drinking, picking up cowboys, raiding the men's sauna. I could get into all kinds of trouble."

Matt smiles. He doesn't believe her.

"Don't challenge me, Matt," she says. "You know I'll only rise to the challenge."

"I can't help it," he says, still smiling. "I just can't get worried about it."

Holly turns over and faces the window. "You are not a nice guy," she says. "A nice guy would be worried about it."

CHAPTER 2

A gathering of midwives doesn't consist of strikingly at-tractive women. Holly had forgotten just how plain they all can be, as she tends to think of the midwives she works with as good-looking. Did the power of affection demolish her objectivity? She and Katrina, who is sharing her hotel room, stand by the glass elevators in the hotel lobby and survey their colleagues. Sensible-looking women, Holly decides, which is probably more practical for the profession than if they were stunning. The older women dress for travel, in white blazers over slacks, while the younger women, who have no history of dressing up to fly on an airplane, schlepp about in khakis and jeans. A few midwives look vaguely hippie-ish, in Mexican dresses and shawls, a bit adrift in the brutal air-conditioning and the Muzak.

Holly smiles at everyone in case she passes someone she's met before but doesn't remember. In the back of her mind works the thought, "One of these people might be able to give me a job someday." She has started to understand politics. Thinking of the future, she glad-hands everybody.

A covey of Air Force midwives, two men with three women, march by in sharp-fitting navy blue plumage. "Birds of a feather," Katrina mutters deprecatingly.

But Holly understands the allure of the armed services, which pay for education, housing, food, and medical bills. The armed services hold you tight while other midwives thrash about in a cyclone of choices or founder in a dearth of them. The Air Force midwives look comfortable in uniform, in a clear, clean identity that answers any and all questions about the person inside the uniform. And Holly likes to take note of the male midwives: men who entered the war machine only to wind up catching babies. She feels a tinge of envy, jealous of their sure footing, as she and Katrina push into the ballroom for the opening of the convention.

The air is galvanized, high anticipation buzzing through the room, as if something extraordinary is about to happen. What's actually going to happen is that the financial status of the American College of Nurse-Midwives will be made public, a no-doubt-depressing disclosure, after which midwives will get to argue about policy.

Holly is hopeful that at least one heated exchange will spice up the proceedings. Midwives tend to be goody-two-shoes, so heated exchanges are often tempered by a veneer of equity and respect. But midwives are feisty, too, goody-two-shoes with opinions, and Holly indulges her desire for excitement, which is a muted, mixed thing. Too many professional disasters crouch, ready to spring, for Holly to be entirely comfortable with excitement. Threats from the insurance companies to decline to renew liability policies. State legislatures requiring that all new nurse-midwives have master's degrees. Sagas of midwifery services that have closed when their physician backup stranded them and no other backup was forthcoming.

Holly buttons up her cardigan sweater. The air-conditioning is rough. The hippie-ish midwives, mainly from the West Coast, have been going around the hotel sniffling and popping Vitamin C, complaining about the recirculated air and bad ions. Only a handful of midwives brave the Nordic blast of Texas-style air-cooling in short sleeves.

The president's gavel drops. Petty business cheats the midwives' hopes of excitement, as the president announces state chapter raffles and schedule changes before reaching the heart of the matter. "I'll now take a motion from the floor," she says, leaning into the microphone more closely than necessary. "This would create a new level of practitioner. A master of nurse-midwifery or a fellow of the college. The language has yet to be worked out, but the idea is to recognize those exemplifying excellence in the practice of nurse-midwifery."

A few midwives, prepared with arguments because they actually read the motion earlier, leap to their feet and appear at the microphones in the two central aisles.

The first midwife identifies herself, then says, "I object to the word *master*, since it could be misconstrued as referring to a university degree, and to the word *fellow* because of the sexism of the term. After all, we're a group of mostly female professionals, and we should be able to find a nonmale term to replace these titles. And doesn't the American College of Obstetrics and Gynecology grant the title of 'fellow' to any dues-paying member? It's a devalued term."

Thoughts run through Holly's mind, ideas she hadn't considered until now but which she is sure are legitimate opinions that must not wither and die in the confines of her own brain. Holly finds herself standing up. Holly is going to speak. Katrina tugs at her sleeve, and Holly slaps her hand away because Katrina is stretching out her sweater.

Katrina hisses, "What are you doing?"

Holly slaps her hand again. Katrina is interrupting the train of thought forming into a whole idea, and she doesn't want to lose the fluent eloquence mentally taking shape, which might possibly last long enough to be transformed into speech. If Holly is going to speak to hundreds of people, she'd prefer not to make a total ass of herself. Her adrenaline charges forth, and row upon row of midwives take on a super-bright appearance, as though Holly is watching them on a Panavision screen.

The midwife ahead of her is putting forth an interesting objection. *Listen to her, Treadwell. Stop thinking about yourself.*

"What kind of peer review would be set up for this mechanism?" the midwife asks. "We don't even have adequate peer review to ensure that the midwives out there are all competent." Scattered hisses, as the suspicion that incompetent midwives might be out there botching their way along, unseen, is considered a breach of faith.

Holly agrees with the midwife at the microphone and says, under her breath, "Go on. You're right."

The midwife, who probably has never been hissed at in her entire life, recovers her poise. "Setting up viable peer review for all midwives, so we don't make the same mistakes as the guys at ACOG, should be our first priority. If other professional groups can't police themselves, we'll be just that much more superior for being able to do it."

A voice in the crowd shouts, "We police ourselves already!" Light applause.

The beleaguered midwife is now inspired. "For this new category of midwife, what mechanism would unearth those midwives working alone out in the boondocks? How would the lone rangers receive their proper due?"

Applause. For the lone rangers, it would seem.

It's Holly's turn, now, and she doesn't look at the midwives who've turned to face her expectantly. She focuses on the president instead, who meets her gaze by studying papers on her desk.

"I'm Holly Treadwell, from New York City. At this point in time" —she winces at her own syntax, what a ridiculous thing to say, *point in time*, but she lurches on, if only to get away from those words—"at this time in history"—equally ridiculous, possibly more pretentious—"when the skill of midwives is still questioned by the public, the one point we shouldn't emphasize is that some midwives are better than others. What we have to get across is that nurse-midwives are all good and safe practitioners, and then we should construct a peer review system to make sure this is so.

"It's important that we stand together and not create elites within the college. We already have an award to honor excellence every year. What we need now are things that pull us together as a united front and encourage solidarity." Holly has hit her stride, and she likes the way it feels. "Let's not encourage divisiveness. I wouldn't want this college to become any more stratified than it already is."

Holly doesn't know she's finished until she is finished. When she realizes that anything said now would only be anticlimactic, she steps back and turns to walk back to her seat as distinct, if mild, applause lifts in the mustard-gold cavern of the room. Her face is flushed, now; her hands are a little shaky. When she was speaking, she'd ridden her own adrenaline and hadn't thought of the crowd. It was as if she'd been in a capsule, or one of the glass elevators gliding up the hotel atrium. Now she's been dropped back to earth to experience a retroactive stage fright, astonished that she pulled it off.

"What are you? A goddamn communist?" Katrina whispers at her. "Don't want no hierarchies? Are you anti-American?"

Four rows ahead is Mrs. Gruener, who has twisted her neck to catch Holly's eye. Mrs. Gruener is in her fifties, and good-looking, with blonde hair in a soft perm that's vaguely World War II in aesthetic origin. Her eyes are both sly and good-natured, and she dresses elegantly, like a European gentlewoman. Today she's in a linen suit, several lengths of pearls, and, as always, good earrings. Not what you'd expect to find in a Houston hotel complex or a Brooklyn housing project. Mrs. Gruener is simultaneously subversive and aristocratic. "I'm of a very old German family," she once sighed. "But let me tell you something, my dear. In this country, you can't count on the upper classes to have any class at all. Poor people almost always outclass rich people." Mrs. Gruener's opinion is of great importance to Holly, so when she waves her fingers at Holly, Holly gives her own fingers a cool flutter, thinking, "Mrs. Gruener approves!"

From the loudspeaker, a voices says, "Holly, I love you." This gives Holly a jolt. Nobody has ever expressed love for Holly in front of a hundred people before. "But I don't agree," the voice goes on. Holly strains her neck to see who loves her. Claire Hanlon, who worked at Howard Street before taking off for private practice. Holly straightens up to look attentive and interested, which she is.

"We live in a credentialed society, Holly," Claire says. Holly finds this personalization of the debate unseemly. "Other professional groups recognize master practitioners—"

"Sexist terminology!" shouts an irritated feminist.

"I'm sorry if the English language has been male-dominated for the last thousand years. For lack of better semantics, let me say that other groups acknowledge their masters by giving them titles of achievement. Such titles of stature will be of great help if and when nurse-midwives are called into court as expert witnesses—an eventuality we should be ready for. We have to compete on the world's terms, and I support a mechanism to recognize excellence in our field and convey that to the world at large."

Holly admits to herself that Claire has a point—not the first time her ability to empathize with opposite sides of an argument has proved to be a troubling hindrance.

A midwife with a quavering voice speaks. "If this mechanism for acknowledging excellence is put through, we should attach a rider that states the mechanism exists to further advance the profession in general, rather than the career of the person who receives the honor."

A lame statement like this, which no one could argue with, sets the restless audience squirming in their seats, bored with the entire issue and embarrassed for the midwife, so earnest about such a minor point. A vote is called, to save the midwife from herself, along with anyone else who might jump up with another useless declaration.

The "ayes" rise scattershot in the air. "Opposed." A loud, unified "No."

Katrina turns to Holly. "Congratulations. You just helped defeat a motion that could possibly be very productive for the college."

"*C'est la guerre.*"

"So it begins."

"What?" Holly asks.

"You come to Convention and speak up at meetings. Soon you'll join a committee and get elected to national position. In twenty years, you'll be up there, president of the college."

"Not me, mate," Holly says, laughing.

"Why not you? Who else?"

"Try Claire Hanlon," Holly says, laughing nervously now.

"We'd fucking draft you if Claire was put up for office."

From the rows ahead: "Ssssh."

"Don't swear," Holly tells Katrina.

"See, Holly? You were just made to fucking rule."

CHAPTER 3

Holly and Katrina steal a cigarette in a parking lot outside, the hot sun and tobacco making their way to Holly's brain when Meg Greenspan opens the door and strides out.

"Shut that door!" Katrina yells at Meg, whom Holly and Katrina know from chapter meetings in New York. "You're letting out the cold air!"

"Don't mind her," Holly tells Meg. "She overreacts to everything."

Meg smiles slightly, grudgingly indulgent. She is tall, thin, and flat-chested in a short-sleeved paisley-print shirt and wraparound skirt. With short brown hair, high cheekbones, and intelligent gray eyes (the kind Holly always pictured the goddess Athena as having), Meg is a woman Holly's mother would call "handsome," which is to say, attractive in a way that's not interested in being cute.

"I liked what you had to say, and I thought you said it well," Meg tells Holly. "How come you never open your mouth in chapter meetings?"

Holly shrugs. "Too pooped to party." The sun has baked her brain.

"You work at Howard Street?"

"I try to, at least."

They walk back into the hotel. After the violence of the noon heat, the air-conditioning is almost humane.

Meg asks, "Are you burned out yet?"

"Is burnout so inevitable?" Holly asks. She really wants to know. "What constitutes burnout anyway? When you start hoping the hospital burns down to the ground? When you lose the ability to get out of bed in the morning?"

"Those are helpful clues," Meg says. "How long do people last there, on average? Two years?"

"One midwife has been there ten years," Katrina volunteers.

"That's one," Meg says. "What about the others?"

135

"I don't know," Holly says. She frowns. "This is sort of a demoralizing discussion, Meg."

Meg turns to Holly, rushing her words. "Well, look-it. I have an ulterior motive to these questions. Maybe you already surmised as much. I'm looking for an experienced, articulate midwife certified to practice in New York."

Katrina looks around. "Where is she?"

"You're recruiting?" Holly asks, having failed to surmise any such thing.

"No lie," Katrina says with a snort, as if all recruiting efforts are basically repellent.

Scared of being overheard, Katrina looks around. The first person she sets eyes on is Mrs. Gruener, chatting up some other ACNM pioneers, who are gazing at her admiringly. Holly is proud of Mrs. Gruener—she's charismatic, able to combine devotion with a peculiar sense of fun, a woman with *presence*. Holly feels an almost physical loyalty to her, as if attached to Mrs. Gruener by an invisible but palpable rope. What other head of a midwifery service goes to her inner-city office in light tweeds and silk blouses because she thinks her impoverished clientele are classy ladies who know how to appreciate a sharp outfit?

But Mrs. Gruener has no significant place on Seven-B, where the whip comes down and burnout strikes. And her charm doesn't help when Holly walks into the clinic to find forty patient files on her desk, forty patients to be got through in eight hours, or when Holly has ten no-shows and spends hours tracking down her absent patients on the telephone.

Holly turns back to Meg.

"The next stop," Meg is saying, "is I buy you dinner."

Holly shakes her head. "I pay my own way. If you have anything to offer me, it's worth it for me to buy my own dinner."

"Don't be an idiot," says Katrina. "Meg's probably got special funds for recruitment suppers."

"Let's argue about this later," Holly says. She looks over to where Mrs. Gruener was standing. Mrs. Gruener is gone, and with her, the physical bond of loyalty. "Tonight then," she says brightly, feeling criminal. "Good."

CHAPTER 4

Hungry midwives swamp the exhibition hall. A pharmaceutical company is giving away free hors d'oeuvres, and Katrina, among others, intends to make a dinner of them. A pamphlet asks, WHY ARE WE ADVERTISING PANTYHOSE AT YOUR PROFESSIONAL MEETING? "I don't care why," Katrina says. "I just want my free sample."

A cluster of midwives gathers around the Air Force recruiting table. The Air Force has sex appeal: flattering uniforms, a general vision of airplanes and flight, the promise of foreign travel. But no interested parties surround the Army table. Who wants to be badly paid while wearing drab green?

The Army officer manning the table bites his nails, legs sprawled out. Army pens, shopping bags, and low, stingy stacks of flyers with outdated illustrations of ludicrously happy people in uniform are set out in too-neat symmetry, as if they've never been touched and he means to keep it that way. The Army recruiter sees Holly watching but doesn't make a move to entice her closer, having already decided that this pretty, intelligent-looking girl isn't going to midwife in the Army. He wants her to keep away. He doesn't want to waste his time or budget passing out a freebie to a nonprospect like herself. Holly stares at him. Feeling like a thief, she takes an Army pen. He stares back. And she turns away, with a chill.

Katrina points to the recruiting table for Midwives Alliance of North America, an organization composed mainly of lay midwives—midwives who have learned their skills informally or in formal programs that don't require nursing degrees. "When are you going to join, Holly?"

"You have some taco sauce on your lip, Katrina."

"You need your consciousness raised, Holly."

"Yeah? Who's going to raise it?"

137

"I am," Katrina says idly, turning to a birthing bar display. "Low-tech specialty. That's the silliest thing I ever saw."

A middle-aged man in a blue blazer demonstrates the bar, which gives a woman in labor something to hang on to as she squats to push. A bed rail would do as well, or a windowsill, a heavy chair, or human arms, but the birthing bar has been invented nonetheless. The man squats stiffly, as if his knees creak, leans his arms on the steel bar cushioned in ersatz leather, and attempts to imitate a woman in labor. Holly turns away. This must be the death of a salesman.

"I'm going upstairs," she tells Katrina.

"But you don't have half the stuff you could get."

"I'll live without it."

"Did you get a little notebook from the Franklin Company?"

A memo pad with a pseudo-Ultrasuede cover. Mighty cute.

"Okay," Holly sighs. "I'll snag one, and then I'm gone."

"Holly, if you want to get the good stuff, you'll have to wade through the patheticos. You're a midwife. You were my goddamn preceptor. You should know that by now."

"I'm on vacation. I don't want to see any patheticos."

"You're at Convention," Katrina corrects her. "And patheticos is what you get."

CHAPTER 5

Upstairs Holly flops onto her bed and flicks quickly through the nurse-midwives' registrar, given to her on registration. She is looking up Meg Greenspan. Meg Greenspan works in Brooklyn Heights. Meg Greenspan works for Dr. Ellen Futterman. Holly shuts her eyes. It all comes clear. Private practice. Progressive woman OB. Brooklyn Heights—shady streets, well-nourished moms-to-be in Laura Ashley shifts, a pleasant receptionist, a clean and calm hospital to deliver in. Meg Greenspan is here at Convention principally to recruit, and Meg Greenspan is recruiting Holly.

Holly throws the registrar across the room so that it strikes the wall and lands on the desk. Then she beats her feet into the mattress. "Yippee," she says. "Yippee."

This is what happens when you speak up in meetings and don't make an ass of yourself. Now that she knows, she'll have to do it again sometime.

Following a swim in the twilit pool, Holly bakes in the sauna, where nobody wears an identifying badge. Half the midwives are in swimsuits while the other half, Holly among them, wear nothing at all. The midwives talk generally, wondering if the administration of the pudendal block—a tricky bit of local anesthesia—will become part of the core competency curriculum that all nurse-midwifery candidates must complete.

One midwife is in the Air Force. Holly must have seen her fifty times before, but out of uniform she looks different—sweet, easygoing. The Air Force uniform may be snappy, but it's hard for a uniform to do a woman justice.

"How are things in the Air Force?" someone asks. "Lots of sections?

CPDs?" CPDs—meaning cephalo-pelvic disproportion, which happens when the baby is too big to pass through the pelvic inlet.

The Air Force midwife sighs. It's not in the Air Force's interest to do sections, as they cost the Force money and mean a doctor must come in on the case. "We're just up to our eyeballs in CPDs," the midwife says. "These American guys marry little Filipino gals, and gals from Guam and what-all. Those Pacific gals just aren't built for American babies."

Holly closes her eyes as the heat melts into her spine. She has to concentrate, imagine what Meg will say to her tonight. What questions should Holly be ready to answer? Questions on birth philosophy, analgesia and anesthesia use, forceps and sections, fetal heart monitors, amniotomy, bonding. Most likely Meg figures Holly's time at Morrison has medicalized her. Holly should come on sensitive, spiritual.

She sits up straight and grabs her towel.

If she's going to go for it, if she's going to move from Morrison, it'll have to be for a place where she can be herself.

Just be yourself, Treadwell, whoever that happens to be.

Spiritually medicalized, she thinks. That's me.

CHAPTER 6

The motel has three restaurants to represent three different levels of cuisine—or prices. The cheapest is The Brass Kettle, where Holly eats most of her meals. One notch up is Chuckles, which the advertisement in Holly's room claims is "a wee bit o' England" in Houston. Then there's the most *haute* of all, The Hunt Club—a wee bit o' posh, as it were.

Meg is taking Holly to Chuckles, which has dark wood and dim lighting to replicate the olde English pub effect.

"Maybe I should let you know where I'm coming from," Meg says, once they sit down in a booth.

"I'd like to know where you're coming from," Holly says.

"I come from Charlottesville, Virginia, first," says Meg. "And the sixties secondarily. Possibly I reversed the order, and it's the other way around."

Meg had been a political activist when a friend of hers became a public health nurse for the Indian Health Services and returned from the desert to tell Meg about social change through midwifery, helping women give birth to babies who'd grow up to be less aggressive, more enlightened than their doctor-delivered counterparts. Midwifery as a hidden influence, a form of crisis intervention. "Social engineering," Meg explains. "Now, fifteen years later, all I do is take care of well-off women."

Holly doesn't know what to say in the face of the death of Meg's political dreams. But she thinks of her own mother, who never received good obstetrical care, and says, "Rich women have gotten pretty screwed over by bad medical care over the years. I guess they're as deserving of decent care as anybody else."

"I arrived at that humanitarian insight myself," Meg says. "Rich women suffer, too. And if those enlightened babies happen to come from affluent homes, that's fine by me."

"You still believe midwifery can do that?"

"Don't you?"

"I don't know," Holly says uneasily. "I'd like to think it's true." Part of what she thinks midwifery involves is what she cannot say out loud. That midwifery involves the saving of souls. That you extend love and care to the mother, who passes it on to her baby...a small, imperceptible chain. But she's not sure if she's only dreaming or not.

"Well, what's your reason for being a midwife?" Meg asks.

Holly doesn't know how to answer; her reasons keep changing. Sometimes she thinks she's in it only for the adrenaline charge, but the professions that might offer stronger adrenaline rushes are countless: skydiving instructor, ER nurse, policewoman...

"I guess I think I'm doing good works," Holly says. "Making birth a positive thing for the mother so she's better able to love her kid. Giving better antepartum care so the baby is strong and healthy at birth..." Holly's voice trails off. There are plenty of reasons for being a midwife. Maybe one of them is that midwifery is the thing she does best in life, and she tells Meg this. "I like being around childbirth. It never bores me."

"If you were somebody else, who'd you want to deliver you kid?"

Holly doesn't hesitate. "Me," she says.

CHAPTER 7

"Did you know I was a lay midwife?" Katrina sits on the edge of her bed and looks eagerly at Holly, who would like to go to sleep, if possible.

"Really? No." Holly slips into bed.

Katrina waits expectantly. "You're supposed to react to that disclosure, Holly."

"Didn't I?" Holly turns on her back and stares at the ceiling. "I always wondered how you got accepted by midwifery school when you didn't have two years of maternity nursing."

"I was their token lay midwife."

"What possessed them to think they needed one?"

"Do you want to hear my story?" Katrina asks, her feet dangling off the side of the bed.

"Must I?" Holly says. "Wouldn't you rather watch David Letterman and forget about midwifery for a bit?"

"I prefer real life to television." Holly, who often prefers television to real life, is humbled. Katrina knows this and starts her story. "In college, I joined a women's health group, and we studied home birth with a renegade medical student. As soon as I heard about midwifery, I knew it was what I wanted to do."

"You had a calling," Holly says dryly. "Destiny." But her heart isn't in her sarcasm. She's always wondered if midwifery is an avocation or a vocation and had given up hope that a person "called" to midwifery actually exists. Holly's skepticism snaps up like a reflex, even though the eternal qualities of birth were what drew Holly to midwifery in the first place.

"I started doing home births with a midwife who trained in England but couldn't be licensed here," Katrina goes on.

143

Holly sits up, awake now. "Maybe you shouldn't talk to me about this," she says. "Home birth scares me. I've been at enough deliveries to know what can go wrong, and I wouldn't want them to go wrong in somebody's house in the woods, that's for sure." Flopping back on the bed, she says, "Home birth is pretty much of a political disaster for us anyway. One reason the medical establishment has always been opposed to midwives is that they're afraid we'll steal deliveries from the hospitals. That's how the anti-midwife feeling got started."

"What are you saying, Holly? That home births make the powers-that-be angry? Or that you don't think home birth is safe?"

Holly scratches her head. "Both." She laughs. "You forget how shaky nurse-midwifery can be. Look at the states that require a doc to be present at midwifery births. Or the hospitals that refuse to grant privileges to midwives for no good reason. Home birth thumbs its nose at the establishment and says, we don't need you. When the establishment is faced with outright threats like that, it reacts in a way that makes other nurse-midwives suffer. The med school or nursing school that sponsors midwifery programs will pull out or refuse midwifery students access to patients. If they decide too many midwives exist as is, they'll arrange it so there won't be any more. Nurse-midwives still have to walk the straight and narrow."

"Oh!" Katrina says brightly. "If we're really good girls and act nice, they'll let us live."

"Why'd you become a nurse-midwife anyway?" Holly snaps back.

Katrina considers the question. "As a lay midwife, no matter how good I became, if my client had to transfer to the hospital, I wouldn't be able to stay with her. I couldn't be happy as a midwife if I had to keep working in the shadows."

"You could have moved to a state where lay midwifery is legal," Holly points out, "where attending a normal birth isn't considered the practice of medicine."

In New York State, both the Board of Health and the Board of Nursing oversee the practice of midwifery. The Board of Health permits the practice of midwifery only by midwives who are licensed by the ACNM and practice with physician backup. Since the only midwives who may practice are, by definition, nurses, midwives are finally governed by the Board of Nursing.

Mrs. Gruener is lobbying for the establishment of an independent Board of Midwifery, which would speak to issues specific to midwifery and not be dominated by potentially competitive or hostile powers. As she told Holly, "A board of medicine regulating the midwives is similar to a pack of foxes regulating the chickens, no?"

Katrina clicks off the light and slides under her covers. "I live where I live, Holly," Katrina says, her voice smothered by her pillow. "New York is my home."

"What's the point of this guided tour through your outlaw past, Katrina? Why are you telling me this?"

"Because I'm still in favor of home birth, Holly, and I want you to be as well. I want you to talk to Sara, the midwife I worked with. She's worked in Africa, in England; she's interesting, and I want you to visit with her."

Holly sits up in the deep darkness of the hotel room. "Risk my neck by hanging out with illegal midwives? No way!"

"Wouldn't you like to see a home birth," Katrina says quietly, "to judge for yourself?"

Holly lies back. When people first meet her and find out what she does, they usually assume that she does home births. She feels like a fraud, sometimes, to be a midwife without ever having attended a home birth. "Katrina, why do you care so much?"

"Because I see where you're going, Holly. You could become an important person in this little world of nurse-midwives. And when you do, I'd hate to see you as closed-minded as some of these women in power."

"Don't flatter me, Katrina. I'm not going to be important. I hate politics and all that stuff."

"Maybe you do. But you jumped up in the business meeting, didn't you? You may loathe it," Katrina says with a laugh, "but that's why you'll wind up in it. Because you react to it."

"I'm going to stop that," Holly says drowsily. "I'm going to learn how to stop reacting to things."

The last thing Katrina has to say is, "I'd like to see you try."

CHAPTER 8

Holly woke up at six-thirty to get to this exercise class, where she hangs over at the waist to skim her fingers over her toes. *You're such a modern woman to be here, Treadwell.* Yippee-skippee. It feels like shit. She's tired of these conference rooms, this aggressive air-conditioning, and the fact that the only place to jog is an interstate highway dominated by rowdy fellows in pickup trucks so that in order to exercise, she's reduced to coming down here for a spot of aerobics with midwives.

She pulls herself up and glances down admiringly at the T-shirt she bought from the Frontier Nursing Service. It's dark blue, with the silhouette of a nurse on a bounding horse, as if they're taking, with grace and control, all the hurdles the midwifery steeplechase has to offer.

"Are you at FNS?" a short woman next to her asks.

"No, I labor in the inner city."

"I was at FNS," the woman says with a wink, as if Holly should get the joke. "Look where being part of history has gotten me."

A midwife with the audacity to wear a cobalt blue spandex leotard at this time of day leaps to the front of the room and gets them working. The class has begun.

The Frontier Nursing Service is less a place than a historic event, the birthplace of nurse-midwifery in America, started in 1925 in Hyden, Kentucky, by an American woman who imported English nurse-midwives at a time when midwives were discredited in this country. As more doctors here insisted that childbirth be conducted in hospitals, midwives were relegated to caring only for poor women and were often their sole health-care providers. Even when midwives were skilled and sensible in practice, they were inescapably tied to the Old World and the old ways, the world of poverty and hardship, in a time when modernity and

146

progress were worshipped. Sporadic efforts were made to train and license midwives, but for the most part they were unlicensed and conducted childbirth as they'd been taught by older midwives.

In contrast, English nurse-midwives were professionally trained and standardized through licensing. An odd marriage—English nurse-midwives caring for dirt-poor women in the Kentucky hollers. But it worked. Visiting their patients on horseback, the FNS midwives reduced maternal and infant mortality and produced statistics to match those for well-off women tended by doctors elsewhere.

When England entered World War II, the nurse-midwives returned home to serve their own country and the FNS was restructured as a school to train American women as nurse-midwives—the first midwifery program in America that required its students to be registered nurses.

The coupling of nursing to midwifery was good public relations, if nothing else. Nursing put a professional polish on a tarnished vocation, and nurse-midwives were recognizably middle-class in a pursuit dominated by poor and immigrant women. FNS midwives legitimized midwifery, as much by their credentials as by their good works.

Holly bought the FNS T-shirt for its logo's romance—many women were first drawn to midwifery after reading about FNS midwives trotting into the hills, hitching up to go catch babies. The midwife as romantic heroine. But inside the romantic logo lies the hard reality: for midwives to be accepted, they had to be nurses, and now they're not accepted because they are nurses, just nurses.

The class is over, and Holly asks the woman next to her how she'd liked it in Kentucky.

"I loved it. I learned a hell of a lot. But you know what they say, ride your donkeys when you're young."

"You rode *donkeys?*"

"Disillusioned? Everyone is." The woman shrugs apologetically. "Where are you riding your donkeys?"

"Morrison Hospital, in New York."

"Oh, yes. Plenty of donkeys to ride there."

CHAPTER 9

Holly figures that if she's getting a recruitment push, she ought to see who else might possibly recruit her. A group of students moves slowly around the recruiting room, hopeful, doubtful, gullible all at once. By traveling in packs, they protect one another from the spiels of desperate services, and one of them is sure to remember to ask the question the others are sure to forget.

Older midwives cruise the recruiting room warily. A certain unhappiness informs their approach, Holly thinks, as if they're caught in bad marriages or have already ditched a bad marriage and are in the market for a new husband. They want to choose wisely, having already failed or been failed, but they're not sure how hard-to-get they should play, how exacting in their choices they should be. Holly catches herself. Do other people see her as a disgruntled wife thinking of taking off?

The public health services appeal most strongly to Holly. Distant outposts in odd corners of America, where midwives work almost autonomously or as part of a close-knit team, braving it out on their own. The lone ranger approach to health care. "We love it here in South Dakota! Could you?" asks a printout.

Maybe. But then there's Matt, of course. In New York.

A pack of students is being wooed by Viv, of the Mudgeville Birthing Center, whom Holly knew from midwifery school, when Viv was not so peaked-looking as she is now. Viv explains that the center was one of the nation's first stand-alone birthing centers and served as prototype for countless others.

One strong-minded student asks directly, "What are the starting salaries?"

"The salaries are commensurate with experience," Viv says hurriedly, arranging her brochures in a dour, hopeless way.

"For a midwife just certified," the student persists, "what would the salary be?"

"The cost of living in Mudgeville is extremely low," says Viv, a transparent evasion that can mean only that the Mudgeville economy is depressed and the clients likely to be depressed as well. Holly would like to let Viv know that her evasion is showing, looming in her eyes.

"Could you give us a figure?" the strong-minded student says, stepping back, sensing that Viv is trying to hide an unhappy truth.

"A ballpark figure," another student says, to coax it out of Viv. It's become a game now.

"Starting salary would be about nineteen thousand dollars," Viv blurts out at last. "But housing is very cheap there."

The students nod sharply as their eyes scan other tables, other brochures, and Viv is left alone.

"Pretty tough?" Holly asks, moving to the table.

Viv sighs, shrugs, sinks onto a gilt-edged folding chair as if burdened by the weight of her curly gray hair. Her shoulders shake in a spasm of anger. "You'd think the history of the center would mean something. That people would be honored to work in a place with our kind of tradition."

A tradition, to appeal, must have an element of romance, which is exactly what's missing from Viv's pitch. "Maybe you could emphasize Mudgeville's rural charms," says Holly. "Highlight the horses and cows and farms."

"Why do I want to talk about horses and cows?" Viv asks, irritated.

"You could attract people who want to live and work in the country without being too far from the city."

"Holly, the last thing I need to do is emphasize that the center is located in the middle of nowhere."

Holly realizes that Viv will resist whatever she says. And she wonders if part of Viv's failure to attract recruits to the center is Viv herself, who wouldn't be much fun to work with, particularly for a new graduate who'd be the most likely prospect at the offered salary. A depressing standard of living to look forward to, on every level. Holly gives up. "Good luck, Viv."

"Good luck to you, Holly." Viv's proud way of saying she doesn't need luck any more than Holly does, but she's wrong. Because Holly doesn't have the air of defeat and fatigue that turns the world away—at least not yet.

In the hallway, an exchange of voices. "Millicent! You're pregnant!"

"For pete's sake, Nancy, I'm not pregnant. I'm just fat. What kind of midwife are you?"

Holly smiles. She feels . . . free, and she and Katrina venture from the hotel to trudge along a scraggly path by the freeway that leads to an ice cream parlor. "Not one of your pedestrian-oriented cities," Katrina comments.

The teenage boys behind the counter are fresh. In every way. After seeing nothing but midwives and baggy old salesmen, Holly is ready to propose marriage. Or a night of passion. Either one.

One of the boys hides his face behind his scoop. "Yikes! It's more of 'em! The midwives that devoured Houston!"

Another counter boy leans on the counter and gazes into Holly's eyes. "I'm in love," he says. "Will you deliver me?"

"You're too late," Katrina says. "Come back when you're gestating."

"I'm gestating now," he says, staring at Katrina. "Will you gestate with me?"

As they lick their ice cream cones in the weeds off the highway, Katrina says, contemplatively, "Texas is all right. I think I like Texas." When she finishes her ice cream, she says, "Maybe we should go back. The ice cream in Texas is all right."

"Yes, Katrina. The ice cream in Texas is all right."

CHAPTER 10

The gala lets the midwives go home with no regrets, as it's as tedious as any other meeting, except for the California wine contributed, as the menu card notes, by a pharmaceutical house. The dumpy, lumpy midwives Holly knows and loves are tricked out, as her grandmother would say, or tarted up, as her father would say, in finery. Midwives seem to dress up only once a year, for the gala, not often enough to get the hang of it. Some older women wear corsages, while younger ones have put on makeup for the first time during Convention.

Holly sits at a table with Katrina and Meg. "The critics' corner," Katrina calls it. At this table, nobody on the podium can do anything right. Mrs. Gruener makes her way to the podium in a sequined ensemble to give the award for excellence and puts forth a history lesson on medical politics, full of dramatic pauses that the midwives respond to by pouring more wine. When Mrs. Gruener is just about to name the award's recipient, Meg says loudly, "They're going to give it to a dead person. I know it. We have one award, and they'll give it to a dead person." And Mrs. Gruener names a midwife who has been dead for years.

The award committee has lost the hearts of most of the midwives present. They have nobody to honor, when all the honor goes to the dead, and they become antsy and moderately boorish.

A drunk midwife at the table next to Holly's screeches, "I want to study the way women sound in second stage and the way they sound during sex."

Yelping laughter. "How you gonna swing that?"

"I'll wire them for sound. I don't actually have to be there!" Gulping laughter. "What's the point? There's no point! I'm just curious! Pass that wine!"

When the guest speaker starts in on a dull-but-worthy speech, midwives stare with glazed eyes at the centerpieces and peel the labels off the wine bottles.

"Bring back the dead person," says Meg.

"Bring on the dancing girls," says a midwife's husband.

"Wrong convention," Holly says.

CHAPTER 11

Holly's bags are packed and propped against her legs as she looks over the convention bulletin board for the last time. She reads an update on a suit brought by the Federal Trade Commission on behalf of a nurse-midwife and her backup physician. After becoming her backup, the doctor was denied insurance by a company owned by doctors, the only one issuing malpractice policies in his state. The physician believed, as did the midwife and the FTC, that the company's refusal to cover him constituted restraint in trade and conspiracy, a way of ensuring that midwives couldn't practice in that state and that no other doctors would follow the backup physician's lead. The last lines of the update read, "Ellie still isn't practicing, Dr. Allen still doesn't have any insurance, but the wheels of justice are grinding—slowly!"

Katrina comes up behind her. "What are you going to tell Meg Greenspan?"

"Don't know."

"You can tell me. I won't tell anyone."

"Think I ought to attend rich women?"

"At least you won't have to do many IUDs." Katrina and Holly both hate inserting IUDs, propping open a cervix with a tenaculum . . . not a painless procedure. Katrina shudders. "Think of all the diaphragms you could deal with. Healthy babies. A real birthing room. You could return to your fold. White upper-class broads like yourself. They'd welcome you back."

"They never knew I was gone," Holly says.

"Whose fault is that?" Katrina wants to know.

Holly's bags are in the locker room by the pool. She's taking one last dip before catching her plane home. It's an overcast day, ready to crack into a Texas thunderstorm. Holly floats on her back and feels the wildness in the air, restless electricity eager to meet, fuse together, and break the sky apart. The wildness sweeps over her, and she feels a part of it.

What do you want, Treadwell?

More, she thinks. Less, she thinks. "I don't know," she says.

She dives down, touches the bottom of the pool, and wonders if she should ever emerge. Without even trying, though, she finds herself rocketing out of the water and jetting into the atmosphere. It's starting to rain.

MORRISON

CHAPTER 1

When listened to in the right way, the corridor sounds like it's filled with noises from the earth's depths. The fetal heart monitors roll thunder into the hallway. The grumble of bowel sounds, roars from the mother that the machinery has caught, churn and wash over the heartsounds of the not-yet-born. Holly likes it when the monitors amplify the glitches and blips. It reminds her of Australian aborigines' music: atonal, arrhythmic, mysterious, but identifiably human.

Sparks tapes a sign above the Cycle-flush hopper: "Urgent and Confidential—Renee Danford, age twenty, due on or around 11/5, received some AP care at Howard Street. If the patient is admitted, contact immediately. Newborn for BCW hold." The sign is from the social worker; the BCW is the Bureau of Child Welfare. What's the problem with Renee Danford? Holly runs a code on the possibilities: junkie, whore, suicidal tendencies, schizo, sex offender. Then she turns away. Maybe Renee will never show.

Holly sits down at the nurse's station desk to log in her first delivery of the evening in the big accounting book. No baby gets born or is truly alive until he has a hospital number and his existence has been validated by being marked down in the Book of Names. A snap and explosion of a monitor cracks the warm air like a thunderclap. An ordinary night.

"You void in the bedpan, darling," Crowley is telling a patient. "You don't know what 'to void' means? Why, it means you make pee-pee." The muted tinkle of the void. To a nurse's aide, Crowley says, "Lots of ketones."

"How can you tell? Can you smell it?"

"It's so dark. I bet it's plus-two ketones."

A ketone level determines if a patient is exhausted or underhydrated.

157

Holly has no doubt that Crowley is exactly right. If Crowley says the urine is +2 ketones, then it is. Crowley is the best OB/midwife on the floor. Holly is sure of it.

"Now, baby, I have to wipe the makeup off your face," Crowley says. An initial protest from the patient fades out. "We have to make you look the way God made you, not that you don't have lovely makeup."

"So do you," the patient says.

"Thank you, baby." Crowley wears purple eyeshadow, mauve lipstick, gold earrings shaped like seashells that work like lamps to light up her rich brown skin. Crowley is over forty-five years old, and usually tired, and her eyes are slightly hooded, but Holly thinks she's beautiful. Jamaican women, at least the ones who work here, including Sparks, are like French women: they seem to age well, with a combination of good carriage, pride in themselves, and a certain dignified sensuality. They also have enough meat on their bones so their faces aren't haggard.

Crowley tells the patient, "We must see what color your face is so when it changes color, if you pale away like a cloud, we can see it go."

Scott moves in for the history. The patient's boyfriend kisses his girl once, twice, until soon her whole face is covered with kisses and their foreheads are pressed together. Not only that, they have started nuzzling noses when Scott asks the patient, who isn't giving him her full attention, "Are you married?"

"No," she answers, not looking up. "I'm single."

When the boyfriend moves in for a long soul kiss, Scott slaps his clipboard against his stomach and stares up at the ceiling. He's a resident and probably suffers from sex deprivation and is jealous, Holly decides, without undue sympathy, as she cuts into the staff bathroom for a minute—a luxury, since some nights she can't make it to the bathroom to pee—and from there she hears something, something that doesn't fit the aural landscape, something cracking up the air. The rough voice of an angry man.

"No man touches her! No man! Do you hear me? No man!"

Holly is pretty sure that whoever the man is addressing can hear him just fine. Now Sparks is answering him, but Holly can't make out the words. Hurrying out of the bathroom, she runs on tiptoe to rescue her chart, sliding it back into the chart rack. Save the records first. Now she's ready to inch around the bend and see which man is exploding exactly, and why.

At the end of the corridor, the swinging fire doors that lead to the elevators are wedged open by a gurney. The gurney is half-coming, half-going, and lying on it, propped up by her elbows, is a very young, pretty Hispanic girl, with soft brown hair pulled back by a barrette save for one braided length of hair with a ribbon woven into it. The girl looks ready for, and about the right age for, confirmation: in a lacy white blouse, blue skirt that looks to have been taken from a parochial school uniform, and a small gold cross dangling from her neck. Maybe she thinks you're supposed to dress up to go to the hospital to have a baby.

Sparks is standing in the doorway that gives way to the admitting desk, spanning it with her bulk, a muscular blockade. Nobody gets by Sparks. By the sheer force of her indignation, Sparks has drawn herself up to a height Holly has never seen her reach before. She must be three inches taller than she was the last time Holly looked.

"Take her away," Sparks says to the orderly who is slouching against the half-open fire doors in a stained white uniform that makes him look like a butcher's apprentice. He doesn't consider Sparks to be the ultimate authority she might think she is, though, and he looks instead at the source of the loud, rough, angry male voice that is knocking Seven-B for a loop.

There's a sense of suspended animation as everyone freezes, waiting for the angry man to make an angry move.

He stands half a foot from Sparks and is not as tall as she is, but compensates for this lack of height by a barrel-chested build and superior battle gear. Sparks is in her old nursing uniform, with washed-out green piping and dulled nameplate and ink stains all over the chest pocket. The angry man has her beat. He's in camouflage-style army fatigues, black army boots (Holly figures he doesn't need to run fast as long as he can kick the shit out of someone with the boots), and a denim jacket shorn off at the armpits over a hooded sweatshirt. An embroidered decal runs across the jacket's back, reading, "Apocalypso," and beneath that is the silhouette of a bird, which was probably meant to be a hawk or some other fierce predator but has been rendered instead as something more soft bellied than rapacious.

The soft-bellied bird doesn't cramp Apocalypso's style. He wears black leather wristlets studded with nails and, around his neck, a full array of chains that bear a wide assortment of amulets, as if Apocalypso needs all the luck he can get: a tiny skull, a crucifix, a shark's tooth, an ankh symbol, a Playboy bunny, and the lead medallion of an Indian chief.

What makes Apocalypso truly scary is his hair. He has scary hair. It's cut in a buzzcut that leaves about as much hair on his scalp as would turn up on somebody else's five o'clock shadow. His head looks, as a result, appallingly round. A long length of hair runs down the nape of his neck, like the tail on an exotic marsupial. Another equally long strip of hair runs down the left side of his skinheaded scalp. The isolated strands of hair look like an experiment in hair-transplant techniques gone awry.

Denise comes up beside Holly and whispers, "Scalp locks."

"Say what?"

"Scalp locks. Like the Indian warriors used to wear right before hitting the warpath."

Apocalypso is shouting at Sparks, "I don't want any guy touching her! Understand?"

Holly flinches. Really angry people, angry down to their bones, make her blood run cold.

"Take your friend elsewhere!" Sparks bellows. "This is a hospital! We have procedures, rules, and guidelines, and when patients come here for treatment, they're treated by *doctors!*" Stretching to see through the swinging doors, she doesn't move her feet a single centimeter, doesn't give up an inch of ground. "You! Ralph!" she shouts at the orderly who is hanging by the elevators now, ready to take off, should the situation warrant a fast break.

"You barked?" he says, standing to.

"Take this young lady downstairs. We can't accommodate her here."

Ralph makes a halfhearted pull on the gurney, the little girl smiles and shrugs, and Apocalypso lunges for the gurney and grabs the other end. Ralph promptly releases his hands.

"Just wait a minute and let's straighten this out," Apocalypso says. "Don't you have a lady doctor here?" he says to Sparks. "Huh? Huh?" Then he slams his fist against a bulletin board—memos on OB conventions and seminars quake and rattle on their tacks.

Holly whispers to Denise to call Security.

"Already did."

"Good girl."

"Ain't no girl."

"Good whatever you are," says Holly.

Holly can see that Apocalypso is wired. If he's not on a drug, then he's rocketing on his own adrenaline. If he's an adrenaline junkie, he'll keep creating scenes to get his adrenaline hit and charge himself up and won't quit until the adrenaline exhausts itself, which makes peacekeeping a dim prospect.

"We have no lady doctor here," Sparks says haughtily. "Take your friend elsewhere. We can do nothing for you here." Sparks's face has hardened, the copper rouge on her high cheekbones cutting across her face like a slash of war paint now that her brown face has paled with anger. The color has drained from her skin and left the rouge behind to hold the fort.

Holly admires Sparks's bravery. In a fight-or-flight situation, Sparks will stick it out and fight. Which makes her a pain in the ass, but courageous as well. "There'll be no lady doctor until tomorrow," Sparks says imperiously. "Perhaps not even then. Come back tomorrow!"

Apocalypso laughs, furious. "Come back tomorrow? Are you crazy? My girlfriend's having a *baby*, lady, a *baby!*" Apocalypso puts a thick arm around the girl's shoulder, exhibiting her. "In this whole, big, famous hospital, you don't have a single lady doctor?" He pouts at Sparks with a hangdog face, transforming himself in a millisecond from aggressor to victim.

Sparks shakes her head to collect her wits. The situation has degenerated to a standoff—the unstoppable force meeting the immovable object—

and Holly knows she has to enter the fray. She doesn't know what she'll say, but she trusts in her ability to think on her feet. Her stomach rolls with something she recognizes as fear, which she doesn't often feel, so she pays attention to it. And the fear is giving her a rush. Adrenaline is a drug in its own right, a power trip of a drug that gives her a sense of self-importance and significance she normally lacks and demolishes hesitation, vanquishes self-doubt, and cuts through confusion. When her adrenaline is charging, things are more clear than they ever are, and Holly moves without questioning herself, her thought processes speeded up and her physical movements going almost as fast. Holly can burn herself out if she pumps up her adrenaline output, depletes her reserves, hyperstimulates herself to no good end. She has to conserve her adrenaline, because when a real crisis arises, adrenaline does more than make Holly feel important. It gives her the power to save people.

This is a legitimate expenditure of adrenaline.

The two adrenaline junkies meet.

"I'm Holly Treadwell. I'm a nurse-midwife." In the universal peacemaking gesture, she puts out her hand.

Apocalypso lurches for her hand, takes it, and yanks her forward so that she falls out of her Dr. Scholl's, loses her balance, stumbles a few feet, and becomes completely aware of just how much unleashed force Apocalypso represents.

"How 'bout that!" he says. "A lady doctor! You can take care of Daisy!"

"She's no doctor!" says Sparks, waving her hand to dismiss Holly. "There's no guarantee she can take care of your Daisy."

Apocalypso looks around, confused, trapped and no longer knowing which way to turn. "What does she mean?" he asks Holly.

"I'm a midwife. That's different from a doctor. I handle normal deliveries, and if complications develop, I refer my patients to a doctor. Male doctors, as it happens."

"No, no." Apocalypso shakes his head. "There won't be any complications. Daisy's a good girl—she does whatever you say!"

"If she needs a doctor to treat her, I'll stay in the room with her to make sure she's okay." A lie. Holly will only stay with her if there aren't any other midwifery patients in labor: an unlikely event. "But the doctors here are very good." Lie number two. Then Holly takes her lie to the hilt. "They're great doctors here," she says, "honorable men." A heavy, intense, and major lie. But a lie in the name of peace.

"Daisy won't need no doctor," Apocalypso says, swaggering to Daisy's side with his feet turned out—a sailor's walk. "You can take care of my Daisy."

The staff has congregated, forming a horseshoe shape in the hall, and now they all watch as Apocalypso bends over to kiss Daisy on the head. The little girl sits up straight, smoothing her hair. The pregnant stomach doesn't seem to belong to Daisy's shining, smiling face. The stomach looks faked. Is this all a joke? Gangland hazing high jinks?

Holly steps forward to take Daisy's hand. This is not a joke. "Hello, kiddo. Welcome to Morrison Hospital and the world of mothers-to-be."

From the rear of the small crowd rises a smattering of applause. Thinking the applause is for him, Apocalypso raises two fists in victory—the middle-weight champion of Seven-B. And Sparks moves, at last, the body she has used to block the doorway and sinks heavily into her seat at the desk.

CHAPTER 2

Sparks sits up very straight at the admitting desk, trying to regain her professional composure. With brisk expertise, she collects the forms Holly will need. Holly usually collects her own papers, but Holly has pulled rank, in front of the whole floor, to reduce her to the status of mere nurse. Sparks will act like a nurse then, with a vengeance.

She turns to Holly, glowering. "I must take the vitals first, before you can evaluate the best management for your patient." Sparks is in quest of complications that would require a doctor's intervention and take control of the underage Daisy out of Holly's hands. "I'll take the vitals," Sparks says, "because I'm in charge of admitting tonight." This is Sparks's idea of irony, as Holly was the one who actually admitted Daisy.

Vitals are the cornerstones of Sparks's world. Blood pressure, temperature, and pulse are the fixed stars in a confusing universe of variables. When in doubt about almost anything, Sparks whips out the fever meter, the pressure cuff, the stethoscope.

Sparks uses a stethoscope with a skill no resident or midwife can hope to match. She doesn't need a fetoscope (the short, blunt stethoscope that has a headpiece with which to press against the mother's belly) to track down a fetal heart rate. A regular stethoscope is good enough for her. "Here, listen to this," she'll tell Levy when a patient is admitted. Levy will listen to a woman's abdomen for a second, then confess, "Miss Sparks, this doesn't work for me—I can't hear a goddamn thing." This pleases Sparks, when it doesn't enrage her.

In a rare, transient moment of friendliness, Sparks told Holly that she'd first begun to listen to people's heartbeats when she was a little girl in Jamaica. Her grandmother was a midwife and used a wooden stethoscope that looked more like a primitive flute than a medical instrument.

"I trained my ears early on," she said, implying it's much too late for Holly to learn with any great degree of skill. Like dancers and pianists, stethoscope masters must start young.

Holly almost never uses a fetoscope—one of her failings as a midwife. She relies on machines to do the listening for her. At the clinic, the midwives use the portable ultrasound devices called Doptones that look like walkie-talkies, operate on batteries, and emit scratchy white noise. To obtain a heartsound, Holly has to slam the instrument into the palm of her hand. All high-tech marvels seem to descend to the down-home level of the old television her parents gave her when they got a new one—a set whose horizontal hold doesn't hold unless she smacks it with a rubber mallet she bought expressly for that purpose.

Like the residents, Holly can't find and sustain a fetal heartsound using just a stethoscope, although she's tried. "You listen to too much rock and roll!" Sparks claimed. "You have the ears of old people!" Maybe Sparks is right. Sometimes Holly thinks the stethoscope has become a stylized medical prop. Like a cadet's saber, its function has become mainly symbolic.

As Sparks works up the vitals, Levy scuffles up against Holly, sliding into her accidentally-on-purpose and pressing against her.

"Oh, Christ, I'm sorry, Treadwell," he says unapologetically.

Holly kicks him lightly in the shins. "Funny how you always misjudge your movements when a young lady is around. And where were you anyway, when the tough got going?"

"I got gone. Doing male doctor stuff. I've seen women get hysterical about pelvic exams, but I never saw a man freak out about one."

"Maybe he'd heard about the group gropes that go on here under the guise of medicine. He probably didn't want his girl subjected to your probing instruments of terror. Meaning your gloved-up hands. Not to mention Scott's."

Levy pulls down a chart from the rack by the board. "If I performed the exam myself, of course, that would be different from Scott doing one."

"You think there's a qualitative difference between you and Scott?"

"Slap my face! There isn't?"

"Levy, I hope you die and return to life as a woman who has to be admitted to Morrison Hospital where a Dr. Levy is assigned to grope for your ovaries."

Looking pained, Levy laughs.

"Or you come back to life and are admitted to a hospital where female residents hover over you and fiddle with your—" Holly stops and breathes deep. She has just set herself up.

Levy smiles. "Don't stop there, Treadwell," he says. "Fiddle with my what? I'm sure there's nothing I'd enjoy more. I have long and pleasurable dreams about just such a nightmare."

Holly throws up her hand. "I give up, Levy."

Denise steps forward, putting both hands on her hips as preface to a declamation. "You guys are whacked," she says. "You don't have the wattage to light a dim bulb. This Apocalypso dog is a control freak. He sleeps with a little girl for control. He knocks her up for control. Is he going to give up his control now to the hospital boys?" Denise hoots with laughter.

"We just been whupped by a nurse," Levy tells Holly.

"Won't be the first time," Holly says.

"Won't be the last," Denise says. "Bet the rent money on it."

Crowley has been on a straightening jag. She's pulled down outdated memos from the bulletin board and organized the Emergency Junk Box that sits on a shelf by the nurse's station. The Emergency Junk Box contained, the last time Holly checked, a grimy plastic cord clamp and dried-up inkpads for stamping newborns' heels and fingertips (long since replaced by disposable pads) and a brochure from the Department of Health on the management of head lice. No one ever runs to the Emergency Junk Box during an emergency. Having Lysoled the telephone receiver, Crowley is free to put her two cents in.

"You are all babies," she says. She taps Holly's hand reproachfully with her knuckles. "Don't you know Spanish men don't like doctors touching their women? Why do you think Howard Street Clinic has so many Spanish lady patients? The other men may not have the bad manners of the young man here tonight, but they feel deeply about their ladies' modesty."

Crowley never says anything unless she has something to say, and when she's said what she has to say, she leaves it at that. She isn't interested in arguing with anyone other than Sparks. Now she sails down the hall, satisfied.

Levy sighs. "In any event, I'm well out of it. Being male and all."

"Cheer up, Levy," Holly tells him. "Maybe Daisy will need forceps."

"Treadwell?"

"Yeah?"

"Time has not been good to you."

Holly turns to Denise. "Hell, he's right."

"I don't know if it's time that hasn't been good to you," Denise says, considering the question. "Maybe it's just midwifery that did it."

"That's reassuring, Denise. Thank you for sharing that with me."

CHAPTER 3

Levy corners Holly. "Let's do an X ray on the baby."

"I was about to ask *you* for something," Holly says. "To bug you for the last time tonight."

"Let's not *try* to run at cross-purposes," Levy says wearily. He lifts his hand to shield his eyes from the fluorescent light. "Let's not actually *work* at it. Let me go first. How about this X ray?"

"Worried about her pelvis?"

"I'm worried that she's a little girl about to delivery a big, bouncing baby. Yeah."

"How about worrying about the big, bouncing baby then?"

A higher rate of leukemia exists in children exposed to X rays in utero than those who were not. The rate is only slightly higher in the exposed kids, and the statistical difference borders on insignificance. But it's there, and the statistical difference isn't insignificant when you actually see a kid dying of leukemia. Then it becomes the essential opposite of insignificance.

Levy shrugs.

"I can palp her and get more data through my hands than through any X ray." Holly waves her hands in his face—a Gus-influenced gesture. "Data in three dimensions!"

Levy swats Holly's hands down. Levy is tired. His skin is coffee colored ("*café au lait*," as Denise describes it), but the rings under his eyes are black. It's the time of night Holly was warned about by a veteran nurse years before, who said, "When the residents get that peaky look, you have to do their thinking for them."

"Pelvimetry is my specialty," Holly says in a soft, conciliatory way. "Honest."

Pelvimetry evaluates the pelvis's dimensions through vaginal and external exams. As a student, Holly had to study all the different kinds of pelvises. There's android, also known as the male pelvis but found in twenty-five percent of women and not the greatest birthing pelvis around. There's gynecoid, wide, well-rounded, and ideal for birthing babies. There's anthropoid, a deep pelvis—almost as deep as it is wide—most often found in black women. And the platypelloid pelvis, which Holly has seen only once—a flat, shallow pelvis that makes vaginal delivery a chancy proposition.

Holly had brought home all her pelvis charts and spread them over the living room floor. When her boyfriend came over and saw those skeletal inlets and hollows, he walked out the door. "I'll come back after you get rid of all those fucking skulls!"

Through pelvimetry, Holly can figure out whether or not a baby can navigate down the birth canal without serious difficulty. Besides not having any side effects, pelvimetry has a distinct advantage over X rays by providing 3-D detail. In deliveries, depth is as important as width.

Levy rolls his eyes and looks up to the ceiling. A sliver of plaster has curled up and now hangs like a stalactite about to drop. Maybe it'll hit him on the head and knock him out for good. Put him out of his misery. These midwives are going to win this war, as a war of attrition. They'll wear him down until nothing's left but a steamrolled ghost of himself.

Holly knows he's conceded the point.

She pats his shoulder. "You need to drink more water, darling. Your eyes are dehydrating."

"You have time to take a piss for me?" He shuts his eyes and leans back into the wall. "Hit me," he says. "Tell me what you want. I need the practice for when I have kids and they start turning the screws. 'Daddy, give me this. Daddy, I want that.'"

Holly is quiet for a moment. "I'm not your kid," she says. "I don't want a Walkman or a color TV. All I want is to put Daisy in the ABC."

Levy snorts without opening his eyes. "Dream on, Treadwell."

"Listen, Levy. She's not going to make it in here." Holly nods toward the labor rooms. "She needs privacy. She needs ambulation."

Ambulation. Holly can't come right out and say "She needs to walk" without losing her medical credibility. Medical people don't seem to take anything seriously until it's been translated into a Latinized version. *Walking* becomes *ambulation* and *newborn* becomes *neonate* and *womb* becomes *uterus.* Only a few words have held their own over the centuries: *labor, breech, stillbirth,* and *midwife.*

Midwife dates back to the 1300s—an elemental word that means "with woman." (Before Holly became a midwife, she thought it meant "middle woman.") Sometimes Holly figures that midwives haven't been accepted because they don't have a Latinate version of their name. As Holly's father said, "That's a terrible name, with that weird medieval association to it." But the obstetricians already took the Latin name for midwife— *obstetrics* derives from *obstetrix,* Latin for "she who is present." *Obstetrics* didn't come into use until the late nineteenth century, when doctors began to take hold of the childbirth industry and wanted to differentiate themselves from midwives. Before *obstetrician* was employed, they were known as male midwives or man-midwives.

"Let's think," Levy says. "You're going into the ABC with a little girl whose only labor coach is a psychopathic headbanger who probably was just released from Attica?"

The alternative birthing center's isolation makes it a bad choice for women laboring alone. Or laboring with a psychopathic headbanger.

"Crowley just called the girl's mother. She'll be here soon. Until then, I'll stick with her, and we can leave the door open."

"I want a spiral in her," Levy says sternly.

"So do I."

Levy does a double take. "You do?"

Holly does. She wants to walk Daisy through labor. Ambulate. Keep her in stir so gravity helps move the baby down through the underage pelvis. Some studies show that walking and squatting can widen the pelvis (which is constructed of bone and ligament) by a few crucial centimeters. The effects of gravity, and the expanded pelvis, reduce the length of labor. If Daisy has an internal monitor in place, she'll be able to walk around the room. With an external monitor belted around her abdomen, she'll have to lie flat on her back, semiparalyzed.

Holly almost never volunteers to insert an internal monitor, as most of her patients never get a chance to ambulate much anyway, and the internal monitor requires that the waters be broken, which carries risks. If the bag of waters hasn't broken, Holly has to rupture the membranes to attach the monitor's spiral to the baby's scalp.

Amniotomy destroys the natural buffer zone between the baby's head and the cervix that the amniotic forewaters create, and there's a greater chance of traumatic injury to the baby without that cushion of fluid. And amniotomy increases the possibility of infection. The sac keeps the uterus and its contents (the baby) sterile. Once the seal provided by the sac is broken, that sterility is compromised as the uterus is exposed to external bacteria. Women with long labors are at greater risk for infection, and the assumption used to be that the longer the labor, the greater the opportunity for bacteria to enter spontaneously. But the real threat has to do with the number of vaginal exams performed on a woman with ruptured membranes when pathogens are introduced into the uterus by someone's gloved hand—picked up in the vagina, possibly, and carried inside. The reason women with long labors are at risk for infection is that they're usually subjected to more internal exams than women with short labors. A woman with a twelve-hour labor and five exams might stand the same chance of developing an infection as a woman with a twenty-four-hour labor and the same number of exams.

Holly tries not to perform vaginal exams just to satisfy her own curiosity about a labor's progress. Sometimes she does exams simply to be able to give a progress report to a patient on the brink of losing faith, who needs a concrete sign that her labor is actually going someplace. But Holly tries to look for other signs to determine progress and does exams about every two hours. Levy, on the other hand, aches to chalk up new numbers on the Board, performing exams every ninety minutes. Holly's patients have very dull labor sagas in contrast, if their stories are judged by the action that hits the Board.

Because Holly is conservative with vaginal exams, she's not overly worried about infection. And Holly has enough faith in herself to believe that another risk of amniotomy—prolapsed cord—won't come to pass either. Daisy is a primap, so her baby's head will be well engaged in the pelvis; it'd be hard even for Gus to dislodge the head when Daisy's bag of waters are broken or the monitor spiral is attached.

Besides, Holly wants to take a look at Daisy's amniotic fluid. If the fluid is thick as pea soup with meconium, she wants to know—the ABC would be the wrong place for Daisy then.

Levy is floored that he doesn't have to pull teeth to get Holly to agree to the internal monitor. Treadwell has acquiesced without a fight to a high-tech intervention! She's thrown him off balance. He has lost his edge.

"She's high risk, Treadwell," Levy says in weak protest.

"I know, Levy, but how's her being stuck in a labor room going to help any?"

Levy thinks for a second. "No doubt she'll be a chandelier case."

"No doubt."

Chandelier cases are the women who flip out during labor, who leap out of bed, charging upward to swing from a nonexistent chandelier. Levy's line of thinking is that a chandelier case going bonkers in the ABC is preferable to a chandelier case crawling the walls in a labor room. At least a Daisy in the ABC won't infect other suggestible patients with her fear.

"She'll probably make quite a racket," Holly says. "You know how these girls can be."

In truth, the very young girls—Daisy is fourteen—are often too frozen with fear to become chandelier cases. If anything, they're compliant to an almost pathological extent. But as Levy has failed to draw this observation on his own, Holly won't call his attention to it now.

"Christ," Levy says, rubbing his eyes. "These girls."

These girls. Holly looks at teen pregnancy by splitting the big lump of the problem in half. There's a younger-than-sixteen group (kids) and an older-than-sixteen group (women). The woman's body is generally ready for pregnancy. With the same levels of emotional support and prenatal care, a sixteen-year-old has just as good a shot at a successful outcome as an older woman. If her body has stopped growing, a female is ready for pregnancy. A girl and her family might not be ready, but her body is.

Holly looks at the mechanics of pregnancy in the context of twenty-five thousand years ago. Evolution hasn't made much progress in the childbirth mechanism since then. The mechanism was devised—by nature, by God—for those hunting-and-gathering conditions. In a brutish landscape of short life spans and high infant and maternal mortality, the survival of the species required that humans not waste any time in reproducing. As soon as a girl came of age, propagation began in earnest.

But the younger-than-sixteen female body isn't of age. It's preoccupied with its own growth, the expansion of its reproductive organs and hormonal and metabolic shifts, and for it to be concerned with a baby is an unnatural strain. Pregnancy in a very young girl is like a house built on shaky foundations, a collapsible structure that threatens to cave in and carry the foundations with it. Even under the most supportive conditions, a young girl is at high risk to develop preeclampsia and complications at delivery.

The young girl is at risk because the young girl is nothing but a kid.

The ABC is off limits to high-risk patients, save those patients with communicable diseases who are essentially quarantined there. But Daisy's high-risk status if just what makes the ABC so important. There, she can be granted some protection against the routines that put even low-risk patients at risk: confinement to bed, close proximity of other laboring women and their audible anguish, the sense of being on public view. The labor rooms are anxious places.

"So what do you say, Levy?"

Levy smooths his forehead with his hand, then rubs his whole face with his palm. A full-face massage. "You get your baby in the ABC," he says, exhausted. The war of attrition has been won by a midwife. "As we say in *español, Vaya con Dios.*"

Go with God.

"I could kiss you, Levy."

Levy shuts his eyes. He leans his back against the wall. He puckers his lips. "I'm waiting," he says.

CHAPTER 4

Holly is working up Daisy Morales's chart. One never lacks for forms. Prenatal record chart (this one is blank or filled with slashes). Labor progress chart. Admission interview chart. Intrapartum problem chart. The index card résumé Holly will stick in her Card-tex flip-file. And because Daisy is fourteen years old, Holly has to fill out an adolescent pregnancy card. This is filed with the city, for statistical purposes, as more bad news from the front. In the war against teen pregnancies, the pregnancies are winning.

Denise hovers by the desk, staring hopefully at a menu from an all-night deli that's taped above the phones. The deli doesn't deliver, and no nurse, even if she had time, would run out into the Brooklyn streets this time of night. The only way Denise can get food from the deli is by enticing an orderly to go on a food run for her. But the orderlies aren't easily enticed. What an orderly would want in exchange is something Denise isn't prepared to deliver. She hasn't reached the point where she'd broker her body for a hot pastrami sandwich. Although she is wickedly hungry. Denise is reading the menu like she'd read a romance. A hot pastrami sandwich is nothing but a fantasy.

"These young ones knock me for a loop," Holly says. "I can't get used to it."

"Were you here when that little twelve-year-old came in?"

"Nope."

"After seeing her, a fourteen-year-old starts looking normal. But that Daisy is a goner. Out of the garden of childhood for good now." Denise lets her eyes falls from the menu. "Is it a full moon tonight?" She squints at the wall calendar half-blocked by Holly's shoulder.

"Nope, the moon is new. A mere sliver."

171

"I figured that the skinhead boyfriend went off because of the full moon."

Holly and Denise speak softly. They both believe that the full moon contributes not to more deliveries, but to more *complicated* deliveries. But they don't have any proof and don't want to be considered superstitious and undereducated by any snotty resident passing by. The full-moon theory is their guilty pleasure, which they share only with Crowley, who concurs.

Denise's gaze sweeps past the calendar and up to the portrait of Martin Luther King, Jr., that hangs above the nurse's station. Then she looks at the cartoon tacked below it—a round-faced kid with a big grin and a caption that reads, "I know I'm good 'coz God don't make no junk." Denise sighs. Idealism. She turns away. For weeks, she scarcely notices that there's anything on the walls at all. Maybe it's best that way.

Holly is busy transferring Daisy's patient number from her ID card to the charts.

"It's a fact," Denise blurts out. "Not a real fact, but something like a fact. That when a little kid gives birth, she's not a kid any longer."

Holly looks up. "You're right. Childhood lost. When you lose your virginity, you don't get thrown out of the garden of childhood. But when you have a kid—"

"You're booted out with a one-way ticket," Denise finishes with a laugh. "*Adiós, muchacha*, and don't come back. But you know what our theme song is around here."

"What?"

"'Careless Love.'"

Holly laughs quickly, but she feels something hit her in her chest. A burning, twisting thing. She looks down at her charts. She loses herself in the slots of information.

"Now don't go getting sad," Denise says. "You got to feel a little bit, and that's good. If you don't, you're just one more hardass in this world. But you got to learn how to feel, Holly. Do it right. You got to learn to feel just a little bit."

Holly looks up and tucks a piece of her hair behind one ear. "Then I won't be able to feel at all."

"I don't see that happening," Denise says, shaking her head. "Maybe you wish it would, but it won't—not for a long time. Your skin is so thin, it'd make Saran Warp look like leather."

Holly frowns, then smooths her forehead with her forefinger. If she lets a frown become a reflex, she'll never stop. Her forehead will keep jumping into a frown, when she's not even thinking about something sad.

"I don't like it," Holly says, standing up. "When a kid like Daisy has a baby, part of her future is written out for her. She loses her potential." And that's a defilement of childhood, she wants to say. She's been at Morrison for two years and has delivered a lot of young girls. But she still believes childhood is sacred. Sacred because most kids have their futures waiting way out there, slow to unfold. When a kid has a kid, a long slab of the future unfolds early and kills off part of the promise.

"Where'd you go swimming?" Denise asks. "In the sentimental pond, old girl, and you came out dripping wet. Don't you know most people have their futures mapped out for them the minute they're born? No. Scratch that. Try, the minute they're conceived."

"We're the products of conception," Holly says in a hollow voice. That's what the textbooks call babies—"products of conception"—just to be on the safe side. For "monsters" can be conceived and delivered as well, freaks of nature that can't quite be called babies. Holly shakes her head to dislodge the morbid train of thought that runs through her mind and threatens to stall there.

"And we don't conceive ourselves," Denise says.

Holly stands up. They've thought on a high and low level long enough. Now it's time for hospital complaints. Holly flips through the charts she's only started to fill out and begins the familiar plaint that comes close to being a ritual. "Paperwork," she sighs. "We get more like secretaries every day."

"The difference is, when we fill in these forms, we know what to do with the information," Denise says. "Those aren't just words to us."

Holly smiles: people always seem to find a rationalization for why their jobs are important. "I wonder if we really know the meanings of those words," she says. "Like 'high risk.' Since everyone is high risk, nobody is."

Denise smoothes down her hair. "I did hear one of the older docs say that a low-risk patient was admitted here once."

"What year was that?"

"The year I was born—1959. But don't lose hope, old girl. They say that by the end of the century, we should see at least one more."

Holly flashes on the image of a genuine low-risk patient. She is twenty-four and married and middle-class, neither tall nor short nor skinny nor fat, and she has never smoked or drunk alcohol or done drugs. She lives in the suburbs, and she sleeps well at night. She's in labor right now in some clean, spacious, quiet hospital in Westchester. She is calling out for help because the labor is getting rough. There are plenty of people to care for her. Or are there? Holly chooses to believe there are.

"High-risk patients are okay with me," Holly says with determination.

"Now you've got it," Denise says. "Morrison midwifery. You have a heart, but you also have some thick skin to keep it in its place."

CHAPTER 5

Holly lifts up Daisy's gown to wash her. When she was a maternity nurse, Holly did this thousands of times. Fill a basin with soapy water. Crack open an E-Z disposable sponge. Swab downward as you block the vaginal introitus with another sponge; you don't want the soapy water insinuating itself inside. Throw out the sponge as soon as it comes into anything that resembles contact with the anus: the object isn't to move pathogens from one place to another.

After the admission interview, Sparks decided to drop her "mere nurse" pose—too intolerable—and let Holly do the scut work. After all, Daisy is an extraordinary admission, let onto the ward only through Holly's intervention.

"I believe you want privacy," Sparks said to Holly.

Holly thought for a moment before she caught Sparks's meaning. Sparks meant, "Scrub her yourself, you bitch."

But Sparks had given in to scut work made manifest: drawing Daisy's blood. This was easy to do, as Daisy's veins run so close to the surface that they dance when she moves her arms even slightly. If Holly has to start an extra line for an emergency transfusion, it won't be hard to tap a vein STAT—and because it'd be so easy to do so, Holly will probably never have to. It's a midwife's law that the only patients who need transfusions are the ones who have no veins. Patients who've used up their accessible veins by drug habits or prior IVs. Patients whose veins are hidden by folds of fat. Patients who have gone into shock, their veins constricting and withering up when inadequate blood supply can't keep the veins pumping and filled.

Holly has never prepped a patient as young as this, and Daisy's physical childishness upsets her. Her pubic hair is sparse and thin, just barely there, and the pigmentation phenomenon called the linea nigra,

174

the dark line peculiar to pregnancy that bisects a woman's torso and usually winds up lost in a mass of pubic hair, here has nowhere to hide at the end of its run, which strikes Holly as fundamentally wrong.

Holly isn't supposed to get judgmental, even in her mind. That's part of her professional posture. When she starts thinking judgmentally, that criticism seeps into the suggestions she makes, the tone of her voice, the look in her eye. But Holly can't accept that this just-fourteen little girl is about to be a mother.

Don't get sad, Treadwell.

Too late. Sadness is in the door. If she doesn't allow herself to feel sad, what will go next? Maybe happiness won't penetrate either. Besides, if there were ever a justifiable reason for sadness, this would be it. A childhood tossed away.

Holly is afraid she'll never strike a balance between feeling too much and feeling too little, which Denise claims she's mastered.

Sparks pokes her head in the door. "Your baby has a nice hematocrit."

"No kidding."

"Spun crit is thirty-one."

"Perfecto."

It takes only three minutes to get a hematocrit reading. A small tube of Daisy's blood is put into the desktop centrifuge in the medicine room. The centrifuge spins, the tube settles, and the red blood cells are separated from the rest of the plasma. As a process, it reminds Holly of making butter in a blender; when the cream separates, the buttermilk flies off and a clump of butter is left behind. The layer of red blood cells is measured with a ruler specifically designed for 'crit readings, and the reading is given in terms of the cells' length.

"You're a healthy girl, Daisy," Holly says, shaking her hand. "You should be proud of yourself."

But Daisy doesn't look proud. She looks in pain. "Aiiiee!"

Her arms fly up in a modified chandelier clutch and lasso Holly's neck. Daisy's thin arms, which had looked before as if they were without muscle, which had looked like flower stems, now resemble nothing so much as taut cable, locked about her neck in a primeval grasp.

Holly drops the prep kit on the floor. NURSE STRANGLED BY TEEN MOM. Stop the presses. In terms of strength, Daisy has Holly beat because her fear is greater than Holly's and her adrenaline is pumping faster. As an adrenaline warrior herself, Holly knows she has to give herself up to Daisy's superior adrenaline production. She has no choice but to be clutched at.

"Easy now. Breathe deep. Slow, slow." Holly is sputtering.

The contraction subsides. The arms loosen and drop. Holly breathes a cleansing breath. She needs it. That was a tough contraction. Now she has to compress a whole series of childbirth classes into the few minutes between the last and next contraction. She can't afford to be strangled. Would worker's comp cover accidental strangulation by a patient? Thinking of Apocalypso—does it cover intentional strangulation, for that matter?

And Daisy needs help. Most likely she's an early bird, only at a fingertip, and nobody can afford for her to be a chandelier case this early on in labor.

"Daisy, what's your favorite place in the world?"

Daisy scrunches up her face, taps her forefinger on her temple, and looks suspiciously at Holly. "Why?" She acts as though Holly is planning on packing her up and sending her there.

"I want you to imagine that place. To shut your eyes and collapse like a wet noodle."

"A wet noodle?"

Holly jumps up to demonstrate, letting her body go limp. She looks more like a hunchback than a wet noodle, but she doesn't realize that. "Like a rag doll," she elaborates, straightening up.

Daisy throws herself back on the bed. She is all angles of thin arms and sharp elbows and knobby knees. A geography teacher in elementary school once ordered everybody in Holly's class to lie down on the floor and work themselves into the shapes of all the South American countries. Daisy looks more like a geometry figure than a young girl in labor pretending to be a wet noodle. Daisy distinctly resembles Honduras.

"When a contraction comes, go with it and picture your favorite place. . . ."

Holly teaches her to take cleansing breaths (deep breath, big sigh, so she won't hyperventilate after breathing quickly during the contractions) and how to distract herself by directed breathing: hee hee hoo.

"But I feel like I'm going to split in half!" Daisy protests. It'll take more than "hee hee hoo" to distract her from that sensation.

"Listen, kiddo—everyone feels that way. Big ladies feel that way. But it's not going to happen. I've helped a thousand girls have babies, and none of them has ever split in half, even ones as small as you. My patients don't split in half. I won't let them."

Holly palpates Daisy's abdomen. Holly has gotten pretty good at estimating fetal weight. When she was a student, she'd go to the nursery, unwrap the babies from their swaddling clothes and diapers, and take hold of their heads and legs to guess their length and weight, putting them on the scale afterward to test out her "guesstimates."

The nursery nurses permitted Holly's invasion of their territory only because she diapered so many babies in the course of her extracurricular studies. They thought she was silly. But by lifting, feeling, and weighing all those babies, Holly's hands learned how big the head of a six-pound baby is, how long an eight-pounder's feet are. Her hands learned it all. All her hands had to do after that was learn how to palpate babies when they were still in utero, packed in skin, muscle, and amniotic fluid.

These are skills you can't pick up from a book. Holly's hands learn by doing, by doing repeatedly and repetitively. Like the hands of a pianist, they remember things by muscle memory and learn in a different way from her mind. And, like a pianist's, a midwife's hands ultimately become more intelligent than the mind that initially taught them. When a midwife's hands get smart, a midwife gets hand skills.

Hand skills are what make or break a midwife, because she has to trust her hands. When they're not catching babies, they act like spies that go where her ears and eyes can't go and report back from reconnaissance missions with their gathered intelligence. When a midwife learns to trust her hands, she trusts them more than almost any other instrument.

Holly trusts her hands now, and they estimate that Daisy's baby weighs a little less than six pounds. The delivery will be easier with a small baby than with a big baby, but Holly would rather feel a porker of a baby, even if it means that Daisy has to go c-sec for CPD. Holly likes big babies.

A baby under five and a half pounds is considered low birth weight or "small for gestational age" (SGA). SGA babies are susceptible to hypoxia, the loss of oxygen that can cause lesions in the brain and mental deficits ranging from minor learning disabilities to severe retardation. And an SGA baby, no matter how easy his birth, might experience retarded physical growth later on, for reasons that aren't known yet.

Holly doesn't like SGA babies. "Grow a watermelon," she tells the girls in Clinic, who think in graphic, visual terms. "That's what we like to see. You grow them, we'll get them out."

Now Holly has to do an internal exam—a tricky undertaking with a very young girl. The paradox prevails that a young woman about to give birth can also strongly resist being examined. Just because she's going to be a mother doesn't mean she's comfortable with her body or her sexuality. The hospital counts on the fact that most women who resist being examined will give in eventually and submit, thinking they have to. But when they do, they underestimate their own freedom. If a woman is bent on not being examined, a clinician can do nothing about it—short of a kind of medical rape that even rough-and-tough Morrison is loath to commit. Holly has yet to see a woman forced down and shot full of tranquilizer, which is what the staff would have to do to complete an exam on a truly unwilling patient.

Most patients who refuse examination eventually warm up to the idea, once Holly succeeds in winning their trust as the labor wears on and the initial modesty wears off. Holly once managed an entire labor and delivery without ever examining the patient. As the baby descended through the pelvis, Holly never knew its station, and she couldn't confirm the presentation until the moment of birth. She had no idea about the dilatation status—although it became pretty obvious when the woman started to throw up and shake that she was passing through transition. That delivery had been a revelation, proving what Holly had always thought: that many if not most vaginal exams have more to do with impatient midwives and doctors satisfying their own curiosity than with satisfying a medical need to know.

Examining Daisy for dilatation status is not the real reason Holly needs to "go in." She has to rupture the membranes, if they haven't broken on their own, in order to twist the internal fetal monitor electrode into the baby's soft scalp. To find out if Daisy has ever been examined before, Holly asks her what clinics she's visited, even though Daisy already told her that she didn't have any prenatal care.

"Only King's County," says Daisy.

"You went to King's County?"

"Just now. Before we came here."

The picture comes clear to Holly. Old Apocalypso must have gotten them thrown out of King's County before they came here.

"Did they examine you there?"

"No, we were only there a little while."

Holly explains the exam and tells Daisy to think of her favorite place, intoning monotonously in the hope of being relaxing in a hypnotic way. Sometimes she succeeds at this, but usually she gets the feeling she's only providing her patients with comic relief. She keeps eye contact with Daisy until her eyes are closed.

Holly figured Daisy would be nothing but a fingertip, but when Holly feels for the cervix, she can only just find it: it's so dilated and effaced as to be barely there. Eight centimeters.

Daisy has done good. Therapeutic ambulation at its best: a long walk on the city's sidewalks for most of early and active labor. Holly won't have to walk Daisy through labor, as Apocalypso has already done so, his maniacal demands accidentally performing a great service, depriving Daisy of health care just when she needed to be deprived of it.

Levy appears in the doorway. He looks jaundiced. His light skin, wearied, now unfamiliar with sunshine after hundred-hour working weeks, imparts new meaning to the old term "high yellow."

"What's afoot, Levy?"

"You don't want to know. But I'll tell you anyway. Out here." He looks up and down the corridor uneasily, as if he would like to be elsewhere, in a big way. "Here's the deal," he says, narrowing his eyes. "I want the delivery in the DR. And I want a blood glucose."

"A blood glucose. Sure." A blood sample is taken from the baby's heel to test the baby's glucose level as a hypoglycemia screening. Of the different indications for a blood glucose, the only two that might possibly apply to Daisy's case are low birth weight and preemie status, since nobody is sure of the baby's exact gestational age. It's a silly request to make this early, and a silly request to make of Holly, since the blood glucose is generally taken an hour after delivery by one of the pediatrics residents downstairs in the nursery. Levy's thought processes must be jaundicing as well.

"The delivery in the DR, Treadwell," Levy says.

Holly tries to assume a perfectly neutral, disinterested air, which means erasing any sort of expression from her face. Neutrality takes to her face unflatteringly; Holly doesn't realize that no expression is a kind of expression in itself. Looking cold and hard, her face dead white and without charm, she says, "We move to the DR if there's mec staining? Or end-stage decels or something?"

"No, Treadwell. You move into the DR no matter what. If God's in his heaven and all's right with the world. No matter what the contingencies." Levy studies her mistrustfully. "Do you get the picture, Treadwell? Should I put this in writing? I have a feeling I'm missing some loophole here that'll let you weasel your way into delivery in the ABC. Why do I get that feeling? Don't even try it, Treadwell. Hear what I say. Don't even think it."

Holly searches his eyes and forgets all about professional disinterest. "Why the change of heart, Levy? Chickening out?"

Levy slaps his clipboard rhythmically against his leg, like an impatient drill sergeant. "Treadwell, we don't play chicken in this hospital. We follow protocol. A high-risk, episodic-care adolescent belongs in the DR." He looks at her for a moment, and Holly can see Levy visibly soften. His air of authority lacks conviction, and that's the loophole.

"I'll draw all your bloods for you for the whole week, Levy, if you let me stay in here."

"She's a little girl," he says, almost pleading now, as if he'd like nothing more than for Holly to let him off the hook.

"You can give me any pain-in-the-ass patient you want until I go back to Howard Street, and I won't bitch at you about it."

Levy shakes his head. "You'll probably have to cut a huge episiotomy. You'll get a freaking backache sewing her up on that bed in there."

"Since when do you worry about my aching back?"

It's frustrating, but tears have started to well up in Holly's eyes, and a big knot has tightened in her throat, without her even realizing it. She turns for a moment to the wall. It's not just that she's sad about having to move into the DR. Confrontations have the insidious power to bring tears to her eyes, and the tears only sometimes get her what she wants. Morrison has turned Holly into something she never was before: a crybaby.

She swivels, clear-eyed, to face Levy.

"Christ, don't worry about *me*. I'm all right. It's a young girl who deserves quality care that you ought to worry about."

Looking at her moist face with alarm, Levy gently puts his hand on her shoulder. "Do we understand each other then?" he asks softly, almost afraid to touch the source of all this passion.

"I don't know if you understand me, Levy, but I'm pretty sure I understand you."

CHAPTER 6

Crowley has an easy, motherly way with young girls, and Holly's glad she's in the room, working a Chux pad (which closely resembles a sky blue Pampers) under Daisy's bottom.

"This doesn't hurt, darling," Crowley tells Daisy as she breaks open the packet containing the Amnihook and offers it, like an extended cigarette, to Holly to extract. The white plastic hook looks just like the crochet hook Holly's grandmother used to make baby blankets for the grandchildren produced by Holly's more settled, fertile cousins.

Having inserted her forefinger and index finger up near the cervix, Holly slides the hook in and uses those fingers as a guide on which to rest the hook, as if she were setting up a shot in pool. She doesn't have the luxury of anticipating good news, and she braces herself for a gush of green-tinged fluid that would mean, according to Holly's own personalized protocol, a move to the DR. Meconium-stained fluid is what you expect for a fourteen-year-old brought in by a scalp-locked bruiser—the outward sign of lost grace.

Holly angles the hook through the cervical opening and snags the bulging forewaters, pulling her fingers out quickly as she gives the membranes a fast rip. Her fingers just make it out as fluid streams onto the blue Chux pad and disappears without a trace.

"That is very lovely," Crowley says, patting Daisy's hand. "You're a good girl, aren't you?" Although being good has nothing to do with clear fluid.

The first time Holly performed an AROM was during her second semester at midwifery school. Her site instructor had teaching principles that could best be categorized as belonging to the give 'em enough rope school. She followed her students with a keen, permissive eye and gave them a long leash and plenty of sharp yanks to reel them back when they strayed too far afield. Holly was an intimidated student who was rarely emboldened to push on independently—the instructor made pointed remarks about Holly's good-nurse persona. Holly had failed to retool her personality to fit the demands of her chosen profession.

"What do you mean, I'm too much like a nurse?" Holly asked.

"You're scared to take authority. You passively accept scut work without a peep. You almost never volunteer to do any new skills."

"I'm worried about being safe. I'm thinking of the patients first."

"To me, that sounds like you don't trust yourself. Because you're just a cute, happy nurse who don't know nothing about birthing babies, Miss Scarlett. Now, why don't you do this amniotomy?"

"Who? Me?" Wrong choice of words for someone who has to prove herself a capable, responsible, metanurse personality.

The instructor, of course, mimicked her. "Who, me? What, me worry?"

"Sure, I'll do it," said Holly.

Which only went to show that coercion through ridicule isn't an exclusively male province.

As a maternity nurse, Holly had seen countless amniotomies, and as a midwifery student, she'd studied the procedure in textbooks. She was as ready as she'd ever be, but instead of pulsing with confidence, she entertained the alarming thought: "What if the baby is in a face presentation, and I poke his eye out?" An intimidating image.

As with most fears surrounding new things, this specific fear dissipated as Holly moved shakily into genuine action. Her fingers found the forewaters, and Holly realized that an amniotic sac is really a water balloon that exists in order that Holly might burst it. The only way she could possibly maul the baby would be if someone happened to crash by and violently jostle her arm, which was an unlikely event in the out-of-the-way labor room.

When she slid in the Amnihook, Holly committed the one mistake that only a greenhorn can commit. She ducked her head. This wasn't based on any procedural logic, as she wouldn't be able to visualize what she was doing no matter how hard she looked. There was nothing at all to see. Lowering her head was sheer, outmoded instinct, her head going where her hands did, as if the two couldn't be parted or she didn't trust her hands to go it alone. Maybe she half-expected to hear what happened inside, as if when the bag of waters ruptured, there'd be a definite pop or whoosh to let her know that she'd accomplished what she went in for.

Holly didn't realize that when she ruptured the membranes, she'd know what she'd done by the feel, the sudden give and the sense of penetration. She learned this when she snagged the membranes, the membranes ruptured, and her lowered head caught a spray of fluid that spurted up and spit her straight in the face.

A hand passed her a paper towel. The first thing Holly did was blot out the little beads of amniotic fluid caught in her lashes so she could look up and see her instructor gloat above her.

"You knew!" Holly said.

"Of course I knew. I know everything. Baptism by fluid. Nothing like a face full of fluid to teach you where to put your head! You won't do *that* again. This is what we call hands-on experience."

Holly has caught plenty of fluid in the face since then, all of it brought up by the babies themselves. Fluid full of baby hair, fetal cells, urine (fluid the baby has swallowed in utero and excreted), bits of vernix and lanugo (the down that covers the baby's body), and, most uncomfortably, meconium—sticky, viscous meconium. "Whale babies" is what Denise calls the babies who swim out of the womb with a mouthful of fluid they feel obliged to spout in a midwife's face: "We're here! Splat!"

Holly screws the fetal monitor spiral in place on the soft center of the baby's scalp, then plugs the spiral into the monitor lead, which she tapes to the inside of Daisy's thigh.

"Hit it, Miss Crowley!"

Crowley switches on the monitor, bringing out the ghostly gallops of the baby's heartbeat. Fetal monitoring would provide an apt soundtrack for a chiller thriller or a movie version of "The Tell-Tale Heart." What would Edgar Allen Poe think if he were here now to listen to one of his worst nightmares come to life?

Crowley and Holly stand stock-still, heads tilted, ears cocked, harkening to the monitor and studying the etched-out tracings.

"One-thirty baseline," says Holly, picking up the strip. "The numbers like us."

"We like the numbers," says Crowley.

A woman in a yellow visitor's gown pokes her head past the door, her face worked up in a tentative expression. Visitors to Seven-B always have a lot to worry about, at first. That they'll walk into the wrong room at the wrong time. That they'll do something wrong and be sent away. That they won't have a chance to put a quarter in the parking meter. Worried for the well-being of the woman they've come to see. Worried about the moans and groans from almost every room. That they have to wear a weird, unflattering smock on top of all this doesn't help their worries much.

In a few hours, the visitors become more selective about their worries. The ward's strangeness is eroded by familiarity, and they grow accustomed to the laboring women's moans, even to the yellow visitor's gown.

But they almost always start their tours of duty in just this way: by peering into a doorway, ready to take off if the room they're peering into is the wrong one.

Holly knows right away that the visitor at the door is Daisy's mother. Not because of the family resemblance, which is strong, but because a bright look of recognition and relief spreads across her face as she glances down and registers Daisy's presence with her eyes. Her daughter may be on the brink of splitting in half, for all she knows, but at least she found the right room.

"You're in a private room, Daisy!"

At last, someone has appreciated the ABC for what it is: a private room.

"Mami!"

It's always good to see a mother at labor. Boyfriends may be good guys, but they're often inept guides through the dark woods of labor, the best coaches being people who have been through labors themselves. Holly remembers a couple who came in a few months ago. Thrown by the oddness and femaleness of the surrounds, the boy was a nervous attendant from the start. Just because he'd gotten his girlfriend pregnant didn't mean he was comfortable with women in intimate circumstances. During exams, he left the room to smoke. Coming back the first time, he returned to the wrong labor room, where a resident was doing an exam. The woman's gown was hiked up, her bottom settled on an inverted bedpan, and the boy turned tail and fled to his girlfriend's side, looking terrified. When labor turned hard and fast, he was scared. If his girlfriend was frightened of splitting in two, like a tree struck by lightning, he couldn't relieve her fears. For all he knew, she was about to crack apart and die. Her fear was strong enough to pull him into it, like a riptide dragging them both offshore, neither of them having any idea where they were heading or how long it was going to last.

When the girlfriend moved into transition, her face became changed by the pain and power of the rushing contractions. Her mouth moved down, her forehead moved up—like a facial contradiction in terms—and then her mouth moved up as her forehead crunched down and she called out, "Mommy! Mommy!" The boyfriend was no longer able to reach his girlfriend, wasn't convinced she'd live through this thing or ever return to the way she used to be.

He flew out of his seat and to the waiting area by the elevators to find the young woman's mother. The grandmother-to-be sat staring into space, smoking cigarettes patiently, legs crossed, back straight, waiting for the precise moment when a boy could not do a mother's job.

At her daughter's side, the woman started to speak, her voice something real the girl could hang on to, a lifeline thrown out and grabbed. In terms of power, only a mother's voice was a fair match for the contractions—a voice that could penetrate through the Demerol and the storm of labor, the voice that would make sure she was all right. This voice knew best. This voice would protect her. This voice wouldn't desert her, ever.

Daisy's *mami* is just a few years older than Holly—a pretty woman with long shiny hair like her daughter's. She wears a white T-shirt that says in large, block letters: CHOOSE LIFE. A happy sentiment for a labor room. "Nice to see you, Grandma," Holly says jokingly. Mrs. Morales is pregnant. From the look of it, seven months or so, with a belly about three fingerwidths above her umbilicus. When Mrs. Morales sees Holly's glance, she pats her stomach and says, by way of apology or explanation, "I didn't even know about Daisy when I started this baby." Then she looks at Holly out of the corner of her eye. "Maybe I knew a little bit. Maybe I was jealous. We both drank our milk together. My little girl . . ."

"Your little girl is great. What I want to know is, who's going to boss around who? Is Daisy's baby, being older, going to boss around her new uncle or aunt?"

"No, I am going to boss around all of them."

Denise stands in the doorway, her hand on a jutted hip. Just as nineteenth-century stage actors had a repertoire of gestures to signify distinct emotions—one gesture for Fear, another for Joy, one for Melancholy as opposed to Grief—so does Denise. The position she has just assumed is Exasperation. "How long until the girl is ready to go?"

"She hasn't reached transition yet—she'll probably be ready to deliver in an hour and a half."

"I need to know because a couple of multips are ready to go out here, and I want to get a handle on the DR traffic before we start gridlocking."

"Well, we won't contribute to gridlock, because we're doing the delivery in here."

"Say what? No, you won't."

"Let's talk outside."

Holly pulls on her white lab coat. The mantle of authority that gives her opinions a bit more clout. These are desperate hours, when Holly feels compelled to draw it on to talk to her best friend on the floor. But she senses that Denise is ready to shift her position from Exasperation to the far more dangerous Pissed Off.

"Girl, did you lose your universal joint?" Denise hisses at her. "You can't deliver that baby primap in the isolation chamber."

"Why not?"

"It's dangerous, that's why."

"Where's the danger? Tell me."

"I have to tell you the dangers?"

"Quit stalling, Denise. If you have a good reason for why I shouldn't deliver in here, I'd like to know. Otherwise, let me go."

"I can't believe you have to ask me about the dangers," Denise says, tapping her Nikes on the floor. A foot tap is a harbinger of Pissed Off. Looking disgusted, she says, "The PDs are going to have to be in on the delivery and you know it."

In a hard voice, Holly says, "I know it, do I? I'll tell you what I know. Clear fluid, good variability, a nice baseline. No temp and good blood pressure. That's what I know, Denise."

"You're courting disaster—with the little girl's health and with the administration. I think you're just doing this to pull Levy's tea bag."

"Pull Levy's tea bag?" Holly says with a disbelieving laugh. "What does that mean? Is that like grabbing him by the balls or something?"

Denise is not amused. "You're just trying to work his nerves."

"Denise, if there's an obstetrical indication to move to the DR, we'll do it. But otherwise, we're staying."

Denise looks torn up, frowning in the involuntary way that brings long lines together in the middle of her forehead—knitted brows. It's not a gesture, but the kind of frown seen on women during childbirth and one that is hard to duplicate just for effect. Only real distress can make that frown appear.

Holly realizes that Denise is genuinely worried and afraid.

Denise bites off her words. "I never expected this of you. Of all the nasties in this nasty hospital, I didn't think you'd risk your patient's health just to work Levy's nerves. You can't beat the residents, Holly. You're not going to fucking win in the end. Maybe if you had a chance, I could make some sense out of this monkey business of yours." Denise lifts her head high and juts out her jaw. "Maybe you think you can get over on those others, but don't try and get over on me. You're just doing a job on those little ones. Why don't you think about the girl and her baby?"

"I am thinking of my patients," Holly says, ready to cry again. "And since when did you start believing that the DR is such a safe place? Why are you falling for that line?"

Shutting her mouth tightly, Denise gives the sign that the fight is over. Denise has hit a plateau, and she won't move back or forward or to the side. The only way for Holly to keep going is to move around her.

Sparks and a nurse's aide pull out of a labor room with the first of the two multips, and Denise and Holly watch them silently as the multip is wheeled into the delivery room.

What is that place? Why is that place so safe? What makes that place a sacred sanctum?

Turning to Denise, Holly asks her, "Can you get all the delivery stuff ready for me on a cart?"

Denise extends her hand for Holly to shake. "It's been real nice working with you, Holly Treadwell. Now I'll see you in the next life."

"Be my friend," Holly says quietly.

Denise turns and walks away and says, "I work with you, Treadwell. I don't have to be your friend."

Friendship, hereby reduced to the status of an irrelevancy, cracks and falls in tiny pieces to the ground. Holly moves on.

CHAPTER 7

During the deceleration phase of labor, dilatation slows up as the contractions come quicker and harder. It's the roughest point in labor, moving from nine centimeters to ten, and it can last an hour, that last bit of dilatation. But Daisy has found her rhythm. She's on top of it all—the hard, rough contractions—or maybe way below it, so underwater that when a huge wave smashes down, she can handle it. She breathes through the contractions with her eyes shut, her head back, her face still, her mouth ajar. Her hair, loose from her barrette, spills around her face. She looks like Snow White in a deep, impenetrable sleep, in stop-time captivity.

Everybody speaks softly; they're scared to break the spell. When good magic comes to Morrison, you step back and let it move as it will. Daisy stirs and cries only when noise pushes in from the hallway—an orderly shouts, the hopper starts up with a muted roar. The noises sound far-off to Holly, but Daisy winces, with her eyes closed, at any noise.

"She's very calm," Holly says quietly to Mrs. Morales.

Mrs. Morales strokes her daughter's forehead and says, "When we were in Puerto Rico, staying with my mother, she slept through a hurricane. A boat came out of the ocean and stopped right near the house. Then a tree by her window crashed down to the ground. She never woke up. Not until morning and the hurricane was over."

Crowley slips a fever-meter into Daisy's mouth. She doesn't need to tell Daisy what to do. With her eyes still shut, Daisy closes her lips around the thermometer.

"She was on a McDonald's double-dutch team," Mrs. Morales whispers. "They went up to Massachusetts for an exhibition," she adds proudly.

"Did she jump when she was pregnant?"

"Every day. She didn't know for a long time." Mrs. Morales shrugs. "Is that bad?"

"That's fine. The baby can take it. She must be very disciplined."

"Oh, yes, she does everything right, most of the time."

"You gonna make sure she stays in school?"

"She'll keep going to St. Agnes," Mrs. Morales says, nodding. "I'm just going to have twins, that's all."

Holly pats her arm. "You're a good mom."

Mrs. Morales looks at Daisy. "I never was this good," she whispers. "I had Daisy by cesarean."

Neither of them wants to jinx the run of good luck, so they stop talking. Holly considers that what makes Daisy so good in labor— passive acceptance of forces stronger than she is, bending to wills stronger than her own—is precisely what got her pregnant to begin with, when she gave herself up to Apocalypso, left resistance to the side, whatever pain there was in it accepted in the face of its unavoidability.

Holly started this labor thinking she'd have to walk Daisy through every step of it, but now she and Crowley have come to trust Daisy implicitly. Daisy Morales knows what to do, if she's left alone to do it. It's hard to understand why Levy, Denise, and the rest really believe she's in danger here. There are no medical grounds for believing this, and Holly figures that what's created the sense of danger is that she's broken with Morrison ritual. She's messed with Morrison magic.

In midwifery school, Holly took an elective course on birth in different cultures, an anthropology seminar that taught her that every culture establishes its own rituals for the way childbirth is conducted. Every culture believes that its childbirth rituals are the only ones that can provide safe-conduct for the mother and child. To break with a child-birth ritual is, as Denise said, to court disaster. Holly didn't believe that her own culture was susceptible to ritualistic beliefs; she thought that this anthropological law applied only to primitive cultures. But three years at Morrison have been enough fieldwork for Holly to draw the conclusion that the American medical community isn't immune to the pull of childbirth rituals. It clings to plenty of rituals—draping, prepping, confinement to bed, stirrups, separation of mother and child after delivery, prohibiting visitors and fathers from the delivery room—that have no medical foundations. Masking, for example, is classic ritual gear for all major life transitions—birth, weddings (the bride's veil), death (the covering of the dead person's face, the mourning veil). And so, while masking at deliveries doesn't influence the rate of infection one way or the other, everyone does it anyway, because not to would be courting disaster.

The hold of the childbirth rituals must be the reason that Levy objects to delivery in the ABC. After all, the ABC is only thirty yards from the nearest delivery room. Moving Daisy there wouldn't take longer than half a minute. Holly runs a mental check of disasters that might require a move. Second stage arrest and the need for forceps would be easy to manage. Fetal distress and the need for a section would be handled as it'd be handled in a labor room—by heading for the OR. Respiratory distress in the baby could be dealt with as easily in the ABC as in a delivery room. There's oxygen here, a DeLee mucus trap as well, and intubation by the PDs could be performed here as well as anywhere else.

What, exactly, is the danger?

The danger is that she's broken protocol, and Holly suddenly knows that having broken with the magic, she is going to be punished. Heretics are always punished in a big way. If she delivers Daisy in the ABC, she realizes, she is probably going to get fired.

To which prospect she says, as heretics always say: "Good. Come and get me then." And in the back of her mind, she thinks: "Meg Greenspan. Brooklyn Heights. I'll chance it."

Daisy is into transition. Toes curled, hiccups, then throwing up into a basin held by Crowley, her head held by her mother, who apologizes. "It's only seasickness," Crowley says, shrugging.

Holly is almost impatient with the elemental calmness of this labor. Her reflex now, as developed by Seven-B's frantic pace, is to manage labor, to care for more than one patient at a time, to actually do something. She's not used to sitting hard by a patient, working as an *accoucheur*, one who sits by the bed. She's been a midwife for three years, but she's never really learned how to labor-sit. Maybe she's never learned how to be a midwife either. Maybe all she is is a second-string obstetrician. Maybe the passive vigilance of a noninterventionist midwife is beyond her now.

"Holly."

"Aw, hell," she mutters. She looks up, and there's the long, stringbeany figure of Scott the Sightseer seeing the ABC sights. "Speak," she says.

"I hear there's going to be a delivery in here."

"You heard right," Holly says, standing up and heading for the doorway. "Who'd you hear that from?"

"Denise. Her exact words were, 'Sightseer, you want to check out some sights, go check out the birthing room.'"

"It's all true. They'll probably have my head on a goddamn platter. So be it."

"I'd like to be here for it," Scott says, shuffling his feet. "I've never seen a bed delivery."

It's hard communicating with someone so much taller. Holly has to squint when she looks up at Scott's face, which is framed by a bank of fluorescent lights. "Where were you when Levy delivered the hepatitis B case last week?" Holly asks suspiciously.

"I wasn't on then."

When are you ever *on*? "Why do you care about bed deliveries anyway?"

"I'm thinking of becoming a family practice man. You know, some-place rural. Wouldn't be a bad idea if I had a couple of bed deliveries under my belt."

Holly smiles ruefully. She can piece a full-color picture together in her mind. Scott jumping into a Jeep, riding roughshod to a measles case, to an isolated farm to catch a baby. It's not as if she doesn't entertain the same fantasies—the Frontier Nursing Service T-shirt currently in her hamper attests to as much. It's just that she feels a bit violated by the discovery that someone as seemingly graceless as Scott would have the same dreams that she does.

"Scott, the whole point of doing the birth in the ABC is so that a whole mess of strangers doesn't suddenly appear to turn the delivery into a public event."

Scott turns away in his familiar miserable shamble. He hates it here. He wants to practice in some other way, some other century. No wonder he is drawn down all the time, into insatiable sleep.

"You're so defeatist," she says, addressing his back. "Why are you giving up without even a fight?"

"I'm sick of it," he says, shaking his head.

"You can be a spectator," she says, and he stops in his tracks. "But not without a price." He revolves around slowly and nods for her to go on. "You defend me later."

"To whom?"

"To anyone who asks. The chief."

"Holly, maybe you're not aware of this fact, but I'm not exactly considered to be one of Morrison's brighter lights. Why would you want me to defend you? Talk about defeatist."

"I guess I'm desperate for allies," Holly says, smiling.

He laughs. "I think we're about to share the same doghouse," he says.

"Move it on over," Holly says. "Mean old midwife is moving in."

CHAPTER 8

The collection of spectators that the ABC is supposed to discourage has not been discouraged. Scott, Denise, and a pediatrics resident talk quietly, hovering by the doorway, as if awaiting a distinguished professor to give an important lecture.

Holly is masked and capped—one ritual she's not breaking with. She's gone far enough for one night.

"She's so quiet," Denise murmurs. If she's not forgiven Holly, at least she wants to oversee Holly's downfall. "Did you do her up with Demerol?"

"She did herself up. She's a genius."

"You telling me that little girl is a *genius*?"

Holly says nothing as she prepares the large-barreled syringe of Lidocaine.

"The baby must be tiny, for such a serious needle," Denise says.

The pudendal block is the forerunner to the episiotomy Holly is planning to cut. Holly plans episiotomies only for SGAs and LGAs. For an SGA, an episiotomy hurries delivery and lessens the stress on the baby's head, which is more sensitive than the head of a larger baby. When Holly cuts an episiotomy, she usually goes for a midline 'pis—a small cut that runs straight down from the posterior fourchette (the vagina's lower rim) to the middle of the perineum, right above the anal sphincter.

But Holly is planning a mediolateral tonight—this slants off to the side, heading down from the posterior fourchette at a forty-five-degree angle. Holly prefers midlines because they're easier to repair, quicker to heal, and less painful than mediolaterals, as a midline cuts through tissue that joins two mirroring sets of muscle together while a mediolateral cuts through muscle and against the muscle's grain.

The advantage of a mediolateral is that it reduces the chance that the baby's body will extend the episiotomy cut into the sphincter. A midline can sometimes just *go*—just as a cut piece of fabric is more inclined to keep tearing if pressure is applied to it. Because Daisy's perineum is very short, the threat of a midline that continues to tear is too great a risk.

For most episiotomies, Holly administers a bit of Lidocaine a few minutes before delivery. Even when she plans an episiotomy, she never is completely sure she'll actually cut one, but waits to see instead. Local infiltration with Lidocaine acts fast but also swells the tissues slightly, making suturing more difficult and less accurate than it is when done with a block. Lidocaine also wears off more quickly than a block, and sometimes Holly has to give a second injection.

Holly often cuts an episiotomy with no anesthetic at all. Right before the head delivers, the perineal tissues are so stretchy and thin that to cut through them is almost like cutting through dead skin, and the burning sensation a woman may feel when the baby presses against the perineum in his descent is actually a built-in mechanism to numb the perineum.

A pudendal block numbs the whole perineal area, as the anesthetic injected into the pudendal nerve literally blocks the transmission of pain as it travels from the perineum to the spine. If pain signals travel a stream, a pudendal block is the dam that collects them and won't allow them to pass. Pudendals last an hour and a half, so that pain relief is supplied for the episiotomy, delivery, and suturing. Holly is giving Daisy a pudendal so that the pain of delivery will be reduced and her concentration and control maintained, and so that Holly will be able to do a top-notch episiotomy repair, with tissues that are not as swollen as with Lidocaine. All patients are equal and deserve equally good treatment. But some patients are more equal than others, and Daisy is one of them.

Holly never gives a block casually—that is, she's always nervous when she does one. She most often uses a block to repair fourth-degree tears—ones that extend up into the urethra and into the rectum—which shows how noncasual she is. Holly's give-'em-enough-rope instructor taught her how to do a pudendal block. It's a tricky procedure, as discovering the pudendal nerve, which is way back in the birth canal, and then differentiating it from the pudendal vein, where the anesthetic must not go, isn't easy.

The instructor gave her students very little rope on their first blocks. "Are you on the spines?" she asked Holly. Holly had nervously guided the five-inch-long needle across the patient's vagina, having found what she thought were the spines—the ischial spine, not the spine in the verte-brae sense, but the bony projection from the pelvis that is the standard landmark against which a fetus's station (or position in descent) is measured and the takeoff point for a pudendal block. The syringe should enter the body right below the ischial spine.

"Yes, I'm on the spines," Holly had answered.

"Look me in the eye and say that."

Holly looked her instructor in the eye, then pulled the syringe out, felt for the spine again, knew it was not anything else but the spine, and guided the syringe back in. Holly looked her instructor in the eye again and said, "I'm on the spines."

The barrel of the syringe is deep and wide and holds quite a bit of Lidocaine. Before the Lidocaine is released, Holly aspirates—draws the syringe up—to see if she's accidentally set the needle into the pudendal vein instead of the nerve. The sight of blood zooming up into the barrel of the syringe is a caution. Holly has done it twice in her life, and she felt her stomach turn each time. "Are you on the spine?" she asks herself, and then goes. In a few minutes, Daisy will be numb. Then her baby will be born.

"Miss Crowley, we need a bedpan."

Holly isn't used to delivery in bed. The main difference between delivering on the delivery table and in bed is that the bed gives with the mother's weight, her bottom sinking into the mattress. But Daisy is so light, she makes almost no impression on the mattress at all. Still, a bedpan, to keep her up.

Crowley hands Holly a stainless-steel bedpan that is still wrapped in brown paper.

"Don't we have any rubber ones?"

"No. No more rubber ones."

The pan is hard and cold beneath the paper, and Holly puts it to the side. No bedpan then.

Daisy sits up, her knees bent, hands tucked under her thighs, pushing. Holly wonders if she should have used the pudendals. Daisy had been a genius at all this, but the numbness only seems to have thrown her off. Daisy can still feel the contractions, but she can't connect with where the baby's head is, and she's confused. She's crying now, as if fear recaptured her: she made it through the woods, came to a clearing, only to be bagged by fear.

In part, Daisy wasn't prepared for this, and that's Holly's fault. With young primaps who don't know what to expect, Holly can spend the whole labor chattering at them, to take them into the next step. But Daisy seemed so in control that Holly didn't want to break the spell, instill fear without realizing it, upset her concentration. Now it's too late.

Scott and the pediatrics resident stand against the wall, tall and masked and fearful in appearance, if you didn't know they were just scared boys themselves underneath all that gear. Holly cuts half of the overhead lights. A true birthing room would have incandescent instead of fluorescent lights, but Morrison isn't very ideological when it comes to birthing room standards. The hospital pretty much just wants to have a birthing room so that it can say to the public that it has a birthing room. Holly snaps on the lamp at the end of the bed.

"Almost home," she says.

Both hands on a cart, Levy leans into the room. "I got a trolley here, express to the DR. All primaps aboard."

"She's crowning, Levy!"

"Crowning's no problem. We take crowning ladies."

Holly looks up, sees Levy, then decides to look down again. Levy is useless. She figures that out in an instant. Holly wonders when she should cut the episiotomy. She feels around the perineum, checking the degree of bulging. A few centimeters of the baby's head show, and Holly is at a crisis point—she has to choose whether to go for the mediolateral or the midline. She'd decided on the mediolateral, but she's not sure now. If Daisy can control the delivery of the head, they might get away with a small midline, because the baby's head doesn't seem that big. And yet the perineum is so short.

Just go, Treadwell. Make your move.

The head will be born in a few more contractions, and if Holly waits any longer, the purpose of the episiotomy will be negated. Holly wishes she had someone to consult, someone she trusts, but there's nobody here whose advice she'd take willingly or confidently. Levy's standing by like a smartass orderly, while Scott's hanging back like a student in an OR theater.

But then there's Crowley. "Miss Crowley, please." For all her bulk, Crowley is light on her feet and reaches Holly's side in a flash. "What do you think?" Holly asks her. "The head size?"

Holly doesn't look up but hears Crowley say, under her breath, right by her ear, "She's okay. She can do it with a snip."

Holly picks up the scissors and enters the perineum from a vertical position. She snips. One snip is all an episiotomy should take; two snips and you can create a jagged tear before the baby is even born. With that one snip, Holly cuts a midline episiotomy.

She wills the slight stretch of the skin *not to tear* and stanches the bleeding, of which there is little, with a gauze square. Then one, two, three... the head is born. Easy. Easy.

The shoulders are delivered.

The cord is cut, fast. Holly doesn't know enough about Daisy's history to allow an exchange of blood between the mother and baby that a delayed cord cutting would create.

"It's a girl," she says. Somehow that seems right. Daisy should have a girl.

It must belong to the pediatrics resident, because that's whose arms reach out to take it.

The trip that began with Apocalypso is ended. The little girl on the cart, who looked ready for confirmation, doesn't exist anymore, because something has happened. She's lost years since she first came in here. In the half-light of the birthing room, she looks like a girl who's stayed home from school because of a bad fever; her mother is kissing her forehead. She's too young for sex, for babies. She's ready, maybe, for her first boy–girl dance.

Under her bottom, the soup of birth. Fluid, blood, excrement. Crowley rolls her to the side, almost with one hand, and replaces the Chux pad. Her mother plumps her pillow. Her hair is damp, so her mother draws it back with a rubber band she found in her purse. Daisy's drier now; her teeth chatter. She's not pregnant anymore. Now she's a mother.

CHAPTER 9

Lighting up a cigarette, Holly keeps it clenched between her teeth as if she were smoking a stogie. She's in the locker room, her own *sanctum sanctorum*. Of course, it's open to everybody, which makes it something less than *sanctorum*. She puts both her hands on the glazed glass windowpanes, through which a heavy, steel-gray light passes. Morning. The glass is cool and damp. Holly presses against the window hard, arches her back, then leans all the way in to place her forehead against the glass. Retracting her head, she rolls her neck and dives down to touch her toes. Then, glancing around to see if anybody else is in the room, she goes behind a bank of lockers, props a chair against a locker, and arranges herself in it so that her feet are pressed against the upper part of the locker and her head dangles from the seat of the chair. A modified headstand. Blood rushes to her head, and she has reversed gravity, for a moment. Fear rushes out. For a moment, everything is fine. What could be wrong?

Until someone stands before her. "You look Chinese like that," Denise says.

"So do you."

"Don't bother to get up."

"I won't."

"You lucked out, Treadwell."

"Think so? Think I got away with murder, do you?"

"Uh-huh."

"I don't suppose I could persuade you"—Holly gasps for breath—"that the reason everything turned out all right was because Daisy Morales labored and delivered in the ABC."

"Uh-uh."

Red-faced, Holly walks her feet, still in their soiled blue booties, down

195

the locker, then wheels herself upright. Pushing back her hair and widening her eyes, which are a good-natured blue despite her smudged mascara and the possibility that she might get fired, she remakes herself into the animated, happy midwife. This is, constitutionally, a tough act to pull off. She is just barely squeezing into her role.

Smiling she says, "I thought I wasn't going to see you in this life."

"You're not," Denise says, looking down at her, not smiling. "It's the next life already. You're here. You're an outlaw, girl."

Denise swivel-hips her way out of the locker room.

At least Denise walks just like she did in the old life. Holly sinks way down into the hard wooden chair. The question is, is that the only thing that'll stay the same?

A new life as an outlaw. A vigilante midwife who takes the protocol into her own hands.

"You're nothing but a pansy nurse, Treadwell," her old instructor used to say. Give them enough rope.

Holly has taken the rope and jumped. Funny how just because you want to stop falling doesn't mean you can. When Holly finally lands, where will she be?

CHAPTER 10

On Holly's dresser, Matt has left a pile of things cleared out from his pockets. Candy wrappers, bank receipts, tokens. Sometimes Holly thinks he is more like a brother than a boyfriend. In an effort to make it seem as though he does his bit around the apartment and pitches in, he's pulled the bedspread over the mussed-up bedclothes. Straightening up, he'd call it.

"Hello, bobcat," says a note on the pillow.

That's romance.

Holly collapses onto the note. At least Matt still wants her.

She gets up, heads into the kitchen, and thinks, "Coffee or beer?" She opens the refrigerator and pulls out a beer, heads for the bathroom, takes off her clothes, and swigs at the beer while she's in the shower. This makes her happy. Whatever happens, she can always do this: drink a beer in the shower.

Romance. Sex. Once, Holly asked her mother how nurses had ever become such sex objects. Mrs. Treadwell skipped over the implications of the white uniform and the subservience built into the role of nurse and jumped to, "It used to be that nurses were the only women who really knew the facts about sex. I suppose they were considered experienced and in-the-know because of it."

Midwives, in-the-know to the max, have yet to establish any sort of sex-object aura. That's a pity, Holly thinks. Of course, this is the price you pay when feminism rather than subservience is built into your profession's structure, and when the bodies you're exposed to all day long are women's rather than men's.

Sometimes Holly forgets that her profession is all about sex. That sex is how babies get born. The reasons women have sex are various and multifarious and universal. They have sex for love or lust, out of a will to be powerful or an instinct to be submissive or an urge to be powerful through submission, to make babies or to make money. Holly always understood why women have sex, but it was only during her first year as a maternity nurse that she realized why women might not want to have sex.

During that first year, she temporarily misplaced her sex drive. She thought she'd lost it forever. When she shut her eyes and waited to fall into a sexy blur as she made love with her boyfriend, a gallery of graphic pictures strayed into her mind and stayed there, no matter how strongly she willed her intellect to turn off and set her body free. Vivid images of women in delivery floated through her mind and lodged there, wouldn't budge, couldn't be avoided. Images of squinting, wrinkled, wet babies just born and bent out of shape in the process. Images of nurses shaving women with a flick of the wrist. Puckered episiotomy scars. Bulging vaginal walls and swollen labia. Lacerated cervixes. Sometimes it helped not to shut her eyes at all but to move through the motions with her eyes wide open and her body stiff and disconnected.

In the past, she'd somehow half-imagined that her sexual parts were designed with the idea of men's pleasure in mind. The body as a work of art, most valuable and valued for its aesthetic uselessness. What she had once seen as romantic had become deromanticized, with the sense of aesthetic uselessness supplanted by a crass functionalism.

If, as she grew up, everything in her life had constructed an image of women's bodies as being bits of fluff and flesh and fun, life on the labor and delivery ward was deconstructing that image. The body seemed insanely strong, obsessively utilitarian, an instrument whose every component had a definite purpose. Her idea of herself as unique fell by the wayside as she saw that the important qualities of her body were shared by almost every woman in the world. Like theirs, her body was a vessel, a baby machine that just happened, because of modern technological achievements, to be inactive. The idea that sex was a recreation, with no thought of procreation, struck her as bizarre. The body as an aesthetic piece of living sculpture seemed to be a huge mental delusion under which most of the world managed, through blindness and ignorance, to operate.

Holly had to ask a friend already in midwifery school if she ever felt . . . "put off by sex, you know?"

"No. I don't. Do you?"

"Well, sometimes." Mostly, now.

"How come?"

"It all seems like a sham, mating game, some pathetic, primitive thing. The woman dances around and shows off her bright feathers or whatever so that a man comes along and fucks her and propagates the species. Except that we dance around and the man comes along and fucks us and we don't propagate the species. What's wrong with this picture?"

Her friend sat her down. "You tell me. What's wrong with this picture? It sounds good to me that I can shake my feathers and not get pregnant because of it."

Holly rolled her eyes. "It's just a farce, don't you see?"

"Of course the mating game or dating game or whatever is a farce. That's why it's fun, you dope. Put on the feathers, dance around with your tail wagging. That's the whole shooting match."

"I can't stomach it. Why don't people just fuck and get it over with? Skip the preliminaries. Just hunker down and couple." Holly shuddered, repelled, surprising herself.

"Maybe nature meant sex to be fun so we'd keep going at it the way we do," her friend said. "If nature throws some fun my way, I'm going for it."

"But it's procreation," Holly said, slowly and insistently. "We treat it like recreation."

"It's both, Holly. Sex is like eating. You'd do it to survive, but it's fun and social, too. Nobody in his right mind eats just to subsist, purely from necessity. Nobody sits down at the dinner table and says, 'This is just a farce. I'm just eating to survive and everyone is acting like it's a recreation!' At least, I don't. You shouldn't either."

Holly broke into tears. "Well, how do I get these nasty images out of my mind?" And she told her friend about the labor and delivery visions that swamped her head as she tried to settle down into lovemaking.

"Prepare a fantasy beforehand. Elaborate on it. Make it stronger than the other images. Do I have to tell you everything?"

Holly sips her beer, lying in a sunbeam that crosses over the bed. She arranges herself so she's lying diagonally on the bed, the sun washing over her body, her face in the shade. She looks at the note—hello, bobcat—and runs through the fantasy she has kept locked in her mind for three years now. Sometimes it shifts this way and that. But it's always the same, strong and clear. Before she finishes it, she has fallen asleep, dreaming of nothing.

Holly is dreaming of something. The phone rings right in the middle of a dream Holly does not want to leave. She is standing in the middle of a field, and the sky is blue, the clouds are puffy; she can even feel a breeze across her face. All around her, like daisies or some other pretty flower that grows without effort and grows everywhere, are babies. Pink babies naked in the grass, stretched out in the sun, rolling around. Holly is counting them to make sure they're all there, but she doesn't know how many are supposed to be there. This doesn't trouble her. By the time she finishes counting, she'll have gotten it all figured out.

"Hullo." Her voice is croaky.

"Holly, this is Marge down at the clinic."

Marge, the head clerk at Howard Street Maternity, is the prototype of the burned-out civil servant who pushes on, despite her burnout. She is so burned out, she does not know how burned out she is. She is sixty years old and utterly devoted to Mrs. Gruener. Marge is so burned out, she laments the passing of *The King Family Christmas Special.* "I'd like to know how all the kids turned out," she once told Holly.

"Hi-ya, Marge. What's up?"

"Mrs. Gruener would like to see you in her office before you report in to work tonight."

Holly is jolted into complete wakefulness. "Is this big-time seriousness or what, Marge?"

Holly can almost hear Marge evaluating the trouble Holly is in as old Marge breathes heavily—thoughtfully—at the other end of the line. "I'd say it's pretty serious, hon," Marge says at last.

Holly is getting fired.

"Any clues, Marge? Did you have to pull my file or anything?"

"No, hon. I don't think it's terribly bad, as bad as all that."

"Just moderate bad, huh?"

"Moderately bad. That's how I'd put it, hon."

In the face of stress, here's what you do. Pull the covers over your head and sleep for as long as you can. Which is precisely what Holly Treadwell chooses to do.

CHAPTER 11

The eight-block walk to the Howard Street Clinic from the subway is cold in the winter and scary at night. But it corrects any egocentric ideas of self-importance Holly may have managed to conceive. Sometimes her patients grow too fond of her, and it goes to her head. They invite her to their babies' christenings, to weddings, to high school graduations. By walking through their neighborhood, she reminds herself that she only skims their lives. Their lives are there: in the crumbling tenements, seven stories high and no elevators (hell for a woman at term, lungs scrunched up by the encroaching uterus, groceries in her arms, and two more flights to go), and in the housing project where the clinic was built.

Most clinic patients come from the project, and the fact that the clinic looks a lot like their own apartments puts them at something like ease. The clinic has the same windows that open out at an angle and speckled black-and-white linoleum and eight-foot-high ceilings. On a good day, the clinic waiting rooms remind Holly of a small-town doctor's waiting room, with everyone seeming to know everyone else.

The clinic's official name is the Arnold T. Lansing Clinic, but nobody calls it that. Even the mayor of New York calls it the Howard Street Clinic, which makes more sense, as the place belongs more to the people of Howard Street than it does to Arnold T. Lansing, whoever he was. People who know only that Howard Street is Morrison's satellite clinic presume that it's a black hole in miniature, but the neighborhood people like the clinic, which gives neither very good nor terribly bad care, while hating Morrison, a mile to the south. If the clinic feels like it belongs to them, Morrison belongs to someone else entirely.

Holly gets this feeling herself. Returning to Howard Street after a month at Morrison is like leaving the muck of the trenches for the reserve lines. There, she marshals her energies, musters her forces, out of the line of fire. It's strange to be going back only in order to stand fire. She snorts as she remembers Denise's final comment last night. "What do you care if you get fired or not? You be a good-looking, albeit palefaced, specimen of femalehood. You have a rich father. Why don't you just snag yourself a husband? Are you whacked? Don't you have a clue about what to do?"

"No," Holly said. "I don't."

Whacked or not, she doesn't want to leave, Meg Greenspan and Brooklyn Heights be damned. She belongs here, even if she is a paleface, and she likes the clinic. Coming back, she realizes that Morrison's dilapidated condition depresses her, with its peeling paint, harsh lighting, and overcrowded rooms with so much space lost in the high ceilings—she's surprised the administration hasn't put in bunkbeds yet, to take full advantage of the unused space. It could be called upper-level care. Howard Street is a sunny place that hasn't suffered a hundred years' abuse to become seedy beyond redemption. And the clinic, only four stories high, doesn't have the out-of-control feeling Morrison has, or its haunted quality.

Holly walks quickly through the halls, not wanting to meet anyone on her way to see the boss, and, with only half an eye, takes in the paintings tacked to the yellow walls, done by kids at the day-care center across the street—rainbows, suns with smiling faces, Easter bunnies, flowers painted in manic, clashing colors. Holly doesn't want to become attached to them if she is about to be fired.

Holly usually likes to return to Clinic so she can have a boss again. Not something to admit out loud, but sometimes she misses Mrs. Gruener, a complicated person she likes and respects and who actually guides her. Mrs. Gruener views the political status of the American nurse-midwife with almost detached bemusement, as if American resistance to midwives is a national quirk deriving from wrongheaded childishness. Her tactic in getting the medical establishment to accept midwives is to beguile her opponents and take them in hand as if they were silly children, and to do so charmingly. "The only way to make it in this country," she's explained to Holly, "is to make these docs see that a midwife is not just a diminutive OB. A midwife is a specialist in normal birth, the OB a specialist in pathological birth. That's how it is in Europe and how it must be here. We separate. A horse of a different color."

Mrs. Gruener doesn't believe in quick change. Any sudden gesture might turn the powers-that-be against midwives and shut them out of the hospitals for another half-century. Mrs. Gruener thinks in terms of decades. "Don't think like an American," she will tell Holly. "Think *historically*. We must infiltrate *slowwwly*." Holly knows she's in for just this kind of talk this afternoon.

Despite her dread of a dressing down and the threat of being fired,

Holly still wants to hear about Mrs. Gruener's five-year plan to remove the prefix *nurse* from the midwifery services at Morrison and Howard Street, replacing *Nurse-Midwifery Services* with plain old *Midwifery Services*. The dehyphenation of midwifery. Some midwives, not wanting to be identified with lay midwives, will disapprove. But Mrs. Gruener has told Holly, "As long as we are nurses, we are nurses." And, because she looks to the future, "What sort of midwifery education might there be in ten years? Direct-entry education that doesn't require a midwifery student to be a nurse? Let's keep a door open for the midwives of the future, shall we try?" Mrs. Gruener thinks in decades.

Holly's adrenaline is on the move as she walks through the bright hallways and ducks past Marge, who is busy filing. Possibly, Marge spends eighty percent of her time filing. Holly breathes deep before knocking on Mrs. Gruener's door. She's never been fired, and she can only dimly imagine how it'll feel. "A new experience," she thinks reflexively, the power of positive thinking flickering through her mind like a tic. But she loses heart when Mrs. Gruener answers Holly's knock on her door with the words, "At least you're prompt."

Mrs. Gruener is struggling with the window's hand crank as Holly slips into the hard-backed chair in front of Mrs. Gruener's desk. Artifacts on the wall testify that Mrs. Gruener has been in league with, and done battle against, powerful forces. A framed declaration from Congress pronouncing Nurse-Midwifery Month. A letter from New York's then-mayor congratulating Mrs. Gruener on the opening of the Howard Street midwifery services. A copy of a bill, and the pen the governor used to sign it, that mandated third-party reimbursement for nurse-midwives by insurance companies.

When Holly first came to Howard Street three years ago, she sat here for the first time and told Mrs. Gruener, "I'm not very interested in politics." Mrs. Gruener had smiled knowingly and said, "But politics is interested in you, my dear."

Now Mrs. Gruener spins about from the window, waving a piece of paper. Her hands don't do births anymore, and her long nails are polished a pearly mauve. An administrator's hands.

"What is a nurse-midwife?" she asks, her blue eyes chilly.

Holly opens her mouth, but Mrs. Gruener puts up her hand.

"Stop. I don't want an answer, because I don't think you know what a nurse-midwife is. What the dynamics of her role consist of." She pushes up the sleeves of her beige cashmere sweater. "A nurse-midwife catches babies, but she is also an educator, a communicator, and, in the hospital community, an agent of change. In an environment inhospitable to change, how should a change agent behave?"

"Very carefully," Holly says, smiling awkwardly.

"You laugh, but that is correct. So why do I hear otherwise about you? You argue with the residents. You're disputatious. The residents find it impossible to work collaboratively with you. You're not part of the team, but from an opposing team."

"Mrs. Gruener, you know all that stuff about collaborative teamwork is so much PR hype."

"Then why don't the other girls have these problems? We go through this every time." Turning to the window, she says, in a high-pitched whine, "'The world is a bad place, Mrs. Gruener. I'm the only good person left, Mrs. Gruener.' That is nonsense." Mrs. Gruener swings around. "You must get over your perpetual discovery of the wickedness of the world and learn to function as a change agent. A change agent must provide a role model, must suggest alternative routes of behavior. A change agent must not confront. Why? Because the institution will come smashing down and crush the little change agent. Holly, I was considering you for a supervisory position, but no longer."

Holly draws a sharp breath. She doesn't lust after promotion, but she's stung to learn she's not promotable.

"This has nothing to do with your baby-catching skills," Mrs. Gruener says sharply. "On those grounds, you are eminently qualified. But your leadership skills and ability to function in an organizational structure are childish." She waves the piece of paper. "Here's a note from Dr. Farber."

Dr. Farber is an attending OB Holly hasn't laid eyes on in months. What would he have to say about her? She doesn't have long to wait, as Mrs. Gruener isn't pausing for an answer, but emphasis.

"He said you delivered an adolescent primap in the birthing room although both delivery rooms were vacant. Is this true?"

"Who told him that?"

"We're not in girl's school now, are we?" Mrs. Gruener says, sighing. "Is this true?"

"I delivered a frightened adolescent primap in the ABC—"

"Is there any other kind of adolescent primap?"

"Mrs. Gruener, the delivery went perfectly. What's the point of the birthing room, if it's used only for infection control? It was one of the nicest births—ask anyone who saw it."

Mrs. Gruener shakes her head, shuts her eyes, and lets Dr. Farber's letter flutter to her desk. "Holly, I have tried to hammer and knock a few simple historical facts into your girlish head about the politics of midwifery. I have emphasized that a midwife's position is very precarious. Yet you persist in thinking—correction—in dreaming that you're a little girl whom everyone adores and forgives and forgets. You are what a midwife should not be. A child. A child delivering children delivering children."

She turns to open another window and mimics a little girl's voice as she says, "'Oh, Mrs. Gruener! Can't we have what the other children have? I want to deliver in bed like other children do at other places!'" She swivels about to look piercingly at Holly. "You have no concept of how things work. You are naive."

Holly straightens up. "I know as well as anyone how things work at Morrison Hospital."

"No!" Mrs. Gruener shouts. "You know how things work at Morrison Seven-B. But you don't know how things work if they are not visible to you. If you don't see it, it doesn't exist. You think the world is a reasonable place, but you are wrong. The world is not reasonable, it does not love you, and it does not love midwives."

Mrs. Gruener sinks into her creaky wooden swivel chair and slips on her reading glasses, rubbing her forehead with the back of her hand. "You have no sense of how slowly we must move," she says quietly. "Yes, at some hospitals, midwives deliver in bed. But at other hospitals, midwives don't exist at all. You don't believe it, but it's possible that midwives won't exist at Morrison soon. A glut of medical students, a lower birthrate. What does that equation add up to? Yes, the midwives will have to go, so the medical students will have enough patients. They have a reason now to do it—the midwives are breaking protocol. I can hear how it will go." Her voice deepens and lowers: "'These midwives have their own interests at heart and not the hospital's interests. They must go. We'll get five residents to take their place.' How easy that will be for them."

Mrs. Gruener moves to her filing cabinet and draws out a folder. "Come here," she orders, and points at a list of the city hospitals and the number of midwives in each. "Where are the South Dutchess midwives, Holly?"

"There are none."

"The number of midwives is not zero!" she snaps. "It's negative five. There were five midwives there, but they walked out after the docs wouldn't let them deliver in bed."

Holly looks skeptically at Mrs. Gruener.

"You think I'm making up a fairy tale? An object lesson?" Mrs. Gruener says sharply. "Is this too convenient to be true? I never lie to my midwives. The truth is bad enough to be good enough. The midwives walked out in protest and expected to walk back in, forgiven. The midwives here said, 'What a brave and noble thing the South Dutchess midwives are doing, standing up for their principles!' But South Dutchess said, 'Fine, good-bye, we can get along without you.' They meant it, too."

Mrs. Gruener slips into her chair as Holly eases into hers.

"You have to admit, Mrs. Gruener, they had guts."

Mrs. Gruener points a pencil at Holly, and Holly flinches, half-expecting it to fly in her face. "Guts is what it takes to stick things out when they don't go your way," she says gravely. "The South Dutchess midwives accomplished nothing for midwifery in general or midwifery in particular. Guts is the patience to change things *slowwwwwly*. Become a guerrilla warrior, Holly. That's how we'll win this war. By never declaring it. As soon as they know we're at war, they'll bring out the big guns and we won't stand a hope of a change, because we won't be here. So no more declarations of war, Holly."

"Mrs. Gruener, I didn't declare war—I delivered an eighth-grader in the ABC!"

"You declared war!" Mrs. Gruener flings down the pencil on her paper-strewn desk. "Actions have meanings. Delivering in a bed is a declaration. Understand?"

"Yes, Mrs. Gruener." Holly takes a deep breath. She has just been dressed down and has paid for her transgression; she's escaped being fired, and she understands Mrs. Gruener. Relief washes through her, and she loses her presence of mind for a moment and simply stares at Mrs. Gruener's pearls. Very old pearls that look lit from within. "Gorgeous pearls, Mrs. Gruener."

Glancing down, Mrs. Gruener picks up her pearls with her long fingernails. "I'm a subversive in pearls. The only way. Guerrilla warriors must wear their pearls at all times. Remember that, Holly." She drops her pearls and sighs. "Sometimes I'm absolutely convinced I'm a genius. What do you think, Holly?"

CHAPTER 12

Holly is slightly disgusted. A new poster has been hung above the nurse's station, showing a little kid on a chamberpot with a caption reading, "No job is finished till the paperwork is done." It's hard enough to do paperwork without mentally equating it with wiping your tail.

There's a freeze on, and the freeze affects Holly exclusively. Since the ABC misadventure, Holly has been shunned on a petty scale, given the cold shoulder, made to feel as though a circle has closed and Holly has been purposely left out of it. Nurses have started to fall back on Sparks's old trick: they pretend not to hear what Holly asks of them, so Holly either does the thing herself or demands it of them in a high, forceful voice. Because Holly doesn't like to be strident, particularly when she gets the idea that everybody hates her, she winds up doing little, time-consuming things, like going down the hall for more tape for an IV catheter, things that a nurse ought to do.

Small clusters turn their backs to Holly, telling jokes, gossiping. When a nurse got married, a collection went around for a gift from the floor, but nobody included Holly in the collection, and when the time came to give the nurse her present, everyone but Holly gathered in the nurses' lounge, with Levy at the center of it all, and laughed. Of course, nothing sounded more alluring and contemptuous to Holly than that laughter, and her ears burned.

The freeze is on such a minor level that Holly is too embarrassed to mention it to Matt. What would she say? "They order Chinese food and don't ask me if I want anything." But Holly had never known how important it is to get goofy among your friends at work. Being unpopular is a new, disagreeable sensation. It's as if the room temperature has dropped by ten degrees—the cold isn't intolerable, but there's always a slight chill.

Maybe the nursing staff thinks Holly is a known troublemaker about to get fired, the kind of malcontent nobody wants to get involved with. But she's already been chewed out by Mrs. Gruener, and Mrs. Gruener would have told her if she were on the way out. So Holly tries not to think about this coolness, and thinks about it all the time. It'll blow over someday—it has to, doesn't it?—and Holly will somehow crawl back into everyone's good graces. Crawl. Tonight, on her way to work, she stood in front of an Italian bakery for a few minutes, wondering if she should buy some fancy pastries as a treat for the floor. *Redemption can't be bought, Treadwell*, is what she told herself then. But now she's not so sure. Could pastries really go amiss at a time like this?

Having poured herself a cup of coffee, Holly shimmies up onto the counter in the nurses' lounge. In the back of her mind, she can hear her mother screech, "Get down from there! You're going to crack the linoleum!" But nobody here cares if she cracks the linoleum. In the far corner, nurses sit on folding chairs in a half-circle, talking in low tones, West Indian voices lifting and lowering. Even during the best of times, Holly feels her aloneness, her apartness, when she pauses for a break; midwifery keeps her on the outside, as she's neither doctor nor nurse, but occupies a professional limbo, a gray area. When she's with a patient, she and the patient create their own circle. But when there's slack time, even when she's in the nurses' good books, circles close and Holly is left out, a circle unto herself. It's easier working days, when two midwives are on duty.

At the best of times, Holly can talk easily with Crowley and Denise, but she's not comfortable sitting in a circle of nurses. In the hospital hierarchy she is, for all of everything, a superior, and she knows from her own experience that the presence of a superior when you're trying to relax induces a chilling effect. Holly doesn't like being a chilling effect, the kind of person who makes conversation go tepid and lifeless just by joining in. For this reason, she never wanted to be part of "management," which is just as well, now that she's been deemed unpromotable. Right now she has none of the benefits of being management but all the drawbacks.

So Holly sits to the side, on the counter. She's not that much of a superior that her presence in the same room disturbs the nurses' ease, as long as she keeps to herself. The nurses studiously avoid her; if they're hostile now, they express it through their indifference. *Brrrrrr.*

Indifference has its virtues. It's restful to be among others in such a passive way, relaxing in other people's murmurs. All Holly has to do is listen. Nothing else is asked of her. No reason to pay close attention.

"You'd let your daughter become a nurse?" Denise asks another nurse in horror.

"She wants to become like her mother," the nurse says quietly, dipping her head.

"I'd never let my daughter become a nurse!" Denise declares. "I'd lock her in her room and play loud music so she couldn't study."

Shaking their heads scornfully at Denise, the nurses stand up and wash their hands, wiping them dry on sterile gauze pads. They don't use gauze because it works well or improves sanitation, but because the coarse brown-paper towels the hospital usually supplies are out of stock. The hospital always seems to be broke, and the liberal use of expensive, sterile goods is prodigal. But nobody cares. The entire staff, from the docs down to the orderlies, feels that they owe the hospital nothing—if anything, Morrison owes them for stealing their lives away. Petty theft and extravagant use of supplies ensure retribution, although it is not enough. "Steal from them before they steal from you," as Denise said once, slipping a bottle of ampicillin into her scrubs. When Holly looked at her questioningly, Denise said defiantly, "Look, they're for my mother, all right? She's sick!" Holly had nothing to say, particularly since all her coffee cups at home came from the dinner trays of postpartum patients.

The nurses abandon Denise as they shuffle back to work, crumpling up the wax paper from their sandwiches and rinsing out their Tupperware. Denise slumps down in the Naugahyde chair stolen from the administrator's office. That's an unlucky chair: Holly never sits there.

She meets Holly's eyes, wary. "What about you? Would you let your daughter become a nurse?"

"I'd bring her up to go her own way, I guess."

"Aren't we open-minded." Denise then says, "What would you say if she wanted to become a nurse?"

Holly thinks for moment. "I'd probably say what my parents said."

"What'd they say?"

"Have you thought about medical school, dear?"

They both laugh bitterly. Denise gets up without a word, and Holly is stranded.

CHAPTER 13

The freeze is on.

"Patsy, did you call the labs earlier about Hodges's CBC?" Holly says, following a nurse fresh out of school, who lives for quitting time and walks silently and sullenly through her shift.

"They were busy," she says, hurrying away.

"Hang on—the phone was busy, or the lab was busy?"

"The phone."

And Patsy moves on. Holly had wanted to be able to tell Hodges if she could go home tomorrow, so that she could call her parents tonight and arrange for a ride to their house in New Jersey. But now the lab is closed until morning. This is the sort of minor shunning that has begun to drive Holly bonkers. Nobody takes the extra step for her anymore. Nobody will try the lab again after the first try brings up a busy signal.

Crowley swings around in her seat. Holly hasn't decided whether or not Crowley has joined the general drift against her. Crowley is an awfully well anchored person, Holly thinks hopefully. She's not inclined to float this way or that as the tide shifts. But it's hard to tell with Crowley. For all Holly knows, she disapproves of what Holly did as well. Her big, strong face is impassive and serious now. "That was Triage on the phone," she says.

Holly stares at the face and regrets that she can no longer assume that Crowley is her friend, her protectress, her mother figure.

"What's up?" Holly says in a sweet voice that pleads, Don't abandon me, Crowley, the world is too cold for that.

"A lady presenting downstairs. They can't find the fetal heartsounds."

"Is she at term?"

"I think so. Yes. A nice lady, they said."

"Oh." Holly comes over to the admitting desk and crouches down beside Crowley. She clasps her hands, puts them on the desk, and rests her face on her knuckles. She peeks upward. "I haven't gotten used to this."

"Nobody gets used to a stillbirth," Crowley says, organizing some papers.

"Crowley, tell me the truth. What would you think of me doing the stillbirth in the ABC? Where it'd be quiet and private..."

Crowley thinks for a moment, staring at the wall, and says mildly, "A good idea, I think."

"Will everyone hate me for it, though?"

Crowley stops her with a wide hand held up just inches from Holly's nose. In a former life, Crowley must have been either a crossing guard or a high priestess. Shaking her hand as if ridding herself of an invisible gnat, Crowley says, "That's not of concern. You are not of concern. The lady has lost her baby. . . ." Crowley shrugs. "It's a good idea," she says finally.

She turns to Holly and gives her a light slap on the back and a smile that gives Holly courage. To Holly, that look means: Don't be scared, protect your patient, dignify her grief, help bring out her dead child with love.

Fetal wastage. That means the lady has lost her baby.

Bibi Velez's exhaustion is as deep as any Holly has ever seen. Her face has an Indian touch to it: high cheekbones, eyes set far apart, a broad forehead. Her eyes are expressionless; a social worker would call this a flat affect, meaning in part that she cares beyond caring.

On the table beside the bed in the ABC is a familiar-looking orange slip. Special Consent for Surgical Operation, the consent form for a tubal ligation, signed by a doctor two months ago. Bibi was to have her tubes tied after this baby, but she won't have them tied right now, not even if she wanted to. No doctor would tie the tubes of a young woman who has just lost a baby. Bibi has a five-year-old daughter at home. Two years ago she had a spontaneous abortion. This baby was planned.

Bibi's husband, José, stands at the window. He looks down at the dark hospital courtyard. Dirt paths, cutting across what are meant to be lawns, are lit up by the steel-gray lights of the lamps in the yard. Holly notices for a moment that he has a beautiful face, a face almost made for grieving: wet brown eyes and a mustache. It's a poet's face. He wears Sergio Valente shoes with the company logo of a ram's horns on the buckle, Sergio Valente striped jeans, and for all Holly knows a Sergio Valente shirt.

"Uhhh," Bibi says. She's in the pushing stage, the second stage. In a multip, this stage should last only fifteen minutes or so. Bibi has been pushing for that long already. Holly wonders if babies that are already dead slow up the second stage, as labor is stimulated in part by the baby's adrenal glands. There's no adrenaline from the baby to fuel this labor.

The door of the room is open, for ventilation. When the baby comes, the heat and smells will overwhelm them without an open door. Denise has put up a screen in front of the door, for privacy, and most of the nurses have stopped talking loudly directly outside the door. Having been in the delivery room when the Velezes arrived, Sparks stood outside the screen and demanded loudly, "Who's in here?" and moved the screen to the side to give her wide self a generous margin of clearance as she marched into the room. "You're in here again?" she said to Holly, appalled.

Crowley, who has risen to the occasion and been everything that Holly ever wanted her to be, the heroine that Holly needs, ran across the hall from the admitting desk with her hands flying out to the side; Crowley has an oddly graceful run that reminds Holly of little girls, the way they keep their arms and hands high up as if they're paddling through water. "Miss Sparks, I beg your pardon, but it's very important I speak to you."

"This room is seeing a lot of action," Sparks said, before turning to confer with Crowley. Once Crowley had a word with her, Sparks did not come back.

Out in the hallway, in lowered voices, there's laughter and horseplay. In the ABC, hushed voices and a sense of apprehension, of dread. When Bibi cries, it's sharp and pained. "Ohhh!" A keen, as if she'd forgotten and then suddenly remembered and the understanding cut right through her, the understanding joining with the contractions to create an immense pain, the pain of labor and grief. Holly can't imagine that kind of pain. And the redeeming virtue that Holly has always given to labor pains—that they bring the baby out, that each pain takes you a small step toward seeing your baby—doesn't apply.

Bibi shuts her eyes and lets Holly hold her hand and massage her shoulders. Denise, who can be stealthy and sleek as a weasel, shimmies into the room in the slight space left open between the curtainlike screen and the wall. She peeks underneath the sterile blue drapes at the items on the delivery tray at the end of the bed, to make sure everything is there, then breaks open a packet that contains a blue plastic apron.

"Holly." She holds the apron up, and Holly stands up and lets herself be gowned by Denise. Holly often finds it odd to be gowned by a nurse; the master/servant relationship comes to the fore and makes Holly uneasy. But now she feels more like one friend being taken in hand by another. Denise claps her on the back when she's done tying the apron from the back. With that clap, all the coolness of the past few days falls away, like ice cracking off a rock and melting.

Holly's eyes shut as she remembers the last, desperate, cruel search for a heartsound when the Velezes first came in. Holly had put in an internal monitor, hoping the baby was hiding in a place that the external monitor couldn't reach, accepting as a possibility that this was an ectopic pregnancy and that the baby had grown in the abdominal cavity, where the external monitor couldn't find it. But there was no mistaking the sutures of the baby's head on an almost fully dilated cervix or the white noise that the monitor gave out and the perfectly flat reading etched on the strip. Holly had ripped off the monitor strip and stuffed it at the back of Bibi's charts, writing on it the time of the monitor reading, the nonreading that said in essence, "This isn't a record of life."

"Do you remember not feeling your baby moving for a while?" Holly whispered.

The woman shook her head. That could mean anything. That the baby had died after the stress of labor. That the baby had died before and that she hadn't noticed the difference.

Funny how the process of labor pushes on. The fundus of the uterus squeezes the body of the baby so that the baby straightens out of its fetal ball-shape and descends, flexed, for labor. All that can happen with a dead baby. . . .

The baby is crowning. Holly speaks softly to Bibi, while José comes to sit by the side of the bed. "Uhhhh!" Bibi cries, her face a grimace. She's only twenty-four years old, but now she looks aged. She might be thirty-five years old. She might be forty.

Holly doesn't know what to do with her hands. She pulls the baby out of the curve of Carus with the same delicate yet strong motions she usually uses, but the delicacy exists only for the purpose of style now. It doesn't matter how hard she pulls at the baby's hand or how roughly her hands clamp around the baby's torso as she guides the baby out and into the world of the living. It's all style, no content, but her hands use the same gentle pressure they always use, as if they couldn't do otherwise.

The baby is a boy, and when the Velezes see him, Bibi sitting up with José's arm around her, their faces collapse like a mountain caving in, an avalanche of grief. None of it was true, really true, before this. José lets out some kind of animal sound. If a man has a core or a spirit, the sound came from there. "Ohhh!"

Holly takes a quick snatch of air and swallows hard. With that moan from José, tears have sprung into her eyes, and a great hollow bubble moves up from her stomach and into her chest to rise into her throat.

Denise is behind her now, touching Holly's shoulder as she sits on the end of the bed and holds the baby in her arms. Bibi cries, in a normal, sad way that seems familiar to Holly, with her mouth turned down, her face buried against her husband's arm. Holly clamps the cord and cuts it, as Denise takes the baby, dries him off, and wraps him in a receiving blanket. She stands next to Bibi, and Holly says, "Do you want to hold your baby?"

Bibi looks up and wipes her eyes with her hands. Holly quickly reaches over for a box of tissues and gives them to José to hold. He nods, as thanks. He remembers his manners, as if bad manners would be particularly bad now.

"Can I look at him?" Bibi asks in a soft voice, checking with Holly to make sure it's all right.

"Sure, you can look at your baby."

Even if he's dead, he is still your baby, she wants to say.

Bibi unwraps him, and José leans over. The baby is stained with meconium, dark-green blotches on his rag-doll body, which is now a gray-white color.

It's his face that is so inexcusably, so unbelievably, so inescapably dead. The little mouth is a slack hollow, which is all wrong. The mouth is a newborn's most active part, so you normally don't notice that babies fresh from the womb are thin-lipped, that their mouths are plainly just orifices. But here it's too clear, as the mouth slumps open and stays that way. The eyes shut, and the nose is a nub of flesh that has no meaning.

Bibi draws her fingers along his chest and glances down for a moment at the baby's penis and testicles, then looks up at the face again, abashed, as José combs the baby's hair in one direction with his index finger.

Holly tries to take the cord blood, milking the umbilical vein and the two arteries into a small tube. The circulation stopped too long ago, and the veins have collapsed. The blood has thickened and almost clotted. Holly will take blood from the placenta instead.

She touches Bibi's leg. "You must push now," she says, almost whispering. To José, she says, "Dad, you can hold your baby." This is an order. Holly knows he will take it as an order. José's job now is to hold the baby. But it's a command she has phrased in a certain way so that an almost imperceptible look of surprise crosses José's face when she calls him "Dad."

Do you mean me? that look said. If the baby is dead, am I still his dad? And Holly has meant for him to stop and think, I'm still the dad, even though my baby's dead.

The placenta delivers with very little effort. Holly examines it. It doesn't look healthy, but spongy and colorless. Whether this is a function of the fact that the baby has been dead for hours or whether the placenta's poor functioning resulted in the baby's death, Holly can't begin to know on her own. As Denise holds the tubes open, Holly draws blood out from a placental vein with a needle and then ejects the blood into the tubes, then lets the placenta fall back into the basin.

Holly asks Denise, "Do we have any of those transport medium tubes?" Denise finds a long tube containing the colorless liquid that keeps samples hydrated and sealed from the air. Holly swabs the grainy maternal side of the placenta with a long cotton swab, and then the fetal side, less glossy than most, with another, both swabs going into separate tubes filled with the transport medium.

"I never seen this before," Denise murmurs, leaning over Holly's shoulder.

"Placenta culture. Maybe it can tell us what happened."

"Uh-huh. Maybe."

Denise knows as well as Holly that most miscarriages and stillbirths can't be accounted for. Possibilities always abound, but definitive answers are the exception rather than the rule. Answers. José has turned to the window with the baby, where the early morning light has started to break into the room. Holly turns off the examining lamp and the overhead lights, and now there's only the white, calm light of early morning, when the sun is striking the other side of the building.

After Holly gives Bibi the thirty cubic centimeters of Pitocin, she asks her if she wants to wash her baby. José hands Bibi the baby, still wrapped in his receiving blanket, as Holly finds a plastic basin with warm, soapy water. She tests the water: too hot. Does it make any difference? It makes a difference.

With the basin balanced on the bed, Bibi sits up and unwraps her baby. Holly notes the peeling skin, the blotted meconium splattered across the baby, the slash of meconium on the baby's brow.

To care for a baby's corpse is the dark side of ordinary child-care. The same motions, the same thoroughness, but now it's all symbolic. Bibi scrubs the baby's belly as if she's ironing, moving back and forth with careful, deliberate strokes, scrubbing extra hard at tough bits of meconium that won't budge. Meconium is a bad stain, and Denise tells Bibi softly, with a touch on her shoulder, "That's won't come off, dear."

Without looking up, Bibi nods and studies her baby, washes his face, and presses hard on the small, thick pools of vernix that won't wash off. Tears stream down her face—it's frustration, that the stuff won't come off—and she wipes her eyes with the back of her hand.

"The stuff that looks like cream is almost impossible to get off, dear," Denise says now, but Bibi keeps scrubbing, dipping the sponge into the basin, rinsing it out carefully, swabbing the baby with a stubborn concentration, putting everything she has inside her into this last act.

At the nurse's station, Holly asks Crowley for the key to the bottom drawer of the admitting desk, where the Polaroid camera is kept, and Holly finds it and brings it back to the birthing room. It seems cruel to most people—all this bonding with a dead baby, the pain and loss driven home, without giving the parents the chance to escape it. And Holly used to think it was. But now that it's actually happening, she sees why all these mechanisms are in place, even in a hospital as insensitive as Morrison. This is an event that asks for completion, some kind of physical resolution. This demands proof that the death and birth actually happened and that nobody ignores it or pretends it doesn't matter.

When Holly returns, José is watching Bibi wash—she is at the baby's toes now—and a rush of grief runs across his face, just like a storm, and he lets loose a sob and turns to face the window again. When he recovers, as Holly is making sure the camera is working, he asks Holly, "Can I see that?" His head gestures at the placenta in the basin.

"Sure," she says, putting on fresh gloves to pick it up. "Have you ever seen a placenta before?" He shakes his head no. When Holly did her intrapartum coursework in school at a hospital where fathers were allowed at deliveries, she found that most men were interested in the mechanics of labor, the machinery of pregnancy, the connective parts of a woman and her baby. As she shows José the placenta, she realizes how much she's missed this—guiding a father into the netherland of internal organs and the body as exquisite machine, vanquishing ghosts and prejudices as the men understand, at last, what women do.

"This is the mother's side; this is the baby's side. See what I mean? This side was attached to the mother, this side faced in at the baby."

José nods and studies it and thanks Holly.

Holly asks Bibi if she'd like a picture.

"Wait till he looks nice," she says.

But he never is going to look nice, Holly would like to say, because what's wrong is that motionless gaping mouth and those red gums and the white color of his skin and the fact that it doesn't matter if Bibi accidentally moves him around a bit brusquely, as she just did, before catching herself. It doesn't matter that his head isn't supported; it wouldn't matter if . . .

"He looks nice now," Denise says. "As long as the face looks clean, he'll look nice in the picture. The picture will be your keepsake."

Keepsake.

Bibi's face crumples up, and tears well up in her eyes as Denise leans over to wrap the baby up. She bundles the baby so that all that's left to see of him is his tiny white face, asleep in his blanket. She gives Bibi the baby as Holly takes a picture.

"Now, you, Dad," Holly says.

José sits on the edge of the bed, and both he and Bibi stare at the baby's face. Click. Got it. Human instinct to bear witness and testify. We were here. This is what happened.

Holly puts the film on the windowsill. It doesn't belong to her now. It comes to life in the morning sun. Denise and Holly clean up Bibi, wash her perineum, dry her, place fresh pads and two maternity pads under her bottom, straighten the sheets, wheel off the delivery tray, open the window a crack to let in fresh air.

In real life, Bibi is pretty, sometimes beautiful, with almond-shaped eyes. Holly thought that Bibi had been looking at her baby when she took the picture, but Holly got it all wrong. As the photograph sharpens and settles, Bibi is staring straight into the camera; her face is exhausted with anger.

How did this happen? Who are you? Where is my baby? What is my baby?

"Would you like me to take the baby yet?" Holly asks tentatively.

"No." Bibi shakes her head vigorously.

"I'll leave you two alone for a while," Holly says.

But are there three of them in the room? And Holly's not sure they want to be left alone. As she pulls the delivery tray out of the room, José looks closely at the photograph of him and his wife and his baby and he bursts into tears.

Now that it's in a photograph, it is all true.

"I'm wiped out," Holly says, sitting at the desk at the nurse's station.

"It doesn't get any easier," Crowley says in the briskly gentle way only she has mastered. "I'm sorry."

"I got to get one of those death certificates."

Crowley passes her one. Certificate of Spontaneous Termination of Pregnancy—Stillbirth. And then Crowley passes her another form, one that combines two consents. "Authorization for Autopsy of Fetus" and below that "Authorization for City Burial of Fetus."

"Don't forget to enter the baby into the log," Crowley says, tapping the huge register of births, the domesday book that lists every new citizen, dead or alive. Velez, baby boy, the date, the time, Comments: Stillborn.

That's easy enough.

"Miss Crowley, would you please explain to me about the city burial business?"

"Holly, have you not done this before?"

Holly realizes she has. She just needs a pretext to talk to Crowley now, to hear Crowley be her strong, maternal self. Maybe Crowley realizes this as well, because she sighs, as if she's starting a familiar old story, and says, "It's a respectful burial, but the grave will not be marked, and they will never know where it is."

"It's a mass grave, actually," Levy murmurs, coming up from behind.

Holly swings around. "They use coffins, don't they?" she asks, startled to think it might be otherwise, to think it might be what the term *mass grave* conjures up.

"Yes, they use coffins," Crowley says. "Quiet down, Dr. Levy."

"Are all the babies in one place?" Holly has to know. How else will she know what to recommend to the Velezes?

Crowley frowns, as if sizing up just how shook up Holly must be to ask these questions. "You mean in the graveyard, child? No, there's no special place for the babies. They go wherever there's room in Potter's Field. Do you have any other questions, Holly?"

"Mmmm, no." Holly lets a strand of hair fall over her eyes. One masks at transitions, for life passages. Because all the spirits are out and about, and if you're masked, maybe they won't notice you. Maybe they'll just pass over you, like a cold wind.

Sitting on the edge of the bed Holly explains the city burial. "The burial is respectful, but the grave won't be marked. You won't be able to go visit him."

The Velezes look down at their baby, who lies in Bibi's lap.

"The disadvantage of a private funeral is that it can cost a lot of money." Holly is embarrassed to mention this.

But the Velezes aren't offended.

"Now, do you want the baby baptized?" If they're Catholic, Holly will call up the priest who serves the hospital community.

The Velezes nod.

"Can we name him?" Bibi asks anxiously.

A rush of sadness sweeps down Holly's back. She hadn't thought to bring up the matter of naming the baby earlier. "Of course you can name him." As if she can dispense the right for the Velezes to name their son and they must ask her permission.

Holly explains that Bibi will stay on the eighth floor, with post-op patients with minor complaints. "Then you won't be around the mothers. . . ." Holly says. The Velezes get the picture right away. "The social worker will talk to you. To let you know that if you want to talk to her, she's available." Because the Velezes might interpret the social worker's visit as a sign that Holly thinks they're screwed-up or crazy, Holly adds pointedly, "She talks to anyone who has lost a baby, to let them know she's there."

They nod.

"Now, there's one last thing, which you have time to think about, just as you have time to think about what kind of burial you want. That is, whether or not you want an autopsy on the baby."

The Velezes look down at the baby in Bibi's arms. Autopsy.

"What's good about an autopsy is that it might tell us what happened to the baby so it won't happen again."

"Does it cost anything?" Bibi asks.

Holly shakes her head and puts her hand on Bibi's shoulder. This is the saddest question. The autopsy, does it cost anything? It costs everything.

"I'll give you a few minutes more with the baby."

Denise is standing in the hallway and Holly grabs her by the arm. They both head into the locker room, and Holly pulls a pack of cigarettes down from the top of a locker, where she stashed them, and passes one to Denise.

"When we finish these cigarettes, you call transport and I'll bring the baby out."

"Right," Denise says.

The cigarette makes Holly's head light. The day shift has begun to straggle in, changing into their uniforms, not knowing what Holly has seen. This makes Holly feel alone. She glances over at Denise.

"Denise?"

"What?"

"Friends?"

Denise squints at her. Holly squints back.

"You paid your dues," Denise says.

"Are you sure?"

Denise weighs this in her mind. "Sure."

"Okay then, let's go," Holly says brusquely. She drops her cigarette and squashes it with her sandal.

"I'm not finished yet."

"Let's go."

Things are back to normal, in a way.

Holly finds her standing orders pad, with its checklist of antibiotics and analgesics. She checks off vitamin C, Dalmane, and codeine. Codeine. Let Bibi sleep it off, stay high for a few days, so the death of her baby swims in and out of her mind like dark clouds, instead of collapsing on top of her like a caved-in mountain.

The transport orderly arrives. "From the morgue," he says, shuffling his feet. He doesn't like this job.

Holly heads into the ABC. José is studying the Polaroid shots, while Bibi stares at her baby and cries quietly.

"I have to take the baby now," Holly says. "Would you like to kiss the baby good-bye?"

José and Bibi look at each other—is it all right?—and José leans in and kisses his son good-bye. The baby is not warm.

"Ahhh!" he chokes out and turns to the window, where the sky is white with the morning light.

Bibi looks down and kisses the baby on the forehead, and Holly reaches down and takes the baby away forever. Forever. When she walks out the door, she feels as if she's taken away the last beam that held up the sky, and now, without that beam, the sky has fallen, and she can hear an inaudible crash.

CHAPTER 14

Crowley and Holly are on the elevator, heading home. "Holly, baby."

"Yes, Miss Crowley?"

"Are you very tired this morning?"

"I am, very."

"Look down at your feet, darling."

Holly discovers she is still wearing her blue paper booties, with her jacket and her blue jeans. "Oh, dear." Standing behind her is a resident she's never seen before. He laughs. "Be quiet and hold still," she says, balancing against him, holding his shoulders while she pulls her booties off. "You can laugh now," she tells him.

"Good night, Holly," Crowley says, getting off the elevator. Holly stays on, to retrieve her shoes upstairs. "Sleep well."

"Good night, Holly," the resident says. "Sleep well."

"Sleep well, all," she says, going up.

CHAPTER 15

Holly browses sleepily through her log of births. Matt is the only person who knows the journal exists. It's a secret. If she needs a reason for its secrecy, there's the legal angle. What if it were subpoenaed during a malpractice suit and mistaken for a clinical journal? What Holly likes about the journal is its inaccuracy and subjectivity, and the freedom it gives her to speculate and abandon the objective approach she's been trained in. In court, her hindsight interpretations of labor and delivery could be read as misdiagnoses and her second-guessing construed as an assumption of guilt. Her journal is a secret. It doesn't exist, really.

But notice, anyway, how her handwriting shifts according to her moods, the rounded schoolgirl style giving way to an angular half-script. She's never learned doctor's script, with its absurd slant, as if a powerful wind pushes all the letters down, and its proud illegibility, as *y* and *g* can just barely be told apart. Holly has tried to learn it, hoping to purchase a soupçon of respect through a more authoritative handwriting, but her letters always wind up clarified and upright. A script that is quintessentially a midwife's.

The log's entries range from telegraphic hints at a delivery, marked down in exhaustion, to inquiries into the spiritual aspects of birth—could she call them "metaphysical quests"? she wonders—and social work reports on her patients.

What should Holly write about the stillbirth? It seems far away now, as she lies on the bed and listens to the refrigerator hum. That's a good thing. Still, she's not ready to shut her eyes yet.

The past few years, metaphysical quests have been on the wane. Morrison is not a hospitable medium for the spirit. A sociologist would have a happy time analyzing Morrison as an example of the industrialization of childbirth. Seven-B as a production line, designed like a factory to produce and package the most babies in the shortest length of time with the least expenditure of manpower. Holly protests this arrangement but is part of it. User-friendly, but a piece of the machinery anyway. Instead of spiritual aspects, there is paperwork and Friedman curves (which chart out patterns of labor and rates of production to which patients are encouraged to conform). When the work is done, Holly would rather smoke a cigarette and think of nothing—the greatest luxury, thinking of nothing—than mull over the mysteries of birth. She doesn't realize it, but her emotions are overloaded, and her spirit, whatever and wherever it might be, strains after rest and nothingness. There it feels free.

Holly plumps up the pillows and sits back with her log and the pen she keeps tucked inside it—it's a ritual always to use the same pen—and writes, "When will I get used to being in a career that deals with life and death?" She pauses and thinks. "I'm so tired after a shift, I think something is wrong with me. Then I realize this work takes a lot out of anyone. Even Gus. The only cure is sleep. The delivery tonight was eventful because the baby was dead." There, she thinks, I said it. "I guess I should quit saying *delivery* and start saying *birth*."

Holly puts down her pen and considers the semantic rebellion against the old medical language. Midwives don't deliver babies: the mothers do the work. Midwives only catch. The word *delivery* reflects the whole obstetrical game of power and control, the reduction of the mother to a passive pawn and the construction of the doctor or midwife as savior, hero, deliverer.

But Holly can't give up thinking that she delivers babies. Her work is too much of an emotional, intellectual, and physical investment for her to think she only helps, like an interested passerby. It would be like a fireman coming home from work, exhausted, covered by smoky film, to tell his wife, "I helped put out a fire today."

Yet a woman's work, to deliver her baby, is different from a house burning down, and far more of an emotional, intellectual, and physical investment than Holly's can ever be. Holly is only a watchdog, a catcher of babies pushed into the world by their mothers' tremendous efforts.

"I caught a stillbirth tonight," she writes. A gust of wind sends the curtains billowing. "*Stillbirth* is a very old word. *Stillbirth* is an accurate word."

She shuts the journal, closes her eyes, and listens to nothing.

CHAPTER 16

Holly wasn't able to sleep during the day. At the end of a month working nights, she's usually found her rhythm, just when she has to return to a day shift. But going to Convention threw off her inner clock, and now her daytime sleep is just a string of naps. She misses the deep, restorative, mind-resting, bone-melting sleep of a full night under the sheets. She's tired now, at the start of her shift, and noises go through her, as if her skin were made of paper. Katrina's high-pitched voice rubs Holly in exactly the wrong way as she changes into her scrubs.

"Please call Sara," Katrina is saying, standing much too close for Holly's liking. "It'd mean a lot to me."

"I'm really not in the mood for the lovey-dovey, hippie-dippie, artsy-fartsy midwife stuff right now. Is that okay with you?"

Wounded, Katrina picks up her bag to go. But before she does, she says, "What are you scared of, Holly?" and lifts her head high, which makes her look like a little girl asking an adult a question. "Why are you so threatened?"

"Please don't psychoanalyze me right now, Katrina."

"Think, Holly," Katrina says, narrowing her eyes. "Think about what's really bothering you." And pushes out the door.

Holly sits down on the card table. Maybe her perspective on midwifery has hardened, calcified. The longer she works at Morrison, the more closed-minded she becomes, as if she can't stand to hear about truly gentle birth because it's so inaccessible. Is that why she feels nothing but hostility toward lay midwives? Maybe she thinks about lay midwives the way doctors think of nurse-midwives—unskilled upstarts who fumble and bumble, not competent to handle the delicate business of birth on their own.

But Holly thinks her position is more valid than a doctor's. As long as lay midwives are unregulated, some will be ill trained and will botch births, propound arcane ideas, and reflect poorly on midwifery in general. Nurse-midwives and lay midwives are, involuntarily, twins. The public sees one and mistakes it for the other, or views the both of them as essentially one and the same, coming from the same family and background.

Holly stows her clothes in her crowded locker and shuts it slowly, realizing that there's another reason she disapproves of lay midwives. For once in her professional life, Holly and the docs are on the same side, with a common enemy in lay midwives. She likes that feeling. And as a nurse-midwife, Holly has more support and power than a lay midwife, and she likes that feeling as well. If lay midwives didn't exist, Holly would never taste power at all.

"I guess this is what being co-opted means," she says to herself, staring out at the orangey sky of the Brooklyn night.

"Think about what's really bothering you," Katrina had said. Shoot, what else is Katrina right about?

CHAPTER 17

Holly steps out of the labor room. "Miss Crowley!"
"What is it, baby?"
"My patient in there has been shaved. All the way."
"Maybe she was very hairy," Crowley suggests.
"How hairy could she have been?"
"Some of these ladies can be very hairy. Don't worry, Holly. It's only hair."

The operating principle behind a total prep has long since been debunked: a bald *mons pubis* doesn't decrease infection or increase visibility. The prep is a holdover from the turn of the century, when lice were a problem and arcane practices in infection control (the days when doctors felt that a handwash in hydrochloric acid was sufficiently aseptic) were guiding principles.

The routine remains, like an example of decadence: the form remains without any useful or living content. Does the prep really have no content to advise its form? As far as Holly can tell, a denuded pubic area does a good job of desexualizing a woman. "Symbolic castration," as the birth activists think of it. At any rate, the total prep is one way of telling the patient just who is in charge.

Protocol dictates that multips, like Holly's patient, receive minipreps. Poodle cuts, but Holly winces at that term. The miniprep means that only the perineum below the vagina is shaved, the idea being that hair "down there" interferes with episiotomy cutting and suturing. But Holly always sutures from the inside, so outside hair doesn't matter. And with multips, Holly starts with the presumption that they won't need an episiotomy at all.

Holly doesn't mention to Montgomery that her full prep is superfluous and useless. She appears to have expected it, and there's no point in telling her that her discomfort was and will be in vain.

In vain. When Holly did her postpartum clinical work in school, almost all her patients had been fully prepped. When the ladies came in for their checkups, they had to face the wall, embarrassed by their own indelicacy, to scratch themselves: pubic hair burns and itches when it grows back in. Holly realized something then. That women are proud of their pubic hair, even without realizing it. They don't know how proud of it they are until it's gone. And when the hair grows back, it doesn't have the rich gloss it once had. Holly had explained this to Matt once.

"How come these hospitals are so slow to change?" he'd asked.

She could have given him her psychology-of-institutions theory— institutions are only in service to themselves—but she gave him the consumer-pressure theory instead. "These ladies are poor," she said. "They can't threaten to take their business elsewhere. Morrison is the court of last resort. The ladies put up with what they get. 'Put down that razor or I'm taking my Blue Cross elsewhere.' Change comes from the outside. From the consumer. Money, honey."

"Some change comes from within the hospital, doesn't it?"

"Matt, watching change come to Morrison is like watching a glacier proceed down a continent. Half an inch each decade."

"So Morrison is still in the Ice Age, huh?"

"Yeah, but the dinosaurs will have to die out one of these days." A high school teacher once told Holly that the only people in history who ever accomplished anything had been optimists. All Holly's instincts move in a pessimistic direction, but she works herself into optimism, through a stubborn will.

Holly tells Crowley, "Maybe it's only hair, but it's her hair and she might have wanted to keep it."

"One does become attached to one's hair," Crowley says. Then she sighs. "Still, that patient might have been very hairy."

Crowley has a stubborn will as well.

CHAPTER 18

A nineteen-year-old nullip has arrived on the floor, flat on her back on a gurney. Sparks lunges out the door and grabs Ralph, the orderly, by the collar. This alarms Ralph.

"How many times must I tell you not to bring these ladies up here flat on their backs?" Sparks barks. "Don't you have a brain in your head?"

Lying flat on the back interferes with the blood flow to the placenta, as the uterus's weight is pressed against the inferior vena cava, one of the body's main arteries. It is what you don't want to have happen with a patient like this one.

The nullip, Richardson, had presented downstairs in ER with a blinding headache. "I feel like I got a nail running through the middle of my head. And I can't see nothing. I want some medicine for my head."

Blood pressure at 160/110. Gross edema in her extremities. Diagnosis: preeclampsia, the cure for which is the termination of pregnancy, the expulsion of the trophoblast, a PET (Preeclamptic Toxemia) induction, which means magnesium sulfate to prevent convulsions, lactated Ringer's solution to maintain hydration, and Pit to induce labor—all bagged and hanging from an IV pole.

Gus, the king of carnage, has done a Bishop score to arrive at an evaluation of the cervix—fifty percent effaced, two centimeters dilated. PETs have quick labors; their musculature is hyperflexive, and their uteruses are easily irritated, therefore easily stimulated. A baby in eight hours or bust.

"Do it, do it, do it, do it," Gus says to Levy. Gus is scratching his head with a packaged tongue depressor. "Fit for a fit," Gus says, holding it up

to the light as though it were a new development in medical technology instead of the sterilized Popsicle stick it essentially is.

"Good, Gus. Go to it."

"Yeah, man, it's a go."

"Yeah, man, it's a groove," Levy says. "You waiting for me to light the
rockets under your tail or what?"

"Levy, it's like this. She doesn't have veins."

"Oh, no? What do you call those blood vessels circulating blood
through their constricted passageways?"

"Well, hey, she has veins. They just happen to be three feet deep.
Have you seen her edema? The layers of fat sandwiching the edema? To
take her pulse, you have to dial the overseas operator. Know what I
mean, jelly bean? Her veins are on a different continental mass."

"Hey, man, it's a go," Levy says. "That girl is ready to go off. Let's do
it, do it, do it."

Gus doesn't move.

"Hey, jelly bean, what's holding you up?" Levy says.

"I think she's hostile to me," Gus says, nodding. "I think she needs
the kind of TLC a guy like me just can't give."

"Who do you think can give the TLC exactly, Gus?"

"I'm not sure, but . . ."

Richardson is in the hot seat, Labor Room 1, bed A. The bed most
visible to passersby. The bed that keeps one eye on the exit. Holly picks
up Richardson's left arm, which is as big and heavy as Holly's left leg.
She just holds the arm for a second and looks at Richardson's eyes.
They're bulging: hypertensive eyes. "You're surprised to be here, aren't
you?"

"Yeah, it's a big surprise. For sure."

"We'll take good care of you."

"Sure."

Richardson's mother is as big as Richardson, who is big enough to
dwarf the labor bed. Holly turns Richardson's arm over, looking for veins,
when she gets thrown by a weird sense of claustrophobia that sweeps over
her and traps her, like someone has just thrown a mosquito net over her
head. Christ, I'm burning out, she thinks. "Excuse me," she said, and
heads for the hall.

It's cooler in the corridor, and there's more fresh air working its way in
through the swinging door at the hall's end, so the walls no longer seem
like they're moving in on her.

The labor rooms had originally been one large labor ward. In the days
of insult and injury, as opposed to these days, bed upon bed of women
filled the ward. In the 1960s, it was cut up into the three labor
rooms—stingily designed blocks of space, with no plan for the addition
of fetal monitors or labor couches. They've never lost their feeling of
subdivision, of an expansive stretch of space having been chopped up

into cells. Holly shuts her eyes, envisions the big room that once stood there, and tries to absorb some sense of expanse. Of elbowroom. Of fresh air. She feels contracted, constricted, hot, sticky. Her month here is almost up.

Holly picks up Richardson's left arm again. Not a vein to be found. "Make a fist, honey." Richardson's hands are puffy and almost without definition. They remind Holly of the huge, inflated hands on the balloon cartoon characters in the Macy's Thanksgiving Day parade. The diminished output of urine—oliguria—is also a characteristic of preeclampsia, as fibrin, the product of blood clotting brought on by hypertension, is deposited in the kidneys and interferes with the kidneys' functioning. Fluid comes into the body but does not willingly leave it, and Richardson must be catheterized and an account taken of her urine, as Crowley does now.

"You little ladies do a lot of poking about," says Richardson's mother.

"We poke, poke, poke," Crowley says. "It's our job."

Holly runs her eyes down Richardson's mammoth thigh to her feet. The old Fats Waller song goes, "Up at Harlem at a table for two, they sit four of us—me, your big feet and you," with a declamatory line that runs, "Your pedal extremities are simply horrendous!" Richardson's pedal extremities look like unfinished sculpture, clay mounds that haven't been carved out yet. The sculptor went out to lunch and never came back.

"I hope you're big-boned," Holly tells Richardson.

"I think I am."

The only way Holly is going to work an IV catheter into this patient is if Richardson's ankle bone is dominant enough to extend beyond the mound of edema fluid. "Flex your foot, dear. Pull your toes back." The vague outline of a vein running across her ankle bone snakes onto the surface. Don't go away, Holly tells it. Crowley hands her the needle, and Holly taps in, blood runs off, tubes fill with blood. Oh, blood! Don't roll, she tells the vein. The catheter in, Holly tapes it with more tape than she has ever used before. She doesn't want that catheter budging a single millimeter. "Turn over on your left side, kiddo," Holly says. "And don't move this foot."

As she moves the IV pole down to the end of the bed and watches the fluids drip into Richardson's ankle, Gus appears in the doorway. "We're cooking with gas!" he says.

"Yeah, some of us are, I reckon."

Holly keeps watch on the edge of Richardson's bed. There is plenty to look for. The slight twitching of her face that signals a convulsion. The hyperflexed, almost paralyzed expression, the hard stillness that tells you the patient is on the brink of a seizure and that her going off is inevitable. Holly has to make sure Richardson lies quietly on her left side, to increase placental perfusion. With blood pressure this high, the blood has a hard time making its rounds through constricted veins. And

Holly is also watching to make sure Richardson doesn't thrash around and dislodge the catheter.

"I'll take over now," Gus says, "I can boogie with the PET."

Richardson is sleeping, and Holly has lost the will to fight. This is his patient, after all.

"Boogie slow. Don't boogie too hard," she says. In the corridor, she leans her head against Levy's arm. "I'm getting out," she says wearily. "I'm starting a private practice." When Levy puts his hand on her hair, she jolts back. It feels too good.

"Go to Utah," he says, smiling, looking into her eyes. She looks away. "Highest birth rate in the union," he says. "Mormons. But there's a catch."

"What's that?"

"You have to live there."

CHAPTER 19

Ralph is back. This time with a patient on a stretcher. On her side. "I have a parcel for you, Miss Crowley." He bows to Crowley, who has never barked at him.

On the stretcher is a known previa. She's been to Morrison twice before with a placenta previa. The placenta migrated down the slope of the uterus to land near her cervix. In her seventh month, she presented at Morrison with bleeding and was admitted to the AP ward for bed rest. Bed rest at home seemed out of the question: she had four kids, and her husband worked double shifts. She stayed on the Ap ward for two weeks, prone, motionless, and the bleeding stopped.

But she checked herself out against medical advice (or AMA, the hospital equivalent of AWOL). The same reasons that she couldn't get bed rest at home were the same reasons she had to get home. She was back in a month, with a second bleed worse than the first, and the docs were adamant about her staying put. The threat was, stay or lose your baby.

"It's a free country, Dr. Levy, and that's how it goes in the USA," was how she replied to the threat.

Now Mrs. McGrath, on her own recognizance, is back.

"Mrs. McGrath!" says Crowley.

"I'm bleeding again," Mrs. McGrath says in a bored, pained voice.

"Maybe we'll dispense with the patient interview at this time," Crowley says kindly. Arms swinging, Crowley trots into Labor Room 1 and grabs Levy by his arm. "Mrs. McGrath is back. Bleeding. Her third."

"Talk about a known previa!" Levy says, alarmed. He pulls off his gloves and heads out the door. "I'm scrubbing. I've had enough of this. Meet you there."

"Scrubbing, Dr. Levy?" Crowley says.

"She's at term, isn't she?" He looks startled. He trusts Crowley's opinion, too. If she doesn't favor a section, he wants to know why.

"Oh, yes, she's ready."

"I'm scrubbing then. Beep the Sneaker."

"The Sneaker?" Crowley doesn't share in the floor's enjoyment of disparaging nicknames.

"Whatever that creepy anesthesiologist's real name is. I don't know!"

Holly comes out of a labor room to find Mrs. McGrath alone on the stretcher. "Mrs. McGrath, you're back!"

"I'm bleeding, goddamnit!"

"No shit," Holly says, under her breath. The third bleed is known as the fatal bleed. At thirty-six to thirty-eight weeks, the bleeding usually doesn't stop. Holly pushes the stretcher back toward the nurse's station, and with Crowley's help, she pulls off Mrs. McGrath's stretch pants, which are soaked by now.

"Nurse!" Holly calls to anyone. "Let's start a line here!"

"It's up to you," Crowley murmurs.

"Give me a bedpan," Mrs. McGrath moans.

"In a minute, darling," Crowley says.

"I got to go. I got to make a bowel movement."

Crowley is trying to work Mrs. McGrath's pants down, but she's a heavy woman and it's a struggle. Holly finds a catheter and an IV needle and a bag of DW5, the dextrose solution used to start IV lines on almost all occasions.

"Don't push," Holly cries.

"I got to go," Mrs. McGrath says, persistent, irritated.

"Just hold it in. Miss Crowley, please put down that bedpan. She can't go now, while she's bleeding. Give Mrs. McGrath an informed consent, please." Holly starts the line as she says, "You're going to be sectioned. All this will be behind you."

"I know," Mrs. McGrath says, very cranky now. "But I want to go to the bathroom first."

"When was the last time you had anything to eat?"

"A few hours ago. I knew I wouldn't get anything in here, goddamnit."

"Hang on. You knew you were coming here, Mrs. McGrath?"

"Sure. I was in labor."

"Mrs. McGrath, you're supposed to come in as soon as you feel anything!"

"It wasn't much of anything, Dr. Treadwell. Nothing that an old horse like myself can't handle."

Holly groans. Then Mrs. McGrath does a funny thing. She bends her knees, grunts, and delivers the head of her baby. Holly drops the catheter and needle. She's not even gloved up, yet here she is, right by the admitting desk, delivering a baby who has a placenta on his shoulder. "Christ!" Holly says. "Christ!"

Crowley, who has been standing by with a consent form and a pen, puts those things down neatly on the counter. "Oh, my word," she says.

"Nurse!" Holly cries to no one in particular. "Let's get a line going here."

Because after she delivers the rest of the baby, there's a gush of blood. Blood that doesn't quit. Blood flowing down onto the floor and dripping onto Holly's sandals. Holly wants to massage the uterus, stimulate contractions to stanch the bleeding, start a line, but her hands are full of baby.

Crowley takes the baby and hands her to a nurse's aide crouching by Holly's left side.

A nurse in white is to Holly's right.

"Nurse, let's go with the IV here. Let's zap this lady now!"

The nurse Holly has just ordered around is none other than Sparks. Crowley runs down the hall for the Pitocin.

"I can't find the right thing," Sparks says, rummaging through the supply shelf. "You people never put things in the proper place."

"I don't care if I have to open her jugular with my teeth," Holly says. "Let's get going. Give me some scissors. I got to cut this goddamn cord."

Denise appears. "What's going on here?" She sees the baby. "Shoot." Then breaks precedent by galloping to the supply closet and galloping back with clamps, cord scissors, and gloves. She snaps on the clamps for Holly, and Holly, who usually strips the umbilical cord back so that it won't spurt blood, as an electrician strips the coat of rubber on a wire, skips this step and cuts right into the cord. Blood shoots out, joining all the other blood.

Holly massages Mrs. McGrath's belly. There's nothing there. No tightening, just a high, flaccid uterus. Holly will have to go in for a bimanual palp. "I'm not even gloved up," she says aloud. She's dislocated, her bearings lost, as she doesn't know where to reach for things here in the nurse's station. Denise whips a packet of gloves from her pocket, tears them open, and forces them onto Holly's upstretched hands. "You're a genius, Denise."

"She's bleeding out, Holl."

"I know."

Sparks has worked the catheter into the back of Mrs. McGrath's limp arm. She doesn't often do this, and Mrs. McGrath is a heavy woman without prominent veins. Sparks is rising to the occasion.

"She must be up to six hundred ccs," Denise says urgently. A blood loss of five hundred cubic centimeters is the definition of hemorrhage. Blood loss beyond that is the definition of disaster.

"Oh, fuck, I don't want to lose her," Holly says. "I'm going in." She makes a fist with her right hand.

"Go in, Holl," Denise urges.

"I'm going."

Holly puts her fist into Mrs. McGrath's open vagina. She puts her left hand on top of the abdomen and tries to make her hands meet, pressing down with her left hand and keeping her right fist still in the middle of the uterus. Nothing goes. No contractions, blood keeps coming. "Denise, hit my hand." Denise puts two hands over Holly's left hand. "Press hard." Blood keeps flowing. "Shit," Holly says. "Get Levy STAT."

Levy runs down the hall as Sparks takes Mrs. McGrath's blood pressure and shakes her head.

"Shocky?" Holly asks.

Mrs. McGrath's white skin pales away, clammy and bloodless. Crowley finally has piggybacked a small bag of Pitocin onto a larger bag of DW5.

"Crowley, honey," Holly says in despair, "we need Ringer's!"

"Ringer's?"

"Leave it," Holly says. "Just get it going."

Levy bounds forward, a syringe in hand, gloved up to his forearms, scrubbed and ready for a section. No section now. "Methergine," he says, coming behind Holly, and shoots the needle into Mrs. McGrath's left buttock. Methergine, derived from ergot, gives one long, sustained contraction, as opposed to Pitocin, which stimulates intermittent contractions.

"I don't feel a fucking thing!" Holly says.

"You'll feel it, baby, you'll feel it!"

Holly presses hard on the abdomen to force the uterus to clamp down on the placental site. Levy's hand joins her, and he presses down, kneading into her hand. "Go," he says, urging the uterus. "Go!"

Holly feels the Methergine kick in, the uterus move on its own. Mrs. McGrath returns to some kind of life with the violence of the contraction. "Oof!" she says. The uterus is going now. And there isn't any more blood gushing out.

"Should I stay in here?" Holly asks Levy. "I think I'm in the way."

"Stay a little while," Levy says, feeling all around Mrs. McGrath's abdomen.

"She's zapped now."

"Then get out and let it go."

Holly pulls out her hand. Her forearm is coated with blood. She shuts her eyes. Christ!

"I'm getting the blood," Levy says, taking off. "We're transfusing!"

"How're you feeling, Mrs. McGrath?" Holly shouts, leaning directly over her face.

"Was it a girl or a boy?" Mrs. McGrath speaks out.

Holly widens her eyes. Fuck! This is a personal first—delivering a baby whose sex she doesn't know.

"I can't remember," she says, aghast, turning to Crowley.

"A beautiful little baby," Crowley says, evading the question.

"You had a little boy," says Scott's voice. Holly turns around. There's the baby, swaddled, capped, a small baby. After all, the placenta's sufficiency is questionable. But he looks even smaller because he's in Scott's arms, the tall young man with the tiny critter in the hook of his arm. Holly can't remember ever seeing Scott holding a baby like that before. His good-looking face has softened. He's bringing the baby to its mother, and it suits him.

Holly leans against the wall and remembers to breathe.

CHAPTER 20

Holly is uptown, to meet Matt at his office for lunch. She is almost asleep standing up. "Sleep in subatomic particles," as Levy calls it. The subatomic particles sweeping through the mind in a wave of unconsciousness, like a passing dust storm. Then she wakes up, her brain having been empty for a few seconds, to find she's in Matt's office. Matt looks older and more competent here than he does at home, giving no sign of the small fears and large ones that possess him there. Seeing him for an instant through the eyes of a stranger, Holly thinks he's more handsome in this setting, but not as lovable. She couldn't love a man for his successes alone.

"I want to show you something," he says.

"Give me a kiss first, creep."

"Not here, Holly! If they find out I'm in a happy relationship, they'll think I'm not working hard enough."

Pulling Holly into a nearby office, Matt introduces her to Jim Hoffman, a clone of all the other lawyers Holly has had the dubious pleasure of meeting. Reaching over an ocean of papers, Matt grabs a big wheel of names and addresses. "Jim's our medical liability specialist," Matt says. "Check this out." He flicks through the Rolodex so Holly can see. After almost every name on file is an "MD" or a "PhD."

"Quite a credentialed society you have here, Jim," Holly says politely. She looks quizzically at Matt. "What's your hidden agenda, buddy?"

"Jim, tell her what you call those guys on your Rolodex."

"Whores. We call them whores. Now give me back my stable," he says, reaching out his arm.

"Holly, these guys will sleep in any bed as long as you have the right stuff, monetarily."

"Hey, hey, hey!" Jim protests.

But Matt goes on. "They're not called whores for nothing. They'll testify to whatever we want them to."

"So there's always an expert witness who'll testify the way you want him to," Holly says. "What's that got to do with me?"

"How many nurse-midwives are there practicing right now?" Matt asks.

"About two thousand."

"Nurse-midwives, huh?" Jim perks up by leaning back and giving Holly a closer look. "Not too many suits against you girls yet."

"No, not yet. And you won't be seeing too many of us in the future either."

But Holly wonders if she's so sure. Nurse-midwives mostly serve undereducated, ill-informed patients like the ones Holly sees at Morrison. Not litigious people. They don't expect good care, and they don't know when they haven't gotten it. But Holly wonders what will happen as more nurse-midwives press into the bread-and-butter world of the middle-class patient—that huge, litigious tribe.

"We're safer than doctors," Holly tells Jim. "We do fewer interventions. Are less negligent. Have a better rapport with our patients."

"Well, I guess no one ever sued a good girl before," Jim says, smiling. "Start building your own list. That's what I'd advise. Feather your bed with your own whores. I don't think any of mine are particularly interested in coming to the defense of a nurse-midwife."

"We can't buy a list," Holly says, cringing. "We're poor girls. The only people who sleep in our beds are the folks who love us."

Jim swivels his chair to face his desk. He's lost interest. "Try and get the right people to love you then," he says. "Because love is the shortest list-builder of them all." Looking up matter-of-factly, he says, "See you in court."

CHAPTER 21

Holly has been assigned a walk-in: a pretty Puerto Rican teenager, with her sister as labor coach. A walk-in is a patient who's had no prenatal care at Howard Street and whose only medical history is the one she keeps in her head and then transmits in Spanglish to the Triage residents, the admitting nurse, and now Holly.

History-taking is a time-consuming ritual, a catechism run through with all the verve of any much-read litany. "Any hypertension? Any of your close family have high blood pressure? Any diabetes? Anyone in your immediate family had diabetes? Any thyroid disease? Kidney problems?" Zzzzzz.

When Holly began at Morrison, she figured walk-ins would be the hardest cases: unknown quantities, powder kegs about to go off, walking time bombs ticking away with undetected medical catastrophes. Continuous-care patients, who'd come to Clinic, would be different: known quantities, bombs the clinic had defused, with explosive powers quantified and thus made manageable.

But it isn't so. A string of prenatal visits at the clinic doesn't prevent complications, while no AP care doesn't doom a walk-in to disaster.

In fact, walk-ins are often easier for Holly to handle because in theory they're put under midwifery management after proving themselves to be somewhat low-risk in labor—assessed in the context that matters most. But patients who've been to Howard Street are managed by midwives no matter how badly they react to the stresses of labor.

No matter how complicated their labors become, the midwives stick with the clinic patients until the delivery requires an obstetrical hand—forceps, section, or manual removal of the placenta. But even after a

238

clinic patient is referred to a resident, the birth statistic is officially credited to the midwife.

Midwives' detractors often claim that midwifery's birth statistics are skewed in favor of midwifery because midwives pass complicated cases to doctors and so are able to take credit only for the less complicated cases with better outcomes. This isn't true at Morrison, where the midwives play the game like baseball, where the starting pitcher takes credit for a win or a loss, as long as he's stayed in the game for at least five innings.

Holly shouldn't have the walk-in she has. There's been a mistake. Something is wrong with Lita's amniotic fluid volume here. The problem is, there's not enough. It's too easy to differentiate the baby's limbs and head as Holly palpates the girl's abdomen. Holly can barely elicit any "thrill" at all as she runs her hand down the belly. An at-term abdomen will usually jounce like a firm waterbed when you squash your hand against it. Lita's doesn't.

Holly's adrenaline is pumping.

"You say your waters broke?" she asks.

"My panties were *soaked*."

"Yes, they were," her sister Angie attests.

"When was that?"

"This morning," Lita says.

"At nighttime," Angie says.

"In the wee hours of the morning?"

"That's right," they say in unison.

"You didn't go to a clinic anywhere to see a doctor at some time?"

"Angie told me what to do," says Lita. "The vitamins."

"The milk," Angie puts in.

"The iron supplements," Holly adds dryly.

"Yeah! The iron supplements!" the sisters say cheerfully.

They have no idea anything is wrong. They look at each other, full of nervous energy, smiling, as Lita lies on the narrow labor bed slapping the patient's rights booklet against her bare thigh. Angie half-sits on the radiator's edge and reaches forward to pull a tiny bit of lint off her sister's gown—the hospital-issued, ass-backward kimono with a pattern of spiky little white stars against a dark blue background.

Lita slaps her sister's hand. "Don't!"

"I'm just—"

"Sssh." Lita points furtively at Holly, and the girls giggle as Holly bends over to examine Lita's belly and keeps hitting too many hard things too fast.

"Lita, please turn on your left side and move your right leg up a little."

Holly sits on the side of the bed. What Lita is presenting with is oligohydramnios—which translates literally from Greek to mean "little water." At term, the amniotic sac is usually filled with almost a quart of fluid. Here, there seems to be less than half a liter. Bad news. Lita is going to have to stay on her side for most of labor, because with oligohydramnios comes the risk of cord compression and cord prolapse.

"Did you notice any of the water leaking before his morning? Wetness?"

"A little, but I don't know."

"You didn't know if it was pee-pee or not?"

"Yeah."

"That's right," Angie affirms. "She didn't know."

"It was colored," Lita says.

"What color, approximately?"

"Green, kind of. Wasn't it, Angie?"

Angie wrinkles her nose. "Yes, it was."

Meconium-stained fluid. Meconium is a danger sign. It's passed during a hypoxic event, when the baby is deprived for a moment of oxygen and the baby's sphincter relaxes as a result. There are two possible dangers associated with meconium: that damage was done during the hypoxic event and that the fetus will aspirate meconium in utero.

All babies inhale—or aspirate—in the womb. Fluid aspiration gives the lungs practice in expansion and contraction: fluid is essential for lung development. (One reason that vaginal delivery is preferred over cesarean delivery is that most babies benefit from having their torsos squeezed during the birth process—it helps empty the lungs of fluid.)

When aspirated meconium is lodged in the lungs, larynx, or trachea, it can be nearly impossible for the baby to breathe at birth unless vigorous suctioning or intubation (suctioning in the larynx) is performed. Meconium is sticky, gluey stuff. The effect of meconium on the lungs is about the same as that of Elmer's glue poured into a bellows. With a little glue, the bellows may still be able to expand and contract. But with a lot of glue, the bellows will be clamped shut.

What's tricky about meconium passage is that the hypoxic event that triggers it may also stimulate a reflex that causes the fetus to aspirate even more deeply. The increased respiratory activity following a hypoxic event does nothing to bring the baby more oxygen, but produces an in utero gasp that serves only to draw in the just-passed meconium.

Meconium—or mec, as the Seven-B crowd puts it—is pretty average business, and most babies with mec-stained fluid come through fine. But an oligo case changes the variables. When there's a normal amount of fluid, the passed meconium will become diluted, tinging the fluid just slightly. But when there's little fluid, the meconium stays in a semisolid state, thickening the fluid so that any aspiration contains a higher ratio of meconium to fluid.

And while meconium aspiration is more serious in a oligo case, it's also more likely, since oligohydramnios increases the chances of an hypoxic event. As there isn't much fluid to serve as a buffer between the baby and the umbilical cord, particularly during contractions, the chance of cord compression or prolapse increases.

The simplest, and most complex, reason for oligohydramnios is postterm pregnancy—oligohydramnios is the chief danger that postterm pregnancy poses. In a normal-term pregnancy, up to forty-two weeks, the amnion (the amniotic sac's lining) will keep producing fluid—even during labor and after the membranes rupture. It's believed that as the placenta ages, the amnion loses its ability to produce amniotic fluid.

But reduced amniotic fluid volume (or AFV) doesn't necessarily mean postterm pregnancy. Oligohydramnios can also mean the baby has no kidneys, and therefore no means of processing and flushing out the fluid he's swallowed in the uterus, as all fetuses do swallow fluid. Another explanation for the oligo might be that the baby has a blocked urethral path: ingested fluid can't exit from the body. In both cases, fluid that belongs in the sac and is normally recycled from baby to sac to baby is trapped inside the baby.

Of all the possible reasons for the oligohydramnios, the worst, the most awful—for Holly, the unthinkable—is that reduced AFV has been a problem from the start, due to some defect that resulted in the sac having never produced enough fluid. Holly's mind reels. She doesn't want to think about this right now.

Whatever the case, oligohydramnios increases the chance of birth trauma. The baby, already compromised, doesn't have much cushioning to protect his head from being struck against the cervix—in ninety percent of all labors, his head will be cushioned, at least at the start of labor, by the bag of waters. No fluid keeps him suspended in the womb or mitigates the intensity of the contractions closing around him. Even in a labor with ruptured membranes, backwaters usually surround the baby's body toward the top of the uterus, as the sac keeps producing fluid and the baby's head acts as a seal to prevent the fluid from escaping through the cervix.

Months ago, a mother brought her daughter in with PROM and told Holly knowingly, "She's going to have a dry birth." But the girl had plenty of amniotic fluid to spare. No matter what the reason for it, this birth will be a true dry birth. This won't be a happy birth.

A midwife's law goes: Think obvious, think stupid, think simple. What is the simplest explanation for the presenting problem? This is the point of departure. Maybe Lita has been leaking for weeks (the bag of waters will sometimes spring a leak, then seal up on its own again) and her production of fluid hasn't kept up with the amount that's escaped.

"Did you notice if your belly has gotten smaller these last few days?" Holly asks Lita.

Lita glances questioningly at her sister, who shrugs.

"You understand my question?" Holly says, somewhat patronizingly.

"I was born in New York," Lita says, with her slight Puerto Rican accent, and stretching across the bed, teasingly slaps her sister's thigh with the booklet. "I know English!"

Postmaturity is the next point of departure. Lita may have gotten her dates wrong—this population of patients is notoriously bad recordkeepers of their last menstrual periods and length of menstrual cycles. Holly asks Lita if she knows when her last period was and when she conceived.

"I knew it the minute it happened, didn't I, Angie?"

"Yes, you did. You told me all about it."

"I said, that's it, I'm pregnant now."

"When was that exactly?"

Lita looks at Angie. "January," Angie says. "Definitely January."

"Do you remember when in January?"

"Do you remember, Lita?" Angie asks.

Lita narrows her eyes, thinking. Holly pulls our her estimated date-of-delivery calculator. The standard formula for determining dates—Naegele's formula—was discovered in the nineteenth century. Some researchers think that it might be time for a new formula, that old Naegele was a bit stingy in his calculation of the ideal length of gestation. Holly's EDD calculator—a cardboard wheel—is good enough for her purposes now. She'll take a rough estimate of a date and work out another rough estimate. She might be off by a month or so, but what the hell?

"Did you have your period in January?" Holly prods. "Do you usually have it at the end of the month?"

"The end of the month," Lita answers quickly, but Holly thinks she may just be echoing the question, to make things easier on herself.

"At the end of January or the beginning of January?"

"The beginning," Lita echoes, with the tentative yet fast way of answering that Holly recognizes as belonging to a patient eager to come up with an appropriate answer that'll bring the line of inquiry to a close.

In short, Lita doesn't know when her LMP was.

According to Naegele's rule, if the last menstrual period was January 7th, you add seven days, which takes you to January 14th, and then you subtract that date by three months: $1/14 - 3/0 = 10/14$. October 14th was the due date. What if the LMP was December 7? The due date would then be September 14th. It is now October 20th. Either way Holly plays it, the baby is past due date. But with these kinds of dates, it doesn't make sense to play it at all.

CHAPTER 22

Holly nabs Levy in the corridor and steps into a role that she pulls out in desperate moments and that she can play for only a few minutes, being physically incapable of prolonging it. The role of midwife as supplicant, subordinate, slave girl, geisha, bowing her head in deference to a powerful, educated man. She remembers she has dimples and uses them. The impact of this mental reconfiguration of herself is that she looks like an actress in a B-movie playing the role of a psychotic nymphomaniac. All the same, Levy has been known to fall for it during his weaker moments.

"Levy, honey, I got to hand you back the Puerto Rican primap and take another." She bats her eyelashes wildly.

"Tough, Treadwell. We're fresh out of Puerto Rican primaps right now."

"Does the word *oligohydramnios* mean anything to you?"

"Treadwell, the primap was triaged downstairs. Did they find anything to concur with your findings?"

Holly's attempt to play the geisha-midwife has lasted less than a minute. "Even you have to admit that your brothers downstairs are lucky if they bumble their way into finding a cervix."

"Don't you ever quit, Holly?" Levy asks, astonished. "Don't ask a favor of me and then launch into a midwifery rap. Why don't you just give it a rest? You've pulled it so many times that I can run the antidoctor party line as well as you. Just tell me when you're about to start, and I'll play the whole thing out for you—you can save your breath."

Holly is abashed. "I'm sorry, Levy, but I'm nervous, sort of."

"I'm nervous sort of, too. I have a preeclamptic about to go over the top, and I'm pulling the new intramuscular mag sulfate regime. I stick her every hour for four hours. Then I have a multip with a cardial infarction history—she's like a model of a cardiology pathology class."

"Let her push when she wants to push," Holly advises. "Then she won't strain her heart."

Levy rolls his eyes. "You came to *me* for help, didn't you?"

Holly bows her head.

"What am I goïñg to do with an oligo that you can't do yourself, Treadwell? How is my expertise, which I know you hold in such high esteem, going to take care of that business?"

"I had a crazy idea that I'm supposed to manage normal births. Refer out, don't you know?"

"Dream on, Treadwell. Don't cop a midwife's plea on me. You're not going to turf an uncomfortable situation because it makes you feel a little nervous, sort of. I'm hip to you, Treadwell. When it's convenient, you handle normal birth. When you're interested in handling pathology, you do that." He mimics her in a high-pitched voice that meets some mental standard of a woman's voice but in fact doesn't resemble, even slightly, her own voice, which is more Peppermint Patty than it is Blondie Bumstead. "'I can do it as well as you can, Levy.' Now your story is different. You can't do it as well as me. You want to wash your hands of a dirty job. No can do."

"Cripes, Levy, you're right." Holly wants to go home now.

"Of course I'm right, Treadwell. I wish you wouldn't say that. It implies that I'm wrong sometimes."

"Well, I'm scared, Levy."

"What you scared for, little girl?" asks Levy, his long lashes dipping over his soft brown eyes. He thinks for a second, then says, "I wish Gus were here. He could deal with this."

"Gloomy Gus," Holly says gloomily.

Holly mentally wills the return of Gus, CNM: certified nutty madman. The carnage addict whose scrubs always look like a butcher's apron. He's taken a one-week leave of absence to attend his father's funeral in California. As Denise put it, "These satanic rituals take a long time to complete."

"He wouldn't mind if the kid was born with flippers," Levy says with a snort.

Holly's heart stops. She opens her eyes wide and jabs a finger in the direction of the delivery room at the end of the hall. She whispers hoarsely, "That kid is not going to be born with flippers."

"It happens, baby doll."

The final solution—the horror option. That there's been oligohydramnios from early pregnancy on. When the embryo develops normally, the fluid acts as a barrier between it and the amniotic sac. But with early oligohydramnios, the sac may stick to the developing embryo, throwing off its genetically determined development, shearing off scarcely formed limbs. . . .

Holly's blood doesn't run cold very often, but it does now—a shiver in her veins. Her mind flashes to Lita and Angie as they tease one another in their companionable way, excited and nervous about labor, sharing pregnancy in a way that most couples only hope to.

No, God. You hear me? Somehow Holly doubts it. This isn't the first time she's worked under the impression that Morrison is godforsaken.

"Hey, baby, we're tertiary care," Levy says, putting his hand on her shoulder. The blood having rushed out of her face, her eyes feel permanently widened. She stares at Levy as he says, "What were you expecting, kiddo—Mrs. Cleaver giving birth to Beaver?"

"She might have been leaking fluid a long time," Holly says, with desperate optimism. "She could just be post-dates." Postmaturity syndrome is starting to look good to Holly.

"If you don't like flippers," Levy says, stepping back, as if drawn into the center of his own mean streak, "you can worry about fetal pulmonary hypoplasia. Just to give you a choice."

Slapping her hands over both sides of her face, Holly opens her mouth in a noiseless scream. In the early stages of the lungs' development, aspiration of fluid plays an important role in their growth, by maintaining them in a state of expansion. Without enough fluid, the lungs never learn to expand or develop to their fullest, resulting in pulmonary hypoplasia, a condition which is usually not compatible with life.

"Levy, did you make this patient to order for me? Is this the creation of your warped imagination?"

"I'm just giving a midwife full rein, full responsibility, just like you always wanted. That's all I'm doing."

"My ass, Levy. This is a revenge fantasy."

As Holly heads back to the labor room, Levy calls, "Treadwell, talk to me after you've run a twenty-minute strip. Let's check out the baseline and decels. If nothing's happening but early decels, she's yours. But if the decels aren't swinging right, she's mine."

"Forget it, Levy," Holly says, putting her hands on her hips.

"Don't be difficult, Treadwell."

"How are you going to manage her labor differently from me?"

Pressing his clipboard under his arm, Levy lifts his arms. "How indeed?" He shakes his head, disbelieving. "You're such a chump for reverse psychology! Threaten to take a patient from you, and you hold on for dear life. Hell, woman, it works like a charm."

Holly hides her face in her hands and steps forward. "I promised myself this wouldn't happen, Levy. I told myself I wouldn't be a patsy any longer."

"Best-laid plans, Treadwell..."

"I got tired. I forgot."

"Don't forget, Holly. As soon as I assigned you that patient, you should have come tearing out of there to thank me. Then I would have taken her off your hands. Now, we got the rules straight?"

"Sure, Levy."

"Back to our respective corners then," Levy says. "Bong. And, Treadwell?"

"Yes?"

"Don't take my worst-case scenarios to heart. They're just . . ." Levy is at a loss for words.

"Revenge fantasies?"

Levy pauses for a second. "No," he says coolly, turning away. "A moment's indiscretion, that's all."

CHAPTER 23

Holly unfolds the scroll of monitor strip. The fetal baseline, scratched along the strip in a herky-jerky way, hovers around one hundred forty beats per minute. The baseline is variable. You can see that right away—the line waving, dipping, rising. Holly hates a flat baseline, which reminds her of a desert: lifeless, bleak. A flat baseline is what a floppy baby gets, the kind whose nervous system is so inert, it doesn't even react to the stresses of labor. A variable baseline means a baby responding, moving, thinking, *alive*.

The strip, as Levy seemed to foresee, shows early decelerations. Two lines run along the strips in waves. The top wave is the fetal heart rate, the lower one is Lita's contractions—it shows the onset, peak, and "decremation," the point when the mother no longer feels them. When the contractions start, the baby's heart rate slows up: an early deceleration. The fetal heart rate swoops down just as Lita's contractions swoop up, and the two lines form a mirror image, a set of matching peaks, a pleasing symmetry. The baby reacts to the contractions clenching about him by slowing his heart rate—that these decels are a quick, immediate response to the contractions means the baby is in decent shape, his reflexes properly tuned, that he isn't sluggish.

What Holly has to look out for, and what are associated with cord compression, are variable decels, which take all different shapes, start at all different points during the contraction, and don't maintain any kind of standard form. You can tell with a glance when there are variable decels, because the eye doesn't make sense of what it sees. A variable deceleration pattern is no pattern at all.

Holly would like to have X-ray eyes so she could see just where that cord is and where it lies in relation to the fetus. The coexistence of the cord and baby is too close. With so little amniotic fluid, the easiest thing in the world would be for the cord to be crushed between the baby and the uterus when the walls close in. Holly feels a weird sense of claustrophobia just thinking about it. But the monitor's tracing has cheered her. The baby is tough. The baby is all right.

Denise sticks her head into the labor room, and Holly asks for a 18-gauge IV catheter.

"A garden hose?" Denise asks in disbelief. "You?"

"Wasn't there a time, not so long ago, when nurses were silent, obedient handmaidens?"

"I'm not that old," Denise says. "I wouldn't know."

"I'll get the catheter myself."

Holly normally uses 20-gauge catheters, which are small and relatively comfortable for the patient. The catheters are pliable, and when the woman moves around, she can't traumatize a blood vessel with a catheter as she would with a straight needle. The catheter acts as an analogue of the vein itself, while a straight needle simply serves the function of pouring fluid into the patient. The 18-gauge catheters, the garden hoses, are a favorite among residents with a worst-case mentality. Garden hoses, being larger, are better for blood transfusions. Garden hoses are the catheter of choice for pessimists.

Holly feels pessimistic enough to follow Denise into the corridor. She leans her head against Denise's shoulder.

"Call my dad and tell him to come and pick me up and take me home," Holly says. "I've had enough."

"Forget it, girl," Denise says, stepping away abruptly so that Holly loses her balance. "You're in for the duration. Now, what do you want with a garden hose, gentle midwife?"

Holly shrugs. "The girl had no AP care at all."

Denise's jaw drops. "I'll be! And to think that all this time I thought I was working on Main Street, USA. No prenatal care. Imagine that. Isn't that the gol' darndest thing you ever heard in your entire life."

"Denise, I happen to think the baby's in bad shape."

"You scared about what's on the way out of there?"

"Do I usually go around singing the bad baby blues without provocation?"

"Holly, what's a bad baby got to do with you? Do yourself a favor and pull yourself out of the stupid pond where you've been swimming. What you do is get on the telephone, call the PDs, tell them you've got a bad baby coming in a few hours and they should come and pick him up. When the baby spits out, you cut the cord real quick and throw it at the PDs like a hot potato. That's what you do with a bad baby. You ain't no perinatalogist. All you got to do is get the baby out of there. What happens next is none of your business. Don't even look!"

"That's cold! That's callous!"

"The first law of nature is self-preservation," Denise sings out. "If you don't like the show, change the station. There's nothing you can do for a bad baby but to buff and turf. Hoe your own row, honey, and leave the bad babies to the bad PDs."

CHAPTER 24

Holly is tired of dealing with human beings. The patient is always two humans. It's a riddle: what comes into the hospital with two legs and leaves with four? A maternity patient subdivided on Seven-B.

Holly sits down on Lita's bed and takes her hand, feeling maternal, wanting to set everything right with a stroke of her hand. It must be painful, Holly thinks, to know you can't protect your daughter from the world. It must hurt to be a mother.

"There's not much fluid in your uterus," she explains. "That could be bad for the baby."

Childbirth is the first time some people really frown. Now Lita's forehead crumples up, and Holly watches it go with a strange fascination: the birth of the frown starts in the middle of the brow and runs two furrows down into the nose. Then the frown goes underground and resurfaces at the mouth, to pull it down in despair.

Holly shakes Lita's hand, letting it flop about on the mattress. "Your baby is probably fine," she said. "Its heart sounds good. Very good." *Because thinking makes it so.*

"It's all dry in there? That's not good?"

"The baby could be fine, but there is a chance."

Holly wants to pull away. She doesn't need to give specifics—pulmonary hypoplasia et al.—but a woman has the right to know, to prepare for what might happen, for the fact that her baby might be whisked away after birth by the pediatricians, that her baby might die.

Holly stays with Lita to undo the damage she's done. Bad news brings fear, fear brings tension, and tension brings pain, and Holly has to try to draw it out, not leave Lita alone with her fear and her body constricted with tension.

She gives Lita an OB backrub, pressing hard into the base of her spine, where the baby knocks against the lower back in its descent. Then an abdominal rub, which Holly doesn't normally do. The intimacy and sweetness of the gesture of an abdominal rub makes the staff uneasy; they are compelled to make cracks about it, and the fear of being "snapped" by the staff makes Holly tense at first, until the circular rubbing relaxes Holly as well, and she just doesn't care.

An abdominal rub is effective medication. Its physiological purpose is to increase circulation to the abdominal tissues, to get the blood vessels, constricted by contractions, to dilate more and so to bring more oxygen to the tissues. More oxygen means less tension, less pain. Holly rubs harder when she gets to the lower abdomen, which bears the brunt of labor pains.

As with any massage, the abdominal rub has a psychological function. Lita lets her head fall back, her eyes shut, her mouth open, relaxed. This is what the human touch does. Childbirth takes body and soul for a ride.

Holly shows Lita how to do effleurage, putting her hands on Lita's as they run feathery circles around the girl's too-small belly. "Think of feathers running around. Shut your eyes and follow the circle in your mind." The Lamaze technique is a psychological tactic to distract a woman from her discomfort. Holly happens to hate the word "discomfort," which sounds like a lie, a promise made that is soon broken. But the word "pain" doesn't appeal either, as it's too charged with the power of negative suggestion and people seem obliged to live up to it. The middle ground between discomfort and pain, which many women in labor occupy, is an undefined district of sensation.

Maybe that'll be my contribution to midwifery, Holly thinks as she rubs Lita's stomach; I'll invent just the right words. As the Eskimos have all their words for snow, Holly will find at least ten words to pin down all those feelings, keep them captive in the mind, articulated without doing harm to the woman who has to experience them.

The longer Holly stays with Lita, the better she likes her. She feels pity, as if pity is an instinct put in place by nature to make sure people don't abandon each other. Pity may be an instinct, but the urge to walk away is a reflex that Holly feels as well. But she's a midwife. That means she stays put.

CHAPTER 25

"The price of admission to the delivery room for a primap is a half-dollar" runs the L&D adage— that's how much of the baby's head should be visible before Holly makes her move. She collars Levy and asks him to call the PDs for her. For some reason, she's shy.

"Treadwell, as far as I know, the protocol for using the telephone system is the same for midwives as it is for residents."

"Levy, you have more clout than I do. You have that . . . that voice of authority," says Holly, the geisha-midwife.

Levy has fallen for it, because there's something in Levy that makes him want to fall for it. "In that case," he says, picking up the phone.

The PDs are here now, trooping down the hall in a band of three, with a male pediatrics nurse in tow. Holly has met all of them before, but they introduce themselves. It's part of their act. You can't stop them from introducing themselves. One is a perinatalogist. Another is a neonatalogist. "What are you?" Holly asks the third.

"I'm a good-byologist," he says.

Levy knows them all by name. "Hi, Curly, Moe, and Larry," he says.

"Hi, Shemp," they say in unison. "Nyak, nyak, nyak."

Kids caring for kids having kids.

The PDs are a merry team, an offbeat clique. When Holly was in college, there were computer nerds and engineering wonks, artsy types versus premed grinds, unidentifiable loners and rock-and-rollers, frat princesses and football jocks, preppies and hippie-dippie types. There was always one group, composed mostly of guys, that spanned all the others. They were the practical jokers who ran labrador retrievers for student council president; won poetry prizes after getting drunk, stringing togeth-

251

er nonsense words and forming epic poems; and sponsored mock hoote-nannies, "black turtlenecks only." Sometimes they had surprisingly sweet girlfriends. They walked the thin line between funny and stupid, often fell over the edge and made complete assholes of themselves, but always picked themselves up and kept stumbling on. These guys, as far as Holly can tell, grew up to become pediatric residents at Morrison Hospital.

The PDs don't practice self-censorship in their language and curse a blue streak. Because their patients don't generally understand language, they've never had to develop the inelegant variations to straightforward swearing that the OB residents and midwives have. If Holly ends up muttering, "I'm up to my ying-yang in this muckola," the PDs come right out and say, "I'm up to my ass in this shit."

It's unsettling to see a bunch of big fellows hover over a tiny baby and start to curse. "Where's the fucking endoscope?" one mumbles to the other when they are visualizing the vocal cords of a baby with suspected meconium aspiration. "I can't find a fucking vein in this whole fucking baby." If they curse in front of Lita tonight, Holly will have to get them to quit.

That won't win you any friends, Treadwell.

It's a little late in the game to start worrying about staying popular with the pediatrics boys.

The PDs are definitely crude, but they have a sweet side that Holly sometimes thinks she is only imagining. Sometimes, when they calm down a little, endearing expressions of concern sweep over their faces and their hands move along a baby's body deftly, with care. At least, that's how Holly interprets their lowered eyes and their slight frowns.

The PDs look like they belong together because they all have long hair, as though they've been laying low in an isolated part of the world where the fashion reports haven't been able to reach them. Nobody ever told them long hair is out of style. It's been out of style for so long, Holly is glad to see it's back. Their hair isn't extremely long, but just long enough to roll out from under their surgical caps when they suit up to stand watch in the delivery room. This makes them look sort of dashing, as if they stepped out of portraits of young noblemen in Renaissance Venice. That is, until they open their mouths to speak.

As the PDs wash up in the scrub room, they tell Levy that the head of pediatrics, the king of the herd, is on his way.

"What's he doing *here?*" Levy asks.

"Maybe he got in a fight with his wife and decided to sleep here tonight," says Moe or Larry or Curly. Holly can't tell them apart.

"How bad could a conjugal fight be for him to take such a drastic measure?" says Levy. "Hasn't the man heard of hotels?"

"He's like our dad," one of them says. "He's Fred MacMurray, and he wants to be with his three sons."

Dr. Laughton is like a dad. He reminds Holly of her father—same age, same World War II generation. "Those guys are going to die off soon,"

Holly once sighed to Matt. Most of the partners in Matt's firm are of that generation, and Matt doesn't choose to sentimentalize them. "Not soon enough," he said. Holly is nostalgic because she almost never sees men that age anymore—not in her social life, her nights at Morrison, or her days on Howard Street.

Dr. Laughton has a private practice and isn't around Morrison much. He's a big man, almost six feet six and thick around the middle, a characteristic Holly thinks is prototypical of that dying generation. He probably drinks bourbon, too, Holly thinks, just as her father does.

When Holly first met him, she figured the man's bulk would intimidate the kids. But the kids have been reconditioned by Mr. T, and think his size is a scream. When Dr. Laughton strolls down the pediatrics ward, he's like the kindly king from a fairy tale who descends from his castle to mingle with his miniature subjects. He is extremely amusing, playing basketball with rolls of gauze and trash cans. No matter how far off his shots go, he always calls out, "Swish!" This sets a bad example for the restless, hospital-bound youth. For days after one of his visits, all manner of objects surround the trash can on the floor, aimed at with cries of "Swish!"

As if by agreement with the hospital, Dr. Laughton picks up and swings at least three children per visit.

This upsets the nurse, who is reduced to playing straight man and stands by to reproach him. "Dr. Laughton!"

"A little dizziness never hurt an appendectomy, nurse!"

"But he's not an appendectomy, doctor! His ribs are broken!"

Dr. Laughton is a scream, the big howl that governs all his howling charges. Affability is Dr. Laughton's game, and he involves himself as little as possible with the nuts and bolts of his department, which runs just fine without his interference.

So why is the genial giant prowling Seven-B at three in the morning? It's middle-aged high jinks, middle-aged menopause, a caprice, a conceit. Weird, to be sure.

"You're the midwife!" Dr. Laughton says gleefully, swinging through the doors at the end of the hall. His white coat is a bit tight and resembles sausage casing, buttoned close against his paunch. Holly had been about to swing into the labor room to transfer Lita to the DR, but first, here's Dad.

"Holly Treadwell, CNM, at your service," she says, with the spunky, good-soldier attitude her dad always liked.

"I just love the idea of midwives. Just love it!"

Dr. Laughton, slightly red in the face, takes Holly's arm and leads her to the alcove near the narcotics chest. His voice is low and soothing, and he says, "Now, Holly, we're not going to have any problems tonight, are we?"

He's Dr. Affability, but he knows what he's doing. He's Fred MacMurray having a heart-to-heart with Rob's new wife. He's a different Dr.

Laughton from the happy fat man who gives sick little kids rides on the top of his head.

This is authority, as Holly used to know it. She's had many authorities in her professional life, but few have fit the model she'd been trained since birth to view as definitive authority. Dr. Laughton is that gray-haired, well-educated, middle-aged, white-male model.

The authority figure has just spoken softly, with an intimacy that Holly immediately intuits as intimidation. She's not sure how she made the equation, but she knows it. Intimidation. Dr. Laughton is expecting her to answer that he shouldn't worry, that there won't be any problems tonight, but Holly has no idea how he expects her to give him the assurance he's waiting for her to give. She has no idea what he's talking about.

"I don't think we'll have any problems," Holly said, taking a small step backward. She doesn't like to stand too close to authority figures or feel their breath on her face. But she smiles, pushes her hair behind her ears, half-expecting Dr. Laughton to criticize her for letting her hair fall out of place, and asks cautiously, "What problems are you thinking of, exactly, Dr. Laughton?"

"I'm speaking ethically, Holly. No problems ethically."

Holly looks at the floor. She is in a stupor, coming head to head with this authority figure, but slowly her brain finds its way to the word *ethically* and then takes the next step to arrive at *euthanasia*. Euthanasia always sounds to Holly like a lost continent flooded by the Caspian Sea or something. Mercy killing. But mercy is an old-time concept that doesn't have a life of its own in the hospital world anymore. Patients' rights have supplanted mercy as a concept. Haven't they?

Holly shakes her head to collect her thoughts. When she finally remembers that Dr. Laughton isn't her father or her boss, and that she answers only to Mrs. Gruener, Holly finds her footing and her voice.

"Dr. Laughton, I'm not sure I understand. What problems, ethically speaking, do you mean?"

She'd like to hear from Dr. Laughton himself. It's too tricky to make assumptions on the basis of a conversation as coded as this.

"It's not the best time for withholding treatment," Dr. Laughton says, tilting back his head, "if that's what you or your patient has been considering. I'm hoping the whole subject will drop right here."

"Dr. Laughton, the subject never even crossed my mind. That's not the kind of decision I'm involved in—"

Dr. Laughton puts up his hand. " 'Nuff said," he says, with a wink.

But Holly has found just the right tone of voice to talk to Dr. Laughton with, establishing a dicey balance that doesn't presume as if she's on equal footing with the head of pediatrics but makes it clear she's not as subordinate as a nurse either. She can't stop now.

"The patient isn't a very sophisticated lady," she says. This is code to mean the patient is uneducated and not extremely bright. "She's just a sweet kid." Code to mean she'll do anything Holly and the hospital tell her to do, as long as they put it in a nice way. "I doubt it's even occurred to her that she might withhold treatment for the baby." It hadn't even occurred to Holly, after all, who supposedly benefited from an expensive education.

Dr. Laughton looks at her with an expression that is more amused than impressed. When she was talking, he was not really listening, but looking at her face, the face of a pretty girl, and that was all. "I want you to know," he says, "we are ready for any eventuality."

"At any price," Holly says. She means emotional cost, but she knows he'll take it in the venal sense. He thinks she's talking bucks.

Dr. Laughton sighs, and the white jacket he's wearing over a button-down shirt swells up as his chest heaves. "Not nearly as much as it'll cost if the federal government decides to cut off our funds if it finds Morrison isn't up to snuff, ethically speaking."

Holly gets the whole of his drift now. No controversies, no Baby Does here. Give the baby the works, no matter how futile or expensive or painful the effort.

"I see what you're saying," Holly says, falling back into her good-soldier voice. "Full steam ahead. Stop at nothing. Heroic measures." Heroic for whom?

"Good girl."

As they walk down the hall, Dr. Laughton says, "You don't mind that I call you a girl, do you? It's just affectionate."

"I don't mind," Holly says. It's the 1980s. Too late to fight these tired old fights. She sighs, switches onto automatic pilot, and says what he wants to hear. "I don't mind as long as your team is there to catch the baby after I catch the baby. The mother to me to the PDs. Triple play."

"That's right, Holly," Dr. Laughton says, beaming at the sports metaphor. "A triple play."

Holly returns to the labor room. She's a girl because she can play with the big boys and knows when to back off and turn into a woman again.

CHAPTER 26

Holly is a good midwife. She's on the side of life. She can't let a baby go without a fight. That's her instinct. The ability to stay hands-off in the face of disaster is an intellectual concept more at home in the classroom than in the delivery room.

Holly remembers her first disaster clearly. She was in a large municipal hospital about to catch the baby of a large municipal woman who waited for delivery with curious detachment. She seemed to think that labor would go on with or without her and moaned in a low, inconspicuous way, as if she didn't want to draw attention to herself.

"Here's the baby's head," Holly called out with a peculiar lack of verve. She couldn't remember the woman's name for an instant—a sign of fractured rapport. With Hispanic ladies, Holly just calls them *señora* if they're over twenty years old or *señorita* if they're not so old. But you can't call an American woman miss or ma'am under the circumstances; that's too cold.

Holly had given up any hope of establishing a rapport with . . . Anita. Anita seemed a thousand miles away, the hospital's policy of excessive draping adding to this impression. Under all the drapes, all you could see was Anita's head and the vaginal introitus, like a conceptual art work to illustrate the mind/body split or the mechanization of the individual in the modern world. Either way, it wasn't a nice picture, and gave the delivery a bad feeling. Anita was reduced to being a decapitated head at the end of the delivery table. If she was passive, maybe she had a right to be, considering all the action was "down there."

For Holly, Anita was a geographical place. Focusing on the place where the baby would emerge was like looking down from an airplane, distinguishing the ridges and plains. Holly felt detached and at ease in a weird, cool way as Anita was reduced to a specific locale, a place, an exitway, an entranceway. The square opening at the pubic area was the only thing that mattered, and nothing upset Holly's concentration. Certainly not Anita, who, as a head at the other end of the drapes, had been split in two as if by a magic trick.

At deliveries, Holly's adrenaline was usually pumped up to the point where she was ready to implode or explode, but it was neither then. She trusted herself, which struck her as strange. After all, she was still a rookie, and nervousness came with the territory—it kept her on her toes. She didn't know if her confidence was the result of more experience or the fact that she didn't really care about Anita and couldn't work herself up into feeling otherwise. Whatever, she'd never felt so humdrum before, waiting to catch a baby.

"So this is how it feels to be a professional midwife," she thought then, frightened. "You just do it and don't really care either way. It's like being a toll collector or something."

She tugged firmly at the baby's head, then delivered the shoulders, and then saw that something wasn't right. There was something that would prevent her from taking the baby in a football hold, cradled in her arms. There was something wrong with this slippery, sliding bundle of protoplasm who was the point of this anxiously nonanxious exercise.

Bang. Something's not right.

This was a spina bifida baby. A neural tube defect. The spinal cord exposed right in the center of its back. A long, hot-pink strip of tissue. Holly's body saw it first, moving before her conscious mind did. Her stomach plunged, and blood rushed from her face like a bucket of water tipping and spilling in a flood. Her arms and knees went limp. Then her mind saw it. She cut the cord while holding the baby with one hand. As now, she didn't like cutting a cord while it still pulsed on as a live, useful thing, exchanging blood even when the baby has made his last exit.

But Holly didn't go sentimental. She held the baby under his shoulders, carried him to the warming table and laid him on his stomach. He was breathing in a slow, raspy way.

A nurse passed by. "Holy shit."

"Call the peds," Holly said brusquely. "Code three."

"I'll say."

Holly reached for the dressings on the shelf above the table. You put the ointment on, then gauze, and you protect this exposed spinal column from the world at large. That's what you do. That's what you do.

The nurse came back. "Hey, take it easy," she said softly.

"What do you mean?" Holly said, as the baby gave a low, ominous grunt.

"He's almost gone," the nurse said gently. "You never heard this from me, but let him go. Don't try too hard."

Holly looked up and stared, stunned, into the nurse's eyes. They were sweet eyes, not cold eyes, and Holly's mind almost froze with confusion—

the nurse telling her to let the baby die was a sweet person, a caring person. That didn't make sense.

Holly wiped the baby's face and legs. He was bluish and floppy, and his face was floppy too. She could see the baby was going. That was clear. He was checking out. Bailing out. Giving up the ghost. Slipping away. Passing on.

The pediatrics resident clattered into the room in what had to be the loudest shoes Holly had ever heard. She was staring at the baby when he elbowed her to the side, flicked back his long hair as if by a nervous twitch, and checked the dressing as the nurse's hands snapped the ID bracelets onto the baby's wrist and ankle.

"Christ," the PD said. Then he wrapped up the baby and stole him off.

Then Holly had only one patient. Anita, who was no longer a place, no longer cut in two, but a whole person covered in blue drapes and a green gown, spoke up in an enervated voice. "Something's wrong with my baby." She spoke so definitely. Usually mothers—even when they know how bad things are—will put the statement as a question: "Is there something wrong with my baby?" Anita sounded too tired to hope.

"Yes, I'm sorry, there is. . . ."

Holly stepped to the end of the table to wait for the placenta, and realized in an instant that this dispassionate bullshit, the view of the mother as a place, an exit for a baby, wasn't going to work.

Holly felt wildly guilty, as if her indifference had caused this to happen, as if the fact that she hadn't cared had produced a spina bifida baby who probably wouldn't live. Spina bifida, a neural tube defect, a genetic scheme blitzed out early in pregnancy—but Holly felt responsible, and she was responsible now to answer to the mother as a person, not just a head on the table meters away from the real meaning of the delivery. Holly had to see that the mother was everywhere, all over the table.

Holly wanted to be with Anita at the head of the table, but she had to monitor the placenta. She couldn't just let it fall, the blood loss left unmeasured and the condition of the placenta unexamined before its fall.

But let it fall. Holly went to the head of the table and met Anita's eyes. Anita was still in the lithotomy position, head flat against the table and no eye contact with Holly. This was the last time Holly would use the dorsal-recumbent position. From here on in, the table would be cranked up so the mother was almost sitting—not just to increase the pull of gravity, but so Holly would never lose complete sight of her patient. And she'd never drape a patient like this again either. The risks of infection weren't as great as the risks of cutting a woman in two, as Anita had been.

Holly's most detached patient now searched Holly's face. For a clue? As to whether Holly could be trusted or not? Why should she trust Holly? But her eyes seemed to say—or was it Holly's sentimental hope that they did?—"You're a good person. Help me." Maybe trust is another instinct of self-preservation: when you have no choice but to trust, you put your faith in anyone or anything. . . .

"Your baby has something called spina bifida. The spine is exposed."

Anita frowned. "That's not right." She had to twist her head uncomfortably to look at Holly, her legs still high in the stirrups. "That's bad, isn't it?"

"Yes, it's bad. I'm sorry. It is."

Anita shut her eyes. "I dreamed the world turned upside down. I dreamed everything was topsy-turvy. We walked on the ceiling, and the lights were on the floor." Holly stared at Anita's face and saw this vision herself. It was a true vision. "So now what's in is out," she finished.

"You're right, Anita. I'm so sorry."

Holly returned to the end of the table in time to catch the placenta. Another bundle of warm protoplasm. It was almost living. It was perversely whole. It was pristine, complete, and precisely as it ought to have been.

Holly would like to grab Dr. Laughton's arm now and tell him, "I don't let babies go easily. I'm not built that way. I try to save everything and everyone. I'm too much like that. You don't have to worry about me in that department."

But what would be the point? On some things, you just stay quiet.

CHAPTER 27

Holly is scrubbing up. In the DR, the Three Mousketeers huddle in the far corner, gulping with laughter. Denise is organizing the delivery tray, setting out the Lidocaine and needle for local infiltration. Holly will probably cut a 'pis on the frightened primap with a baby who might be sick. That baby has to move out fast.

"Denise, are you circulating now?" Holly asks as Denise passes by.

"I'm orbiting," Denise says.

"Well, help the pushing effort, will you?"

Holly talks as if she's biting off something with a sour tang. Because Holly has stage fright. She's about to deliver a kid in front of an audience.

She's already masked and capped, as she always is before she scrubs. In her costume, she feels secure and professional. How many babies has she delivered now? Oh, hundreds, hundreds of babies of all shapes and styles. Bad babies, good babies, floppy babies, blue babies, sick babies, beautiful babies, even a baby with two teeth (loose, wobbly things the PDs pulled out before the baby had the chance to swallow them). Holly is a pro. Which doesn't stop her from feeling performance anxiety, as if this were the first delivery she'd ever done.

Levy has screwed up publicly a number of times, to Holly's best recollection. Once, when the PDs were here, Levy almost dropped the baby immediately following a delivery. Thanks to manual dexterity he claims he learned playing table soccer in college, he caught the kid by the feet at the last possible second. "Way to go, Levy," the PDs had said with a laugh. "Good reflexes." Another time, also in the presence of the PDs, Levy cut an episiotomy that extended into his patient's rectum. That wasn't quite as laughable.

Holly doesn't intend to screw up in front of the PDs. As a midwife,

260

she's a member of an embattled minority. That means being good enough isn't good enough: she has to be better. She has to be flawless. She can't create the slightest opening for her technique or skill to be criticized. She needs grace under pressure.

Scrub time is time to run through the management decisions. She doesn't want to cut too large an episiotomy too soon. If she waits it out, though, Lita might tear, and Dr. Laughton and the PDs will spread the word that midwives let their patients tear. She decides to go with the Lidocaine as soon as she's in the DR. If Lita hollers with pain when she cuts the 'pis, the docs will claim that midwives—dogmatic natural childbirth fanatics all—make their patients suffer.

The big question is, will Lita control her pushing well enough to push only between contractions when the head is delivered? A slow, controlled delivery would be a nice object lesson for the boys in the peanut gallery. Yet Lita might flip out when the perineum starts burning as the baby's head pushes out. Did Holly describe that burning to her? Flipping through her mental memory file, Holly accesses the moment when she told Lita about the sensation of burning. She's reassured, then worried. She nearly forgot describing it—will Lita have forgotten, too?

Holly looks up. Denise is draping Lita, and Lita is getting restive, rolling her head back and forth. In a moment, she's going to lose it. The Three Stooges stand in their corner, laughing.

Get out there, Treadwell. Don't abandon her.

I'm going, she tells herself.

Sometimes you need a goddamn kick in the tail.

Holly shakes her head. Is she becoming a schizophrenic midwife? The three faces of a CNM.

Dr. Laughton enters the DR with Crowley chasing after his thick, bearish figure. "Dr. Laughton, dear, would you like some gloves?"

"Gloves? Hands-on, eh? Thank you, nurse. Who have we got here, the Bowery boys?"

"Hi-ya, doc," say the Bowery Boys.

Dr. Laughton reminds Holly of what she's doing there. What they're doing there. Anticipating the worst. The transport unit is plugged in, warmed up by the door, a racing car in the pit. Holly's adrenaline is charged, but there's nothing for her to do but get the baby out with the least amount of trauma.

Of course, midwives who work in birth centers and doing home births find Holly's concept of a nontraumatic birth nothing but a farce. The bright lights of the delivery room, the slight chill in the air (as the delivery room is only about seventy-two degrees while the labor rooms are all about eighty degrees), the presence of strangers who haven't been introduced to Lita, and the absence of her sister, Angie, the fetal monitor still blipping as the spiral remains attached to the baby's head, the pretty midwife with the smudged mascara and the blonde hair now looking unfamiliar and strange behind her cap and mask. Nobody has told Lita that Holly would look this way.

All this is filtered in through a blur of fear, of not knowing what it'll feel like when the baby is born and of knowing that something might be wrong with the baby. Something wrong inside. Yeah, this nontraumatic birth is a laugh. But everything belongs to a context, and this is the context in which Holly works.

The show has started. Denise cranks up the table to a forty-five-degree angle, putting gravity on the side of the baby. The peanut gallery has quieted down, as the Bowery Boys move in to study what Holly does and Denise stands at the head of the table with her arm around Lita's shoulder. "Almost finished now, girl, almost done." The pledge of all *accoucheurs*.

"Now, Lita, remember that burning sensation I told you about," Holly says, as she unscrews the spiral of the monitor from the baby's scalp. She's sick of these things—whirligigs on the skulls. Holly has never been the groovy kind of midwife. She's never hated medicine or mucked around with herbal treatments, and she's smoked in defiance of common sense, as if to abuse her body with a vengeance. But she's sick of screwing gimmicks and gadgets of metal and wire onto and off the world's most pure, most human things. Back-to-nature comes to Holly as a dream, of paradise lost or some heavenly future, where there'd be none of this: the gray walls of the delivery room, the harsh lights deflecting off the shiny metal and glass of the cabinets to the side, the grown men standing at attention before a lady's vagina, murmuring as they observe the exhibition.

Nontraumatic birth. Hello, baby. Are you ready to be blinded? Are you ready to be pained? Welcome to the world, baby. It's a smack in the face, isn't it?

Holly puts her left index and middle fingers into the vagina and presses out, to move the perineum away from the baby's head. Her thumb feels for the anal sphincter, which is a must to avoid, and with her right hand holding the scissors almost vertically, she poises to make her cut. She adjusts them so that when she makes the cut, she'll have gone just far enough. There. She's hit it right. She sponges away the trickle of blood, moving the fingers that hold the perineum out even more in order to see how far her incision has gone on the vagina's interior. The perineum isn't a flat plane, like a stretch of cloth, but more of a slope, with the muscle built up on the interior like the side of a hill. At this point, Holly doesn't view the vagina as a vessel—a passive orifice that accepts a penis, a canal for the baby to spill out of—but as a structure of active, flexing muscle.

Holly devised a mnemonic method to remember all the muscles in and around the perineum. Dumb People Instigate Great Stupidities, I Believe. Darling People In Great Shape In Burbank. Deep transverse perineal muscle, pubococcygeus muscle, iliococcygeus muscle, gluteus maximus muscle, superficial transverse perineal muscle, ischiocavernosus muscle, bulbocavernosus muscle. The bulbocavernosus muscle contracts the vagina and can make it small again after a baby has stretched it out. The deep transverse muscle supports the whole vagina. The ischiocavernosus keeps the clitoris erect. Dangerous People Insinuate Great Schemes in Bolivia. Indeed.

Every woman is a muscle.

Holly feels the taut hymenal ring running right around the immediate interior of the vagina. She can only feel that in primaps; the hymenal ring is one reason that primaps need episiotomies more often than multips do. With her next child, Lita won't have that ring, with its jagged, torn edges.

Holly quickly dabs at the cut to stanch the blood, but she doesn't need to, since the baby's head is pressing hard against the cut and stanching it for her.

Holly quietly tells Lita to push. "Come on, darlin', push. You got it now. Easy. Easy. Slow. Slow. All right, pant now. That's a good girl."

"Come on, baby, come on home," one of the PDs calls out.

Let's see you, baby, Holly thinks, let's see what a sick baby you are, what pediatric wonder you prove to be.

Her whole being is galvanized, as if a current of energy and power is shooting up and down her body, pulsing. With adrenaline like this, Holly feels she should be doing major efforts. Lifting pianos. Carrying bodies out of burning houses. Instead, she waits, one hand on the crown of the baby's head.

Holly pulls off the top layer of her gloves, which may have been soiled by contact with the rectum, and drops them on the floor, scooting to the right side of the table. She moves her right hand under Lita's bent leg; if she works above it, Lita might kick or jerk her leg and send Holly's hand flying when she does. With a flicker of awareness, Holly wonders if the PDs have seen this position before. If they haven't, they will now. But then awareness of the PDs burns out, her stage fright a useless exercise, because she doesn't care about them anymore. This is the moment when Holly's energy and awareness focus into one strong beam and the rest of the world drops away.

The baby has lots of curly black hair, which Hispanic babies often do.

From the back, one of the Three Stooges can't refrain from calling out: "Come on, push! Push!"

At this stage in the game, Holly can't take her eyes off the perineum. But if she could, she'd shoot the offender a dirty look for shouting. She knows that he's eager to be a participant and that he's compelled to take an active role, but this is her turf and this is a quiet birth.

So much for principles: as soon as Lita hears that foreign male voice, she becomes agitated and invigorated and energized. She winces and grunts and pushes hard, the voice having jolted her somehow, and the top of the baby's head pushes forward to give way to a brownish forehead the color of a plank of wood.

Holly's left hand controls the birth of the head. Slowly. Then it's out. Definitively, permanently *out*. No turning back. The head is a small, brown face stuck between Lita's legs. A face with shut eyes and pursed lips, indifferent to everybody who is looking on. A head attached to a body that is not its own, so that Lita has become a body with two heads. For how long in a woman's life is she a two-headed body? Minutes, that's all, if she has many children. And seconds, only, if she has just one.

It takes less than half a minute for restitution. The shoulders tuck in under the pubic arch as the baby turns, knowing just where to go, getting itself placed just right in the curve of Carus. The head turns slowly, almost creakily, to the right to face Holly.

"Hello, occiput anterior," Holly says softly. "Hello."

The baby's head has a caput—swelling where the head has become edematous—because the head provided pressure on the cervix that the bag of waters normally provides.

"Hello, caput."

Ordinarily, Holly would bring down Lita's hand so she could feel the top of the baby's head and affirm that the baby really is here. But Holly anticipates grief, and she wonders how celebratory this birth should be. What if there are still flippers in there? She'd forgotten about the flippers until now, because she didn't really believe in them, those stunted implications of legs that existed mainly in Levy's mind and revenge fantasies. Holly's mind depends upon the idea of wholeness, as if it's wrong to presume anything else. The baby will be well, and to think otherwise is to be fatalistic and defeatist. It's like when Holly plays poker and she crosses her fingers before picking up a card dealt to her, hoping it'll be the one she wants. What good, once the cards are shuffled and dealt, to cross her fingers? Nothing can change then, but she does it anyway. Wishing hard. Her mind just moves that way.

The baby's head stops rotating, and Holly wipes his brown, wrinkled face and starts to suction the mouth. There's almost no fluid, but the baby's face is splattered with meconium.

Go on, Treadwell.

Holly puts her hands on both sides of the face, her hands steering clear of the neck, where the nervous system runs its vulnerable route. She presses only what can withstand pressure.

"Now pant all the time, Lita. You're doing great!" Down and up, Holly applies this pressure. Way up, aim for the roof. Her bottom hand moves down to bring out the shoulders as she controls the baby's arm and elbow lest they tear the perineum or leave skidmarks. While she controls the shoulders with the palm of her hand, her ring finger and index finger create a track on which the arm can glide. Amazing how much of the limb just one hand can control. Holly loves this feeling of having gotten hold of a baby.

She knows the other shoulder will sweep right out, and it does, as she's got most of the baby in her hands. Her thumb is on the back, her fingers opened and pressed against the chest, the baby's neck cradled in the fingers of her other hand, its head supported by Holly's wrist. Holly puts her top hand down the baby's back, and she slips her index finger between the baby's legs until she has the baby by his ankles. Ankles. These aren't flippers, Holly registers, these are legs. Baby, you are here. You are all here.

Holly catches both of the baby's feet between the fingers of one hand, all her fingers gripping the little extremities. Then the entire baby, a girl, rests in her arms. Holly's hand cups the head and neck as she slips the body onto her arm.

"A girl!" a PD stooge shouts, and Dr. Laughton calls out, "Wonderful, lovely!"

Holly recovers her stage fright, as if it were part of the earth to which she's returning, as if she'd been in a glider, flying through high white clouds, but had bailed out, barely aware of making progress toward the earth before suddenly hitting ground.

She's here now, thinking of stage fright, as the beam of concentration that held her for the duration of delivery breaks and shatters and scatters. A PD steps up to clamp and cut the cord, and a spray of blood sprinkles across the drapes. He takes the baby in his gloved arms. The baby is out of Holly's hands. The baby has been effectively turfed to Pediatrics. Holly's hands are a transport system, part of the machine to turn the baby over to the PDs.

But that's what her hands always were: a transport system, a funnel, a wagon.

"You did great, Lita," Holly says.

Her baby isn't pretty. The baby has no vernix on it, and it's brown when it should be as pale as the moon. A creature from a dry environment whose skin is tough and leathery, like an old sharecropper's hands. Holly draws the cord blood as the PDs bundle the baby, with its wrinkled skin, tough as shoe leather, into the transport unit. Ah, it's all over. For Holly, at least. She is doing as Denise suggested she do. "Leave the baby to the peds. Your patient is the mother."

While the PDs move out with the wasted-looking baby, the patient, the mother, the woman, the teenage girl calls out, "Let me see!" Lita is sitting up, straining her neck to see past the blockade of bodies surrounding her first child.

"Fellas, can't she see her baby?"

"Yeah, sure," they say, flustered, and wheel the unit toward Lita. And then, regretting the concession: "Only for a minute." Lita bends down to stare at the small, wrinkled brown face of her baby.

"That's your girl," Holly says. Maybe she doesn't know that the baby doesn't look as it should. Maybe she thinks this is how all babies look.

"That's my baby?"

"Didn't you see her come right out of you? Isn't that your baby?"

"Yeah. My baby," Lita says, pleased.

"Let's go," the PDs say to each other, addressing Lita only indirectly.

"Say *adiós, muchacha*," Holly says.

"Adiós, muchacha," Lita says faintly.

Dr. Laughton slaps Holly on the back on the way out.

"Thanks, Dad," she says under her breath. To Lita she calls, "You're doing great. You're doing great."

And if before Holly had resented the intrusion of so many people in the DR, now she feels deserted. There's nobody there but Denise and Holly and Lita. And Holly is at the end of the table, far away from Lita. Lita is all alone. She shivers in the clammy confines of a world apart. How could something that took so long be over so fast? That's life, Holly thinks. That's the way it goes.

CHAPTER 28

Holly lies on her bed, listening to *Donahue* and looking at the slip of paper Katrina gave her with Sara's phone number and address. The more she thinks about it, the less inclined she is to call, particularly since Katrina told her that Sara is opposed to a credentialing process for lay midwives.

"Sara says that word-of-mouth is a better standard to go by than a bureaucracy is," Katrina told Holly.

Holly thinks this is malarkey. A lay midwife, having studied a few midwifery books, might attend fifty deliveries with no problems. But what if the fifty-first delivery careers off track and switches into pathology mode, as one in fifty births will do? The midwife's status as a medical outlaw makes consult with a doctor nearly impossible—the very problem that propelled Katrina toward nurse-midwifery, as she herself admitted. If the lay midwife were credentialed, she'd have greater access to medical resources. To Holly, the vaunted self-reliance of the lay midwife is a curse reconstructed as a virtue. When human life is at stake, self-reliance is a sentimental notion. At least nurse-midwives admit their interdependence on and with other medical powers.

"Sara says that certification by a board doesn't guarantee that a practitioner is competent," Katrina said. "The only thing certification promises is that some lay midwives, even if they're skilled, will be excluded because they don't have the specific skills some board wants them to have. The midwives who do pass the licensing procedures will have control over the birthplace. Sara believes that nobody should have that control. Nobody except the woman giving birth. It's her choice whether to call in a shaman, a surgeon, a high priest, or a midwife."

The more Holly thinks of her, the more she hates Sara. She puts the slip of paper on the night table, turns off the sound on the television, and stares blankly into the screen.

"Sara doesn't think midwifery is a science," Katrina had said. "She thinks it's a domiciliary art. An art of the home."

Katrina had looked questioningly up at Holly, waiting for some kind of response.

Holly's response was, "This game of 'Sara says,' Katrina—does Sara actually say these things, or do you say them?"

"Sara says them," Katrina answered, smiling slyly, "and then I say them."

"Well, tell Sara that all medicine is an art, a science and an art. A good internist works the same way. He listens to his instinct, and he lays on his hands."

"Why don't you tell Sara yourself?"

"Won't that spoil the game?"

Holly looks at the slip of soiled paper with the upstate telephone number on it. She is tempted to call and tell Sara just exactly what she thinks of her. But instead she writes in her journal, describing Lita, and wonders, as she falls asleep, what Sara is doing out there on her own, catching babies outside the law. She's just curious, that's all.

CHAPTER 29

A rough case, this Edna O'Toole. Most of the hardcases—the streetwalkers, the junkies, and the homeless—that Holly sees at Morrison are either black or Hispanic, and while she sympathizes with them, or tries to, at least, she can always keep them at a safe emotional distance, as long as they're of another race. Is this racism? Maybe, but it's also tribalism. They're women, always, just as she is, but not of her own tribe.

Being half-Irish herself, Holly can't say this of Edna O'Toole. That Edna is Irish makes Holly think, "There but for the grace of God go I," in a way she doesn't when she sees other women who have hard luck and haven't stood up to it well. If Holly were an alcoholic, or had been kicked out of her family or abused by her parents, or hadn't had a good education—well, it's not likely, but it's possible that Holly would look a lot like Edna O'Toole.

Edna has pasty white skin and small, tired, hard blue eyes. Crowley is washing off Edna's makeup now, and it's an effort—Edna must have spackled the pancake onto her skin with a spatula. After Crowley cleans Edna up, a weasel's face stares angrily out from the white pillow, with small, sharp features and quick, suspicious eyes. Her skin has a sick quality and seems to hang loosely from her bones, while her body, with the exception of her belly, is thin and brittle. Holly has noticed that black skin ages better and survives malnutrition with more grace than northern European skin. The skin of a black woman who has been through hard times loses its gloss and luster, while white skin seems to show all of life's lumps and bumps on its surface and to break down, as if it wants to molt and abandon the roughed-up body it's hanging from.

It's Edna O'Toole's skin that tells Holly she's either an alcoholic or a junkie. Alcoholic, to judge by the broken blood vessels around her nose

269

and eyes, the hooded eyelids, and the dehydrated state of her skin. Either alcoholism or drug addiction would give her body this brittle look, as if all the calcium has been prematurely leached from her thin bones and they're ready to snap.

When Holly introduces herself, thin-lipped, thin-skinned Edna O'Toole snaps, "I ain't going with no midwife."

"Oh, no? Why not?"

"Everyone knows midwives put you in a room by yourself and don't give you nothing to ease the pain."

"Not me," says Holly. "I put you in a crowded room and give you Demerol if you want. You know Demerol?"

Still lying flat on the gurney in her street clothes—blue jeans with a stretch waistband and a short-sleeved green velour sweater that does nothing for her anemic pallor—Edna lifts her head, as broken-looking strands of red hair run behind her, and mutters, "Yeah, I know Demerol." Then she flops back.

"Next of kin or someone we can contact for you?" Crowley offers, hovering over her.

"Geez louise, how many times I got to tell you?" Appealing to Holly, she whispers, "I told the colored fella downstairs there wasn't nobody, and goddamnit if I didn't mean it."

"I think I'll just walk away now," Crowley says.

In the corridor, by the admitting desk, an older man stands with a big-boned girl. She's about five feet ten, with thick, long legs like tree trunks and a round, sweet face that would make her a suitable wife for the man in the moon. She speaks no English and no version of Spanish that anybody can understand, but some mountain dialect home-grown in Honduras, according to the man who brought her in. The presumption that the middle-aged man with the thin mustache, wearing an overcoat pulled over a T-shirt, and carrying the girl's overnight case, is her father is quickly disabused.

"She's my neighbor, she's from Honduras, she has no one, her husband is in Honduras."

The young woman ducks her head, fiddles with her wedding ring, and smiles at Crowley.

"My wife told me to bring her. It's the least I can do for the girl. I haven't done this for years. My kids are all grown. I can't stay." His face is white, and beads of sweat collect on his brow. He is in a state.

"That's all right, love," says Crowley.

"No, you don't understand," he says, sinking into a chair by the desk. He pulls his T-shirt out with his hand and flaps it. "I have to go. Downstairs." He throws his head back.

"Dear, are you all right? Would you like a glass of water?"

"A heart condition. My heart . . . a heart attack," he gasps.

The CODE cart is currently parked in the ABC. Fibrillator, electrodes. It'll stay parked there. Pulling a CODE on a suspect CI isn't a mainstay activity of admitting nurses on Seven-B.

"You, there!" Crowley shouted at a passing orderly. "Don't you move." She eases the man into the wheelchair that the young Honduran woman has just vacated. Ashen and damp-faced, the man slumps there as the orderly runs off with him.

The Honduran girl looks stricken. "Sit," Crowley tells her. Seeing the worried look on her face, Crowley says in Spanish, "Don't worry. Men are nervous people."

The girl may not speak mainstream Spanish, but she understands it. "Ah, sí, sí," she says with a smile, nodding.

CHAPTER 30

Holly says, "You seem to have a vaginal infection, don't you?"

This is the understatement of the month when applied to the condylomata warts on Edna's perineum. They look like barnacles—dry and breakable and stubbornly stuck. Pregnancy aggravates preexisting condylomata, and the only somewhat successful treatment is tincture of podophyllin, which is contraindicated for pregnant women as it's been linked to "fetal wastage." When the warts spread over the perineum like a lumpy-textured mold, all a pregnant woman can do is wash with soap and water—a low-tech treatment of a low-life organism.

"Trich," Edna O'Toole volunteers.

Trich? No, not quite.

"You were diagnosed with trichomoniasis?" A sexually transmitted disease (STD) that limits itself to internal inflammation and discharge. The external devastation that Holly is looking at isn't trich, even if Edna O'Toole thinks it is.

"I was taking Flagyl till I got pregnant."

"Then you quit."

"I was in Philadelphia at the time."

Holly is startled. "You're from Philadelphia?"

"Yeah."

"So am I."

Edna O'Toole studies Holly critically. "Yeah," she says.

When Edna's baby arrives, he'll be bound for the suspect nursery. Edna bought him a ticket there, with unknown quantities and kinds of disease. Holly doesn't like putting a baby on the suspect list, which works up a baby with eye cultures, throat swabs, and nasal smears—any part of the baby that might harbor bacterial growth.

When Holly is through with Edna's workup, she'll head downstairs to the lab and ride tail for a fast bloods workup—in particular, her VDRL (Venereal Disease Research Lab) and hemoglobin, the stuff within the red blood cells that transports oxygen, the lack of which creates anemia. As with most of the patients here, Holly puts in for a cross-match—plasma on hold for transfusion—because the more anemic the patient is, the more she's inclined to hemorrhage and the more dangerous hemorrhage is for her, as she is least able to afford any loss of blood.

Holly is worried about chlamydia—the organism of the 1980s that makes herpes, the virus of the 1970s, seem like smooth sailing. Herpes is easily diagnosed and has easily identifiable outbreaks, and its recurrent outbreaks (which don't necessarily ever occur) aren't usually as severe as the first one. But chlamydia is hard to diagnose. You have to take a clean sample, going straight up the endocervical canal with a swab and then pulling the swab straight out without touching anything en route: vaginal discharge, blood, fluid. And even with a clean culture, one-third of the results are false negatives. Chlamydia was such a sneaky STD that Howard Street started taking chlamydia cultures only a year ago. In any case, it's too late to test Edna for chlamydia because what's prominent in her endocervical canal right now is a baby's head.

Knowing whether Edna has gonorrhea or chlamydia makes a difference in the kind of eyedrops the baby will be administered after birth. The state mandates silver nitrate eyedrops, or, as an alternative, erythromycin, which is gentler than silver nitrate and burns the baby's eyes less. Both eyedrops are meant to combat STDs, but silver nitrate is more effective against gonorrhea while erythromycin works better on chlamydia.

Deciding which eyedrops to go with in a walk-in case like Edna is a gamble, and no matter which course Holly takes, she'll think it's the wrong one. Like other conservatives nervous in the face of risk, Holly sticks with the status quo—silver nitrate, which is no choice at all, since that's what is immediately available on a shelf in the delivery room. Erythromycin is in the corridor supply chest. The decision is made almost by default.

It won't be easy to extract information from Edna. Crowley already asked her if she had any STDs, and Edna, a capricious witness, said no. Now here she's just confessed to a dose of trich.

"You didn't mention to the nurse that you have a sexually transmitted disease, did you?"

Edna glares at Holly. "What was I gonna do? What would she have done then? Besides, what I got is a vaginal disorder. It don't have nothing to do with sex."

"Have you ever been treated for any other STDs?"

Rolling her eyes, then squinting at Holly, Edna looks about forty years old, although she claims to have been born in 1953. "I've had 'em all," she says, lifting her chin. "So, satisfied now?"

"Do you have any active STDs now?"

"Hang on. I got a pain." Edna squeezes her eyes tight, and Holly takes her hand. When the contraction passes, Edna yanks her hand out from under Holly's. "I'm cured," she says. She smiles, disclosing a stretch of top teeth that are little more than brown stumps. Holly has seen teeth like these in anorexics, junkies, speed freaks—a combination of malnutrition and no dental care. "Besides, I learned a trick or two so I won't catch any of them diseases anymore."

"What tricks are those?" Holly asks with interest.

"What tricks are those?" Edna mimics. "You put something up your box. It's a trick. For tricks. You probably never seen it."

"What do you put in your"—Holly stumbles—"in your box?"

"Aren't you gonna call it a vagina?" Edna asks slyly.

"I don't live in a convent. I'll call it a box. What do you put up there?"

"Toilet bowl stuff. A thousand flushes."

Holly takes it back. She lives in a convent. She's shocked. "Hey, girl!" she says. "That's no good!" She tries to picture the pH status of a vagina that holds a Tidy-Bowl or some such cleanser, and fails.

"Yeah. Right," Edna says, staring at the ceiling. "It's no good. But who are you to say?"

Who am I to say? I'm a clinician. A nurse-midwife. Certified by the state to treat STDs. I know about these things.

Somehow, this strikes Holly as a less-than-persuasive pitch, and she's speechless.

Edna seems aware of the fact. As Holly reels herself in from her shock, Edna says, with a crooked smile, "So, you got that Demerol for me?"

"Is she an addict?"

Levy has just asked a sensible question.

"No tracks," Holly tells him. "No repressed respiration. Pulse is okay."

"I don't like giving Demerol to a working girl. Just because there's no tracks . . . maybe she snorts the stuff. You know how junkies are when they come here. They know we won't give them anything else so they dose up on their own medication at home."

"I can tell she's got a low pain threshold," Holly says. "And everything bugs her. We need the Demerol. With a perineum like that, we can't do an epidural."

Epidurals, the spinal anesthetics that numb the patient from the waist down, are rare on Seven-B. This is due to three staff factors: mistrust of the Sneaker and his *compadres* in anesthesia, the fact that epidurals require too much effort, and the fact that, no matter what epidural advocates say, epidurals screw up the pushing mechanism, which is triggered by the baby's head applying pressure to the perineum, pressure an epidural patient can't feel. It's important for Edna to be in control of her pushing, because Holly has to have an easy delivery.

"If she doesn't come through this tear-free," Holly says, "we're going to have the kind of suturing that made the lacemakers in medieval France go blind."

With a condylomata-infected perineum, the tissue shreds and falls apart as you run even the smallest needle through it, and any hope for a stretchy, tissuey perineum has to be abandoned. An episiotomy is out of the question, because, as a minor midwife's law goes, don't cut what you can't sew.

"What's Demerol going to do to the kid if she's been drinking?" Levy asks.

"Won't be the first time a depressed baby woke up in time for delivery," Holly says. She's surprised by her own callousness. Tomorrow is her last night here. It's time. She's turning into a resident.

Levy thinks for a moment. "Start her out real low. Fifteen milligrams. Give it to her in a couple of hours. Keep an eye on the strips. If you have to pull the Demerol, blame me if you want to. Tell her the mean old doctor made you do it."

"Thanks, baby," Holly says, turning toward the labor room.

"What did you just say, Treadwell?" he asks, with happy surprise.

"I said, thanks, chump."

"That's what I thought you said."

CHAPTER 31

"Wanna see midwifery grace under pressure? See how it's done?" Holly asks Levy, by way of inviting him to the delivery of condylomata-ridden Edna O'Toole. "Left-lateral position."

"I'm always up for spectating delivery gymnastics."

Holly has caught only two babies from this position: woman on her left side, right leg bent and raised off the left leg by a wedge made of a rolled-up towel or the right leg pressing against someone's hip.

Each time Holly has delivered this way, she did so over an intact perineum with less-than-average blood loss. Claims have been made that this position decreases perineal tension and, with it, the need for episiotomy and the incidence of tears.

Left-lateral also makes for a full view of the perineum. The dorsal position—the woman on her back with her legs bent—provides only partial viewing; the patient is lying on a good deal of it. Lithotomy—the feet in stirrups—gives total visualization of the perineum, but would guarantee tearing tonight. Holly needs good visualization not only to study the impact of delivery on the delicate, breakable perineum, but to trace the movement of the baby's head closely so she'll be in complete control at the moment of delivery.

Another benefit of the left-lateral Simms—as it's also called—is that the side position prevents supine hypotensive syndrome (usually precipitated by the woman lying on her back) and allows the baby to profit from optimal oxygenation. This baby needs it.

When Holly administered the promised fifteen milligrams of Demerol, the fetal baseline flattened out, meaning that the baby's nervous system, which controls the heart rate, was depressed or in some way not up to par. As the Demerol wore off, variability returned in a mild, halfhearted way. A slow heart rate means a depressed baby, and Edna's sluggish kid needs all the oxygen he can get.

Levy makes his way into the delivery room. Taking one glimpse at Edna's condition, he curses under his breath. "Holy shit."

"Pipe down," Holly says, elbowing him. "I can't take you anywhere."

Levy starts for the door, and Holly trots to catch up with him. "Where are you going, tough guy?"

"I'm calling the Stooges down in PD."

"How come?"

"If that's what's on the outside, Treadwell, I hate to think what's on the inside."

"Well, don't fret. I called them already. They're going to see left-lateral birth as well." She didn't want to do it, but she did it, going against the shy, self-reliant, private grain that most people don't see in her. "I'm doing my job as a nurse-midwife, to serve as a role model for all you physician-types. A change agent, as it were." She smiles in a saccharine way she means to be ironic, but which not everyone perceives as such. She takes Levy's arm. "Come on, my man, the Three Stooges are going to see just how easy it is to suction a baby in left-lateral."

"How's that?" he asks, tying on his mask.

"You got an occiput anterior, right? Born facedown? Well, check it out. Visualize that facedown being born to the side, and what do you have then? The baby faces out, just waiting for suction."

Holly follows Levy's brain waves as he shuts his eyes and pictures the OA baby coming out with the mother lying on her side. His eyes move behind his lids, like someone in REM sleep, and Holly knows he's getting the picture.

"Now, are you going to spectate or are you going to coach?" she asks.

"Hey, I'm a doc, not a coach. I'm going to spectate."

"You're going to coach," she says. "You have better things to do than engage in continuing education here in the DR."

"You invited me and I accepted," Levy says. "Are you going to be a charming girl or a hardassed bully?"

"Both," she says. "That's the secret to being a charming girl."

CHAPTER 32

My Three Sons are missing Chip. "He had homework to do," says one of the PDs.

"Don't lie, Robby. He has a date," says the bespectacled PD who must be Ernie.

"She's teaching him how to dance so they can both go to the junior prom and have a good time."

Levy is masked, gowned, capped, and supporting Edna O'Toole's right leg with his hip, into which her foot is pressed.

"What ho!" says the PD, as he comes in the door.

"Left-lateral Simms," the other says. "Very progressive."

"Going light on the drapes, too," says the first one.

"Drape-lite, the new lo-cal sterile field."

"Keep it down, fellas," Levy says. "There's people working here."

"Aw, Dad!"

It's true that the drapes have been kept to a minimum. One drape under Edna, another over her left leg. The first time Holly delivered in this position, she put a legging drape on the right leg, which wound up bunched around the patient's ankle.

Holly has to brief the nurse, Patsy, on how to help out Edna. She is the prototype of the well-trained, greenhorn nurse who still thinks obedience is the key to success. She hasn't learned yet that if she thinks for herself, she'll come out ahead of the game.

"We don't want her pushing real hard at the end," Holly explains, as Patsy nods every five seconds. "We want it to go real easy. Don't shout at her to push unless I tell you to. The main thing is to help her pant." Patsy nods and nods. "Don't tell her to pant and stop there. You have to pant with her. You follow me?" Nod. Nod.

Edna's rear end is close to the left edge of the delivery table, and Holly keeps a close eye on the speckled perineum. Suddenly she's nervous about her hands. Her hands might get confused in this position, since the baby's head won't be quite where she expects it to be and her hands are caught in a muscle-memory program designed to catch dorsal deliveries. She's scared she'll be disoriented and botch it in front of the PDs.

You won't botch it, Treadwell.

I will.

No, you won't.

"FAS, right?" says a PD standing behind Holly.

FAS being fetal alcohol syndrome, a syndrome with a host of symptoms, of which the baby may suffer a few or all—low weight, small head circumference, congenital heart defects . . .

"I don't think so," Holly says, putting her left hand ever so gently on the perineum to support it. She doesn't quite know if pressure on the perineum will hurt or help. What if support of the perineum causes a tear on this brittle stuff? But if she doesn't support it . . . r-r-r-rip.

Both of Holly's hands work under the right leg, which is held aloft on the siderail now, using Levy only as marginal support. Edna has her right hand, blinking with the polish of her pearlized pink fingernail polish, clamped about her thigh. She's not actually controlling her pushing this way. It's more as if she's finding her bearings.

"It's not FAS," Holly hears herself say, annoyed with the macho medical tradition of talking about one thing while doing another. She wants to concentrate. But she can handle it. She can do two things at once, three things at once. Anything they can throw at her, she can do. So says her adrenaline. "The baby's head is too big for FAS," she says. She wishes it *were* smaller, if only for ease in delivery.

"Let the lady work, Ernie," Levy says, surprising Holly with his protectiveness.

Holly told the PDs all about Edna O'Toole on the phone, but she supposes they need to be reminded. "Flattened-out baseline after Demerol," she murmurs, so Ernie can be ready for a floppy baby. "When I say go, suction."

"Lean right in?"

"Yeah, go for it."

Holly talks to Edna—"Here it comes"—and Patsy and Edna keep panting, as Holly puts the flat part of her fingertips on the head as it crowns. Her adrenaline soars as she guides the head out and puts pressure on it so that it just skims the perineum, rather than popping out with its chin extended, which would tear the fragile fabric.

"All right," she says to the PD as the baby is born with a spill of fluid. "Go!" As she delivers the shoulders, the PD, now positioned in front of Levy, dives in and suctions the baby's face. With her left hand, Holly clamps the cord, strips it, and cuts it. The baby is free. It's bluish around the edges, its mouth is loose, it gulps and coughs in a faint way, then rasps out a gasp. *Arrrgh.* Not good. It's a girl. Her skin is loose, her limbs are long and stalklike, and she must weigh about five pounds. She's not in good shape.

"Give me," says the PD, arms stretched out.

"She's yours," Holly says.

Holly has priorities. She looks down at the perineum and finds it unscathed. . . . That's what matters.

You're a cold bitch, Treadwell.

I'm getting that way.

Your priorities are fucked up.

I know.

But you can't care about everything, all the time.

I know.

Edna's eyes track her baby and the baby disappears with the PDs. A transport unit is standing by, but it's a waste of time. It's quicker for the PD to trot down the stairs with the baby, bundled up in its receiving blanket and cap. Tracking a baby: that's an instinct. Even Edna O'Toole is entitled to maternal instincts. That's the beauty of it.

"A girl. Wow." Edna is now lying on her back, looking out the vacant doorway into the empty hall. "Welcome to the goddamn world."

Holly is trying to sew up a tiny tear that occurred as the baby's right shoulder was delivered. Just slightly scathed, that's all. It's an internal tear, distinct from these lumpy condylomata warts. Warts that look like sea parasites that have found a host, homeless, roving organisms set down. On Edna O'Toole. Spores landing on a spore.

Edna pulls a hand through her wavy red hair. "That's over, huh?" She bites her lip. Then she brightens up. "Now it's over. Hey!"

"Holly's my name," she calls up from her suture work. "Midwifery's my game."

"Yeah. Right." Edna tilts her head to squint at Holly. Holly guesses she's nearsighted. "So. Hey. Umm. The baby. Was that baby colored or was it white? They all start out pretty white, huh?"

"Yeah. They do."

"So this baby, wasn't it a colored baby?"

"Well, she had pretty dark hair." Holly knows a black baby—or a mixed-race baby—when she sees one. "Is the father black, Edna?"

"I'm not sure. That's why I'm asking."

"Well, if the other possible father is white, I'd say that this baby's father is black."

"Okay," Edna says, hitting her head back. "I'm dealing wit' it." Long pause. "What about those clowns who took the baby? They okay, or what?"

"They're okay. They're good docs. I wouldn't go out with one, but medically they're okay."

The way the PDs took off with the baby reminds Holly of the gypsies her Irish great-grandmother used to tell her about. "They come sneakin' and crawlin' in the dead o' night, masks and scarves all about their faces, lookin' this way and that, and when nobody is watchin', they snatch the pretty babies, and the little pretty Irish babies, they grow up as gypsies, too, and come back home to steal another 'un."

"Well, she got dealt a shitty hand," says Edna O'Toole.

"Who's that?"

"The baby."

Holly doesn't know how to answer this, particularly as it appears to be true. "Not necessarily so."

"Sure." Edna stares at the light over her head. "I'm callin' her Tiffany. Maybe she'll grow up to be rich." Her face goes hard, her eyes go dead, and then she says, "What else do you give me now? You give me some Demerol now?"

CHAPTER 33

In the corridor, the Honduran girl, the mother of a plump, thick-legged, nine-pound boy, lies on a cart. Her time is almost up. Soon she'll head down to Postpartum. Her baby sleeps soundly in the Isolette below her cart. And tapping at the crib's Plexiglas window is the neighbor, the suspect CI victim. He's not in a wheelchair, his color has returned, and he is cooing to the baby.

"Sir, you're up and about!" Holly says.

He stands up, claps his hands, shrugs. "I didn't pass on tonight! I don't know why!"

"And you didn't go home either. You bring your neighbor in, you think you might have a heart attack, and now, five hours later, you're singing to the baby."

"Meant to be! Wasn't my time!" He opens his arms up to fate. "Destiny!"

The young Honduran mother smiles her big moonbeam smile. Lying on her side, tapping lightly on the Plexiglas, she points at the baby. "American," she says. "American."

"Named after me," the man says, smiling.

The maternity ward, people say, is a happy place. Everyone smiles. Everyone sings.

"American!"

CHAPTER 34

att has gotten away from work early, so he can eat dinner with Holly before she leaves for work at seven-thirty. She's making dinner. How do you cook dinner in a hurry? You're supposed to cook breakfast in a hurry, not dinner.

"You know, Holly, it's an accepted principle in this city that a two-career couple is more interested in saving time than money," Matt says, knocking back a beer and unloosening his tie. To Holly, he looks like he's in rehearsal for a beer commercial. This Bud's for you at Miller time. "The restaurant business is booming in this town for good reason. It's ridiculous for you to spend so much time and effort cooking dinner."

"I'm tired of restaurant food," Holly says, bending to baste the chicken. "Portions controlled just as they want to control it, food cooked just as they want to cook it, and brought to you just when they want to bring it to you. I get tired of just sitting there waiting. I'd as soon get up and fix it myself."

"I thought the first law of midwives is, never refuse help."

"The first law is, if the baby's stuck, change position."

"Ah, nothing like a little birth metaphor as dinner appetizer."

"Besides, I'd hardly call us a two-career couple. It's not as though we pool our income. And my twenty-eight thousand a year doesn't exactly buy the high life in this city."

"No, we don't pool our income," Matt says thoughtfully.

He sits down at the kitchen table and slips off his shoes. He looks very handsome there, and it doesn't make sense to Holly that he'd still want to stay with her. She's always tired. She's always running late. She's not home nights—at least, one of every three months, she's not. Her nerves are ready to snap.

She leans her forehead against the cool refrigerator door, and the only thing she feels is her hair, oily against the side of her face. She's almost thirty, and yet she still wears her hair as she did in the ninth grade. Her hair has become an obsession. She's serious, she's strong-minded, she's deep feeling, she's obsessed by the state of her hair.

Without even knowing it, she is starting to cry.

Matt stands up and moves behind her, arms around her waist.

"Nerves," she says.

"Nerves," he says, putting his chin on the top of her head.

She turns around. "Do you like my hair?"

"I love your hair." He studies her. "I do love your hair," he decides. "You know what? You're taking your job all wrong."

"How's that?"

"You should view your job the way I view my job."

"A pain in the ass that sucks out your life's blood?"

"For sure. And that it's not going to last forever. See this as a kind of residency. You got out of midwifery school, you needed some hard-core experience, so you work a few years at Morrison and leave with a hundred years of midwifery under your belt."

"It's not even midwifery," Holly says glumly, letting out a cloud of steam as she checks the broccoli. "It's obstetrics."

"All to the better. You have a lot of obstetrics under your belt and still have a lot to learn about midwifery. You don't want to know it all at the age of twenty-eight."

"Do you see your job as a residency?"

"Absolutely! Do my time. Pay my dues. Earn my wings. Then find someplace a little more congenial—but nobody can say I went into some twerpy little firm because I couldn't hack it in the big time. Sure, I want to get out of there. It's no fun representing a multinational conglomerate that'd be represented just as well by some other jerk attorney."

"But it's different for you, Matt. You're replaceable."

"And you're not dispensable? People will have babies without you. How do you know that the midwife who takes your place won't be just as good as you?"

Holly is stung. "Don't say that!"

"All right—almost as good as you?"

"You talk as if I'm definitely going."

"I'm posing alternatives, Holly. You're not as trapped as you make yourself out to be. You're a free agent. You can get out any time you want. You're not beholden to that place, Holly. Better midwives than you have taken off."

Holly chops up some green peppers and glances at the kitchen clock: six-fifty. She frowns. "You don't have to be mean about it. Going on about these midwives superior to me."

"I'm not being mean about it," Matt says, lifting his beer in salute. "I'm offering you your freedom."

CHAPTER 35

Bundled up in her toggle coat and boots and jeans, Holly gets off at Six before heading up to Seven-B. She wants to see Edna and reinforce what the CNM who saw her in the morning must have tried to convey. That the condylomata might affect the baby later on; when she's two years old or so, she might develop bronchial or laryngeal condyloma. Edna will have to take the baby for regular checkups, and if warts are found then, have them surgically removed with laser surgery. Holly has to drill this information into Edna now, because she's the kind of lady who'll disappear as soon as she steps out the hospital door.

Edna is sitting up in bed, reading the *New York Post*. The Honduran woman, mother of the first American, is asleep in the bed next to her, snoring heavily, with Spanish-edition pamphlets on baby-care and contraception scattered in the hollow made by her flexed legs.

"She's like a bull," is the first thing Edna says, jerking her head in her direction.

"Maybe."

Edna has her makeup on now, but she still looks green and sick. She's spiking a slight fever, and as if to prove just how susceptible her immune system is, both her hemoglobin and white blood cells are at levels too low to permit medically approved discharge for at least a week. She's wearing a turquoise nightgown that accentuates her pallor, and she looks like she's been lit up on the inside by an aqua-colored lightbulb.

"This the way you look normally?" Edna asks, assessing Holly.

"Some of the time."

"The schoolgirl look. Men like it. Some of 'em." She shrugs. Not impressed.

After Holly has reiterated to Edna what the midwife explained that morning, Edna puts down her newspaper and says, "I was gonna give that kid up if it was white. I figured, it's white, it'll be adopted. That's what you hear, anyway. They always say white babies get adopted."

"Other babies get adopted, too. It's the older kids who have the hardest time. But the babies don't have such a hard time of it. And Tiffany is mighty cute."

"Well. Yeah." Edna looks up and says suspiciously, "They said she had respiratory distress."

"Her lungs weren't working so well at the start, but she's off the ventilator now."

Edna shrugs. "I guess they know all about it." She smiles. "They took my picture today. They tell ya?"

"No. Who did?"

"Them. The doctors or whatever. Took me down to an office and took a picture of my pussy. I guess it's gonna hang in the hall of fame." She looks slyly at Holly. "What would you have done, if they'd asked you? Forget I asked. I know what you would do." Edna laughs through her sharp, small nose, with its broken blood vessels crawling all around the sides. "I asked them for money, but they said the picture was for research. Yeah. Right. Like they don't pay for research." She picks up the newspaper. "Can't even get a goddamn cigarette," she says, speaking into the front page. "How can I think about these things if I can't get a goddamn cigarette?" She throws the paper down. "I don't know what you put down on my prescription, honey, but you tell them that Tylenol with codeine just ain't the same as Percodan. You tell them Percodan. You know, I got these big decisions to make, and I can't even smoke a goddamn cigarette!"

Holly and Edna are sitting in the nurse-midwifery office on Seven, outside the labor and delivery ward, near the darkened rooms of the antepartum ward, which is filled with hypertensives and bed-resting placenta previas and hydrated hyperemisis gravidarum cases.

"Milk comes out anyway," Edna says, opening her cobalt blue robe and checking the front of her nightgown. "Stuff they give you don't even work. Disgusting."

"It's the way of the world. Been like that for thousands of years."

"People been shitting for thousands of years, too. Doesn't make it nice." Edna wraps the robe around her, hunches in her seat, and inhales a True Blue. "Bless your heart. Where's an ashtray?"

Holly passes her an empty mason jar with the label TREADWELL'S FRESH AIR FUND. "The girls gave it to me because I was always bitching that there's no fresh air in this place. They said they'd chip in and buy me some, but all I got was that jar full of fresh air."

"Ain't fresh anymore," Edna says, tapping a long ash into it.

"You have sixty days to decide, Edna."

"Decide what?"

"Whether or not you want to keep your baby."

"I know that. The social worker's been to see me."

"You can take your baby home and see how it goes."

Edna laughs. "Oh, I know how it'll go. It'll go the way my pussy goes. The way the whole rest of it goes. It'll go fucked up." She shakes her head. "I can't believe I went and had a little colored girl!" She snorts.

"Maybe you could call her black, now that she's your little girl."

"Naw." Edna shakes her head fast and hard. "She's colored. I'm in her someplace, and she's not black all the way through. Nope." She stubs her cigarette out in the mason jar. "Here, honey. Here's your fresh air."

CHAPTER 36

This is Holly's last night on the floor, and she's glad of it. Four days off, and then she starts at Clinic.

"Good luck, honeybunch," says Levy. "You've got whale meat."

"What are you talking about?"

"Whale fat." Levy smirks. "Blubber."

"What he's trying to tell you," Sparks says, "is that you have an obesity on your caseload."

An obesity. In other words, a profanity.

The hospital staff is prejudiced against fat people. Sparks herself is fat, but Holly guesses she considers herself an exception.

Holly is helping her patient onto a bedpan when Gus the Butcher bursts in, blood on his white coat.

"Whoa, mama!" he cries. "Wrong bedpan!"

And he flies out again.

Holly's patient has yanked her gown down with reflexive modesty. It's hard to remember that modesty is a right, like any other right.

Gus finds the patient he's looking for and tries to insert an internal monitor. His patient squirms.

"Steady yourself, for God's sake!" he says. "Settle down!"

The patient is wincing, but the wince has nothing to do with pain and everything to do with modesty.

"Come on, you little sucker," Gus mutters as he works the spiral onto the head of the not-yet-born baby.

Gus is cursing now, and Holly wonders why. She figures he's dehumanizing his patient, diminishing the body as an aesthetic or sexual experience, working the body out of personhood and reconstructing it as a thing, a problem, machinery, as something less than the sum of its parts. He works the fetal monitor up his patient's vagina, through her dilated

288

cervix, onto the baby's scalp. He's putting his hand into the part of a woman that is most charged with meaning, trespassing into the territory considered most sacred and most profane. That's his business. That's what he does. He puts his hand in the place invested with more emotional significance than any other place. And the only way he can do this is by shedding that place of mystery and mystique and taking the soul out of nakedness. To do what he does, he disassociates the vagina from the body, the body from the woman, and the woman from the context in which she lives: her life. He curses. His patient is not yet wired.

"You're connected," he tells her. "You're wired for sound. You're beeping. You're blipping. You're bleeping. You're bleating."

Holly chases him into the hall. It's her last night, and she'll bug one more resident so he doesn't forget what a pain in the ass she is.

Gus is still wearing his gloves, which are slightly moist from amniotic fluid.

"Can I talk to you one second?" Holly asks.

"What's the deal, banana peel?" he says, wiping his hands on the legs of his scrubs. Then he runs his hand through his hair. He's taken off his gloves by now, but for a moment Holly hadn't realized this and her stomach lunged in disgust.

"I wanted to remind you that some of these ladies have a strong sense of modesty and privacy. It's good to be a little delicate with them when you can."

Gus throws back his head and laughs. "Thanks for the tip."

"I know it doesn't sound important, but—"

"Oh, no. No! No! It's rich! It's important! You're chock-full of helpful hints. Thank you, Miss Midwife, thank you!"

He bows, then heads down the hall, his hands shaking at his sides as if he's making a very emphatic statement.

When Holly returns to the labor room, Gus's patient asks her, "Miss, was that my doctor?"

"Yup."

The woman nods. "All right," she says. She nods again. She takes it all in. She is preparing herself. That's my doctor. Now she knows the worst.

Holly doesn't feel so good. She'd like to take a shower now, and lie down, and shut her eyes.

CHAPTER 37

Holly is ready to go home, and she stands in front of Edna O'Toole's room in her toggle coat. It's dark, and its only occupants are the Honduran girl and a sleeping black woman.

"Where's O'Toole?" she asks a passing nurse.

"Gone," she says, staring blankly at Holly.

"Gone? What do you mean, gone?"

The nurse looks at her wearily. "Gone, as in she pulled on her shoes and coat and walked out."

"She just walked out?"

"What's wrong with you? Haven't you ever heard of a walk-out?"

The walk-in walks.

"What about her baby?"

"What about her?" the nurse says. "The baby's in the NICU. The baby can't walk."

Holly scuffles downstairs to the NICU and bursts in, into the world of the tinies. Exposed little creatures. Wired-up and mute.

"Hey, you! Put on a gown!" A nurse grabs her by the hood of her coat. "For heaven's sakes, girl, what's got into you?"

Gowned up, Holly stands before the O'Toole baby, female, who is lying under a bank of bilirubin lights, purple like the lights used to cultivate African violets. Her skin is browning. She's asleep, a mask over her eyes, and bundled up tight. She's warm; she's two days old. O'Toole, female.

"Didn't the mother name this child?" Holly asks.

The nurse waves her hand. "That child doesn't have a name!" Tiffany O'Toole is no more, if Tiffany O'Toole ever was. Holly crumples up her paper gown and heads for home.

CHAPTER 38

"They're letting you out!" Holly says as she steps onto the elevator going down.

"What kind of getup is this?" Levy says. "How come you don't have those little leads for your mittens so you don't lose 'em? How come you're not wearing red rubber galoshes?"

"Well, where do you think you're going? Skeet shooting?"

Levy is prepped out in brown corduroys, Timberland boots, a navy blue down jacket, and a Cambridge scarf.

"I guess not everybody can get into Harvard," says Levy, who did.

"I guess that's something to be grateful for," says Holly, who didn't.

The door opens onto the lobby. "How come you're leaving so early?" Holly asks.

"Celia wants to take off early, so we're switching. And I thought, what the hell, I'll take off early and chase Treadwell's tail into Manhattan."

Holly looks around to see if any big-eared, big-eyed nurses are about, listening in on their banter. A come-on from Levy in scrubs is something different from a come-on from Levy in his Ivy League casuals. A come-on from Levy in his civvies can't be interpreted strictly as a tension-breaker. Can't be interpreted as anything but a come-on.

They push silently through the nonfunctioning automatic doors into the blinding light of morning.

"I never saw you in daylight before, Treadwell."

"I try to limit my appearances to the flattering fluorescent lights of Seven-B."

"I've noticed that attractive green pallor those lights give you. Everyone comments on it. 'That white girl sure is green,' they say."

"We're off duty, Levy. We don't have to bust each other's chops anymore." Holly feels a sadness about O'Toole in the pit of her stomach.

291

It makes her bones feel tired. She looks up and down the street for a skinny lady with red hair.

She starts toward the subway, squinting against the light and bending over slightly as she faces the wind. The morning shift is trudging onto the hospital grounds, picking their way around the potholes in the sidewalk. Every person seems to take the potholes as an inconvenience that afflicts them in particular.

"Hang on!" Levy shouts. "I'll give you a lift."

"You got a car, Levy?"

"No, a troika pulled by three midwives. Come on!"

"We're here," Levy says.

"I don't live here, Levy," Holly says, looking out the window.

"I do." He glances at Holly. "For a drink. For a minute. Come on—it's your last day. I won't see you for a whole month."

"That ought to please you."

"Follow me, Treadwell."

"You live here?"

"Sometimes. But mainly I sleep here."

Five flights up, a one-bedroom railway flat, that New York City housing curiosity in which an apartment has no hallways. To save space and cram as many people as possible within the confines of one apartment, the rooms are joined together, opening into each other, strung along like a railway car. Once you step into the front door, you're in the kitchen, then the parlor, then the bedroom. The bedroom faces the courtyard behind the buildings, where branches snake around the windows. It makes the room green, and Holly likes it.

"I wouldn't object if you took off your coat, Holly."

"I'll keep it on, thanks."

"Want a drink? Some cocaine?"

Holly turns. "Is that why you're so wired at work?"

"I didn't say I did it on the job."

"Do you?"

"I made an offer. You can say no if you want to."

"No."

Holly takes in the bareness of his room. There's a boxspring mattress with the sheets in a jumble, and cardboard boxes filled with kitchen equipment, records, books, and clothes. A wrapped box of clean clothes from the laundry stands by the radiator.

"How long have you lived here?"

"Two years," Levy says, pouring a glass of vodka.

"I guess you're not in any hurry to settle in."

"Baby, when I come home, I walk from the door to that bed and don't look back. This is the place where I flop. I live at Morrison. Then I wake up, hit the shower, and walk back out the door. That's as settled as it gets. Now drink this and at least take off that foolish-looking scarf."

The vodka explodes inside her, sending warm currents to her brain, to her limbs, to her spinal cord, where it seems to run up and down her back. A drink has never felt so good. Then again, she doesn't remember ever drinking this early in the morning before.

She unwinds her scarf and unbuttons her coat. She drops down on the bed, only half-conscious of inviting him to join her. The other half of her unconsciousness feels how heavy her legs are, how tired her feet.

Levy stands in the doorway between the bare parlor and the bedroom. "You look better in jeans than you do in scrubs," he says finally.

"I like you all right in scrubs."

He steps forward. "I like you all right in scrubs, too." He sits down by her side.

"No," she says.

"Don't tease, Treadwell."

Holly's will pulls her down, to lie down on the bed, to lie next to him, but she stands up anyway, walks across the room, and shimmies against the wall until she lands on the floor.

"Clandestine sex isn't my style," she says.

"Well, my thing is clandestine sleep." He stands up, pulls down the shades, lies back on the bed, unlaces his big boots, and throws them across the room, where they land with a thud. He shuts his eyes.

"Levy?"

"What, Treadwell?"

"I want to know why you went into OB, of all things."

"I like the ladies. What do you think?"

"Do you really?"

Levy puts his hands under his head and opens his eyes. Holly lies down on the rug by the boxspring mattress and looks up. "I always wanted to be a doctor. Not just the big bucks," he says. "I wanted to be a doctor when I was a little kid, before it even occurred to me to go after the bucks. I wanted people to call me Dr. Levy, and I wanted to have a black bag, and I wanted to be like those guys on TV."

"But why OB?"

Levy shuts his eyes. "I don't like death. I don't like working with it. I don't like seeing it. I don't like smelling it. I never felt that as a physician, I could stop it. Death. Some guys, they think they can stop it, but I never felt like that. I always felt like that little kid in the story, who put his finger in the dam—"

"In the dike," Holly corrects.

"In the dike and holds it back that way. Sooner or later, it's going to give. You can't hold it back."

"But, Levy, even in OB some of your patients are going to die. Ovarian cancer, metastasized cervical cancer."

"But most won't," he says in a rough voice.

"Well, how come you didn't go into plastic surgery or dermatology—some field where the patients really almost never die?"

Levy snorts and turns on his side to face her. "I'm not saying I have a pathological fear of death, Treadwell. I just don't like to be knee-deep in the shit. All right? I'm not a frivolous coward-slime, no matter what you think."

Holly lies on her back, shutting her eyes. She listens to a branch scrape against the window in the breeze. She likes the sound and listens for it again.

"Why'd you bother becoming a midwife, Treadwell? A girl from a nice family. You could have done anything else."

"Because I thought I could do it better than the docs," she says, her eyes closed. "Because I get a rush from that moment when the baby passes from one part of life to the next."

"That's a pretty short moment in time, Treadwell. You live your life for that?"

"That's why I keep coming back. I always want more. I never get enough."

"Neither do I."

Levy swings up from the mattress and brings the bottle of vodka to the bed. He takes a swig and passes it down to Holly.

Holly says, "I always wanted to know, Levy. How does it feel to touch a woman, making love, after you spend your whole night touching women?"

"I don't touch women at work," he says. "I touch patients."

"Aw, Levy, that's not right."

After a pause, Levy says, "Come on up here, Treadwell."

"I don't want to, Levy."

"You can sleep with your head down where my feet are."

"That doesn't sound like a very seductive proposal."

"Yeah, but I have to put up with your feet as part of the bargain."

"It's comfortable down here," Holly says from the rug.

"It's nice to sleep during the day when it's cold out," Levy says sleepily. "Outside, everyone's cold and miserable, but here it's soft and warm. . . ."

"Aw, hell," Holly says, staggering up. Still wearing her coat, she lies down next to him and looks into his warm brown eyes. "Levy, you're like a brother to me."

He shuts his eyes. "Treadwell, that's not a very nice thing to say, even if you meant well."

In a minute, they are both fast asleep.

Early evening, and it's rained during the day. Holly trudges home, sidestepping puddles, weaving around people coming home from work.

Levy had left for the hospital by the time Holly awoke, disoriented and sweaty in her heavy coat. She found her scarf folded up beside her with a note that read, "You can darken my door anytime, anywhere. Dr. Levy. P.S. I stole a kiss."

Holly wonders if he did. She can't say she'd mind if he did.

HOWARD STREET CLINIC

CHAPTER 1

The Howard Street midwives stumble into the supply room as soon as they come in to work. They don't even glance at the stacks of folders Marge has set on their desks. Nobody goes home until her folders are done, until she's seen all the patients who are reduced to charts and forms and piled on the desk. In the supply room, they warm up their hands and brains drinking coffee and smoking. They sit on high metal stools in white coats and smoke the cigarettes they otherwise never, ever smoke.

Holly is glad to be with the other midwives. One of the toughest things about working nights is that the midwife on duty works alone, while on days, there are two midwives on duty at Morrison. Denise and Crowley are serviceable companions, but their camaraderie is limited. When Holly comes back to Howard Street, she realizes what she's been feeling over at Morrison is loneliness.

Mrs. Gruener designed the rotation schedule with burnout in mind. Just when a midwife—like Holly—thinks she can't take it anymore at Morrison, she's bumped down to the busy yet secure confines of the clinic for belly checks, contraception consults, and the other midwives' bad jokes. To be back with the young women who are not yet in labor, patients who are not in pain. And when a midwife gets bored processing patients through the clinic mill, she's bumped over to Morrison to catch babies and wrangle with the residents.

"We're cracked to smoke," says Paula as Holly walks into the supply room. She examines her cigarette. "Ya know why we do it? Because we never see sick people. We see pregnant girls, and we figure, well, we can smoke because we're not pregnant. That's why we smoke."

"You smoke because you're a weak-willed and mean-tempered old midwife," Holly says, by way of hello.

"I know. The girls faint when they see me over at Morrison. 'Holy shit, Mrs. Kwiatkowski, you're gonna deliver me?'"

Paula is the mother-in-residence at Howard Street. She plays this role for everybody—the docs, the midwives, the patients, Mrs. Gruener. She is as stubby as a sawed-off shotgun, with a pouchy face and pudgy features, orangeish makeup and penciled-in eyebrows, a raspy voice and bleached-blonde hair in a bouffant that has never been allowed to deflate.

"I smoke in the morning to get a buzz on," Pam says. She's Holly's age and has a big-boned but sweet face, and flaming red hair. Holly has never seen anyone as freckled as Pam. Freckles on her eyelids and ears and covering her forehead so thickly that her forehead is almost brown, although the skin where the freckles aren't is chalk white. It's easy to imagine her picking potatoes in the fields of County Clare. "There, I said it. I get high from a cigarette this time of morning. Now, excuse me, but I gotta go out there and tell the kids to keep away from all them nasty drugs."

Holly's heart sinks when she sees Barbara in the corner. Holly doesn't like Barbara. Holly has noticed that wherever she works, there's always one person she really doesn't like. She's not sure if this is her personal failure or if those are life's odds: ten nice people to one pain in the ass.

Barbara is pedantic, humorless, and literal minded. She's no fun. She never smokes, not even for the ritual morning cigarette, which would be an understandable lapse on anybody else's part, but is completely inexcusable in Barbara.

Barbara's the kind of woman who gloats when another midwife misses a diagnosis. She hoards gonorrhea culture swabs in a locked box in a locked drawer of her desk so that when another midwife runs out and asks her for a loan, she claims not to have any. Barbara doesn't smile easily when she talks with a patient, and these patients need a lot of smiling. She's stingy with expressions and affection, and doles out both in wooden little parcels. Barbara has a fine-boned face, with the skin pulled tight across those fine bones, flat, expressionless eyes, and thin lips.

"She doesn't have any sex appeal," Paula once complained.

"What do we care about that?" Pam said, studying Paula, who does not fit into the boy-toy category herself.

"She has no sense of fun," Holly had answered. "That's what Paula means."

"Heard you broke protocol," Barbara says now, looking up from a bunch of lab slips. "Your procedure functions didn't pass."

"Really? That's what you heard?" Holly turns to Paula. "Did you hear that, Paula?"

"I heard you got ants in your pants and wanted to dance," Paula says with a shrug. She seems to shrug with her whole body—torso, shoulders, forehead, eyes. "Other than that, I didn't hear nothing. How about you, Pam?"

"I heard Levy cornered you and chased you around the hospital and you bailed out into the ABC to escape, taking a primap with you for protection."

"That's what happened," Holly says. "You heard it right."

The midwives tap their ashes into medicine cups with milliliter markings on their sides, cups that are normally used for urine specimens but are now filled with water.

Pam turns to Holly with her broad face and demands, "Easiest birth of the month. Name it."

"Isn't easy birth a contradiction in terms," Holly says, "like army intelligence?"

"Holly, please!" Pam says, tossing her cigarette in the medicine cup, where it sizzles out. "We're midwives. We take a positive view toward childbirth, and don't forget it."

"I forgot," Holly says. "I've been down at Morrison. Maybe you noticed."

"Easiest birth of the month," Pam demands again.

"Mrs. Ortega."

"The one with the crimson red stretch pants?"

"The same. Had her baby in the bathroom of her apartment. Nobody did a thing. Her husband cut the cord with a—"

"With a machete," Paula finishes for her.

"Is that an ethnic slur?" Holly asks.

"Naw, that's what they use. Machetes."

"Paula, that's what they use in the jungles of *Nicaragua*," Pam explains. "New Yoricans like the Ortegas don't use machetes."

"Maybe they used a Vegematic." Paula shrugs. She turns to Holly. "Some people save their machetes. My father saved his saber from the Polish cavalry—"

"Come on, kids," Pam says, pulling on her white jacket. "It's showtime. Our first number, for those who break protocol, is a Jackson Five number."

"Ethnic slur!" says Paula. "That wasn't an ethnic slur?"

"ABC," Pam says. "Remember that old song, Holly?"

CHAPTER 2

The examining room is what Holly thinks of as her office, but it isn't hers and it isn't precisely an office. Holly uses this place only six months out of the year. To the left is an exam table with a curtain around it. To the right is her desk. The phone numbers written on the wall over the phone aren't at all familiar. She called one of them once and got the Off-Track Betting results line. What midwife plays the horses?

To put her own mark on the office that nobody owns, Holly tacks up a picture of Matt on the bulletin board over the desk. There he is: on a beach, in a black sweater, his cheeks red, his eyes bright, and his hair whipped back. Tiny Matt, flanked by the numbers (written in bright red ink) for the blood labs, the OBs and Morrison Seven-B, from which Holly has just, in the nick of time, escaped.

Next to the desk is a mound of dusty diaphragms. Holly wonders if it would be a better tactic to hide these rubber domes. She doesn't have many candidates for a diaphragm anyway. The only women she ever bothers pitching it to are women who are married or living with a man, women who are mentally adjusted to the idea that they'll have frequent sex without being coerced into it, and women who are comfortable with their own bodies. Such women compose only about a tenth of the Howard Street practice.

The rest seem to be women who never know when or if sex is going to happen and are so shy with their own bodies that they've never even used tampons. "I don't like sticking anything up there!" In any case, those sooty diaphragms aren't anything you'd want up there, that's for sure. The Howard Street crowd goes in for the Lippes loop, birth control pills, and "surprise conception."

On the wall is a chart of sexually transmitted diseases and a big poster of a pregnant woman smoking a cigarette as her baby coughs in the womb. Subtlety is lost on most of Holly's patients. In your message, you go for the jugular, the concrete, and stay away from the mood-message posters, the ones that show a young woman staring into a sunset, her hands clasped on the mild slope of her belly, and have a caption reading, "Plan for the future." That's no kind of poster! A baby choking in the womb—now that's a poster!

CHAPTER 3

Cleopatra Pitts is twenty-eight weeks gestation. She's had a peculiar history. Except with very obese patients, Holly and the other midwives can pick up fetal heartsounds with a Doppler at about fourteen weeks. But by Cleo's twentieth week, nobody could hear a thing, even though a simple fetoscope ought to have been able to pick it up. Cleo hadn't felt the baby move either, and quickening, when a mother first feels her baby stir, usually takes place at twenty weeks.

Just before Holly was to go on Morrison duty, she saw Cleo in her twenty-second week. "Maybe we'll hear the baby today," she said, "but don't get your hopes up." The Doppler brought nothing but scratches and rumbling, and Holly asked Paula to help. "She has better ears than me," Holly had said to Cleo.

"Even if I am an old bat," Paula said.

But even Paula couldn't pick it up, with her old bat's ultrasound ESP.

"I can't even palpate the uterus really, and she's skinny," Holly said, consulting with Paula later.

Paula squinted in a way that reminded Holly of Popeye. "Size/dates discrepancy is what you got there."

"I wish. She came in for a pregnancy test a week after she missed her period. If anything, her LMP is earlier than she said, not later."

"Hmmmph." Paula's face curled and collapsed in thought. "Silent uterus. That's what you got there."

"It's pretty quiet," Holly agreed, meaning that the fetus was most likely dead. "We did another HCG test last week, but she has pretty high levels."

HCG is produced by the blastocyst—the microscopic ball of cells that will develop into the embryo. It takes a little longer than a week

302

following fertilization for HCG to appear as more than a trace in the blood: HCG production doesn't start in earnest until the blastocyst implants itself in the uterine wall, which takes about that long. Two weeks after conception, the quantity of HCG is pumped up high enough to be excreted in the urine and can be picked up by urine tests. But HCG found in the urine doesn't prove that a pregnancy is still intact; it can linger in the system following a miscarriage.

Paula shrugged. "She might have miscarried the day before, and the levels were still high."

"Paula, what do you think of an ectopic pregnancy?"

A pregnancy with the fetus implanted in some other part of the body—the fallopian tubes, the ovaries—would still, in the first trimester, enlarge the uterus so that it could be palpably discerned as pregnant, thanks to the hormones set off by the blastocyst.

"Naw." Paula waved a thick hand at Holly. "She got abdominal pain? She got pain during pelvics? She got diarrhea? She got slight bleeding? She ever had an IUD? No, no, no! She doesn't have anything like that. Don't talk to me of ectopic pregnancy. She got high HCG—forget it, baby doll, an ectopic isn't going to have a high HCG. She's pregnant in every way but the fact that the fetus is nowhere in sight. That happens. A silent uterus, yeah, but maybe not forever. You'd be surprised. Make an appointment for sono next week. Let them play hide-and-go-seek with the embryo. The more I think about this, the more I get the feeling it's just size/dates. She's a skinny kid, and she's woozy and nauseous, and she's eating maybe one piece of dry toast a day. Maybe she's scared her mother will find out she's pregnant and hasn't touched a bite for four months. How much has she gained so far?"

"Six or seven pounds."

"Measly little shrimp. You tell her to spend the whole week doing nothing but eating. Go ahead—scare the daylights out of her. Tell her the baby's hungry. Tell her you can hear him crying." Paula leaned forward with a wicked grin.

"Paula, I can't do that. If it's a miscarriage, she'll think she killed it. You yourself said the uterus was pretty silent."

"I got a hunch I was wrong. The more I think about it, I bet you two McDonald's gift certificates that you hear the baby beating next week."

"I don't eat at McDonald's."

"So frigging self-righteous. As the kids today say, get outta my face."

Having made a sono appointment for the following week, Holly told Cleo to stop in for a visit with Paula first. "I'm going to have a picture of my baby?" Cleo said, her face lighting up.

"Oh, you young people," Holly sighed. "All you want to do is get a picture of your baby.

"I just want to know he's in there!"

So does every other Howard Street patient. Even when they're thirty-six weeks and their babies are leaving bruises on their skin from kicking so hard, they want to see their babies, to make sure everything's all right, to get some visible, tangible proof of their existence and well-being. The number-one question at about the sixteenth week is, "When am I getting a picture of my baby?"

Holly has to disappoint the majority of them. The Howard Street midwives don't routinely order sonograms, their policy being that technological intervention is justified only when indicated and that the financial cost and health risks of each intervention have to be outweighed by the benefits.

One problem with ultrasound and sonograms is that they can give a midwife a false sense of confidence, as she relies too much on the sonographer's abilities, which may or may not be up to par, on the fitness of the machine itself (there are no set standards for how long the machines may be in service before becoming inaccurate), and on the sonographer's interpretation of what he sees. It's like a weatherman flying through some clouds. He has to be able to say what those clouds mean and which clouds to look for—otherwise he just returns to ground with a report that there are clouds in the sky.

In the early stages of pregnancy, a sonogram doesn't do much good unless there's a specific question it's been asked. In Cleo's case, the questions are: is the fetus lodged in the uterus and not elsewhere, are there any gross abnormalities (which is the only kind of abnormality the sono would be able to pick up now—or later), are there any fetal movements?

Before Cleo was to go to her sono appointment, she arrived at Paula's office. She stepped on the scale, three pounds heavier than she had been, and Paula picked up the FHT with a fetoscope. "I felt it," Cleo said shyly. "Like a little feather inside."

"They say black people got rhythm, but I don't know. You don't gain weight, and now you gain three pounds," Paula said.

Cleo giggled.

"I'll make a diagnosis," Paula said. "You don't feel like eating a thing. But now you got to plump up. Fatten up. Drink milkshakes. How's that for modern medicine? Are you on WIC yet?" Women, Infant, and Children nutritional supplements.

"I just got on," said Cleo.

"Good. Now you got no excuse. Milkshakes. Cheese sandwiches. Tuna fish. I'm going to chase you down the street with an egg cream. I'm Catholic, but I'm a Jewish mother, an honorary Jewish mother." She pinched Cleo's cheek. "Eat, bubulah, eat!"

Now Cleo, after her three-pound jump, has gained only three more pounds. Her fundal height—the length of the uterus from its top to the symphisis pubis—is only twenty-five centimeters. The rule of thumb is that the fundal height should be equal to the number of weeks gestation. At thirty weeks, Cleo is still shrimping out.

Cleo would have to take in three thousand calories a day to meet the dietary requirements for her own body and that of her baby. When a teenager eats for two, consumption can become a full-time job. The two she's eating for both happen still to be growing. If Cleo is a picky eater, she could be eating only fifteen hundred calories a day, and maybe most of them in junk food.

Holly sits her down now and starts getting bossy. "I'm writing up a dietary plan for you because your baby is hungry. He's not growing fast enough, and that's the truth. You understand?"

Cleopatra, who has beautiful, almost Oriental eyes and who could in fact be the queen of the Nile, nods solemnly.

"Now, do you know what protein is? Protein is the stuff that makes your baby grow. You have to work on getting a lot of protein. That's your job now. The most important job you'll ever have, understand? Because how you treat your baby now will affect him for the rest of his life."

Holly pauses and gets eye contact with Cleo, and Cleo nods again.

"Treat him good now, and he'll be sweet to you later on." Holly writes out a list. "You go to McDonald's?" Cleopatra nods. You have to figure that fast food holds an unconquerable position as a source of nutrition in these patients' feeding schemes. "That's all right. You can go there. But forget the french fries, the apple pie—nothing good for your baby there. Go for the chicken nuggets, the fish sandwich, the quarter-pounder with cheese, the milkshakes. You like pizza? Go for pizza, with double cheese on top. When you're at home, eat peanut butter sandwiches. Cereal is good, lots of milk on it. What's your favorite cereal?" Cleo shrugs. "You don't eat cereal, do you?"

"No, not really."

When Holly talks too fast, a sweet-tempered girl like Cleo will just let her go on to be polite and never interrupt or correct her.

"I want you to keep a list of everything you eat," Holly says. She pulls out a little spiral notebook to which she's affixed a label that says MY BABY'S NUTRITION. This gives it that official touch, plus hammers home the notion that her patients are eating for the baby, not themselves. Under the label is space for a name, and Holly very importantly writes in the name of Cleopatra Pitts, Team A. (All APs belong to Team A or Team B. They see only midwives from their team, and when they go to Morrison, if there's more than one midwife on duty, they'll be managed by the midwife from their team, whom they will already have met.) None of the other midwives have these notebooks or these labels. They come out of Holly's own pocket, and Holly must admit they work only half the time. Asking some of these young women to keep track of their food intake is not particularly effective.

Cleopatra takes the notebook carefully.

"Write it all down so we can make sure your baby is getting enough to eat. Next time I see you I want you to be five pounds heavier." Holly fixes Cleo with her eyes and tries to look stern. Then, softer, she says, "Have you had any other problems?"

"I had a cold last week," she says in a low voice. "I didn't know, does the baby catch the cold?"

"Cleo, we want to hear from you when you're not feeling well. Why didn't you call?"

"Who am I supposed to call?"

Holly grabs the nutritional diary, opens it to the last page, and scribbles her full name, followed by the word *midwife* and the clinic phone number as well as her own number. "That's my home phone. If you can't get in touch with me here, I want you to call me at home."

Continuous care. If it's good enough for well-off ladies, it's good enough for Cleopatra Pitts.

Cleo smiles slightly. "You'll remember who I am?"

"I've only known one Cleopatra in my life and that's you."

Cleo makes a foolish, pleased face and takes back the notebook.

"Are you going to eat a lot for me and Paula?"

Holly recalls what an instructor told her in midwifery school. "Compliance to the AP plan increases when you show you care."

"How do you show you care?" Holly had asked.

The instructor had answered, "By caring." The big questions are, how do you care and how much do you care when you do care?

"Who's Paula?"

"The grandma in the next room."

Cleo giggles. "Yes."

Everybody wants to please Paula.

"You got your WIC supplements? Your vitamins and iron from the pharmacy downstairs? If you don't gain weight next time, we'll have to take your bloods in the lab. If you do gain weight, no bloods." An effective threat. "Just hugs. Got it? Tuna salad."

"Okay," Cleo says delicately, and slides out the door.

Except for obese teenagers and women who become gestational diabetics, Holly has yet to see a teenager who gained too much weight over her forty weeks. As one of the army of women who gave birth in the 1950s, Holly's mother had been told by her doctor not to gain more than twenty-five pounds over the course of her pregnancy. Luckily for Holly and her brothers and sisters, her mother hadn't been able to hold to the doctor's regime. Now a principal part of Holly's profession is the fattening up of pregnant women.

During childbirth classes, Holly wishes she could forgo the discussions of fetal heart monitors and Amnihooks—much as these discussions reduce fear and confusion—and just hold serious pig-outs instead. "Pig-Outs for Teens," she'd call them. Huge tubs of salad with big chunks of tuna and chicken and cheese, standing next to tanks of buttermilk dressing and sunflower seeds. Urns of banana milkshakes, pots of peanut butter. Holly's dream: no girl would be allowed to leave until she'd scarfed down at least fifteen hundred calories.

No more low birth weight. No more babies in that limbo zone between

2500 grams and 2999 grams—not so tiny that they go into intensive care, but so small that their rate of mental retardation and neurological deficit is much higher than that of babies over 3000 grams. A severely mentally retarded baby will cost the government at least a million dollars now. And what price is the loss of a human life that could otherwise contribute to society?

Holly pokes her head out the door. "Cleopatra, eat!"

Holly slinks into Paula's office. "It makes me sad, Paula," she says, remembering Cleo's sweet face. "Four months with hardly any growth." Holly thinks of those early days of embryonic growth, when the cells geometrically increase and lay the groundwork for the human being to come. What was the lost potential—the truncated cell division and replication, the process weakened by malnutrition? Holly should have stepped in more forcefully earlier on. For all she knew, there was a fifteen percent decrease in brain cells—a whole lifetime of lost potential.

"Hey, you! I know you're into saving souls, but leave the souls to God," Paula says, punching her lightly in the arm. "So the kid won't win the Nobel Prize. Fatten him up now, and he'll still make a good obstetrician."

CHAPTER 4

"They's too much. They's too much. You, LeMoyne, sit back down here." LeMoyne is climbing up on the examining table. Tanya is crawling under the examining table. The littlest, Natasha, is in Holly's arms.

Holly looks down at Natasha and says, "She's just as cute as the day I delivered her."

"She's pretty, isn't she? She better not get into trouble. You hear me, Natasha?"

"Wait until she's a little bit older."

"That's what I'm afraid of. You, LeMoyne, get down from there!"

Didi is eighteen years old. "Now, listen, Holly, I got to do something. Birth control—it just don't work for me. I tried that loop, and it didn't work for me. All of it—it don't work. I want to get my tubes tied. I can't have any more of these crazy little babies. It's too much."

"Didi, Medicaid won't pay for a tubal ligation until you're twenty-one."

"Say what?" Didi grabs LeMoyne by the belt hooks of his pants and yanks him toward her. "That can't be. How much do it cost? They paid for all of the delivery and the midwife and all that business. Can't they pay for this?"

"The law is designed to protect you, so that nobody tries to force you into having your tubes tied when you don't know any better."

"But I know better!" Didi cries. "How can't I know better with all these crazy animals running around me? Holly, I can't have any more. I just can't. And I do not believe in abortion. No, I don't."

"Why don't we try the loop one more time? As soon as it starts to feel funny or you're not happy with it, you call me up right away. How about it?"

"Holly, I think I am pregnant now."

"You do?"

Didi nods gravely. "LeMoyne, get back here, you little motherfucker!"

Five minutes later, Holly confirms that she is.

Shit.

CHAPTER 5

Pam pokes her head into Holly's office.

"Come on out and say hello to the time-lapsed twins."

The Birth of the Time-Lapsed Twins was Pam's act of rebellion on Seven-B, a year earlier, and her equivalent to Holly's ABC Rebellion. The time-lapsed twins are as much a political feat as a natural one.

The first twin was delivered in the delivery room. After an hour's wait, when the second twin hadn't appeared, Pam moved the mother into Recovery so as not to attract the residents' attention. The mother's cervix closed, labor shut down, and she slept in Recovery until labor started up again, on its own. Then Pam moved her back into the delivery room just as Holly came on duty.

"Come in and catch a twin," Pam called to Holly when she waved from the doorway, and so Holly did.

The residents never picked up on what was going on. Only Crowley knew that Pam was delivering twins, which was against protocol—a mutinous act for which Pam had to stand trial and be dressed down by Mrs. Gruener. Now Pam and Holly are drawn together in a kind of rebels' elite. They know that Mrs. Gruener's arguments are realistic, and they are contrite, and yet... when they're together, they think of themselves as freedom fighters.

What the time-lapsed twins are to Pam is what Daisy's baby will be to Holly. Happy endings that make the fight worthwhile.

In the hallway, Pam stands with the mother and the two pocket-size twins in their double stroller. They're about a year old, but they're still small enough to ride together in one stroller. The mother is proud of their twinhood.

310

"Which one was yours?" she asks Holly, smiling.

"I would know her anywhere," Holly says. The one Holly delivered is the smaller one, with the delicate, beautiful head and the soft, mocha skin. A little princess of a baby. "This one," Holly says.

"That one," the mother says, nodding, "is the dreamer. She lies in the crib and dreams, dreams, dreams."

CHAPTER 6

Holly's mother did not expect, did not want, and did not believe that Holly would actually become a midwife. But now that Holly is one, her obstetrical secrets and questions press out, like steam escaping from a leaky pipe. The confessional mode doesn't come easily to Mrs. Treadwell, and the only way she can access this arcane mode is by being on the telephone. There, her spirit flies free. Sort of and almost. She says things on the phone that she's never said aloud before.

Tonight she calls Holly at home. Holly can picture her pulled-together mother, hair set, straight backed, busy doing something else while talking on the phone. Or sipping a drink—a finger of bourbon, two fingers of water, no rocks—or Fresca, if she's dieting, which she often is, in a thick glazed crystal glass, with ice, while talking to her oldest daughter in New York.

"Your father is utterly triumphant," she says in her husky, semilockjaw style. "He beat Gordon James at singles yesterday, and now there's no stopping him. He's ready to take on Ivan Lendl." A pause. A clink of ice cubes in her drink. Fresca. "Did you know, Holly, that when your brother was born, they made such a big cut, they sewed it up all wrong?"

To extract the most information possible from her mother, Holly scarcely breathes and is completely quiet. She doesn't want her mother to be reminded that she is talking to her daughter. If she remembers, she'll clam up, and Holly doesn't want her to do that. As the invisible midwife-confessor, Holly speaks quietly, neutrally. "What was wrong?"

Pause. "Well, I can tell you I wasn't very happy with your father for quite some time."

Holly translates this roundabout speech to mean: dyspareunia, pain in intercourse, which might follow a badly repaired episiotomy if the OB had been too zealous in stitching her up.

"What happened?" asks Holly.

"Well, Holly." Pause. "I thought it was *me*. That I . . ."

Mrs. Treadwell doesn't have to go on. In fact, Holly isn't at all sure now that she's ready for the details of her parents' sex life. But her heart sort of pushes out, while her voice says the words that are sure to bring her mother's confessions to a close.

"Oh, Mother."

"Anyway." Brisk now, Mrs. Treadwell abruptly changes tone, disconnecting the confessional mode. She is back on cleared land, having pushed through the bramble of her past. Yes, here she is, in the familiar if boring turf of her own backyard. "Do you remember that lovely woman we had in for the cleaning? She went back to Georgia, where it turns out she's quite a landowner. . . ."

CHAPTER 7

Gloria, an AP, puts her hand over Holly's and looks earnestly into Holly's eyes. She is about to go to the lab for blood tests, and there's something she wants to say.

"You know, I was adopted."

"No, I didn't know that."

"I know about my father just one thing."

"What's that?"

"He was a drug addict." She pronounces *addict* like "addick."

"Oh, I'm sorry."

"They say it's inherited."

"Are you afraid you're going to become a drug addict, too?"

"Me? No!" Gloria pounds her chest with her fist. "The drugs, from my father," she explains, "they stay in your blood."

"You think you might have drugs in your blood that you inherited from your father?" Holly says, catching on.

"That's it!" Gloria says, relieved that Holly understands. "Write it down, that my father was a drug addict and it's in my bloods."

"You ever take drugs yourself, Gloria?"

"No, never! It's from my father! It's his blood I inherited!"

And this is how a sixteen-year-old disinherits her own blood.

CHAPTER 8

Holly steps out into the waiting room to call her next patient, but on her way she becomes involved in this exchange.

FIRST GIRL: When are you due?

SECOND GIRL: This week.

FIRST GIRL: You don't look it.

SECOND GIRL (proudly, throwing back her head, putting a bangled hand on the mild slope of her belly, and striking a pose): I know. I can fit into all my old clothes.

FIRST GIRL (admiringly): You do pregnancy right.

HOLLY: Hey. We want big babies around here! Big bellies!

FIRST GIRL: Yeah? And who's gonna buy me some new clothes? You?

SECOND GIRL: (Laughs.)

HOLLY: (Laughs.) We only want big babies around here, even if you have to wear your aunt's old housedress.

FIRST GIRL: And that's just what I have to do.

Holly wants to grab each girl by the scruff of her neck and shout: "That's not just your stomach. There's a baby in there!" But she understands, too, that a girl would want to fit into her clothes.

Most of the Howard Street patients can't afford maternity clothes. It's demoralizing for them to have to wear dowdy clothes passed down by an aunt, to squeeze into badly fitting skirts given to them by their mothers, and to stuff themselves into matronly housedresses bought at Woolworth's for nine bucks.

Like this girl who passes by in the hall, on her way into Paula's office: she shuffles along in flip-flops like an old housewife, breathing heavily, in

315

a cotton shift with a print of huge bananas on it. Who wants to go forth into the future looking like that?

Holly thinks that state and federal funds ought to allot money for the wardrobes of pregnant girls. If the welfare state is going to look after the health of these girls, how about looking after the psychological distress as well? The right to two flattering maternity outfits would be guaranteed by law, according to Holly's fantasy.

Or maybe she could start a charity drive back home on the Main Line—drive around the neighborhood, filling up the trunk of her mother's Lincoln Continental with the Lady Madonna outfits cast off by the well-to-do mothers who've already had their two planned children and have vowed never to get so fat again. Better yet, Holly could approach the antiabortion groups. "You wanted them to have their babies," she'd say with compelling indignation, "now give them a break!"

Holly would never actually talk about the clothes issue, because no matter how she phrased it, she'd wind up sounding frivolous. But she still believes that if a teenager were more positively inclined toward her pregnancy, she'd be more positively inclined toward her kid as well.

It asks too much of the adolescent mind to believe that pregnancy is a beautiful thing, when everything in a girl's life proves that in fact it's kind of ugly. When girls look bad during pregnancy, it eases the way for them to resent their unborn babies, anger that then takes the form of poor nutrition, cigarette smoking, drug taking, and drinking—things young girls are prone to anyway, since they have a hard time imagining the long-term repercussions of what they do.

Holly is sure that a clothes allowance would help society in general. Adolescent pregnancy is associated with health problems that affect the babies' development, the emotional and financial costs of which are then put upon the society at large—and those health problems have a large psychological component. A bit of preventive wardrobing might reduce the psychological component, hence reducing the health problems and the cost society eventually has to absorb.

Preventive wardrobing might encourage pregnant girls to stay in school longer, thus increasing the number of employable single mothers. The trouble is, the system in the main is still not geared to attacking adolescent pregnancy with the mind-set of adolescence incorporated into its offensive plan.

The social workers know it, the midwives know it, plenty of docs know it, but does the government know that adolescent mothers are more adolescent than they are mothers? Pregnancy may throw girls out of childhood, but it doesn't kick them out of adolescence. Their abstract thinking isn't yet developed, their cognitive development is still lurching toward completion, and pregnancy drags the body, but not the mind, into the world of the adult.

The adolescent mind can't skillfully field abstract arguments or easily visualize what isn't immediately and tangibly *there*. Elegant logic isn't nearly as persuasive to them as what is real, concrete, and before their eyes. Holly thinks that efforts to prevent teen pregnancy fail when they don't calculate a teenager's sense of invulnerability into the plan. Most girls really do believe "it won't happen to me," with the same sense of immunity felt by teenage boys who drive too fast or drive drunk when they should know better. It's not stupidity as much as the natural limitations of minds that are not yet adult. The threat of pregnancy, before it actually happens, is a lot of words, an abstract hypothesis like everything else learned in school, occupying the same sphere as algebra problems, the atomic bomb, and one nation indivisible. Not quite real.

Howard Street girls, who risk pregnancy and catch it, disapprove of abortion or expect to become pregnant at a young age. While they may not expect it to happen to them, they're not surprised that it has. Half of them don't want to be pregnant, while the other half see pregnancy as a coming-of-age rite. They hadn't planned it, but here it is. (Fewer teenagers seem to get pregnant with the goal of going on welfare and moving into their own apartments, contrary to popular belief. Most stay at home, with their mothers.) And with the same failure in abstract thought, they can't picture the reality of their futures either.

For girls who think in concrete terms, one of the main problems of pregnancy is its high-visibility status. Pregnancy enters their lives just at the time when they become hyperconscious and hypernervous about their appearance, when they are anything but at ease with the changes occurring in their bodies. Despite their obvious experience with sex, they are usually not the slightest bit comfortable with their sexuality. They are just as bashful and ashamed and exhibitionistic all at once as any other teenage girls.

They need nice things to wear.

Holly knows that any Dress Up a Pregnant Teen drive would be doomed to failure. Who wants to make pregnancy easy for young girls? No public figure would want to do anything that could be interpreted as condoning or rewarding adolescent pregnancy, or encouraging girls to give a repeat performance or even to feel good about being pregnant. This is the country's loss, as a young mother who feels good about herself is the best health bargain the government can buy.

"All right," Holly says to herself. "Bring on the next surprise conception case." She goes out into the waiting room, filled with pregnant teenagers who are pregnant for all kinds of reasons, and calls out: "Desiree Hodges!"

CHAPTER 9

Desiree has just found out she's pregnant. There are plenty of false negatives for pregnancy tests but fewer false positives. The pregnancy kits the Howard Street midwives use work just as the over-the-counter test kits on sale at drugstores work, gauging the levels of HCG in a urine sample.

"Yup, you're pregnant, all right, kiddo. How do you feel about it?"

Desiree, very dark-skinned with shy, bright eyes, breaks into a grin. "I feel glad."

For all of Holly's despair over teen pregnancy, there are always more than a few girls who view their pregnancy cheerfully and hopefully. To them, sixteen years old isn't too young to start a family. Holly is glad to see them approach pregnancy cheerfully and hopefully, if they have already approached it. Now, if there were some way for all that cheer to extend into the baby's actual existence, for the hope to press on for longer than nine months . . .

"I'm glad, too," says Holly, "that you came in this early." For one thing, one of the most frustrating problems in dealing with a young population, and an older population that is not very well educated, is correct dating of pregnancy. Deciding when a gestation is postmature is more complicated than looking at the dates and making a decision from them. Because the dates given by Howard Street patients are not known for their reliability.

If Holly can get some blood out of Desiree, she can find out the precise HCG levels and see how those values stack up against the dates of last menstrual period and conception given by Desiree. This might be one of those rare occasions when the clinic knows the exact gestational dates. Holly is excited.

318

Desiree smiles some more and peeks mischievously at what Holly is writing. Holly looks up at her with a smile, and Desiree ducks her head down. "It's all right to read what I'm writing. This is your chart. By law it belongs to you."

"Thought we weren't s'posed to look at it."

Holly playfully gives Desiree a push with her arm. "Look at it all you want and ask any questions you want." As if Holly is about to smack her across the face, Desiree comically puts up her arm to block the blow. Which is when Holly sees her left forearm.

It's speckled with little circles of dark, shiny scar tissue. Cigarette burns, they might be. Holly's stomach sinks. But Desiree notices nothing. She leans onto the desk and asks, "So when do I get to see a picture of my baby?"

Careful, Treadwell. You don't press directly against some subjects, but walk around them instead, as though you're stalking deer. If you stomp toward the deer, she takes off, white tail waving, bounding into the forest of the neighborhood, to turn up again eight months later, a walk-in at Morrison Triage. Circling around her subject, Holly pushes in closer as she wedges in the question she wants answered between a question on childhood diseases and the patient's history of hospitalization. Nonchalant, she asks Desiree, "Hey, how did you get those scars on your arms?"

"What scars? Oh, yeah. Cigarette fell. I guess I fell asleep."

"The cigarettes always fell in the same place?"

"Just about. I guess so. I never really noticed."

"I guess you're not smoking much in bed anymore."

Desiree declares staunchly, "I ain't smoking nowhere anymore because of the baby."

"Good." And Holly asks the hospitalization question, a question on what pets Desiree has, and then lets drop, "You know, sometimes when people get scars like that on their arms, it means they do drugs."

Slipping down in her seat, Desiree looks up over the curl of her hair. "You think I'm druggin'? I ain't druggin'."

Tilting her head thoughtfully, Holly says casually, "It's just that I've known girls with marks like that who skin-popped sometimes. You know what skin-popping is? It's when you shoot drugs up just under the skin."

"I know what popping is," Desiree says sulkily.

"They didn't know they were pregnant or anything when they did it, of course. They wouldn't do anything to hurt their babies."

Folding her arms and sitting up a bit straighter, Desiree says staunchly, "I don't do no drugs. That's for fools."

"Plenty of people who do drugs aren't fools. They just get into it, that's all. Then they have to get out of it. Okay. So you were never in the hospital for appendicitis or kidney disorder? No thyroid disease? No diabetes?"

At the end of the interview and exam, Holly tells Desiree that she needs to come back in a few days. "There's a test I don't have here that

I'll have then"—a deer-stalking lie. Holly doesn't want Desiree to get too far afield, drift off, bound off. She'll circle Desiree. She'll stalk this girl. She's not going to let a girl who's both happy about being pregnant and skin-popping float away, untethered. "You don't have to make an appointment with the receptionist. You just be here at one o'clock on Thursday and come right in."

"I need a note for school," Desiree says sourly, her eyes angry, a different girl from the one who almost skipped in the door.

On a prescription pad (chosen for its official look), Holly scratches out: "Desiree Hodges has an appointment at the Howard Street Clinic for Thursday, November 8, at 1:00" and signs her name with her telephone number running beneath it.

"How come you're no doctor?" Desiree asks after reading the note.

"Because I'm a specialist in normal birth. Doctors are for when you're sick. You're not sick."

"That what I am, a normal birth?"

Holly looks her straight in the eye. "Yes, that's what you are."

CHAPTER 10

Holly starts the schlepp home, waving good-bye to Mrs. Gruener, who pulls out of the small parking lot in her beat-up Volvo. She wills herself home instantly, ready to zone out on the couch watching television. The most boring conceivable fantasy consumes her brain. This is what Howard Street has driven her to look forward to.

Then somebody blocks her path. "I ain't no addict," says Desiree, dressed in a thin, shiny windbreaker, jeans, and long, pointy, boatlike flats. "How come you want me to come in Thursday? You gonna do a test to see if I'm drugging, ain't you?"

"Naw," Holly says. Midwifery as the art of deception.

"So why I got to come back?"

Holly looks down at the sidewalk and then straight into Desiree's eyes. The eyes are angry, and Holly feels the same way she felt when she told Matt she loved him, scared that her honesty will drive Desiree away and send her scurrying for cover. But she'd done it with Matt and survived, and she'll do it now. "I wanted to give you time to think," Holly says. "To think about whether or not those marks on your arms are cigarette burns. Or if they're something else."

Being an authority figure is hard. Holly can't be afraid to be self-assured or to impart an air of higher wisdom—an attitude to inspire confidence. But at the same time, if she pushes too hard, becomes authoritarian, she loses her patient. She's seen it happen. The eyes wander off. The ears shut down. Appointments are missed. A wall falls between them. A patient lost. And when Desiree is seen next, she's at Seven-B Admitting, dosed up on her medicine.

"Shit!" Desiree says. She stamps her foot and looks with exasperation

321

at the housing project across the street. "Well, I ain't gonna do it anymore."

Holly's stomach flutters. This is a confession. This is sacred.

"Skin-pop?" Holly asks. She keeps her eyes steady, no emotion. This is how you're supposed to elicit information. Pretend you're not shockable or excitable or judgmental. Pretend you've expected this to happen all along, while conveying that you value that it's happening. Holly's eyes go heavy with the exertion of compressing all this into a single expression.

"It was a while ago, before the baby," Desiree says, continuing her confession.

"I know you don't want to hurt the baby," Holly says. "I could tell that today."

"You could tell that?"

"You seem like the kind of girl who wants the best for her baby."

"I take this serious. I'm serious like a heart attack."

"Come in tomorrow and let me introduce you to the social worker."

"Oh, please, social worker! Forget it! I don't even want to hear about it."

Holly starts to walk toward the subway, Desiree by her side. A kind of power play to let Desiree know she has to make an effort to reach Holly, that she's here for Desiree, but Desiree has to push on if she wants Holly's companionship.

"Here's the deal," says Holly. "The social worker knows a lot about how to stay in school, how to deal with your folks—"

"Folks! What folks? Hey, is she going to tell my mother about this?"

"No way. This is strictly confidential."

Desiree kicks a can off the sidewalk. "I don't need no methadone or anything like that. I'm no junkie."

"You don't seem like a junkie," Holly says. "So, are you going to come see me on Thursday?" Desiree looks at the ground and says yes. "Now look me in the eye and say that, girl."

Desiree looks her in the eye. Sweet, shy eyes.

"Now smile and say that," Holly says.

"Do I got to?" Desiree says, smiling.

"Sure. Smiling is good for the baby. You'd be surprised. I'll see you Thursday."

As Holly heads up the street, Desiree calls, "Yo, miss! I got a question I got to ask."

"Shoot."

She turns, and Desiree runs up to her. Breathless, she says, "You think my baby's gonna be messed up?"

Holly thinks for a moment. "No."

"How do you know?"

"I can't promise anything, but you have a long time to make a good baby—eight months—and I think you'll be able to do it. Understand?"

"I understand." Desiree walks away and then says, tilting her head shyly, "What's your name again?"

"Holly Treadwell."

"That's a funny name. *Midwife* is a funny name, too."

"Maybe it is."

When Holly reaches the subway, she sees a red-haired woman standing by the bodega lighting a cigarette. She's hunched over her light and tosses the match away furiously. Then the woman looks up. It's not Edna O'Toole, and Holly heads down the stairs.

CHAPTER 11

Matt lives in Park Slope, in Brooklyn, and when Holly agrees to meet him there for dinner, the agreement means she'll spend the night at his place. They're meeting at a Japanese restaurant. Sushi has finally made it to the Slope, and the place is crowded with couples who look a lot like Matt and Holly: nonnative New Yorkers who bring the standards of non–New York— politeness, low voices, and naturally blond hair—to the rough-and-tumble world of ethnic New York past.

Holly is dressed in her corduroys and wool sweater, and she feels out of place in clothes that are rough and unsophisticated in contrast to what other people in the restaurant are wearing. Her hair, which she just got cut a week before at the corner unisex shop for twelve dollars, is her continued obsession. It seems too collegiate for a professional New Yorker. Holly is still pretty, but it's time for a change. She wants to give in to the sophistication she has started to feel inside.

Besides, she feels she's not keeping pace in a world of pacey people. Matt's no longer the pretty boy, with red cheeks, holes in his sweaters, beat-up running shoes, and hair that falls into his eyes. He's what Holly understands is considered a fast-tracker. Keeping pace has never been Holly's ambition. She's never wanted to be a fast-tracker. But she doesn't like being left behind either. It's times like these she starts to think about Meg Greenspan and making a move, out, up, away.

When their sushi arrives, Matt fiddles with his chopsticks. "Holly, I know it's a financial strain for you, living in the city, paying rent on that overpriced place of yours, and paying back your school loans."

"I'm doing all right," she says. She's on the alert now. This is a preface Matt is framing, an opening statement. Holly catches a glimmer of the meat of the matter and squelches it fast. The specter of decision-making looms before them. Matt is going to propose. Propose marriage. Or, being Matt and circumspect, propose that they think about his proposing. That sounds more like it.

So Holly jumps in. "Matt, I'm eating! Finances don't go with raw salmon!"

She's scared of what he'll say, because she doesn't know what she will say. And when they walk home, she knows she hasn't escaped it when he draws her to his side and gives her a squeeze. "I'm really happy with you, Holly. You know that? I really am happy."

"That's good. I'm happy, too."

Another block and he says, "We can't go on like this forever. Living in different apartments. It's getting tedious."

It *is* extremely boring. The love commute. Holly has to pack a gym bag with her diaphragm and clean underwear and change of clothes. She always forgets some little thing: vitamin C or contact lens solution. They try not to argue about whose place to go to, using means of persuasion before actually quarreling: "My place is a mess." "So is mine." But then they'll give up on politeness and burst out: "Why do we always go to your place?" and "Why do we always stay at my place?"

Of course, moving in together as a solution has always been just around the corner.

"But, Matt, could you live with a midwife?" Holly asks, trying to joke her way out of it.

"I almost have, haven't I?"

"No, not really. You haven't seen me after I've been up for fifteen hours, when everything else seems trivial compared to what I've gone through. I get burned out, and it takes me a long time to recharge my batteries. My emotional energy gets depleted. I don't know if I'd have anything left over to give you."

Matt stops on the street and pulls his arm away.

"But you're always going to be a midwife, aren't you?" he says, looking at her seriously. "And are you always going to feel that way, that you don't have enough energy left over to give your... your mate?"

Holly looks down the street, at the sulphurous orange light of the streetlamps and placid-looking brownstones. "I don't know," she says quietly.

"Does this mean you're never going to be able to get married?"

"Matt, you're starting to sound like my mother."

"I happen to have a vested interest in the question."

Holly starts to walk again. "I'm tired now. Let me think about everything."

Matt puts his arm around her. "Holly, I don't need coddling," he says. "I'm busy, too. My energy gets depleted. I'm not the kind of guy who needs a lot of fussing."

"I know," Holly says.

But she doesn't know. He probably is that kind of guy, actually, like most men are, needing reassurance in a subtle kind of way. Most of her working hours are spent giving reassurance and tapping in and out of emotional involvement. It's hard to come home and repeat the entire process, particularly now that Holly has come to think of men as being even more delicate and vulnerable than women.

She's cold and moves in closer to Matt. What if she's chosen a profession that's not compatible with a good relationship? That's what she's scared of, she realizes. That's what she doesn't want to find out.

"We could get a big apartment," Matt says, eyes lit up on the dark street. He has this imagined in his mind; he's formed a fantasy that not only includes her but places her at the center. She's touched. "You could have a den," he goes on. "I could bring you a beer after you've come home from birthing all day and hand you the evening paper."

She lets herself fall into this fantasy of his. A big apartment. A separate bathroom where she could take long showers, crouched down, taking pulls from a beer as she soaks in the steam. Come out, find Matt there. It sounds like the life they already have. Maybe she's living a fantasy and doesn't even know it.

"New Yorkers don't have dens," she says.

Matt hugs her tight and feels her resistance fall. "We will have a den. We'll be the exceptions."

"I'll sleep on it."

Matt says nothing. He's fast-tracking, and with strange contrariness, settling down is part of the course. He has the rest of his life to settle down in, but he wants to do it tonight. He wants everything resolved, his life tidied up so he can get on with it. He's impatient for his dreams to come true. And if she isn't ready, he'll go on alone. But then again, maybe he loves her. That's always a possibility.

CHAPTER 12

R egina is a seventeen-year-old who looks twenty, acts thirty, and has just married her boyfriend, who, Holly figures (to judge by the amount of money he flashes around), is in an illegal line of business. Regina is a modern gangster's moll—sexy, hard-edged, and determined to put her looks to any financial advantage just this side of prostitution. She is at thirty-eight weeks.

Holly usually hates to see a pregnant girl marry her boyfriend and move away from home into a life where she has nobody to talk to, nobody to advise or help her. When a pregnant girl leaves home, she loses her support network just when she needs it the most: when she has to learn how to keep house, live with a man as lost and confused and frustrated as she is, organize a budget, learn to be a mother. Marriage for a pregnant teenager seals her in, cuts her off and puts her in an isolation tank.

Compared to a teen mother who stays at home, a married teen mother has less chance of finishing up high school or entering a job-training program, since there is rarely someone around who can care for her baby. Because of this, and because there's nobody she trusts to take care of her baby if she goes job-hunting or takes a job, married teen mothers stay on welfare longer than unmarried teen mothers. And the illusion that a teen marriage will produce a dual-wage-earning unit is shattered, not only when the uneducated, untrained teen mother fails to find a job even if child-care is available, but when the marriage falls apart, as seventy-five percent of teen marriages do. Parents who put pressure on a young daughter and her boyfriend to marry do nobody any favors.

Holly has a different feeling about Regina. Regina is the exception. She is selfish, driven, willful, unsatisfied. If she doesn't like a situation, she tries to change it. Regina might be an awful person, but she probably won't be defeated before she has a chance to start out in life.

Like most teenagers, even precocious Regina loathes internal exams, and Holly had promised her that she'd only "look at you outside today." But now Holly has to break her promise because Regina has little pimples around her vulva. They don't look like syphilis chancres, and they don't look like herpes.

"Do you know why you have those tiny little bumps down there? Have you noticed those?"

"Aw, I washed my underpants in bleach and they made me break out and itch," she says in her husky voice, lifting her head. She has long peroxided hair, which makes her a favorite among the guys on the street. Her hair dangles over the table like a thing apart.

"You know what? I'm going to have to culture these and do an internal culture."

"Aw, shoot. What for?"

"Because when you're in labor and you go to Morrison, the staff might think these little bumps are herpes. You might tell them you got them from bleached underwear, but they're not going to believe you. And once you're at Morrison, there won't be time to do a culture to prove you're right, and the docs may decide to deliver your baby by cesarean. But if I do a culture now, we can put it loud and clear on your chart that your rash is just a rash."

In her husky, Brooklyn honky-tonk voice, Regina says, "No offense, Holly, but the hospital has its head up its ass."

"Well, you won't be the first to say so."

CHAPTER 13

Holly pokes her head through Mrs. Gruener's doorway as she knocks at the doorjamb. "Can I talk to you a minute, Mrs. Gruener?"

Mrs. Gruener looks up from some papers and raises her eyebrows. "You seem to be in a fairly unstoppable frame of mind so I suppose, yes, you may."

Holly slides into what she has come to think of as the Supplicant's Seat—the hard-backed wooden chair that faces Mrs. Gruener's wide desk. "It's about fetal scalp sampling."

"Good," Mrs. Gruener says, taking off her eyeglasses. "I was afraid you were going to tell me you're pregnant."

"Mrs. Gruener, I have a strange feeling that working here renders women infertile."

"Good. Just as it should be."

"Besides, if I were going to tell you I was pregnant, I would have said, 'I have good news and bad news. I'm pregnant and I'm pregnant.'"

"Now I know," Mrs. Gruener says with a nod. "What about fetal scalp sampling?"

"I'd like to learn how to do it," Holly says, pushing her hair behind her ears. "I'd like to do it."

Mrs. Gruener drums the side of her face with her beautiful fingers. She tilts her head and says, "Wait. Wait until the residents go on strike."

"The residents are going on strike?"

"I didn't say that," Mrs. Gruener says with a slight smile. "The only time you will learn how to do fetal scalp sampling is if and when the residents choose to vacate the labor suite. Then, and only then, will the midwives perform fetal scalp sampling at Morrison Hospital. Otherwise, to do so, you as a midwife will have to go to North Central Bronx or an

329

Eskimo outpost. For a midwife to learn something new, the system must find it expedient for her to do so."

"It's not expedient for midwives to learn fetal scalp sampling at Morrison?"

"What would Morrison gain from midwives learning scalp sampling techniques?"

Holly snorts and slumps down in the Supplicant's Seat. "Well, how about a reduction in the rate of cord prolapse?"

"Ah, you're so sure that only residents can cause a cord to prolapse?" Mrs. Gruener shuts the door. "You're so positive that every one of our midwives, Paula and Pam and Barbara and Kathleen and who else I have forgotten for the moment, could do a safe job of scalp sampling after one or two tries?"

"As safe as any resident after one or two tries, yes."

"As safe, Holly? That doesn't sound like much of a guarantee to me. Not quite expedient enough. How many fetal scalp samplings are performed in one night at Morrison? Two or three? Each takes only ten minutes to complete. A resident can handle that. There's no need for the midwives to perform scalp sampling."

"But if we do the scalps ourselves, we can provide continuous care to our patients."

"Maybe you can administer general anesthesia to your patients when they're being sectioned as well," Mrs. Gruener says. "Oh, and what about forceps? You can provide continuous care by doing forceps deliveries, too."

"Yes, Mrs. Gruener."

"You are supposed to be a specialist in normal birth." She slaps her desk with her palm. "Now what do you need to do sampling for?"

Mrs. Gruener believes in a Socratic method of teaching. A cutting irony runs through all her questions. She knows the answers; she knows that Holly doesn't know them. She asks questions that Holly will respond to with lame, pathetic answers. A caustic exchange.

"So we can see if the birth is normal or not. Just as we insert internal monitors."

"I believe you want to learn scalp sampling so you can show those rotten residents just how much better you are than they. So restrain your idiotic impulses, Holly. The demand for any clinicians other than the residents to perform fetal scalp sampling is minimal. Remember this rule: Expediency creates change. No expediency, no change. Don't let the basic principles of supply and demand escape you. Until there is great need and demand for scalp sampling, midwives will be deemed unsuited to the task.

"Here's the history lesson of the day. Before World War II, nurses were considered unequal to the challenge of giving intramuscular injections. But when the war started and millions of men needed IM shots, nurses were considered more than capable enough." Mrs. Gruener shrugs. "History, all right? You learn a little from history. Is that too painful for you? So. Our degree of skill has a shifting market value that rises and falls, depending on how expedient it is for the system to use our skills. You understand?"

Holly knows this is all true. In communities with populations greater than five hundred thousand, only half of working nurse-midwives perform manual placenta removal; in communities of less than ten thousand, more than three-fourths do. In large communities, only about a tenth of nurse-midwives do breech deliveries, and in the smaller communities nearly a quarter of them do. This is because there aren't as many available doctors in these smaller, more isolated places. There aren't as many residents chafing at the bit for experience, limiting the midwives' procedures as they carve out more territory that belongs to them, to the exclusion of the midwives.

Of course it's true, but that doesn't stop Holly from looking sulkily at the ground. "In the meantime, the residents go wacko."

"Do you have any proof of that?" Mrs. Gruener asks sharply. Her eyes have gone very cold and piercing, and Holly feels slightly sick to her stomach.

"Proof?" Holly isn't sure, for all her defensive medicine, what constitutes proof in terms of malpractice.

"I'd be very careful of what I say in public, if I were you. This country has libel laws that are in place to very good purpose. I've been victim of character defamation myself, many times, and I don't take disparaging remarks lightly. If you believe that residents are invulnerable animals at whom you can take potshots anytime and anyplace, then you had better work somewhere else, where you have colleagues whose rights you respect."

"I'm sorry, Mrs. Gruener. I forget sometimes that my words could have any power."

"Words, even from a midwife, have power." Mrs. Gruener slips her glasses back on, and she leans back in her chair, staring out at the low, dark clouds scuttling over the housing project. "You're a bright girl, Holly," she says quietly. "Now when are you going to start using your brains?"

"Mrs. Gruener, sometimes I think if I have to use my brains any more, they're going to break from the strain."

"That's when you use them even more. You're in the second stage now. Keep pushing."

"Do I have to smile?"

"Smiling helps reduce the pain," Mrs. Gruener says grimly.

CHAPTER 14

Holly did it. She called Sara. She'd thought that Sara's voice, as befits a lay midwife working in the backwoods and backwaters, would be of the groovy, peace-be-unto-you variety. What Holly got instead was a tense, ironic voice that bit off its words.

"I have a couch you can bunk on, if you really want to." Sara's idea of an invitation. Then she laughed in a dry, short way. "What if I get busted while you're here? That should make for an interesting field trip."

It's clear enough that Sara doesn't like nurse-midwives, who collaborate with the medical establishment that outlaws Sara's identity as a midwife and discredits the principles by which she lives. To Sara, Holly might be the equivalent of a Nazi collaborator planning a weekend stay with a French resistance fighter.

Holly calls Matt. "I made a date with a lay midwife," she says. "I'm going up this weekend."

He groans. "I don't want to hear about it. When you need a lawyer, you know where to find me. Until then, I never heard anything about this."

Holly can count on Matt to strike at the heart of the matter. What a great way to look at the world, she thinks: everything legal or not legal, right or wrong. But into the world of the outlaws she will go.

A few minutes later, Matt calls her back. "Are you going away this weekend to run away? Because of what we talked about?"

Holly doesn't know. *I don't know what to do—about anything.* But she says, "I just want to see what's out there."

"Oh." He considers this. "You're running away," he says.

CHAPTER 15

Friday, and Holly's last patient is pregnant and doesn't want to be. She's sixteen and wants an abortion. She and Holly talk over the alternatives—giving up the baby for adoption, keeping the baby—but the girl isn't moved. It's Holly's moral responsibility to mention the alternatives, but it's easy to tell when the argument isn't going to penetrate. It's not penetrating.

Holly is sorry that abortion is a midwife's concern. She tends to think of midwives as concerned mainly with catching babies, instead of encompassing all the problems of the reproductive process. Holly doesn't like to think about abortion, but she practices well-woman gynecology in a country where abortion is legal and performs pregnancy tests on women who don't want to be pregnant. She is her patient's advocate, and she'll support whatever decision her patient makes. Holly calls a nearby abortion clinic and makes an appointment for the young pregnant girl.

"After this, we don't want you to get pregnant until you want to. Am I right?" Holly asks.

"Right!"

"Are you going to come back for some birth control?"

"Sure," the girl says, looking out the window.

"Look me in the eye and say that." Holly withholds the slip of paper with abortion information until the girl turns, looks her in the eye, and says, "I'll come back for birth control. I promise." And Holly hands over the information.

If Holly helps whisk girls to the abortion clinic, it was not always so. She dove into the issue of abortion and underwent a sea change to arrive at the point where she is today.

In college, she was pro-choice (although the movement in support of abortion rights wasn't called "pro-choice" back then). If anyone had asked, she would have said, "I don't think there's anything wrong with abortion." An embryo had less feeling than other things that were killed—calves for veal, cattle for steak, rabbits for experiments, ducks in hunting.

As a maternity nurse, she witnessed the gruesome spectacle of a second-trimester abortion. Stillbirth by design: labor induced by prostaglandin suppositories to bring forth the "product of conception," knowing it wouldn't survive outside the womb. The product of conception in the second trimester wasn't an embryo, wasn't microscopic, and didn't look amoebic and inhuman. It was a baby, like other babies, and differed only in its size, unfinished look, and the fact that it hadn't reached the age of viability. Second-trimester abortions were grueling for the hospital staff and the would-be mother herself. The woman went through labor to bring forth death, and Holly could think of few conditions as wretched as that.

Holly remained pro-choice, but became less pro-abortion, wondering if second-trimester abortion should be legal at all, except when necessitated by dire medical situations. She still thought that if she became pregnant, she'd have a first-trimester abortion, as many of her friends had. But she'd have it with guilt, fear, and pain—it wasn't nothing anymore.

Did a fetus have a soul? Holly didn't know. She wasn't even sure she had a soul. She was sure an embryo had no consciousness, suffered no pain, and had no notion of its existence or of the threats to that existence. But she was sure, too, that an embryo had a life force that stirred its cells around and then distributed them according to a sacred design to form a new life.

When she started studying how pregnancy really worked in midwifery school, "termination of pregnancy" began to seem like a brutal abruption. A work-in-progress destroyed. The crude demolition of something elegant and fine. It was contradictory to be a midwife—someone who viewed pregnancy as the workings of nature—and to be in favor of abortion.

But the first time she came head to head with the problem of abortion was when she started working at Howard Street.

"Yes, you're pregnant," she told a young woman, trying to be even-handed and nonjudgmental. *Ask open-ended questions, Treadwell, no leading ones.* A good midwife was not supposed to clue the patient about what kinds of answers she wanted to hear. "How do you feel about it?"

The girl was eighteen years old and had just started an accounting course at City College. "Not too good," she said, picking lint off the border of her sweater. "I feel bad."

"Why do you feel bad?"

The girl cocked her head to the side, swallowed, and said, "I feel ashamed. But it would be too much. Just too much."

"You don't have to feel ashamed with me," Holly said. "You're safe here to feel whatever you want to feel."

The girl nodded without looking up.

"Do you know what you want to do? Have you thought about your choices at all?"

"Uh-huh," the girl said, nodding.

"Tell me what you've thought about so far."

"I don't want it," she said. She dropped her head to her lap and rested her forehead on her knees for a moment before straightening back up.

"You don't want to go through with the pregnancy, or you don't want to keep the baby?"

"I don't want to go through with it."

Holly's back stiffened. She nodded. "I'll be right back." She stood up and walked to the door. "Stay right there."

She pushed through the crowds of people milling about the waiting room and hurried to the bathroom, reached into her pocket for a cigarette, and lit it with her hands trembling. She stared at her hands, not believing they were so corny as to shake under strain. She had hokey hands. There they were: trembling so badly she could hardly hold a match up to the end of the cigarette.

She hadn't expected this. She'd told her roommate, "I wouldn't choose abortion for myself, but everyone has the right to make her own decisions. My feelings won't really affect how I treat my patients." The virtuous Holly.

That was a lie she didn't even know was a lie until she hid out in the bathroom, scared. Maybe the girl would have a change of heart. Maybe she'd get tired of waiting and split. Maybe her pregnancy test was a false positive.

Maybe Holly was just flipping out.

A midwifery instructor had told her class that people with religious objections to abortion should transfer abortion consults to other midwives. Step back, walk away, and leave the dirty work to someone else. But Holly didn't think she could spend her life as a midwife turning tail on patients who came to her for help. Besides, she knew there was another kind of moral crime and murder of the soul—encouraging a woman to have a baby she didn't want, then doing little or nothing to help the woman and her baby after the baby was born.

Holly stamped on her cigarette, picked it off the floor, and tossed it into the trash can marked FOR PLACENTAS ONLY, stolen, no doubt, from Seven-B. It didn't belong here, in the staff bathroom at Howard Street. Nothing was in its right place in the world.

Holly needed Paula.

Paula was Holly's friendliest supporter. When Holly asked questions that struck other midwives as obvious and exasperating, Paula literally took Holly by the hand, patted it, and said, "These little things are confusing when you're just starting out."

But Paula's friendliness wasn't why Holly wanted to see her. Paula was a midwifery rarity—she was middle-aged. A nurse for twenty years, she mortgaged her house to raise money for midwifery program tuition. ("I waited ten years for someone to start a midwifery school in my state, and the day they did, I headed over to the bank for a mortgage, a loan, and an Alka-Seltzer.")

Being middle-aged meant she had some kind of wisdom anyone with a sweet heart might accumulate over the years. But most important, Paula was a Roman Catholic. She'd had to wrestle with abortion—she must have—but she was still here at Howard Street, helping women arrange them.

Holly knocked on the door of Paula's office, swinging it open at the same time. Paula looked up. "Name it," she said. "Name your problem."

"Abortion," Holly said.

"For abortion, we shut the door." When Holly did, Paula said, "Midwives don't perform abortions, in case you hadn't noticed. So what's your problem?"

"But we recommend and arrange them—and I can't do either."

Paula rolled her tongue in her cheek. It moved behind the skin like a trapped animal lodged in her mouth. "Religious scruples?" she asked.

"Some kind of scruples—I'm not sure they're religious."

"We don't have time to talk about this now," Paula said. "You know, what's religious and what's not? Is God alive? Is God dead? Are any of our girls pregnant by immaculate conception? Let's play musical patients instead. We'll shoot the scruples breeze later. I take your patient, you take mine. She wants to know the yings and yangs, the ups and downs, the blacks and whites of the rhythm method. Your scruples should be up to that."

Holly stayed late that evening to join Paula in her office.

Paula leaned back in her chair and drummed a pencil on her desk, sizing up Holly in a silent assessment. She leaned forward suddenly and stared Holly in the eye. Holly had always seen short, stubby Paula as a semicomical caricature of a Polish peasant woman, but now Paula came into sharper focus. Holly said to herself, "You're a fool, Treadwell. Why'd you think someone like this, who went back to school when she was forty years old to become a goddamn midwife, would be an airhead?"

Paula leaned back, her assessment finished. "You're young, Holly, and you don't know what's what. You don't know the half of it. You don't even know the three-eighths of it."

Holly nodded, hands in lap, ankles crossed, as if ladylike manners would see her through life's trickier confrontations. Being chewed out struck her as good therapy. Being chewed out was a learning experience.

"I wish you were an ER nurse twenty years ago," Paula said with a half-smile. "Women, not bad women, nice women, maybe someone you know, for all you know, would come into the ER. One of 'em might have been me. Anyone. Anyway. These women would come in, wouldn't say what's wrong. You can tell right away what's wrong. No color in their faces, blood dripping down their legs, spiking mean temperatures, vomiting. Knew right away. Not a heavy period. 'I'm miscarrying,' they'd say finally. Miscarrying with a punctured uterus? With a lacerated cervix? With a punctured embryo still inside? That wasn't any miscarriage, believe you me. In our ER alone, a dozen women would come in to die each year. Just to die. Another dozen would come in to die but didn't die. Infected, infertile, needed hysterectomies, but didn't die. Can you imagine that, or do I need to imagine it for you some more?"

"I can imagine it," Holly said quietly.

"I have my RC scruples. You bet. I got six RC kids to show for it, and they all go to mass, every last one of them, even if it's only hangover mass at one o'clock. They go. But, Holly, when those ladies came into the ER, did I think I was in the presence of sinners? No, because I was a nurse. The sin was in what was done to them, the way they got mauled by who knows what kind of ape with a dilator and curette. To me, that's sin."

Paula rubbed her face. Her skin was loose and folded in her fingers like a length of vinyl.

"The Church teaches you plenty of good things," she went on. "But it doesn't teach you that people have their own reasons for doing things and sometimes one law doesn't work for all of them. When abortion was legalized, I said, Good, I won't ever have to see that again. The sliced-up wombs. The shocky women bleeding out on the ER floor. But when I became a midwife, the same thing happened to me that's happening to you. 'What, me, a good Catholic, advising on abortion? That's going too far. I'm pro-life.' "

"How did you change, Paula?"

"I didn't *try* to change. I just started seeing things. The girls who come in here, twenty years old, two kids at home, hooked on drugs. What chance does a baby have under those conditions? Is that a life you'd wish on a fellow human being?"

"But the poor are always with us. It's not up to us to decide what kind of existence is good enough for a kid to have."

"That's right. It's not up to us." Paula leaned forward, put her hand on Holly's, and shook it hard. "It's the woman's decision. She doesn't wish that existence on her baby, and she knows better than you do. She doesn't want an unwanted kid."

"But we can't just monkey around with existence. Decide who should live and who should die."

Paula lifted both her pudgy hands, then dropped them onto her white slacks. "That's right," she said, with a curl of her lips. "We can't. That's why everyone makes her own decisions now."

Pumping with her short legs, Paula wheeled herself on her chair to a cabinet she unlocked with a key from a key chain that held about fifty other keys and pulled out her old leatherette box of a purse. "Holly, kid, you're not going to settle this today. You're not going to settle this tomorrow."

"What do I do until I do settle it?"

"Refer all your abortion cases to the abortion counselor."

"We have an abortion counselor?" Holly asked in disbelief. "And here I've been going bonkers about what I was going to do about abortion counseling."

"Relax. I'm just trying to save your professional tail, so you don't run outta the room crying every time a girl sputters out that she doesn't want to keep the kid. There's no abortion counselor. *I'm* the abortion counselor. Graduated from the school of hard knocks. That's the school you're entering now."

From her pro-abortion views of college and the anti-abortion feelings of midwifery school, Holly has arrived at her present position: pro-life and pro-choice at once. And it doesn't seem like waffling to feel this way.

"If you have any questions, you give me a call." Holly writes down her name and number. "I'm calling you in six weeks if you don't call me."

"What for?"

"To see how you're doing. Because the next time you get pregnant, it's going to be because you want to be."

The young woman nods.

"You're going to like that, I think," Holly says.

CHAPTER 16

H olly carries her bag with her change of clothes for the visit with the midwife. She's leaving two hours early, and Pam is taking over her charges. "Mental health leave, Pam," she said.

"I know you," Pam said. "You just want to drive someone else crazy."

As Holly walks by Mrs. Gruener's office, she sees Mrs. Gruener pacing back and forth, clicking her heels loudly on the linoleum. When Mrs. Gruener gets angry, there's something inescapably comic and operatic about her. That is, when she's not angry with Holly. She gets angry in a dramatic way that seems completely at odds with her Nordic elegance. Mrs. Gruener, with her golden hair and transparent white stockings glistening in the fluorescent light, shakes her head furiously and mutters sporadically. As she stands in the hall, looking at Mrs. Gruener, Holly realizes that Mrs. Gruener would have left Germany whether or not there was Nazism or a war, because Mrs. Gruener actually has a Latin soul. Mrs. Gruener is as much a Carmen as she is one of Wagner's Valkyries, despite her ice-goddess looks.

"Mrs. Gruener?" Holly ventures.

"Ah!" She stops dead in her tracks and flaps her arms to her sides. "Come in and shut the door," she says, as if she were waiting just for Holly. "It's that Dr. Pollard." The head of the clinic's pediatrics department.

"What about him?"

Dr. Pollard's most recent infuriating proposal is that the pregnant teenagers, who share a waiting area with teenagers who've come to the clinic with "presenting complaints" other than pregnancy, be cordoned off in a waiting area of their own.

"I've received complaints," he'd told Mrs. Gruener. "Mothers are worried that the pregnant adolescents are providing a bad example to the nonpregnant adolescents."

"Let me see these complaints," Mrs. Gruener had demanded.

"They're not in writing," Dr. Pollard had replied.

"How many complaints are there?"

"Quite a few."

"What does that mean? Four mothers? Eight mothers?"

"What difference does it make?" Dr. Pollard lashed back. "They raise a legitimate point. These pregnant girls—"

"These pregnant young ladies didn't get pregnant by other pregnant young ladies. You tell your quite-a-few mothers that."

And when Dr. Pollard brought his complaint to the board of governors, the true number of complaining mothers emerged. There had been two mothers, sisters, who had complained together. Mrs. Gruener viewed Dr. Pollard's complaint as a nuisance suit—to divert Mrs. Gruener's energies from her true business and to establish Dr. Pollard's power over her.

"What has he done now?" Mrs. Gruener asks Holly in a high-pitched voice. "Is that your question? I'll tell you. He now believes that all the adolescent teenagers, the young ladies under eighteen, should be under the jurisdiction of Pediatrics, since they are still children. He doesn't understand—or he does understand, he is just trying to drive me insane—that midwifery includes pediatrics within its range of treatment, but that pediatrics does not include midwifery. Fancy that, my midwives having to report to Dr. Pollard."

Mrs. Gruener is steamed and stalks her own office.

Holly leans against the wall and says, "Don't pregnant girls, by becoming pregnant, forfeit the right, to some degree, to be treated as children? Isn't their condition a condition that is, by definition, adult?"

Mrs. Gruener looks thunderstruck. "Yes," she whispers and pats Holly's arm. In her high heels, she scuffles to her desk and grabs a pen. "Say that again, just as you told me." As Holly tries to repeat herself (more clumsily this time), Mrs. Gruener nods enthusiastically. "I like that. Forfeit the right. A condition, by definition, adult. Lovely. Lovely." Holly is in a state of shock. She has just advised Mrs. Gruener. This is astonishing. She puts down her bag.

Mrs. Gruener slips into her seat, slides on her half-lenses, and gets on the phone. "Dr. Pollard, you listen to me one minute." She holds the paper up before her eyes, straining to find her focus. From across the room, Holly can hear Dr. Pollard's unintelligible barking rasp out of the receiver.

"You listen to me, Dr. Pollard. Do not pregnant young ladies, by becoming pregnant, forfeit their right, to some degree, to be treated medically as children?"

More scratchy yells from Dr. Pollard.

"I have one thing to say to you, Dr. Pollard, and that is, go to hell very fast."

Holly searches her mind for more eloquent perceptions to fuel Mrs. Gruener's fight. But, alas, her brain has done its work for the day.

Mrs. Gruener's calm seems to be restored. Sitting straight-backed in her chair, she graciously dismisses Holly. "Thank you, my dear. You have been of the greatest help, as always."

Holly leaves the room like an Indian servant, walking backward. She does not want this to stop, but she'd better leave before she says something wrong. Then she straightens up and runs out of the clinic, before anyone can stop her.

She'll be among the outlaws soon.

CHAPTER 17

The Puerto Rican bodega near the subway is a kind of neighborhood center. Old men in little hats gather there to sit on milk crates and conduct obscure business. Young people line up to use the pay phone just inside the door. Bananas and plantains hang on a washline in the window to ripen; the only way the neighborhood people will concede to buy them is when they're on the verge of turning black. A young mother steps in, pulls down a bunch of bananas, and, surrounded by three kids with bookbags, tears off a banana for each of them. The kids scuffle off in the direction of the playground, peeling their bananas as they go, when, as if on cue, they double back, give their mother a kiss, and tear off again.

Following the woman out of the bodega is a certain young black woman whom Holly knows and who knows Holly and who doesn't see Holly as she steps out, because she's too busy ripping open a bag of Doritos with her teeth.

When Desiree looks up and sees Holly, Desiree hides the chips behind her back and smacks herself on the head.

"Busted! I'm busted!"

All Holly needs to do is grin threateningly at Desiree, and Desiree backs up, putting herself into reverse, and moves into the bodega. "I'm buying some milk, all right? See? I'm going?" To the woman who bought the bananas, she wails, "I'm busted, you know, by my midwife."

"Midwives are like nuns," the woman said, shrugging. "They got eyes in the back of their heads."

Holly stares Desiree down. "I'm watching you, Desiree. I will always be watching you."

Desiree shudders. "Oooh," she says. "You're scary."

Scary is an all-right way to start a weekend.

AMONG THE OUTLAWS

CHAPTER 1

Night has fallen when Holly's bus from New York grinds into the bus station in Castleton, where Holly settles in on a wooden bench to wait for Sara. College boys also wait, in letter jackets and short haircuts with long bangs that seemed dipped in peroxide. Boys were never this pretty when Holly was in college—she wonders if they use facial masques and hair conditioners. Next to them, she feels tired and old.

Holly knows she doesn't look old. The man next to her on the bus thought she was a college student returning to school.

"No, I'm a midwife."

"A midwife? Can you make a living from that?"

"Most of the time."

He assumed she was a home-birth midwife. Can you make a living from that?

The age she feels is emotional; she looks young, feels careworn. Bringing life into the world is a wearing occupation. But nothing else makes her feel so high. Next to a birth, almost everything else seems trivial. Most likely Sara thinks of midwifery this way, too. Why else go through the hassle? The only way Holly will get along with Sara is by bringing this bond to the fore.

The station doors swing open, and friends of the college boys rush through. The boys heave their bags over their shoulders and go laughing through the doors. Below their neat, stylized haircuts, they have the smoothest necks Holly remembers ever seeing. They don't even know how supple their necks are. As far as they're concerned, their necks will always be this way. And Holly feels a sudden desire to sleep with one of them in a lust that's not really sexual, but a desire to leave her thoughts behind, to make love in the blank, hopeful way she did when she was younger. To run out of her hard, ragged life into something as smooth and easy as the boys' glistening necks. "This is how middle-aged men look at me," she realizes, swallowing and squelching the sudden lust. "Not as a sex object but something else. As youth. A simpleton. A smooth neck."

A slight figure moves toward the station doors, and Holly jumps up. *Don't let her catch you sitting down, Treadwell.* Holly doesn't quite know why not.

The woman who must be Sara is in an old suede jacket and a flannel shirt over jeans, and her hair is auburn. She looks mercurial, hot, flickering. Holly knows she'll have to keep on her toes—mentally, if not physically—the entire weekend.

"Holly?" Sara stands by the door as Holly lurches forward.

"You must be Sara. I'm Holly Treadwell."

"Car's outside," Sara says, turning. Brusque. Quick.

When Holly has slid into the front seat of Sara's 1960s Rambler station wagon, which is just like a car Holly's parents once had, Sara says, "All right. Explain to me why you're really here."

"Katrina McLeod thought I should see other ways of birth. If the midwives of the world can sit down together peacefully, we can all see how alike we are." Holly speaks in an ironic way, as if she sees the futility of the effort before even starting.

"What do you think of lay midwives?" Sara says. "I've always wanted to know what nurse-midwives think of us."

"At our most negative, we think that most lay midwives aren't well trained. Enthusiasts who don't know as much as they think they do. Hobbyists. We figure a lot of them aren't safe. That there has to be some certification process to ensure a certain level of competence."

Sara laughs. "Who'd decide the certification process? The ACNM? The docs? The board of medicine, the board of nursing, the Catholic Church?"

"I don't know," Holly says. "But I'm not a policymaker in the lay midwifery movement."

"Well, I am, and the answer is, all of the above."

After a bit, Holly says, "What's your take on nurse-midwives?"

"This is a mouthful! That you're conditioned by the medical establishment. You see birth as a pathology. You rely too much on high technology. You're obedient to the hospital hierarchy, and because doctors look down on you, you look down on us. The physics of oppression: oppressed people need someone else to scorn. Nurse-midwives have a nurse mentality. You're handmaidens to the OBs—"

Holly laughs. "The OBs wish it were so!"

Sara goes on. "You've been brainwashed to believe a hospital is a safe place for childbirth even though all the facts prove that hospitals are actually dangerous." Sara is ready for Holly; she must have rehearsed all this.

After a few quiet moments, Holly says, "At least we have one thing in common."

"What's that?"

"We both take midwifery to heart."

With much wheezing, the car climbs a winding road up a steep hill, and Holly has the eerie, spacy feeling that she'll be trapped forever in this car, trapped with a bitter lay midwife who hates her. This is the special hell God designed especially for her. Driving along for eternity with Sara. Holly shudders.

"Let's call a truce," Sara says, to Holly's relief.

They're going to a birth, and the woman in labor is named Seashell. "I know it's a time warp," Sara puts in quickly. "She should ditch the name, for sure. It makes her sound more mellow than she actually is. Her name really misrepresents the case."

"What role do I have here? Am I your assistant or what?"

"You're a what," says Sara as she parks in front of an old barn, set off from the road by about fifty yards.

"Are the clothes I'm wearing all right?"

Sara glances over at Holly. "I can't see what you're wearing. What's wrong with it?"

"I thought maybe I needed some clean clothes or something."

"Unless you plan to examine the lady yourself, Holly, I trust your germs."

Sara called Holly by her name. A certain thaw is under way. When Sara cuts the car lights, the barn becomes a ghostly old mass, lost in the fog. She explains about Seashell's husband, Bruce, who scrapes out a living by doing odd jobs and growing marijuana in a geographically unspecified field.

"Underground economy situation here, all the way. He intimated he'd pay me with his cash crop, but I intimated back that I wasn't amenable. Midwifery is illegal enough as is. If word got around that I get paid in pot—well, that's a good excuse for the authorities to go after me. Besides, how much pot can one beer-drinking midwife smoke? The payment problem is always touchy. Some people—well, Bruce mostly— act like money turns childbirth into a crass affair when it should just be this sacred, spiritual deal. But I have rent to pay. My fee is only four hundred dollars. Think that's too much?"

"I think that's too little," Holly says.

"It includes everything. Prenatal, postpartum, the birthing. Obviously I'm not in this for the money, but some people imply that's what I'm up to."

"How many births do you do?"

"About three a month. But it's rare that I ever get the full four hundred dollars."

Through the murky night, Holly makes out a screen door hanging off its hinges on a doorway of the barn. Sara squints into the darkness. "The more I know of Seashell and Bruce," Sara says thoughtfully, "the less happy I am about attending their birth. Not just because they're deadbeats." She glances almost timidly at Holly. "I get bad vibes about this, and they're not coming from you."

A creepy sensation steals over Holly, the kind she used to feel when everyone told ghost stories around a campfire when she was a kid. Bad vibes, a dark barn, a home birth. Certain relief in that the bad vibes, evidently, aren't emanating from *her*.

The smell of wet earth, the screeching crickets, and the rustling trees move Holly. She wishes Matt were there, as Sara pulls her midwifery bag out of the trunk. An oxygen cylinder is held fast in the trunk by a wooden girdle bolted to the side of the trunk. The bag is a big canvas sack covered with stickers that say, SUPPORT YOUR LOCAL MIDWIFE and MIDWIVES DO SPECIAL DELIVERIES. Sara apologizes: "My sister. She buys these things at conferences on alternative birth. She's a birth groupie."

"A birth groupie?"

"A birth groupie knows the answers to everything, while the midwife only knows the right questions. A birth groupie thinks mother nature is this sweet lady who looks like Joni Mitchell. A midwife thinks that nature is more like the sky. It's not blue all the time." Sara slams the trunk shut. "Hell, you're a midwife. Am I right?"

"You're right, except sometimes I don't know the right questions."

Sara opens the door and shouts hello, and they climb narrow wooden stairs to the apartment, one large room under the eaves, with a cubicle filled with toys in chaotic disarray and another with a workbench strewn with tools in an equally chaotic state. Holly thinks, it's hard to trust a man who doesn't respect his tools.

A wood stove blasts forth waves of heat, as reggae music drifts from one corner and wind chimes tinkle in another with the breeze created by their entrance. Indian prints line the walls, and Holly is time-warped back to a commune at Brown she'd visited in the early 1970s, which looks just like this. To seal the time-warp effect, Holly walks straight into a pocket of pot smoke that seems to hang in the air in a self-contained mass, so that by the time she catches a whiff, she has already walked through it, as if through a low-lying cloud.

A heavily bearded man stands by the wood stove and stares at Holly with unabashed curiosity. *Stoned again*, as they used to say in the old days. This must be Bruce, with hard, emotionless eyes that don't fit in with the rest of him, so that he looks like a narcotics agent posing as hippie. Holly smiles nervously, and he returns her smile with a smarmy one that comes dangerously close to a smirk.

Seashell is sprawled on a big bed in a T-shirt and underpants, gaunt and bony with a washed-out complexion, narrow gray eyes, and dirty blonde hair. She looks like a sharecropper photographed by Walker Evans during the Depression, her enervated appearance suggesting she's subsisted on turnips for years.

Seashell's daughter, Maya, sits on the floor. With tangled blonde hair and pale skin, she looks like a restless version of her mother and gazes up blankly at Holly before setting back to the work she'd been busy with: yanking the clothes off a smudged, gritty Barbie doll.

"How are you feeling?" Sara asks, pulling a fetoscope from her bag.

"All right," Seashell answers in a tired voice more reluctant than serene.

Palpating the abdomen, Sara finds that the baby's head hasn't engaged, but is floating above the pelvic inlet. "The baby's not real big," she concludes. "It should fit just fine."

Hovering over the bed, Bruce asks, "Why wouldn't it?"

"Sometimes if the baby is real big, it has a hard time sliding through the pelvis."

"Why would that happen with Seashell here?" He looks down at Sara with hard, watery eyes.

"I don't think it will."

"But you brought it up, right?"

If Bruce were at Morrison Hospital, Crowley and Holly would Siberia him to the elevators, along with all the other coaches who bring bad vibes to the proceedings. But they're in Bruce's house, this is his turf, and Sara can't send him anywhere.

Sara scrubs up at the kitchen sink. "Midwifery texts say you should scrub for ten minutes before delivery," she tells Holly, who has followed her with studentlike obedience.

"So did mine. But we rarely do."

"Too much scrubbing is detrimental. It washes away the skin's protective covering and leaves it more susceptible to infection. Three minutes is long enough. I haven't infected a client yet."

Holly doubts this, and she's relieved when Sara pulls a familiar-looking if small bottle of Betadine from her bag.

Seashell shimmies out of her underpants as Sara works a clean towel beneath her bottom and spritzes her with what Morrison nurses would consider a stingy amount of Betadine. When Sara breaks open a pair of gloves, she saves the sterile paper they're packed in and opens the vagina with her left hand. Holly mentally notes: Vag. exam skills okay.

"How far along am I?" Seashell asks wearily.

"About six centimeters. Pretty good. But you should sleep while you can and keep up your strength. It's still early yet."

"I can't sleep in labor. I never could."

"You weren't home then. You were in the hospital. Maybe you can sleep in your own bed." Seashell shrugs, unmoved by Sara's logic. "Who's coming to stay with Maya?" Sara asks.

"My sister was going to, but she split for Maine."

"Where does that leave Maya?"

"She's a big girl now," Bruce says. "A self-sufficient little lady. She wants to help. Like she's into it."

Sara suggests she and Bruce talk in the kitchen, where she tells Bruce, "Maya's only eight years old. You have to put all your energies into what's going on with Seashell. So do I. A birthing is a rough passage for everybody. Strong emotions go down, and someone should be around to help Maya get through it."

Scratching his beard and running his finger along his lower lip, Bruce says coolly, "Maya's stronger than you think. Even stronger than we are, because she's not as fucked up."

Sara throws back her hair, which looks like it'll burst into flame, and says, "A child is a vulnerable creature. Just because she's an innocent, unfucked-up kid doesn't mean she's immune to confusion or distress. She's a little kid, and she needs someone to help her through this."

Bruce picks up a hammer off the kitchen counter and pounds its head into his palm. He says casually, "We can't get anyone now anyway."

"No neighbors or relatives?"

"We can't call anyone—the phone company cut the juice."

Sara rolls her eyes. "One of my few definite rules is that I have to have a phone. We talked this through when your phone was disconnected half a year ago."

Swinging the hammer into his hand, Bruce says cavalierly, "Nothing's going to go wrong." Then he loses his grip, and the hammer falls with a thud onto the unfinished floor.

"Yeah, right."

"Sara, you're real negative, aren't you?" Bruce is evidently concerned for Sara's mental health.

Sara shuts her eyes briefly. "Let's see if everything else is in place. Do we have enough food to keep up our strength?"

Bruce opens the kitchen cabinet and flourishes at the food on the mostly empty shelves: chick-peas, brown rice, spaghetti.

Sara looks angrily down at the floor. She says finally, "Seashell will need to be energized. And I can't keep alert if I'm hungry. Food is a necessity, not a luxury."

"You know how it goes," Bruce says, laying the hammer on the counter. "The labor seemed to come on so suddenly."

"Bruce, you had nine months to prepare. The point of home birth is so you don't put yourself in someone's hands and say, 'Do with me what you will.' Now I have to tell you what to do. Let's go through the list to see what you do have ready."

Olive oil, to soften and elasticize the perineal tissues before delivery. Hydrogen peroxide, for perineal tears and the baby's umbilicus. Linen, baked in the oven for an hour at 250 degrees, then sealed in plastic bags.

The labor wears on. Holly plays go-fish with Maya, both cross-legged on the floor. Sara encourages Seashell to walk, she refuses to walk, and Sara and Holly step out for some air.

Sara glances at her watch. "It's midnight," she says. "They used to call midwifery the midnight industry."

"Your midwifery is a cottage industry," Holly says.

They circle the barn, tall grass switching at their ankles. "I guess this birthing gives you the wrong idea of home birth," Sara says.

"You mean Bruce? There are jerks wherever you go. You have pain-in-the-ass husbands. I have pain-in-the-ass residents."

"My best births are with Leos. They aren't afraid to take center stage, to let the world revolve around them. They're also aggressive; they don't just sit back and see how things turn out."

Holly, a Pisces, wishes she were at home in bed with Matt. She is tired of Seashell and Bruce, and she misses the hospital's diversity, where she has more faces to set her sights upon when she becomes tired of her patient. It's quiet midwifery here—maybe true midwifery, but it's claustrophobic, too.

"Slow labor, for a multip," Holly says, hinting at her restlessness. "At my hospital, a multip has to move at a one-centimeter-per-hour pace or she's Pitted out."

"Second-time moms have funny contractions. This baby's real little. There's not enough pressure for the cervix to pull back. And Seashell won't stand up enough, damn her." A lone car speeds by on the narrow winding road, then is gone. Quietly, Sara says, "What I like best is the magic of birth and to facilitate that magic as best I can."

Holly thinks of birth as magic, as transformation, process, faith in the not-yet-seen. A rabbit produced from a hat. She wonders if the appeal of that standard magic trick is its symbolic parallel to the birth process: the white creature pulled from the black depths.

"I don't want to wrangle with husbands." Sara kicks at the ground. "Oh, well. I just have to free up my energies so I can help Seashell now. She seems to think this labor is somebody else's problem. Like the labor will take care of itself if she keeps her hands off it."

"A laissez-faire attitude," Holly muses. A train snakes its way along a distant hill. She wishes she were on it, barreling home through the night.

They gaze out at a stone wall that has collapsed in disrepair. Despite the Robert Frost poem that regrets man's inclination to make walls at all, Holly thinks she'd like the hard, relaxing work of mending walls, fitting the stones in place and working with things that have no feelings. She was wrong when she told Denise she didn't like to deliver stones. You can let a stone drop, roll down a hill, drown in a lake. You can throw a useless stone away. A stone doesn't complain.

"I lied to Seashell after that first exam," Sara says, looking up at the sky. "She was only four centimeters. At the time it seemed...expedient. Therapeutic. I figured labor would move faster if she wasn't disheartened."

"But did your tactic work?" Holly asks, an unkind question, because they both know it didn't work, and without answering, Sara pivots and saunters back to the old barn.

CHAPTER 2

The sky has slid out of darkness into a steel-gray color. Dogs bark. Holly's stomach grumbles. From a distance, roosters crow and screen doors bang. Even at Morrison, morning sounds can trigger a woman in labor, as if she knows she's part of nature and she should start stirring, with the rest of the world. Morning gives an extra kick, like a hint of Pit.

Sitting at the rough wood table, Maya digs into a plate of spaghetti, which Holly cooked in olive oil appropriated from Seashell's perineal massage stash. That Seashell's uterus might turn hypotonic—the exhausted womb tiring of contracting and giving out—falls like a film of gauze between Sara and Holly. They are both thinking of this, but neither is talking.

The presenting part has descended far enough for Sara to actually touch it—the baby coming into view, more or less—and what Sara touched wasn't a skull or a brow. "I felt an ear," she tells Seashell. Poetic justice that the presenting part should be the one most closely resembling a shell.

"What does that mean?"

"The baby is malpresenting."

The baby has abandoned nature's efficient packaging method, declining to pack itself into an oval mass. Its response to being crunched by the uterus walls is to arch its neck rather than flex it under, against its chest. This is the quirkiest malpresentation Holly has ever seen. A face or brow presentation is odd enough—both slowing labor, as neither the face nor the brow puts efficient pressure on the cervix. But an ear presentation means the logistics are way off.

Holly is worried. The mechanics of the baby's head passing through the pelvis are comparable to those of moving a large sofa through a narrow doorway. The couch has to be angled just right to squeeze through. If the head doesn't rotate right, the baby might get stuck. A legitimate case of failure to progress and cephalo-pelvic disproportion.

Bleary-eyed, Holly glances up from a cup of herbal tea, which she realizes too late is specifically designed to lull people to sleep, and she puts the cup down fast. Her adrenaline fills in for caffeine anyway—as heroin might take the place of methadone, the real thing substituting for the milder imitation. There's little to do with buzzing adrenaline in a situation like this, though, other than to let it stir about and make her empty stomach churn. "Was it only an ear?" she asks Sara.

"Some brow, but mostly ear."

Holly frowns in a quick, involuntary way, feeling the full force of the lay midwife's essential isolation. At Morrison, advisers lie in every direction. Second opinions spring from nowhere. Comments are shouted, hissed, accepted, rejected out of hand. Here in the barn, the exchange is slow and quiet. They're in outer space. Sara can rely only on herself, which Holly finds both gutsy and foolhardy, just as Sara's style of working is enviable and frightening.

What's most seductive about home birth is what they have here in the backwoods that the hospital doesn't have. Time. Holly is used to working with a stopwatch running, and it runs here, too, with Holly hearing it in the back of her mind when she worries about hypotonia. But it doesn't tick loudly, whirring instead in the distance like the hum of white noise you can hear only when you listen for it.

Sara asks to consult with Holly, and they stand amid the clutter of Maya's bedroom cubicle. "Isn't there anyone you can consult, other than me?" Holly asks, feeling inadequate to the role.

Sara stares out at the narrow road, where cars rush by, windshield wipers slapping at the almost-rain of the mist. She doesn't answer. Her answer must be no. Cows sway on a hillside: spotted white things on a gray-green background. Free things. She sighs. "Seashell's uterus must be more pendulous than I thought, and the baby a lot smaller. The baby is swimming in there. I have a solution, but you won't like it." Turning to Holly, she says mockingly, "It's not a nurse-midwifery option. But I'm going to maneuver it."

"Maneuver what?"

"The baby's head. If Bruce and Seashell consent—well, forget Bruce— if Seashell consents, I'll tuck in the baby's chin before he can move down any farther."

Holly's constructs a worse-case scenario straight away. Holly hauled into court, the reluctant martyr of the alternative birth groupies. Then she considers the risk to Seashell. Seashell bleeding out in this backwoods coven of counterculture relics.

Holly swallows hard. "Christ, I can't be involved in this. I'd be liable, legally. . . ." She'd like to call a Yellow Cab and catch the next bus to

New York City. Leave all this behind, just like that. She feels like one of the "refrigerator midwives" she detests, who step into the fray long enough to pull down a paycheck for a new refrigerator, then cut out as soon as their shift is up, abandoning patients to indifferent personnel. But she doesn't care. She's outstayed her shift. It's time for a new shift. But she can't call a cab. The telephone is dead. Holly is stuck for the duration.

Contemptuous, Sara shakes her head and spits out, "Yeah, right. Liable. But you're liable now, Holly." Sara's face goes hard, her lips looking thinner and her eyes narrowing. "You're an accessory already. This is a conspiracy, and you're part of it. And your paranoia doesn't help the situation a whole lot."

Holly is ashamed. "Sorry, I'm trained to think defensively."

"You said it. I didn't."

Bruce plays with Seashell's long ponytail and speaks for her. "What are the options?"

"You can call the OB you've been seeing or risk the internal version deal. I go through the cervix, reach the baby's head, push it back a bit, and ease it down. I don't use force."

"What are the risks?"

Sara looks off to the side. "I apply too much pressure to the baby's neck or perforate the uterus. Neither is likely." Although Bruce is asking the questions, Sara now answers Seashell, looking straight into her drab gray eyes. "I have good hands, and I've done more complicated manipulations in Africa, including turning babies completely around in the uterus. There's still a lot of amniotic fluid, so the uterus will be buffered from"—Sara stumbles for the words—"from any jostling by the baby."

Sara doesn't mention what Holly sees as the gravest risk. Cord prolapse—the baby's head, dislodged from its perch, clearing the way for the cord to fall. Holly doesn't have the faintest idea how close the nearest hospital is, but she hopes it's near. In some states, home-birth regulations stipulate that the place of childbirth must be only fifteen minutes away from a hospital. But this home birth is outside the law on all levels. Regulations do not apply. If the cord prolapses, Holly can do nothing but stand back and watch.

"It'll be painful," Sara goes on. "Going through your cervix will hurt. But if we're doing it, we should do it now, before the baby moves down any farther."

"Let's do it," Seashell says firmly, without expression.

The manipulation, which a few minutes earlier belonged to the realm of hypothetical options, is moving precipitously into the arena of actuality. Holly's not used to aggressive interventions by a midwife, and her mind oscillates in panic. After hours of doing less than a nurse-midwife, Sara is about to do more, following a protocol of her own devising.

By the stove, Holly calls Sara in a strained voice. "Can I speak to you for a moment?" And then Holly asks, because she can't think of any other way to stall the manipulation, "Have you thought of calling a backup?" Holly is lunging at last-ditch efforts, suddenly afraid for the baby, who seems to have no advocate to represent him.

Sara laughs curtly. "Holly, get real! If I call the doc, he'll knock her out in a minute flat and section her like a tangerine before you can count to ten. *If* he doesn't yank the baby out with forceps."

"A section is a reasonable option at times." Holly doesn't like the way she sounds—priggish—or that she's in the weird situation of pressing for an obstetrical operation. She feels traitorous and right at the same time.

Exasperated, as if Holly were slow-witted, Sara says, "This isn't a face presentation. My hands can do this. They've done it before." They both look down at Sara's long-fingered hands. Digital instruments. "I've palpated that baby up, down, and sideways. I know how far to go with this and what that baby can do."

"For the record, remember that I tried to dissuade you."

"Ah, yes. Legally liable. Your disclaimer is taken. You're just a visitor, aren't you?"

"I guess so," Holly says meekly.

"Yeah, right. A visitor. Who the hell would believe that?"

Wham. Holly feels like she's been smacked in the face. She's paralyzed, because she can't stop Sara now, but she can't work as a midwife either. She's a powerless spectator, and she feels like she's going to explode.

"Holly's used to working in hospitals," Sara explains to Seashell and Bruce, who look at Holly with something uncomfortably like pity.

Holly's face reddens, and she turns to the wood stove, which heats her up more: she doesn't like being talked about as if she weren't right there.

Gloved-up, Sara presses back Seashell's labia with her left hand, placing her right hand on her abdomen to hold the baby's feet still so they won't slide back when she applies counterforce to the baby's head. "Breathe deep and easy," she tells Seashell. "It may hurt, but it won't last long."

Holly mentally follows Sara's steps. Pressing the baby's ear, her fingertips push the head up and away from the cervix so that it's "floating." Concentrating, staring at the wall and sticking out the tip of her tongue, Sara walks her fingers up the slope of the baby's head to the crown of the head, pulls it down, and flexes it.

Seashell's face contorts with a grimace, the kind she'll wear when she pushes the baby out. "Jesus, Mary, and Joseph." The bed crackles as she rhythmically pounds the mattress with her fists: that's the plastic mattress liner to protect the mattress from the rush of bodily fluids released by labor and delivery.

"It wants to come down," says Sara. "The baby wants to be all tucked in." Seashell dares to open her eyes, then shuts them fast again. Sara keeps her fingers inside until the next contraction, then turns to Holly and asks her to take the fetal heartsounds with the fetoscope. The one midwifery chore Sara has asked of Holly is the one she feels least at home with. Why should anything start to go right now?

"I can feel the fontanels and sutures," Sara says brightly. "All the familiar landmarks in place." When she withdraws her fingers, she says, relaxed, "Labor should run smoothly now." In an instant, Holly understands that Sara snapped at her because she was almost as nervous as Holly—or more so. After all, she had more to lose if things went wrong.

Exhausted, Seashell lies back in a bed of pillows that Bruce plumps loudly for her, the bones in her face rising out of her damp skin like gray driftwood. She reminds Holly of the Laplanders—those caucasian people with Indian bone structure, faces that ought to be Eskimo but are actually fair skinned and blue eyed. Maya, who'd been sent to her cubicle for the duration of the maneuvers, emerges warily, like the little matchstick girl creeping in from the cold.

"Maya should have been here," Bruce complains.

But Seashell shuts her eyes. An unspoken consensus rules: what Bruce thinks doesn't matter. And everybody ignores him.

CHAPTER 3

en in the morning, and the room is flooded with white light. A laboring woman gives off heat, and Holly strains her body to meet the breeze sneaking through an open window. Seashell is semi-sitting on the bed, one foot pressed against Sara's hip and the other against Bruce's. "I've come all this way for a dorsal lithotomy position," Holly thinks, actually relieved to see anything resembling a normal delivery. There's been enough flukiness already, for one outing.

Sara runs her fingers over Seashell's perineum with olive oil warmed on the wood stove. "Did you massage every night?" she asks Seashell.

Bruce answers for her. "Religiously."

With eyes closed, Seashell says, "Makes the sheets greasy. Uhhh!" And pushes, her arms stretched out to the side, her back curving down, pushing against a wall of human beings.

Holly holds Maya's hand, the debauched Barbie dangling from Maya's free hand. Holly is now Maya's guide through the wild world of birth. Pointing at the bulging perineum, she says, "Under that skin, that's where the baby is."

"That bump?"

"That bump."

The sterile blue paper that the surgical gloves were packed in is given a second life as Sara drapes it over the old towels meant to absorb fluid and blood. Bruce sits behind Seashell with his legs around her hips, and Seashell, her T-shirt off now and her small breasts as full as they'll ever be, leans back with her head cupped in the hollow of his throat. A photogenic position, but not practical. Seashell is doing exactly what her baby did—extending her head instead of flexing it, arching her back instead of rounding over. She has ceased putting her back into it.

The baby crowns. The object of Holly and Sara's calling is here. The

357

moment of birth and revelation as the unseen becomes seen and the idea becomes real and what has only been imagined materializes. Dark becomes light, water becomes air, and the most significant passage in the world is about to take place. The moment of truth, Holly thinks, on every possible level.

Sara delivers the head with a spill of clear fluid. An adrenaline rush hits Holly like a rough, warm wind, as everything seems hyperclear and hyperreal, and she wants this moment to go on forever. The baby's face appears reddened and puffy, his eyes swollen shut.

"It's here," Sara says, taking hold of the baby's shoulders and lifting him out of the dark warmth for good, forever. Pure and wet, the baby enters the land of the living.

"Maya!" Seashell calls, and Maya hops to her mother's side.

"Jesus, he's fuckin' lookin' at me!" Bruce greets his son.

Maya stares at the baby as Sara lifts him to Seashell's chest, wiping his face. His hair is like blackbird feathers. "This is the way it happens then," Maya says, astonished. "It happens just this way."

"The Africans I knew thought that babies come from the land of the ancestors, a place of the spirit where people go when they die. I was with my granddad when he died, and the vibrations were just like the ones at a birth, the same release of spiritual energy when pure spirit fills the room for a split second. If you could take that moment, distill it, and expand it a zillion times, you'd get the atmosphere of heaven."

Heaven, Holly thinks: spirits in motion, life force that has nothing to do with time or space.

Holly and Sara sit cross-legged on the floor, waiting for the placenta.

"Where you work, too many energies move around," Sara says. "You can't feel the birthing energy anymore."

Who is to say Holly doesn't pick up birthing energy at Morrison? "Babies get born anyway," Holly says finally. That's a chant, a mantra, an article of faith. "Babies get born."

From her bag, Sara extracts a syringe and an ampoule of Methergine, the ergot derivative that, like Pitocin, is an oxytocin but is more practical for a hemorrhage—the drug of choice for a bad situation—as it sustains one long contraction rather than produces a series of contractions. Methergine is what Levy hit Mrs. McGrath with when she was about to buy the farm in the Seven-B corridor. It's also a controlled substance.

"A midwife friend got this from a sympathetic doc," Sara says. "He figured home births would happen with or without it, and that it'd be better if we had Methergine than if we didn't. All the midwives I know stash Methergine."

The Methergine is the specter at the banquet; it puts an edge on the birth. After this tiring night, Seashell's uterus may be too exhausted to contract anymore, having stretched in and out too many times for too long. The baby, swaddled and in his receiving cap (a clean white sock cut in half, the sock's heel serving as the cap's crown), is breast-feeding, which diminishes the chance of the uterus giving out: breast-feeding stimulates natural oxytocin production.

When the placenta delivers, with a swift little stream of blood, the smell of childbirth fills the room. It's a yeasty, musty smell, as what belongs within the body's confines hits the hot, dry air. The strong smell of the placenta mixes with that of urine voided during pushing, fluids secreted by the vagina, amniotic fluid tinged with fetal cells, bits of feces already disposed of, crumpled in the blue paper that had been below Seashell's bottom. There's the smell of bad breath, too, as nobody has yet brushed his or her teeth, and the baby smells as well, of baby, of still-moist warm skin.

The smell of childbirth is an acquired taste, a good argument for keeping fathers up at the head of the bed. A midwife learns to like the atmosphere she'll work in, but before Holly was used to it, the smell moved in a thick cloud and sent her head swimming, made her woozy. An emotional smell most people smell only a few times, when they are born and when they give birth.

Sara and Holly admire the placenta in the basin. That's the midwife aesthetic, too, and Holly is envious. She almost never sees such a firm, bright placenta at Morrison.

Bruce looks over their shoulders. "Do you know people who eat it?" he asks.

Holly's stomach gives a lurch. She doesn't want to even think about eating a human organ.

"None of my clients do," Sara says. "In Africa, they took it to the outskirts of the village, dug a deep hole, and buried it."

Seashell looks up at Bruce apprehensively. "I don't want to eat it," she says.

"There's good stuff in there for you," he protests.

"That hunk of meat has done its job," Seashell says, shutting her eyes. "I don't much care if I never see it again in this lifetime."

Sara slips the placenta into a plastic bag. "Freeze it until you know what you want to do. Or take it frozen to the dump and give it the heave-ho there."

They can leave in an hour, when Sara is sure that Seashell won't hemorrhage, and they wait it out like zombie midwives. Sara sits in the lotus position, meditating, in Maya's room, among a sprawl of broken toys, while Holly meditates, too, in her own undisciplined way, in a rocking chair by the stove. The Seashell-Bruce family has collapsed on the big bed like...piglets. Piglets? Holly's mind traces back the image, to piglets she saw once on a farm, piled atop each other around the mound of warm mother.

Maya, curled up like a kitten, stares at her brother through heavy-lidded eyes. His eyes blink open. Bright blue newborn eyes, staring out from the cave of his mother's breasts, soaking in his sister's eyes. Holly has heard that siblings who attend deliveries are less prone to sibling rivalry than other kids, because the baby doesn't appear, out of the blue, to vie for the parents' affection. This baby belongs to Maya as well as to her parents. A bonding process, kids meeting babies, eyes imprinting on eyes.

Maya seems puzzled, as if she can't quite figure out the baby's existence. She saw how he got here, slipping out of her mother, but how did he come to be here, really, when he hadn't been here the day before, or the day before that? Why did the baby start to live today?

Holly is so sleepy, her thoughts come to her like dreams. "The mystery of birth," she thinks. At Morrison, babies arrive in the middle of obstetrical hurricanes, and things spin around. The atmosphere is charged, and Holly rarely has the chance to absorb what she's felt and seen. She processes information instead, spews it out onto charts and in wisecracks, or sidesteps everything, when she kicks back into her adolescent personality in the locker room, dragging on stolen cigarettes and purposely thinking of nothing. You don't think a lot about the mystery of birth at Morrison, and when you do, you don't admit it.

Go ahead, Treadwell. Think about spiritual meanings now. It's all right. She gives herself permission to flake out.

Accepting a birth, she thinks, is like accepting a death. At first, both are unreal, and acceptance is impossible, as the permanence and finality of both states are almost beyond fathoming. In grief, the mind runs about in circles, looking for a way out, an acceptable resolution. "This can't be true," it insists, taking off in search of a solution that proves the death isn't real. But each cerebral twist and turn produces the same undeniable answer. "This is the only truth. He's dead and gone forever."

When a baby is born, the mind stumbles about in a similar, less panicked way, to absorb what can't be absorbed, the existence of a brand-new person. "Here he is, never before seen. He wasn't here ten minutes ago, but he's here now." The mind boggles.

And there's a loss, as pregnancy, a way of life for so long, slow-moving and lumbersome, disappears. In contrast to the supreme permanence of the baby itself, pregnancy seems like the most fleeting condition.

Because the baby is superior to everything. Nine months to create an intricate piece of work. Cells reproducing, charging up and down the embryo to form a toe, a pancreas, a palate. The precariousness of this makes pregnancy uneasy, a mother's fears formless and sharp edged by turns. What if the blueprint is mangled and the cells go awry? The coffee I drank, that bump on the belly... But what's ridiculous is how relentless the growth is. The cells, despite their delicacy, almost always go where they're meant to. Despite the cup of coffee, they don't back off. Blobs sharpen into hands, and clumps are sculpted into legs.

Gestation won't be rushed. It's persnickety, perfectionistic, and puts impatience in its place. It's not a modern movement, but classical. The element of spirit that makes one baby different from another is where the romance enters into it.

The forty weeks' gestation is for the parents, too. The baby starts as fantasy in their minds, develops into theory, and, at term, is almost eclipsed by the plans for labor and delivery, as when wedding plans overwhelm a bride and groom, who seem beside the point in the face of the event itself.

Then, bang. The baby appears with an unimagined suddenness, and the nine months seem like a crude, inadequate stretch of time. Holly wonders if one's own death works that way. She'd always thought she'd be ready to go when she was in her eighties. She'd be tired of life, and old age pains would make her ready to give it up. But what if on her deathbed, she winds up thinking, "Is it over now? It went so fast. Give me more time."

Holly nearly bolts out of her chair, resolved to live life to the fullest. Let me at it! She sits back. This is life, too.

Is anyone ready for anything? Life has to give a shove, as labor pains make a mother want her pregnancy to be over with, make her want the baby to come into the world more than anything else in the world, more than life itself.

Holly falls asleep, her head dropping forward, her eyelids falling like shutters. A wisp of a dream drifts across her mind. A little kid—a girl at first, then a boy—runs toward her. His arms stretched out, his eyes bright. "Mom! Mom!" Holly scoops him up and can feel the curve of his back, his soft, almost-baby hair. She hugs him tight. Then her arms are empty, and the boy is gone.

"Holly," Sara is saying. "It's time to go."

Seashell, Bruce, Maya and the baby are huddled on the bed like piglets—or was it puppies?—and sleeping their way into a new life.

CHAPTER 4

Holly is asleep, in a sleep that seems beyond dreams, below dreams. Now she has to swim up from that level, because someone is knocking on the door. Holly pushes through yards of mental cobwebs to reach the point where she remembers where she is. Right. She's at Sara's, in the living room, and someone is knocking on the kitchen door. Now all she needs to do is remember where Sara's bedroom is. Should she walk around dressed as she is, in her underpants and one of Matt's soccer shirts? She pulls on her jeans, staggering to the staircase, hits her shin on a chair, and glances at her watch. A bit after midnight, it feels like the dead of night.

She calls Sara from the foot of the stairs. A stunned voice shouts, "What?" Sara is pushing her way through her own cobwebs.

"It's me—Holly! Somebody's at the door!"

The hall light flips on, and Sara charges down the stairs, looking about twelve years old with her auburn hair flouncing against a flannel nightgown. A match for Katrina, who always looks about twelve years old herself. Katrina and Sara would have a cumulative age of twenty-four. Maybe lay midwifery keeps you young.

Sara peers through the gauzy curtains on the kitchen door. "Geez, it's Peter Zimmer," she whispers, opening the door.

Peter Zimmer is an Amish man in round-brimmed hat, with a thick beard and strong blue eyes, cautiously avoiding actually looking at Sara, who is, after all, in dishabille, even if her nightgown is more modest than Holly's jeans and jersey. "It's time," he says, gazing at the kitchen table as a resolution.

"Else isn't due for another two weeks."

"Her mother is visiting and must go home in a few days. Else wanted the baby to come before the mother goes back."

362

Sara tells him her apprentice and she will gather their things, then follow him out to the farm in her own car. She shuffles out to the stairwell, Holly following. "Mennonite. He drives a car but doesn't have a phone. Go figure."

"I thought delivering without a phone was against your principles."

"They'd use a midwife, phone or no phone, and the midwife may as well be me. Besides, nobody's going to prosecute me for attending a Mennonite birth. Midwifery is their legal right. As a midwife, I happen to be part of their religious principles." She ransacks a battered dresser for clean clothes.

"Is your equipment sterilized?"

"I didn't even unpack my bag." Sara runs a brush through her hair. "I usually bake everything in the oven at 250 degrees for an hour, but now we don't have an hour. Those Mennonites don't cry wolf. If Peter Zimmer says the baby is on the way, I take his word for it. We'll boil the equipment when we get there."

"I always wanted to hear a midwife shout for boiling water," Holly says.

"You're going to hear one now. A time warp of the first degree. You're in charge of the boiling water."

"These Mennonites keep themselves in the best physical shape," Sara tells Holly, as they follow Peter Zimmer's car past moonlit fields. "How often do you see bodies that have never touched liquor or junk food or cigarettes or drugs?" Try never, Holly thinks. "And the Mennonite ladies aren't scared of being strong."

"They don't have their own midwives?" Holly asks, shivering. The Rambler is strong on nostalgia value, but lacks amenities like heat.

"The Mennonite community here has only three families, with the rest of their people elsewhere. Don't ask me why. You don't get too inquisitive with these guys. The hippie types out here like them." Sara glances at Holly. "Were you ever a hippie?"

"I'm too young to have been a hippie."

"There are hippies here who are only twenty years old."

"I'm too nasty to have been a hippie, then," Holly says.

"Yeah," Sara says. "That sounds about right."

Peter Zimmer's car turns into a long driveway. There's almost a full moon, and a farm as idyllic as Holly has ever seen takes shape in the darkness. Horses shuffle behind a gate, their glossy coats catching the moonlight. Behind the shut doors of a barn, a cow lows softly, as if talking in her sleep or clearing her throat. Old trees creak in the breeze.

"We should have come by horseback," Sara says, swinging out of the car. "That'd be a dream come true."

The house, with no shutters and dark windows, seems to glow in the moonlight. Is anyone at home there? A woman laboring inside those bare white walls? Holly knows what Denise would say. "Keep your eye out for Cujo, girl. You know those country folks are whacked."

Sara and Holly follow Peter Zimmer into the house, walking through a dark dining room with a long table and straight-backed chairs—Holly's mother would declare them "darling Shaker chairs, just charming"—and into a bedroom just off the parlor. The sick room, Holly thinks. The architectural equivalent to the A bed, the hot bed, in the labor rooms back home in Morrison.

In bed, her hair back, and wearing a white flannel gown, Else looks plain and unflinching—at least, that is what Holly makes out by the light from the kerosene lamp on the night table—with the covers pulled up to her shoulders and sweat collecting on her forehead and neck. Else's mother sits by the bed in a dark, calf-length dress, her hair in a cap that reminds Holly uncomfortably of the hairnet she wore when she worked in the college cafeteria, which embarrassed her whenever a good-looking guy happened by.

"How'd you get your labor to come on so early?" Sara asks gently, sitting on the bed.

"Herbs." Else reaches under the bedclothes for a bottle of capsules that contain pennyroyal, blue cohosh, raspberry. Holly wonders if the Mennonites' purity makes them susceptible to herbs. Holly senses that her body, abused by beers, junk food, and cigarettes, would resist their too-gentle powers.

"Some crazy herbs," Sara says.

"I did what you told me, too," Else says, inching closer to Sara. "With the bosoms."

"Ah." Sara understands. "Now I know it works."

Else is talking about nipple stimulation, rubbing each nipple for five minutes to trigger the natural production of oxytocin and induce contractions. Holly has heard of nipple stimulation used to run a stress test, to see how well a baby will withstand the stress of labor, but never knew it could actually induce labor. Where there's a will...

Else takes a contraction by shutting her eyes, mumbling, snorting, and opening her eyes, then Sara clears the room for an examination that is chaste, Victorian, and conducted entirely under the tent of Else's nightgown, with Sara staring into space.

"I thought of breaking the waters," Else says. "If the herbs and the other thing didn't bring on the pains."

"Never do that, Else. It's not good for the baby or for you. How'd you think you'd manage it?"

"My mother would do it. She knows about these things."

"Let the waters break when they break. Everything in its own time." Then Sara looks up at Holly. "Boiling water," she says. Holly likes the way those words sound, and she knows she could have lived an entire life without ever having heard them at all.

· · ·

Peter Zimmer stokes the kitchen stove as Holly spreads Sara's instruments on the kitchen table. Cord scissors, mosquito forceps, eyedroppers, bulb syringes, metal Amnihook. Else is at nine centimeters and not a hair out of place. Maybe deeply religious women think of God watching them as they suffer in labor and try to please Him by their calm and strength. What would God think of old Holly? she wonders. It's not one of her grander moments—watching a pot simmer and percolate en route to a boil.

Holly drops the instruments into the water, allows them to bubble about, then wraps them in a clean towel and hurries back to the labor room, only to be exiled to a high-backed .chair in the dark parlor. Silhouetted against the bay windows across the room are two women, their ages impossible to tell in the dimness, and both are dressed in long skirts, aprons, and the little cap that reminds Holly of the loathed hairnet. They are thick swift-moving silhouettes, whoever they are, and they are folding linen.

Holly is about to doze off, but she feels so serene, she thinks, "This is better than sleeping," as if she were on a retreat, away from the world, by a cool stream. These religious people must know something she doesn't to live in peace like this. *They know God, Treadwell.* Oh, yes. That's it.

Sara has been exiled as well. She and Holly sit side by side, across the room from the three-dimensional shadow women, and Holly listens to Sara's rhythmic breathing. "Your breathing is putting me to sleep," Holly complains.

"That's because I *was* asleep."

"How can you sleep now? Aren't you keyed up?" Holly asks, though she lacks the usual adrenalinized birth rush herself.

"Are *you* keyed up?"

"No."

"All right then," Sara says. "Let me sleep."

But Peter Zimmer opens the labor room door. "Come, Sara."

Sara uses the proper expletive under the circumstances. "My goodness! The baby is almost here, and you didn't say a word!"

"We wanted you to be here," says Else.

"Thanks a lot!"

Else's face, wrenched out of its smooth calm at last, winces as she bears down. Sara has pulled up her nightgown, and by the lamp's flickering light, Holly sees the baby's head start to crown.

"Holly, hot compresses, please."

The compresses will loosen up the perineal tissue to protect against tears. Holly grabs a small towel from the stack of linen by the bed, hurries to the kitchen, dips the towel into the still-boiling water, and charges back to the labor room. She feels imbalanced, rushing with adrenaline in a peaceful place like this.

Sara applies the compress as Else sits back with her nightgown hiked to the waist. "Easy, now, dear," Sara says. "No pushing."

The baby's head is shiny, and Holly now sees why. The baby is still inside the bag of waters. Holly always ruptures the membranes as the second stage begins, to check for meconium staining. She's never seen this before. What if the fluid's full of meconium? Babies born in the sac run a greater risk of pneumonia—they have a better chance of aspirating meconium. Sara always goes a step beyond the point where Holly will go. *You know new things scare you, Treadwell. You're just like the others at Morrison.* Maybe so, she considers, and her fears give way to the clinical pleasure of seeing what she's never seen before.

"A caul baby," she murmurs to Sara. The opening of *David Copperfield* reads, "I was born with a caul," and Dickens describes how the caul (the amniotic sac) was put up for sale as a charm to protect the owner from death by drowning. Like placentas today, Holly thinks: a magic potion.

"Caul babies have good luck," Sara says, running a gloved finger along the curve of the vaginal outlet to coax it to give. "They're cushioned as they move down the birth canal," she says, for the benefit of Else's mother and Peter Zimmer. "Less affected by birth trauma."

Holly taps the bed frame, knocking wood and bringing her heathen superstitions into the religious house. She doesn't feel she has a choice, since Sara has talked about good luck when the baby isn't even born yet.

Streaks of white appear on the perineum—Holly would cut a small episiotomy now—but Sara doesn't move. A trickle of blood as the perineum tears, and Holly winces. The baby's head retracts back. "Pant, Else," Sara says. When the baby's head pushes forward, Sara snags the membranes with the Amnihook. Gush. Then she hooks the baby's double chin, which holds the baby back, over the perineum.

With the double chin, Holly's fear rises up. Fear and adrenaline are part and parcel. Without fear, no adrenaline, and without adrenaline, no hyperawareness of what might come next. It's bad luck not to have some fear at birth. The fates will punish them for complacency, for failing to will the baby out with every fiber of their being. The presumption that everything will go fine is pleasant, but to Holly, it's disaster—an attitude that permits your brain to doze off.

Besides, transition into life is meant to inspire fear and joy. That's the meaning of awe. That's what comes with meeting life face to face.

Sara peels the membranes from the baby's face, and the baby snorts, wrinkling his nose, looking disdainful of the whole process. The big-cheeked, fat-headed potentate of a baby is comical, and everyone laughs, as the baby is here and it's almost over. Pause, as they wait for the baby's restitution and the slow clockwork turn of the head. But the baby doesn't give.

"All right then," Sara says. "Here you go." She slips her hands inside Else, who gasps, and presses firmly on the baby's shoulders. The baby moves slowly, with strain. "Okay," Sara says tensely, because everything is not okay. She has just completed the ninety-degree rotation that the baby couldn't complete himself, and Holly sees it all clearly. Shoulder dystocia. The shoulders packed in tight. "Push with the contraction, Else," Sara tells her.

Holly wipes the baby's face, and the baby winces, but no one laughs this time. How long does it take for laughter to shift into fear? Maybe ten seconds. Fear to joy, joy to fear, a rocking back and forth until the baby is born. The baby isn't born.

Sara checks to see if the umbilical cord is keeping the baby reined in, being too short or wrapped around a leg. But the cord has plenty of slack, and Sara says authoritatively, "Push with the contraction, Else. Holly, grab Else's leg so she pushes against your hip. Peter, follow Holly."

Holly takes Else's foot in hand and clamps it to her hip. Human stirrups. "Home birth is a disaster waiting to happen," she can hear Levy say, although shoulder dystocia happens all the time in the hospital, where Holly and Levy would be just as helpless.

"Push now!" Sara speaks as loudly as Holly has heard her speak. Sara wants Else to dig in and know this is the most serious thing in the world. "Push!"

Else grunts, with the animal grunt that sends babies into the world and seems to come from someplace other than the woman about to deliver. A primal noise, a mother-grunt of the ages, that gives women access to a power they can draw on only at the moment of birth. A physical inspiration. "Uhhh!"

"Let me cut a 'pis," Holly pleads, knowing Sara won't.

Sara thinks for a second, then hands her the scissors. "Go."

Holly isn't gloved, but better an infection than this... what might happen. Grabbing a flashlight from her bag, Sara spotlights the perineum as Holly searches for the course of the previous tear, hoping to follow it with her cut. But the baby blocks her view, and she slips two bare fingers behind the perineum, snips a long midline, and prays the cut won't rip to the rectum. All babies get born, and this baby will get born, she promises herself, even if Sara has to break his clavicle to get him out.

"I'm going to press on it," Holly tells Sara.

"Go."

Standing over Else, Holly presses down hard, above the pubic bone, hoping to lower the baby's shoulder so it clears the pubic arch, as Sara does firm head traction, pulling the head without yanking or twisting it. But the pressure does no good. Holly's adrenaline is pumping in earnest, and she could pick up the bed and carry it outside if that would help, but it won't, because this is shoulder dystocia and the baby is going nowhere.

Midwife's law: When the baby's stuck, change position.

"Let's get Else on all fours," Sara says bluntly.

"All fours?" Peter's face is white with fear.

But Sara can't explain. She and Holly help Else roll onto her knees, Holly gathering up Else's gown and piling it on her back and Else facing the wall above the headboard, her head lowered. Sara scoots below Else, like a mechanic under a car, and works at the baby to unscrew him as if twisting out a cork.

Holly is shaking, her hands want to move, and she shuts her eyes in one long blink. When she opens them, the baby's anterior shoulder, the one closest to the opening, to life, slips out.

"Here it is," Sara says. A shoulder out, and Holly's own shoulders fall with relief. "Two shoulders. The whole baby. A fat baby girl."

The shift from terror to joy is too quick, and everyone is stunned. All-systems-go for catastrophe, they now have to go into radical reverse and double back, to happiness. Nobody can do the trip in ten seconds. Half a minute, possibly.

Tears pool on Else's face, and Peter kisses the top of her head, then straightens up and turns a moment to the wall to cry.

"All right, baby, let's hear you holler," Sara says, slapping the baby's toes and blowing in her face. The baby is bluish but cries loudly. "A nice cry," says Sara, voice muffled from her odd position under the bridge of Else's body. "Now we have to get out of here." Else lowers onto her side as Sara shimmies out, passing the baby, whose cord isn't cut yet, to Else, while Else's mother rushes forward with a blanket and a towel.

Pained, Peter glances first at Sara, then at the floor. "She's all right then?" he asks, meaning Else or the baby or both.

"All fine. Say hello with a great big kiss." Sara turns to Holly. "It looks like you bought yourself a suture job, apprentice," she says.

"That would be my pleasure," Holly says. At last, her hands will move.

Sara and Holly eat by candlelight at the long dining room table. Whole-wheat bread with fresh butter, smoked turkey, carrot cake, unpasteurized milk. The room is washed blue by the almost-morning light. "I could live a long and happy life on food like this," Holly says. "I didn't know bread and butter could taste so good."

She replays the delivery in her mind. What did Sara not do that Holly might have done in a hospital? An earlier episiotomy may have helped, but the one Holly did cut hadn't done much good.

"Thank you, God," Holly says out loud.

"Thank you," Sara says.

Holly had never sewn up an episiotomy without anesthesia before. She'd hesitated, but Sara had said, "The tissues are anesthetized as is. But the longer you wait, the less they are." When Holly considers Else's stoicism, it's hard to tell just how numb those tissues were.

The Mennonite ladies sweep into the room, ghostly attendants, and put down a pitcher of cider that's just about to turn. It's the best thing Holly can remember drinking.

"I feel like we're the meeting of the sacred and profane," Holly whispers. "Where I work it's loud, bright, godless. Where you work, it's

quiet, dark, religious. I live on hot dogs and Coke. Here, you have this."
And she points to the Mennonite food.

"I have my profane moments," Sara says, looking at Holly curiously.

"What?"

"I'm making out the features of a convert on your face."

"To Mennonitism, or whatever it's called?"

"To home birth."

From the labor room, the baby lets out a cry, gurgles, falls silent.

Holly's not a convert. She dodges the question by saying, "I never saw that all-fours method before."

"You risk urethral tears, but it's worth the risk."

"How come you don't believe in episiotomies?"

"Tearing is more economical. A woman tears only what she needs to tear. An episiotomy may cut more than you need. And suturing doubles the trauma—puncturing already traumatized tissues."

If anything, Holly is converted to natural foods, she decides. The sky lightens. Mist hangs in the trees and in pockets on the field, like dust balls. She peers at Sara's watch. "What time is it?"

"That's not the question," says Sara.

"No?"

"The question is, what century is this?"

When they both laugh, their breath blows out the candle in front of them. The sun is up.

CHAPTER 5

Holly is glad to be home, and she stares at Matt in the dark. All she can really see is the gloss of his eyes.

"I feel like I know you," she says. "You're like my family. You're like a brother to me."

"We're close," he agrees, staring back at her. "I tell you things I don't tell anybody else."

She lies back and rests with her head under his arm.

"Is that offer still open for us moving in together?" she asks, because when she was away, she missed him. She is tired of missing him.

He props up on his elbow. "Sure." Then he says, tentatively, "We could do more than that, you know."

Holly knows what he means. He's talking about marriage.

"Do you think so?" she asks, wanting to know.

"I think so," he says. He breathes deeply. "I'm too old and tired to have a girlfriend."

"Matt, you're only thirty years old."

"I'm too old and tired anyway. Dating sucks."

"I wouldn't call what we do dating."

"When are we going to move in together so you can be a bitch full-time?"

"April or May. When we'll want to change our lives. Before it gets too hot. I won't want to move in if it's too hot."

Matt lies back. "Good," he says. "It's really happening then."

"It's starting to happen," she says.

"Good," says Matt. "I'm glad."

HOWARD STREET

CHAPTER 1

Holly is back, taking everything slow, as she is in as much culture shock as her person can stand. She moves slowly, says little, lets time readjust for her.

There's the weekly meeting of the midwives in the conference room, and Mrs. Gruener holds up her hand for silence among her followers. "Fundal height," she says.

Glances bounce around the room. Paula to Holly to Pam. Paula rubs her hand over her rubbery face. "Fundal height," she repeats. "What about it?"

"No more of this 'normal for dates' business," Mrs. Gruener says. "What is 'normal for dates'? Nothing. What is one midwife's normal compared to another midwife's normal? There is such a thing as a tape measure. A standard measure recognized all over the world. And on the tape measure are marks for centimeters. Please feel free to utilize these centimeters."

At each AP visit, a patient's belly is measured from the top of her *symphisis pubis* to the end of the fundus. At twenty weeks, the fundus is a finger width below the patient's navel. At twenty-four weeks, a finger width above. When everything checks out, the midwives casually mark on their charts "FH—NFD," which translates as "fundal height—normal for dates."

But as a check on fetal growth, that kind of measurement is useless, unless there's a gross size/dates discrepancy. The only way to monitor fetal growth is to compare one fundal height measurement with the previous one. If the midwives don't mark down exact measurements, the only point of comparison with the previous visit is the vague and subjectively interpreted finding of "normal for dates."

Mrs. Gruener clasps her hands. "Do you understand me? This is the riot act, ladies. Do you know what that means?"

"If we misbehave one more time, we get the can," Paula growls.

"Paula understands plain English," Mrs. Gruener says. "Now, fundal height. Measurement technique. We are going to standardize it. When you utilize these tape measures, which the clinic supplies in abundance, I want you to consider the standardization of technique, so all the centimeters arrive in the same place. Some of you, when you use the tape measure, hold it out from the abdomen and do not follow the curve of the fundus."

Mrs. Gruener looks about the room for those midwives who subscribe to this method. Nobody looks up.

"We are not going to do it this way, and Marge has provided a new page in the protocol to this effect. You are to run the tape measure along the fundal slope to the very end. In my view, this is considerably more accurate."

"Mrs. Gruener," Barbara says, back stiffening.

"Yes, Barbara."

"I was taught that you get a more accurate reading if you don't follow the slope exactly." Barbara waits expectantly. Mrs. Gruener says nothing. "We could do it one way for a while and see what the overall impact is," she adds with a jerk of her head.

"I suppose we could," Mrs. Gruener says, matching Barbara's stiffness. "But we won't."

"What about the girls over at Seven-B?" Paula puts in. "How're they gonna learn to do it right?"

"I'll explain when they come in."

"I can't believe you want to put these finger widths to sleep, Mrs. Gruener, after serving you so well all these years."

"Oh, Paula, you may keep the finger widths. Just give me centimeters in the box on your AP charts in addition to them."

Like a queen finished with a press conference, Mrs. Gruener leaves the room first. Then the midwives explode.

"Talk about nitpicky!" Pam says. "Maybe we should make sure all the tape measures are from the same company so we can really *standardize.*"

"Oh, come on, Pam," Holly says. "You know we get lazy. Ballotte the uterus, then mark down NFD."

"Not me," Paula says, shaking her head.

"What do you do then?" Pam asks.

"I eyeball it," Paula says, padding out of the room.

"Naw, she doesn't eyeball the fundus and then decide it's normal for dates," Holly says. "No way."

Pam looks her in the eye. "Oh, yeah?"

"Think in thirty years I could do that?"

"Hell, I can do it now," Pam says, lifting her chin.

"And you do," Barbara says, collecting her pad and pencil and scooting out the door.

"Do you?" Holly asks.

"Hell, no, I eyeball it, then measure it by fingers. Of course, I'm always right."

"Except when you mistook that obese girl coming in for an IUD for an AP case."

"Extraordinary circumstances," Pam says, and sweeps out the door.

Holly follows her. "It was extraordinary, all right, when you asked, 'When was your last period, dear?' and the girl said, 'Three days ago.'"

"She was three fingers into thirty-two weeks, Treadwell," Pam snorts. "I don't care what you say."

"Your fingers were sleeping, Donnelly."

Barbara winces. "We don't talk in fingers anymore." A Sparks follower. That's the key. That's why Holly doesn't like Barbara. She's a whiter, thinner, younger Sparks. But she's Sparks, all right.

"Centimeters." Holly nods. "I guess I'll feel free to utilize them now."

CHAPTER 2

Marge knocks on Holly's door. "There's some school principal on the line for you."

"Did they catch me smoking in the hallway?"

"Sounds like it," Marge says, retreating.

It's Edgar C. Dawkins, of Monroe High School. "I'm calling in reference to Desiree Hodges."

For a moment, Holly figures Desiree is busted, Desiree is dead, Desiree burned down the school building. Holly's hatred for school principals is less vestigial than she thought. She now tries to squelch it, but that's hard to do, listening to Edgar C. Dawkins's pompous voice. Is there a school principal who doesn't think he commands an entire nation of pathetic underlings?

"She's a patient of yours, I believe?"

"Yes."

"And you want her to leave school in the middle of the day for a third appointment? Two appointments in one week? Just what is a CNM, Miss Treadwell?"

Cantankerous Nuisance Maker, Mr. Edgar C. Dawkins.

"Certified nurse-midwife, Mr. Dawkins. We're the primary clinicians at the maternity services here at Howard Street."

This might be of interest to you, Mr. Dawkins, considering almost a quarter of your female students get pregnant every year.

"And just what does a CNM do?"

Patient advocate, counselor, school liaison, social worker, crisis intervenor, family planning adviser, labor-sitter, baby catcher . . .

"We're specialists in normal birth—prenatal care, intrapartal care, et cetera."

"Don't three appointments strike you as excessive? We don't want to set a bad example for the rest of the students. If because a girl is pregnant, she thinks she can skip off in the middle of the day—"

Skip. Yeah, right.

"Mr. Dawkins, we don't really consider pregnancy to be a minor affair. It's a major event, and some of these young women are not in the best of health—"

"Still, when a student takes off in the middle of the school day, she becomes an object of envy and admiration—"

"Mr. Dawkins, the reason we have frequent appointments with some of these younger women is to make it clear that pregnancy isn't a lark, to reinforce the seriousness—"

"Can't you schedule appointments after school hours in the future?"

"I'll try, Mr. Dawkins, but it isn't always possible."

"I'd appreciate as much."

"Mr. Dawkins, maybe you'd like to come down here to visit one day? Meet with the head of the maternity services and—"

"I'm sure that would be very nice," Mr. Dawkins says, and hangs up.

And talk about one of the most serious problems facing your population today, Mr. Dawkins. I'm sure that would be very nice as well.

Holly looks at the phone receiver, thinks, "I was right to hate school principals," and slams down the phone.

CHAPTER 3

Dr. Pollard comes racing up the corridor from the elevators, his wide tie and white jacket flying. He looks like a refugee from a college campus circa 1972 with his big beard, gold-rimmed glasses, and longish hair. By never altering a thing about his appearance, he also never seems to age.

"Beatrice!" he says to Mrs. Gruener in a rushed, anxious voice. Holly can't stand it when Mrs. Gruener is called that. Mrs. Gruener has one proper name, and that is Mrs. Gruener. "King's County just called. They have a fourteen-year-old girl there who was raped by her uncle. She won't let anyone examine her. I told them to send her here. Can you handle it?"

Mrs. Gruener looks with satisfaction at Holly, because this is Dr. Pollard's way of showing confidence in the midwifery service, as well he should. Confidently, Mrs. Gruener turns to Holly and says, "Can you handle it, Holly?"

Holly fails to feel the same confidence. Hesitatingly she says, "I don't know the rape protocol. Maybe Paula should do it."

Mrs. Gruener's eyes flash at Holly. "We can handle it," she tells Dr. Pollard.

When he has rushed back to his office, Mrs. Gruener turns angrily to Holly. "Don't you ever do that again."

"What?"

"Show the slightest bit of doubt in front of Dr. Pollard. Express your doubts in private. Do you understand?" But before Holly can answer, Mrs. Gruener has stormed off to tell Paula to get ready.

Incest and rape as a career opportunity. Holly is a coward. She doesn't want to see it.

Last year, she had a rape victim. An unreported, unconfessed rape victim. She was thirteen years old, came to the clinic alone, was completely devoid of expression, and wouldn't let Holly examine her. Holly called Hilda, who stayed with the girl for her first few visits. In a case like this, the patient has all her appointments with one midwife, rather than rotating midwives on a team.

For the second visit, Holly inserted only a Q-Tip.

"That doesn't hurt, does it?" The girl shook her head. "I promise not to hurt you," Holly said. And during the third visit, she inserted her finger. "That doesn't hurt, does it?" This was to build up trust—Holly said she wouldn't hurt her, and she lived up to her promise. The girl could trust Holly. When at last Holly did examine her, she found lacerations, streaks where whoever had had intercourse with her had punctured the walls. It had taken Holly a while to recover. The girl's eyes had gone dead. Holly couldn't recover from that.

Maybe Holly hasn't recovered at all.

When the ambulance arrives with the raped girl and her mother, Holly can hear the girl crying in the hallway and Paula's voice subduing her. "Mami! Mami!" Holly hides out in her examining room and feels her stomach sink in sickness.

"I want a job where I can laugh it off," she says out loud. Then lowers her head on the desk. She could stay like that forever.

CHAPTER 4

"I'm not coming out," Holly says, punching down the files Marge has put on her desk. "I have a caseload of twenty patients, and I'm not coming out to see no good-time girl gloating over me."

"She brought some delicious pastry," Pam says. "Croissants and all that French garbage."

"I don't want to." She pounds her caseload with her fist. "Check it out—how am I going to get through them all? I pray for no-shows. Is that a pleasant attitude for a midwife to take?"

"Don't be a problem child. Five minutes won't kill you. Just because Gina is rich and beautiful and happy doesn't mean you have to hide out in your office."

"Hey, I'm beautiful and happy."

"Looked in the mirror lately?"

"Give me a break—you mean I'm not beautiful?"

"You look okay. It's the happy part I wonder about. Anyway, if you don't come out, she'll know you're jealous and gloat even more."

Holly considers this. "I'll be out in a minute."

She pulls her hairbrush and lipstick from her desk and brushes her hair, glides on the lipstick, glances in the mirror. She looks tired and plain. "I could have sworn I used to be pretty," she tells herself. As an afterthought, she pulls out a compact and smacks some powder on her face. "Chalk face," she says to herself.

Gina is the fallen angel, the angel who cracked. She was seduced, she tumbled, she fell, she became happy and rich working for big money, in a huge bank, doing something international and incomprehensible. She told all the midwives that she was going to look for a job in the private sector.

"The what sector?" Paula said. "What's that?"

"Doing what?" all the midwives asked.

"Something where I can work nine to five and make a lot of money."

"You wouldn't be happy doing that," Pam had said, shaking her head.

"I'm not happy doing this," Gina had said.

And Holly knew this was true, as she was with Gina when she broke out of her orbit, in orbital decay, which occurs when you stay too long in the same orbital groove—the motion abrades the mass that maintains the orbit, the motion alters the mass's shape, and the mass sails off course, crashing into anything that stands in its way as it falls.

The day she blew off course, she had burst into Holly's office while Holly was examining a patient and screamed, "Getting a history out of these people is like doing veterinary medicine! Stamp two times for yes and one time for no! I can't take it anymore!" And then, in a Spanish accent, she said, "I doan remember the pill I took, Miss Gina. It was big. It was red. I took 'em three times. Maybe ten times. I doan remember." And then, in an American black accent, "He tol' me if we did it standing up I wouldn't get it. Pregnant, I mean, Miss Gina. Or was it the whachmacallit, the gonorrhea?" And then, loudly, in her own voice, "I can't take it anymore."

A rather impolitic performance considering a young black woman lay on the examining table, whom Holly had to leave as she escorted Gina into the supply room. "Easy on the racist stereotypes, Gina. This isn't exactly Klan country, you know. I mean, that stuff doesn't go down here."

But in the supply room, Gina had broken down—crying and shaking. "It's not racist. If these were a bunch of dumb white folks, I'd do the same. Believe me, I worked in Chicago, and those white people weren't much better. 'Miss Gina, maybe I should head on back to Kentucky and have my li'l baby there. In the outhouse.'"

"Gina, you have a gift for accents. Maybe you should give all this up for the stage or something. Or take a long vacation."

"Try a permanent vacation." She blew her nose and unraveled an entire spool of nitrazine paper, tearing its ten-foot length into little bits. "I dream of being a normal person. Get up in the morning, go to work, come home, eat dinner. Meet nice guys."

Holly nods. "Sounds good to me."

"Think that's impossible?"

"Two hundred million Americans can't be wrong, and that's how many aren't midwives and seem to survive."

"But I'm twenty-nine years old. How can I just change careers now?"

"People do it all the time, Gina. When you're fifty years old, you'll look back and see how young you are," said Holly, who was then twenty-seven and had a hard time remembering that she was young.

"Think so?" Gina sniffed.

"Sure. You're a free agent. This is a free country. Do whatever it is you really want to do."

Gina laughed through her tears. "I want to make money. That's what I want to do."

And according to all reports, Gina is thriving, which is not how the story is supposed to end, is not the object lesson she is supposed to illustrate for the midwives left behind. Burnout victims are supposed to cut loose, wander about the earth, and live bereft of real purpose or meaning, then return to the fold, calmer, serene, devoted. They're not supposed to find happiness in jobs that involve huge transfers of money, puts, calls, zero sums. They're not supposed to give the impression they've done the right thing.

The waiting room is a roar of little children, chatting mothers-to-be, laughing clerks. "Hi, Holly," a patient calls out. "Holly!" another one calls. They're fighting over her hellos, waiting for her to show a favorite. That's more like it! She loves them, too. *Fancy that, Treadwell, they actually want to see you.* Holly wants to see them, too. It's Gina she doesn't want to see. "Back in a minute, fans," she says, and they laugh.

Gina looks well maintained. Her hair is permed and cut nicely. Her skin looks fresh. Her eyes are bright. She's in a light skirt with a linen blazer and wears what no midwife in her right mind would wear: high heels. Her stockings are not support hose. "Holly!"

"Gina!"

"God, you're same as always!"

"That's me—same as always!" Holly says brightly, furiously. "You look great! The private sector suits you."

"It suits me all right. My burnout days are over."

"Watch out you don't get burned in—what is it? Investment banking?"

"No, the firm gets burned, I keep my nose clean."

Laughs are traded. When Gina quit two years ago, her skin was blotchy, and her hair long and scraggly. She broke into tears easily, and she snapped at patients. Now she looks resplendent and collected and prosperous and calm, holding out a box of almond croissants.

Holly doesn't know what to say, and neither does Gina. It's as if Gina wanted to show that she'd made the right choice. And now that she's exhibited herself, there's not much to say.

"So nothing's really changed?" Gina asks, pitying them all.

Paula shrugs. "There's always some new little girl who got herself knocked up," she says. "That's change."

"But really?"

Holly considers for a moment. She's changed. She's become a more confident midwife. Her skills improve by the day. She's become more sure that being a midwife is how she wants to spend her life. Even if she is tired and plain that day.

"You don't count on anything changing out there," Holly says, gesturing with her head toward the waiting room. "You count on things changing in here." And she taps her head. She doesn't know what she's talking about, but it's impressive enough for Pam to say, "Amen."

"Well, the place still smells of Lysol," says Gina, by way of a joke.

"We don't use Lysol," Paula says, sinking her teeth into an almond croissant. "Too expensive. We use the generic brand. A big tub with black letters saying 'Industrial Cleaner.'"

"If budget cuts keep up," says Pam, "we'll be using it instead of Betadine."

"I guess budget cuts don't really affect you anymore, Gina," Holly says. "I guess the economy is treating you okay."

Gina gives her a piercing look. "Right. I don't give a shit what happens now, as long as it's good for the company."

"I'm sorry," Holly apologizes. "I thought you were somebody else."

"Who did you think I was?"

Holly opens her eyes wide, trying to make sense out of herself. "I don't know."

Pam and Gina look at each other and say, *"Burnout!"*

CHAPTER 5

Holly is stacking the gym mats from childbirth class when a tall figure in brocade slippers appears in the doorway. That's Regina. Regina is at term, but that doesn't mean she doesn't do it up in striped capri pants and sandals with pink socks. Her rich hair is in a thick ponytail that sways as she moves as a real pony's tail would. She intercepts Holly as Holly drags the mats into the corner.

"I gotta talk to you, Holly," she says in her husky voice.

Holly looks up, as if she hadn't seen Regina come in. "God, Regina, you do an incredible job with your makeup. You should give me some pointers." Regina's face does not look pregnant.

"Your palette is out of date," Regina says flatly, like a policeman informing you that you're parked in a no-parking zone.

"My palette?"

"Look, when I open my own shop, I'll send you a card. Now come over here." She pulls at Holly's arm and leads her to a table by the door. "I have something in my purse," she says when they are both seated. "A hundred dollars. My due date was yesterday. A hundred dollars for you, Holly, if you take my baby today." She surveys Holly's face. "And I'll help you update your palette."

Stunned for a second, Holly laughs. "It'll take more than a hundred bucks for you to induce me to induce you!"

Regina nods. She was expecting as much. "That was my first offer," she says in her heavy Brooklyn accent. Her boyfriend, a thick, muscular guy, is standing in the doorway with a flowered overnight bag in his hand—for the hospital, Holly guesses. He looks like a hitman, a Mafia soldier, an enforcer, and Holly wonders if he'll threaten to break her kneecaps if she doesn't induce Regina. Holly decides to go on the presumption that he won't lay a hand on her. "One hundred fifty," Regina says. "Final offer."

Holly has to nip this whole bargaining process in the bud. "Regina, it's illegal to induce a patient just for her convenience."

"It doesn't have to be illegal. You could say there's something wrong with me. And there is, Holly! I'm gonna be so neurotic if you don't do this. I'll be a psychological case." Zipping open her little pink purse, Regina takes out an envelope full of bills. "Two hundred dollars. My final offer."

"No go, girl. Look-it, you don't want to be induced, believe me. It's a pain in the ass. Labor hurts more, takes longer, and if your cervix isn't ripe and ready to go, the Pitocin won't do anything but put you in a world of hurt. What's your hurry anyway?"

"We have plans, that's all," Regina says, glancing toward her boyfriend and stuffing the envelope into her purse. "But if you can't help me, I'll find another midwife who can. I'll tell them I've been pregnant ten months." Regina scrapes her chair back.

"I don't think you'll find another midwife who'll do it. We're all in this together."

Narrowing her eyes, Regina says, "You're all a bunch of liars. You tell a person the baby is going to come on such-and-such a day. Then the baby don't come, and you don't do anything about it. I call that a lie." She tosses back her ponytail and plows into her boyfriend, who blocks the door. "Two hundred dollars!" she exclaims in the corridor to her boyfriend. "And she turned me down!"

Holly rests her head on her forearms. The estimated due date is out of hand. The estimation part is not getting through. The notion of a two-week margin of error isn't hitting home. Maybe the midwives ought to add a week on to all the patients' due dates. That way, nobody would feel betrayed. And of course, nobody would be ready either, and if perchance they had to go to another hospital, they might be mistaken for premature labor cases. But something has to be done.

Holly has never been offered a bribe before. Two hundred dollars. What an insult! She runs into the corridor and calls out to Regina.

"What?" Regina says, enraged.

"Ten thousand bucks," Holly says. "And we'll talk."

Regina glances at her boyfriend, then turns and starts walking.

THE FUTTERMAN PRACTICE, BROOKLYN HEIGHTS

CHAPTER 1

There are premium ice creams. Premium potato chips. Premium bonds. Then there are premium babies and premium births. By extension, there must be premium midwives. "I must be one of them now," thinks Holly.

Most definitely, she now works in a premium neighborhood of the somewhat less-than-premium borough of Brooklyn. That Brooklyn Heights occupies the same land mass as Morrison Hospital is a geographical principle Holly hasn't quite absorbed. This is another Brooklyn.

Old, well-kept brownstones with wide stoops and wrought-iron rails are set way back on the broad tree-lined streets. In spring and summer, facades the color of dirt are charged up by windowboxes brimming with petunias and geraniums. Flowers wave like flags in the breeze. There always seems to be a breeze here, down by the harbor. The brownstones may be worth a million dollars each now, but they don't have the pretentious, off-putting air, which so much affluent housing has, of trying to be grander than they are. These buildings weren't built for millionaires. They were built for families.

During the day, Brooklyn Heights has the emptied-out, lazy feel of a workday in Bryn Mawr. What's left, after the morning exodus into Manhattan, are old women sweeping the sidewalks in front of their houses and mothers and West Indian nannies pushing bundled babies in strollers. On weekends, the professional parents stroll themselves, the fathers appearing serene as they haul their children's heft about in brown corduroy Snugli's. So many people here actually stroll and glide on the street, it's as if a local ordinance prohibits aggressive struts or defensive shuffles.

Holly isn't hard-pressed to imagine her own mother here. In tennis dress and sneakers, she'd slam the station wagon door and call, "Okay, kids, how about a hand with these groceries!"

An October wind blows, and the leaves sound brittle as they stir in the breeze. Holly sits on a bench on the promenade overlooking New York Harbor and Manhattan, and eats a salad-with-feta-cheese sandwich, wrapped in the whole-wheat shell of pita bread. As a premium midwife, she is now engaged in premium health habits. She almost never smokes now.

Working for Dr. Futterman has made her look more collegiate than ever. She doesn't have to apologize—in any way—for being an Ivy League girl from the Main Line. This is not the relief she thought it would be, although her background does work to her advantage, as most of her patients seem to come from similar ones, as do Meg and Dr. Futterman. Holly is now among her fellow tribespeople, and she can be herself, whether or not she likes it. Why then does she miss Crowley and Denise and Levy, who all come from worlds entirely different from Holly's? Without them, Holly feels a little . . . bereft.

The wind whips Holly's straight blonde hair back over her green sweater. She's wearing corduroy jeans and tennis shoes just like the ones she wore in college. If she were still in college, an observer would see that she's too thoughtful looking to be a fraternity princess, too outdoorsy to be a grind. Intelligent preppy: that's her look, and it's out of place in the 1980s, now that preppies look sleekly professional.

Holly thinks a lot about clothes these days. If she wore different clothes, she might pass for one of her patients, the women Holly might have been—investment bankers, lawyers, advertising executives—if Holly had gone to business school instead of midwifery school. What would Holly have become if there were one more atom of materialism in her composition or in her—what would you call it?—her soul.

These patients are what makes Holly's life as a midwife enviable to other midwives. They don't eat junk food, shoot heroin, or get pregnant at fifteen. To the contrary, almost thirty percent are nullips over thirty-five: career women with deferred dreams who are high-risk because of their age but highly *motivated* and *compliant*, which is to say, they eat well, follow instructions, and know what to do when Holly asks for a fresh catch.

They are used to the best of everything. The best apartments and jobs, the best freshly ground customized coffee mixtures and the best cheeses, the best restaurants and the best movies. They have come to Dr. Futterman's practice for the best obstetrical care and with concern for their future children. Midwives get you through with the best baby in the end: babies born without drugs who will be smarter and better-looking and more athletically competent than babies delivered in the old be-nighted way.

When these patients don't enclose themselves in blue suits and bow ties, they have lovely clothes, which Holly jealously observes.

"I'm a Dumpy," Holly told Matt.

"A what?"

"A downwardly mobile professional."

While most of her patients seem to be prototypical young urban professionals, they usually emerge out of their cliché after the second visit, to become individuals. But when they don't, Holly wonders why they decided to come to a midwife to begin with. Holly entertains the idea that some of them consider going to a nurse-midwife to be the social equivalent of discovering a new restaurant or the perfect unspoiled Caribbean island that will soon be stampeded by less desirable types who inevitably jump on the bandwagon they've set in motion. A hidden advantage. A secret privilege. Which they then go out and broadcast to everybody they know. To Holly's ultimate advantage, of course.

This was the specific benefit to which Holly alluded during the awful meeting with Mrs. Gruener when Holly had to tell her she was leaving. Holly wished she could just chuck a brick with a resignation letter wrapped around it through Mrs. Gruener's window and take off, breathless, not looking back.

"I'm leaving," Holly said in a surly, defiant way, not looking up, but staring so hard at the familiar black-and-white linoleum tile that her eyes began to water. "For a private practice in Brooklyn Heights. Meg Greenspan works there."

Mrs. Gruener threw down her pencil. "Why become a midwife at all? To make money? If that's the case, why don't you simply join Gina on Wall Street and be done with it?"

"Mrs. Gruener, you know most midwives don't stay here more than a few years."

"Ah, there's the justification then! 'But it's what all the other midwives do, Mrs. Gruener!'" She stood up and marched about the room. "Fine, you are as good as a doctor now. You use poor women for your experiments, then you leave for where the money is."

"Mrs. Gruener, it's not about money!"

"Then exactly what is it about?"

"I'd like to actually practice midwifery, as it's meant to be practiced!" This was an insolent way of phrasing it, and Holly knew it. It was as if her mind moved in the direction that would most irritate Mrs. Gruener and Holly could do nothing to call it back from its obnoxious slide.

"Ah! Do tell me, please, I'm so interested—how is midwifery meant to be practiced?" She slipped into her seat and cradled her face in her hands. But when Holly didn't answer, Mrs. Gruener said in a flat, cold voice, "They don't need you down there in Brooklyn Heights. That's the truth." She shrugged. "You'll see."

"They need midwives in Brooklyn Heights," Holly had said, remembering Meg's arguments. "Dr. Futterman's patients are media people. Pacesetters who start trends. What they do filters out to the rest of the country. Being a good midwife in a practice like Dr. Futterman's is good public relations."

"Oh, I see," Mrs. Gruener said, nodding vigorously. "Midwifery as public relations now. I understand."

"Affluent women deserve decent health care, too," Holly said lamely.

"Oh, and I'm glad you'll be there to make sure they get it. Poor things." Mrs. Gruener picked up a pencil, held it up to the level of her eyes, then let it fall, in a casual, listless say. "Good-bye," she said, looking mildly at Holly.

That had been the worst. The utter indifference. The illusion of specialness shattered. Mrs. Gruener had rendered her insignificant and dispensable—a feeling she had not yet recovered from. Holly is beginning to wonder how many more hard lessons she will have to learn.

"Don't think," she tells herself now. "You're on lunch. And you always think too much."

But she can't stop thinking, remembering how much she'd hated Mrs. Gruener then: Mrs. Gruener's complete certainty in her own opinions, and the truth that rang in what she said, in the German accent which, that day, Holly found loathsome for the first and last time. What had catalyzed Holly into giving notice—after calling Meg and meeting Dr. Futterman on the sly—was that sense of dispensability and insignificance that had been allotted to her in small, infuriating doses. What had moved her to leave Howard Street was not strictly burnout, but the fact that the illusion she was Mrs. Gruener's favorite midwife had collapsed.

Mrs. Gruener had appointed Pam to a new position, which Holly thought she herself not only deserved but was best suited for: midwife-counselor to adolescents.

The new position was the result of a tenuous pact between Mrs. Gruener and the pediatrics head, Dr. Pollard. The Adolescent Midwife, as Holly came to think of the role, would be available from two-thirty to six as a one-woman information center whom teenagers could approach with any and all questions on contraception and pregnancy. While the Adolescent Midwife might do some exams, she would exist chiefly as a confidante and oracle available to any teenager who had worked up enough courage or interest or fear.

As much as Holly liked Pam, she thought she was more sensitive and insightful than Pam was, more adept at skating over the thin ice of adolescent rapport.

While still feeling wounded at being overlooked, Holly could understand Mrs. Gruener's choice in appointing Pam as Adolescent Midwife. What she couldn't understand and would never forgive was the choice for second Adolescent Midwife, the midwife who would stand in while Pam was pulling Morrison duty. That midwife was none other than Barbara. The cold fish, the stingy-hearted, the tense and charmless midwife who turned haughty when a seventeen-year-old chose not to breast-feed, who asked young women questions on their history of STDs while they were accompanied by new boyfriends, and who made Howard Street patients terrified of birth control pills by overemphasizing the pill's side effects. Barbara. What frightened young girl opening a door in search of kindhearted guidance could possibly find it with the stiff-necked Barbara sitting there like the reincarnation of a hanging judge from the Salem witch trials? How could Mrs. Gruener have chosen Barbara over Holly?

The only explanation was that Holly was being punished by Mrs. Gruener, who was still angry about the ABC incident, Holly's indiscreet complaints about Gus, and Holly's bush-league tentativeness when Dr. Pollard announced that King's County was sending down a rape victim. Mrs. Gruener was teaching Holly a lesson in humiliation, in the capriciousness of power, in the worldly knowledge that the powers-that-be are not always benevolent and can reduce an individual midwife to a nonentity if they so choose—even a power-that-is like Mrs. Gruener could do such a thing.

The lesson had been learned, and Holly took it to heart. She had always been lucky in love and, in a fashion, lucky at work. The Adolescent Midwife debacle was the first time Holly had ever been overlooked and made to feel insignificant by someone she cared about. The truth was, Holly nearly idolized Mrs. Gruener, the adversarial Socratic examiner who could help Holly discover her own principles. Mrs. Gruener hurt Holly, and Holly found out she couldn't bear to work in a place not just where she was punished, but where the person she trusted and admired most had turned against her. That was the catalyst which sent Holly to the phone to call Meg, which drove Holly into Mrs. Gruener's office to say a sullen good-bye and which placed Holly here, on the promenade in Brooklyn Heights.

The Manhattan skyscape is beautiful, a bit brutal in its mass. The Staten Island Ferry steams along in a steady, prosaic push. It takes nighttime and a glittering skyline to transform this car-laden barge into something romantic. Beyond the ferry is the Statue of Liberty, which still excites Holly. As she eats her sandwich, she actually says to herself, "I really am here, here in New York!" For a moment, she feels that same sense of possibility and expectation of adventure she brought with her when she first arrived. But the feeling passes.

She tosses her sandwich wrapper into a garbage can, then leans against the promenade railing to study the view. Her career is like the skyline. From the outside, exciting and impressive. But from within, it's frightening, irritating, exhilarating, and confusing.

Just as the city is the big time, so Holly seems to have made the big time in midwifery. She has just about peaked. She's at one of the city's best practices with some of the city's best patients. She has a beeper that she carries when she's on call, which reinforces her sense of nurse-midwifery as a profession. And she's making thirty thousand dollars a year. Holly is almost as far up as a midwife can go, and she's only thirty years old. Odd to peak when you're so young.

Holly jogs back to work down quiet streets of leaves turning and about to turn, then bursts into a sprint, slowing to a trot and almost stopping as she suddenly realizes that she's dying for something she can't have. A sense of endless possibilities.

CHAPTER 2

Lynn, the office secretary who likes to speak in French as much as possible but only has a handful of French phrases under her command, leans over her typewriter to hand a "While You Were Out" slip to Holly. *"Voilà,"* she says.

It is easy to mark Lynn as a nonmidwife civilian by the insupportable length of her immaculately polished fingernails. Long nails are not the privilege of a working midwife, who must actually reach inside people, who must grope in search of unborn babies, who must make an effort not to lacerate the clients. The other visual cue that tips off Lynn's civilian status is her extremely well set hair, another distinction that most active midwives can't lay claim to. Holly now spends a third of her life on call, which means that the pursuit of sleep lies somewhere between a quest and an obsession, and just thinking about waking up an hour earlier than she has to, in order to curl her hair, makes her want to fall to the floor and collapse. Holly's beauty secret for hair care is summarized in one word: shampoo.

Lynn is diligent in her labor after beauty. Facials, manicures, coordinated outfits. Sometimes Holly becomes worried and upset that Lynn goes to so much trouble to come to work at a place where she doesn't meet any available men.

"Wouldn't you rather get a job where you can actually meet unattached fellows?" Holly once asked.

"Don't you like me?"

"Of course I do. But do you like it here?"

"I like it here," Lynn declared. "I like the stories."

Lynn likes a disaster. Cradling her chin in her hands, she stops everything to listen, wide-eyed, to the details. She thrives, in the most benign way possible, on complications: vicarious misadventures in an uneventful life. She listens ardently, with just a slight smile of pleasure, as each and every story unfurls. Now and again, a frown appears on her face as a show of sympathy for the absent players. She feels for them and is always the first to cry. To Lynn, a cry is as good as a laugh. Or, almost. Usually, a cry has the edge on a laugh.

"Julie Varney called and said please, whatever you do, when you call back, if she doesn't answer, do not, repeat, do not tell whoever's at the end of the line that the midwife is calling."

"Guerrilla midwifery," Holly says, in homage to Mrs. Gruener. "Surreptitious midwifery."

"Are you offended?"

"Her mother's probably staying with her. A mother who has midwives pegged somewhere on the lunatic frontier of fringe medicine between astrologers and acupuncturists. Julie probably isn't up to defending midwifery to her mother, and I don't blame her. A disapproving mother is a no-win situation. A disapproving mother can always out-argue you."

Lynn sighs knowingly. *"Je sais,"* she says.

"In case I ever have an affair with a married man, at least I'll know how to make furtive phone calls."

"Don't make *le* jokes about *le* married men in *le* midwifery office," Lynn says, wagging a manicured finger. *"Le* married men are not *le* joking matter."

"Je sais, chou-fleur, je sais."

This morning, Holly saw *le* married man at his most painfully extreme. Roger, reluctantly accompanying his wife, Christina, to an AP visit, slouched on a seat in the examining room, bored by everything: the pregnant woman who is his wife, the Matisse print on the wall, and the copy of *Forbes* magazine he'd curled up into a baton.

At least half the married men who accompany their wives to the Futterman practice are, by all appearances, devoted guys. But another fraction—perhaps not half, but too large, at any rate—seem to have been knocked for a loop by pregnancy and all that it means.

Roger appeared to be one of them. He was heavy with eye contact, languorous bedroom-eyes looks. Very experienced stuff, so that Holly couldn't even flatter herself that he was exceptionally smitten by her and was assured only of the fact that he was an expert at undressing women with his eyes. Holly wanted to punch him in the nose. Didn't he realize that his wife was beautiful in her cumbersome, lumberous state?

Other men act this way, but usually more covertly. To Holly, the roving eye seems to have less to do with sexual desire than with fear. *Le* married man as a guy wondering what he's gotten himself into as he falls, irreversibly, into a fathomless pool of lifetime responsibility.

Holly understands why a man might want to turn and run or why he might be attracted to her when his own wife is seven months pregnant. Not because Holly is irresistibly attractive but because she represents freedom, which is, for a man running scared by an overwhelming sense of responsibility, the ultimate in seductiveness. Holly is everything their wives are not: in control of pregnancy rather than controlled by it, single rather than married, slim rather than gravid, and attached to nothing. In contrast to their confused, needy, demanding wives and futures, Holly is a blithe spirit. From the looks of her, at least.

"Listen up, buddy," Holly had wanted to tell Roger this morning. "Here's my boyfriend's number. Call him up and ask just how free and easy being a midwife's lover can be." Instead she asked him if he wanted to feel his baby's feet. Sighing, Roger hauled himself up, brushing almost imperceptibly against Holly, and pressed his hand against his wife's abdomen with bored, heavy-lidded eyes.

"Do you feel it?" Christina asked desperately, straining to look her husband in the eye, *le* married man who was so expert with his eyes. "Do you feel it?"

"Yes," he said in a lazy, dull voice, without looking up. "I feel it, Christina." Then turned away.

Holly did, too. What could be more terrible to watch than a woman asking for love from a man who refuses to give it

Holly now says to Lynn, "No, I don't make *le* jokes about *le* married men."

Lynn takes a call. "Take the number two train from Manhattan," she explains. "It's very safe. Brooklyn Heights is nice!" She hangs up and asks Holly, "Why are these women so scared to leave Manhattan?"

"It's the unknown wilds."

Wary patients start their AP visits by arriving in taxis. Once emboldened by the neighborhood's peacefulness, they chance the subway for the next few visits, only to take taxis again by the last trimester. In the thick of pregnancy's general miseries, springing for a cab is the most reasonable of extravagances.

"Well, I suppose Manhattan is the known wilds," Lynn says huffily.

The offices take up a floor-through of an old brownstone. If Holly cranes her neck out a rear window on a clear day, she can make out a view of the harbor in the wedge of space left open between two tall buildings across the courtyard. "Sliver view," Meg calls it.

Dr. Futterman's office is a class act. The waiting room couch is upholstered in a beige, nubbly fabric that Holly could not identify.

Lynn was quick to inform her. "It's linen," she said, "real linen! Very tasteful."

"Oh."

The end table is stacked with creased copies of *Parents* magazine and, for snob appeal, to prove that this Brooklyn Heights outpost is every bit as upscale as a Park Avenue practice, copies of *Town & Country* and *Forbes*.

"Why don't we get *American Lawyer*?" Holly had joked to Meg after she saw her third lawyer of the day.

"Their firms get it," Meg answered seriously.

There is a rack of brochures on one wall, crammed with booklets about baby-care, "those special nine months," and information on breast-feeding put out by—a dubious source of information—formula and baby-food companies.

The wall art consists of a framed print of a Mary Cassatt painting of a mother breast-feeding her baby (Holly has seen this same print in more than half the private midwifery and progressive obstetrics services she has ever visited) and framed photographs of little kids tumbling about together in dewy grass: black and white, Oriental and Hispanic. These prove that the Futterman practice has its heart in the right place, even if most of the babies it delivers are white ones.

The most significant piece of art is the bulletin board overpopulated by hundreds of pictures of babies brought into the world by the hands and under the management of the Futterman practice. "This is Jason, at nine months!!!" Corny announcement cards with storks carrying bags full of babies in their beaks. Upscale announcement cards engraved by Tiffany. And babies, babies, babies. Instamatic, Polaroid, or Nikon, all the babies come out the same. Babies.

Baby pictures taken by fathers who have hidden behind lenses and fiddled around with f-stops right at the vital moment of delivery. It has occurred to Holly that picture-taking has become a modern ritual related to the anthropological rule that during the moment of significant life passages and transitions, the participants must wear masks. The camera has become a mask, particularly now that the Brownell Hospital birthing room, where the Futterman practice delivers, doesn't require masks or gowns at delivery. The camera has filled the void.

Besides, a man with a camera in hand has a purpose beyond just supporting his wife—which is an important contribution, but ultimately an intangible kind of assistance. With a camera, the father bears witness as official recorder of the event. He has something purposeful to do with his emotions when other outlets don't seem up to the job, when all words and most gestures seem like pathetic understatements.

And maybe the event of childbirth is too awesome and overwhelming for a man to face and absorb on his own. So the fathers invent their own rituals and use the cameras to catch the overflow of emotion. The viewfinder frames and reduces the mother and baby to manageable size, and squares them off into a controllable package. And later on, when the father tries to describe what he saw, and words fail him, he can pull out the photographs to rescue him from his inarticulateness.

Meg emerges from her office to tack a baby picture up on the photographic breeding ground.

Holly peers over her shoulder. "Whose baby is this?"

"The Reynolds kid."

"Maybe they shouldn't have used birth as a photo opportunity for this one, Meg."

The Reynolds kid has a severe case of molding. The soft, unformed bones of the skull, flexible by design, have overlapped as the head squeezed through the birth canal. In addition to the molding, which shapes the head like a football, is a caput succedaneum—swelling on the part of the baby's head that presented first. A caput is usually the result of early rupture of the membranes, when no cushion lies between the head and cervix. Edema fluid then fills the space between the baby's skull and skin to compensate and ensure some kind of protective buffer. A caput is scary to mothers, and has to be watched by midwives, as it can also look like cephalhematoma, or intracranial bleeding. A caput's swelling is normally generalized, while a hematoma is confined to a specific range.

Meg examines the picture. "I forgot how bent out of shape he was. Think this will scare off the clients?"

"Well, it doesn't inspire confidence."

"If the Reynoldses ask, maybe we can pretend we never received this."

"They'll only send another. They probably don't realize he looks extraterrestrial. And when you caught the kid, you told me he was really cute."

"I was punch-drunk. After a two-and-a-half-hour second stage, he looked cute, believe you me."

"Weren't you afraid of hypotonia, letting a second stage go on that long?"

"Sheer stubbornness," Meg says. "My blessing. My curse."

"I would have marked her for transverse arrest." With transverse arrest, the head is blocked in the pelvic cavity.

"It was just a matter of time. Besides, can you imagine that baby with forceps marks on top of all that molding?" Studying the picture, Meg says, "This baby has been through the mill. We are under a professional obligation to pin him up even if he is momentarily and somewhat monstrously misshapen. I will hang up his picture in this very top corner where most of you shorter folks would never be able to see."

"High and outside."

"A tad obscured by the other cards," says Meg, "but on the board nonetheless."

The board. Holly flashes on the Board at Morrison Hospital. The numbers. The times. Scott's handwriting. But now the board only means a flurry of baby pictures held in suspended animation. Holly shuts her eyes for a moment. Then opens them. She is here now. She is safe.

CHAPTER 3

Lynn's hand cups the phone. "Cutler's on the line. Emergency."

"Pull the file," says Holly.

"Details, Lynn, details," Meg says.

"Can you give me a few specifics, Fran?" Lynn listens, then stabs the hold button. "She's bleeding?"

"Bloody show?" Holly asks, glancing hopefully at Meg.

Meg doesn't answer. Her seniority shows in the way she takes authority without hesitation, pulling the phone from Lynn's hand. She must hear the complaint from Fran Cutler herself and write it down as Fran has stated it. For the chart, you make no assumptions, jump to no conclusions, and interpret as little as possible. You leave unproven opinions to discussion . . . words that cling to nothing and evaporate after a few months.

That's how risk management works. Treat the file as a legal document, as if you know for a fact that it's going to be submitted to a court of law. Information that Fran Cutler has passed along to Lynn, who has passed it along to Meg, is hearsay, with all that hearsay implies: a broad margin of error and misinterpretation. You don't practice defensive medicine by making a working diagnosis from data gathered by a secretary whose only skills are fifty-words-per-minute typing, a pleasant phone manner, and "I'm a people person. I like people." That doesn't play in court. Not to your advantage, at least.

As Meg gets on the phone, Holly waves a pencil at her, making scribbling gestures in the air. "Take notes!" she hisses. Lynn hands Meg a pen and Fran Cutler's chart.

They're covered defensively now. Fran probably thinks her chart is pulled so that Meg can cull pertinent data and make an informed

400

diagnosis. But the chart hasn't been pulled to extract information from it, but to enter information into it. Legally, no treatment or advice has been given unless it's marked down on the patient's chart—the only proof that will stand up in court.

"How heavy is the flow? Have you used more than one pad? Is there any pain? No pain down on your lower abdomen?"

Glancing up at Holly, Meg shakes her head. Not a mucus plug. Nor a placenta abruptio either, which would make the uterus tender to the touch.

"Fran, we think you ought to come down to Brownell for an ultra-sound," says Meg. "We're not alarmists, but when there's bleeding in the last trimester, it's no time to pussyfoot around. You might just have a cervical irritation that's causing some bleeding. Or the baby's head might be applying pressure so some blood vessels are breaking in the cervix. But it's also possible that what you have is a placenta previa—the placenta may have moved down or grown around the cervix. So take it easy, lie down, and I'll call Sono to fit you in this afternoon."

Meg hangs up. "Holly, you call Sono."

"Why me?"

"Because you're new. Sono still likes you. I'm *persona non grata* around there since I gave them hell for telling Liza Bailey that her kid was a boy when it turned out to be a girl. There's nothing like handing over a newborn to a mom who says, 'It was supposed to be a boy!' Ultrasound!" Meg snorts. "What a concept! I'll use it for bleeding, a real severe SGA—that's it."

"*C'est tout,*" Lynn translates.

"Their machine is old," Holly says apologetically.

"That's why you're calling. They like you, Holly, because you cover their ass for them."

Holly calls Fran. "Three-thirty, fifth floor, Brownell. Got it?"

Silence, except for the distant sound of a siren passing outside Fran's window. Fran says finally, "But that's so soon."

"We don't take our time with bleeding. If it's nothing, we want to know it's nothing."

"But Ernie can't get off work until six o'clock."

"The Sono office closes at five, Fran."

"Couldn't I come in tomorrow morning?"

Holly speaks carefully. "We strongly advise that you don't wait until tomorrow. We really insist you come in this afternoon," she says, mentally reviewing what she's said for legal correctness. It's Meg's turn now to make frantic scribbling gestures. Write it down! Advised against waiting! "When there's bleeding at this stage in the game," Holly goes on, "we consider it an emergency. We also advise that you take a taxi to Brownell Hospital."

Fran is impervious to the legal beauty of Holly's argument. "But Ernie and I do everything together," she says. "This is our pregnancy. It's important that he be with me."

Meg rolls her eyes. Ernie is the most impassive of all the involved husbands. He seems devoid of curiosity. Dragged to each AP visit, he stares at his hands, never asks a question or comments on anything Holly or Meg does. Ernie has been shanghaied into togetherness.

"There ain't going to be any pregnancy if she doesn't haul ass to the hospital," Meg hisses at Holly.

"Fran, I'll meet you at Sono. Will that be all right?"

"Holly, you'd be there?"

"For you? Sure."

Holly hangs up, grimacing. "Nothing I like better than to spend an afternoon holding a grown woman's hand."

"Come on, Holly. That's our job," Meg says, sliding Fran's chart in the file cabinet. "We're supposed to hold our patients' hands. Remember those extra little TLC touches? Besides, a previa is frightening. I'm surprised she didn't freak out more than she did."

"I thought we were supposed to encourage patients to take responsibility for their own health and their own decisions. She can't keep running to someone to hold her hand for the rest of her life."

Meg smiles slightly. "Some people do, you know."

Sometimes Holly feels like her grandmother. "Have you noticed how much everyone complains these days?" her grandmother used to complain. Holly wishes for a world of no tears, no fears, no fighting, no biting. A little more stoicism, please! Yet stoics can make the worst labor and delivery candidates. Bite-the-bullet resistance can resist everything, including childbirth.

"I don't mind being a nurse," Holly says gruffly, "but I don't know if I can cope with being a nursemaid."

"It doesn't happen all that often, Holly."

"If this bleeding is just a friable cervix dripping away, I promise you, the next time Fran Cutler calls me complaining of heartburn, I'll—" Holly stops to invent a threat. Over the years, she's noticed that she's slightly impoverished when it comes to colorful oaths available to her—a cultural disadvantage of being a girl from the Main Line, where all the curses are ridiculously adolescent. As she tries now to imagine a fate suitable for Fran, she regrets that her background is so bland.

"You'll what, Holly?" Meg asks, smiling.

"I'll go to med school, become a physician, and refer all these stupid calls to my nurse." A true WASP curse. She slaps her head. "Shoot, I forgot to tell Fran that they'll keep her at the hospital if she's a previa."

The orderlies will slap Fran on a stretcher, lifting and lowering her like a stiff board, and send her to the postpartum wing, which always houses a few antepartum cases. The orderlies will be directed not to jostle old Fran, lest they set off the placenta previa's hair trigger and give the placenta the last push into complete displacement and disaster: hemorrhage, STAT section, preemie baby.

Analysis of Fran's conditions will take place externally, the chief examining tool being ultrasound to determine how far the placenta has slipped down, whether or not vaginal delivery is still feasible, if the placenta appears to be migrating back to where it was, and whether or not Fran can go home and join her beloved Ernie. All this gets decided with Fran flat on her back.

"Hell, Holly, ain't no way she could prepare for a bed rest stay anyway. Don't fret it."

"Besides," Holly reasons, "she's got Ernie."

"For sure. She's got Ernie."

CHAPTER 4

Brownell Hospital is ten blocks from Dr. Futterman's office: a pleasant walk. Holly thinks that maybe the excitement she used to feel in Manhattan was really just agitation and anxiety in disguise. She feels none of that here. Here, there are trees, quiet and calm, and cars that wind slowly through the streets as drivers crane their necks on the lookout for kids. Kids are out and about, as they aren't in Manhattan: playing stoopball, heaving pink Spaldeens at the stoops of the old brownstones. They're well trained, looking both ways on a one-way street (you never know) when they give chase to an out-of-hand ball.

Brownell, a small hospital, used to be St. Barnaby's Hospital, which is how neighborhood people still think and speak of it. Many of the older Jewish people in the neighborhood resist going there, as it used to be owned and operated by the Catholic Church, and all the nurses were nuns. "Not that I have anything against the nuns, but it's my personal choice, personally, not to go there," an old lady told Holly in a coffee shop.

"But the nuns aren't there anymore," Holly explained.

The woman shrugged, unconvinced. "The more things change . . ."

In theory, Brownell is tertiary care, but it's only tertiary care under duress, which makes it ideal for maternity care. Small in scale, with nurses who are neither overworked nor underpaid and congenial residents (all New York hospitals are, to some degree, teaching hospitals) who never see quite as much action as they'd like and are slightly antsy as a result but ultimately not nearly as crazed with fatigue and stress as the Morrison residents were. And in the postpartum wing, the rooms look out on New York Harbor—the same view Holly had from the promenade: a good place to jump into a new life from.

What Holly doesn't like about Brownell is the sono office, run by the house radiologist. Holly doesn't trust him. Radiologists don't necessarily know a thing about performing or interpreting sonography, and Holly wonders how Bill picked up his skill: by trial and error, hit or miss, hunt and peck? When Bill was in school, ultrasound fell into the casual curriculum placement of "elective," rather than being an academic requirement. Holly figures that sonography is something Bill picked up along the way. Now here he is, determining fates.

Ultrasound works on the same principles a bat does, operating as a blind thing that uses percussion to sound out depths and mass. The transducer emits high-frequency currents of sound into the belly, and the sound bounces back. How far the currents have traveled before striking something solid determines the presence and shape of the mass that it hits. In essence, the shadows that compose the picture sonography creates are really echoes, sound translated into form. Which is, after all, how sonography got its name: it's sound made readable.

There is a large margin for error in this method that jumps from one sense to another. Echoes become shadows, and shadows are . . . well, shadows, without the differentiated detail of real vision. And the unknown quality of the sonographer is a variable entered into an already unstable formula. The as-yet-undetermined long-term effects of ultrasound on fetuses, and the chance that it might cause genetic damage that won't be definitively revealed for another ten years, catalyzes the sono equation into an anxiety-producing mix for many midwives. Holly included. But use of ultrasound for something like this—determining the position of a possible placenta previa—is the one endorsable function of technology that had been designed, fittingly enough, during World War II for the tracking of submarines underwater.

"Holly, you're here!" Fran reaches for Holly's hand, which Holly gives her a bit reluctantly. Fran has big round eyes that Holly thinks are the eyes of a silly goose. As if to reinforce the silliness of these silly goose eyes, she has silly goose hair: a tumble of bleached, permed curls that fall around her round, rouged face. Fran looks like an overanxious, aging child who has had too much milk and cookies.

"Hi-ya, blondie," Bill says, glancing up for a moment. He runs the transducer across Fran's abdomen in quick strokes, like a minesweeper, and returns his eyes to the ultrasound screen. The quick sweeps of the transducer are supposed to help compile a three-dimensional picture. Holly studies the screen, too. She'd like to learn ultrasound herself, particularly if sonographers are as unreliable as so many docs and midwives claim. Holly studies his technique, although the technique seems to be the easy part. The tricky stuff is the interpretation of what turns up on the screen.

"I don't think you have a thing to worry about, my dear," Bill says to Fran.

Good. You can let go of my hand now, Fran.

Fran looks up at Holly, having failed to pick up Holly's negative vibration. "I haven't had any bleeding since I called you," she says. "Maybe because I knew Ernie couldn't join me. I knew this wasn't the time for this thing to happen to me now. I just willed it away, Holly, with positive thinking."

"Ah, positive thinking," Holly says, nodding.

The radiologist puts a thick arm around Holly's shoulder. There's always a lot of physical contact in this sono office. "Now see here," he says, pointing at the screen where white and black blobs are fused together. Blobs, nothing but blobs. I have to learn this, thinks Holly, but it's tough with the jerk's arm around me. *But he won't teach you otherwise, Treadwell.* Holly stands still, somewhat glumly.

"There's the placenta," Bill says, pointing at an emerging blob that hugs the edge of the uterine slope. It's located in a completely different milky way than the cervix or the fetus. It's planted in the wall. It hasn't slipped or migrated or abrupted. Even Holly can see that. "If I were you," Bill says in a growling voice, with a salacious touch to it that Holly can't quite identify, "I'd look somewhere else for the source of the bleedings."

Bill is supposed to be the impartial radiologist who, as so many women have comforted themselves thinking, has seen a million naked women. By now he must be entirely inured to the sight and feel of them. But in fact, he's a thirty-year-old man who deals mainly with older cancer patients whose radiation therapy hasn't treated their bodies kindly. Bill is not immune to noticing or enjoying the bodies who enter his office so fearfully.

To "look somewhere else" for Fran's problem, stated so vaguely lasciviously, reflects the titillation many people feel just imagining a vaginal exam. It's a titillation Holly often forgets exists. She forgets to lower her voice in restaurants when talking about a bad case of trich. She forgets to lower her voice when saying the words *vagina* and *cervix* in public. Bill brings her thought processes back in line with the standards of the rest of the world.

Holly ducks out of the curve of Bill's arm. "Hey, Fran, you'd better come back to the office with me and let Ellen take a look at you."

"Can I sit up?" she asks, as Bill wipes the gel off her belly, as thorough as a minesweeper, but slower. She makes doe eyes at Bill. "Can I?"

Like other nurse-midwives, Holly often resents having to be bound to physicians as a subordinate. But now she's relieved she can pass the buck to Dr. Futterman without feeling as though she's delivering her patient into dangerous hands. Holly's responsibility is to recognize pathology when she sees it and to make proper referrals when she does. This wasn't her role at Morrison. But it is now.

At the Futterman practice, they follow the protocols. All questions on what constitutes midwifery care are answered by the elaborate protocols kept in a thick binder on Lynn's desk, as accessible as a fire extinguisher.

Vaginitis, cervicitis, and syphilis are all midwifery-treatable. So are pregnant women whose age is over thirty-five. Postdate pregnancies that require Pit inductions, premature labor, breeches, and twins are shifted to physician management. (But one of these days, Holly is going to get her twins!)

The protocols are outlines listing the steps for every problem. They start with the most obvious solution, as when you go to fix a lamp that isn't functioning, you first make sure that the lamp is plugged in and turned on, and that the lightbulb works. The final suggestion for fixing a lamp is to take the lamp to a shop. That's how the protocols work. The last line, which the midwives may not cross, reads: "Consult attending physician." Following a protocol is like following a labyrinth until you arrive at a wall. Then you give it up.

Holly has followed the protocol for third-trimester bleeding step by step. The last step is an either/or equation. Either the placenta is previa, in which case the doctor is consulted. Or the placenta is not previa, in which case the cervix is examined for friability. Holly will follow neither of these options. Dr. Futterman will check out Fran. You can't fail the protocols by consulting the attending physician too much. You fail them only when you consult too little.

"You think it might be just an irritation on my cervix?" Fran asks anxiously as they stand on the corner of one of Brooklyn Heights' least busy streets, hoping that someone will drive up to the hospital in a taxi that they will then grab. "It couldn't be from my baby?"

"No, your baby is fine."

"It's funny to see you here, Holly. Out of school." Fran's round face beams up at Holly's in the brilliant sun. Fran looks almost blindingly bright, in a big pink jumpsuit (which will be ideal for breast-feeding—a zip, a breast pops out). She reminds Holly of a tropical fruit.

"It is a little like a school outing, isn't it?" Holly says, smiling, feeling less than cheery. She's sweet, Holly thinks with forced affection, she's just a kid. *She's older than you are, Treadwell.* Holly is scared that she'll wind up either as one of those falsely bright nurses she'd always hated ("How are we today?" "Miserable, go fuck yourself," Holly always wanted to say) or one of those perennially cranky bureaucrats like Sparks. It's hard not to let your feelings show. As a midwife, Holly can evince concern, but not fear, doubt, anxiety, or impatience.

This is true of many professions, but it's especially true in midwifery, where much of your appeal is based on the depth of feeling, your reservoirs of compassion and sympathy. Holly can never release the insidious feelings of contempt that sometimes creep up on her when she's tired and doesn't have the energy to field any more frivolous complaints. Sometimes she misses her Howard Street patients. At least you could tell them off, as long as you were good-natured about it. But these Futterman patients don't roll with the punches the same way, and they don't swing back.

A cab rolls up to the hospital, a woman unfolds herself from it, and Holly lunges for the still-open door. "Ernie and I were talking," Fran says, settling herself into the seat. "We were wondering if there's some way you could *definitely* be our midwife when the time comes."

"Oh, Fran, that's very nice of you," Holly says, on guard. It's not nice at all. It pits Holly against Meg and puts her in the uncomfortable role of being the favorite. A moment's flattery isn't worth discord at work. "You know Meg and I rotate our shifts and appointments. There's a fifty-fifty chance it'll be either one of us doing your delivery. And Meg is the midwife's midwife. The midwife every midwife wants at her delivery."

"I'm sure she is," Fran says, quickly, without conviction. "But we'd feel just so much more comfortable with you."

"I'm flattered," Holly says, just as quickly and with just as little conviction, "but the whole purpose of prenatal visits rotating between Meg and me is for you to feel comfortable with both of us."

"Well, Ernie and I thought maybe we could call you *directly* when the time comes. We could give you some kind of *bonus* or *retainer* for doing it." Fran stares at Holly with her big, blank eyes.

Look, you silly goose, if you think I can be bought, if money is what I'm after, would I, an Ivy League graduate with good connections, have bothered becoming a midwife?

Holly sighs. "No go, Fran. And we're here."

The cab stops, and Holly pays the fare. *Get that back from petty cash, Treadwell.* She's not after money, but she's not into throwing it away either.

Fran pulls herself from the taxi, trying to locate a center of gravity that has momentarily escaped her. Holly takes her arm until they are both standing solidly on the sidewalk outside the office. Holly admires the stately brownstone. How can brown stone look so cheerful? Dr. Futterman has a brass nameplate drilled into the wall beside the door at the top of the stoop, which Lynn periodically polishes. Lynn is very scrupulous. Nobody had ever asked her to polish it. It was her own idea, and polishing this short length of brass takes about fifteen minutes, which makes Lynn wonder how long it takes Lynn to do her nails. Holly smiles to think of poor Lynn laboring over her nails, which few men will ever see to admire.

She turns to Fran and says, "I'm sorry, Fran, but your idea is just not viable. You and Ernie will just have to work on feeling more comfortable with Meg so that you'll have a good time no matter who attends the birth."

Fran sighs. She appears to deflate her round, bright self into her round, bright jumpsuit, and her round, bright eyes sink sadly as she shuffles up the stoop in noticeable defeat. This makes Holly impatient and irritated. After all, the woman had a close shave with a previa, ran a strong chance of losing her baby, of bleeding out in a hemorrhage, and now she's upset that she failed in bribing Holly for her services? Fuck them all, Holly thinks.

She leans her head way back and stares straight up into the October sky. It's clear blue as clouds race on a cool north wind. "I believe I'm falling in love with the absurdities of life," she thinks. And she's glad. From here on in, she's determined to make life into a good laugh, even if she has to work at it day and night. That's a laugh, too, and she laughs as Fran disappears behind Dr. Futterman's door.

CHAPTER 5

Holly is sitting with an AP who has the first signs of pregnancy-induced hypertension. Linda Altman is not ready for this. She's not programmed for health problems.

Holly has started seeing patients in her gym. There they are, little beached whales heading for the pool, taking yoga, taking calisthenics classes.

Futterman patients know what to do. They fight stress vigorously, and usually they win. When they lose, it's because the ammunition they use has turned against them. Aerobics and long runs take a toll on ligaments, knees, arches, the minuscule bones in one's toes. Futterman patients hobble out of enough taxis and into enough sports medicine clinics to compose medical histories that read like the uphill sagas of world-class athletes. Sports injuries harm the sense of immunity that Holly and her well-off patients enjoy. They aren't, after all, exempt from pain. But their ailments are the product of a privileged life. If in the nineteenth century, there was gout, now there are stress fractures.

They have elaborate insurance plans and incomes generous enough to provide for specialists their insurance doesn't cover: nutritionists and hypnotists, psychotherapists and masseuses. But when their bodies fail them, when their health takes a nosedive or goes into a tailspin that can't be immediately righted or reversed, these people are thrown for a loop, act like people who've been ushered to balcony seats although their tickets make it plain they're meant to sit in the orchestra below.

What makes things even worse is the way they have swallowed the notion that people bring sickness upon themselves—by being repressed or anxious or by abusing their bodies with what they consider poor nutrition (a candy bar every two weeks). While this thinking might have protected them in the past—others make themselves sick, but this won't happen to them—when actual problems strike, they come down hard on themselves.

"What am I supposed to do now?" Linda asks, glum, anxious, a thin, well-dressed advertising executive with short, highlighted hair that she throws back for emphasis. "It's not bad for the baby now, is it? I have to cut down on salt, I guess. What salt? I don't even *use* salt."

Linda's blood pressure has risen twenty points on both the systolic and diastolic scales since her first visit. Now that she's at about twenty-five weeks' gestation, she is certifiably PIH. If the symptom of protein in her urine appears and is factored into the equation, she'll be diagnosed as preeclampsic. Right now, her urine is free of any trace of protein.

Preeclampsia used to be diagnosed when a marked rise in blood pressure and proteinuria was accompanied by edema, swelling in the extremities. But now, edema, which afflicts most women during pregnancy, is accepted as a simple symptom of pregnancy, not a sign of a pathological development. And preeclampsia is diagnosed only in the presence of hypertension and proteinuria. When preeclampsia explodes into maternal seizures, the pregnancy is threatened, and termination—by section, at that point—is done as soon as possible.

At Morrison, too many patients accepted their hypertension as their destiny ("Well, my mother has it and my aunt has it and my grandmother has it") and a high percentage of the adolescent patients—twenty percent—suffered from it. But someone like Linda is likely to be insulted by it.

"I can't believe it. I never had anything like high blood pressure. It doesn't run in my family. I exercise every day. I don't eat animal fat. I don't smoke." Linda juts out her jaw and strains her neck in the useless exercise of finding out more reasons for why she can't be hypertensive. The fact is, she is.

"Linda, the women most at risk for pregnancy-induced hypertension are first-time moms. Nobody knows why. It seems to be a weird adjustment to pregnancy—an inappropriate response—and we're not so sure that salt or animal fat has anything to do with it. I know this is anathema to you, but maybe the way you should relax now is the old-fashioned way: to lie down, take naps, rest."

"Turn into a couch potato?" Linda asks, revolted.

"The main thing to do is to try to keep this in hand. How's your protein intake?"

"Does high protein cause it? Because I don't eat too much protein." Linda thinks this is another reason she shouldn't be hypertensive.

"Actually, a high-protein diet seems to help sometimes."

Looking disappointed, Linda says, "I'm on an athlete's diet. Low protein, lots of complex carbs. Low fat, high energy."

"Well, you can't be an athlete right now," Holly says. "Cottage cheese. Yogurt. Eggs. Hard cheese."

"Eggs? Cholesterol!"

"Linda, you're thirty-two years old, you don't smoke, and a little bit of cholesterol isn't going to kill you. You're only going to be pregnant four more months. So eat protein, take lie-downs, because if this gets out of hand, we might end up recommending bed rest."

"Bed rest? Oh, come on!" If hypertension is unbelievable, invalidism is unthinkable.

Holly peeps out the window. Linda trudges down the street in a long black slicker and high red boots—her despondency is stylish. She'll have to give up her athlete's diet, along with her athlete's body. The body that she nurtured with the maternal instincts she'll soon have to turn over to her baby. The body that's had the best of everything is turning against her without just cause. The perfect pregnancy is no longer hers.

The imperfection would be more tolerable if it were caused by something more dramatic. High blood pressure is for sedentary, overweight, cigarette-smoking, pork-eating couch potatoes who live way beyond the outskirts of the charmed circle of good health. Being deprived of a perfect pregnancy by something as proletarian as high blood pressure is just squalid. It doesn't make for good conversation. It has no romance, no drama, no class. Like arthritis, hemorrhoids, and eczema, it has zippo sex appeal.

Once the baby is belted into the Aprica stroller, Linda will be all right. But pregnancy is the pits.

CHAPTER 6

Dr. Futterman taps Holly on the shoulder. She is a short, practical-looking person, with brown hair parted in the middle and pulled back, off a plain, smooth face. Dr. Futterman is a sensible doctor, but she could use a sense of humor. Holly always feels kind of inhibited around her. She's scared to make jokes—what if she makes one, and Dr. Futterman fails to get it? Having been here for over half a year, Holly still doesn't feel that she knows Dr. Futterman at all, and what may be worse, she doesn't particularly want to.

"Did you tell Fran Cutler she had a tipped uterus?" Dr. Futterman asks now.

"No," Holly said. "At the start of her visits, I told her I didn't think she did have one."

"She said she thought the bleeding was caused by her tipped uterus."

"Where would she get that idea?" Holly asks. As soon as Holly looks in Dr. Futterman's eyes, she knows Dr. Futterman thinks Fran got that idea from Holly.

The tipped uterus is one of Fran's obsessions. She'd had a septic abortion when she was still in college. The doctor who'd performed the abortion had visited her in the hospital and said that nothing like this had ever happened before (Holly had wanted to ask Fran, "What did you expect he'd say? That these things happened all the time?") and that he thought Fran's uterus might be tipped, making it slow in expelling debris. The doctor's visit was successful, as Fran was effectively persuaded the septic abortion was her fault.

"Do you think my tipped uterus will complicate my pregnancy?" Fran had asked Holly at the first appointment they'd had together.

"I don't think your uterus *is* tipped," Holly had said. The empty uterus

413

flops over on itself, to the front or to the back, but during pregnancy it expands and stands up straight. "It's certainly straightening out now."

Holly hadn't been as persuasive as the doctor who performed the abortion had been, though, and the tipped uterus fallacy is still with them.

Dr. Futterman's eyes narrow. "You're sure you didn't mention anything about this?"

Holly's eyes widen. She is being accused, and her face flushes, as if she's guilty. "I'm sure."

Dr. Futterman returns to her office.

That Fran Cutler's scapegoat is her tipped uterus is a certainty. That Holly is about to become Dr. Futterman's scapegoat is only a probability. And her resolution to laugh everything off breaks in two, like a twig under her feet.

CHAPTER 7

At a party. Holly rubs her eyes as cigarette butts from an ashtray are dumped into a fireplace and the smoke heads straight for her eyes.

"Wow, you're a midwife!" a girl is saying.

"Yep. That's me. I'm a midwife."

The girl keeps nodding. "Wow."

"Yup," says Holly. "Wow."

"I was having this talk with my astrologer, you know? And he said, go ask my mom did she remember any funny stuff pulled on her at the hospital when I was born, you know? And so I did. And my astrologer is so amazing. I mean, he just *knew*. Like my mom explained to me how the doctor who delivered me wanted to go on vacation but I wasn't born yet and he was getting real impatient, you know? So he gave my mom some drug to get the labor going so she'd have me, you know? So I told my astrologer this, and he figured out that I wasn't a Pisces at all, I'm an Aries. I mean, I was conceived to be an Aries and all. And he said he knew that right away, that I was supposed to have been an Aries but I got interfered with and got born a Pisces. I guess that happens all the time, huh?"

"Maybe some of the time," Holly says, waving the smoke out of her eyes.

"That could really screw you up, you know?"

"Yeah, I bet."

"But you're a midwife and you'd just let it happen, right, so that wouldn't happen to other people, getting born under the wrong astrological sign, right?"

"We just let it happen, pretty much of the time," says Holly, nodding. "Yeah, we do our best to get people born under the right sign."

"Yeah, really, because you can really screw somebody up if they think they're a Pisces but they're really not. I mean, now that I know I'm an Aries, everything makes a lot more sense, you know?"

"Yeah, I guess it would," Holly says. "I'm a Pisces."

"Yeah, but are you sure?"

Holly thinks for a second. "Oh, yeah," she says. "I'm pretty sure."

CHAPTER 8

"I'm thinking of visiting Viv at the birthing center in Mudgeville," Holly says to Meg in the little kitchen off the reception area.

Meg cocks an eyebrow. "Leaving so soon? But you just got here."

Holly ducks her head. "I'm not looking for a job, Meg."

"Well, if I were you, I'd avoid birthing centers. Birthing centers are on the way out." She pushes her coffee cup across the small table in the corner to Holly. "Here," she says, "have some germs."

"I'm a midwife," says Holly. "I don't believe in germs." Holly rests her head on her crossed arms. Her disciple position. Mrs. Gruener always imparted bits of political wisdom when Holly sat in the Supplicant's Seat. Lately she's noticed that whenever she asks Meg a serious question, she curls up like a little kid, trying to duplicate that experience. *It's a disgusting display of the search for a mother figure, Treadwell.* A self-criticism Holly accepts. "But with a mother like mine, who could blame me?" she thinks.

"Why aren't birthing centers going to last?"

It seems that Meg has considered every birth issue and can always be prevailed upon to supply an answer. The only trouble is, Holly doesn't trust her as she trusted Mrs. Gruener. Otherwise, the relationship is ideal, as Meg is more than glad to take Holly on as her protégé idiot.

"Birthing centers served a function when hospitals couldn't offer what the birthing centers do," Meg says, leaning back. "But they're no safer than a woman's home, really, as long as the woman lives about as far away from a hospital as the birthing center is. A birthing center has all the drawbacks of a home but few of the advantages. It's a nice, centralized convenience for the midwives, just as a hospital is for doctors.

417

But otherwise, it's just a hospital without medical facilities. So what is it? An inferior tier of health care."

Holly considers all this. "What's wrong with having a place where midwives can all work together, consolidated? At a birthing center, they're not as isolated as they'd be attending a birth in someone's home. They can consult with each other. And they don't have to take the crap we do in hospitals."

Meg shrugs. "How often do you consult with me when you're at Brownell?"

"I have," Holly says doubtfully.

"Once or twice. And over the phone." Meg draws herself up. "Look-it, people go to a birthing center for midwifery care because they're nervous about delivering at home and have an illusion that a birthing center is safer than the home, or they're afraid of hospitals for being places where sick people go. But then there are specific things to be nervous about at the birthing center. About being screened out at any point or being transferred... For most women, a birthing center doesn't make much sense. As hospitals compete for patients, they're going to have newer and nicer birthing rooms, and if we midwives hang on long enough, we'll be in those birthing rooms. You can already see it outside New York, all the aggressive advertising. 'Come to us and have birth your way.' Why would anyone bother with going to a birthing center? To have a home birth in somebody else's home?"

Holly can't give Meg the real reason that she wouldn't want to work in a birthing center. The rigorous screening of each birthing center client means that women at the slightest risk, who might benefit the most from birthing center care, are screened out. And Holly wouldn't be able to bear transferring a client to the hospital and having to sit back and watch someone of possibly inferior skill deliver a woman who'd been promised superior care.

She'd be indignant on behalf of her client and feel cheated on her own behalf. She can't be content anymore with the narrow spectrum of normal birth—her supposed specialty. Morrison has ruined her: normal birth is no longer interesting or challenging enough to her now—Holly needs more. But Holly can't explain this to Meg, can she? "I thrive on adversity, even if it does burn me out."

Holly stands at the windowsill and looks out at the geometric fragment of sky visible through the tall buildings across the way.

Are you ever going to be content, Treadwell?

She doesn't know. This makes her sad.

CHAPTER 9

Holly is lying flat on her stomach on a Nautilus machine, when she realizes she is looking directly at one of her patients. Usually she avoids meeting any of her patients here. Enough already! When she is caught, she'll smile politely and act as if she's in a terrible, midwifery-inspired hurry. But Danielle Greenhouse, thirty-eight weeks, on the machine next to her wearing a huge T-shirt with a silk-screened greenhouse on it, is an exception.

"Nice shirt," says Holly, who is in one of Matt's soccer shirts and running shorts.

"This pushy young artist is always making me T-shirts to try to get into my good graces."

"Is it working?"

"He needs a T-shirt outlet, not a gallery."

"You're not lifting much weight, are you? Don't get too anaerobic. Keep your oxygen up."

"I'm controlling myself," Danielle says, standing up.

When not pregnant, she's a triathlete—swimming, running, and bicycling to the verge of collapse and beyond. A very determined woman, and very funny, too. That's why she's the exception. She's only a little over five feet tall, and her nonpregnant weight is about one hundred twenty pounds, all of which is muscle, "except for my boobs, which were purely decorative elements and weighed ten pounds each." Danielle runs an influential art gallery, so that Holly gets to read all about her in various newspapers and commentaries on the New York art world. She has yet to read a serious quote of Danielle's.

"I'm going to row some," Danielle says. "Want to go? I'll be your coxswain. I'll sit behind you and hurl insults and be abusive generally while rowing sort of lackadaisically myself."

On the rowing machines, they catch each other's rhythm, and when Holly starts to get lazy, she hears the clack of Danielle's rows behind her and keeps pace.

Two girls in leotards and ballet slippers are stretching out nearby.

The first girl says, "Dan wants to get married."

"Oh, God, that's great."

"But he wants to have kids."

"Oh, forget it."

"Can you imagine being ugly for nine months?"

"I couldn't stand it."

"Ugly for nine months."

"I can't imagine. Forget it."

So this is what pregnancy means to some women, Holly thinks. Ugly for nine months. Forget it.

"This is your coxswain speaking," Danielle's voice behind her says. "I'm going over and pull the hair out of those scrawny putrescences. Then I'm going to throw carbolic acid in their faces. What do you say? Are you with me?"

"Forget them," Holly says without turning. "You look great, and you're going to have a great kid, and they're not."

"According to the amnio, I'm going to have a man child."

"You're going to have a man child," Holly says, "and when those girls are old and gray, they'll be lonely and bitter and rue their words."

"Keep rowing," says Danielle. "You lie."

Holly rows until her arms ache and her back and front are slick with sweat. She looks up and sees Danielle standing in front of the scrawny putrescences. She stretches up, then lifts her T-shirt to scratch her huge smooth belly. She drops the T-shirt, yawns, and proceeds out.

The scrawny putrescences exchange looks, laugh, and bend in two like folded lengths of rubber.

CHAPTER 10

Meg stumbles into the office, haggard and bleary-eyed, her hair lank and limp. She needs a day in the sun, an afternoon at Elizabeth Arden, a good night's sleep.

"Rough night at the office, *cherie?*" asks Lynn.

Meg holds her head and staggers into the kitchen, where she opens the freezer door and sticks her head into the cold vapor.

"That bad?" asks Holly.

Meg slams the freezer door shut and slumps against the refrigerator. "You know how they tell you to keep your eye on the perineum at all times?"

Holly nods.

"Take it from me," Meg says, reaching into the freezer and pulling out two ice cubes, which she applies to both eyes, "do it."

"Did a baby take a flyer?"

"The baby flew to London, express," Meg says, pitching the ice cubes into the ferns on the windowsill. "The baby was a square peg through a round hole. Fifteen hours to second stage, and then two hours in second."

"Could be worse," Holly says, wondering how much worse it could be.

"She couldn't get with it. Why can't some women get the hang of pushing? I figured there were at least fifteen minutes to go before she delivered, and Frischling was hanging around—"

"Frischling? In the birthing room?" Frischling is the chief resident at Brownell.

Meg sighs. "He was interested in watching a real live midwifery birth, and I figured, here was our chance to do a little role-modeling for the benighted medical man." Meg is in pain. She buries her face in her hands, then looks up. "I turned to scrub up, then I heard a scream.

421

Bloodcurdling. I swung around. There's Frischling holding the baby with his bare hands and this stunned look and about five liters of blood flushing out on the bed."

"Oh, no."

"Oh, yes." Meg shakes her head. Her eyes are swollen into slits. Meg looks . . . Slavic. "I do not know what took that woman over. She shoved that baby out of there like a shot-putter hurling a discus."

"Hurling a put," Holly says.

"Whatever, she was doing it. The baby flew. Third-degree tears."

"Urethral tears, too?" These are the toughest to repair in terms of suturing skills, and the easiest to screw up.

"A bit of everything. It took me two hours to do it all. She was ripped to shreds." Meg bites her lower lip. "If it weren't my fault, I could deal with it." Meg's eyes look hooded and small, like she'd like to hide behind her face and never come out again. She leans on the windowsill. "What bugs me is that I told her later that it was my fault. If I'd been smart, I would have persuaded her she was to blame for losing control of the bearing-down mechanism. Scolded her as soon as it happened. 'How could you do that, Dana?' Instead, I did the worst thing. I said, 'I'm sorry.'"

"That's sort of an admission of guilt, Meg," Holly says.

Meg kicks the cabinet door under the sink. "I should have done what Dad always told me to do. Never apologize, never explain. Act like every primap tears this way."

"You'd have had a hard time convincing her that all primaps give birth when the midwife's back is turned."

"Yeah, that might have been pretty hard to pull off." Meg shakes her head.

Stepping into the kitchen, Lynn says, "Dana's husband, *il est dans la phone.*"

Meg glances fearfully at Holly. "Not wasting any time initiating the lawsuit, I see." She picks up the phone, and after a buzz of conversation, hangs up. "What's the name of that head nurse in Postpartum?" she asks Holly.

"What day is it?"

"I don't know," Meg says. She calls out to Lynn for the day.

"It's Thursday, *mesdames*, you flakes."

"Robin," says Holly.

"I have to disabuse Robin of the notion that visitors aren't allowed in Dana's room when she's feeding the baby."

"You can deal with that," Holly says, heading to work.

"That sort of stuff I can handle," Meg says. She looks up at the ceiling. "By the skin of my teeth. Maybe nothing will happen."

"Just pray the sutures hold," says Holly as she leaves. Crossing the reception room, she hears Meg's answer: "Oh, fuck!"

CHAPTER 11

The married man who disheartened Holly weeks before is back with his wife, Christina, who is eight and a half months pregnant. The last time he passed the half-hour exam by sweeping Holly with his eyes, but this visit it's clear that both women bore him. He sits with crossed legs, jiggles an impatient foot, looks blankly at the wall and studies his Rolex. Holly's bruised ego ("What? Bored with me even?") has pegged him now for a bounder, a bolter, a bad egg.

Christina sits up on the examining table, swinging her feet. She has a new, trendy haircut, very short, that she is not used to yet; she pulls uneasily at the short bits of hair behind her ears. "Roger says sex is bad for the baby," she says breathily, glancing nervously at Roger.

"Christina!" he says sharply, and Christina drops her head.

As the mollifying midwife, Holly assures them, "You can't hurt the baby now. In fact, the baby might even enjoy it. And at the end of term, before the waters break, sex might even help bring on labor."

Roger looks disgusted, as if he's just swallowed something bad. "It's all repellent," he snaps. "This entire thing." He stands up. "I'm late for work. I'll see you later."

And he's out the door. A bolter.

"I don't think he's ready to be a labor coach," Christina says apologetically.

Roger has always been about as compliant as a caged panther. Throughout the talks on what the mucus plug looks like and how the waters break ("Is it just a huge gush or is it a trickle?" "A huge trickle," Holly had answered), Roger had yawned and released sighlike whistles. Roger never promised much as a labor coach.

"He was brought up in Europe," Christina goes on. "They expect their women to be ladylike."

This might be true, but Holly knows other European men who let their ladies bleed, have mucus plugs, and go to the bathroom. Holly's disagreement must have spread to her face, because Christina elaborates. "He was brought up in *England*, you see. The men can be very repressed there, in England."

"I see," Holly says with a nod. "I understand, because the men are very repressed where I come from, too."

"Where do you come from?"

"Bryn Mawr, Pennsylvania."

CHAPTER 12

Holly is in the Education Room at Brownell to pitch the practice to prospective AP clients, serious browsers who must decide who to entrust their deliveries to—a decision they'll have to live with and live with and live with. Every hospital has a room like this one, with watercolors of a mother and baby, a table messy with half-drunk cups of coffee and soiled brochures, and dusty props on the radiator—a plastic pelvis, a smudged doll, gym mats for childbirth exercises, and posterboard diagrams of the cervix in all stages of dilatation.

Holly examines the doll she uses in her childbirth classes, when she puts the doll in a cloth bag (the womb) that's closed with a drawstring, then pushes it against the drawstring closure, to show how a baby causes a cervix to dilate. Then she slides the baby through the dusty plastic pelvis to create a full picture of dilatation, rotation, and descent.

Last week, Holly squeezed the baby through the pelvic inlet, explaining how the tightest fit is at the pelvic midpoint, the obstetric conjugate, and said (lyrically, she felt), "It's bone through bone. But don't worry—the baby's made for it." Her class was sufficiently awed by the tight squeeze, when the doll popped out of the bag, flew through the pelvis, and fell to the floor with a thud. Not auspicious. Now Holly is superstitious enough to approach the doll with extreme caution, wondering if she should tape some padding to the doll or just spring for a doll with greater cranial circumference.

The first orientation couple enters the room, and Holly, a bit embarrassed, quickly slides the doll to a seat beside her. This couple is sweet looking and walks through the door holding hands, breaking apart only to take a brochure Holly holds out for them, then clasping hands again. She's in a frontier-style dress, and he's in a flannel shirt and Levi's—the kind of

New-Age-hippie–inspired clients that people expect midwives to have but that Holly, here in Brooklyn Heights, sees only occasionally.

It's an uneasy time, because Holly's instinct is to talk with the early arrivals. But if she does, they'll ask the same questions the later arrivals will, and everyone's time will be wasted. Yet Holly doesn't want to seem cold. The brochure, which Meg wrote before Holly joined the practice, describes what a midwife is, how the practice practices, what noninterventionistic birthing means (not, as the brochure explains, knee-jerk objection to all technology and medication). It's supposed to occupy the early arrivals but only consumes five minutes, even for slow readers, and Holly doesn't know where to look when a couple has finished with the brochure. She'd just as soon read a book, but that might make her seem uninterested and discourteous, so she fumbles with her list of prospective clients, reads through the brochure for the hundredth time, and glances a lot at her watch.

A man in a trench coat enters. "Did you bring someone pregnant with you?" Holly asks. Everyone laughs, and the pregnant someone, in a Burberry coat herself, appears a moment later, rushing from another subway, another office. They are not the Seidners, about whom Lynn warned her. "Watch out for them," Lynn said ominously.

"Why?"

"Mrs. Seidner kept asking questions I couldn't answer. I kept telling her that I couldn't answer them and that they'd be answered at orientation. She kept asking, and I kept not answering, and she kept asking, and I kept not answering—"

"I get the picture."

Lynn wanted to reinforce the picture. "They're trouble with a capital T," she said, hugging herself against the chill of the Seidner specter. "I feel it in my bones."

Holly felt it in her bones as well. Lynn's assessment had some credibility, since Lynn is not imaginative enough to invent these things out of whole cloth.

"And, Holly," Lynn called out urgently, "I forgot to tell you—they're both lawyers."

Holly does not ever want to see the Seidners.

A gorgeous Italian girl steps in with a jangle of gold bracelets, in a green suede suit, silk blouse, and blue suede boots. She has hair the color and thickness of a lion's mane. Holly is in awe of the burnished look only the European upper classes can achieve, and she suddenly feels not as if she belongs to the American equivalent of the ruling class but as if she's straight off the farm, in overalls with hayseed in her hair. The Italian girl tosses back her hair, brushes the brochure with her eyes, and promptly stares at the ceiling. Holly would like to get to know this Italian princess, which she imagines she is, but she doubts she will. A princess will go elsewhere.

Next, a bland-looking couple with a bland name, Thomas: they seem dependable, people who'd remember to water your plants if you asked them to, and they rush in carrying bundles, worried they're late. They're not late. They won't have an easy time at delivery, Holly decides—too tense and polite at the same time, not go-with-the-flow types. But she's often wrong. . . .

This leaves the Colliers and the Seidners, and Holly is hopeful. It's ten past seven. Maybe the Seidners will just bail out.

Arguing voices resound in the hall, then hush down, and a man and woman in their late thirties appear in the doorway. They can only be the Seidners. Mrs. Seidner takes a brochure with a snap of her hand as Mr. Seidner flings himself down on a seat, slapping his knee with a newspaper to emphasize a point he hasn't made yet: a hefty guy who fills out his pinstripe suit in a way that makes Holly uncomfortable, with his sleeves riding up and his trousers inching down. Mrs. Seidner, with dark hair in a French roll and wearing a black suit as shapeless as her husband's, collapses onto a seat separated from her husband's by a small table. She might have taken the empty seat next to her husband, but no, the body language must speak of resentment and the kind of unhappiness that likes to spread itself around.

Go elsewhere, Holly chants in her mind. *Go elsewhere.*

"We passed a chapel on the way in," Mr. Seidner says loudly.

"Ah." Holly smiles in her polite, off-putting way. Orientation hasn't officially begun, and Holly isn't ready for comments from the floor, particularly ones from the Seidners.

"Is this a religious hospital?" he asks.

"The chapel, like most hospital chapels, is nondenominational. Brownell used to be affiliated with the Catholic Church, but no longer." Why does he ask? Is he afraid nuns will serve as nurses, extreme unction administered to his wife against her will? Maybe, like the old woman in the coffee shop, they personally would like to go elsewhere. In which case, Holly thinks, feel free.

This isn't his point.

"What would you do if something is wrong with the baby?" Mrs. Seidner asks in an untraceable European accent.

"Aren't we jumping the gun here?" Holly glances at the other couples, who are as startled as she is by this gloomy question. The husband of the very young woman puts a protective arm around her as she rests her head against his chest. The mild-mannered Thomases, eating homemade sandwiches, look up in confusion. The Italian girl surveys the Seidners with open distaste and then looks down lovingly at her beautiful suede boots.

"A legitimate question," Mr. Seidner says. "What would you do if something is wrong with the baby?"

The question is a medicine ball flung at Holly's chest when she wasn't looking. She expects a good percentage of flaky questions—"I have to have my B-twelve shot every day. I'll never get through labor without one. Can you give me one in labor?"—but few are this gruesome this early. If Holly doesn't answer, she'll anger the Seidners and appear evasive. But answering the question doesn't work to the common good. Holly will be able to cover ground of general interest—what early discharge is, what medications the practice uses, if a couple can videotape the birth—if she can cut the Seidners dead.

"Can you be more specific?" she asks, looking straight at both Seidners. *I'm afraid of nothing,* she wants them to know. *I can take whatever you fire at me.*

Mrs. Seidner rolls her eyes in search of the appropriate term. "The Baby Doe case, for instance."

"Ah."

"Yes. Ah. What would you do?"

Mrs. Seidner wants to know that Holly won't do anything the Seidners don't want her to do, and that the Futterman practice will let their baby die, if that's what they want. Holly can't give them this reassurance. Not because the practice philosophy doesn't subscribe to the right to die in extreme cases, but because by the time the baby is diagnosed, the midwives and Dr. Futterman no longer control the baby's care. Babies who used to be clearly hopeless cases are no longer so, and cases that seem hopeless to the Futterman practitioners may not seem so to the parents. In any case, nobody is in a position to judge right after delivery. Holly mentally sounds out what she's about to say before she lets the words escape through her lips.

"After a baby is born, I do everything to help him," she says. "If a baby is sick, he's under my care for only a minute before the pediatricians take over. I'm not equipped to evaluate a baby in those few minutes, and my protocol—the steps I always take—is to do everything I can until the pediatricians take over."

The Seidners exchange glances—smirks, really—as if Holly has just admitted to grave incompetence.

"And later, if we want treatment withheld?" Mrs. Seidner demands. "This hospital was associated with the Church. Won't they initiate some kind of stop order to counter our wishes?"

"Brownell has an ethics committee of doctors, clergymen of all faiths, and specialists in disabilities that weighs all the information and makes recommendations. Something family members wouldn't be able to on their own, especially in a time of grief, and in the end, families know that whatever has been decided is the right thing."

Mr. Seidner snorts. "Just what the world needs—ethics by committee. Legislation of morality!"

"Morality is legislated all the time!" Holly says, forgetting she's supposed to remain coolheaded during orientation. "That's what law is." Remembering that both the Seidners are lawyers, she cringes in embarrassment, sits back in her chair, and smiles with understated apology at the other couples, who smile back weakly, sympathetic. It's an Us against Them situation now, unpleasant but possibly useful in terms of recruiting the other couples to the practice.

Holly is satisfied she's said it all. But for the benefit of the alarmed group, she adds, "The likelihood of having to deal with this is"—she fumbles for the word—"so unlikely."

But the Seidners can't be stopped. Holly hasn't even explained what a nurse-midwife is, but the Seidners ask if their own pediatrician can care for the baby in the hospital. Not unless he has privileges to practice here. How can he get privileges? He'd have to submit an application to the head of pediatrics, the credentials committee, possibly the board of directors: not a viable scheme, and the grant of one-time-only visiting privileges is rare.

"Ridiculous!" Mrs. Seidner says, clapping her hands. "My own pediatrician can't examine my child? Don't I have the right to have my own child examined by whomever I choose?"

"If all goes well, you can leave the hospital in less than twenty-four hours and take the baby to the doctor on your own." This is Holly's introduction of the early discharge concept to the group. She doesn't like its unhappy context.

"If I don't want to wait twenty-four hours?"

"Have him see your baby informally," Holly suggests, "as a friend might see your baby. By coming into your room. But he won't be able to prescribe any medications or draw up orders."

"Isn't that ridiculous, Albert?" Mrs. Seidner turns to her husband, who is sprawled in his seat, legs parted. He shrugs.

"The policy protects the patients," Holly says, exhausted by exerting her defensive oratory skills. Holly would like to articulate a certain phrase to the Seidners, and the phrase is *Fuck off*. But she goes on. "If a physician could walk in and draw up orders without the hospital's approval of his credentials, standards couldn't be upheld, and the hospital has ultimate responsibility for what happens here."

"They're responsible for what happens at my delivery?" Mrs. Seidner asks.

Holly thinks Mrs. Seidner must not be a very good lawyer. But she's not surprised. "If it turned out I was an uncredentialed nurse-midwife, the hospital would be negligent for permitting me to practice here."

There's a pause, a calm, and Holly hopes to move on to her mild-mannered, reasoned-out introduction to midwifery in a modern hospital setting. But she's afraid it's too late. The Seidner interrogation has brought a malign feeling to the proceedings.

"Have you had any of these cases?" Mr. Seidner asks thickly.

We're back to this then. "What cases?"

"These Baby Doe–type cases."

"I've had sick babies on my hands, yes." The Italian girl has now pulled out a date book and is reading it for amusement. "I used to work in a high-risk setting, where I delivered a few babies incompatible with life." Holly says this quietly, hoping the other couples won't hear. But they all hear.

Mrs. Seidner laughs. "A funny phrase. Incompatible with life."

"An accurate one," Holly says tensely.

"What happened?" Mrs. Seidner asks.

This is prying now, Holly thinks. Her sense of privacy is offended. "They died," she says.

"What did you do?"

"When they died?" Holly asks. Now she laughs. She'd like to know, when did you first lose your mind, Mrs. Seidner? "Let's follow up on this discussion later, Mrs. Seidner. We have a lot of ground to cover of interest to everyone." Holly has the paranoid flash that the Seidners were sent here by a cabal of obstetricians as agents provocateurs to break up the meeting of midwives and prospective patients. What do the Seidners want from her exactly?

"You tried to save them because you'd be accused of negligence if you didn't," Mrs. Seidner says challengingly.

"I tried to save them until I knew that I couldn't." Holly's integrity has never been questioned in front of a group before. In private, yes. In public, it's unacceptable. It's intolerable. She looks up. The last couple, the Colliers, stand in the doorway, out of breath from rushing, bright eyed, pink cheeked, panting through their smiles.

"Sorry we're late," they say, spilling through the doorway. Their faces are eager and bright, and they look excited by pregnancy, by life. Holly wants to fall to her knees and bless them.

But she stands, welcoming them. "You must be the Colliers," she says. "Now we can begin."

CHAPTER 13

Holly is walking her fingers over the abdomen of the managing director at an investment firm. A big job, Matt told Holly, although she doesn't have the faintest idea what it is Carla does. Carla is always in a hurry. She likes abbreviated visits. For this visit, Carla has kept on her black knit dress, rolled it up like the leg of a stocking up to her bra, her dark slip rolled up with it, like the filling in a jelly roll. Carla has kept on her pantyhose by rolling them down in the opposite direction. Holly almost expects her to develop a shorthand code by which she can communicate with the midwives and not waste any time. Most patients come to the Futterman practice because the midwives take their time with them and don't whisk them through. Carla may like the quality of care, but she could do without the birthing blather. What's most on her mind is hopping a taxi over to Water Street, in the financial district.

"Carla, did you choose this practice because it's located in Brooklyn Heights rather than on the Upper East Side?" Holly asks as she measures fundal height. Carla's at thirty-two weeks, and the height is right for dates, the top of the uterus almost but not quite reaching the line where her breasts start. "Did you decide to come here because it's near Wall Street and you won't get caught in a traffic jam leaving here?"

Carla studies Holly disapprovingly, as if she's put off by Holly's impertinence. Holly is about Carla's age, but Holly has a hard time viewing Carla as a peer. Carla has a very authoritative aura, which Holly feels compelled to try to dispel. She just wants Carla to turn into a normal young woman.

"I came here because," Carla says, drawing out her words uncharacteristically slowly, "because you'll support me in my decisions."

431

"Yup. We aim to please."

"So when can I have my section?"

Carla's pregnancy has been streamlined, as she planned. No muss, no fuss. She has carried a vertex all through pregnancy, but now the baby has inched around and become a breech. Tall, tense Carla has a tall, tense baby who runs up and down the length of the womb.

"Feel the feet, there?" Holly says, guiding Carla's hand to where the head—movable, palpable—usually is, right above the *symphisis pubis.* But this mass is immovable, characteristic of a breech.

"I don't want to press too hard," Carla says, lifting her head with its long, graceful neck and looking down, her sharp chin almost digging into her chest.

"Don't be scared. You can't press too hard. This is very well designed packaging."

Carla presses tentatively, then draws her hand back quickly.

"I felt it," she says. She's completed her chore. She looks at Holly. "So, does this mean a cesarean?"

"No, this means we've got to get him turned around. You can get up now, Carla."

As Carla pulls up her pantyhose and rolls down her dress, she asks, "So how do we do that, Holly? Get the baby turned around?" She's all business. "Besides screaming at him, I mean." That's the closest thing to a joke Holly has ever heard from Carla.

"Screaming at him won't hurt," Holly says. "Mentally, I mean. If you shut your eyes and picture the baby turning around and will it to happen..."

Carla scratches her neck distractedly as Holly talks, snapping open some lipstick and smoothing down her hair in the mirror. This doesn't sound much like *doing* something about the problem to her. Holly can see that the sensitive, holistic methodology is not going to take.

Holly says staunchly, "We recommend that you take an ironing board, prop it against a bookcase about three feet high, and lie on the board with your feet up for two hours a day in one-hour intervals." There, that's doing something. "We've had good results with that."

"Holly!" Carla is facing her, handbag over her shoulder, shoes on, hands on her hips.

"Carla! What?"

"I don't have an ironing board."

"Don't you?" Holly doesn't have an ironing board either. When she irons, she clears off the kitchen table, puts a towel down and irons there. But she lives in a tiny apartment. Carla draws down big bucks and lives in a townhouse with her husband, who also pulls down good money. How come they don't have a whole phalanx of ironing boards?

"I never iron," Carla says flatly.

Next to Holly's mother, Carla is the least wrinkled person Holly knows. "What do you do then?"

"We send everything to the cleaners. What do you think?"

Ah, of course. But even Holly's mother, who's made it her life's work importing poor black women from the Philadelphia inner city to clean her house and do her laundry, has, on the odd occasion, found herself doing touch-up ironing jobs in the utility room.

"Don't you have anything like an ironing board?" Holly knows these guys. She knows what they have. "Do you have a sit-up board?"

"Actually, Tom does."

"Lie on that then. Two hours a day or longer, if you're so inclined." Holly laughs. "That's a joke, see—*inclined*, on the board. Get it?"

Whether or not Carla gets it is beside the point. She'd just as soon not get it. "I've got the sit-up board, but where do you think I'm going to get two hours a day?"

Holly washes her hands. "You'll just have to find those hours. Think of it as investment for a very large return." Holly remembers a story by an Irish writer about a Catholic priest who preached to his constituency of businessmen entirely in business terms. That was the only way they could understand religion and take it to heart. Holly will have to keep this in mind and do the same with Carla.

"You'll waste so much more time if you wind up having a section," she says. "Besides, lying with your feet up will do a world of good for your appearance, not that you don't look wonderful now. All the blood will rush into your face and give you a pink, healthy look."

Most of Carla's appeal lies in her face's angularity, her fine bone structure and her pale skin. A pink, healthy look is the last thing she needs.

"An investment of two hours?" Carla says, thinking aloud as she picks up her briefcase. She narrows her eyes. She's calculating. "Maybe I can listen to self-hypnosis tapes while I'm at it. Learn how to relax for the labor."

Carla knows how to capitalize on an investment.

"If all else fails," Holly says, "you can shout at the baby." Holly smiles, to show she's joking, as if to say, all that mystical gobbledygook isn't for us rational ladies. Holly will act in almost any way to keep her patients' trust, and she doesn't want Carla to think she's a flake. Holly would make a very pragmatic missionary.

It's too late to say anything, because Carla is out the door, to churn money, or whatever it is she does, on Water Street.

CHAPTER 14

On her way to childbirth class, Holly takes the long route through the hospital to the Education Room. She likes to walk through the hospital in the evening. Dinner trays are stacked in the halls. Small televisions twang out the news and reruns of *The Odd Couple*. Visitors, easing their way into good-byes and out of rooms, seem both reluctant and relieved to leave. Holly no longer works day in and day out in a hospital, and she likes the feeling of just passing through.

She particularly likes walking through Pediatrics. The hospital combined two buildings by a labyrinth of corridors, so Maternity and Pediatrics is MacMillan Five. Holly likes to reach Maternity by swinging through Pediatrics.

For every badly sick child there, one is tearing up and down the hallway singing the Superheroes anthem at the top of his lungs while another one, in a head bandage, tries to teach a nurse the proper way to imitate a Smurf. Wending her way through Pediatrics puts midwifery back in perspective. If childbirth sometimes becomes an end in itself, Pediatrics proves it's only a means to an end, and the end is something like this: a kid with his arm in a sling spinning down the corridor just to make himself dizzy. For all Holly knows, she might have delivered some of these kids, in another hospital years ago.

Holly wishes she could recognize all the kids she's ever delivered, so she could pick them out on a playground to say, "I know you. I brought you into this world." She wishes she could brand a small *HT* on the back of her babies' necks, so later on she could spot the tattoos and say, "You're one of mine." How can she keep track of all these babies when they're scattered over the face of the earth?

Sometimes Holly dreams about becoming a pediatrics nurse-practitioner, so she could treat the babies she catches and follow them into the world.

Even then, she'd have no proprietorial rights, no custody. When the mother of one of the first babies Holly ever delivered came to say good-bye because she was moving to Ireland, Holly was shocked. "You're taking the baby with you?"

"I'm not leaving him behind after all I've been through."

One of Holly's babies was moving to a completely different continent. Soon Holly's sphere of influence will extend beyond landmasses. One of her Howard Street patients told her daughter, "Be nice to Holly. One day she'll be your nurse, too." Holly looked down at the little girl and thought, "See you in ten years, kid."

Soon Holly will be crossing generations.

She pushes through the door to Maternity, which is marked with a big STOP sign that even a kid meandering away from Pediatrics can understand. Meg, her hair in a bandana and wearing a plastic apron, has just finished a delivery and is standing in the middle of the corridor. She gives Holly a big grin.

"Having a good time, Meg?"

"A blast. I love multips. The Woods. I told her she could start pushing. 'I don't want to push,' she said. 'I can't go through that again.' First time, she pushed for an hour and a half. 'You're a second-timer now,' I said. 'It won't take so long as before.' 'Don't make me push,' she begged and asked for a bedpan. I told her I didn't think that was her problem, considering the castor oil she took before labor, and the enema later. 'I think you're about to have your baby.' 'No, I have hours to go,' she said. 'Give me a bedpan.' Then, bingo, there's the kid. Intact perineum. She was happier about not having to push for hours than she was to see the kid. 'I don't have to push?' she said. I asked her what the baby was doing here if she had to push. Multips. They're the greatest. Eight-pound boy. Huge ears. Maybe he'll grow into them. So, how come you came in that way? Through MacMillan?"

"I like to go through Pediatrics and see the kids." Meg makes a face, and Holly empathizes. "Pediatrics makes you sad?"

"Lord, no. I'm just not all that crazy about kids." Meg glances about furtively. "Babies just don't appeal to me. They don't turn me on."

"But you always say how cute they are."

"I'm glad to see them after labor. I like childbirth, I like women, I like men, but kids . . ." Meg shrugs.

Holly is shocked. But why should she be? Meg doesn't hate kids—it's more of a general disinterest. And after all, they're both midwives and chose childbirth over child-care, keeping the time they spend with real, live babies down to a minimum.

And yet, a maternal instinct always seemed part and parcel of midwifery. Holly wonders if Meg doesn't feel the elemental urge to have a little creature pull at her finger, a child she can give unconditional love to.

Meg pulls off her plastic apron, unties her bandana, ending a job well done. Maybe it's just as well she doesn't want children. It doesn't do Holly much good, to be twenty-nine years old and feel an almost palpable void where children should be. She should just unlock her unconditional love, pour it onto Matt, give it to the world instead of holding it back, keeping it in stir.

But there's a catch. Only a baby can unlock something as deep as unconditional love. Maybe Meg is well off, Holly decides. It's hard waiting for a baby to unlock her love. It's hard waiting to be released.

CHAPTER 15

Holly teaches one childbirth class a week. The tuition for a six-week course is one hundred twenty-five dollars per couple. Tax-deductible, she points out, when she collects fees at the first class. At five couples per class and five sets of classes each year, Holly's extra income, after the user's fee for the Education Room at Brownell and film rental fees, is a bit over twenty-five hundred dollars a year. "Just enough to boost you into an obnoxious tax bracket," as Meg has said.

It's tiring work, since she has to repeat so much of the same material. The most common worry that crops up is the nuchal cord fear. A universal fear of strangulation. Is a midwife skilled enough to deal with an umbilical cord around the neck at birth? "The cord around the neck is a last-minute problem you detect just as the baby's head is being born. It happens in nearly a third of all deliveries—" The class gasps. "But it's one of the easiest to handle. You either sweep the cord over the head or cut it right away, which is fine, too." No matter how often Holly explains this, she senses she's fighting a losing battle. Her reassurances fail to root out the deep fear. If Holly mentions that a patient needed an emergency section, someone always asks, "Was the cord around the baby's neck?"

"What kind of training do midwives have?" someone always asks apologetically, too shy to ask this in the office, where it may seem to doubt the midwives' abilities. It's the kind of question that troubles clients late at night when they sit bolt upright wondering, what have I gotten myself into?

"A midwife is a registered nurse, has completed a nurse-midwifery program, sat for boards before the American College of Nurse-Midwives." *Sitting for boards* has a professional sound that eases her patients' minds.

Then Holly whips out her own credentials, which are even more reassuring.

"I got my B.A. from Brown, my master's in nursing from University of Pennsylvania, and my certification in nurse-midwifery from Penn as well."

After she flashes her credentials, visible signs of relief and trust and respect pass over her clients' faces. An Ivy League midwife. Yippee-skippee, Holly thinks, remembering Pam and Paula and other midwives who got their RNs through diploma programs and could only attend certification midwifery programs, instead of master's programs, at non-Ivy schools. They wouldn't pass muster here, under the scrutiny of Holly's status-oriented childbirth class.

One of Holly's friends has gone back to school for her Ph.D. in nursing. "The only way we're going to get accepted, Holly, is if we're all doctors. We have to get those big degrees."

"You know a degree doesn't mean a thing when you're on the floor," Holly said. "The best midwives are the clinicians, working in the field. Besides, the people I'd like respect from right now are the nurses I work with."

"That's the idea. Nurses see us as nurses with airs. If we all have Ph.D.s, they'll accept us as superiors."

"That's not a very nice attitude," Holly said.

"It's not a very nice world."

Couples begin classes seven weeks before their due dates. A few couples are conspicuous by their absence toward the end, and Holly tells birth stories to the most avid listeners in the world. She's careful about the gory details she spills, censoring the stories to neutralize fears and accentuate the positive. "Joan had her baby. A boy. She went into premature labor and had to have a section, but she's fine now and so is the baby."

"Awww." *She missed out on the birth experience.*

"Oh!" *This does happen, and it could happen to me.*

"Ahhhh." *I wish it were over for me, too.*

"I'm having a girl," says a patient who's had amnio.

"Let's make a match with Joan's baby!" her husband says.

And the class is off again.

The primaps obsess on labor. They apply their high standards of achievement—they all seem to be ridiculously high achievers—to a part of life where these standards are positively detrimental. The things that have served Holly's clients well over the years—ambition, self-control, discipline—are at odds with labor's peculiarities. Her clients are too prepared, have learned rules for a situation where no rules apply, intellectualized labor when labor won't be intellectualized. The more sure they are of how labor is supposed to be, the harder time they have, when the intellect is rendered useless by the body and, in essence, the body tells the intellect, "You can't do anything about this, I'm in charge here as I have been for thousands of years, and you're no exception."

At this last class in the series, Holly gives her final pep talk. "The way to control labor is to give up the idea of control," she says, knowing she sounds like an ersatz Zen master. "Give yourself up to it." She'd like to tell them to go with the flow, but that would tip her over the edge into guru flakiness.

Holly's never sure if she should dash these people's hopes. The couple, for instance, that has put together a birth tape, an orchestrated cassette of Mozart, Philip Glass, and Talking Heads, to pack in the big gym bag they'll take to the hospital. Once labor comes hard and heavy, most women prefer silence. Music becomes an irritant, a noisemaker, ultimately irrelevant. "We even have birdsongs on the tape," the father-to-be said excitedly at the start of class.

Holly would have liked to say, listen to Talking Heads when you pace the apartment, dilating slowly, or stretching out, ten hours postpartum, but forget it for the rest of the time. But she can't bring herself to say it. They'll learn, as all primaps learn, and when they do, all they need to do is press the boom-box button that says STOP.

Most of the couples are, reasonably, drawn to Leboyer's gentle birth. Holly can supply the hushed tones and dim lights, but the bath for the baby right after birth is the butt of midwives' jokes, a symbol of unrealistic romanticization and wishful thinking. Because when the baby is finally born, and well enough not to have to go to the nursery, what father wants to pull the kid off the mother's chest, where he's already started to nurse, to sink him into a bowl of warm water? Leboyer made it seem like the most natural event in the world, but nothing seems so artificial when the time actually comes.

In a private practice, a midwife is supposed to respect her clients' wishes and carry them out whenever possible. So when a husband now asks about Leboyer baths, Holly answers, "People often think they want the baths, but they're so happy when the baby gets here, they forget all about it." This has a ring of truth that actually seems to pierce the heavy gauze of the couples' dreams, and Holly is sure that only a few couples will haul the little baths to the birthing room, without Holly having to be overly discouraging.

Fran Cutler blows into childbirth class, red in the face, looking as if she's about to burst. Something has happened. "I was in line for a token, and I thought I lost my crotch. I thought I was going to lose it all right there. Baby, placenta, kidneys, bladder, bowels, my breakfast. Forget this, I said. If I'm going to lose it, I'm going to lose it in a cab."

"Fran, kiddo, your baby just dropped."

The class, excited, sits up and studies Fran. She is closing in on the destination. She doesn't look any different, but is just as frowsy and blowsy as ever.

"So that's why I could breathe as soon as I got into the taxi. I thought it was incredible, what a difference a cab could make."

"Lightening can produce slight incontinence," Holly tells the class. "Or, at least, frequent urination."

"I find that hard to believe!" Danielle Greenhouse bellows. "I could not possibly pee more than I do now."

The class laughs nervously. The women sip juice through straws, their shoes off and their feet up, and they don't look as if they're taking this deadly seriously. They are. The nervous laughter gives away just how serious they are. Their bodily functions have become conspicuous to the max—could it become worse?—and their laughter is sheer nerves, springing to the surface.

Lightening has a quaint sound. But it's deceptive. Nothing lightens. The weight only shifts. The ability to breathe more easily, as the fundus sinks a few inches and doesn't poach on the turf the lungs use to expand, comes at a price: pelvic discomfort, vascularity in the vagina, a squashed bladder.

"God, that's the story of my life," Danielle says. "Shifting the bulk from one place to another."

"Mine, too," says Holly. Then she announces, "You're allowed two labor coaches in the birthing room. These may be your astrologer, masseuse, ex-husband, any prepared child who appears to be over eighteen years old, your former obstetrician, your parents, your parole officer. Any questions?"

Danielle raises her hand. "Can I bring my dog?"

"No, Danielle! No dogs allowed!"

"He's like family!"

"Next time, give birth in a kennel."

"Holly, you're mean."

"Yeah."

Holly warns her students that the classes are misnamed. "These classes can't prepare you for childbirth. You don't know until you're there what it's actually going to be like. You may think you know, but you don't. Not really."

The couples nod, and husbands and wives exchange glances. No matter what Holly says, they still think that Holly's disclaimer is for some other pregnant people.

Danielle and her husband, Paul Stolz, stay behind. "I bought a bra the other day," Danielle says. "It's rather immense, and I'm thinking of selling off one cup as a condo. Perhaps you'd be interested."

Holly thinks for a moment. "How much?" she finally asks.

CHAPTER 16

"A Gallup poll in the newspaper today said that lawyers and doctors are the least trusted professionals in America," Holly says. She's eating dinner with Matt.

"You live with one and work with the other," Matt says. "What does that say about you?"

"I'm a sucker and a chump."

Matt says nothing. Holly glances at him. Tired eyes, hair standing up at the forehead, showing he's passed his hand through his hair, while thinking, at least one hundred times since this morning.

"What's eating you?" Holly asks.

"I don't know how you stand it," he says, pushing his plate away. "Your line of work would blow me out of the water."

"Yeah, I know. What's happened? Did you deliver a baby today or something?"

Matt leans back and shuts his eyes. "Worse," he says, gloomily. "I got put on my first malpractice case today."

"Really?"

"Christ, it's repulsive. You don't want to hear about it over dinner."

"All right then, I'm through with dinner."

"No, finish your dinner."

"No, I'm through."

"Holly, you don't have to be nice to me."

"I'm through with my dinner. If I was being nice, you'd be the first to know."

"Well, digest for a while then."

"Matt, tell me!"

"All right. I had to depose a lady. A sick lady." He stands up. "Holly, did you ever hear of a recto-vaginal fistula?"

"That's what she's got?"

"I had to hear all the gory details. That's the point of a deposition."

A recto-vaginal fistula is the unnatural communication established between the vagina and the rectum. The artificially, accidentally constructed canal is usually caused by some trauma. The complications are horrendous, as the contents of the rectum leak into the vagina—the definition of an unwholesome condition.

"What was it? A bad episiotomy?" Holly asks. "I've almost done it a few times myself. Push the needle in too far and you hit the rectum. If you don't catch it—well, there you go."

"Holly, shit came into her cunt!"

"Matt, can't we be a little professional here in our working vocabulary?"

"I've been professional all day long. I don't think I can stand it anymore."

Matt paces up and down the living room. He stops, kicks the rug back, folds the border over on itself with his foot, then straightens it out, kicks it back, straightens it out. . . .

"Do I dare ask which side you're representing?" Holly asks.

Matt gives Holly a sardonic, slack-jawed stare. But a second later he looks sad and defeated. "Who do you think a firm like ours represents?"

"The doc," Holly says quietly.

Matt throws himself down on the couch. "Christ, this perfectly nice lady has shit in her goddamn vagina, and I'm representing the wrong side. The Gallup poll is fucking right, fuck it."

Holly gets up and lies next to him, half on him, on the couch. "Don't worry," she tells him. "This is just your residency, like you told me."

He looks in her eyes. "This isn't right, Holly. I'm supposed to be the one reassuring you. You're supposed to be the one who's fucked up and doesn't know what's going on."

"That's all right, Matt," she says, resting her head on his shoulder. "I'll never know what's going on. Or if I do, I'll get it all wrong. You can count on me. I promise."

CHAPTER 17

Wednesday mornings are conference sessions. This is Lynn's favorite part of the week. She buys muffins and brings Meg and Holly and Dr. Futterman coffee, and sits in a corner of Dr. Futterman's office, listening to the stories, running out to answer the phone when it rings.

Dr. Futterman's office is filled with pictures of her two children. The kids on a sailboat, the kids on a ferryboat, the kids on the beach, the kids hanging upside down from monkey bars. They are well-documented children.

Meg and Holly flop into the long couch placed under a bookshelf. It feels like a clubhouse under there. Dr. Futterman sits before a stack of files on her desk—the active AP files.

"Carla Fedders," she says, opening the file.

"Breech—thirty-four weeks."

Dr. Futterman raises an eyebrow. "That doesn't look good."

By this time, the baby has usually grown too large to move around and get itself into a vertex position on its own.

"Ellen, how about external version?" Holly broaches tentatively. "Dr. Lehmann at Brownell is really the master now. . . ."

Dr. Futterman taps the side of her cheek with her fingers. "No. Carla Fedders is too—"

"Neurotic," Meg puts in.

"Maybe next year, Holly," Dr. Futterman says kindly, "when more results are in. I don't want to do our first chancy procedure with someone like Carla Fedders."

How could external version, performed with ultrasound, to make sure the placenta isn't dislodged in the process, and performed in a hospital setting, be chancier than the problems of a breech birth?

443

"You've never seen Ellen do a breech," Meg says. "It's inspiring."

"In any case," says Holly, "I've got her lying at an incline. Just in case."

"Call her up and encourage her to do it," Dr. Futterman says. "She's—"

"Impatient," Meg says.

"Busy," Holly says.

CHAPTER 18

Holly is ready to leave the office. "Cheers then," she says, pulling on her old denim jacket.

"Got your beeper?" Meg calls from the file cabinets.

Holly smacks the side of her purse. "Yes, Mom."

"Let me hear it."

"I just changed the batteries yesterday, Mom."

"I want to hear it."

Holly digs into her purse and dislodges her beat-up copy of John Cheever's collected short stories (good for reading during a long labor, with stories short enough to finish in a fifteen-minute break and interesting enough to stand rereading), her makeup kit, and a clean pair of underpants (to reduce the postpartum grunginess factor). She pulls out the beeper, holds it up, and switches it on. Beep-beep-beep-beep.

"Okay," Meg shouts. "Don't stay out too late. Have fun on call."

Have fun on call. When Holly first took the beeper home—or, as she phrased it then, when she *got* to take the beeper home—she had a lot of fun. She'd never admit as much to anyone, not even Matt, but the beeper made her feel . . . grown-up. What could be more upscale? Its aura of importance and power seemed to radiate from her pocketbook. As she walked home, she was always aware of its presence. When a clamor of trucks and cars passed, she imagined she heard it go off, then stop. Opening her bag, she put her ear to the hollow of her purse, listened for the beep-beep-beep, and was disappointed when she heard nothing. Nothing was happening in her pocketbook.

She wasn't planning on doing anything that night but washing "fine washables" and sleeping, but she realized that if she stayed home, the answering service could reach her by telephone and never have to resort to beeping her. She corralled Matt into going to a movie he didn't want to see. "I'd better take an aisle seat," she said, picturing herself squeezing by rows of viewers time after time as she was beeped.

"Aren't we big-time," he said.

She kept her bag on her lap, the flap unzipped so she wouldn't miss a beep, and could barely keep her mind on the movie for wondering if she'd be called away. What would it feel like? If the beeper went off and Holly called the answering service, who told her there was an emergency, would she leave the theater without going back to tell Matt? Was this the start of a lifetime of half-viewed movies?

The beeper didn't beep.

"Looks like you're still here," Matt said when the movie ended.

They went home, and at eleven, she hit the hay. "God, I never knew how good a bed could feel," she thought, stretching her legs out over the clean sheets. "This is the best feeling in the world."

This was exactly when the phone rang, of course, and the precise moment when she learned what it means to be on call.

When you're on call, your time is not your own, even though it has a deceptive similarity to your own time. Being on call is not about catching babies. When Holly first came to the practice and attended two deliveries with Meg, to get a lay of the land and observe the Futterman way of birth, Meg had called her from the hospital. Those calls had awakened and startled Holly, but she hadn't had to think at all. She'd just pulled on her clothes and gone.

Being on call has more to do with screening problems over the phone: a nerve-racking exercise in communication. Holly felt as if she were learning how to do pelvic exams all over again, groping around in the dark, her voice exploring where her eyes and hands couldn't go, and she lacked confidence and felt awkward and fumbling. What if I say the wrong thing? Make the wrong suggestion? She took notes at bedside in a self-styled shorthand that she couldn't interpret in the morning and so had to re-create her conversations from memory—extremely poor risk-management practice—to put them down in proper chart form when she got to the office.

That first night, her only call was a diagnosis of false labor. Although false labor often leads to genuine labor, these were just sporadic Braxton-Hicks, as the uterus flexed its muscle cells in preparation for the real thing.

"How strong are the contractions?"

"Pretty strong."

"How long are they lasting?"

"I'm having one right now."

You don't have to be a master telephone communicator to figure out that if the patient is talking through contractions without much effort, she is either in false labor or early labor, and that in either case, what she ought to do is try to go to sleep.

When Meg first told Holly that she'd be paid three-quarters of her hourly wage for her time on call, Holly was struck by the practice's generosity. To get paid for sleeping, eating dinner, and going to the movies! (On top of which, she'd get paid time-and-a-half for the time spent on hospital duty, including travel time, to and fro.)

But then Holly came to understand that the sleeping, eating, and movie-going you do when on call bears only a surface resemblance to that which you do when you're not on call, and when she realized how being on call alters your entire experience, so that every facet of your life is penetrated by On-Call Consciousness, Holly was no longer overwhelmed by the Futterman largess.

Her sleep is tainted by On-Call Dread. She never quite gives herself up to sleep, a punishing state of affairs since she needs as much sleep as she can get, when she's on call and might be called out in the middle of the night to work through morning, then have to do a full day's work the following day and go on call again the next night. Holly has fewer patients than she did at Howard Street, but she never counted on the energy drain created by the On-Call Life.

Holly and Meg are on call in two-day rotations. Holly is on call Monday and Tuesday, Meg is on call Wednesday and Thursday, and they split Friday, so that whoever pulls weekend call duty has to take Friday night as well, letting the midwife with the free weekend really have a free weekend—completely free of midwifery. A weekend of sleep.

Being on call makes all phone calls suspect. And sometimes Holly finds herself answering the phone just as she's answering it now that she's home and changed into her gym shorts. "Yes?"

It's the service telling her to call Danielle Greenhouse, the triathlete. Holly smiles as she calls. Holly would like to catch Danielle's man-child.

"I'm lying in my bath like a manatee," Danielle says. "Those are those tubs of lard with mustaches that nearsighted sailors used to mistake for mermaids, in case you're interested in getting the picture. I think this is it. I think I got the nesting instinct you were telling me about. I piled up a whole bunch of antique quilts worth thousands of dollars in the corner of the loft and just nested. Now I'm nesting in the tub."

"Danielle, the nesting instinct these days usually takes the form of cleaning up the house, washing clothes, storing up food."

"So, I'm primitive. My nesting instinct is old-fashioned. It comes from the reptilian part of my brain. I make a real nest. The nest just happens to be worth half a million dollars. Hang on. Shit. Here it comes again." Holly hears a splash of water, the sound of something plastic falling to the ground, and water running.

"I'm back," Danielle says. "I go underwater for them."

"Contractions?"

"Yeah."

"Don't hold your breath for too long," Holly tells her. "Don't make bathing into an anaerobic event. Did you lose your mucus plug?"

"Did I lose it? I damn near lost it on one of the antique quilts."

"It's probably happened to those quilts before."

"Damn, that's right. Babies must have been born in those quilts. Maybe that's why I pulled them out. I smelled birth in them quilts. Maybe I have the smell instinct."

Holly tells her to take her temperature, to look out for leaking fluid, and to call her if her water breaks, and says that she will call back in an hour.

Before Holly became a midwife, she'd never been able to nap. Her incapacity was a point of pride, the basis for a modest boast.

But Holly's spiritual growth has included the discovery of the nap's virtues. Naps are the prudent behavior of well-organized professionals. To deprive oneself of the opportunity to sleep is a prodigal waste tantamount to tearing out your wits, tossing them to the wind, and declaring, "I want to be punch-drunk in a few hours. I want to fall down on the job. I am so eager to see my client's labor over and done with that I won't give a damn what happens as long as I can get home to sleep." For Holly, nap-taking has become a responsible act.

Getting under the covers is too much of a commitment. She'll resent having to wake up. So she falls on top of the bedspread, mentally repeats, "relax relax relax relax" to herself, listens to her own breathing, then falls asleep.

CHAPTER 19

"Have you ever worked in a hostile environment before?" Meg asked when Holly had just joined the practice. "Morrison was very hostile. A place where ninety-nine percent of the patients are high-risk. . . ."

"I mean, the nurses."

Holly thought of Sparks. She was hostile, but Crowley and Denise balanced her out. "The nurses resent midwives over at Brownell?" Holly asked.

"They sure do. We're new arrivals."

"You've been here a year."

"A year ain't nothing," Meg said. Apparently this long-term view of institutional change was a feature of pragmatic politicians like Meg and Mrs. Gruener. "It'll take more than a year to get the bugs out."

"How long do you suppose?"

"Try three to four years, minimum."

"Shoot, Meg, can I wait that long?"

"Do you have a choice? There are nurses at Brownell who have been there fifteen, twenty years. Never met a midwife in their life, much less thought about them. They're isolated. Half of them don't know what to make of us, don't know what to do with us. What you got to do is show them the way in a kindly fashion. The other half feel we're nothing but nurses with an attitude. They think we ought to do all our own nursing. At Morrison, did you do all your own nursing?"

"No, that's what nurses are for," Holly said. She had spent half her time at Morrison worrying that she was just a junior obstetrician without any of the power of an OB, and that was how most of the staff viewed her: nobody really saw her as a nurse. She didn't feel like a nurse over there. More like a little sister bullied around by older brothers—she had to be scrappy all the time and stick up for herself.

"You'd think it hadn't occurred to some of these nurses that our clients pay just as big a hospital fee as any other private client on the maternity floor and deserve just as many services. When you need a nurse to do vitals or walk three steps to hand you something, she's not going to be there. Just wait till you have to ask a client's husband to open up an Amnihook package for you. And when you don't want a nurse sticking her nose into everything, that's when she'll appear. These nurses are like the guardian flames of hospital protocol, and when you start stepping off that protocol, they come down like a buzzard on a dead mule. If you happen to leave your client alone for a minute, you'll come back and find her enemaed up to the patootie, catheterized, prepped."

"How about the residents?"

"The residents maintain their cool. We're sort of the geeks in their carnival. An object of amusement and derision—from afar. It's the nurses you got to handle."

"How do you handle them?"

"You ever do any horseback riding, Holly? You know what happens when you don't show the horse who's boss? Well, you got to show them who's boss. You don't win any popularity elections, that's for sure."

Holly figured that maybe Meg had a tough time because she took a kind of superior posture that escalated resentment from low-lying to full-fledged. Maybe this wasn't a professional problem at all, but Meg's personal problem, which she rationalized as being professional so as not to blame herself.

But the more Holly has worked on Five, the more she sees the truth in what Meg had to say. What's frustrating is that Holly appears on Five only sporadically. She never has the day-in, day-out presence that wears down resistance, that gives the sensible nurses a chance to get to know, respect, and like her. Holly gets to prove herself only once or twice a week, and what she succeeds in proving, mostly, is that she thinks she's above the rules because she's a hotsy-totsy midwife.

Holly pushes past the door from the pediatrics ward, heading toward the locker room, when the head nurse, Annie D'Angelis, or Anna Bananas as Meg calls her, blocks Holly's path. Annie can be one hundred seventy pounds of pure hostility, twenty of those pounds nothing but pure hatred of nurse-midwives. The problem, so banal, so tacky, is this: Anna Bananas wants to be queen of the floor. With the advent of midwives at Brownell, she's deprived of that power about three times a week.

"Holly," Annie says in a low, threatening way.

"Annie," Holly says, mimicking her.

"Your patient. Greenhouse-Stolz. Has a hyphenated name."

"Yes, Annie, she does. But not normally. It's just so the hospital doesn't wind up giving the baby her last name."

"You know what I say about the Hyphenated Names. When a Hyphenated Name admits, prepare for a section."

Holly laughs. A certain element of truth here. The Hyphenated Names plan too well, are too prepared, too logical. Sometimes the Hyphenated Names are just plain uptight. But Danielle Greenhouse isn't a true Hyphenated Name.

"Did they bring extra pillows, Holly?" Annie asks suspiciously.

"I don't know."

"Are they bringing a videotape getup?"

"No, Annie."

"Are they bringing a tape cassette with the sounds of the ocean?" Annie asks, apparently in reference to another telltale clue that spells trouble.

"I don't know, Annie."

"Well, let's hope not." Stepping to the side as brusquely as a prison matron, she says, "Okay, you can go now."

Danielle Greenhouse's husband, Paul Stolz, walks down the hall carrying a big cardboard box. "Excuse me, sir," Annie says, moving toward him like a defensive tackle. "What's in the box?"

"A time bomb. I'm going to blow up the hospital." Paul smiles, but Annie doesn't smile back. "I guess this isn't a joking matter, as they say at the airport. It's just a fan."

Suspicious, Annie lifts the flaps on the box and peers inside. It's a fan. "All right," she says reluctantly, and waves Paul on.

Turning to the head nurse, Holly says, "Really, Annie, is that necessary?"

"I have to know what's going on on my floor," Annie says, marching to her office to oversee the goings-on.

Danielle is blowing out. Strong exhalations. Psyching herself. "Stamina." Blow. Inhale. "Energy." Blow. Inhale. "Stamina." Blow. Inhale. "Energy." When she sees Holly come in, she says, "So, tell me, is labor harder than the marathon?"

"Probably. Can be."

"Is it harder than a triathlon?"

"How long a triathlon?"

"The Iron Man triathlon in Hawaii."

"No," Holly says with confidence. That's ten miles of swimming, one hundred twenty-five miles of bicycle riding, and then a marathon. "It's probably not harder than the Iron Man triathlon in Hawaii."

Two hours later, Holly is about to reevaluate her triathlon assessment. Danielle is pacing up and down the room, her labor moving slowly. "Christ, I can bench-press one hundred fifty pounds and look at me." She sits on the edge of the bed. "I'm all done in by labor. Girl's stuff."

She's wearing a nightshirt that says on the front, in small letters, LIFE IS SHORT, and on the back, with stretched-out letters, ART IS LONG. Holly tells her clients to bring a nightgown that they don't mind never seeing again. "It can get pretty gross," is all she has to say. People seem to get the point. The more frugal clients bring their old things, but other women see the loss of their nightgown to the onslaught of what-is-internal-becomes-external as part of the price of intrapartum care.

"As your trainer would say," Paul says, smiling, "'Don't be such a *girl.*'"

"Fuck that," Danielle says. "I am a girl. I'm a girl."

"Danielle, I know you think this is wrong for me to say," Holly says hesitantly, "but sometimes a little Demerol takes the edge off. If later..."

"Holly, I've run a marathon. I'm a triathlete." Danielle beats her breast, signifying her profound confidence in her own body—which Holly is scared might get her into trouble. Athletes train their bodies to do what they want them to do, using them like instruments. But during labor, the body calls its own shots and plays its own tunes. Danielle eases back on the bed. "You're looking at a girl who can deal with a little edge." She falls back. "Ooofff!"

"You're in the home stretch, Danielle," Holly says. "You're really into hard labor now."

Danielle looks up with tired eyes at Paul and says, "I sentence you to twenty years of hard labor for this. You men have got to feel this. I don't want a kid. I changed my mind. I want to go home."

"Stamina. Endurance," Paul says. "Discipline."

"Where are my drugs?"

"Try to hold out a little longer, Danielle," Holly says. It's too late now for Demerol.

"Just kidding," Danielle says. "I wanted to hear how you try to talk people out of it. You do a lousy job. What would you do if I screamed?"

"I'd smack you in the mouth," Holly says.

"Let's walk."

Danielle drapes her arms around Paul's and Holly's shoulders. Danielle and Paul have both read Michael Odent, who is to the eighties what Leboyer was to the seventies. Odent methodology wears out midwives, as it advocates labor and delivery from a squatting position. Holly thinks nostalgically of the birthing bar displayed at Convention. If she'd known she'd be here now with one hundred forty-five pounds pulling down her shoulders, she'd have bought one with her own money.

Danielle's legs buckle beneath her. "I want you to carry me like I'm the queen of Sheba."

"Forget it, get back on the bed," says Paul.

Danielle looks down at her T-shirt and then walks around the room chanting, "Labor is short. Kids are long. Labor is short. Kids are long. Labor is short. Kids are long...."

"You're so verbal," Paul says. "Why did you go into the art business when all you do is talk?"

"So I can talk down to artists," says Danielle, leaning against the wall.

CHAPTER 20

Danielle has been in labor ten hours, and she is only at nine centimeters. It's a slow crawl to ten centimeters.

"Danielle, I know you objected before to an enema, but I think we might as well give it a shot now. What do you say?"

"Anything. Anything. When I told you I didn't want an enema, I'd never been in labor before. I don't care what you do now."

Paul leaves the room during the enema. ("That's too much," he says.) Holly uses a Fleet enema—warm, soapy water. "Okay, kid, hit the toilet." Holly helps her up, supports her on her arm as she shuffles across the floor, and watches as she lands on the toilet all right, then turns away to give her some privacy.

From the bathroom, Danielle calls, "Holly, am I the funniest patient you ever had?"

"Without question."

"Can I stop being funny now?"

"Even if you don't make another joke, you'll still be the funniest patient I ever had."

"I want to stay in here for a while." Her voice sounds muffled because she has bent her head and is speaking directly into her lap. "Holly. I'm going to throw up. I can't stand up. God can take me now, but I hope he waits until I'm off the toilet. I don't want to die on a toilet."

"Oh, I want to push. I like this part. It's a fucking bitch."

Danielle has been waiting to push. Here she feels free. She can actively apply her strength, instead of having to make jokes as labor sweeps over her. Knees flexed, hands gripping her thighs, putting her back into it, she applies her weight-lifter's knowledge to the effort.

"Grunt it out," Holly says. "Grunt it out. Short, hard pushes. Go with the contractions."

With each contraction, the baby's head applies pressure to the pelvic floor, which induces the urge to push. By sitting up, Danielle has increased that pressure as well as helped the baby stay a straight, narrow course.

Between contractions, Danielle breathes deep. "Fuckin'-ay."

"No big weight-lifter's exhalations now," Holly tells her. "Short little grunts—little expirations. Uh. Uh. Uh."

Danielle has been exhaling in a sweeping *huh*.

Except for pushing, weight lifting hasn't done Danielle's labor a whole lot of good. It's Holly's personal belief that the worst candidates for labor are those in the best shape and the worst shape. Triathletes and dancers, smokers and couch potatoes, beware. For one thing, Holly thinks there's something about constant exercise that reduces levels of relaxin. This is strictly personal conjecture, for which she has no proof except clinical observation. Not much is known about relaxin, the hormone that softens the cervix, but women with high estrogen levels seem to have more of it. If exercise reduces levels of estrogen... well, it's a wild suspicion, borne out only by the fact that athletic women seem to take longer to efface and dilate. What's worse is, the more athletic they are, the better they think they'll be able to handle labor, and they are shocked that they are, like other women, just women.

Danielle has strong abdominal muscles capable of increasing the force of the uterine contractions by contracting themselves, on top of the uterus. But this additional power is met by another facet of her muscularity—the internal muscle mass is so well built up that the birth canal is more resistant to stretching out with the descent of the baby. Toward the end of term, a woman starts to sway and waddle as hormones relax the ligaments that hold together the parts of her pelvis, in anticipation of being stretched out, and the pelvis may expand by a few centimeters. Holly tries to remember if Danielle swayed less than other women at term. It seems that her ligaments are as strong as steel cable. They just don't give.

Weight lifting has also thickened Danielle's pelvic floor. This will be great in her recuperation postpartum and in supporting her pelvic organs in the long-term future. But it's lousy right now, as the baby's head pushes against the perineum to thin it out—that's how the mechanism of delivery is supposed to operate. But if an average woman's perineum is like a length of fabric, Danielle's is like a strip of leather. The fabric will give faster, stretch out more easily, than the leather. Holly will probably have to cut an episiotomy.

"Talk to me, guys," Danielle says, her eyes shut after a contraction. "Let's hear some chatter out there."

That's what Holly's uncle used to say when he played softball with Holly and her brothers out on the lawn. "Let's hear a little chatter out there." And they'd all start smacking their fists into their baseball mitts and chattering. "Come on, baby boy." "All right, easy catch." "Make the easy look hard, and the hard impossible."

"Don't be a girl, Danielle," Paul says. "Put up or shut up."

"Fuck off," Danielle says, taking a deep breath, going into the equivalent of a one-hundred-fifty-pound bench-press.

"No pain, no gain."

And Danielle grunts, her thick perineum bulging.

"Labor is short, the kid is long," Paul says.

"Let the man-child out," Holly says.

"Huh-huh-huh."

"Use it or lose it," Paul says directly into her ear.

"Fuck off," Danielle says, sweat dripping over her forehead into her eyes, her hair stiff with old sweat. "Get this off me." Paul pulls off the T-shirt, which is damp to the touch.

"All right, it's skins against the shirts," Paul says. "Get out here and do it, you wimp. You sissy."

"Damn you."

And that's how the baby gets born. Just like in the gym. But this time Paul is coxswain, hurling abuse, as Danielle is rowing home alone, in the Iron Man triathlon.

CHAPTER 21

"Personally, I think it's disgusting that they don't mask for delivery. It's not sterile technique."

Which is what Holly overhears when she scoots to the nurse's station for a birth certificate and to log in the delivery. Hyphenated Man-Child Greenhouse-Stolz. Annie D'Angelis is holding forth to a young nurse, who nods attentively. "Sssh," the young nurse says, gesturing with her head toward Holly, whose ears burn.

"I don't care if she does hear me," Annie says loudly. "I'm entitled to my opinion."

Back off, Treadwell. Get your papers and leave.

There is going to have to be some sort of peace talks, a reiteration of policy. According to both Meg and Dr. Futterman, the one protocol requirement that their practice is obliged to fulfill is a twenty-minute external monitor strip at admission. If the strip shows heartsounds within normal limits, the practice is free to manage labor and delivery according to its own protocols.

Holly finds a birth certificate and is ready to leave as Annie says, "They let the husbands deliver the babies. *Without gloves.*"

Holly sighs loudly, stands up from where she was crouching by the desk, and faces the wall. *Clam up, Treadwell.* "I can't," she tells herself. *Do it. Hold your tongue. Rise above it.* "No, I can't," she tells herself. But maybe she can. . . .

"They're setting OB back by a century," Annie says loudly.

"And a good thing, too," Holly says just as loudly, facing the wall. *Ignorant, uneducated fisthead!*

"What's that?" Annie says too quickly, spinning around, revealing herself as someone spoiling for a fight, someone who has set the bait and has been waiting for Holly to pick it up between her teeth, as Holly just did.

Holly turns around and says with a smile, "Baby boy, ten pounds, hyphenated name, all's well." She waves the birth certificate and smiles. "That's what I said. Greenhouse-Stolz. The kid is hyphenated."

CHAPTER 22

Christina doesn't look well. Her skin is mottled and haggard—the mask-of-pregnancy pigmentation reaction having swept it—and without makeup, her small features look plain, pained, pinched, like smoke is perpetually flying in her eyes. She's in white overalls, and her short, sculpted haircut is in bad need of a trim. This is the time in pregnancy when women often start looking bad, because they don't sleep well and haven't hit the hormonal high of at-term that makes so many of them start to glow. Mainly, it's not that Christina looks pregnant. It's that she looks unhappy.

Christina is eight months pregnant, and Roger is gone.

"He'd always had affairs," she tells Holly, hiding out behind her bangs. "But it was as if he wanted me to find out this time. His girlfriends would call up at the house and wouldn't even hang up when I answered. Why would he want to do that to me?"

Holly doesn't know. She can understand, without condoning it, why a man might get turned off sexually when his wife becomes pregnant. But Roger seemed less confused and anxious than simply cruel. Holly runs through a humanitarian exercise anyway, dutifully trying to discover his psychological motive, his emotional excuse. Like he's terrified of the commitment of fatherhood, testing her love. Flattering reasons for why a man is cruel to a woman. But most likely Roger is "wicked," as Holly's grandmother would say, and his behavior is inexcusable. The man's a cad, a jerk, an asshole. Holly is pretty sure that Christina is better off without him.

"I don't know, Christina, I just don't know," Holly says, then digs into a pitch for Christina to get some kind of counseling. Refer out. Holly hands Christina the name and number of a Brooklyn Heights psychologist. "Think about it. Really think about it." Christina nods dully. "You haven't been sleeping well," Holly says, abandoning the open-ended line of inquiry she's supposed to take.

"I've been sleeping too much. I think I'm getting narcolepsy."

"That can be a response to stress."

"I realize that," Christina says, pushing her bangs back. "But I don't care anymore about me. I just care about my baby. I don't think it's good for the baby to be under that kind of strain."

It's a hopeful lie. I don't care, I don't care, I don't care. . . .

Humiliation and despair create a lousy maternal environment for the fetus to grow in. The strain of living with Roger would be intolerable. It must have been like life during wartime; women in war-torn countries, or countries under siege or threat of siege—Israel and Northern Ireland, for example—have higher rates of certain birth defects. Stress alters the body's chemistry and the rate at which certain hormones are produced, interacting with unknown genetic predispositions and environmental factors to create damage in a way impossible to follow. Stress is one of the reasons poor women are at risk during pregnancy. Poverty, and its living conditions, are stress. A caddish husband is stress. Living alone when eight months pregnant is stress.

"I'm glad I told him to get out," Christina says, miserable.

"That must have been a rough decision."

Christina looks mean, as mean as Roger ever did. She flicks back her hair. "No," she says hollowly.

CHAPTER 23

"Brava, Carla," says Holly. She looks down at Carla's Renaissance face—her arching high eyebrows; her sharp, intelligent, shrewd eyes; her Italian nose that curves slightly downward. She hadn't believed that Carla would really take the time to get her breech baby turned around.

"I could feel him moving," Carla says. "I ordered him to. You thought I wouldn't do it, isn't that so?"

"You can sit up now," Holly says. "I'm not going to do an exam this late in the game, because an exam might bring on premature rupture of the membranes."

"In that case, examine me, by all means."

Holly waves a fist at Carla.

"Well, at least tell me some tricks so that labor won't take too long. Dish it, Holly." Carla sits up and pulls her dress down.

"Carla, labor is labor-intensive business. Any efforts to speed it up, other than walking around and squatting, usually result in decreased quality levels. Decreased profitability." Holly fumbles around for business language, adjusting to what she thinks is Carla's sensibility. "It's like all the other great crafts—knitting, cabinet-making. When they're mechanized, quality plunges."

Glancing impatiently at the door, Carla says, "Don't be ridiculous. I'm not asking for mechanization. I'm asking for tricks of the trade."

"When you start going into labor, try to get some sleep. And if you can't sleep, start moving around. Keep gravity on your side."

Carla looks appalled. "That's the best you can do?"

She pulls a Filofax, the one-hundred-fifty-dollar book/organizer that about half of Holly's clients seem to use, from her briefcase and flips open to a page marked by a card. "Look here. This is my due date. The day before I have to make a presentation in Washington. It's a fifty-million-dollar account, and they don't give you two chances. You make it or you lose it. Three days after, I have another meeting down in Washington, with the World Bank. I need to do both things. I need a short, uneventful labor and delivery on those three days."

"Maybe you should give birth in Washington," Holly suggests.

Carla yanks up her pocketbook impatiently.

"Carla, my dear, you're one of the best brains in the entire country. Why then do I have to explain to you what I used to explain to the illiterate fifteen-year-olds over at Howard Street? Due dates are approximate things. Labor can take place two weeks before or two weeks after. The odds that you'll actually deliver on your due date are very slim. Only twenty-five percent of women deliver in even the week of their due date."

Carla shuts her Filofax. "My labor is going to be on time. What about inductions?"

"Oh, Carla, please. You know this is the wrong practice to ask about inductions. For one thing, elective inductions for the convenience of the patient or the doctor have been illegal in this country for two decades. An induction is much more painful than ordinary labor, longer, more traumatic for your baby, and more likely to fail and result in a section. Is that what you want?"

"I read in the newspaper that eighty percent of Brazilian women have elective cesareans."

"Good," Holly says. "Move to Brazil."

"You could stretch out my cervix. A friend's doctor did that for her, when he was about to go on vacation."

"Good, go to that doctor then."

"Your integrity is really excessive," Carla says, pulling on her black silk jacket. "At least tell me what I can do so that I won't have the baby before the due date then."

"Carla, you're being silly."

"Fine. I'll be silly. What can I do?"

"Don't have sex. Don't have orgasm."

"That's easy enough," Carla says, smoothing back her hair. "Inflicting myself on Tom at this point would be akin to a war crime. I'm an atrocity. What else can I do?"

"Nothing else." Put yourself in a frightening situation, Holly might have said. Fill your soul with fear to keep that cervix clamped shut.

"You're not telling me everything."

Visualize the cervix shutting, locking the baby in, visualize a brick wall across the cervix How evil this would be, Holly thinks, to sow negative mental suggestions.

"I'm telling you to protect your investment by willing it to leave," Holly says. "Roll over your investment at term."

If other women wait for Holly to give them permission to leave, Carla always hears the wind-down small talk of an appointment that has come to its end before it actually happens. Opening the door to the examining room with a bored expression, she says, "Holly, stop with the business metaphors. It's bad enough to treat the body as a glorious machine. Let's not treat it like an antiquated cottage industry."

"Gosh, you're tough, Carla," Holly says, slightly wounded, having thought she was so clever to hit on the business lingo approach.

"I'm sure it'll work well for somebody else," Carla says diplomatically, and in her streamlined pregnancy, she races off.

Meg is at the kitchen sink in the office, drinking a glass of water. Holly steams in. "I don't understand that woman," she says, scooting up onto the kitchen counter. "Carla, the demon banker of Wall Street. Why did she come to this practice at all? She might have found a doctor to do an elective section for her. She could have timed it out, had an epidural, studied her graphs and papers on the operating table, been on the phone to Europe in post-op."

"She's scared," Meg says, shrugging. "Aren't all addicts? Workaholics? Whatever? She's a woman living in fear."

"What does she have to be scared about?"

"Who knows? A woman as shut off from her feelings as she seems to be is usually scared of something. Maybe of herself."

"She's just ambitious," Holly says without conviction.

"Maybe it sounds unfeminist of me, but women as driven and ambitious as she is are running scared from something."

"How do you help someone that scared?" Holly asks. She stares out at the courtyard. The leaves are off the trees now, and the garden furniture has been brought inside. Rusting grills and boxes covered in plastic are all that remain out there. It's a cold, sad, abandoned place, and Holly feels the rush of melancholy she gets only in autumn, the sense that the whole world is lonely and scared. "Especially someone scared in that inaccessible way," she says.

"Women like Carla aren't as easy to help as a person like Fran, who gets scared in an obvious, babyish way," Meg says. "You can't really help Carla, because she isn't going to let you. Your role is to give good health care with the baby in mind. Think of the baby—Carla will take care of herself. Maybe she knows that. Maybe she's scared that if she went to a doctor who let her get the things she wants—an elective induction or section—she'd wind up hurting the baby. Maybe she chose this practice so that she'd find people who'd take care of the baby and stop her from doing the things she wants to do."

"People are strange," Holly says, scooting off the counter.

"People are interesting," Meg corrects her. "Life is strange."

"People are strange," Holly says again.

CHAPTER 24

The Seidners have decided to favor the practice with their patronage. Having just marked down the date of Mrs. Seidner's first AP visit, Lynn looks up at Holly. "In a word, *cherie*," she says, "Seidner."

"Why oh why oh why oh don't they go somewhere else?" Holly jumps up and down in front of Lynn's desk, stomping like a spoiled child, except that she'd never have gotten away with this kind of behavior when she was seven years old. She'd started out jumping up and down as a joke, but now she can't stop. She's into it. She's jumping and stomping like she's in the throes of a religious inspiration.

"It's so reassuring to see midwives responding to adversity with reservoirs of grace, compassion, and calm," Meg says from the doorway that leads to the examining rooms.

"Oh," Holly says, turning to Meg. "I'm busted."

She takes a deep breath, which she could use, and turns to look out the window and erase the last minute of her life and everyone else's from her brain. The yard is filled with ailanthus trees, the city trees that start out as weeds, planting themselves in sidewalk cracks and among the roots of other, more established trees, and then, against the odds, grow into recognizable trees themselves. Ailanthus trees are into mass production. They can't be stopped. In New York, you search out nature to soothe the nerves and find ailanthus trees.

"What's your problem, Holly?" Meg asks from the doorway. "Unless that's an unfair incursion into your hysteria."

"The Seidners. The two lawyers I told you about They've decided to have their baby here, with us. Of all the obstetricians and midwives in all of New York, they decide to come to us."

"Holly, sometimes I don't understand why you wanted to go into private practice. Didn't you have undesirable patients at Morrison?"

"Sure, but they had to go to Morrison. They had no other place to go. These people have so many choices. It's a personal attack that they choose to come to us." Holly turns to face Meg. "Does my attitude need some adjusting?"

Meg shrugs, meaning yes.

Holly follows her down the hall, locked into a staccato-style rant. "Maybe Ellen should up our policy coverage. I mean, the Seidners are both lawyers. They're looking for a premium birth. For premium births, you have to pay a premium." Holly gulps down a breath of air. "They're looking for Mr. Goodbaby. Forget good baby. Try perfection. Try convincing people that nature isn't perfect, especially when they've never had any real contact with nature. They think everything is solvable. You don't hear people say what my grandmother used to say anymore. 'It's God's way.' You don't hear people say that much in New York City."

"No, you don't." Meg looks at her strangely. "Do you want a glass of water?"

Holly stops. She comes to her senses. She realizes she's been on a rampage.

"I think I'm getting a grip now," she says, blinking her eyes.

"Yes, Holly, try to get a grip."

Holly slumps into the chair by Meg's desk, her adrenaline roused. She is ready to go a full twelve rounds. But she lacks an opponent. Where is a callous resident, tangled bureaucracy, or ludicrous protocol when she needs it? She has to shadowbox the adrenaline away, joust with an invisible opponent. Her enemy is an abstraction: the prospect of a malpractice suit brought against her and the practice by Two Lawyers. Before the Seidners walked in to Holly's life, a lawsuit never seemed quite so threatening before, never so possible. It's as though she's heard talk of an imminent war for years and has finally seen tanks amassing at the border. She just wants to pack up her belongings and take off in the opposite direction.

"I guess private practice has its peculiar stresses," Holly says glumly, looking into her lap. She plucks at her corduroy skirt. "I guess I didn't completely anticipate them before. I guess I got sort of out-of-hand out there."

"That's all right," Meg says, still studying Holly. "But when you decide to rant and rave the next time, it's a good idea to do it in a room with a closed door."

"Right."

Holly straightens up and looks stern to show she's in command of herself again. The last thing she needs is for Meg to question her ability to stay cool in a crisis, since Meg has never seen her at work in a crisis and has no hard evidence that Holly won't flip her lid or become... unglued. For all Meg knows, Holly might fly off and shatter into a hundred pieces when the going gets rough. This makes Holly pretty miserable. She's never flaked out in public before, at least, not without having proved herself first. Holly says nothing now, because any fervent apology will just reinforce the memory of the transitory hysteria that struck Holly for a few minutes before passing on, like a tropical storm.

"I'd better get back to work then," Holly says, hopping out of her seat and smoothing down her skirt. A lesson from her mother: looking pulled together helps people think you *are* together. And when embarrassed, leave.

Back in her office, Holly finds an old cigarette in her desk and lights it up. She's never smoked in here before. She certainly has never smoked and lain down on the examining table either, which is what she does now. She swings off the table, ripping the paper beneath her, and pulls her aerobics shoes from the bottom drawer of her desk.

Baby-catching shoes. Designed for lateral movement, sashays across the gym floor, and high can-can kicks. They are, in short, ideal for maternity ward work.

They were her going-away present from her friends at Morrison— Denise, mainly—and had been wrapped with a note that said, "Now you can deep-six the clogs!" Whatever luck her Dr. Scholl's had brought her wasn't transferable out of Morrison. In the future, Holly would have to make a new kind of luck.

She couldn't bring herself to pitch the old Dr. Scholl's. That would have been too much of a slap in the face of the fates, like she was telling the most powerful amulet of her life, "I've used you all I can, and now I'm getting rid of you." She slipped the sandals on top of an out-of-the-way locker, so they could radiate a dim kind of luck onto the floor without her.

Looking at the shoes makes Holly homesick. This is disturbing, not because she's afraid she made the wrong decision in moving to the Futterman practice, but because she's worried that maybe she's a perennial malcontent, someone who is never satisfied, who always needs something more and never knows what it is she needs.

She likes it here. Who wouldn't? With Meg and Lynn and Dr. Futterman and the nubbly beige couch ("Real linen!"), the advertising execs and magazine editors, patients she can speak to in college-level English, who invariably understand her. As Holly's mother puts it, "They're your social equals, dear." Holly has yet to see a nasty case of condylomata warts, and she can practice midwifery according to her own lights.

But something is missing. She has less effect here. There are no skin-popping teenagers to rescue from junkie hell, no small-for-gestational-age fetuses to plump up. Everything that makes the practice good is what makes the practice...lacking. The patients Holly sees here could get good care somewhere else, and Holly feels superfluous. As a possible defendant in a future negligence suit, Holly feels more at risk than they are.

But is it the needy patients she misses? Yes. But that's not quite what bothers her either.

Turning her aerobics shoes over in her hand, Holly reaches a frightening conclusion. What she misses most about Morrison and Howard Street— even more than the young girls who need her, or fooling around with Denise, Crowley, and Levy, or being subjected to Mrs. Gruener's pointed guidance—is the wicked, abusive presence of Morrison itself.

The crises Holly tried to finesse on Seven-B had as much to do with protecting her patients from the abuses of the maternity ward protocol as they did with intervening in high-risk situations. Without those abuses to counter, Holly's importance, her sense of virtue, has shrunk. It's hard to be a good person among other good people. It's hard to be good when goodness is expected. Holly has lost her superiority and self-righteousness by coming here. The only thing she has to fight against, besides her own impatience, is the pushy yet ultimately manageable head nurse over at Brownell.

What is it she misses? Her ability to do good, in the sense of helping women in need? Or the fight that wore her down and burned her out? Can it be she misses battle fatigue?

It's time for her next patient. She drops the aerobics shoes into the drawer and slams it shut.

She'll have to find some other fight, if only to survive.

CHAPTER 25

Danielle Greenhouse has many fans, fans with access to extravagant florists. Her room on the postpartum wing of the fourth floor bursts with huge arrangements of flowers that seem to be alive, more alive than the baby in the cradle by Danielle's bed, and telegrams and cards are mounded on the night table, next to the postpartum instructions on the care of episiotomy stitches. It's a happy room. The view of New York Harbor, the flowers, the telegrams, the Greenhouse-Stolzes themselves, particularly the man-child Greenhouse-Stolz.

"Holly, knock some sense into this boy," Danielle Greenhouse says, pointing at her husband, Paul. Danielle is out of bed, in a long T-shirt that reaches her knees and shows a neon pink baby, with a caption in block letters that says JUST CRAWLED OUT OF THE BUSH. The Man-Child is, as babies at this age usually are, asleep. Paul leans against the wall and watches as Danielle touches her toes gingerly, exploratory movements that Danielle uses to test out the extent of damage childbirth has wreaked on her triathlete's physique.

"I hardly think I could succeed where you failed, Danielle," says Holly.

"Talk to him about circumcision."

"Ah." Holly leans over the man-child's cradle. "Just what is the name of this baby?"

"We're debating," says Danielle. "It depends on whether his last name is Greenhouse-Stolz or just plain Stolz."

"For the record, so I'm not accused of sexism," says Paul, "I like Greenhouse-Stolz."

"I like Stolz, for the record," Danielle says.

"We thought we'd call him Holly," says Paul.

"But we decided against it."

"Maybe Treadwell," Paul suggests.

"I like that," Danielle says, musing. "Treadwell Greenhouse-Stolz." She hobbles with her legs wide apart and eases herself down on the bed. "Treadwell, explain to Paul Stolz why Man-Child shouldn't be circumcised."

"It depends on if Paul wants to talk about it or not. Do you?"

"I'd better say yes."

"I'm biased against circumcision," Holly says, sitting down on Danielle's bed, looking up at the lanky man with the flattop hair.

"I want my son to have the same dick I have," Paul says. "That's the whole argument. I don't want him fighting his way through every locker room in the country."

"We'll send him to school in Europe," Danielle says. "As soon as he's old enough to start flashing it, we'll pack him off to France."

"I don't even know how to keep a foreskin clean," Paul says to Holly.

"I can show you, and give you the booklet that explains."

"Besides, the kid is Jewish!" Paul goes on. "He has to be circumcised."

"Paul, I'm Jewish," Danielle says. "You're not. Circumcision isn't part of your religion. It's part of mine. And I don't want it."

Paul leans his forehead against the window and lines up perfectly with the Statue of Liberty. "Go ahead, Holly. Tell me why we shouldn't circumcise the kid."

"I'll try to restrain my biases," she says.

She explains that circumcision first became popular in this country in the late 1800s, when it was purported to prevent masturbation later on. It never became popular in Europe.

"Surgery for prudes, Paul," Danielle puts in.

"Save it, Danielle," he says.

When birth moved into the hospital, circumcision became standard procedure, presented as modern and hygienic. Once one generation was circumcised, the next had to be as well, so that boys would look like their fathers. By the middle of the twentieth century, most people believed circumcision, like eyedrops or PKU tests, was required by law—a belief Holly encounters still, all the time. Medical theories favoring routine circumcision—that men with uncircumcised penises increase the chance of their wives' developing cervical cancer, that they're more susceptible to penile cancer and venereal disease—have all been debunked. The remaining objection to the abolition of routine circumcision is a cultural and aesthetic one. The aesthetic standard has shifted so that circumcised men view an uncircumcised penis as relatively loathsome—mainly, Holly thinks, because they have little idea how to care for an uncircumcised penis and imagine it to be more disgusting than it actually is.

"Circumcision is basically cosmetic surgery," Holly says. "It alters the shape of a bodily part to conform to cultural standards. In 1975, the American Association of Pediatricians said there was no medical indication for routine circumcision. And circumcision isn't painless or without risk, so there are contraindications for it. But the cultural reasons for wanting a son to be circumcised are legitimate, and you're in good company if you decide to go ahead with it."

Paul looks at Danielle. "Holly talks about penises very well for a girl."

Danielle nods. "Holly is definitely great."

"But I don't know," Paul says, hands in his pockets.

"Paul, if you ever wondered why American men are so much more fucked-up than European men, here's your chance to redeem yourself," Danielle says.

"I don't think American men are so fucked-up," says Paul.

"I don't either," Holly says. "Not really." Well, possibly, she thinks.

"Thank God we agree," Paul says, turning to her. "I feel like I died and went to a hell full of feminists."

"There are worse hells," Holly says.

"Maybe," he accedes.

CHAPTER 26

Holly is heated up. Her neurons are going crazy, and her brain is on fire. "My skull cannot contain my thoughts," she tells herself as she charges up the stoop into the office.

She considers that Brooklyn Heights does not appreciate an adrenaline high and stops for a moment on the landing at the top of the stoop. Taking a deep breath, she believes she is now calm and bursts into the office. She walks quickly by Lynn's desk and, as she does so, unknowingly brushes paper clips out of Lynn's paper clip tray with the raccoon coat she bought a week before at a thrift shop.

"Say good morning like a decent person!" Lynn shouts from the floor, where she is picking up paper clips.

"Good morning like a decent person!"

For a few months, Holly has eaten breakfast at a coffee shop that's halfway between her apartment and the office. After living with Matt for almost half a year, she'd come to the unhappy conclusion that she doesn't like to talk in the morning. "I'm very thin-skinned in the morning," she explained. "I need time for my skin to thicken."

"Is that an unattractive process?" Matt had asked.

"I believe it is."

"You'd better eat out," he said. "Here's two dollars. It's probably worth every dime."

Eating out was a good move, but she committed a gross error in judgment to think that a thin-skinned person like herself should start her morning by reading the letters section of the newspaper—the literary contributions of those even more thin-skinned and touchy than she is. Holly rarely has any kind of grip on the issues that stir these thin-skinned writers to heights and depths of epistolary skill, so she can usually sit

470

back and watch the intellectual scuffle with the amused distance of a thin-skinned but untouched observer.

Her mistake was to think that the issues would always fail to touch her. Until this morning, that was the case. But today, a letter jumped up and bit her on the nose, before she was at all thickened, when she was still so thin-skinned as to be almost flayed by what she read.

The headline read, A DEATH OF THE FAMILY.

The letter's author was from an outfit that sounded suspiciously like a think tank. "Bernard D. Collins, Director, The Richards Institute." He is the head of either a think tank or a reform school.

"You should be hauled off and shot, Bernard D. Collins," Holly said aloud at the luncheonette counter.

"Delivering babies getting you down?" the waitress said.

"Delivering babies doesn't get me down. Babies aren't idiots with opinions. They're idiots without opinions."

"You're cranky," the waitress said and went away.

What Bernard D. Collins said made sense, in a way. His letter deplored a welfare system that discouraged the formation of families by making it financially advantageous for young pregnant women not to marry.

"The single-parent family, which is endemic in many of our inner-city neighborhoods"—a code way of talking about black people, Holly thinks, without taking responsibility for pinpointing any racial group—"destines its members to that most vicious of traps: welfare dependency. A structure that lacks stability, the single-parent family is deprived of the financial relief afforded by the presence of another wage-earner in the family."

As far as Holly is concerned, the resolution to this whole problem is to intervene before the single women have babies, to make a dent in the high fertility rate of black teenagers. Because once these girls are mothers, it makes no sense to pack them off with husbands. Two sixteen-year-olds married! Disaster!

Holly threw down a dollar for her coffee and marched out onto Atlantic Avenue in her raccoon coat, which, as it turned out, is ideal for thinking. Like a snail shell, it's a portable home, a private place to live in in public.

Holly is going to tell Mr. Bernard D. Collins *off*.

"Holly, do you think you could bestir yourself to see a patient now?" Meg asks, popping her head past Holly's door.

Teen marriage means more child abuse, more wife-beating, more isolation, more despair, a divorce rate of eighty-five percent. "The case for teenaged mothers staying at home," Holly scratches out on the back of a prescription pad. "Their families take care of the kids while they stay in school or enter job-training programs. The families offer some (albeit limited) guidance when the young mothers need it the most."

Holly glances up, in a fog of indignation, and makes out Meg's inquiring, disapproving face. "Say what?"

"Fran Cutler is here and ready to be seen."

"Meg, am I hotheaded?" Holly asks. She knows she's thin-skinned.

"Of course you are."

"If I write to the newspaper and explain that pregnant adolescents shouldn't marry, would the world think I was crazy?"

Meg considers this. "Having teen mothers stay home isn't a solution. It's a stalemate. If you write to a newspaper, you have to propose an alternative. It's nihilistic just to negate someone else's theory."

Holly bites down on her pen. A stalemate. Nothing moves. Nobody loses. Nihilism. Things torn down. Nothing built.

Holly's adrenaline takes off without her, leaving her earthbound, heavy, feet of clay. Holly is surprised: Meg is completely right.

Meg says kindly, "Look, youngster, your patient is waiting. As an expert in pragmatic activism, I advise you to see your patient and then change the world."

"I'll see my patient," Holly says dutifully.

"Then write your letter," Meg orders.

CHAPTER 27

D r. Futterman isn't the progressive OB Holly had hoped she'd be. Fran Cutler is now at forty-one and a half weeks, and Dr. Futterman has scheduled her for automatic induction at forty-two weeks. Holly doesn't want Fran Pitted out, induced labors being rough on the mother, even rougher on the baby, who might, being post-dates, be at risk already, and they have five times the section rate, three times the forceps rate of spontaneous labor. And Fran's cervix isn't ripe enough, soft or effaced enough, to promise a fruitful induction. A routine induction is something worth fighting against.

Holly isn't used to fighting with Dr. Futterman. When Holly fought the powers-that-be at Morrison, she felt she was fighting an unjust system, rather than an unjust person. Dr. Futterman is the system here, and the arguments are trickier, more personal, and don't have the bantering give-and-take that Holly almost enjoyed at Morrison. And Holly doesn't know quite how far she can go, fighting with her boss.

She already lost the fight to replace the oxytocin challenge test (OCT) with a nipple stimulation stress test (NSST). The OCT uses Pit to induce contractions for a short time while the fetal heart rate is monitored to test the baby's responses. The NSST works exactly the same way, but the oxytocin is produced naturally by nipple stimulation, as Else produced it on the Mennonite farm, while carrying less risk of hyperstimulation (which would stress the baby out) and using no IV. Even if the NSST failed to induce contractions, an OCT could still have been administered and nothing lost by trial.

Holly can only figure that Dr. Futterman resisted something as benignly innovative as the NSST because of a medicalized mentality, and she has begun to feel about doctors the way some women she knows feel about men: "They're all rats, down deep." Holly doesn't know much about the ratishness of men, but as for doctors . . .

Now Dr. Futterman and Holly are arguing the merits of a biophysical profile—an ultrasound exam of the fetus and placenta. Holly doesn't see much point if Fran is definitely going to be induced. A biophysical profile should be the means of discovering whether or not an induction is necessary at all. But if Holly opposes the profile, she'll have no evidence to present to Dr. Futterman as an argument against induction, while if she speaks in favor of it, she'll only fuel the notion that all post-dates pregnancy is pathological.

"I just read that third-trimester bleeders are inclined to be post-dates," says Meg.

"Maybe that's because the woman gets scared by the bleeding and is afraid to let go," Holly says.

Meg shrugs, and Dr. Futterman ignores Holly.

"How were her NSTs?" Dr. Futterman asks, meaning the nonstress test, which monitors the fetal heart rate whenever the baby moves.

"Reactive and good," says Meg, "as are her fetal movement counts." Meaning the number of times the baby moves when Fran is still for an hour.

Holly is stuck in Flaky Midwife Mode. "I think she's just scared to let go," she persists. "The bleeding frightened her." Fear and anxiety are thought to reduce the production of circulating catecholamines, the chemicals that work on the nervous system and are believed to help instigate labor.

"Holly, I'm not willing to risk a postmaturity on the grounds that Fran is scared," Dr. Futterman says with a sigh. "Fear is hardly unique to Fran."

"Besides, she went to a hypnotist," says Meg.

"Did she?" Holly didn't know this.

"One who specializes in fear of childbirth. She stares into her fingers and then drifts off."

"Maybe she's drifting off too much," Dr. Futterman says briskly. "We're scheduling her for induction next week." She pencils this into her thick date book. Then looks up, wrinkling her brow. "For your benefit, Holly, I'll settle for forty-two and a half weeks. Will that make you happy?"

"I'm happy," Holly says gloomily.

"But the price for bought time is biophysical profile," Dr. Futterman says. "You can set it up for her, Holly."

"And go with her," Meg says, smiling wickedly, "and hold her hand."

CHAPTER 28

Holly sits on the counter in the office kitchen, a legal pad on her lap. "Cosign this with me," she tells Meg, who's at the small table by the window.

"I don't want reams of hate mail."

"Maybe I shouldn't emphasize the prevention of teen pregnancy," Holly says doubtfully, even though she thinks this is the heart of the issue.

"Explain the hazards of teen married life," says Meg, "then launch into how you propose to prevent teen pregnancy. That's the hate mail part."

"A nurse-midwife and clinic in every high school where more than a quarter of the girls get pregnant."

"That's the indecent proposal that'll make it impossible for you ever to convert to Catholicism. But block your critics' arguments. 'While this may appear to condone teen sexual activity, teen sexual activity will persist whether we condone it or not.'"

"And that every pregnancy prevented will pay back the clinic costs," Holly says, imagining it all. "If the clinic costs fifty thousand dollars a year to run, one pregnancy and birth of a welfare-dependent child will come to that much at least. Right?"

"You're on your own, hothead," Meg says, studying her newspaper.

Holly drops her pencil. "Meg, I'm in private practice. Who am I to make any kind of proposal, indecent or otherwise?"

Meg tosses back her hair. She's indignant. "This is America," she says. "You have that right. And you know this issue, from personal and professional understanding. You're in an enviable position. You can write this letter as an individual without having to speak for an organization."

But that's what bothers Holly. If she cares so much, why is she here, commenting from a kitchen in Brooklyn Heights?

"You don't just have the right to express your opinion," Meg says. "You have a responsibility. If you don't work for change, who will?"

Sitting in a hard beam of sunlight, Holly pulls her feet up to the counter and props up the legal pad. A responsibility. "This clinic would not only dispense information on contraception," she writes, "but provide emotional support for those who want to practice abstinence and give a realistic evaluation of what a baby will mean once it arrives. . . ."

Foresee the arguments and cut the detractors off at the pass. Should she explain a nurse-midwife's merits as well? High rate of patient compliance, rapport . . . Holly stares at the ceiling and tries to picture her detractors out there, waiting to critique, waiting to blow a fuse.

Lynn pokes her head through the doorway. "You've got a new AP out here," she says.

"Pragmatic activism will wait," Holly says to Meg, scooting off the counter and out of the hot sunlight, into the shade.

CHAPTER 29

Holly is on the phone with Fran, who says, "My bags are packed. I made a lot of spaghetti sauce for Ernie. How much can he eat in three days?"

"Give yourself a break," Holly says. "Let him live off it for seven days. You're not going to feel like cooking."

"I vacuumed and washed the windows today. Maybe I'm feeling the nesting instinct you talked about."

"I bet you are," Holly says hopefully. "Now, let's see what else you can do. How's your love life?"

"Sex life?" Fran laughs. Holly is actually starting to like Fran. Maybe the hypnosis is eradicating the desperate neediness in her personality. "Ernie is . . . a good sport," she says finally.

"Are you enjoying yourself?"

"Sure."

"Now, Fran, I have something important to tell you."

Fran sounds alarmed. "What?"

"It's kind of personal," Holly says.

"I can handle it."

"Get Ernie to feel you up a lot."

Fran laughs with relief. "Okay. I'll tell him you said so."

"I never thought this would be part of my job," Holly says. "But do it, do it, do it."

CHAPTER 30

Danielle Greenhouse and Man-Child Greenhouse-Stolz have left the hospital after twenty-four hours of incarceration. Danielle calls Holly from home, where she is perched on an exercycle, building up her strained musculature.

"You thought my perineum was thick before," she says, out of breath. "Ha! Wait until next time!"

"Danielle, your episiotomy stitches . . ."

"Stitches, bitches. I have something really important to say. My stretch marks are still here. When are you going to take them out?"

"Sit-ups, Danielle. Get off your bicycle and do sit-ups. What does your lochia look like?"

"It looks like my period, to the max. Red. Not to gross you out, but I'm a bucket of blood. I was lying down, then I got up—a flood of blood."

"Which stopped? The blood collects in your vagina when you lie down and then it spills out."

"Birth is so beautiful," Danielle says wispily. "I'm just like so into its awesomeness." Then she barks into the phone, "Listen up, you told me I'd lose ten to twelve pounds after delivery. I'm still a manatee."

"You should lose five more pounds this week. Fluid and blood."

"Blood! More blood!"

"You get hypervascular during pregnancy. You'll be back to normal soon."

"I don't even get to keep the blood after this ordeal? Well, at least my vagina isn't gaping open like the Lincoln Tunnel anymore. The tunnel of love. I didn't like that, Holly," Danielle says sternly. "You should do something about that."

"*You* should, Danielle. Do your Kegels."

"I'm in a permanent state of contraction. I'm a nonstop Kegeler."
Pause. "That man who is my husband wants the foreskin off. 'I know I'm
an asshole, but I want it done anyway.'"

Having come on so strong about circumcision, Holly had worried a
little that she'd used undue influence in imposing her own opinions on
what was ultimately the most personal of decisions. Evidently her powers
of persuasion are something less than mesmerizing.

"But I want Meg to do it," Danielle says. "You've both done this
fabulous—simply *fab'lous*—job, dahling, so if she says she can do the job,
she can do the job."

Holly tells Danielle that it's good for the baby to have a parent with
him during the operation.

"Does the little guy cry?"

"Yeah. He'll probably cry."

"Is it painful to look at?"

"Yeah, it's painful to look at."

"Then Paul can go."

"Won't he feel guilty?" Holly says.

"Good," Danielle says. "He can feel guilty." She hangs up the phone.

CHAPTER 31

Tonight Holly is on call. She and Matt have made love, and now they lie on top of the bed, their bodies sliding into each other.

"I feel like I'm on a raft, a boat," says Matt.

"That's nice."

"Just drifting along."

"Yeah, me, too." Her eyes are getting heavy, so she gets up and organizes her clothes before she falls asleep. She has a specific organizational principle to follow. Her jeans are the first layer to go on the chair by the bed, then her shirt, then her bra, then her underpants. She puts a sock in each sneaker and her purse by the side of a chair.

She used to change in the bathroom when she had to leave. But she's learned to change in the bedroom, so that even if Matt is asleep, he can absorb the information that she is changing to go and her leaving doesn't come as a shock as it did when she changed in the bathroom and deprived him of his unconscious understanding.

Her clothes arranged, Holly climbs back onto the bed.

"So how do you like living with a midwife, Matthew Dailey?"

"I like living with you," he says. "It's like living on the edge . . . of abandonment."

CHAPTER 32

The first thing Holly does is turn to the clock for reference. Where am I, in time? It's three in the morning, and Holly has to climb up the steep path out of deep sleep. She had contracted for a full night's sleep because this night she's not on call, so this phone call makes no sense. It's a violation of her contract. It's violent.

Matt sits bolt upright and says savagely, in the darkness, "You're not on goddamn call tonight."

"Ssssh, go back to sleep." She strokes his hair with a sweep of her hand and he falls back like a stiff board.

Maybe the answering service mixed up the rotation schedule and called Holly instead of Meg. Or there was a disaster at the hospital—or two women have gone into labor—or—

But it's Tom Fedders, and he's calling from a place where voices speak in Spanish, where bursts of laughter mix in with the clattering of footsteps. Not-so-distant sirens cut through the muddle of noise. He's calling, as Holly is just barely able to extract, from a hospital. Tom is numb, and scared, and at Morrison Hospital.

"That's a good hospital," Holly says forcefully.

"Yeah, right," Tom says bitterly.

No hospital is good now.

Holly is dialing the car service. She knows the number by heart now, its seven-note melody, and punches the number into the Touch-Tone phone.

"What?" Matt asks.

"A car accident, one of my patients."

She's picking up her clothes, which are all scattered on the floor. Sometimes she likes to undress like this, pulling off clothes as she walks and letting them drop, particularly when Matt is waiting for her.

481

"Why'd they call you?"

"They wanted me. This is different."

"Is everything all right?" he asks cautiously, knowing that nothing probably is.

"Carla went through a windshield. Her husband was driving."

"The demon banker?" Matt has been following the demon banker. Holly thinks he almost has a crush on her, without ever meeting her, because Carla is so many things that Holly is not, and that's the kind of woman a man in a happy relationship gets a crush on. Someone he will never really know, someone he admires from afar.

"Try and sleep."

She sits down beside Matt, feels the bulk of his body under the covers and presses her face against his back. This is the best place anyplace. Right here. Then she runs downstairs, where the cab, the only occupied car on the street, is waiting.

The cab speeds down the street, bulldozing into potholes and flying over bumps. Good, she thinks, drive like a maniac. The shut-up antique shops on Atlantic Avenue are gated and dark, and the only things that move on the street are the herky-jerky figures of junkies lurching about to stay warm in the cold night air.

Holly is a professional, and she believes in modern medicine. This doesn't mean she doesn't bargain with God. As her father used to say, there are no atheists in foxholes. "Please, God, I'll go to church every Sunday if..." Regular churchgoing used to be such a potent promise when Holly was a kid. Now it's pathetically inadequate. God isn't going to save Carla just to get Holly back into church. God wouldn't operate that way.

The automated doors leading into Morrison are still not fixed, and Holly pushes her way in. A city hospital is like a casino, paying no mind to the outside world, to real time, to real weather. Like a casino, it's a world apart, with high-pitched activity, bright lights, and throngs of people who seem indifferent to the late hours and hover tensely, like cumbersome hummingbirds, put into perpetual motion by anxious compulsion or nervous energy. Whether it's morning or afternoon, the staff wears the same look of fatigue, and everyone rubs his or her eyes the same way. And, as in a casino, the paying customers watch, wait, and study the roulette wheel when it spins. Like Holly, they make bets and bargain with God.

The first person Holly sees is Pam. She's smoking a cigarette, hand on hip, wearing green surgical scrubs (thereby flouting the regulation that prohibits personnel from wearing scrubs off the floor they work on), and squinting up at a cute black orderly. Her black mascara sticks out from her pale, freckled skin like hairbrush bristles. She laughs and shoots out a plume of smoke, drops the cigarette, and does a twist-and-shout number as she grinds it out with her aerobics shoes. When she laughs, her eyes are lost as her face swells up, leaving nothing behind but the spikes of eye makeup and the rust-colored eye shadow floating like smoke up to her eyebrows.

"Pam?"

"Holly!" She puts a hand on Holly's arm. "I been waiting for you, believe it or not. If you didn't show in a minute, I was gonna hightail it up to Seven."

"Waiting for me?"

"I've been on the Fedders case. I heard all about you. The darling midwife. No one else will do. They're all right people, the Fedderses. She's kind of hoity-toity"—here Pam sticks her nose in the air—"but she's people."

"How is Carla?"

Pam waves her hand. "She got banged up. She blacked out. But she's okay. So, Holl, here you are at Morrison, where the elite meet and all roads lead. Or all roads end. For your friends, at least."

"What's Carla's diagnosis?"

Pam screws up her mouth. "*Nada.* No concussion. No subhematoma. Did a goddamn CAT scan, too. Nothing."

"But Tom Fedders said she went through a windshield."

"Yeah, but the windshield got smashed up before she had the chance. It shattered at the moment of impact, as you'd say, and your lady was thrown forward after the glass was already broken. She caught a gash in her forehead and a pellet of glass in her neck. A lucky girl."

"A pellet of glass in her neck?"

"That's just part of the lucky part. A piece of glass aims for the jugular and just misses."

"How about trauma to the abdomen?"

Pam squints at Holly and pokes her in the chest. Holly had forgotten that the midwives at Morrison are . . . physical. "Good question," Pam barks. "Didn't you give your patients lectures about not riding around in cars without seat belts?"

"Sure, in the classes."

Pam laughs shortly. "Maybe they missed the class. Maybe they thought a seat belt would be worse for the baby. Better for her to go flying instead." Pam stamps out the cigarette. "Blunt abdominal trauma. Nothing there either, but who knows? There's no way to pick up intracranial hemorrhages in babies before birth."

"Christ, there could be a cranial bleed right now?" Holly feels something she figures is dread—a woozy washing-about in her stomach, clamminess on the back of her neck, trembling in her fingers. Adrenaline that hasn't been converted to action that circulates through her system and just stops, like a metal weight, somewhere in her bowels.

"Sure." Pam studies Holly warily. Holly knows that if she still worked here, Pam would make a wisecrack about her ignorance. But Holly's company now.

"Was your friend ever pissed off when she was brought in," Pam goes on, lighting a cigarette, which Holly steals out of her fingers and smokes herself. "You know how it goes in ER: first things first. See to maternal stabilization first. Nobody gives a damn about the baby when an auto case like theirs comes in. That'd make sense, if these ER guys knew what shock looks like in a pregnant woman. But they don't know the blood values. You know how hypervascular a woman is at term, and how fast she loses blood. But they wouldn't know if she's lost a lot of blood because they can't remember what kind of blood volume a lady at term has. A lady's systolic will dive down to one hundred and the docs think that looks fine, even if she was up at one-seventy before the accident. They don't consider maybe she was hypertensive because of the pregnancy and that one hundred is a shocky-looking number. They don't remember that there's a pulse increase of fifteen beats per minute in late pregnancy, so they don't factor that in. The lady has to go into irreversible shock before they wise up that maybe she's in trouble. Then they put these little butterfly lines in, when they should get in some big lines, and hook up DW5, when they should start with Ringer's. And you know the incredible urine output in pregnant ladies? The ER docs flip when they see that. They figure you're overloading her."

Good old Ralph, the big man on the hospital campus, passes by. "Pussycat, come back home to purr?" he calls.

"Maybe to scratch some eyes out."

"Oh, you're an alleycat, ain't no doubt." He looks around. "Legs—everywhere I go, all I see are legs! No wonder I can't sleep nights—women! Grrrrrrr!"

Pam lights another cigarette. "The ER docs always go the wrong direction. They take the complaint as part of pregnancy when it's due to trauma. They take trauma as an associated part of pregnancy when it isn't. We had a pregnant lady in here the other night with a seizure. Of course they jump to the conclusion that she's eclamptic and send her up to Seven-B to be magged out. Only when she's awake and coherent do we realize someone clubbed her on the head with a blunt object. I always know which way to go—the opposite direction they're going in.

"These days, I tell the Triage nurse to call me and me only when a pregnant lady presents with a nonpregnancy complaint. Not just because they don't know how to deal with pregnancy, but because she's going to hit the anxiety ceiling—she's worried about her baby, and no one else seems to be. The first thing a pregnant lady asks, just like your lady did, is whether the baby's all right. But no one can tell her how it's doing."

Holly wants to see Carla. She wants to see the Carla who asked, before anything else, "How is my baby? Is my baby all right?"

Holly and Pam move swiftly by the rows of tired, anxious people. The television is still playing a bad psychedelic movie from the 1960s, locked in perpetuity in the TV Trash Zone. They move past a curtained-off cubicle, where an old lady is propped up on an examining table. She is staring down the front of her paper gown in search of an ailment. Past a cubicle with a young black woman in stirrups, who is searching the face of a smooth-skinned resident for the answer to her ailment. He searches between her legs for some clue, some working diagnosis he can put down on a chart. Then, behind a curtain, lies Carla.

Her black hair is loose and spreads out like a fan about her face, which is white save for the bandage running across most of her forehead and the small cuts flecked across her skin like Chinese characters on white silk. An ultrasound transducer is belted across her abdomen, and Holly sighs with relief as she hears the heartsounds move forward in what sounds like a hundred-beats-per-minute rhythm. Tom, in black tie, hair ruffled, face pale, stands at the top of the table, looking down, not touching Carla, not holding her hand. Holly thinks it's too terrible that he's in evening clothes. It's too bitter. Too terrible.

"Holly!" Carla cries sharply.

Holly had always wanted to see Carla get real, become just an old girl like Holly, but tears spring to Holly's eyes to see her there, where she shouldn't be. Carla is right. She should be in Washington, D.C., making a presentation—angular, beautiful, sharp-eyed. Carla's smooth face crumples up like a piece of paper, a marble statue that cracks before Holly's eyes. Holly puts two fingers on Carla's forehead, running them across the skin where there isn't any bandage.

"Carla, the baby sounds good," Holly tells her, leaning her face near Carla's. "It really does."

"The kid's doing swell," Pam says.

"But they didn't even care about the baby before!" Carla mutters. "They didn't, and I got him turned around according to your instructions and—"

"Sssh," says Holly. "Sssh."

"Oh, God, this is awful," Carla says, sounding like her old self and twisting her neck around. "This is disastrous. It's not acceptable." Then she bursts into tears.

"It's all over now," Holly says, taking one of Carla's hands in hers, shaking it. "It's all right."

"They did an X ray," Pam puts in. "Look-it." Holly turns. "See, the baby just smiling there, floating around in the fluid."

"Amniocentesis as well," Tom says. His blue eyes shine out from bloodshot whites. He is guilty, his eyes say, and he's not guilty, they also say.

Pam says, "That was just to see how mature the baby's lungs would be."

"They didn't even want to do an ultrasound at first," Carla says.

"Well, you know, they got to make sure you're okay first," Pam says, putting a hand on her shoulder. "You're top priority. That's the rules."

"Sweetie, you did need a dozen stitches," Tom says, frowning, venturing to put his hand on her other shoulder. Carla is not a woman Holly would imagine being called "sweetie." But there's a lot about life, and other people's lives, Holly doesn't know yet.

"They might have waited," Carla says, staring at the ceiling. Carla is fuming.

"Carla, they couldn't have waited."

"Hmmmph."

The ER resident shuffles in with a clipboard and spies Holly. "You look familiar," he says boisterously.

"I used to work here."

"That's not it. Didn't you go to Brown?"

"You goddamn Ivy Leaguers," Pam says, disgusted.

The resident pulls Holly to the side to explain that Carla should have continuous fetal monitoring for another twenty-four hours. "You know, there might be a delayed abruption," he says quietly.

"Have you talked it over with the Fedderses?"

"No, I thought I'd wait for you, after what they told me. I didn't want her to freak with the possibility."

"She's a grown-up woman. She can handle it." Holly turns to Carla and Tom to explain that the trauma to the abdomen might have dislodged the placenta from the uterus, that there might be a placenta abruption which is sometimes delayed for twenty-four hours.

"Oh, fuck," Carla says, furious now.

"I can understand if you want to transfer your friends to the hospital where you have admitting privileges," the resident says quietly—a not so coded way of saying that Tom and Carla have money and good insurance coverage and that if they can bail out of Morrison, they should do so.

As the resident prepares the transfer for hospitalization papers, Holly steps outside with Pam.

"Who ordered the X ray?" Holly asks tersely.

"Honey, don't look at me," says Pam. "I can't order a glass of water down here, much less an X ray. They couldn't be stopped. They didn't even want fetal monitoring at first. I had to remind them that maybe there was internal bleeding and that they'd find out if the mom was getting shocky if the baby was getting tachy. But once they got hooked on the baby, I couldn't get them off it. I tried to get the portable sono down from upstairs, but they said there wasn't enough time. So they took pictures. Sorry."

Holly blanches and stares at the floor. The door opens, and a blast of cold air hits them.

"When I suggested an amnio, they all said, 'What's the point?' They have to ask me, me with a CNM? I figured if something went wrong, as things sometimes do, it'd be nice to know if we should section the baby the hell out of there or let your friend ride it out for a while. A shake test from the amnio would be useful."

The amnio draws out a sample of fluid for an L/S test, which determines the levels of lecithin and sphingomyelin in the fluid, clues to how mature the lungs are. When the baby's lungs are developed enough to expand and contract on their own power, lecithin appears in the fluid in almost equal concentrations with sphingomyelin. When the lungs are mature enough to inflate and deflate in the respiratory exercise without sticking together, lecithin appears in the fluid in much greater proportions than sphingomyelin. The purpose of the L/S test, and its less accurate diminutive form, the shake test, is to calculate the L/S ratio and evaluate the fetus's viability—or ability to live outside the womb or respirators. The shake test takes only about fifteen minutes, as the fluid sample is put in a tube with other reactive agents.

"Holly, you'd have been proud of me. I put forth the proposition in their flipping language. 'A shake test will be useful in analyzing the risks and benefits so we can decide whether or not to intervene in or terminate this pregnancy.'"

"I *am* proud of you, Pam." Holly rests her head on Pam's shoulder. She's missed Pam. She didn't know it until now.

"Guess who had to do the amnio?" Pam asks with a huge grin.

"No." Holly knows, from Pam's smile, that it had to be Levy. "I don't believe it."

"Levy. Down here in ER they can't deal with putting a needle in a lady's belly. They sew limbs back on. They pull out coils of bowel the length of a football field to look for a bullet lost in inner space. But as soon as they hear the word *amniocentesis*, they quake, cower, and moan. 'I can't put a needle in there. I'll hurt the baby.' They don't even have a portable sono down here. We had to tell Levy to bring ours down with him. Can you dig it?"

"I'm digging it," says Holly, "in a big way."

"Getting Levy to do the amnio right was like teaching a blind man to thread a needle. He was aiming the needle right into the baby's side. Great, catch some membranes, why don't you? So I tell him, 'Go suprapubic.' You know, Holly, the kid isn't engaged yet, so you have all that nice fluid in the big cavity right above the *symphisis pubis*. Levy didn't take the suggestion kindly. He just about smacked me in the face."

"Levy's feathers are easily ruffled."

"You know how it is. With him, it's brother and sister time. I pester him and tag along behind him and generally get in his way. He acts like I'm bugging him, but he really likes it. It's our shtick."

Holly's back stiffens. Christ, she thinks, I'm jealous. She'd imagined that what she and Levy had between them was special, that Levy was hers, when all was said and done. But Holly salvages her pride by reasoning that Pam is just a substitute, the closest thing to an attractive, irritating, pain-in-the-ass midwife named Holly he can find. I miss Levy, she thinks, the cretin.

"Yeah, Levy's nice to me in private, and in public he treats me like a subhumanoid," Pam says with a sigh. "Sound familiar?"

Holly smiles tightly. She wishes she could see Levy. She wants to meet his eyes. She wants to bitch at him. She wants to be with him. Holly rubs her eyes. I must have kind of been in love with him, she thinks.

"Anyway, Levy wound up taking three taps," Pam goes on.

"Three taps?" Reality gives Holly's nostalgia the shaft. Three taps are a lot of taps. Each tap increases the risk of infection and the chance of puncturing the membranes, the baby, or the placenta.

"Leave it to Levy to draw blood the first time. Maternal blood. She moved, he tells me. She was perfectly still, and I don't know what he hit on the way in, but he came back with a barrel of nice red fluid. Second time, he drew a lot of meconium, too much for an L/S test. Throws the values off."

"Meconium?" Holly's heart sinks. "Why did I imagine the tap would come clean? Was it heavy?"

"Yellowish. A mere tinge. Holly, get real. That's not evidence of fetal compromise. We don't know when or where that meconium is from. Maybe it happened a week ago. Besides, your friend blacked out. Maybe some meconium was passed then. These things happen a lot, but most meconium births have happy endings. Don't you remember that much?"

"Yeah, I remember," she says, laughing. "What happened with the third tap?"

"Levy got a nice clean sample. We got our results. Of course, I had to ride their tails for that, too. The baby's borderline. I wouldn't section. I got to say, Holly, it's a pleasure to see one of your patients. A big, healthy baby in a big, healthy lady. When I first saw her, I thought she was at term already."

"We grow 'em big down in Brooklyn Heights."

"I don't envy you on this one, though, Holly." Pam looks at herself in the reflection of the doors leading out to the street and unsnaps her barrette, drawing her red hair back. "Man, slippage. Good-looks slippage. You do everything. Manicure, facial mask, hair conditioner, and at the end of a night here, your hands are dry and chafed, your hair is stringy and oily, and check this out! In these lights, my hair is the color of a nectarine!"

"You look great," Holly says, hurried. "Why don't you envy me, Pam?"

Pam looks serious. When she looks serious, her entire face droops. She is just on the brink of looking middle-aged. She needs a vacation. "Those two are upset," Pam says in a raspy voice. "They don't seem to be the types who'll quit being upset either."

"They're not alarmists," Holly says protectively.

"No, I guess not," Pam says uncertainly. "Funny, they probably don't even need to be in the hospital for evaluation at all. They'll probably evaluate each other like crazy on their own. But at least they'll be in a halfway decent hospital, instead of trapped here in the iatrogenic capital of the world."

Iatrogenic means doctor-caused. Some statistics claim that one-fourth of the ailments treated in hospitals are iatrogenic in origin.

When Holly thanks Pam, she says, "Next time you're in Brooklyn Heights..."

"Shoot, Holly, I'm only in Brooklyn Heights in my dreams."

CHAPTER 33

The cab ride to Brownell Hospital is the most miserable ride Holly has ever taken. Gloomy, glum, hateful, as if the baby were already dead and they're transporting it to the hospital for a cruel, useless experiment.

Carla had refused to take an ambulance, and now they're crushed into the back seat of the taxi, the Fedderses aching with every jouncing motion of the car, the emotions thick and wild and inarticulate. If a psychic, sensitive to auras, were in the cab with them, she'd be overwhelmed by the vibes: tense, edgy, electric, sending out sparks.

They are all thinking furious, dangerous thoughts. When Holly broods about something at home, Matt says, "What are you thinking about over there? I can hear you all the way across the room."

They listen to each other think. This makes a terrible sound.

The cab driver's tape player spills out Middle Eastern music. It whines and keens its way into the back seat: unintelligible, praise to an unknown God. A thick stick of incense, stuck into the dashboard, clouds up the car. They're in a foreign country. No one has the energy, can make the slightest effort, to ask him to turn down the music, put out the incense. No one can speak.

No one can speak, because the opportunity for self-incrimination is too great. If Tom or Carla or Holly breaks down, admits his or her own guilt, that guilt will stick, impossible to escape, ever, once it's articulated.

Blame, too, is just an inch away. Just the slightest slip of the tongue and everyone would blame everyone. But blame would be unthinkably cruel.

Everything is unspeakable. Everyone is at fault, everyone guilty.

Tom had been driving the car when he lost control and spun off the road, crashing into the lamppost, totaling the car, sending Carla flying.

But Carla hadn't worn her seat belt because . . . Holly doesn't know why she didn't wear her seat belt.

But Holly figures she hadn't worn it because she hadn't told her to.

Holly finally knows what the burden of guilt feels like. It feels like three hundred pounds and wedges into the pit of her stomach because it won't fit anywhere else. The guilt comes from the fact that Holly didn't lecture Carla on the importance of seat belts. Holly doesn't like to sound bossy or school-mistressy, like the girls in school who were always made proctor or crossing guard. But in childbirth class, where Holly often has to turn in a crossing-guard performance, she states that any seat belt is better than none, even the old-fashioned airplane kind, which can be worn loose below the abdomen and across the pelvis. "They must have missed that class," Pam said.

But Holly hadn't pressed the point with Carla, because Holly was tired of being a deadbeat around Carla. Holly should have ignored her social instincts and followed her midwife's instinct for once. Then, when Carla had gotten in the car tonight, she might have said, "Seat belts are a pain in the ass, but I'll use it anyway," and strapped herself in, and she wouldn't have gone flying. It was Holly's fault, really.

Breaking the silence, Carla says at last, "I want to have a cesarean as soon as the baby's ready."

Holly turns from the window, where the gray mist of dawn shifts into the hard white sky of morning. She tries to meet Carla's eyes, but Carla stares straight ahead, into the incense smoke.

"I want to get it over with now," Carla says. "This not knowing."

"Carla, there's never been any guarantee. It's always been not knowing. Besides, no matter how the baby's doing, he'll do best if he's born at term, when he's strong and healthy."

Carla looks old, for the first time in her entire life. Her features seem to have fallen—everything about her depressed—and Holly can almost see the nerves go dead, retreating from having to feel, emotions on a long slide underground. The inaccessible Carla hides out again.

Holly realizes that Carla and Tom aren't preparing for the worst. They're assuming it.

The cab driver has turned down his Middle Eastern music so the wails are confined to the front of the cab, and Holly feels as if she's come out of a dark tunnel into something resembling daylight. The Fedderses' confusion and despair had drawn her in, but now she's free of it. How did that happen? When she realized she's only an observer in this drama, no matter how much she cares. She settles back on the seat, the pressure of Carla's arm against her, and sighs deeply.

"It'll never be the same again," Carla says.

"It'll be different," Holly acknowledges. The baby is even less an object of desire than it had been. Now it's the source of anxiety, and everything has shifted, pessimism falling over their lives, cold and wet. "You still have a lot to look forward to, Carla."

"That's easy to say, isn't it?"

"You can believe things will turn out for the worst, or you can believe they'll turn out for the best. Medically, both feelings have equal validity. You have good reason to decide the baby will be fine. The fetus is well protected, you know. Cushioned by a thick abdominal wall and amniotic fluid so that what shakes you just jostles the fetus."

"Don't call my baby a fetus," Carla says coolly.

Holly is defeated. *Is this how you comfort a miserable person, Treadwell, with a lecture on the power of positive thinking? Why not just tell her to go home and aerobicize?*

The taxi pulls up to the hospital. The worst ride in Holly's life has ended.

Maybe you've learned something from this, Treadwell.

Yeah, but what?

Here, at Brownell, only the worst-case scenario can be revealed, only a disaster detected. Good news will wait. The best-case scenario hangs back, in the ambiguous future, and waits to be seen. The same ambiguous future is what holds the Fedderses back. They couldn't get much farther back than they are right now. That's what Holly hopes, of course.

CHAPTER 34

When Holly comes home, Matt is in the shower.

"Shit," she hears him say. No doubt he's trying to save time by shaving in the shower, and now that he's cut himself, he'll finish up shaving at the sink, peering into the fogged-up mirror like other men.

Holly lies on the bed, picturing him in the oblivion of masculine ritual. Her practice is supposed to be family centered, meaning that the husband is involved in the pregnancy. But midwifery is still a woman-centered profession: of women, for women, and about women. For Holly, being with a man is a happy change. A man she loves is a holiday.

Sometimes during a labor, Holly will think, in quick, visual flashes, of a man's body. Its bony, hairy, muscular hardness. The fantasies aren't exactly sexual, which is not to say they're not sexual either. When Holly pictures Matt, he's just existing in male nakedness, which is so drastically different from the female nakedness Holly always sees. *Vive la différence.* Her mind wraps itself around the image, then the image blows away.

Holly wants to be with Matt now, not because he's a man, but because he's innocent of everything that's happened tonight.

Dripping across the bedroom, he leans over and kisses her with a steamed-up face.

"I'm clobbered," she says, "I'm beat."

"Get up and go to work, girl."

"Must I?" she asks.

"Did anyone die last night?" he asks.

"No. I don't think so."

"Then you have to go."

"Oh, Matt, don't you want to make love?"

493

He buttons his shirt. "I want to make money," he decides.

"You're fooling me, aren't you, Matt?" Silence. "Aren't you, Matt?" Silence.

Then he comes and lies down with her, for a while.

CHAPTER 35

"**I**s this your first experience with maternal trauma?"

It's ten-thirty in the morning, and Meg is studying Holly's face. Dr. Futterman leans back, watching the both of them. Holly has the unsettling feeling she's engaged in a group therapy session she didn't sign up for.

"I've had gone-to-ground gravidas before," Holly says. Falling down in the bathtub cases. Falling down the stairs cases. Bumping into wall cases. But she had to come to private practice before dealing with a violent case of maternal trauma.

Holly glances up at Meg, who sits on the windowsill of Ellen's office, legs crossed, and waits with a patient expression that Holly doesn't trust. Maybe Meg thinks Holly jumped into Meg's territory, when the Fedderses called her before calling anyone else. Maybe Holly should have called Meg before she did—which was when she admitted Carla at Brownell. Holly suddenly realizes she blew this, politically.

"I guess I haven't seen a real trauma all the way through," Holly admits at last, knowing this is the confession Meg and Dr. Futterman have been waiting to hear. "What can I expect from it?"

Meg glances at Dr. Futterman, to see if she should field the question. Dr. Futterman gives the nod, and Meg says, "Expect grief." Meg likes to teach; she's good at it. She has the air of authority that Holly always associates with firstborns like herself and that she keeps waiting to grow into. "With grief there's denial, distancing, blame, guilt, feelings of failure, ambivalence."

"I think they skipped the denial phase," Holly says.

"Don't be too sure," Meg says sharply. "You don't know what they're thinking and not thinking."

Holly heard them thinking. They're afraid to hope; they're scared to talk to each other. In all of Holly's serious relationships with men, a make-it-or-break-it point has been reached, a moment of crisis resolved either by a rift beyond repair or a bond that resists breaking.

Tom and Carla are at this point now, the fork in the road. Holly thinks Carla may end up taking one road and Tom the other, and then they'll only be able to meet on the dry, barren ground that divides them.

"What do you mean by distancing?" Holly asks, so that Meg can have the pleasure of telling Holly things she doesn't know.

"They might step back and act as if this is someone else's problem, that it's all the same to them. It's a defensive mechanism. Then there are feelings of failure. They'll wish they never got pregnant. They'll prepare for the worst."

"Shoot, Meg," Holly says, hardly able to keep her eyes open and forgetting for the moment that Dr. Futterman is watching her. "They went through all those stages last night."

"Expect to see more of the same. If they were all full of plans for labor and delivery, like figuring out what stuffed animals to take with them or whatnot—"

Holly snorts, remembering Carla's Filofaxing of her labor. How could Meg get Carla so wrong?

Meg ignores her. "All those cute little things just won't matter anymore. They won't talk about it, but those things just fall by the wayside."

Holly stopped listening at the stuffed animals part. She shields her eyes with her hands and says, "I didn't tell them about the meconium. They were so bummed out as it was."

"I told them," Dr. Futterman says with a nod. Dr. Futterman arrived soon after Carla was admitted at Brownell.

"So there's nothing more for me to do," Holly says, half-questioning, not quite believing it.

Neither Meg nor Dr. Futterman says anything, and when Holly looks up, they're studying her, almost critically. She feels as if she's been caught in some embarrassing pose, scratching her crotch or something, and she wonders what. Oh, yes, she understands now. There was never anything for her to do. This is out of her hands. Why had she thought otherwise?

She has transgressed. She stands up. "Back to work," she says, bright and hard, just like her mother.

CHAPTER 36

As she attempts to grow thick-skinned over breakfast at the luncheonette, Holly opens the newspaper to the letters page, as she always does these days, and scans it for the headline that ought to be there, the one that reads, MESSAGE TO TEEN MOMS: STAY HOME. When she sees that her letter isn't there, she loses heart and folds the newspaper. She's becoming ill informed because she hasn't read the newspaper for weeks, but opens it, then shuts it in defeat.

It's a big city, Treadwell. Lots of thin-skinned letter-writers.

She never knew how much she wanted to shake sense into the world at large, but maybe it's too large a world to shake.

Before she heads in to the practice, she stands at the top of the stoop and glances up and down the street. It's a kind of mental tic, looking for Edna O'Toole. It's not that Holly thinks she can save her anymore, but it seems that when a person is all alone in the world, someone has to try to find that person, fish for that person, send out a line to that person to reel her back in, if she wants it. Holly guesses she thinks she can save that person after all.

But there's nobody on the street except an old woman sweeping her square of sidewalk, and suddenly Holly realizes that Edna O'Toole is dead. She doesn't know how she knows this or why she knows this. But she knows this. Edna O'Toole doesn't exist anymore. Holly doesn't have to look anymore.

With the newspaper under her arm, Holly pushes the door open and moves in, out of the cold.

497

CHAPTER 37

Meg pokes her head past Holly's door. "You were unhinged the other day about these Seidner characters. Remember?"

"Yes, Meg. I remember." Holly hides her face in her hands. "I don't know why I overreacted like that. I can be coolheaded sometimes." She looks up to see if Meg forgives her.

Instead, Meg pushes a letter into her hands. "I'm beginning to believe that maybe you had a point."

The letter reads:

Dear Dr. Futterman,

This is to confirm the decisions reached in our telephone discussion.

As we agreed, any medical procedure proposed by any health-care provider, in practice with you or in practice independent of you, to be administered to Mrs. Sandra Seidner, will be discussed in full with both Mr. Seymour Seidner and Mrs. Seidner prior to such administration.

This discussion shall include the purpose of the procedure, a thorough calculation of its risks and benefits to both Mrs. Seidner and the unborn child, the procedure's known monetary cost or a reasonable estimation thereof, and the health-care provider's knowledge of and experience with said procedure's administration and side effects.

In the instance of Mr. Seidner's unavoidable absence or in the instance of a medical emergency, such discussion shall be conducted between Mrs. Seidner and the health-care provider to the exclusion of Mr. Seidner.

Such medical procedures may include any and all prenatal testing techniques, not excluding ultrasound examination or any method of any electronic fetal heart monitoring, prescription of any and all pharmaceutical medications, administration of any and all anesthesias and analgesics and any and all surgical and obstetrical procedures, including episiotomy and cesarean section and not excluding forceps delivery or any other invasive procedure.

No procedure shall be administered without said discussion. No procedure shall be administered without the full and formal consent of Mrs. Sandra Seidner.

As a general outline for Mrs. Seidner's course of treatment, the Seidners request treatment that requires a minimal number of medical procedures. This is left up to the discretion of you, any other health-care provider and the Seidners. Mrs. Seidner shall be informed of all discussions among the health-care providers that pertain to her obstetrical care. The Seidners shall be apprised at all times of the health status of their unborn and delivered child. The health-care providers willingly agree to share any and all knowledge regarding the health of the child with the Seidners as the health-care providers are apprised of information regarding the child.

The decision as to which health-care provider shall be in the main responsible for the intrapartum care of Mrs. Sandra Seidner will be the exclusive and sole decision of Dr. Ellen Futterman.

I hope this letter satisfies any questions you may have regarding our telephone discussion.

The letter is signed by Seymour and Sandra Seidner.

Holly looks up. Her fear of the Seidners is justified. She wishes it hadn't been. "Does this mean we get sued if we lay a hand on her?" Holly asks. "Or do we get sued if we don't?"

Holly and Meg stare at each other, agog. They are in the presence of the malpractice beast made manifest.

"She's pretty old," Meg says slowly. "Maybe Ellen will take her on exclusively."

"I don't even want to think of the Seidners. I'll think all wrong. Do I have to report what I think about them? What if my opinions are all wrong?"

"Does this mean we can't use a Doptone?" Meg asks, walking out of the room with Holly following. "Do we auscultate by fetoscope? What about a tape measure? Can we use a tape measure?"

"Meg, you are panicked and confused."

"I am bonkers," Meg says, nodding slowly. The Seidners have started to register. "Those people can do that to you." She turns to Holly, dazed and wide-eyed. "I forgive you for your outburst." She looks down at Lynn and lays the letter on her desk. "Here, dear. File this manifesto under M. I think I'll flip out now." She jumps weakly up and down three times and says, "Why oh why oh why oh?"

"You know the French word for midwife?" Lynn pipes up.

"No," says Holly.

"*Sage-femme,*" Lynn says, pleased.

They both look at Meg, who has resumed hopping.

• • •

Before the Seidners, Holly managed not to obsess on the specter of malpractice. Malpractice was a game, something you played at dodging. It's a new thing for her, as for most nurse-midwives, to dwell in the realm of the litigious. If Holly's patients aren't lawyers themselves, they have a close relative or friend who is, and the possibility of a malpractice suit is lodged in their minds as threat and consolation. Like divorce, it's what you do when things don't work out: an unpleasantness undertaken when faced by even greater unpleasantness.

Holly's patients have high expectations, low tolerance for bad luck, and little experience with things not going their way. Holly sees the rise in litigation as part of a religious crisis. Her clients don't seem to take shelter in prayer or refuge in church, or to place their trust in God. Holly should know, as this description fits her well. Her clients aren't particularly existential either. They believe in cause and effect, in logic, and resist the idea that random chance often plays a part in how things turn out and leaves no one to blame. Holly's clients are the kind of people who must place blame somewhere.

What bothers Holly the most about the malpractice epidemic is that it's only harmed health care. The hackers still hack, and defensive medicine is a new, legally creditable kind of hacking.

A slew of unnecessary tests, ultrasound, overliberal use of cesareans and inductions and IVs can all place pregnant women at greater risk. Defensive medicine medicalizes childbirth and pathologizes pregnant women, as clinicians turn them into medical patients to ensure that their care-giving is beyond legal reproach.

Holly never felt she had to be this way, but she no longer feels immune from being sued, as she once did. "People who bring suit have had their trust broken by doctors," Meg reassured her when she joined the practice. That midwives don't betray their patients' trust, Meg's theory ran, would shield them from being sued.

Midwives don't come in at the last minute as many doctors do, let other clinicians make labor evaluations for them, or act without informing their clients of the ramifications of their actions. By explaining things, they establish a rapport that won't be abandoned in tough times. If clients are given all the information a midwife has, the theory runs, they won't become paranoid or feel like abused objects.

But the statute of limitations is twenty-one years. How long does a good rapport last? Eighteen years from now, Holly might be seeing Fran Cutler in the courtroom. Who can divine the future?

And any sense of immunity deriving from the low number of suits brought against nurse-midwives—only six percent have been sued as opposed to seventy percent of OBs in the early 1980s—is specious, as this rate reflects in large part on the different pools of patients the two groups care for. Nurse-midwives are only starting to penetrate the litigious middle-class, and a practice like Dr. Futterman's is still an anomaly. That a disadvantaged population hasn't brought many suits (a poor woman on a witness stand might easily be made to seem guilty for any birth defects herself) hardly proves midwives are immune from suits brought by better-equipped, -educated, and -defended women.

There is one theory Holly subscribes to that she admits to no one. In the final analysis, she has a personal sense of immunity, a psychological defense that posits that she won't be sued because she's better than others: safer, more intelligent, better skilled, and even better liked. Maybe it's arrogance, but if she didn't believe that she was those things, she'd bail out of midwifery altogether, leave the aggravation behind to some other idealistic chump, and cut out to the leafy pastures of the Bryn Mawr Tennis Club to be bored out of her skull—but safe, at least.

The Seidners knocked Holly off balance, but only for a moment, just one moment in a (touch wood) long life. Now Holly's back. "Come and get me, coppers," she says out loud. "I ain't scared." She laughs when she realizes she's lying.

CHAPTER 38

"Why don't you come with me?" says Meg, who is on her way to the Greenhouse-Stolz circumcision. "Wouldn't you like to learn how to circ?"

"I'll never get enough practice to do it well," says Holly. "It's something you really should be able to do well."

"Too bad you didn't learn to do it at Morrison. Easy money. One hundred twenty-five dollars for an hour's work."

"Not the kind of easy money I want, though," Holly says.

"Come watch anyway."

Danielle stands outside the nursery, pressing her nose against the windowpane. Holly, Meg, and Paul are all dressed in visitor's gowns, and Paul is holding his baby. All the babies in the nursery have started to scream, the domino theory of vocalization as illustrated by life's littlest members.

Clapping her hands over her ears, a nurse runs out, screaming, "These babies are driving me crazy!"

Paul observes her. "She's in the wrong line of work, I think."

Meg looks at Paul. "Sure you want to go through with this?"

"Is that a high-pressure or a low-pressure tactic?" he asks.

"It's a last-chance bailout offer," Meg says.

On a clipboard are the consent for surgical operation, the baby's original hospital numbers, and his no-name hyphenated status on a chart to track the progress of the circ. After the circ, Man-Child will spend a few hours in the nursery to be observed.

"Witness," Meg says, passing Holly the pen for the consent form.

In the corner is the light blue Circumstraint, a molded plastic board with Velcro straps for the baby's arms.

"If the baby has a very little penis," Meg says, washing down the Circumstraint with rubbing alcohol, "we refuse to perform the operation, because we don't want to take too much off."

"I'm sure the baby's parents are really relieved to hear that their baby's penis is too small," Paul says.

Meg gives him a glance. "Sometimes we lie. Besides, the little ones grow. Later on."

Meg undresses the baby, save for his diapers, and settles him down on the Circumstraint, snapping his new IDs around his ankle and wrist.

"I guess this thing is blue because it's always for boys," Paul says dolefully, watching his son's arms get strapped down to the side.

"Sometimes a female baby finds her way here," Meg says, "but it's designed for boys, that's true." She opens Man-Child's Pampers and pushes them out to the side. He'll lie on them during the operation as a cushion and so he won't soil the Circumstraint.

His penis looks tiny, exposed, vulnerable, and not at all ready for any kind of surgery. Meg unfolds a sterile blue drape—like any drape, except that this one has a diamond-shaped hole cut into the creases. Meg spreads out the drape and pulls Man-Child's penis through the hole.

"Now we separate the foreskin," she says, putting the cone of the clamp around the glans and drawing the foreskin over it to create a smooth tube of skin. "We'll only take a little bit off," she says, glancing up at Paul, who nods solemnly. "Now we put this clamp on," she says, sliding a stainless steel Gomco clamp over the penis. It looks a bit like a hole-puncher and caps the glans of the penis with a bell-shaped dome, so the foreskin surrounds it. "We wait about three minutes, so the clamp crushes the blood vessels—hemostasis—which minimizes bleeding and anesthetizes the skin, a little bit."

The baby is red-faced and wailing now. Meg strokes his hair back. "I know, baby, I don't like to do this to you either." Turning to Paul, she says, "You can kiss your baby, Dad." Paul bends down anxiously and kisses Man-Child lightly on the forehead. "Talk to him in a high-pitched voice. He hears those sounds the best."

"Are you mad at your old man, sport? Are ya? Are ya?"

Danielle taps at the nursery window, lifting her shoulders in query. "What's going on?" she mouths.

Holly just waves.

"He's calming down now," Paul says uncertainly, stroking the baby's fine brown hair. "Isn't he?" He checks Holly's face anxiously.

"Sure. He is."

Picking up the scalpel, Meg says, "Some guys just cut around. But we were taught to peel it like a grape." She leans down and begins to peel back the skin. "We don't want to take too much off, or an erection might be painful when he gets older."

"Oh, God, don't do that," Paul says, frowning with distress as the baby starts to cry again. "How come there's no anesthesia?"

"Too risky on such a young one," Meg says. "They used to think the baby's nervous system wasn't developed enough to feel any pain. But they feel it." She studies the isolated length of skin and flesh, bits of the foreskin on the blue drape. "I did a nice job," she says. "That's going to look nice." She unlatches the clamp and tells Man-Child, who is crying only sporadically, like a hiccup, "Now when you go pee-pee, it'll hurt some." She takes off the clamp, and the top of the baby's penis is glossy with newly exposed skin. "Soon all that will toughen up. But right now, it's not so tough."

Paul's lower lip trembles. His eyes are watering, and Holly puts a hand on his shoulder. "He'll be fine," she says softly. He nods without looking at her, on the brink of tears.

Meg reaches for a fresh diaper, unhooks the baby from his Velcro straps, and pulls out the old diaper.

"Don't you bandage him or anything?" Paul asks, as she closes the diaper.

"That just irritates him at this point. Later, you put Vaseline on. But for now..." Meg looks up. "Want to diaper your son, Dad?"

"Guess I better get the hang of this," he says, laughing nervously. This is more like it, what a new dad should do. "Okay, sport, here we go." He looks down at the circumcised baby and gingerly shuts the Pampers.

"It's done," he says.

CHAPTER 39

When Holly comes home tonight, she feels defeated, in a vague way. She bounds up the stairs to her apartment, because a slow trudge upstairs would be an intolerable admission of this vague defeat. This doesn't prevent her from collapsing on the sofa as soon as she breathlessly pushes her way into the apartment.

She opens the mail from her prone position, staring at the pictures of the Himalayas included in a mailing for *National Geographic*, purposely ignoring the American Express bill, glancing through a copy of Matt's *Skiing* magazine, and then finding a letter that is actually addressed to her, by some other instrument than a computer. The return address is *The New York Times*.

Don't get your hopes up, Treadwell.

But when she opens the letter, she finds herself sitting up, standing up, then hovering by the window, pressing her forehead against the glass, staring out at the passersby trudging home looking more defeated than she ever could, lugging bags of groceries in their arms. "I can't fucking believe it," she says into the window, misting up the glass.

She looks around the apartment. There is nobody to tell. Matt is in transit. She can't tell Meg—that might come off as boasting, considering how strained things are between them. Katrina will only scoff. There's nobody to tell that the newspaper wants Holly to restructure her letter and expand it into a piece for the Op-Ed page, where only legitimate hotheads have a say, that her opinions aren't just the het-up remarks of a powerless nut case, but the valid suggestions of a certified nurse-midwife who knows whereof she speaks.

Holly sits down at the kitchen table and studies the morning's coffee left behind in a cup stolen from Morrison Hospital, swirls of milk condensing on its top. She kisses the envelope and the letter and embarrasses herself. She looks up at the ceiling and says, "Mrs. Gruener, what do you think of me now?"

But there's no answer yet.

CHAPTER 40

It's Marge on the phone, from Howard Street. "Some crazy woman has been trying to reach you," she tells Holly. "When we tell her you're not here, she hangs up or asks for your new number. What should I say when this certain individual calls again?"

"Who is this certain individual?" Holly asks.

"An Irish girl. Edna O'Toole."

So she's not dead! Or is she? "When was the last time she called?"

"About a week ago."

She might be dead by now. "Give her my office number," Holly says urgently. She might not be dead. "Give her my home number."

"Holly, we're talking unstable personality here!"

"That's the only kind who ever calls me at home."

"I used to call you at home," Marge says plaintively.

"Well, there you go," Holly says happily.

Holly doesn't know why she cares so much about Edna O'Toole. Maybe Edna is Holly's other, her secret double in life—the bad girl who took flight rather than fight. And Holly's failure to get through to Edna was one of the hidden currents that pushed her out of Morrison. If she knew she couldn't change the world, she'd thought she could, at least, grab on to certain individuals and not let go.

Holly laughs to picture Edna at the Brooklyn Heights office. Her pinched, sharp features, face almost green with anemia, dyed hair as brittle and lifeless as dead grass, her hard blue eyes taking in the huge-bellied, well-mannered women, placid on the nubbly linen sofa in their nice maternity clothes with their briefcases on their laps. What would Edna do? She'd blow cigarette smoke in their faces.

When Edna walked out, something inside Holly just gave up, even though Holly didn't want to give up.

Holly wants to find Edna, because Holly has lost her double.

CHAPTER 41

Holly is saying good-bye to a patient, Betsy, but Betsy isn't ready to leave. "I'm bumping into walls. I keep sucking in my stomach and holding my breath to squeeze by something, but it doesn't work. Nothing moves in. It's ridiculous. There used to be nothing I couldn't squeeze by with a bit of breath-holding and stomach-tucking."

"The reluctant abdomen. It can't be willed away."

"My balance is truly pathetic," Betsy says. "My feet are on another planet. My center of gravity is underwater, floating around. Solid earth has become shifting sand."

"Oh, yes, the lost center of gravity." With each trimester, the number of minor accidents increases. "Your ligaments are stretching. That's good."

"I feel like Gumby. A big rubber ball, just rolling along."

"I don't usually tell my patients this," Holly says tentatively, but she is encouraged by the happy look on Betsy's face as she looks forward to her midwife's confidences, "because of the self-fulfilling prophecy effect. But midwives have a law that goes, 'Third-trimester ladies hit the ground at least once.' It's kind of a rite of passage, to let you know you've really arrived."

"You have to hit the ground to know you've arrived? Arrived where, exactly?"

"On the brink of motherhood."

"Well, I've arrived," says Betsy. "I'm barely into my third trimester, and I've fallen at least a dozen times."

Holly wipes her forehead with relief. "Well, that removes the burden of having supplied you with a negative suggestion. You do fine without me." She sees Betsy studying her. "What?"

"You've never had kids, right? How can a girl like you resist, being around it so much?"

Holly thinks of all the reasons she resists: money, career, not sure she's ready for the responsibility. But the reason she gives seems to make the most sense.

"I resist because the man I live with doesn't want kids yet."

"You know what my mother says," says Betsy.

"No, what?"

"If a woman had to get permission from her man to have kids, the world would be pretty empty out there."

"What else does your mother say?"

"No man ever wants to get married. You want to get married? You've got to turn those screws."

"Thanks, Betsy," Holly says. "Gosh, being a midwife is such a learning experience."

CHAPTER 42

When Holly goes to cash her paycheck, the bank teller, who knows her by name, asks, "What do midwives do for fun?"

"We sleep."

"Don't you have any hobbies?" he asks.

"Yeah. Sure."

"Such as?"

"Sleep," she says.

Sleep. On call. At two in the morning, the phone rings, and Holly doesn't want to answer it.

"I wouldn't mind if you quit this business," Matt mutters into his pillow. "It'd be fine by me."

"You want to support me?"

"I didn't say that."

"Go back to sleep."

Holly's pad and pencil are by the bed, and she sits up long enough to take Christina's name and number from the answering service operator. Holly can't imagine how it feels for Christina to be all alone and starting in on labor. She calls her from the kitchen, lit only by the light over the stove, and paces up and down the cold floor as she talks, in her underpants and T-shirt.

Christina has been in labor for hours and never called. Her contractions are coming every seven minutes for forty-five seconds.

"I forgot to tell you," Christina says. "My waters broke."

"You forgot to tell me? You're supposed to call then, Christina!"

"I'm calling now."

510

"Did they break before or after the contractions?"

"Just before. I did the castor oil. Two tablespoons. It was...unpleasant. I couldn't phone you. I was on the toilet."

"Let me hang on with you until you get another contraction." Holly glances at the wall clock above the kitchen table. "Then I want you to take your temperature."

"Spontaneous ruptured membranes, six p.m.," she writes down as she leans against the humming refrigerator.

"How do you feel...otherwise?"

Christina doesn't answer, and Holly shuts her eyes, imagining Christina alone in a deserted apartment, her bag packed. Holly tried to persuade her to find another labor-coach after Roger took off. She even suggested a childbirth educator she knew, who'd coach the labor for free.

"I'm not going to pay someone to stay with me," Christina answered, stung.

"She'd do it for nothing," Holly had said.

"But it'd be as if I were paying her," Christina said, with a degree of truth. Because the childbirth educator wouldn't be staying with her out of love, but out of pity.

"I can feel that something's wrong," Christina says at last.

"I tell you what," Holly starts to say, because plenty is wrong. A woman is in labor for the first time and completely alone. That's pretty much the definition for *wrong*. "Maybe it's time for you to go to Brownell."

"All right," Christina says, relieved and resigned.

"What if I came by in a cab and picked you up?"

Christina pauses, and Holly listens to her breathe. "That's a good idea," Christina says, and Holly's glad. She is going to save someone.

Christina is only three centimeters dilated. Holly would tell any other client to go home and try to sleep. But no way is Holly going to send Christina home, even if this is a prolonged latent phase. She's just run down to the cafeteria to buy Christina something to eat and has returned with a granola bar. "Why is a midwife's practice like a granola bar?" runs the midwife's joke. "It's full of nuts, flakes, and fruits." Midwife humor lacks something. Humor, possibly.

At Morrison, Holly would have given two Seconals to a woman so long in early labor, just enough to keep her cranky and dozey, but not enough to let her ignore the contractions well enough to sleep. All the Seconal seems to do is take a big bite out of a woman's energy level.

"Get real," Meg told her. "Give them morphine. Accept no substitute. I don't know why, but none of them pharmaceutical equivalents is equal to morphine. Twelve point five Sparing. That's the trick."

Since Holly started at the Futterman practice, she's learned that the real trick to being a midwife is to shift the vibrations of a place. Replace fear with strength, grimness with humor, and disorder with calm. Like what used to happen when Holly and her friends played with a Ouija board when they were kids. Holly didn't believe that spirits spoke through a board mass-produced by a toy company, but the board always managed to spell out messages as an invisible pressure was brought to bear to slide the marker across the board in a purposeful way. That's what Holly has to do now. Apply invisible pressure to make the spirit of the place spell out a different message without Christina knowing how it's come to be spelled out and to let her think that the spirits are in control and that the spirits are good.

Holly doesn't know if she's up to the job. Christina's sadness is like a huge boulder, and Christina must somehow roll it to one side. For this, she needs her strength. She needs sleep. She needs granola bars and morphine.

"Christina, I think we should give you something so you can sleep."

Christina nods, expressionless. Her hair is too short to pull back but too long to do anything but hang over her face.

"If we give you a wee bit of morphine, it'll knock you out for a while and you'll wake up kind of . . . restored."

Take a short leave of absence. Just check out. Wake me when the baby gets here. Christina is ready for all of it.

Holly walks out to the narcotics chest by Annie's desk. A nurse glances up, and Holly lowers her eyes. But it's not Annie, and she doesn't care that Holly is about to hit her patient with Sparing. Why does Holly feel so criminal then? She slowly unlocks the narcotics chest. She'd almost counted on Annie for a wisecrack about having to resort to morphine, so that she could shore up her own faltering faith in what she's doing by a self-righteous argument. Why does she resist doing this? The baby is stable, his variability good, and there's little chance of narcotic depression at delivery.

What's the problem? A deep sleep might be restorative, with Christina working things out while she's under. Holly could take a lie-down herself, now that she's beyond being tired, with almost nothing left to give. It's six in the morning, and noises go through her. Phones ringing, elevator doors opening, chattering voices. A little Sparing, and Holly could take a lie-down.

She stares at the grains of Sparing in the brown vial and remembers what Sara told her. "Labor is a psycho-spiritual process. Some ladies just have to work things out." Holly leaves the vial alone, on the shelf, shuts the narcotics locker and locks it, and tosses her keys into the pocket of her scrub. She and Christina will learn to rest together. They'll work it out. And babies get born. Babies get born.

Holly's shoulders ache from supporting Christina as they spent the morning walking up and down the corridors. "You're surfing on the ocean," a nurse says to Holly, smiling. "Stay on top of it." That's what Holly told Christina as they walked.

"You must have been here awhile," Christina says, holding her son. "I like it," she says. "This is what I was made for."

She was made for this. The moment when the baby was born, Christina stared him in the eye. He stared back. She was crying, as if she'd moved the boulder to the side. She had done it. "I've been waiting for you for so long!" she said. "If only you knew how long I've been waiting for you!"

CHAPTER 43

Christmastime in the corporate world, and Matt's law firm is throwing its annual party in a Manhattan dance club. "To mollify us disgruntled guys," Matt said. Holly hopes to see celebrities there, but Matt tells her, "I hate to clue you, but eight o'clock isn't a big celebrity time."

"If I can convert one celebrity to midwives, maybe she'll go on Johnny Carson and talk about midwifery and influence millions." Her eyes widen as she contemplates the miracle. "Or if a rock star's wife goes to a midwife and lives to tell the tale to suggestible fans? Think of it, Matt!"

"Don't you ever stop thinking like a midwife?"

Holly thinks for a second. "No," she says. "I'll try."

Matt stops in his tracks. "You don't look like a midwife."

"Is that good?"

"I don't want to give you a swelled head," he says.

The dance club has transmogrified the drab, obedient law firm personnel into raging discomaniacs. Leonard from Accounting is spinning on his back, attempting something like break-dancing, while the managing partner flails his arms behind him in a lethal Australian crawl.

Holly isn't on call, which is not to say that she's without her beeper, just in case Meg has dropped dead and someone needs her. But she wonders if she'll even be able to hear the beeper, the tiny ripple of sound overpowered by "Atomic Dog" now pounding through the speakers as big as houses in huge ultrasound waves. Holly lifts her bag to her ear, as if listening to the ocean in a shell, and strains to make out the lost sounds of a beep.

"It's such fun to go out with a girl who tires to make contact with another planet by handbag," Matt shouts in her ear. "Some girls just make contact with their handbags when they need lipstick or mad money or something. How pedestrian. They pale in comparison. Should we try our luck on the dance floor? Maybe you can pick up some interesting waves out there."

Holly and Matt are slumped in leather couches that overlook the dance floor. "I'd like to make out with you," he shouts in her ear, "but at beer four bucks a pop, I'm not drunk enough. Tried tuning in any planets lately?"

Holly shakes her head.

"Let's pretend you established first contact. Let's go home so I can take off that dress for you."

"Is that what a dress can do?" Holly shouts back.

"No! That's what you can do, if you let yourself!"

Her dress has been off for a while. Matt asks, "When are you going to be on call again?"

"Tomorrow."

"I want to ask you something when you're on call, so I can tell our children that I asked you and that your beeper went off so you didn't give me your answer for twenty-four hours."

Holly stares into the darkness. "What if my beeper doesn't go off?"

Matt thinks. "I'll lie to the kids. I'll tell them it did."

"Tell them that you didn't get your answer for twenty-four hours. They'll like that. It's more romantic."

"What's the answer I'll have waited for?" Matt asks softly.

"What did you plan the answer to be?"

"They're our kids," Matt says, "so I guess the answer is yes."

"I guess you'll still have to wait twenty-four hours," says Holly.

"I'll ask you the question then," Matt says, "when you give me your answer."

"I'm glad I'm going on-call tomorrow." Then, after a moment, "For the sake of the children, of course."

"Of course," Matt says.

They agree.

CHAPTER 44

*T*he *New York Times* has given Holly no notice about when her piece will appear, except that it will run sometime in November. The first few mornings of November, Holly woke up before the alarm clock went off: highly irregular behavior. She could barely tolerate the time-consuming ritual of showering and dressing, but tore out of the house with her hair still wet to run to the newsstand, buy a paper, and stand on the corner, ripping the paper open to the Op-Ed page, only to find . . . nothing.

Now she lies in bed with Matt. The alarm clock rang, but she turned it off. Five more minutes. The thought that her piece might be in today's newspaper dribbles through her mind and rolls out again. She's not inclined to leave the warmth of her bed, Matt's warmth, to find out if her name has entered the public record. As the weather gets colder, her desire to become thick-skinned at the luncheonette has waned and her thin-skinned self has learned to accommodate living with someone else. She's glad.

When the phone rings, Holly stares at the ceiling. She knows. She knows what this is. This is the start of it.

"You're not on call yet," Matt says from his sleep.

"Yes," she tells him.

Holly picks up the receiver, and Pam's voice shoots out. "Why didn't you call me and let me help you write that thing? Fucking-ay, Treadwell, you're a traitor! Shit, though, it was good. It was. You're such a goddamn loudmouth, though—"

And Holly is flying out the door with a five-dollar bill in her hand. She is going to buy every newspaper on that newstand.

CHAPTER 45

Holly is standing on the promenade in Brooklyn Heights. There's Manhattan. She feels marooned. Or unmoored. At sea, is how she feels, and alone. It's eleven in the morning and bitterly cold. The day is what she's come to think of as a Canada morning—hard, blue sky, hard, cold wind, hard, high clouds, everything bright and cold and hard, clean and mean. The wind has come straight down the Hudson, as if the river exists as a chute just for the wind, so that it can speed downstate and hit right here, right where Holly stands.

She's moved her life here to Brooklyn, for her work. Her apartment, her boyfriend, her job are all in Brooklyn. She wonders why. She turns her back to the wind, pulls an old cigarette pack from her old raccoon coat, and lights up. Or tries to. It takes six matches for the cigarette to catch, nearly burning the fringe of her collar in the process. She's remembering what she said to a boyfriend in college, when she told him she had to break up with him: "There isn't any easy way to say this. There isn't any nice way to say this. I'm being as nice as I can be, but still it isn't nice. And I tried to prepare you. I dropped clues, but you didn't pick them up."

The clues she had dropped weren't particularly obvious ones—only a paranoid boyfriend would have picked them up—but everything else she said was true. She'd never been dropped. No boyfriend had ever left her in the lurch, drawn back one day and let her feel the electrifying sensation that soon turns into a dull, thudding nausea, of being rejected, of being let go, a superfluous person, an unnecessary accessory.

"I don't like this feeling," Holly tells herself.

What had she said on leaving the office? Nothing embarrassing or angry, she hopes. Nothing that will hurt her chances of getting a good recommendation from Dr. Futterman. She had to get out of that office. She couldn't stand to feel that unreal, sickening sensation in front of other people, even if they were sympathetic, understanding, infuriatingly so.

Transition. The toes curl. You throw up. You can't get comfortable in any position. You don't want to be touched. Your bones chatter. You feel alone, surrounded by other people.

What had she said? "I think I'd like to take a walk, I think I'd like some fresh air."

And Dr. Futterman's anxious glance at Meg and Meg's anxious glance at Holly and Lynn leaping up so that she could gaze anxiously at Holly until she got out the door. "Holl, Holl, are you all right?"

Holl is all right. Holl is a Treadwell, which means she likes to feel pain alone. Holl is not all right. Holl does not want to feel pain alone. Holl does not want to feel pain.

She scuffles along the promenade, sees an old man in a beret faithfully tending to his bevy of filthy pigeons. That's fidelity, to feed birds too stupid to fly south in the winter. That's loyalty.

She had heard it coming, the way Dr. Futterman had prefaced what she was going to say with that look at Meg and the slight nod Meg had given her. Meg had known all along. And Holly felt like a stooge, the victim of a conspiracy. That's how a patient must feel when the doctors have conferred in private, returned with a diagnosis, sprung it on the patient, and produced but one resolution that the patient must abide by. No wonder people sue. No wonder people are enraged.

"It was completely unexpected," Dr. Futterman had said, in her careful, measured way. "Unfortunately, midwives are lumped in with us OB/GYNs now. You're tarred with the OB brush, as they say. Last year your insurance was fifteen hundred dollars. This year it's going up to ten thousand."

"What does that mean?" Holly had asked blindly. For a moment she thought of saying, "My father has money! He'll buy my insurance for you! If you just let me stay!"

But Holly is almost thirty years old now—she feels about eighteen years old, but she is almost thirty anyway—and she's too old for her father to buy her insurance. Fancy that, a subsidized practice. Her stomach turns again.

"The practice can't carry that kind of premium," Dr. Futterman said. "I'm sorry. You've been wonderful to work with."

"Meg?" Holly asked, glancing at tall, collected Meg—a "long glass of water," Holly's father would have called her.

"To tell the truth, Holly, I'm thinking of getting out of OB altogether," Dr. Futterman went on. "Phase out the OB side of the practice by the end of next year. Meg will stay on until then. It's seniority."

Holly nodded, speechless. "I know." Tears sprang to her eyes, and that feeling swept over her, under her, inside her. Why did she feel ashamed?

Why do I feel ashamed? She heads back up the street, past the old mansion with its hedges and still-thick lawn, the grass almost insanely bright on this cold day, a little bronze birdbath stuck in the middle of it, behind a fence of spears painted black. Birdbaths, pigeon-feeding. What is this obsession with birds? Who cares about birds? A garden that pretends to be secret and yet every weekend attracts hundreds of sightseers who stroll by and wonder, "Who lives there?" and hope, "What would I give to live there someday?" It's all insane.

Why do I feel ashamed? Malpractice is out of hand. It's not as if Dr. Futterman is really firing Holly—circumstances are forcing her to. It's like the farmer threatened by foreclosure who has to let go his old fieldhand.

Ah, but that's the thing. If I were really a good midwife, thinks Holly, she would have seen her way clear to keeping me. She would have found a way. She would have asked if I was interested in working part-time, so that I could cut my malpractice insurance in half. She could have asked if I'd stay on to do well-woman gynecology. She could have found a way. And now I'm expected to go back there.

Holly leans against the fence, staring into the bare, classical little patch of garden. That would be pathetic back home, she thinks. That garden would be laughable back home. Only in New York could anyone think that garden was something special. But all things are special when they're rare.

And where else can Holly find a practice like the Futterman practice? How many are there in the entire city of New York—four or five?

A figure appears in a darkened window off the garden, and Holly pulls back. "Just looking," she mutters. "I'm not going to break into your precious garden." She scuffles up the street, past the old-fashioned apothecary with the brown glass bottles in the window, past the chic gourmet delicatessen with its baskets of bread arranged so tantalizingly— bread that has been in the window for months and must be brick-hard by now.

She could start her own practice. Get a loaner from her dad. Find a backup. She laughs out loud. Get Levy to back her up. Become Levy's nurse. Where is Levy now? Still at Morrison, sleeping through his last lap around the academic track. Chief resident Levy.

She doubles back, passes the brownstone where the office is, keeps walking. She'll work something out. She'll find something. She has three months to work it out. Change is good. Change creates opportunity. Life is nothing but change. Transition. On to the next stage. The stage of expulsion.

Then she feels her stomach lurch and a feeling she's never had before—a throbbing all around her head. Oh, yes, she remembers now. She's been fired! She isn't wanted! And she has to go back there today!

"Well," she decides as she stops in for a cup of coffee at the luncheonette. "This is the first time my heart has ever been broken.

How interesting that it's finally happened." Then she runs into the bathroom to throw up.

Holly has gotten reasonable. She pokes her head in to Meg's examining room. "Look, I'm going to be gone in three months, and you know what? That means you have to deliver the Seidners' kid."

"Holly, I could count on you to find a silver lining."

That evening, Meg offers to buy Holly a drink.

"Any kind of drink I want?" Holly asks defiantly. "Any kind of fancy drink I want, the kind that is a gallon of liquid and comes in a canoe carved out of imported cola nuts and the straw is a bamboo shoot and there's a plastic pigmy stuck in the canoe, punting?"

"Somehow I suspect the Emerald Isle on Atlantic Avenue doesn't carry that kind of drink. But if they do, I'll buy it for you."

"And if I want two of them, even if they're called the Monsoon Tropical Storm Hurricane Ring of Fire Special?"

"Yeah. The Monsoon whatever. But somehow I don't think the Emerald Isle makes that kind of drink."

Holly settles back on a greasy chair at a table that is still wet from the previous occupants' beer. "You bring your wronged colleague to a dive?"

"Hey, all the best medical people come here. That guy there, on the barstool, he's one of the best neurology guys going. He's at Brownell."

"He's at Brownell? How good could he be?" Holly knocks back her St. Pauli Girl. So much for Monsoons.

"Hey, watch your bitterness."

"How long did you know?"

Meg scratches her nose. A most unsanitary tic for a midwife, Holly notes. "Only a week, Holly. Swear to God."

"Tell me straight. Am I a good midwife or what? Do the clients hate me? Do they complain about me?"

Meg looks amazed. "Are you off your rocker? The clients make me jealous, they love you so much. You can be sure that if old Meg Greenspan heard a complaint about you, you would have heard it. Maybe you noticed, but I'm forthright to a fault."

"Yeah, but you know how to keep a secret. What is it? Pity? You couldn't tip me off?"

"Holly, it wasn't my place to tell you before Ellen had a chance to tell you."

"Couldn't you guys have let me down easier?"

"Like how, Holly? Strung you along? Told you a couple of weeks ago that there was a possibility one midwife was going to get cut from the great, glorious, Yupped-out Futterman team? Then told you a week later that the possibility was becoming more likely. And then told you today that you were definitely going, when we knew it all along. Is that what you would have wanted? You wouldn't have felt humiliated if we had done that?"

Holly considers this, head dipped, studying the insides of her beer bottle. *You're actually crying into your beer, Treadwell. I'd quit if I were you.* "I am you," she tells herself and looks up, quizzically, at Meg, whom she can barely see in the dim light of the Emerald Isle. Just that tall, straight-backed, forthright Meg who has always told her the truth in the past. "You can trust a midwife," Holly can hear herself explain to a new convert to midwifery, "because midwives don't hold back information. Midwives involve you in your health care. After all, it's your life and your health. Midwives are just adjacent to it."

"Naw," says Holly. "I wouldn't have liked that. But I don't like it this way either."

The man sitting behind Holly tips his chair back and extends a large, oval mass that Holly decides must be his fat face. She could just put her hand over it and shove it back to its own table. But that wouldn't be politic. "My friend and I were wondering if you're a movie star," he says, eyes glowing.

Holly looks at Meg. "Did you pay this guy off?"

"Not me. I don't pay off strange men to flatter midwives."

"You're a midwife? No kidding! I'm a dentist. So's my friend. You ladies mind if we join you?" Both the dentist and his friend, the dentist, are scraping their chairs inexorably in the direction of Meg and Holly's table. "We mistook you for a movie star because of the way you swept in wearing your mink coat."

"I wasn't sweeping in," Holly says, drawing back close to the wall. "I was stomping in."

"That's what I told my friend. She's not sweeping in. She's stomping in, like all midwives do."

"You're midwives?" asks the second dentist, who is a slight, mustachioed man. "Midwives in mink. You must be doing all right."

"Am I doing all right?" Holly asks Meg.

"You're doing all right," Meg affirms.

"That's a second-hand raccoon. That's not mink," Holly tells the first dentist.

"You girls—you ladies—you're like obstetricians, huh? You do deliveries and all that, right? How many deliveries a year do you do?"

Meg gives Holly a glance. *Play along. Let's educate these guys, give nurse-midwifery a good name, help establish a positive image of nurse-midwifery in these dentists, maybe they'll tell their wives, their patients, their friends who became doctors: "Hey, we met some midwives the other night, and they were great ladies!"* Holly nods at Meg. *Comrades. For the moment.*

"We each do about seventy-five."

"Yeah? No kidding."

"I used to do more, before I went into private practice."

"Oh, you were in the wards, huh?" the first dentist says, turning to his friend, who nods at him. They understand quick. "So, how much for the whole delivery package? You do it that way, right? One set fee, am I right?"

"It's sixteen hundred dollars for prenatal care and delivery and postpartum care and a six-week checkup," Meg tells him.

The first dentist lets out a slow whistle. "Ho, boy! You're doing all right!" He lifts his eyes toward the ceiling and calculates. "Sixteen hundred times seventy-five—that's one hundred thousand dollars gross, less say five grand for insurance, twenty grand overhead. You ladies are doing all right!" He looks at them, no longer curious. Now he's impressed.

"Well, it doesn't work that way. We're salaried midwives."

"Ohhh," the first dentist says, nodding at the second dentist, registering this, the last piece falling into place. "You work for a doctor who pays you a salary. I get it."

"Yup," Holly says, taking a long swig from her bottle of beer. "You got it."

"So, you're like my assistant, who pulls down twenty-five grand a year!" he says, amused now.

"Something like that," Holly says.

"Oh, so you're getting screwed, just like she is?"

Holly looks to Meg. What do I say now, Meg? How do I deny this percipient bit of insight?

"Yeah," Holly says, throwing back her mane of movie-star hair. "We're getting screwed."

CHAPTER 46

"But you're going to have to tell your mother some-time, aren't you?" Matt asks. For a moment, Holly wonders what huge change in her life he's talking about. "I told my parents, and they keep wondering if they're supposed to call your folks or your folks are supposed to call my folks."

"I don't want my mother going through a huge Main Line drill of a wedding."

"So you get on the phone and say, 'Ma, I'm getting married, but it's going to be a small wedding up here in New York."

"I would never call my mother 'Ma,'" Holly says.

"Excuse me," Matt says, standing up and heading for the bedroom. "I forgot how upper-crust you supposedly are."

"It was just a statement of fact!" Holly shouts after him, feeling miserable.

The phone rings. And rings.

"I'm sick and tired of answering your calls, Holly!"

Holly picks up the receiver. "Yes?"

"Holly, this is Beatrice."

"Oh, hello . . . Beatrice."

Holly sinks into the couch. It is, by her real name, Mrs. Gruener. Holly is too miserable to be excited by that familiar Teutonic voice. For a moment.

"I read your article in the newspaper, Holly."

Holly catches her breath. "What did you think of it, Mrs. Gruener?" She sits up straight.

"You are growing up." That's a declaration, an opinion, an editorial comment.

"I am trying hard to do so, Mrs. Gruener."

"You are thinking beyond yourself."

Holly bursts into silent tears, because it's not true. Because all she's thinking about is herself.

"You are not so concerned about what's best for little Holly Treadwell."

Her whole face collapses now, and tears stream down the side of her nose. She breathes deep. Then she breathes again. "I'm not so sure of that, Mrs. Gruener."

"You are behaving as a responsible change agent. An inspired change agent."

Holly covers her face with her hand.

"How are things in Brooklyn Heights?"

Holly sits up straight again. "Don't you know, Mrs. Gruener?"

"Know what, Holly?"

"The practice is closing. Well, the OB practice is being phased out. I'm the first phase."

Holly slumps into the couch. Why does this sound like an admission of failure? Because part of her believes the practice is going to continue to exist and thrive, and that the plan to phase out OB is just a ruse to spare her feelings. Part of her feels as if she's lying, because she doesn't come right out and say she's been fired, which is the obvious, inarguable truth.

"I'm sorry to hear that," Mrs. Gruener says. "I'm very sorry to hear that," she says, thinking of something else. Holly would like to know what she's thinking about. "What are your plans now?"

Holly laughs, swallowing hard. "Besides jumping into the river to drown?"

"Ah," Mrs. Gruener says. "Not quite grown up yet, I see."

"Mrs. Gruener, that's justifiable gallows humor."

"No other plans?"

"I'm still kind of stunned. Dazed."

"You'll do all right, Miss Treadwell."

"Think so, Mrs. Gruener?" Holly needs to know.

Holly can hear her thinking on the other end of the line.

"Haven't I always told you the truth, Miss Holly?"

Yes, she has.

CHAPTER 47

Holly is in Bryn Mawr, a week before Christmas. It's her early Christmas. It's her refuge. Stung by the real world, as Holly and her friends constantly referred to it back when they lived in what must have been, by logical extension, "the unreal world." Nursing her wounds.

"Oh, Holly, stay over until Christmas," her mother had said at dinner tonight.

"Mom, you know I can't. I'm on call Christmas day."

"You were working last Christmas too! It's insane!"

"I was working elsewhere last Christmas, and next Christmas I'll be working elsewhere, too, and will probably have to work."

"Let's not be gloomy," her father said.

"If you stayed over Christmas, you could be on call here. It's only an hour and a half to New York. You could jump on a train and be there in just a few hours. In a long labor, that's not much time."

"Mom, I've explained to you that midwives don't do that. We get to the hospital as soon as our clients do. That's the point. And what if there's an emergency? When you're on call you're supposed to get there lickety-split."

Her mother looked despondent. "Anyone can see you look peaked and exhausted," she said.

"Babies do get born on Christmas," Holly's father said to comfort her.

"What a horrible day for a birthday," Holly's mother said. "You look worn out."

"Mother, since when have you gotten so maternal?"

Holly's mother looked wounded, and Holly was scared by how old she looked. "I'm sorry, Mom, I'm snappy, I'm tired."

"I know you are!" her mother said, affronted. "That's just what I'm trying to say!"

Holly is now flopped on the old leather couch in the most comfortable room in the house. It's the den, where her father watches football in the fall, and when *The Preppy Handbook* came out, Holly was sure someone had sneaked into her house and taken down the details. There's the time-beaten banner FOR GOD, FOR COUNTRY, FOR YALE on one wall, the old duck decoy on a low bookshelf filled with Time-Life Books bought to educate the kids, crumpled copies of the *Yale Alumni Magazine* and *The New Yorker*, and a relatively unused sewing box her mother dips into once or twice a year, when she's feeling homey and wants to darn some clothes.

What's different now from when Holly lived here is that her parents have cable television, a box with a zillion channels resting on top of the old color set. Holly's watching MTV, brainless, enervated, exhausted.

"Lucky there weren't music videos when you were a kid," her father says from the doorway. "You'd never have gotten your homework done."

"I got all my homework done," Holly says, staring at the set. "And look where it's gotten me."

Her father steps closer to the television. "Is that Mick Jagger? Is he still around? I thought we'd gotten rid of him years ago. Why would a man with a build like that want to take off his shirt and show it off?"

Holly laughs. "Dad, we had this fight fifteen years ago. Give the guy a break. He's over forty years old."

"He is? My God!" Her father is trying to zero in on her. He eases his way into the room, sits down on the hassock. "Let me turn off the sound, at least," he says, switching off the television altogether.

"Dad, are you going to give me a heart-to-heart now?"

"You know why your mother is really upset that you're not going to be here for Christmas? She's got a list this long of available young men for you to chat up at the Christmas party."

"I've got a young man, Dad." Holly still hasn't given her mother the benefit of the Big News. "It's a job I need now."

"Well, I suppose she has an outdated notion about you marrying some fellow and not needing a job anymore."

Holly winces. "It so happens that I'm a born romantic, Dad, and the idea of marrying some guy for any idea other than love—well, it's not in my emotional vocabulary."

"No, no, I'm sure your mother wants you to fall in love with some of these young guys with means. I'm sure she wouldn't want you to marry anyone you didn't love."

"I know, Dad, I know." Holly feels unspeakably tired.

Her father clasps his hands together and leans forward. "So, Holly, what about his midwife stuff? Thinking of giving it up?"

Holly shuts her eyes for a second. "I don't know. One day I think of giving it up. One day I think of going to medical school, becoming a doctor, and saying, 'Hey, you guys, screw you.' Some days I think about going into practice for myself."

Her father draws back. "How would that work?"

"Get an office, put out a shingle, buy a beeper."

"Sounds like a hard life, out on your own like that."

"Well, I'd have a partner."

"Any candidates?"

Since Holly is considering this idea seriously for the first time right this minute, she doesn't have many candidates in mind. She thinks of all the midwives she knows. There are plenty of candidates in there. Pam. Katrina. Barbara. Barbara? No, not Barbara. "A few," she says.

"What else do you need, besides patients?"

"Physician backup," Holly says, pulling herself up off the couch. "Hospital privileges."

"How do you go about getting that?"

Holly leans back. "I have no idea."

"From what you've told me, there aren't many physicians supportive of midwives."

"There are always a few renegades," Holly says, truthfully but without much conviction.

"What about this medical school idea?"

"Eight more years of school, Dad," Holly says, shaking her head. "If it were three more years or four more years, but eight more years... I can't hack it. I'd be thirty-eight. That's a depressing thought."

"Maybe you need a vacation. Time off to collect your thoughts." Her father looks keenly at her. "Would you like that? If money's a problem..."

"What if I take time off and I don't have any thoughts to collect? What if no answers come to me?"

"Oh, no, Holly. I have too much faith in you ever to think that. Answers will come to you. You'll see."

"Dad, do you mean that?"

He looks at his hands. "Yes," he says, surprised. "I do, actually."

Holly bursts into tears. When she looks up, her father is looking at her, sad and helpless. He doesn't seem to mind that a Treadwell is crying, even though Treadwells don't cry. She is happy, being miserable like this.

CHAPTER 48

Holly and Matt both lie on the floor of the living room in the dark.

"I understand this is good for the back," Matt says.

"Yes."

A parallelogram of light spreads across the couch from the streetlamp below. When the wind blows outside, the branches of the ailanthus tree in front of the house slice into the light, casting wispy scratches of shadow.

"We were talking of the future," says Matt.

"Mrs. Gruener wants me to come back."

Holly had been to Howard Street that morning. She wound through the streets she still knew well. Immigrants just up from Latin America, with little skill at dressing in winter, hurried along. Holly followed a family, all dressed in lightweight jackets, pressed close together for warmth. Plantains and bananas, hanging in the window of the bodega, were still nearly black.

Holly kept an eye out for Edna O'Toole, half-expecting to see the thin figure with the bright red hair listing down a sidestreet. She watched out for Desiree, Cleopatra, and their babies. But she saw nobody she knew until she hit the clinic, and then she understood why each person who leaves always says, when she comes back for a visit, "Nothing has changed!" What it means is that her leaving, which she once saw as such a crucial thing, has made no difference.

But maybe it has. When Holly knocked on Mrs. Gruener's door, Mrs. Gruener stood up and came to the door and shook Holly's hand before she had a chance to slip into the Supplicant's Seat. Holly felt a huge sense of relief to be back with Mrs. Gruener, when she realized for the first time how rare it is to trust and admire another person. Holly had always assumed there'd be someone to look up to—for wisdom and a tough kind of heart. She hadn't known how things really were. She felt like saying, "I'm ready to learn again, Mrs. Gruener. Tell me how the world works."

Mrs. Gruener scrutinized her. She put on her half-glasses, took them off, put them on again. "You don't look the same."

"It's my clothes. I bought some decent clothes."

Mrs. Gruener glanced at her wool dress. "No," she said. "I don't think so."

"My heart's been broken then. I'm calmer now."

"That might be it," Mrs. Gruener said quietly.

A baby Holly had passed in the hallway, held by her mother, an Indian baby with huge eyes who looked like some kind of icon to holy innocence and sacred beauty, now cried out.

"But it's just as well," Mrs. Gruener said, standing up. "That your heart has been broken. Nobody should be in love with midwifery. That's nonsense. You were in love with catching babies. You were in love with being the sweetest girl in the world. But now there's something else. When you're in love, you only care about yourself. I think midwifery has changed you. You are ready to leave yourself behind a little, I think."

"A little," Holly said. "A little."

Mrs. Gruener stood up and turned to the window. Holly admired her profile. It'd be nice to be that good-looking when she got older. Her own mother might have been that good-looking, if she hadn't hardened up with age and sealed out change.

"When I had my first child, I was twenty-nine. That was very old for then, you know, just as it's old for Morrison." She swung around, her necklace swinging with her. She wore some kind of knockoff of a Chanel suit: she looked ready for lunch at the Carlton. But here she was, to put Holly through the wringer again, in Brooklyn.

"I was a baby," Mrs. Gruener said, narrowing her eyes significantly, as if to say, "*You* know what being a baby is about." "A spoiled child. I wanted things to be just right. Not only for myself, because I was a *noble* spoiled child. I wanted things right for the rest of the world as well. The world was very unsatisfactory, you can imagine. I was quite displeased." Mrs. Gruener sank into her old wooden swivel chair. "When I had my first child, I hemorrhaged. I was on all sorts of drugs, because I had the child here, in America." She laughed duskily. "And as I was bleeding, all I could think of was the baby, the baby. It was then that I knew I'd be all right, because I could leave myself behind. I could live without selfishness."

Holly looked down at her lap. "I'm not ready to live without selfishness."

Mrs. Gruener looked at Holly hard. "I have a nice life, a nice home. Am I talking about not being selfish? I am talking about survival, about having a heart for things that do not benefit you, that are not your concern. I learned to be a good soldier."

That was what Holly's father used to call her, when she was a sturdy, steady kid who didn't complain. Good soldier. Holly guesses that you had to live through World War II to call someone a good soldier and mean it as a compliment.

Mrs. Gruener leaned across her desk. "Are you ready to be a good soldier?"

Holly sat up stiffly. "In what war?"

Mrs. Gruener held up a blueprint of what looked like a ship, full of cramped cabins. It was Morrison Seven-B. In her mind's eye, Holly raced up and down its fifty-yard dash, and each of the blue-penciled compartments lodged a figure. Denise. Levy. Crowley. Sparks. The blueprint was a memory palace.

"Forget this," Mrs. Gruener said, letting the blueprint drop to the desktop. "That's the past."

"That's true."

"The future is what's true. We're reorganizing. Knocking it all down. Restructuring. Not me, personally. But Howard Street/Morrison, as a complex." Mrs. Gruener squinted at Holly. "We are being given the greatest gift midwives can get. We are starting from scratch. Maternity services are going to change. Are you ready for change?"

Holly stared at the blueprints whose time was up.

"They finally conceded," Mrs. Gruener said, smiling. "They lost the war. The guerrilla won." She pulled out a lipstick case from her drawer. When she had her lipstick on, she asked Holly, "Are you ready for change?"

Holly's head is on Matt's chest. She can hear his heart pound. "Your resting pulse is seventy beats per minute, I'd wager. That's what you get when a nurse-midwife's ear is pressed against your chest."

"That's not my resting pulse. I don't call it resting when a midwife is pressed against the front of my shirt."

They listen to each other breathe.

"What is it Mrs. Gruener wants you to do exactly?" he asks, running his hand through her hair.

"Structure the new midwifery services. Write up new protocols. Work with the designers for the new Seven-B. Then, when I'm done with that, propose and fight for—especially fight for—the first clinic in a school."

"Piece of cake," Matt says. "When do you catch babies again?"

Holly thinks. "When it's all over."

"It'll never be all over."

"When it's all over for me then."

A car starts up on the street and rumbles out.

"Maybe you'll want to make babies for a while instead of catching them, when that time comes." Matt's eyes look wet and wondering in the half-light.

"Oh, yes," Holly says. "Maybe I will." She's imagined having her own babies for so long that she feels they're almost here, in the shadows, ready to come forward.

"Are you going to become an effective change agent then?" Matt asks, lying on his side, studying her.

"Do you think I should?"

"I think you should always light out for the territory, as long as you don't leave me."

"I couldn't."

"Does the future look good?" Matt asks, holding her.

She listens to his heartbeat. Eighty beats per minute. He wants to know about the future. "The future looks good," she says. "From here."

"Good," he says.

Glossary

ABC—abbreviation for Alternative Birthing Center; consists of private room(s) with homelike atmosphere in which woman goes through both labor and the delivery of the baby (usually in the same bed).

accoucheur—literally "one who stands by the bed"; a midwife.

ACNM—abbreviation for American College of Nurse Midwives; professional organization of certified nurse-midwives; certifies the education and practice of nurse-midwives.

amniocentesis—a procedure in which a small amount of amniotic fluid is removed for laboratory analysis.

amniotic sac—commonly called bag of waters or "membranes"; surrounds the developing fetus within the uterus and is filled with amniotic fluid.

amniotomy—procedure in which the bag of waters (amniotic sac) is ruptured (broken) to release the fluid.

amnihook—small hooklike instrument used to rupture (break) the amniotic sac (bag of waters) and release amniotic fluid.

Apgar scores—a very helpful system of assessing a newborn baby's state of health one minute and five minutes after birth.

AP—abbreviation for "antepartal" which means "before birth" (also known as "prenatal").

auscultate—to listen with the aid of a stethoscope or fetoscope.

bag of waters—another phrase for the amniotic sac which contains the fluid that surrounds the developing fetus.

blastocyst—microscopic ball-like cluster of cells that will develop into the embryo; very earliest stages of cell development.

baseline—the fetal heart rate during labor, between uterine contractions.

Bishop's score—a method of determining the readiness of the cervix (neck or mouth of the uterus) for labor.

bloody show—the bloodstained leakage of fluid from the vagina; a signal that the cervix has begun to dilate and labor is impending.

bonding—the development of a close relationship between mother and baby, and father and baby; a gradual process that begins immediately after birth.

bradycardia—slower than normal heartbeat; in the fetus, a heart rate between contractions of 100 to 119 beats per minute.

Braxton-Hicks—"false labor"; contractions of the uterus which prepare the uterus for labor.

breech birth—birth in which the baby's buttocks or feet are delivered first.

BCW—abbreviation for the Bureau of Child Welfare.

caput succedaneum—swelling of the scalp of the newborn infant because of a collection of fluid (not blood); caused by pressure on the head during a long labor.

caul—archaic term for the amnion; the inner membrane of the amniotic sac.

cephalhematoma—collection of blood that forms in the baby's scalp during delivery; scalp bruise.

CPD—abbreviation for cephalo-pelvic disproportion; situation in which the fetal head is too large to pass through the mother's pelvis.

cesarean section—also called C-section or cesarean birth; removal of the fetus through a surgical incision made in the mother's abdomen; surgical delivery.

CNM—abbreviation for Certified Nurse-Midwife (certified by the ACNM).

contraction (uterine contraction)—the uterus (a muscle itself) tightens then relaxes; contractions help open the cervix and push the baby out.

CBC—abbreviation for complete blood count.

cord clamping—the application of two clamps to the umbilical cord prior to cutting the cord after delivery.

cord compression—the umbilical cord is squeezed due to pressure against it, causing the fetal blood supply (and oxygen) to be decreased markedly, especially during a contraction.

cord prolapse—the umbilical cord suddenly slips down into the vagina causing "cord compression."

CI—abbreviation for cardial infarction (heart attack).

curve of Carus—the cylindrical curve of the lower portion of the birth canal.

DR—abbreviation for delivery room.

D5W—a dextrose solution used intravenously.

dilatation—enlargement (widening) of a ringlike structure; during labor, the progressive widening of the cervix to allow the birth of the baby.

Doppler (Doptone)—portable ultrasound device.

draping—the application of sterile paper or cloth drapes to an undressed patient.

ectopic pregnancy—pregnancy in which the fertilized egg is implanted outside the uterus (usually in one of the fallopian tubes).

edema—swelling of tissue caused by an abnormal trapping or collection of fluid; during pregnancy may be normal or a sign of elevated blood pressure.

edematous lip—swelling of a portion of the cervix during labor, usually due to a woman's pushing before the cervix is completely dilated (open); may interfere with complete dilatation of the cervix.

EDD—estimated date of delivery.

endometritis—inflammation (and usually infection) of the lining tissues of the uterus; most often a complication of childbirth.

EBL—estimated blood loss (during surgery or childbirth).

epidural—a form of anesthesia which involves injecting an anesthetic medication into the lower portion of the spinal canal.

episiotomy—a cut which is made in the perineum at the time of birth to allow an easy delivery and prevent tearing.

external version—shifting the fetus into the vertex (head down into the birth canal) position by applying pressure to the mother's abdomen.

fetal compromise—another term for fetal distress.

fetal distress—a condition in which the fetus shows one or more effects of sudden and/or chronic lack of oxygen; often caused by cord compression.

fetal heart monitor—external and internal: electronic device which detects (and may record) the heartbeat of the fetus.

fetoscope—a specially designed stethoscope used to listen to the fetal heartbeat.

fingers—(slang for "centimeters"); used to measure and describe the extent of dilatation of the cervix during labor; essentially gauges the progress of labor.

first stage—the early portion of labor, from the start of contractions until the cervix is completely dilated.

fontanel—"soft spot" in the head of an infant; areas between the bones of the baby's skull which allow the skull to "mold" (change shape) during labor and delivery, and later on, to grow.

friability—abnormal tendency of baby tissue to be damaged or torn; loss of resistance to tissue injury.

Friedman curve of labor—a graph which outlines the usual length and pattern of labor; used to compare a woman's labor to the median and predict potential problems.

fundus—the body of the uterus.

gravida—a pregnant woman.

HCG—abbreviation for human chorionic gonadotropin; a hormone produced by the blastocyst; the basis for pregnancy tests.

hematocrit—a measure of the concentration of red blood cells in the blood; a laboratory test for anemia.

hemoglobin—the red pigment in the red blood cells; the oxygen-carrying chemical in the blood.

hopper—a receptable for refuse from bedpans.

hydrocephaly—the condition in which there is an abnormal accumulation of fluid leading to an enlarged fetal head.

hyperstimulation—over-stimulation; during labor, excessive use of drugs leading to frequent, abnormal contraction of the uterus.

hypervascular—an increased number of blood vessels in a portion of the body.

hypotonia—abnormal floppiness and softness of the uterus.

L&D—labor and delivery; slang for the labor & delivery ward.

lanugo—the fine downlike hair that covers the fetus and newborn.

lay midwife—a person who attends and assists at births without specific professional training.

left-lateral (left-lateral simms)—a body position in which a woman lies on her left side;

during late pregnancy and labor, this position is safe for the fetus because it allows the best possible blood flow for the fetus.

LGA—large for gestational age; newborns who are in the ninetieth percentile for height and weight, as compared to normal-size infants.

lithotomy position—the position of giving birth in which the mother lies on her back with her legs raised on stirrups.

mag (to mag)—to administer magnesium sulphate to preeclampsia patients to prevent convulsions.

meconium—the baby's first stool, sometimes passed in utero when there is fetal distress.

methergine—a drug which can be administered after delivery to cause the uterus to contract; slows bleeding.

mucous plug—a gelatinous piece of mucus in the cervix that seals and protects the entrance to the womb.

multip—from the word multipara, meaning a woman who has given birth at least twice; informally used for a woman giving birth for at least the second time.

multiple gestation—the conception of two or more fetuses, i.e. twins, triplets, etc.

neonate—newborn infant; infant from birth to twenty-eight days of age.

NICU—abbreviation for Neonatal Intensive Care Unit.

NSST—abbreviation for nipple-stimulation stress test; nipple stimulation leads to natural production of oxytocin, which leads to uterine contractions; monitoring of fetal heartbeat during nipple stimulation can be used to predict fetal response to stresses of labor (fetus's fitness for labor).

NST—abbreviation for nonstress test; monitoring the pattern of the fetal heartbeat during fetal movement, without inducing contractions of the uterus; can be used to detect fetal distress before labor.

nuchal cord—term which refers to the umbilical cord being wrapped around the neck of the baby during labor and/or at the time of delivery.

nullipara—a term used to describe a woman who has never given birth; also commonly used to mean a woman who has never been pregnant.

OB—abbreviation for obstetrics.

OCT—oxytocin challenge test; uses oxytocin (Pitocin) to induce uterine contractions for a short time while the fetal heart rate is monitored to test the baby's responses.

oligohydramnios—an abnormally small amount of amniotic fluid.

oxytocin—naturally occurring hormone that causes uterine contractions; synthetic oxytocin is called Pitocin or Pit.

para—slang for the number of children a woman has previously delivered.

pH—one of the blood gases, pH is a measure of acidity; determining pH level in the blood is helpful in determining inadequate oxygenation in the fetus.

palpate—to examine by touch.

perineum—the area between the anus and the opening of the vagina; an incision in the perineum is called an episiotomy.

pelvimetry—evaluation of the pelvic dimensions through vaginal and external exams (by touch).

PD—abbreviation for pediatric (resident).

PET—abbreviation for preeclampsia/toxemia (toxemia is the older term for preeclampsia).

PIH—abbreviation for pregnancy-induced hypertension.

'pis—slang for episiotomy.

Pit (to Pit)—to administer Pitocin.

Pitocin—synthetic oxytocin; when administered will cause uterine contractions; used to initiate and/or assist the progress of labor and delivery.

PKU—abbreviation for phenylketonuria; metabolic disease in which protein breakdown is defective leading to severe mental retardation; treatable if found early in newborn screening.

placenta—provides for fetal nourishment (oxygen and nutrients), as well as elimination of waste products; the placenta and fetus are connected to the mother by means of the umbilical cord.

placenta previa—condition in which the placenta is attached to the uterus in an abnormally low position, near or covering the cervix.

post-maturity—a group of problems in a fetus which result from decreased placental function; may be the result of prolonged pregnancy.

preeclampsia—a hypertensive (high blood pressure) disorder of pregnancy.

primip/primipara—informally used for a woman giving birth for the first time; formally used for a woman who has given birth once.

PROM—abbreviation for premature rupture of membranes, in which the amniotic sac ruptures (breaks or seeps) before the onset of labor.

pudendal block—anesthetic injected into the pudendal nerve (in the lower back) which numbs the entire perineum and pelvic area.

pulmonary hypoplasia—condition in which the fetus's lungs remain immature or too small.

quickening—sensation of fetal movement, usually occurring around the twentieth week of pregnancy; the time of quickening can help in estimating a woman's delivery date.

Ritgen maneuver—a method of delivering the baby's head in a speedy, controlled fashion during which a midwife applies pressure to the back of the baby's head and the bottom of its face.

rotation—internal rotation is the movement of the baby as it descends down the birth canal, which places the baby in the ideal position for childbirth; external rotation is the forty-five degree turn the baby makes to place his/her body in position for delivery; rotations occur naturally.

scalp sampling (scalping)—a minute amount of blood, similar to a pinprick, taken from the fetus's presenting part (usually the scalp) for laboratory analysis; used to determine inadequate oxygenation of the fetus.

second stage—the stage of labor after complete dilatation of the cervix; also known as the pushing stage or the stage of expulsion.

SGA—abbreviation for small for gestational age; newborns who are in the lower twenty-fifth percentile for birth weight and height.

shoulder dystocia—condition in which one or both shoulders become impacted above the pelvic brim at delivery.

spina bifida—a neural tube defect (birth defect) in which the backbone fails to form normally, often allowing part of the spinal cord and coverings to protrude.

spiral—the tiny electrode of the internal fetal monitor that is attached to the baby's presenting part (usually the scalp).

stillbirth—a fetus which died in the uterus or during labor and was dead when delivered.

suture—a connecting joint found on the baby's skull.

symphisis pubis—the pubic arch.

STD—abbreviation for sexually transmitted disease; venereal disease.

tachycardia/tachy—rapid heartbeat; in a fetus a baseline heart rate above 160 per minute signals fetal distress.

tertiary care—most sophisticated and intensive care available for both mother and unborn/newborn.

transducer—the device used to relay and retrieve ultrasound waves.

transition—the stage of labor during which a woman's cervix becomes fully dilated, leading into the second stage.

transverse arrest—condition in which the fetus's head does not rotate normally as it passes through the birth canal.

triage—the entry point for incoming patients who are then referred to various departments based on their condition and needs.

tubal ligation—a form of sterilization for the female in which a piece of each fallopian tube is removed (or severed) or blocked so the egg (ovum) cannot be fertilized; also called having the tubes tied.

ultrasound—a method of diagnosing fetal problems and development; based on the principle of producing inaudible, high-frequency cycles of sound vibrations that bounce off dense objects and back into special equipment that converts them into images (photographs or films).

variability—the normal ups-and-downs of a fetus's baseline heart rate, the absence of which is a danger sign known as "flattened baseline."

vertex position—commonly called the "head down" position; also called cephalic presentation.

vernix—a thick creamlike coating that protects the baby's skin before delivery.

walk-in—those who have not been seen prenatally and "walk in" for delivery of the baby.